Eating and Stayi

Planning 325–344

Maps 345–356

Index 357–363

HOW TO USE THIS BOOK

Understanding Ireland is an introduction to the country, its geography, economy and people. **Living Ireland** gives an insight into Ireland today, while **Story of Ireland** takes you through the country's past.

For detailed advice on getting to Ireland—and getting around once you are there—turn to **On the Move**. For useful practical information, from weather forecasts to emergency services, turn to **Planning.**

Out and About gives you the chance to explore Ireland through walks, drives and organized tours.

The **Sights, What to Do, Eating** and **Staying** sections are divided geographically into six regions, which are shown on the map on the inside front cover. These regions always appear in the same order. Towns and places of interest are listed alphabetically within each region.

Map references for the **Sights** refer to the atlas section at the end of this book or to the individual town plans. For example, Cork has the reference 351 D8, indicating the page on which the map is found (351) and the grid square in which Cork sits (D8).

UNDERSTANDING IRELAND

The most striking feature of Ireland is the legendary 40 shades of green that make up this Emerald Isle. You may have to put up with the unpredictable showers of its maritime climate, but your reward is the dazzling spectrum of colour on the lush pastures and rolling hills when the sun breaks through. Some 6 million visitors come to Ireland every year to see its prehistoric monuments, castles and high crosses, crumbling monasteries and stately homes. But although the island looks small on a map, don't assume you can tour it quickly. Its winding country roads and beautiful scenery demand a leisurely pace. Besides, it's almost a sacrilege to hurry in Ireland. Take time to chat with the locals, linger in the brightly painted coastal towns or vibrant cities, share a story or a song in a local pub. Through the people, as well as the places, you will discover the magic of Ireland.

WHAT IS IRELAND?

Officially, this North Atlantic island nation goes by its ancient name of Éire. More widely known in English as Ireland, it measures 84,421sq km (32,924sq miles) and is part of the British Isles. The independent Republic of Ireland comprises 26 counties—five-sixths of the island—while the six northeastern counties that make up Northern Ireland are part of the United Kingdom. However, 20th-century political divisions cannot erase Ireland's strong ties to its united past. Its four provinces reflect the island's ancient kingdoms: Leinster in the east, Connacht in the west, Ulster in the north and Munster in the south. Even though they hold no official significance today, they are still important historically and culturally, featuring in regional literature, and often referred to in poetry and song as 'the four green fields'.

Ireland's landscape is surprisingly varied given its size. Much of the coastline is backed by a rim of mountains and sea cliffs, while a limestone plain spreads across the interior, where the terrain ranges from flat pasture to rolling hills, with winding rivers and lakeland regions. Much of the land is agricultural. The ancient oak forests are long gone, but there are still vast stretches of peat bog in the central and northwestern regions.

POLITICS

Although the violent clashes known as 'the Troubles' came largely to an end with the Good Friday Agreement of 1998 (▷ 38–39), peace in Northern Ireland remains the biggest political issue on the island. The problems of the province are often simplified by outsiders as being a religious conflict between Catholics and Protestants, but the reality involves more complex economic, social and political issues. About 60 per cent of the population of Northern Ireland are Protestant. Both the Unionists (who want the status quo of union with Britain) and the Nationalists (who wish for Irish unity) have long historical ties to their positions.

The implementation of a devolved Assembly in Northern Ireland, with the main opposing parties sharing power, has been difficult. Since October 2002, the Democratic Unionists, led by the Reverend Ian Paisley, have refused to sit in government with Sinn Féin, led by Gerry Adams, over concerns that a rogue branch of the Irish Republican Army—called the Real IRA—is still active. Talks took place at the end of 2004 to try to get the power sharing back on track. When these issues are resolved, the Assembly will have legislative powers over social and economic policy in Northern Ireland. Only time will tell if the province becomes part of a united Ireland at some point in the future or remains part of the UK.

The Republic is a parliamentary democracy. The Oireachtas (National Parliament) consists of the president and two houses: Dáil Éireann (House of Representatives), with 166 members (Teachta Dála or TDs), and Seanad Éireann (Senate), with 60 senators. Both are elected through a system of proportional representation.

The president is the head of state and is elected directly by the people for a term of seven years, with a limit of two terms. Although the president does not have an executive or policy-making role, he or she may still influence legislation. Mary Robinson, a lawyer who served as president from 1990 to 1997, championed civil liberties. Under her term of office, homosexuality was decriminalized and divorce was made legal, despite fierce opposition from the Catholic Church. She was succeeded by Mary McAleese, the current president, now in her second term.

The Head of the Government, or Taoiseach (pronounced 'tea-shook'), is nominated by the Dáil and appointed by the President. Bertie Ahern has served as Taoiseach since 1997. The two main political parties are Fianna Fáil and Fine Gael, and there are several smaller parties as well. The last general election, in May 2002, resulted in a coalition government of Fianna Fáil and the Progressive Democrats. The Republic of Ireland is a member of the European Union.

HERITAGE

Ireland's rich heritage stretches back to prehistoric times. Megalithic tombs, cairns and stone circles scattered throughout the countryside are testimony to an ancient and mysterious race. Along with remnants of primitive dwellings, such as ring forts and *crannógs* (artificial islands built on lakes), they lend a sense of wonder and timelessness to an exploration of the island.

Early Irish craftsmen were making impressive weapons and exquisite gold jewellery as far back as the Bronze Age. These skills were enhanced by the Celtic people who came to Ireland from Europe in the sixth century BC. Celtic art features interlaced geometric patterns and stylized animals, often carved on stonework. Its motifs are still used in traditional Irish arts and crafts.

A gift shop on the Aran Islands, selling the famous knitwear (left). Crossing Carrick-a-Rede rope bridge at sunset (middle). Misty clouds hang over the mountains of the Ring of Kerry (right)

The early Christian era gave Ireland some of its most striking architecture. The slender round towers, unique to the island, and tall, elaborately carved high crosses are key features of monastic sites around the country such as Glendalough and Clonmacnoise. From the seventh to the ninth centuries, while the rest of Europe was in the Dark Ages, art and learning flourished in Ireland's monasteries. Celtic decorative arts reached their zenith in magnificent illustrated manuscripts such as the Book of Kells.

The Anglo-Normans brought Romanesque and Gothic churches, and monastic sites such as Jerpoint Abbey. In eastern counties, you can find the ruins of a few of the early Norman castles. Most of Ireland's 2,500 castles and fortified tower houses date from the late 12th to the 16th centuries and are in the west and southwest. During the 1700s and early 1800s, the aristocracy built splendid neoclassical mansions such as Castle Coole and Bantry House, and Dublin acquired the elegant Georgian squares for which it is famous.

The art, literature, music, theatre and culture of Ireland are again in the spotlight, as Cork is one of the cities to be a European Capital of Culture in 2005.

ECONOMICS

Ireland joined the European Economic Community, forerunner of the European Union (EU), in 1973, and by the 1990s it was one of Europe's biggest success stories. The lowering of trade barriers expanded the market for Irish goods, while EU aid helped Ireland to modernize its economy. Between 1995 and 2002, annual growth averaged an impressive 8 per cent, making it the fastest growing economy in the industrialized world. Ireland became known as the Celtic Tiger, and for the first time in decades, Ireland's young people no longer had to seek work abroad. Despite the global slowdown of the past couple of years, Ireland outranks the four big European economies in per capita GDP by 10 per cent.

In the past decade, Ireland has prospered by creating favourable conditions for foreign investment, such as low corporation taxes. Ireland's young, well-educated workforce is also highly attractive to overseas firms—more than 1,000 have moved here, nearly half of them from the US, including leading computer software and information technology companies. Many firms have their European call centres based here.

Around 60 per cent of Irish workers are employed in the services sector, which now accounts for half of the country's GDP. Electronics, pharmaceuticals, financial services and telemarketing are other leading industries. Tourism is one of the fastest growing economic sectors. Agriculture remains an important factor in the economy, particularly livestock production. Prosperity has also brought a boom in the construction industry, not only in Dublin but all around the country.

Ireland enthusiastically embraced the euro as its official currency in 2002.

THE IRISH

The Republic of Ireland is a nation of 3.9 million people. Its population is young, with about 37 per cent under the age of 25. About 1.7 million people live in Northern Ireland.

The official language of the Republic of Ireland is Irish, one of the Celtic languages related to the Scottish Gaelic. Around 35 per cent of the population have a knowledge of it, and it's widely spoken on the west coast, in Gaeltacht areas. The second official language, English, is spoken almost everywhere (▷ 341).

Though attitudes are becoming more relaxed in certain respects, many people in Ireland remain deeply religious. In the Republic around 92 per cent are Roman Catholic (around 40 per cent in Northern Ireland). The importance of religion is noticeable in just about every aspect of life, from conversation and statues to law and politics.

The Irish are famous for their friendly humour and wit. There's no better place to enjoy it than the pub, the hub of Irish social life. Even if you don't drink alcohol, come for the *craic*—the Irish word for fun. This often involves an impromptu session of Irish music, with everyone who is able joining in. Ireland's great literary tradition sprang from its ancient bards, and throughout the land tall tales and good conversation flow as freely as the Guinness. It is a country in which no one is a stranger for long.

Horse traders at the Ould Lammas Fair in Ballycastle (left). A Celtic cross, silhouetted against the evening sky, on the Aran Islands (middle). The majestic cliffs of Fair Head in County Antrim (right)

IRELAND AT A GLANCE

Dublin The Republic of Ireland's vibrant capital has lively pubs, restaurants and nightclubs, and numerous historical and contemporary attractions. It has a population of nearly 1,028,000. Over 40 per cent of the population of the Republic lives within 97km (60 miles) of Dublin.

The East Bordering the Irish Sea, the eastern counties contain some of the country's most visited attractions. North of Dublin, the ancient sites of the Boyne Valley lie in County Meath, while County Louth has outstanding monastic ruins. Inland along the border with Northern Ireland, Monaghan and Cavan are quiet lakeland counties. West of Dublin, Ireland's famous racehorses are bred in the rolling pastures of County Kildare, home of the National Stud. South of the capital are the Wicklow Mountains, with Powerscourt Gardens and the monastic site of Glendalough, leading south to Wexford and its wildfowl reserve. Inland are counties Carlow and Kilkenny, with a fine castle and medieval sites.

The South The bustling city of Waterford, along the south coast, is famous for its crystal glassworks, while the surrounding county has pretty harbours, fishing villages and market towns. Inland, bordering the Midlands and the East, County Tipperary is ringed by low mountains that form the backdrop to attractive river valleys, historic towns such as Clonmel and Caher, and the famous Rock of Cashel. Bordering the West is County Limerick, whose northern boundary is defined by Ireland's longest river, the Shannon. Limerick, Ireland's fourth-largest city and western international gateway, has a historic hub with fine churches, museums and galleries. Many castles, both ruined and restored, dot the rolling landscape that leads to lovely beaches on the coast. Inland are picturesque villages such as Adare, and the Stone Age settlement of Lough Gur. The dramatic scenery of counties Cork and Kerry in the island's southwestern corner makes them among the most visited regions of Ireland. Killarney and Kenmare make good bases for driving the famous Ring of Kerry, round one of several wild, rocky peninsulas that stretch into the sea. To the north, the Dingle Peninsula lies west from Tralee with rugged mountains, stunning seascapes, and fascinating ancient forts and beehive huts. Cork is Ireland's second-largest city, known for its art and music scene. Nearby is the famous Blarney Castle and the picturesque coastal town of Kinsale.

The West Bordered by the Atlantic Ocean, the South and the Midlands, the western counties have some of the most fascinating scenery in Ireland. North of the River Shannon, County Clare is home to the stark limestone plateau called The Burren and the towering Cliffs of Moher. Ennis is its largest town. County Galway's capital is lively Galway City, set on Galway Bay. Offshore are the largely Irish-speaking Aran Islands. Between here and Clifden stretches Connemara, with its rugged sea coasts, mountains and heathlands. Westport is the main town in County Mayo, home to Croagh Patrick and the miraculous shrine of Knock. It is a large county of vast boglands, lonely headlands and dramatic sea cliffs. From Sligo Town visit County Sligo's picturesque coastline, mountains, lakes and forests that inspired the poet W. B. Yeats. There are also many prehistoric sites. Carrick-on-Shannon is the capital of nearby County Leitrim. County Donegal in the northwestern corner borders Northern Ireland. Donegal Town and Letterkenny are the biggest towns in this large but sparsely populated region. Its stunning Atlantic coastline is studded with rocky inlets, towering cliffs and deserted beaches.

The Midlands The defining features of the landlocked Midlands are the many loughs that dot the landscape and the vast stretches of bogland that cover much of counties Offaly and Laois. Clonmacnoise is one of Ireland's finest ecclesiastical sites. The Georgian town of Birr has delightful castle gardens. County Westmeath boasts the region's largest town, Athlone, and the country's largest castle, Tullynally. It adjoins counties Longford and Roscommon; in the latter is Strokestown Park and the Famine Museum.

Northern Ireland Belfast is the province's capital, with attractive city buildings. The coast of County Antrim has some of Ireland's most spectacular scenery, including the famous Giant's Causeway with its dramatic cliffs and volcanic rocks, as well as quaint fishing villages and Carrickfergus Castle. The Mountains of Mourne rise along the coast in the southeast corner of County Down, which has several sites linked to St. Patrick around Downpatrick. The historic city of Armagh is in nearby County Armagh, as is the huge Lough Neagh. To the west is County Tyrone with the Ulster American Folk Park. Enniskillen is the main city of County Fermanagh, a lakeland county with many attractions set around Lough Erne. The walled city of Derry is in County Londonderry, which has a fine stretch of coast.

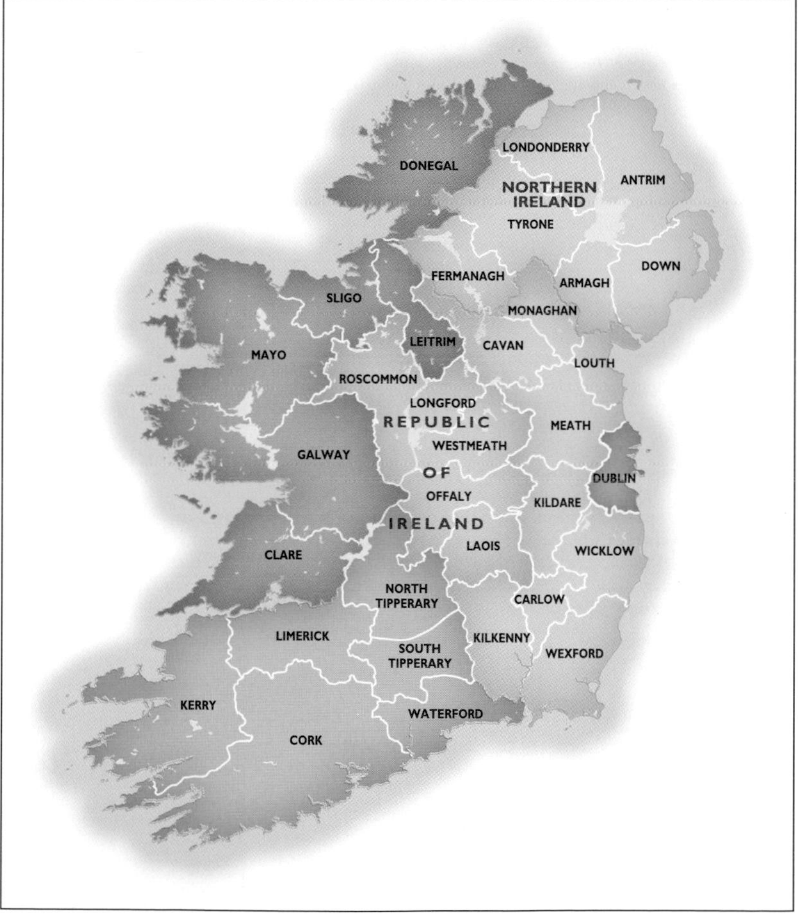

THE BEST OF IRELAND

DUBLIN

Book of Kells (▷ 84, 86) This magnificent ninth-century illuminated manuscript in the Old Library at Trinity College represents the height of Celtic artistic achievement.

Christ Church Cathedral and St. Patrick's Cathedral (▷ 68 and 82) Dublin's two grand cathedrals are filled with monuments to historic figures, from Strongbow to Jonathan Swift.

Dublin Castle (▷ 70–71) Historic heart of the city, the castle has Viking and Norman foundations and lavish State Apartments.

Guinness Storehouse (▷ 73) Drink a pint of Ireland's most famous brew while enjoying the view from the rooftop bar.

Howth Head (▷ 74) Take the cliff walk out beyond Howth Harbour for sweeping sea views over the bay.

Kilmainham Gaol (▷ 76–77) Learn the poignant history of the Irish fight for independence on a tour of the jail where Irish rebels were held and executed.

The National Museum (▷ 80–81) Marvel at the stunning gold jewellery and other treasures that make up the largest collection of Celtic artefacts in the world.

St. Stephen's Green (▷ 83) Do as the locals do—relax on a park bench and watch the passers-by.

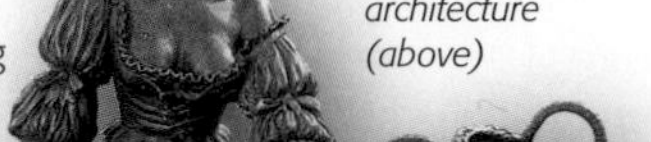

Dublin's Georgian architecture (above)

THE EAST

Boyne Valley (▷ 256–257) Drive through beautiful scenery to visit fine monastic sites and the seat of the High Kings at Tara.

Brú na Bóinne (▷ 90–93) Tour the mysterious passage tombs at Newgrange and Knowth, over 5,000 years old and among the world's most important prehistoric sites.

Glendalough (▷ 94–95) Set in a valley beside two lakes, this is one of Ireland's foremost and loveliest early Christian sites.

Kilkenny (▷ 100–101) After touring the magnificent cathedral, castle and Black Abbey, explore the medieval alleyways and lively streets of this delightful historic town.

National Stud and Japanese Gardens (▷ 98–99) Learn the secret of breeding Ireland's finest racehorses at the National Stud in Kildare, and enjoy the charming Japanese Gardens.

Powerscourt Gardens (▷ 104–105) Enjoy the superb view from the terrace, then wander through the beautiful gardens.

Wexford (▷ 96) See how early settlers lived from Mesolithic to Norman times at the Irish National Heritage Park.

Wicklow Mountains (▷ 242–243) Take a walk along the Wicklow Way in the Wicklow Mountains National Park.

Molly Malone statue (above), one of many fine examples of sculpture in Dublin. St. Fiachra's Garden, Kildare (below)

A pegasus statue at Powerscourt Gardens (left)

Lofty view over Derrynane on the Ring of Kerry (below)

THERE IS NO CHARGE FOR KISSING THE BLARNEY STONE. REMOVE HATS, GLASSES AND SECURE JACKET POCKETS.

THE SOUTH

Blarney Castle (▷ 111) Kiss the Blarney Stone at one of Ireland's most famous castles.

Cork City (▷ 112–113) Explore the picturesque lanes of the old French Quarter, in the heart of Ireland's second city.

Dingle Peninsula (▷ 116–119) Duck inside the curious beehive huts, among the many antique sites on this scenic peninsula.

THE BEST OF IRELAND

Dolphins inhabit the warm waters of the west coast, notably Dingle Bay

Kinsale (▷ 122) Enjoy a seafood meal in one of the highly acclaimed restaurants in this pretty harbour town.

Ring of Kerry (▷ 260–261) Drive the most famous scenic route in western Ireland, but start early to avoid the many tour buses.

Rock of Cashel (▷ 125) Walk up to the top of this monumental fortress church, an impressive sight from above and below.

Sheen Falls Lodge (▷ 314) Relax at this former fishing lodge, now a beautiful luxury hotel on the banks of the Sheen River.

Take a sea cruise to the Skelligs (▷ 274) and spot dolphins and other wildlife along the way.

Waterford (▷ 126–127) Shop for a special piece of glassware at Waterford Crystal.

THE WEST

The Burren (▷ 134–135) Walk out across the limestone and look for the tiny wild flowers that brighten this barren landscape.

Carrowmore Neolithic Cemetery (▷ 133) See the passage graves, standing stones and other remains of one of Europe's oldest and largest prehistoric graveyards.

Cliffs of Moher (▷ 133) Enjoy the awesome view from the top of these coastal cliffs, but expect to share this prime beauty spot with the crowds.

Connemara (▷ 138–141) Mountains, lakes, boglands and a jagged coastline of rocky bays and islets make this one of the most scenic areas of the country.

County Mayo (▷ 264–265) Drive from stunning seascapes to remote mountains to lonely stretches of blanket bog that are amazing in their vastness.

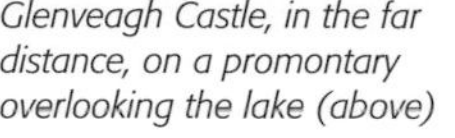

Glenveagh Castle, in the far distance, on a promontary overlooking the lake (above)

A stylized bronze of W. B. Yeats in Sligo town (right)

Celtic crosses, such as this one at Clonmacnoise (below), are a feature of many religious sites in Ireland

Galway City (▷ 142) Bright shop-fronts and medieval buildings line the cobbled streets in this lively university town.

Glencolumbkille (▷ 143) It's well worth the drive to this remote Gaeltacht village to see its excellent folk museum surrounded by beautiful scenery.

Glenveagh National Park (▷ 143 and 250–251) Stroll through the stunning gardens amid beautiful mountains and woodland.

Gregans Castle (▷ 315) Escape from it all at this hotel in the heart of The Burren and enjoy the views towards Galway Bay.

Sligo (▷ 146–147) Base yourself in this lively town, for music and the arts, and the enchanting landscape that influenced poet W. B. Yeats.

THE MIDLANDS

Blackwater Bog (▷ 150) Take a trip on a narrow-gauge train for a close-up look at the boglands and learn how they were formed.

Birr (▷ 151) Admire the splendid gardens of Birr Castle, with plants from around the world, and see the Great Telescope.

Clonmacnoise (▷ 154–157) Admire the elaborate stone-carved high crosses, round towers and ruined churches at this important early Christian monastery.

Strokestown Park and Famine Museum (▷ 158–159) Visit the Famine Museum, where the tragedy of the famine years is movingly portrayed.

Water sports (▷ 160 and 226–228) Take to the water with a spot of fishing on Lough Ree or a canoe trip on the River Shannon.

THE BEST OF IRELAND

NORTHERN IRELAND

Armagh (▷ 165) Two historic cathedrals grace the skyline of one of Ireland's oldest cities, founded in the time of St. Patrick.
Belfast (▷ 166–171) Attend a performance to see the lavish interior of the city's Grand Opera House.
Derry (▷ 176) Walk around the ramparts of the 17th-century town walls and admire the historic buildings within.
Giant's Causeway (▷ 178–179) Walk (carefully) along the volcanic stepping stones of Northern Ireland's most popular sight.
Glens of Antrim (▷ 180) Hike the scenic trails in the glacier-carved glens that wind up from the scenic Antrim Coast Road.
Lough Erne (▷ 182–183) Take a boat trip to White Island to see the strange carved figures on the old church.
Shu (▷ 299) Visit this chic Belfast restaurant and enjoy the relaxed atmosphere as you sample the eclectic menu.
Ulster American Folk Park (▷ 188) Re-live the experience of Ulster immigrants to the New World during the famine years.

The Big Fish on Belfast's Laganside

A traditional Guinness pub advertisement (above)

Two essential ingredients at the Galway Oyster Festival (left)

TOP EXPERIENCES

Attend a *céili* where you can watch reels, jigs and other traditional dances. Set dancing is big in the west and you can even join in!
Brush up on Ireland's literary history on a Literary Pub Crawl in Dublin (▷ 274), and visit the Dublin Writers Museum (▷ 72).
Drink Guinness with the locals in a pub, or tour the Guinness Storehouse and have a pint in the Gravity Bar (▷ 73).
Drive along the Antrim Coast, a spectacular scenic route that begins north of Belfast and runs all the way to the Giant's Causeway (▷ 178–179).
Eat some Galway Bay oysters, wild salmon or mussel soup—Ireland offers excellent fresh seafood.
Experience Ireland's famous passion for horses Attend a race meeting and maybe even place a small bet (▷ 196).
Get sporty Play a round of golf at one of Ireland's many courses (▷ 196), or visit Croke Park to watch a Gaelic football or hurling match (▷ 68).
Hop on a ferry to Achill Island (▷ 130) or to the Aran Islands (▷ 131) for the sense of tradition and timelessness.
Listen to some live, traditional music; some of the best can be found in villages on the south and west coasts.
Marvel at the views Look out from the high ramparts of a castle tower and admire the view, such as that over the River Boyne from the castle at Trim (▷ 106).
Pack a picnic and head for a remote spot on the Beara (▷ 109), Mizen or Sheep's Head peninsulas (▷ 124). They're less busy but just as scenic as the Ring of Kerry.
Party on St. Patrick's Day or at one of the many other festivals around the country.
Seek out Ireland's prehistoric sites The remote, less-visited sites are often the most rewarding and retain a sense of ancient spirituality (▷ 63–188).
Shop for traditional Irish goods such as Aran sweaters or Donegal tweed.
Take a hike From woodland strolls to cliff-top rambles along the coast, there are walks to suit everyone (▷ 241–253).
Trace your ancestors Every region has local offices that can help (▷ 344).
Watch a sunset from the Cliffs of Moher (▷ 133) or any number of scenic spots on Ireland's west coast.

Throughout Ireland, pubs host live music sessions (above). Bright costumes feature in the St. Patrick's Day parades (below)

Living Ireland

Tourists still like to buy leprechauns (far left)

St. Patrick's Day in Dublin (left)

Ireland's famous brew (below)

Hip Hibernia

Belfast nightlife

As Ireland grows more confident and more prosperous, a distinctive sense of style has emerged. Dublin takes its cool image seriously, as a young, fashion-conscious and cash-rich generation demands chic bars, clubs, shops and hotels. In 21st-century Irish style, Celtic meets European with lots of Eastern and trans-Atlantic influences, and local designers are given every opportunity to impress. In Dublin, don't go north of the River Liffey if you want to follow the current style icons, mostly figures from the world of music, like Bono, The Thrills, Ronan Keating and Westlife. These are the new leaders of fashion, and the good causes, artists and restaurants they patronize are sure to be well supported. Organizers of big events in the young, sharp-edged capital will want A-list celebrities like actor Colin Farrell and Rugby Union star Brian O'Driscoll to be present, while ex-Formula One driver Eddie Irvine always attracts attention. Although Dublin likes to think it is the leader of fashion, Belfast and Cork also have boutique hotels, hip clubs, sleek restaurants and designer shops, which highlight local talent and demonstrate individual modern style. Customers may find them less pretentious and not as expensive as those in Dublin.

Celebrity aisle

The Irish have been delighted and a little bemused at the number of celebrities who have chosen to marry in Ireland. Famously, Sir Paul McCartney married Heather Mills at romantic Castle Leslie in Glaslough, County Monaghan, in June 2002. Sir Paul explained that Monaghan was the chosen venue because his mother came from the county. The sleepy village was surprised by the glamorous extravaganza, and by the famous faces who attended. Host for the day was 84-year-old, Sir John Leslie, whose family have owned the property since the 17th century. The couple were married in the private St. Salvator chapel on the grounds and the reception followed in giant lakeside marquees, with a pontoon and a luxury boat alongside.

Westlife's Nicky Byrne and his wife, Georgina (below), daughter of Ireland's prime minister

Traditional food in Temple Bar (above)

Real women, real success

Ireland's most famous fashion designer, Paul Costelloe, claims to get more pleasure from seeing his designs worn on the street than being paraded on the catwalk. His clothes are fashioned with 'real women' in mind, rather than wafer-thin supermodels, and his trademark, timeless elegance has made his clothes sought after in the most stylish stores throughout the world. The 'Costelloe' brand made a significant breakthrough when the late Diana, Princess of Wales, started to wear his creations. Subsequently, Ireland's first woman president, the stylish and charismatic Mary Robinson, made a point of choosing the Costelloe label. Preferring fabrics which must be 'good and fluid', he has repeatedly turned to the special qualities of Irish linen for inspiration, and has based his factory shop at the Linen Green in Dungannon, Co. Tyrone.

***Remnants of Light* by Victoria Rothschild in a Temple Bar Gallery (above). Robbie Williams in concert at Slane Castle (right)**

Pop and politics

Many people in Ireland were intrigued in 2003 when the daughter of the Taoiseach (or prime minister), Bertie Ahern, married a star of the boy band Westlife. Childhood sweethearts, Georgina Ahern and Nicky Byrne wore jeans and baseball caps at a low-key civil ceremony in Wicklow, but four days later exchanged their vows in church followed by a lavish celebration. It was a glitzy affair, with friends of the couple from the worlds of showbiz and professional football, and entertainment provided by the likes of Ronan Keating. Despite the father of the bride's position, there was not a politician in sight. To the disappointment of many, however, the wedding took place, not in a romantic Irish setting, but in a French château.

Rankin's revival

When Paul Rankin and his Canadian wife Jeanne came to Belfast in the 1980s, they bravely opened their chic new restaurant Roscoff (today called Cayenne) in a city which was not previously noted for gastronomy. Rankin quickly acquired a reputation for adventurous and stylish cuisine, always based on the best local produce. The stylish restaurateur, now a television celebrity, has trained a generation of new chefs, including Robbie Millar of Shanks restaurant, and his influence has made the Belfast area a gastronomic hub. His empire extends to airport cafés, Roscoff brasseries, a range of speciality Irish breads, including wheaten bracks, potato bread and soda farls, which are available in supermarkets, and the *Gourmet Ireland* gift hamper selection.

Castle rock

The dashing head of the Conyngham family, Lord Henry Mount Charles, plays host to the greatest stars of world music every summer at his picturesque estate at Slane Castle, the family home for three centuries. And he shares the occasion with 80,000 fans. Since 1981, the elegant Irish peer has brought mega-names to his estate on the banks of the River Boyne. U2, David Bowie, Bob Dylan, The Rolling Stones, Robbie Williams, Queen and Bruce Springsteen have all played at Slane, and in 2004 Madonna headed the bill, causing controversy by playing on a Sunday, a decision not welcomed by all in this quiet, and traditionally religious, rural village. Celebrity guests have coveted invitations to watch the concerts from the castle battlements.

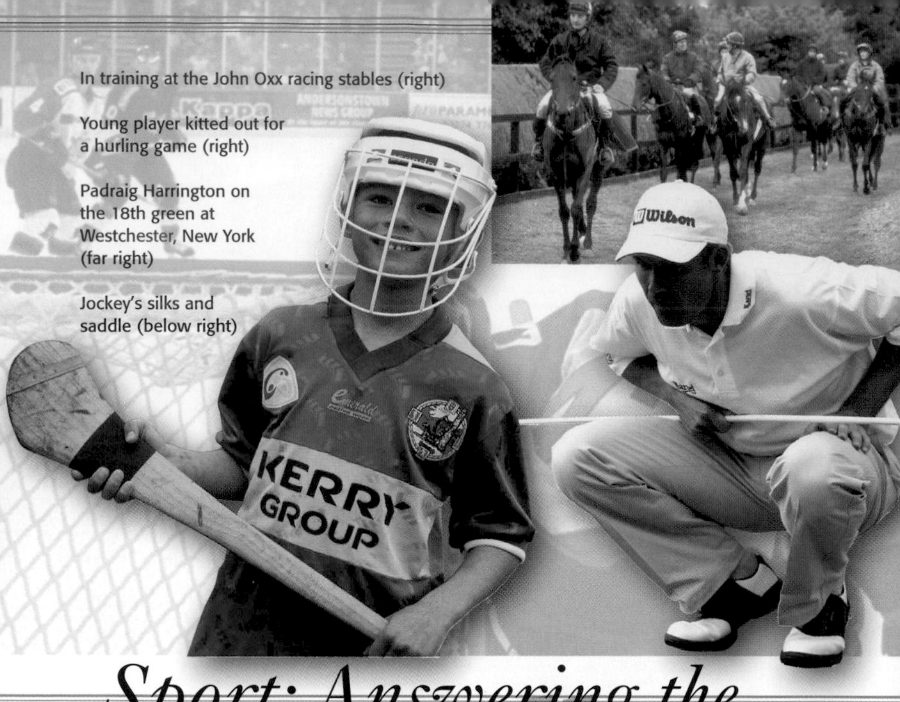

In training at the John Oxx racing stables (right)

Young player kitted out for a hurling game (right)

Padraig Harrington on the 18th green at Westchester, New York (far right)

Jockey's silks and saddle (below right)

Sport: Answering the Call

Sam's your man

Don't be surprised if you hear many references to 'Sam' in Irish pubs through August and September. 'Sam' will be spoken of with considerable reverence, affection and a good deal of nervous anxiety. The 'Sam' in question is the Sam Maguire Cup, the trophy for the All Ireland final of the Gaelic football competition played among the 32 Irish counties (that is, those in both the Republic and Northern Ireland). The passion of the support is intense, and visitors can tell when they cross from one county to another by the change in the flags proudly flown throughout. The victorious county team will parade 'Sam' from village to village, and the trophy has become a bit battered from years of celebration, as serious partying follows every All Ireland success.

Players in the Irish rugby team come from both north and south of the border, and compete as a united country under the flag of the Irish rugby football union. A stirring anthem has been adopted which transcends political divides and before the big international matches at Lansdowne Road in Dublin members of the team lock arms and sing 'Come the day and come the hour, come the power and the glory, we have come to answer our country's call, from the four proud provinces of Ireland . . .'

Many other sporting bodies, including boxing, hockey and swimming, also draw their international teams from both sides of the political border, but others, such as soccer, field individual teams from Northern Ireland and the Republic. The Gaelic sports of hurling and football for men and camogie for women, now thriving abroad, have keenly fought competitions within the country. Prepare to be amazed at the combative style of these intensely exciting, fast and physical Gaelic games—some played without the protection of padding or helmets. Tickets for the major international games and finals are hard to come by, but are easily available at interprovincial and county level.

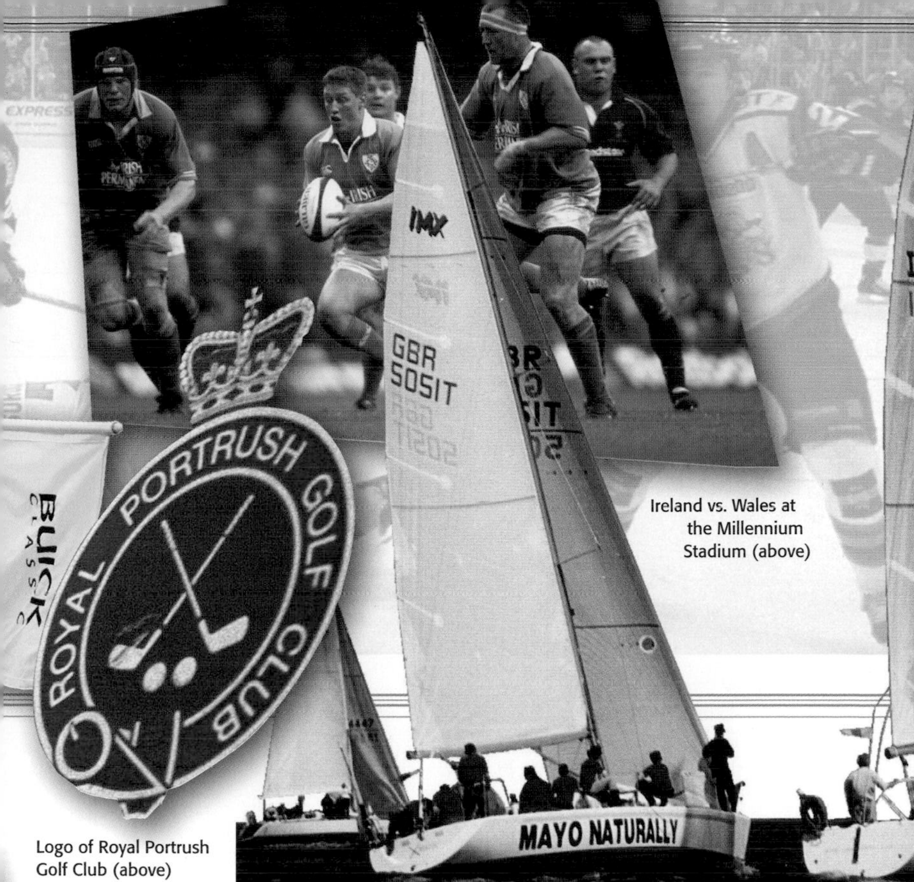

Ireland vs. Wales at the Millennium Stadium (above)

Logo of Royal Portrush Golf Club (above)

The biennial Round Ireland Race (right)

Racing the tide

It was, they say, the idea of a local priest, in 1876, to start one of Ireland's most extraordinary horse-racing meetings, held each August or September at Laytown, about 46km (29 miles) north of Dublin. It is the only horse race in the world, organized under Jockey Club rules, that is held on a beach. The length of the course is an inexact science, laid out in haste as the tide goes out, but it's around one or two miles of an expansive strand. The finish line has a wonderful backdrop of surf, the going can never be said to be 'firm', the grandstand is in the dunes, and the jockeys have to race not only the other horses, but sometimes the tide as well!

Stadium saga

A frustrating quest to build a national stadium for major events has so far failed because of financial problems, lack of agreement on sites and logistics, and the Gaelic Athletic Association's reluctance to share facilities with rugby and soccer, which they regard as 'foreign' games. The Gaelic games are currently staged in a first-rate stadium at Croke Park, Dublin, while rugby and soccer internationals take place in an increasingly decrepit, but much-loved, stadium at Lansdowne Road. Observers wait with interest to see if G.A.A officials will allow the 'foreign' games to use Croke Park while Lansdowne Road is redeveloped.

Bullets

Despite its alarming name, the game of bullets is frightening only if you happen upon it unprepared. This traditional sport is really a form of road bowls. Played in counties Cork and Armagh (but not exclusively), contestants throw iron balls at great speed along country roads, which are often winding and hilly, for a distance of about 4km (2.5 miles). Half the fun lies in the antics of the partisan camp followers who support the contestants. The cry of 'wey-hay' (bullets' equivalent of golf's 'fore!') isn't much use to the unwary driver who happens to be coming in the other direction. The bullets season is in May and June, and local pubs are the best source for information.

Special occasion

Ireland can take pride in the way the Special Olympics were staged in June 2003. The nation was inspired by the ethos of the challenge, 'Let me win, but if I cannot win, let me be brave in the attempt.' Although there were plenty of celebrities—Arnold Schwarzenegger, U2, Nelson Mandela and Muhammad Ali were all present—it was the athletes and their friends, families and trainers, who were the real stars. The whole event went without a hitch and Ireland's corporate sponsors put their hands deep into their pockets. Each nation was hosted by a city, town or village, and the general concensus was that the hosts gained as much out of the experience as their guests.

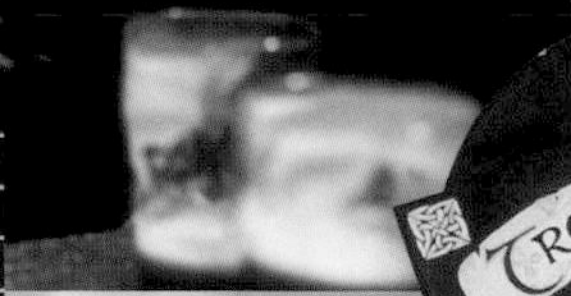

The pub is a popular part of Irish social life (above and top right)

The Harbour Café in Kinvarra (left). Pubs often stage live Irish music (right)

The Craic

To Irish men and women, there is nothing like a bit of *craic*. It's hard to define: Good-natured and relaxed, it involves laughter, conversation and sometimes a drink or two. Stout with a whiskey 'chaser' traditionally fuels many a good night. In Ireland any excuse will do for a celebration; birthdays and weddings are examples, and at many Irish weddings guests are invited to entertain the gathering. *Craic* is very inclusive. 'Wetting the head' of a new baby is another good reason for a night out—usually a party of lads supporting the new father. The Irish tradition of a 'wake' is a strong one: Family and friends meet to celebrate a life that is over. The Irish are great at acclaiming a fine sporting victory in style, but they are just as good at 'drowning their sorrows' in defeat.

Sin bin

Irish Rugby legend Peter Clohessy earned an international reputation as an abrasive and pugnacious prop forward, affectionately known to colleagues and opponents alike as The Claw. He served his province, Munster, and Ireland gallantly for many years, but his unofficial activities in the thick of the game often led to a warning yellow card from the referee and banishment to the 'sin bin' at the side of the pitch. It was no surprise, then, that when he retired from rugby and opened a bar and nightclub in his native Limerick, that he called it The Sin Bin. As the affable proprietor he now hosts many visiting athletes and teams.

***Slainte!* A happy participant of a street festival in Killala (left)**

Many of Ireland's music festivals feature both local and visiting performers (above)

Traditional music and dance at Galway's Oyster Festival (left and below)

The banter

A crucial element of Irish fun is 'the banter', and it's a form of humour that visitors can sometimes misinterpret. Essentially it's a type of teasing. In Ireland it's natural to engage casual acquaintances in conversation but beware of the seemingly innocent question, asked with an angelic smile, addressed to the unwary. The Irish, north and south, have developed a comprehensive vocabulary to identify potential jokers, including 'Are you having me on?,' 'taking the mick,' 'jossing,' 'messing' or 'gegging'. When Irish people 'banter', it can sometimes sound like outright abuse, but this humour is linked to a delight in the ludicrous. Just don't take it too seriously.

Meet your match?

A good way to be sure of finding some fun is to follow the trail to the Matchmaking Festival in the normally sleepy town of Lisdoonvarna, where, traditionally, single farming men and girls came to find a partner. Europe's largest match-making festival retains much of its original character and Ireland's last remaining matchmaker, Willie Daly, still presides over the proceedings, which take place in late summer (after the harvest), but much of the fun is tongue-in-cheek. Afternoon dances are one way to meet the right partner, although today's singles may prefer the organized speed-dating or music bars which go on late into the night.

Café society or alfresco fun

The Republic of Ireland government has followed the lead of New York by imposing a total ban on smoking in most public places, including bars and restaurants. One result of this is that traditional pub culture has spilled out into the streets, with many bar owners providing outside tables, Parisian-style, for those who feel they need a smoke. Although not quite the Champs-Élysées, the elegant Georgian streets of the capital lend themselves to boulevard merriment, and portable gas heaters are often provided to take the chill off the air. One enterprizing publican attempted to dodge the ban by setting up a double-decker bus outside his premises, but officials insisted it was contravening the law.

Whiskey with an e

An essential element of Ireland's pub culture and the *craic*, Irish whiskey is different from Scotch, not only because it's spelled with an 'e'. Irish distillers claim that their whiskey is lighter and smoother than its Scottish counterpart. The Irish also claim to have the oldest licensed distillery in the world at Bushmills (note the word 'licensed': The tradition of distilling poteen, illegally, goes much farther back). Irish whiskey fans will also point out that its distilling process usually takes longer—why rush something so important? And finally, where would we be without Irish coffee? Visitors can decide for themselves in the rivalry between Scotch and Irish whiskey by taking one of the distillery tours and sampling the product.

The Guinness toucan was a popular advertising icon (right)

The Irish Financial Services building (right)
Giant cranes in the Belfast shipyards (background)

Celtic Tiger Still at Large

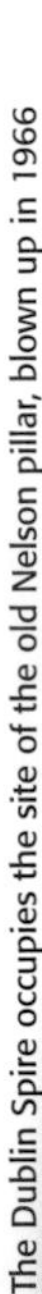
The Dublin Spire occupies the site of the old Nelson pillar, blown up in 1966

Ireland's phenomenal economic success, which in the 1990s earned it the tag the 'Celtic tiger', continues, though at a less meteoric rate. Within the last decade the economy has grown by 80 per cent, and with it has come a feeling of prosperity and national confidence. Growth has been mainly in the service sector, supported by technical investment and the success of an incentive-based campaign to attract multinational investors. A major factor has been Ireland's shrewd policy of maximizing the advantages of European Union membership. Unemployment, for so long a scourge throughout Ireland, has practically disappeared. The infrastructure of transport and telecommunications has improved markedly and Ireland's education system is judged to be serving the demands of the new industrial and technological employers. A very wealthy top tier of society has emerged and demands for a luxury lifestyle have pushed up prices, especially in bars, hotels and restaurants. The price of housing has rocketed, which analysts see as a potential threat to future growth. There is still much hardship, however, and poverty and urban deprivation pose significant social problems. The republic's welfare and health benefits are improving, but sometimes still lag behind those enjoyed in Northern Ireland.

The Spire of Dublin

The Spire of Dublin, in the city's principal thoroughfare, O'Connell Street, was erected in 2003 to replace Nelson's Column, blown up by extremists in 1966. As a monument to celebrate the millennium, it is regarded as a bold symbol of national confidence. A slim needle of stainless steel, 120m (394ft) tall, 3m (10ft) wide at the base and tapering to 15cm (6in), it is designed to look stunning throughout the day. Initial problems with the self-cleaning material and the LED lights at the top, are being addressed, but Dubliners have not lost the opportunity to poke fun at the monument and its environment. Mostly known colloquially as the 'spike', other nicknames include 'the skewer in the sewer' and 'the stick in the sick'.

Waterfront Hall and the Hilton Hotel on Belfast's waterfront (right)

Ian Paisley, leader of the Democratic Unionists (below)

Bertie Ahern visiting Tony Blair in London in 2003 (left)

Tunnel vision

Dublin's notorious rush-hour traffic congestion looks set to be eased by the ambitious Luas tram system—completed in 2004—which links the southern suburbs with the heart of the city. The aim is to supply sophisticated and efficient public transportation for the capital's commuters. Another solution lies in people bicycling to work, and, with 200km (125 miles) of bicycle lanes, thousands of lock-up positions and a relatively flat city, it's estimated that 25,000 Dubliners now choose pedal power. A plan to 'hoover' heavy goods vehicles off the streets by siphoning them into the new and expensive Port Tunnel, has run into an embarrassing problem, however: The 'Leprechaun' tunnel is 25cm (10in) too low for the new generation of monster trucks!

Tower block turn around

Ireland's new wealth has put into sharp contrast the country's acute social difficulties. The problems at Ballymun, a 1960s north Dublin housing estate, had reached crisis proportions by 1985. By then the available housing there, including seven high-rise blocks, had become badly rundown and was used for housing homeless and single people, in an area with limited employment opportunities. The area's regeneration began with a community-led initiative, and now Ballymun Regeneration Ltd has embarked on a radical plan to build a new town, demolishing six tower blocks, and providing housing based on quality design, matched by sustainable local employment, strong links with the nearby Dublin City University, and robust community involvement. The pioneering project at Ballymun has attracted a great deal of international attention.

Ryder riches

Nowhere is the new wealth of Ireland more evident than at the opulent K-Club in County Kildare. Owned by the Smurfit Group, founded by entrepreneur Michael Smurfit, the complex represents the last word in luxury, and has been selected to host the 2006 Ryder Cup. This fiercely competitive golf tournament between Europe and the United States will come to Ireland for the first time, to a course designed by golf legend Arnold Palmer. Art meets affluence here in the Jack B. Yeats room, where a collection of paintings by Ireland's greatest 20th-century artist is held. The golf courses are dotted with luxury villas owned by celebrities, who no doubt appreciate not having to travel far to enjoy the 2006 golfing extravaganza.

Titanic quarter

The skyline of Belfast is dominated by two huge bright yellow cranes, dubbed 'Samson' and 'Goliath' by the citizens of the northern capital. It is unlikely, however, that these monsters of the shipbuilding industry will be in use again, as the order book of Belfast's proud shipbuilding yards has emptied in the past decade. Small-scale refurbishments and work for the oil industry have replaced the proud tradition of ocean-going liners in the dry-docks of Harland and Wolff. The 'Titanic Quarter', however, named after the most famous ship to slide down the slipway, is a scheme to turn the decaying dockland into a vibrant new commercial and residential development, and will extend the exciting urban renewal schemes along the River Lagan.

Trinity College's Old Library (right) has a wonderful collection of historic volumes

The Literary Trail in Dublin is marked by plaques such as this (below)

Hamlet, as performed at the 2003 Dublin Theatre Festival (below)

The Power of the Pen

A plaque on the Brides Close Flats in Dublin recalls *Gulliver's Travels*

Jedi or not?

Ireland has a legacy of wonderful libraries, of which the finest is unquestionably The Long Room at Trinity College, Dublin. Not only does it house the world-famous monastic manuscript, the Book of Kells, it also has the right to receive a copy of all material published in Britain and Ireland. Jonathan Swift, Oliver Goldsmith, Edmund Burke, William Congreve, J. M. Synge, Oscar Wilde and Samuel Beckett all studied here—but did the Jedi? Well, Thomas Burgh's 1732 architectural masterpiece bears an uncanny, some would say identical, similarity to the Jedi Archive in *Star Wars: Attack of the Clones* (2002). Lucas Films have denied any replication, but the suggestion of the cloning of the Library has led College authorities to stock *Star Wars* merchandise in the college shop.

It seems that the Irish have always had a gift for words. The Celtic saints, whose persuasive speech converted non-believers throughout medieval Europe, the bardic poets and the giants of modern literature all form part of a proud tradition in Ireland. Poets and writers are (nearly always) honoured in this country, although in the past, writers such as James Joyce and Samuel Beckett had to go into exile to create their best work. Most Irish writers now live here, encouraged by the tax benefits offered to those who create original works of cultural or artistic merit, and film-makers and screen writers also favour the Republic. The Abbey Theatre, founded by Yeats, still holds a pre-eminent place, and there are good local theatres everywhere. The Dublin Theatre Festival is a lively event, and the works of Marie Jones, a Belfast playwright with a sharp, analytical sense of humour, regularly transfer to London's West End.

Buildings associated with some of Ireland's great writers, however, have not been well preserved, and controversy has surrounded attempts to demolish the homes of W. B. Yeats, Seamus Heaney and C. S. Lewis. Lissadell, the house closely associated with the Celtic Revival, has recently been sold, despite pleas to retain it for the nation.

Film director Jim Sheridan, on set in the US (above)

The Dublin Theatre Festival 2003 included *Sharon's Grave* (right) and *Hurl* (below left)

Nobel laureate Seamus Heaney (below)

A scene from *The Commitments* (below)

Hope and history

Seamus Heaney, who won the Nobel Prize for Literature in 1995, is hugely respected throughout Ireland. A dignified and self-effacing man, he has given generously of his intellect and time to the community. He comes from a farming family in south Derry and his early poetry reflects the rural society of Ulster, while his subsequent work is marked by rigorous analysis and restrained and sensitive beauty. Before moving to Wicklow, he taught at Queen's University, Belfast, where a major literary centre bearing his name has recently opened. An excerpt from his translation of *The Cure at Troy* is often used as an evocation of a national aspiration for peace. He articulates the yearning that once in a lifetime 'hope and history rhyme'.

Hell's Kitchen—Dublin

Hell's Kitchen is familiar as an area of New York, but it's not so widely known that a leafy suburb of south Dublin also has a 'Hell's Kitchen' tag. Screenwriter and director of Academy award winning films, Jim Sheridan, named his Irish-based film production company after the area in New York where he lived with his family. It became the setting for his 2004 Oscar-nominated screenplay *In America* (2003), a treatment of the experiences of an immigrant family, which was to a large extent autobiographical and co-written with his daughters. Never afraid to be controversial, but with a sure directorial focus and a keen sense of humanity, Jim Sheridan has made a number of films that have an Irish theme including *My Left Foot* (1989), *In the Name of the Father* (1993), *Some Mother's Son* (1996) and *The Field* (1990).

Re-Joyce

16 June is Bloomsday, the day Dublin devotes itself to remembering James Joyce's *Ulysses*. Events mark the epic journeys of Stephen Dedalus and Leopold Bloom through its streets and pubs. Many of the landmarks along the way remain unchanged and Dubliners and visitors enjoy the opportunity to join in the spirit of the day and dress up as befitting the age of Leopold and Molly Bloom. At one level it's a serious literary homage to a great work of literature: At another level it's a good excuse for an actor-led pub crawl. And in 2004 Bloomsday got bigger, when the city decided to arrange a centenary festival around the event, starting with a breakfast for 10,000 in the city's principal thoroughfare, O'Connell Street.

Doyle's Dublin

The vitality and pathos of life in a north Dublin suburb is captured with extraordinary accuracy by the perceptive writer, Roddy Doyle. The former teacher delights in letting his vividly real characters inhabit an unglamorous landscape of run-down estates, schools and shopping complexes. His books are funny and popular, and are also critically acclaimed. *Paddy Clarke Ha Ha Ha* was awarded the prestigious Booker Prize in 1993, while the film *The Commitments* (1991), based on Doyle's gritty and hilarious novel, wowed film audiences with its story of a working-class soul band taking on the Dublin music scene. Doyle's historical novel, *A Star called Henry*, features the Dublin inner city slum landscape of the War of Independence.

Traditional rural houses often have spectacular views (far left)

Work at Muckross Traditional Farm (left). Country folk (below)

Rural Identity

The rural Ireland of picturesque thatched cottages and donkey carts, if it ever existed outside the film *The Quiet Man* (1952), has more or less disappeared. Today's Irish farmer is no quaint peasant, but a combination of business executive, environmentalist and agricultural expert, as the demands of European and domestic legislation, landscape management and market forces make the job of farming more demanding. However, almost all farms in Ireland are still family concerns, and are relatively small in scale. Farming families have become skilled in diversifying, through activities such as specialist food production, farmhouse bed-and-breakfast or holiday home rentals and leisure activities.

Because of the history of land legislation and absentee landlords, the typical Irish farmer jealously protects his holding; the ties with the land are strong. In fact, many city dwellers can trace their family back only one or two generations to the land, and rural traditions and practices are carried on in the big towns and cities. Only a small proportion (9 per cent) of the land is farmed for crops; the vast majority of Ireland's countryside is devoted to grass for pasture. It's the predominance of pasture that explains Ireland's description as 'The Emerald Isle', an effect of verdant greenness helped by the legendary amount of rain which waters its fields. Those green fields feed thriving herds of dairy and beef cows that produce top-quality meat, butter and cheese.

Agri-gourmets

As the agricultural industry meets the challenges of a shifting economy, farmers have diversified to maintain their incomes. One of the most successful ventures has been the production of specialist cheeses, made on family farms, from the yield of superb dairy herds, and also from sheep and goats' milk. Most of these delicious cheeses are handmade and wrapped on the farms, using skills that have been passed down through the generations. Look especially for the creamy Cashel Blue and the Camembert-style Cooleeney, which comes from Tipperary, and oak-smoked Gubbeen and Carrigaline Farmhouse from Cork. The taste of the award-winning Durrus reflects the salty conditions of the south-west tip of Ireland, where it is made.

A traditional jaunting car, with the owner's dog in pursuit (right)

Fish are cut open and left to dry on a roof on Aran's Inishmore (above)

Ferbane peat-fired generating plant (below)

Turf accounts

As with many aspects of Irish life, it was the rain that made the difference. High rainfall and bad drainage are the primary causes of the formation of the distinctive native landscape: the peat bog. Now environmentalists are worried about the protection of this extraordinary habitat. Country people have cut turf for burning for centuries, and neat piles of cut turf can be seen beside many farmhouses. The traditional cutting method was with a specially designed turf spade but once mechanization was introduced into the equation, the disappearance of bogs increased dramatically. The demand for peat for horticultural use created an additional threat. Steps have been taken to stop the destruction, and visitors can learn the whole story at the peatland Nature Reserves.

Fishing boats at rest (right)

The urban horse

The Irish passion for horses goes back to pre-Christian times. Even in today's densely populated cities, horse-lovers hold on to this relationship with an amazing tenacity. It's not unusual to see horses in Irish cities. Right in the heart of Belfast, there's a small triangle of grass on which a horse is regularly tethered, and city traffic may have to slow down to the pace of a pony and trap. On the housing estates of Dublin, Limerick and Cork, young men will ride horses bareback with all the bravado and style of their motorcyclist counterparts. Horses are kept in cities for pulling tourist carriages or for competing in trotting races, but more often, just for the sheer love of the animal.

Country meets town

The essence of rural Ireland can be experienced at the dozens of agricultural shows around the country in summer. But the best displays can be seen at the two major shows, the Balmoral in Belfast in May and the Royal Dublin Society (RDS) Show in August. The RDS is a venerable institution, established in 1731 to promote the development of agriculture, arts, science and industry. It still plays a significant role in Ireland's farming life. Both events showcase the latest farming technology alongside traditional crafts. The prize agricultural specimens are paraded, and Ladies' Day is a considerably stylish affair. The highlight of the Dublin Show is the day on which international show-jumping teams vie for the Aga Khan Trophy.

Salmon leap?

As well as the sport of angling for salmon, there are commercial sea fisheries, and locally smoked salmon can be bought in coastal villages. In County Antrim there is a remarkable fishery at Carrick-a-Rede, a tiny, rocky island called 'the Rock in the Road', where the salmon that swim between the rock and the mainland are caught in the nets. Each year the fishermen erect a rope bridge 18m (59ft) wide and 24m (78ft) above the sea, to take them across to the island. It used to be a precarious affair, with rickety wooden slats and one rope handle, but it is now in the hands of the National Trust, and is much safer. It still needs a brave heart and a head for heights to cross it, however.

Bilingual signposting at Kilrush (left)

Children celebrate in the run-up to Cork's installation as European Capital of Culture 2005 (below)

Gaelic Country, European Nation

Cultural Cork

The Republic of Ireland's second city, Cork, has been selected to become the European Capital of Culture in 2005, the smallest city ever to have been awarded this title. Cork has grand ambitions, however. It will not only celebrate its own strong cultural heritage but has launched many initiatives with European partners. A high point of the city's events will be the installation of a pavilion designed by Daniel Libeskind, the architect of the master plan for the rebuilding at Ground Zero in New York. In another project, labelled 'Iris', the Daghdha Dance Company will distribute 10,000 message-laden rings throughout the city. The rings each come with different instructions, and when released 'Iris' will take on a life of its own.

Geographically, Ireland may be on the edge of Europe, but politically and economically it has become integrated into the European ideal. Quick to adopt the euro as currency, the Republic has embraced European institutions with an open readiness. Ireland is modern, cosmopolitan and young. It is also ancient, traditional and still essentially Gaelic, although the Anglo-Irish influence is evident everywhere, and Dublin's gracious residential and institutional architecture dates largely from the Georgian era. Great efforts have been made to retain the Irish language as a living organism, but although its use as an official language is comprehensive, only in the Gaeltacht in the far west and south is it used in everyday speech. Gaelic sport, dance and music are alive and well, though, and city streets and pubs everywhere echo to the sounds of traditional instruments. Ulster-Scots and Gaelic traditions complement each other in Northern Ireland, where the heritage of the planter stock remains strong. Here, the European identity is less evident. The British pound is the official currency, but the euro is often accepted.

Miles or metres?

Visitors to the Republic of Ireland are often baffled by inconsistent distance measurements on signposts. One sign showing miles will be followed shortly down the road by one in kilometres, but soon all signage will be made to conform to metric units. North of the border distances are measured in miles, and observers are concerned that the discrepancy in speed limit signs will cause confusion. Petrol pumps have been standardized to dispense in litres, not gallons, and although shops are required to label in multiples of grams, many customers still ask for goods in pounds and ounces. And a pint is still a pint, not 0.57 litre. In both parts of the island motorists drive on the left, and there are no plans to change that—for the foreseeable future.

The Story of Ireland

Mystery, Myth and Religion

About 10,000 years ago hunter-gatherers crossed a land-bridge linking Britain to Ireland. As the sea separated the two islands, Stone Age people settled along the Irish coasts and rivers. From the fourth century BC neolithic communities began clearing the inland forests and planting crops. Among the few clues to their lives and rituals are traces of walled fields, unearthed from bogland at Céide Fields (▷ 133), and the elaborately decorated passage graves at Knowth and Newgrange (▷ 90–93).

Trade links and immigration spread new technologies—first the bronze industry and then, from around 700BC, the Celts of southern and central Europe brought ironworking skills to Ireland. Last of the Celtic tribes to arrive were the Goidels, or Gaels, who enjoyed a rich culture of music, art and mythology, and whose settlements were grouped into small kingdoms, or *tuátha*. Ireland remained outside the control—though not entirely free of the influence—of the Roman Empire. But the Celtic world was changing, and by the late fourth century AD Christianity was replacing the native Druidic religion in parts of Ireland. In AD432 St. Patrick arrived and established a secure foothold for the Christian Church in Ireland.

Sacred waters

According to Celtic legend, the River Boyne was once no bigger than a well—a holy well, surrounded by hazel trees which shed hazelnuts of knowledge and inspiration into the water every year. Only initiates were allowed to approach the well, but the goddess Boanna, lover of chief god Dagda Mór, let curiosity get the better of her. The waters promptly rose up and washed her away, and the resulting flood became the river that took her name. Water played a fundamental part in Celtic beliefs and similar stories were told about other rivers—such as the Shannon, which was said to have been created when the goddess Sionnain looked into a sacred well.

Display in Adragl Heritage Centre (left). Clouds hang low over Lough Leane (below)

Rathfran Dolmen, near Killala in north County Mayo (above)

Legendary Cúchulainn slays the Hound of Culainn (right)

Kings and kingdoms

For many centuries Celtic society followed the same basic pattern. Each autonomous community, called a *tuátha*, was ruled by a *rí* (king), a worthy warrior chosen from among royal ranks. A *tuátha* was made up of scattered *ráths* (farming settlements), and a strict class system extended from slaves, at the bottom of the heap, to the learned and the royal, at the top. Throughout Ireland there were a hundred or so of these kingdoms grouped into five regions—Ulster, Munster, Leinster, Connaught and Meath—and lord of them all (in theory) was the *Ard Rí* (High King), who sat in state at Tara. Frequent and violent power struggles arose as royal dynasties vied for control of their own territories and, ultimately, of the whole land.

The Mighty Finn

During the third century AD King Cumhal (Cool) was killed in a battle over leadership of the fearsome Fianna warriors. His son, Finn, was brought up in the wild and sent to a druid for instruction. One day the druid caught the Salmon of Knowledge in the River Boyne and gave it to his pupil to cook. In the process Finn burned his thumb and licked it, immediately acquiring great wisdom. He subsequently made his way to Tara, where a demon was wreaking nightly havoc after mesmerizing the townsfolk with enchanted harp music. Finn touched his forehead with the tip of a magic spear, thus blocking the music's effects, and slew the demon, earning the right to be Chief of the Fianna, the strongest and wisest king they ever had.

Language of the gods

Standing stones carved with intriguing lines and strokes are found all over Ireland, Britain and Europe and even in parts of America. These are no abstract decorations but inscriptions in Ogham, the Celtic language named after Ogma, god of literature. Ogham script was in use from the fourth century AD, but according to some theories had been part of Druidic ritual since the first century or earlier. The alphabet is simple but flexible: Straight or angled strokes are placed above, below or through a vertical line to represent 15 consonants and 5 vowels, each letter taking the name of a tree. Ogham script gradually gave way to the Roman alphabet, but some remote communities were still using it as recently as the 19th century.

St. Patrick's adventures

Ireland's patron saint was born to Roman parents in Britain in around AD389. At 16 he was abducted and sold into slavery in Ireland, where he was put to work as a shepherd in County Antrim. After six years he escaped and was reunited with his family. During his captivity Patrick had developed a strong faith, and he subsequently trained as a priest in France. He had a dream in which the Irish called for his help, and this convinced him of his life's mission, so he returned to Ireland to lay the foundations of its Church. Legend has it that while preaching from Croagh Patrick in County Mayo (▷ 136) St. Patrick rang his bell and drove the country's snakes into the sea, a miracle that may symbolize the eradication of paganism.

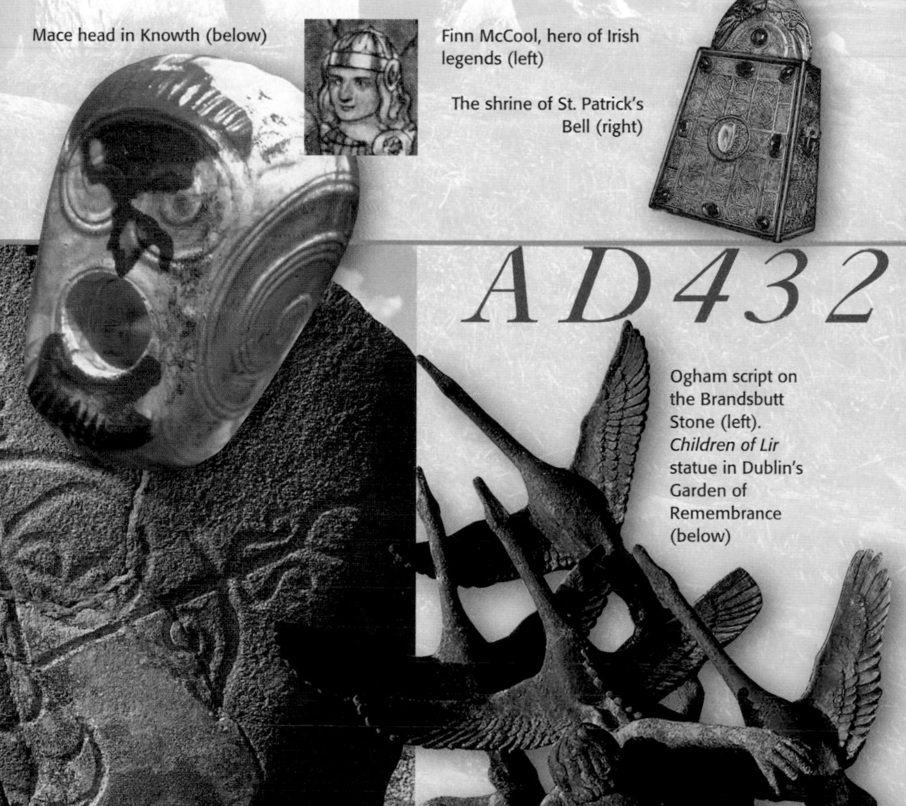

Mace head in Knowth (below)

Finn McCool, hero of Irish legends (left)

The shrine of St. Patrick's Bell (right)

Ogham script on the Brandsbutt Stone (left). *Children of Lir* statue in Dublin's Garden of Remembrance (below)

Monasteries and Missionaries

Christianity took root in Ireland and during the fifth and sixth centuries monastic communities sprang up in valleys and woods and on remote islands and windswept cliffs. Missionaries ventured abroad to spread the word further: Columcille (St. Columba) journeyed to Scotland to found the famous monastery of Iona; St. Brendan the Navigator may have reached American shores, and St. Columbanus developed communities in Belgium, Germany, Switzerland and Italy.

Scholarship and art flourished in the great Irish monasteries, but from AD795 people lived under the constant threat of Viking attacks. High round towers were built to keep watch for, and to provide refuge from the plunderers whose sporadic raids continued. In 914 the Vikings launched an all-out invasion and established themselves in Ireland, building walled cities such as Dublin, Wicklow and Wexford.

Meanwhile the rival Irish dynasties struggled for ascendancy, occasionally using the Vikings as allies in their cause. Brian Borúma (Boru), King of Munster, finally emerged as High King but was killed defeating the Danes at the Battle of Clontarf in 1014. Interdynastic wars simmered on, and in 1169 the exiled King of Leinster, Dermot MacMurrough, summoned to his aid an Anglo-Norman magnate, Richard Fitzgilbert de Clare, known as Strongbow. Troubled by Strongbow's military success, English king Henry II sailed for Ireland, and, backed by the Pope, declared himself its feudal overlord.

St. Kevin (left), founder of the monastery at Glendalough

Columcille and the copyright case

In 561 Columcille (St. Columba) left Ireland and set sail for Scotland, where he established several important monastic communities. But it is thought that the journey may have been prompted by his part in a terrible battle. Columcille was an aristocrat who trained as a scholar and a monk under the tutelage of St. Finnian. The story goes that he copied the saint's book of psalms but refused to hand over his work. In the first recorded case of copyright, a court ruled that St. Finnian, as the original book's owner, had a right to its copy. The dispute was taken up by Columcille's relatives, and the two sides came to blows. As a penance for this horrific turn of events, Columcille went into exile with a dozen followers, and began his famous mission.

AD432

Illuminated page from the seventh-century Book of Durrow (left)

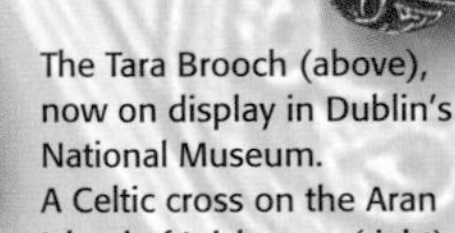
The Tara Brooch (above), now on display in Dublin's National Museum.
A Celtic cross on the Aran Island of Inishmore (right)

The Book of Durrow

There's a touch of mystery to the Book of Durrow, now kept in Trinity College Library, Dublin. Created in AD675, it's Ireland's oldest surviving illuminated gospel and takes its name from Durrow Abbey, County Offaly, where it was said to have been made. But clues have emerged to cast doubt on its origins. Among the tints used for the illustrations is orpiment, a yellow mineral from the Mediterranean. Fragments of this same dye were found during excavations of the hill fort of Dunadd in Argyll, Scotland. This has prompted speculation that the book was actually put together at Iona monastery, which was only 56km (35 miles) from Dunadd and whose monks would have had easy access to the town's imported goods.

The trials of Clonmacnoise

The sixth-century monastic site of Clonmacnoise, on the eastern bank of the River Shannon, suffered more than its fair share of disasters. After its foundation by St. Ciaran in AD545 the monastery earned an international reputation for scholarship, but in the seventh century many students were killed in a bout of plague. The site was destroyed by fire no fewer than three times during the eighth century, and in the ninth and tenth centuries it was frequently targeted by Viking raiders and rival Irish leaders. During his wars of expansion King Fedelmid MacCrimthainn of Cashel burned Clonmacnoise and slaughtered its monks in 832, 833 and 844. On the final occasion, it's said that St. Ciarán appeared and dealt Fedelmid a fatal blow with his staff.

Viking Dublin

In summer 2003 the remains of four Viking warriors were unearthed at South Great Georges Street in Dublin—members, perhaps, of the Norse invaders who sailed up the Boyne and Liffey in the early ninth century, meeting little effective resistance. By 841, Viking settlers were following in the warriors' wake. A thriving port evolved at Duiblinn (Dublin), and coinage was introduced. Within the town's walls the Vikings built windowless houses of wattle and daub, each designed to last about 15 years before replacement. Ships came and went, carrying animals, slaves, wool, fur, wine and gems. And meanwhile the townspeople went about their business in the latest Scandinavian fashions: shirts and long trousers for the men, aproned tunics and silk headbands for the women.

Life of Brian

Brian Boru was a name whispered with dread in 10th-century Munster. The younger brother of King Mahon, he had fled in protest at an alliance with the Vikings, and from a hideout in the woods he and his followers conducted vicious attacks on the Norse settlements. As Brian's fame grew Mahon sought him out, and together they expelled the Norse king. After Mahon's death Brian fought his way to ascendancy over all Ireland's kingdoms and ruled as High King for a decade until, in 1014, the King of Leinster and the Dublin Vikings joined forces against him at Clontarf. A day of terrible carnage passed before Brian emerged victorious, but he was killed by a retreating Viking in his moment of glory.

Brian Boru, Ireland's last High King (below)

The 12th-century church of St. Finghin and its round tower (left)

1169

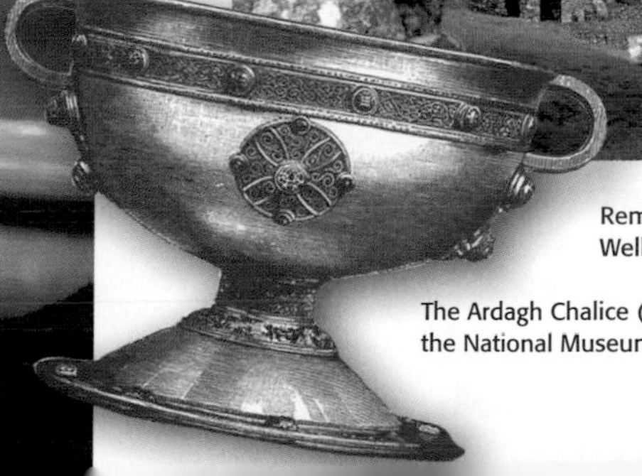

Remains of St. Declan's Well, Ardmore (above)

The Ardagh Chalice (left), in the National Museum, Dublin

Normans to the Flight of the Earls

Henry II failed to extend his authority beyond Dublin and a swathe of land around it known as the Pale. The Anglo-Norman invaders were gradually assimiliated into Gaelic culture and customs, and in the 14th century the Crown tried—unsuccessfully—to separate the two sections of the community with the Statutes of Kilkenny (1366), which forbade the English from taking Irish names, marrying into Irish families or even employing Irish balladeers.

The most powerful Anglo-Irish families embarked on a struggle for supremacy; the Fitzgeralds, earls of Kildare, eventually emerging victorious. When, in the 1490s, Henry VII determined to bring Ireland under his control, he used the Kildares as his agents. As part of this centralizing drive, royal deputy Sir Edward Poynings instigated Poynings' Law, requiring royal approval for the summoning of Irish parliaments.

In the 1530s Henry VIII split from Rome and pronounced himself head of the English Church. Rebellion promptly broke out in Ireland, led by the Kildares, and was ruthlessly put down. In the years that followed a steady trickle of settlers, adherents to the new Protestant religion, arrived from England. Elizabeth I made concerted efforts to establish colonies, or plantations, in Munster and Ulster, provoking several uprisings. These ended in massive land confiscation and in 1607 a number of Irish aristocrats left Ireland for Italy—an event known as the Flight of the Earls.

Mixed motives

The conquest of Ireland served several purposes for Henry II, apart from reining in Strongbow's (▷ 28) ambitions. The King needed the distractions provided by an invasion. In December 1170 the Christian world had been shocked by the murder of Thomas à Becket, Archbishop of Canterbury, by four of Henry's knights. Becket was canonized within a record two years and pilgrims flocked to his shrine. Faced with the wrath of the Vatican, Henry performed elaborate public penances. The invasion was, likewise, calculated to please, as the pope was anxious to bring the Irish monasteries to heel. Henry's Irish campaign was a way of simultaneously asserting power, distracting public attention and restoring himself in the papal good books.

1169

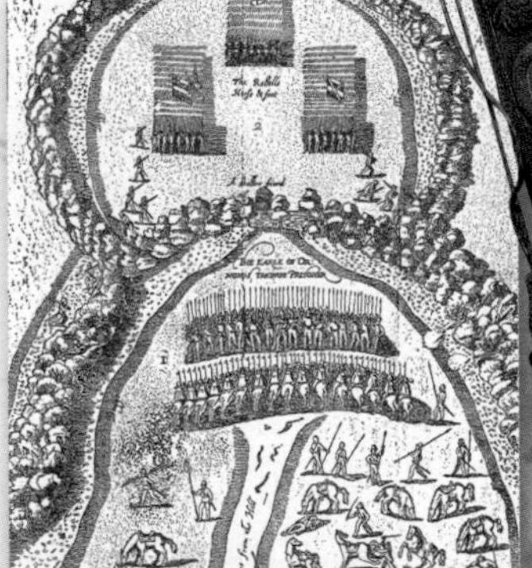

Exhibit from Dublin's Heraldic Museum (above)

Illustration of the capture of the Earl of Ormond by the O'Mores (above)

The Second Great Seal of Elizabeth I (right)

Gallowglass

In 1290 Turlba O'Donnell enlisted the help of mercenaries to overthrow his brother. Contemporary accounts of the event include the first known record of the term 'gallowglass'—an anglicized version of *gallóglach*, Irish for foreign soldier. Between the 13th and 17th century, well-trained bands of mercenaries—some of Viking origin—fought for Irish and Scottish kings. Easily recognizable by their long chain-mail or padded coats and their cone-shaped helmets, they were highly skilled in the use of double-handed swords (claymores) and battle-axes. Some gallowglass families remained in service to the same dynasties for hundreds of years, but with the departure of the most prominent Irish nobles in 1607 these forbidding warriors also disappeared from the scene.

Beyond the Pale

English royal authority was dwindling by the 1400s. Events of the previous century, which included the Black Death and an invasion of Ireland by Robert Bruce of Scotland, had further weakened its hold. The only area loyal to the Crown was Dublin and a belt of land around it known as the Pale (or fortified boundary). This was defended by trenches, forts and guards, but Irish raiders from 'beyond the Pale' still managed to penetrate the area. In 1429 Henry VI offered every Englishman within the Pale £10 to build a castle measuring 5m (16ft) by 6m (20ft) and 12m (40ft) high. Within 20 years the authorities had to call a halt to the building work, as hundreds of castles sprouted across the countryside.

Feuding families

There was constant animosity between Ireland's titled families, and evidence of one particularly stormy period is displayed in St. Patrick's Cathedral in Dublin. A fierce tussle for political power between the Butler family, earls of Ormonde, and the Fitzgeralds, earls of Kildare, erupted into widespread violence in the 1490s. Gangs of their supporters clashed in the Dublin streets, and when the family heads and their bodyguards crossed paths in the cathedral nave more fighting broke out, forcing the Earl of Ormonde to take shelter in the chapterhouse. Eventually a temporary truce was agreed and a hole cut in the chapterhouse door so that the rivals could shake hands. The door and its hole can still be seen, in the cathedral's south transept.

The O'Neill rebellion

Hugh O'Neill (1550–1616) was brought up as an English gentleman, but his true ambition was to rule an independent, Catholic Ireland, and in 1595 he led a full-scale rebellion in Ulster. Reinforcements were sent from Spain to help him, but storms and disease weakened them and in 1601 O'Neill was forced to surrender. He was later restored to his earldom but with only nominal status, and the English authorities continued to treat him with suspicion. In 1607 O'Neill joined several other disgruntled earls on a ship bound for Italy, where he died in exile nine years later.

Catherine, the 'Old' Countess of Desmond (below), is said to have died aged 120 from falling out of a cherry tree!

Three medieval banners from Dublin's Heraldic Museum (below)

Archbishop of Armagh, Jacobus Usserius (left)

–1607

Dunluce Castle (left). Medieval Irishmen attacking a tower (below)

Cromwell and the Conflict of Kings

In the early 17th century land grants attracted some 100,000 Protestant immigrants from England and Scotland to Ulster and Munster. Sectarian conflict was rife in England, where enmity between the largely Protestant parliament and Charles I was escalating into civil war. Ireland's Catholic gentry took arms in the King's name, and during the 1641 uprising thousands of Ulster settlers were slain.

Led by Oliver Cromwell, England's Parliamentarian army gained ground in England, while the Catholic royalists gained almost full control of Ireland. Charles sought their help, but baulked at their demands for independence. Soon after the King's capture and execution, Cromwell brought 12,000 troops to subdue Ireland; Drogheda and Wexford suffered terrible massacres. Within nine months Cromwell had crushed the opposition. Nearly half of Ireland's land was confiscated, and dispossessed Catholics were transplanted west of the River Shannon under the 1652 Act of Settlement.

After the restoration of the monarchy in 1660 simmering fears of 'popish plots' prevented any real reform of anti-Catholic measures. In 1685 James II, himself a Catholic, became king; three years later parliament invited a Dutch Protestant prince, William of Orange, to seize the throne. James escaped to Ireland and raised an army, but on 1 July 1690 William won a decisive victory on the south bank of the Boyne and James fled into exile in France.

Oliver Cromwell (right), still reviled by some in Ireland

Birth of a dynasty

After the 1641 rebellion about a million hectares (2.5 million acres) of land were confiscated from the Catholics and snapped up by English Protestant adventurers. One was Richard Boyle (1566–1643), who, having arrived in Ireland with less than £100 to his name, took on the title Earl of Cork and increased his worth to £20,000 a year. His youngest son, Robert (1627–91), was a scientific pioneer, experimenting with air pressure and advocating the theory that matter was made up of atoms. Richard Boyle's grandson Charles (1676–1731), Earl of Orrery, continued the family's scientific interests and paid inventor George Graham to design a mechanical model of the planets—a device called an orrery to this day.

1607

Ireland's oldest Quaker cemetery, at Mountmellick (above)

British cavalry at the Battle of the Boyne (right)

An unseemly scuffle

The Irish parliament summoned in 1613 had a large Protestant majority, fixed by the creation of 40 'rotten boroughs'. Its first task was the election of a speaker. The Protestant candidate was Sir John Davies; the Catholic choice Sir John Everard. When Davies' supporters filed out to vote, his Catholic opponents grabbed Everard and shoved him into the speaker's chair. On their return the indignant Protestants promptly heaved their own, rather stout man onto Everard's lap. During the ensuing fisticuffs Everard was ejected from the chamber, and the Catholic members walked out. But the incident made its mark—the number of rotten boroughs was cut drastically and several proposed anti-Catholic laws withdrawn.

Leader of the gang

Like most notorious outlaws, 'Count' Redmond O'Hanlon (*d*1681) is an enigmatic figure, whose story is a tangle of fact and myth. Starting out as a footboy, in 1670 he took charge of a gang of Ulster tories (from the Irish *toraighe*, or bandit); according to some he'd been dispossessed of his land by Cromwell. His men were feared throughout Armagh, Tyrone and Down, where they levied 'tributes' from the colonists. A price of £200 was put on O'Hanlon's head, but he evaded capture several times before being tricked and shot by his foster brother, in the pay of the Earl of Ormond. The pricey O'Hanlon head ended up on a spike at Downpatrick Jail.

The Boyne Medal

Some 60,000 men took to the field in the Battle of the Boyne (1690) as William of Orange and James II fought over the right to rule. William won the battle and the throne, but events could have taken an entirely different direction. In the confusion of battle a Jacobite soldier had managed to reach William and almost pulled him off his horse. A certain Major Rogers galloped to the rescue. In gratitude the King commissioned an 18-carat gold medal, possibly the first to be awarded for an act of individual courage. A profile of William III decorated one face; the other depicted Enniskillen Castle, in tribute to the Major's company, the Royal Enniskillen Fusiliers.

The growth of Dublin

By the mid-17th century Dublin was in a sorry state. Many Catholics were expelled after the civil war and in 1650 the plague struck. Dublin's population fell from 20,000 in 1640 to less than 9,000 in 1659. Lord Lieutenant James Butler, Duke of Ormonde, raised from earl to duke by the restored Charles II, commissioned a flurry of new developments. Phoenix Park and St. Stephen's Green were laid out. New institutions such as the Blue Coat School and the Royal Hospital were built, and brick and tile houses replaced thatched dwellings. Trade in wool and linen boomed, a second bridge was built across the River Liffey in 1670 and the city's quays were revamped. By 1700 the population had grown to 60,000, and the prosperity that continued into the Georgian era was under way.

William of Orange (1650–1702)

James II, from a painting by Sir Godfrey Kneller (left)

1690

The Siege of (London)Derry (below)

From Penal Laws to Emancipation

After the Jacobites' defeat, Ireland was firmly under Protestant control. A series of measures passed in the late 17th and the 18th centuries—the penal laws—kept the Catholic majority out of power, forbidding them to hold public office, sit in parliament, vote, teach, inherit land from Protestants or buy land. In 1703, 14 per cent of the land was in Catholic hands; by 1776 this was down to 5 per cent.

Meanwhile trade flourished and Dublin became the hub of Anglo-Irish intellectual life. Protestant thinkers increasingly criticized Catholic persecution. Politician Henry Grattan called for equal rights and limited Irish independence and achieved some of his objectives, but not for long. France was engulfed by revolution, and fear of its influence provoked further repression. In 1798 Wolfe Tone led an ill-fated uprising, and three years later the Act of Union brought Ireland under direct British rule. Ireland sent MPs to Westminster, but only Protestants could take their seats. Rebel Robert Emmet led an abortive attack on Dublin Castle in 1803, but the most effective campaign was Daniel O'Connell's peaceful movement for Home Rule and emancipation. O'Connell (▷ 36) was elected an MP in 1828; his faith excluded him from parliament, but his success had a major impact. The following year the Catholic Emancipation Act extended the vote to all Catholics with a £10 freehold—14,000 in all—and enabled them to sit in Parliament.

Hedge schools

Under the penal laws, education in Irish and of the Catholic faith was banned, but rather than send their children to schools where an English-language curriculum included Protestant instruction, many opted for hedge schools, illicit gatherings—under hedges, on the roadside or in derelict buildings—where teachers passed on Irish history, legends and ballads and the tenets of Roman Catholicism. An 1826 report on education estimated that of 550,000 children registered in schools, 403,000 attended hedge schools. By 1832 the laws had been relaxed and, as new schools became more open to Irish tradition and faith, the hedge schools died out.

Attilbrassil Bridge, site of the Battle of Aughrim in 1691 (left)

Mussenden Temple (above), built in the 18th century

Irish insurgents are led in this picture by Father John Murphy (right)

A way with words

The 18th century was a golden age for English-language Irish literature. Leading the pack was Jonathan Swift (1667–1745), who employed his acerbic wit in satires such as *Gulliver's Travels* and *Modest Proposal* (where the rich end poverty by eating the babies of the poor). George Farquhar (1677–1707) was an actor who took up writing after injuring someone in a stage fight. He had to borrow 20 guineas to write his last comedy, *The Beaux' Stratagem*, which brought him success at the end of his life. Other literary stars were playwright Richard Brinsley Sheridan (1751–1816) and Oliver Goldsmith (1730–74), whose novel *The Vicar of Wakefield* broke new ground with its unsentimental narrative; its success saved him from imprisonment for debt.

The sound of music

Georgian Dublin was an affluent and fashionable city with a flourishing creative life. Among many musicians who came to enjoy its buzz were Italian violinist and composer Francesco Geminiani (1687–1762); Thomas Arne (1710–78), who wrote songs and oratorios; his son Michael (1740–86), an opera singer; and the musical superstar of his day, Georg Friederich Handel (1685–1759). Handel arrived at the invitation of the viceroy, who commissioned a new work for Dublin and within six weeks was presented with the *Messiah*. The oratorio was first performed on 13 April 1742 in the Charitable Musical Society's base, Neal's Music Hall in Fishamble Street. It was conducted by Handel himself, who stayed on to take in the Dublin scene for a year.

The failed revolution

Wolfe Tone (1768–98), a Protestant lawyer from Dublin, was a leading light of the United Irishmen, a society inspired by French revolutionary ideas. He hoped that, together, Catholics and Protestants could overcome the government's 'boobies and blockheads' and enjoy equal rights in an independent republic. After his implication in a plot to encourage a French invasion, Tone sailed first to America and then to France, where he persuaded the government to send troops to Ireland. One fleet was beaten by the weather; the second was defeated in 1798 at Lough Swilly. Tone was among those captured and convicted of treason. He requested a soldier's death—by firing squad—but on learning that he would be publicly hanged, cut his own throat in prison.

Battle of The Diamond

County Armagh was a powder-keg in the 18th century. Catholics and Protestants competing to control the growing linen industry formed armed gangs: the Peep O' Day Boys (Protestants) and the Defenders (Catholics). Both sides notched up a terrible tally of atrocities. In September 1795 a particularly vicious clash in a pub called The Diamond ended in the deaths of a dozen Defenders. To mark the event the victors formed an association and named it after William of Orange, pledging allegiance to the Crown and to Protestantism. The following year, members of the Orange Order paraded in celebration of the Battle of the Boyne (▷ 32–33). The Orangemen's marches continue to this day and remain a contentious issue between the two communities.

Jonathan Swift

Bust of General Humbert in Killala (left)

1829

One of Dublin's famous Georgian doors (above). The mace of the Guilds of Cork, 1696 (left)

Historical re-enactment in Killala (right)

Great Famine to the Easter Rising

By the mid-19th century most of Ireland's 8 million inhabitants were rural poor, living mainly on potatoes. In 1845 and 1846 a fungus ruined the potato crop, with catastrophic effects. About a million died of starvation or disease. Government relief was slow and inefficient, and proponents of free trade were reluctant to intervene. Mass emigration followed, many thousands dying en route to the Americas. Meanwhile, landlords hiked their rents and evicted tenants unable to pay. The famine left a bitter legacy.

In 1858 the Fenian movement was formed, advocating armed insurrection. Alternative strategies were pursued by MP Charles Stewart Parnell and his Home Rule Party, who kept Irish grievances in the spotlight in the House of Commons by talking parliamentary bills out of time. A fragile alliance with Prime Minister William Gladstone fell apart in 1882 after the British Chief Secretary's murder in Dublin's Phoenix Park, and a few years later Parnell's reputation was destroyed by news of his affair with a married woman.

A Home Rule Bill was eventually passed in 1912 but put aside when World War I broke out. Rival Unionist and Republican militias were formed, and tensions mounted. On Easter Monday 1916, Republicans occupied Dublin's major buildings and six days' fighting ensued before their capture. The ringleaders' execution created new martyrs for the Republican cause.

James Joyce statue in Earl Street, Dublin (right)

The Liberator

On 13 August 1843 a million people stood on the Hill of Tara to hear a 68-year-old lawyer. The crowd-puller was Daniel O'Connell (1775–1847), champion of emancipation, land reform and the repeal of the Anglo-Irish Union. The Tara gathering was the last of 40 held across the country. O'Connell was opposed to violence. His peaceful campaigns attracted widespread support, and a final meeting was planned on 8 October, but O'Connell was arrested and imprisoned, and was released six months later only after a national protest.

Daniel O'Connell (above)

1829

Jim Larkin statue on O'Connell Street (right)

Republican banner in Enniscorthy's Castle Museum (below)

Route to power

Among the emigrants escaping the Great Famine in 1848 was a 25-year-old brewer's cooper from Dunganstown, near New Ross. Patrick Kennedy came from a farming family which was facing eviction. Determined to try his luck elsewhere, he boarded the SS *Washington Irving* to Boston, and with his wife, Bridget, set up home in a tenement. They raised three daughters and a son before Patrick's death from cholera at 38. Bridget worked on, eventually buying a grocery store. Their son, Patrick Joseph, did well as a saloon-owner and grandson Joseph climbed farther up the ladder, becoming ambassador to Britain. In 1961 Joseph's son John was elected President of the United States, little more than a century after his great-grandfather's departure from Ireland.

The first Boycott

Charles Stewart Parnell's policy of ostracizing negligent landlords was responsible for coining a new phrase. One of its first targets was Charles Cunningham Boycott (1834–97), an ex-army captain employed to manage Lord Erne's estates in County Mayo. When supporters of the Land League refused to work for him, Boycott faced a ruined harvest and a ruined career. Volunteers from the Orange Order (▷ 35) were hastily brought in, but police and troops were needed to protect them from reprisals as they gathered the crops. Within a month the term 'boycotting' was in use in the press, and the captain had earned his place in history.

Curtain up

Celtic legend and poetry and the political struggle were themes that injected new life and interest into the literature of the early 20th century. At the heart of this revival was Dublin's Abbey Theatre, headquarters of the Irish National Theatre Society. In 1903 Miss Ann Elizabeth Horniman bought the derelict theatre and the former morgue next door and converted them into the Abbey. Poet W. B. Yeats (▷ 39) and his friend Lady Gregory were closely involved in the project, and Lady Gregory wrote *Gods and Fighting Men*, for performance there. In 1907 the theatre confirmed its reputation for staging controversial contemporary works with J. M. Synge's play *The Playboy of the Western World*, which sparked riots among the audience.

City of ships

Writer Stephen Gwynn (1864–1950) noted in 1911 that Belfast's ships were 'marvels of symmetry and strength'. Shipbuilding was at the heart of the city's success and on 31 May 1911 it celebrated the launch of the mighty SS *Titanic*. Harland & Wolff had employed hundreds of men on the *Titanic*, which, along with her sister ship *Olympic*, was the biggest moving vessel of the time. Launched from the Queen's Island and cheered by a big crowd, she set off for sea trials in Belfast Lough. Her 1912 maiden voyage, from Southampton to New York, called at Queenstown, Co. Cork, and carried many Irish emigrants hoping for a new life. Three days later she struck an iceberg and sank, with the loss of 1,495 lives.

A place that spawned a dynasty (below left). Captain Boycott (below)

The sinking of the *Titanic* in 1912 (below)

THE
KENNEDY
HOMESTEAD
DUBLIN AND EAST TOURISM
BRAM STOKER
1847 - 1912
THEATRE MANAGER
AUTHOR OF DRACULA
LIVED HERE
1916

Dublin plaque commemmorating Bram Stoker (below)

Depiction of an all too common eviction (left)

Irish dramatist Oscar Wilde (right), photographed in 1891

The 20th Century

At the 1918 general election the Republican Sinn Féin party virtually swept the board and set up its own Dáil (parliament) in Dublin. After two years of fighting between the Irish Republican Army and the Royal Irish Constabulary, reinforced by the notoriously ruthless Black and Tans, a motley band of mostly ex-soldier mercenaries, the Government of Ireland Act was passed, establishing one parliament for the 26 southern counties—the Irish Free State—and one for the six northern counties. The Free State left the British Commonwealth in 1949 and became a republic.

The IRA remained active in Northern Ireland, where Unionists had their own armed factions, and a pattern of attacks and reprisals was set. British troops were sent in after riots in 1969 and became frequent targets for the splinter Provisional IRA group. On 30 January 1972—'Bloody Sunday'—soldiers opened fire during a civil rights demonstration in Derry (Londonderry) and 13 unarmed protesters were killed. 'The Troubles' escalated, and Northern Ireland's assembly at Stormont was suspended. Bombing campaigns, protests, riots and repression marked the 1970s and '80s. But behind the scenes tentative negotiation was under way. An offer of talks involving all parties was followed, in 1994, by ceasefire declarations from the IRA and the Loyalists. Despite setbacks, the peace process stumbled on, and in 1998 the Good Friday Agreement proposed an elected assembly and the disarmament of all paramilitary groups.

Countess Markievicz

One of the first orders to open fire on Easter Monday 1916 was given by Constance, Countess Markievicz (1884–1927), deserted wife of a Ukrainian aristocrat and daughter of Arctic explorer Sir Henry Gore-Booth. She was a member of Sinn Féin and an ardent activist, commanding a contingent during the Rising. For her part in the event she received a death sentence, but was subsequently reprieved. Countess Markievicz was the first woman ever to be voted into the British parliament, at the general election of 1918. She, like other Sinn Féin members, refused to take up the seat in Westminster. In 1919 the Countess served in the cabinet of the first Dáil, as Minister of Labour.

Countess Markievicz in uniform(below)

1916

GUINNESS
AS USUAL
THERE'S NOTHING
LIKE A GUINNESS

Certain things remain constant (above)

The Red Hand of Ulster, from a Shankill Road mural (right)

A Derry mural (below)

ARE NOW
ENTERING
FREE DERRY

De Valera

Eamon de Valera (1882–1975), the only military commander to escape execution after the Easter Rising, became president of Sinn Féin in 1917. Months later he was imprisoned for treason, but escaped in 1919 and returned to lead the new Dáil. De Valera sent negotiators to London, but rejected the resulting Anglo-Irish Treaty. Civil war raged over the treaty until the 1923 ceasefire. De Valera founded Fianna Fáil, which took power in 1932. Éire's 1937 constitution reflected his ideal of a socially conservative, Gaelic-speaking, Catholic nation. In World War II his government maintained neutrality; consequently Éire was not admitted to the UN until 1955. Summing up his career, de Valera remarked that he should have been a bishop, rather than a revolutionary.

Eamon de Valera

Love story

In his 1939 collection *Last Poems* William Butler Yeats (1865–1939) described Maud Gonne as 'Pallas Athene in that straight back and arrogant head'. He had first met the beautiful radical 43 years earlier, and his unrequited love for her was a constant theme from then on. Having refused the poet many times, Gonne married fellow revolutionary John MacBride, and in his next collection Yeats paid wistful tribute to his lost love. MacBride was executed after the Easter Rising and again Yeats proposed unsuccessfully—first to Gonne and then to her adopted daughter, Iseult. In 1917 he married Georgie Hyde-Lees, an old friend. Always fascinated with the supernatural, Yeats found a new source of poetic inspiration in his wife's talent for automatic writing.

Omagh

On 15 August 1998 the market town of Omagh, in County Tyrone, was busy with Saturday shoppers. At about 2.30pm police received a bomb warning by telephone. The middle of town was immediately evacuated. But there was confusion about the location of the bomb, and shoppers were actually being directed into the danger area. When a car bomb exploded at 3pm, 29 people were killed and hundreds wounded. Sinn Féin leader Gerry Adams was quick to condemn the bombing, and chief negotiator Martin McGuinness described it as an appalling act, designed to stall the peace process. Three days later the Real IRA, a splinter group opposing the Good Friday Agreement, claimed responsibility and issued an apology; two weeks later it suspended military action, but later resumed bombing.

The gravestone of W. B. Yeats in Drumcliff churchyard (left). Troops on Dublin streets during the Easter Rising (below left)

Fame and fortune

Rock band U2 was discovered by manager Paul McGuinness playing in a community hall behind the Clarence Hotel in Dublin. Now the band owns the hotel, along with a string of clubs, bars, media firms and other ventures contributing to its multi-million-euro empire. In 2004 the band was worth over €680 million, making it the fifth richest company in Ireland. Earnings were helped by sales of 85 million albums over the past 23 years, each sale bringing in over €4 in royalties, as well as the tax-free status granted to major Irish artists. Lead singer Bono (Paul Hewson) is a prominent campaigner on Third World issues.

Bono speaking at a Canadian Liberal Party Conference

Red Hand Commando sign (above), Belfast

21st-Century Ireland

The Republic of Ireland entered the third millennium with an impressive record of economic growth. The Dáil is dominated, as it has been since the 1930s, by the rival Fianna Fáil and Fine Gael parties, often relying for power on the support of smaller parties. Northern Ireland continues along a bumpy political road, with disputes erupting between Nationalists and Unionists, and violence flaring on the streets. After a 13-month suspension, Assembly elections were held in November 2003. Sinn Féin won 24 seats and the Democratic Unionist Party—who agreed to participate in talks on condition that the IRA gave up its arms—won 30. These talks stalled, but attempts to restart them took place at the end of 2004.

Ireland in Europe

On 1 January 2004 Ireland took over presidency of the European Union for the sixth time. Since its entry into the European Economic Community in 1972, the republic has enjoyed the benefits of regional grants and tax concessions contributing to a meteoric rise in its economy that earned it the name 'Celtic Tiger'. In 2001 the nation's commitment to Europe was underlined when the Irish punt was replaced with the euro. Not everyone is comfortable with the influx of international business and immigration, however. A referendum on the Nice Treaty, proposing increased European integration, produced a 'no' vote. A second referendum in 2002 reversed this decision and approved the treaty.

Police officer on duty at an EU meeting in Ireland (right)

Hot property

By the new millennium Dublin was capital of a booming economy and the second most expensive place to live in the EU. The average price of a Dublin house rose from €89,032 in 1996 to €298,196 in 2003, and builders toiled to keep pace with demand. New one-bedroom apartments in Smithfield Market were snapped up at €345,000 and nearly 50 new houses sold in a few days at Malahide, each one costing €750,000.

Arms inspections

The decommissioning of arms is a hotly debated part of the Northern Ireland peace process. Arguments about timing, definition and inspection of disarmament have hampered negotiations and led to the suspension of the Assembly. In May 2000 the IRA announced its intention to put weapons beyond use, agreeing to inspection of arms dumps by independent observers. A commission headed by Canada's General John de Chastelain oversaw the scheme. Just before the 2003 election of a new Assembly, the general confirmed that a large number of IRA arms had been destroyed, but Ulster Unionists were sceptical. The hardline Democratic Unionist Party won substantial election victories, placing yet another question mark over the entire issue.

2000...

Waterfront development at Lanyon May, Belfast (above)

Masked Ulster Freedom Fighters in decommissioning talks (right)

Peace monument, silhouetted against the Derry sky

On the Move

ARRIVING

Arriving by Air

BY AIR TO THE REPUBLIC OF IRELAND

The Republic is well served by international airlines, and there are three international airports at Dublin, Shannon (near Limerick) and Cork. There are regional airports on the Aran Islands and in Donegal, Galway, Kerry, Knock, Sligo and Waterford. More than 30 airlines fly into the Republic from more than 55 cities, with an increasing number of budget airlines operating routes from Europe, which means that if you book in advance on a low-cost airline, your flights need not be too expensive.

The national airline in Ireland is Aer Lingus; Ryanair is a privately owned Irish airline, which is the largest low-cost airline in Europe.

You can fly into Dublin and Shannon airports from North America, but if you are coming from Australasia, you will have to connect in another country (for example, London), as there are no direct flights. For more information about flights within Ireland, ▷ 59.

Dublin Airport (DUB) is 13km (8 miles) north of the city. In Departures there is a bureau de change, a pharmacy (open Mon–Thu 6.30–6.30, Fri–Sun 9am–10.30pm), a vending machine that sells stamps, a shoe shine and plenty of cafés. In Arrivals there are several car rental desks, a tourist information desk, CIE (state-run transport company) information desk, an ATM, a café, a bureau de change and a bookshop.

Airlines with flights to and from Britain include Ireland's own (and Europe's largest) low-cost carrier Ryanair. Others are Air Wales, Aer Lingus, bmi, bmi baby, Flybe and BA CitiExpress. Airlines with flights from Europe include Aer Lingus, Air France, Air Luxor, Alitalia, Austrian Airlines, Iberia, Lufthansa, Ryanair and SAS. Carriers from the US include Delta, Continental Airlines and Aer Lingus.

For general information about Dublin airport tel 01 814 1111; www.dublin-airport.ie and www.aerrianta.com

Cork Airport (ORK) is 3km (5 miles) south of Cork in the south of Ireland. Facilities in the main terminal building include a bank (Bank of Ireland) with a bureau de change, an ATM which dispenses euros and sterling, an information desk, a mailbox, a café and a bar. Aer Arann, Air

GETTING TO THE CITY FROM THE AIRPORT

AIRPORT (CODE)	DUBLIN (DUB)	CORK (ORK)
TAXI	Price: approx €20 to downtown Dublin. Extra charges for luggage, pets, extra passengers and on Sundays and public holidays. Taxi stand on the right outside Arrivals hall.	Approx €12 to the middle of Cork.
TRAINS	Aerdart shuttle bus (www.aerdart.ie) to Howth Junction Dart Station (north of the city). Frequency: Mon–Fri every 15–20 min until 11.20pm, Sat–Sun once an hour until 8pm. Journey time: 15–20 min. Price: adult single €4.30, child single €3.	None
BUS	For all buses, turn left outside the Arrivals hall. Aircoach (www.aircoach.ie) to O'Connell Street, Grafton Street, St. Stephen's Green. Frequency: every 15 min. Journey time: 30 min. Price: adult single €6, return €10. Airlink Express Bus number 747 or 748 (run by Dublin Bus; www.dublinbus.ie) to O'Connell Street, bus station *(busáras)*, Connolly and Heuston train stations and Temple Bar. Frequency: every 15 or 20 min 5.45am–11.30pm. Journey time: 30–40 min. Price: adult single €5, adult return €7.50, child single €2. Dublin Bus also operates several regular services (16a, 41, 41b, 41c, 746), which go from the airport to the downtown area, although there is not as much space for luggage as on designated airport services. Frequency: every 15–20 min. Journey time: 30 min. Price: adult single €1.65.	The Air Coach (operated by Bus Éireann) goes to the bus station at Parnell Place in Cork City. Frequency: Mon–Fri from 7.50am. Between 10am and 8.45pm they run every 30–40 min. Journey time: 25 min. Price: adult single €3.50, adult return €5.70.
CAR	Take the M1 then the M50, following signs to City Centre and An Lár.	Take the N27 to Cork City.

Wales, bmi baby, Loganair, Aer Lingus, Ryanair and BA CitiExpress fly in from Britain. Airlines with flights to and from Europe include CSA Czech Airlines and Aer Lingus. Cork airport does not have any flights from North America.

For general information about the airport tel 021 431 3131; www.aerrianta.com

Shannon Airport (SNN) is 24km (15 miles) west of Limerick in the Shannon region in the west of Ireland. Scheduled flights from Britain are operated by Aer Lingus, Ryanair, Flybe and BA CitiExpress. Most European flights (Paris, Frankfurt, Brussels), are operated by Ryanair, although there are other airlines which run flights from destinations farther away, such as Minsk and Moscow. There are many flights from cities in the east of the US. Aer Lingus have flights from Boston, Chicago and New York (JFK), Continental Airlines fly from New York (Newark) and Delta have flights from Atlanta. Note that US immigration officials check your documentation at Shannon airport before you board your flight back to the US.

For general information about Shannon airport tel 061 712 000; www.shannonairport.com

BY AIR TO NORTHERN IRELAND

Northern Ireland is served by Belfast International airport, Belfast City airport and City of Derry airport. Most scheduled

Allow plenty of time for the usual airport procedures

SHANNON (SNN)	BELFAST INTERNATIONAL (BFS)	BELFAST CITY (BHD)
There is a desk in the Arrivals hall where you can hire a taxi. Price: approx €28 to Limerick City or Ennis.	Price: approx £23 to downtown Belfast.	Price: approx £6 to downtown Belfast. Almost all taxis are wheelchair-friendly.
None	There are no rail services directly to the airport. The nearest station is at Antrim, 9km (6 miles) away.	Take the Belfast City Airlink bus number 600 to Sydenham train station (journey time: 3 min, price: adult single 60p, child single 30p), then a Northern Ireland Railways train to Great Victoria Street or Belfast Central station. For Airlink service and train information, see www.translink.co.uk
Service 343 goes to Limerick City bus station. Frequency: irregular service, but at least every hour from 7.15am–midnight. Journey time: 45 min. Price: adult single €5.20. Service 051 goes to Galway via Ennis bus station. Frequency: 9.20am Mon–Sun and 12, 2, 4 summer only. Journey time: between 1 hour 40 min and 2 hours 20 min. Price: adult single €13.50. Service 344 goes to Ennis bus station (and there you can take bus number 051 on to Galway). Frequency: irregular service from 8am–midnight. Journey time: between 45 min and an hour. Price: adult single €5.20.	Airbus service 300 (www.translink.co.uk) goes to Royal Avenue, Castle Place, Laganside Buscentre and Europa Buscentre, although after 9.30pm it only goes to the Europa Buscentre. Frequency: Mon–Sat every 30 min from 7.10am–11.20pm, Sun every hour 6.50am–11.20pm. Journey time: 30–40 min. Price: adult single £6, adult return £9.	Airlink number 600 (www.translink.co.uk) to Donegall Square and Europa Buscentre. Frequency: Mon–Fri every 30 min, Sat every 30–45 min, Sun every 45 min but next bus after 8.15am is 9.45am. Journey time: 12 min. Price: adult single £2, child single £1.
Take the N18 south to Limerick City or north to Galway.	Take the A57 then the M2 to the heart of the city.	Take the A2 Sydenham bypass to downtown Belfast.

flights to these airports are from Britain or the Republic of Ireland and there are no flights to or from the US—you'll need to take a transatlantic flight to the Republic or to London, and then make your way to Northern Ireland. For more information about flights within the island, ▷ 59.

Belfast International Airport (BFS) is 29km (18 miles) north of the city. Services in Departures include internet kiosks, a travel agency, a bureau de change, a café and ATMs. In Arrivals there is an information desk (open 24 hours) that provides information on flights and public transport and a bureau de change. Most flights to the airport are from Britain on airlines such as bmi baby, Eastern Airways (Aberdeen) and MyTravel Lite (Birmingham). EasyJet operates many flights to the UK and also Amsterdam. There is also a large number of charter flights in the summer to European holiday resorts.

For general information about Belfast International Airport, tel 028 9448 4848; www.belfastairport.com

Belfast City Airport (BHD) is 4km (2.5 miles) east of the heart of the city and is used mostly by business people from Britain. Airlines include British Airways, Flybe and bmi.

For general information about Belfast City airport, tel 028 9093 9093; www.belfastcityairport.com

BUDGET AIRLINES

The number of low-cost flights to and from Ireland has increased enormously in the last few years, making Ireland a popular weekend destination for visitors from Britain and Europe. One-way tickets to destinations in Ireland are sometimes advertised for as little as €5 (not including taxes) although you will need to book well in advance and be flexible about when you travel and at what time of day. The downside for passengers is that budget airline collapses are not unheard of and that routes come and go fairly quickly. Flights are inexpensive because the airlines do not provide services such as accommodation or a refund if their flights are severely delayed, for example. The best advice is when you book a flight, always read the conditions of carriage of that airline very carefully. Make sure you also know what identification the airline requires, as there have been reported cases of airlines refusing to allow passengers to board, because they did not have an acceptable type of photo identification.

A number of low-cost airlines serve major European airports

Arriving by Ferry

Ireland has six main ferry ports with services from Scotland, England, Wales, the Isle of Man and France run by different ferry operators. Sometimes more than one ferry operator runs services on a particular route, so it pays to shop around. You should always check crossing times as there are fast and slow services, so if time is short you may want to sail on a faster, if more expensive, service. You should remember that the Irish Sea can sometimes be quite rough, which occasionally leads to crossings being cancelled. Many ferry operators run a reduced service in January, when ships have their annual refit. The information below is grouped under the name of the Irish port and includes details of which ferry operators have services to that port, where they sail from and how long the sailing takes. The section also includes details on how to get from the port to the middle of town.

REPUBLIC OF IRELAND

Cork

Swansea Cork Ferries sail from Swansea in South Wales to Cork in the south of Ireland in 10 hours. Brittany Ferries provide a crossing from Roscoff, Brittany, in the northwest of France, to Cork.

Dublin

Irish Ferries and Stena Line run services from Holyhead in North Wales to Dublin. The journey time on Stena HSS *Explorer* is 1 hour and 40 minutes, or 3 hours on the Stena *Adventurer*. With Irish Ferries the journey takes 1 hour 50 minutes on the fast service or 3 hours 15 minutes on the Cruise Ferry.

SeaCat Scotland has a Liverpool to Dublin service, as does P&O Irish Sea and NorseMerchant Ferries. P&O Irish Sea also has two daily sailings from Mostyn in North Wales with a journey time of 6 hours.

The Isle of Man Steam Packet Company has a service from

the capital of the Isle of Man, Douglas, to Dublin, which takes 2 hours 45 minutes.

P&O Irish Sea also operates a seasonal crossing between Cherbourg and Dublin. When you drive your car off the ferry, be very careful, as you have to drive through an industrial area which is served by freight trains. You must give way to these trains as they cannot stop, and there is no signalling to let you know that a train is coming. For this reason, be particularly careful if your ferry arrives at night.

Dún Laoghaire (South of Dublin)

Stena Line has a service from Holyhead in North Wales to Dún Laoghaire, (pronounced 'Dunleery') which takes 1 hour 40 minutes on the fast service or 3 hours on the slower ferry. From the port it's then only a 20-minute journey on the DART light railway to the heart of Dublin. A return ticket to Pearse station in Dublin costs €3.20.

Rosslare

Irish Ferries run a service from Pembroke in South Wales to Rosslare which takes 3 hours 45 minutes. The company also sails to Rosslare from the French ports of Cherbourg and Roscoff. P&O Irish Sea also have a year-round service from Cherbourg to Rosslare. Stena Line sails from Fishguard in the southwest of Wales to Rosslare. The journey time is 1 hour 50 minutes on the fast Stena *Lynx* or 3 hours 30 minutes on the Superferry.

NORTHERN IRELAND

Belfast

Stena Line has a fast Stranraer (Scotland) to Belfast service which takes 1 hour 45 minutes. There is also a slower service which takes 3 hours 15 minutes.

FERRY OPERATORS

FERRY COMPANY	TELEPHONE RESERVATIONS	WEBSITE
Irish Ferries	1890 313131 (Ireland), 08705 171717 (UK)	www.irishferries.com
Stena Line	08705 707070 (UK), 01 204 7777 (Republic) Ferrycheck numbers provide up-to-the-minute information on sea conditions and timetable changes: 01 204 7799 (Republic), 08705 755755 (UK)	www.stenaline.com
Swansea Cork Ferries	021 427 1166 (Ireland), 01792 456 116 (UK)	www.swansea-cork.ie
P&O Irish Sea	01 407 3434 (Ireland), 0870 242 4777 (UK)	www.poirishsea.com
SeaCat	1 800 805055 (Republic), 08705 523523 (UK)	www.seacat.co.uk
Isle of Man Steam Packet Company	1 800 805055 (Republic), 08705 523523 (UK)	www.steam-packet.com
NorseMerchant Ferries	01 819 2999 (Republic), 0870 600 4321 (UK)	www.norsemerchant.com
Brittany Ferries	021 427 7801 (Ireland), 0870 536 0360 (UK)	www.brittany-ferries.com

SeaCat Scotland runs a service from Troon in the west of Scotland which takes 2 hours 30 minutes and one from Liverpool in the north of England. NorseMerchant Ferries also covers the Liverpool to Belfast route, with a journey time of 8 hours 30 minutes.

The Isle of Man Steam Packet Company (SeaCat) runs a service from the Isle of Man to Belfast, which takes 2 hours 45 minutes). The SeaCat terminal on Donegall Quay in Belfast is just a 5-minute walk from the Laganside Buscentre and taxis are available at the port.

Larne (North of Belfast)

P&O Irish Sea operates two services from the west of Scotland. The Superstar Express service sails from Troon to Larne in 1 hour 49 minutes and the Cairnryan to Larne service takes 1 hour on the *Superstar Express* or 1 hour 45 minutes on the *European Causeway* or *European Highlander* superferries. The same company also has a crossing from Fleetwood, Lancashire, in the north of England. If you are a foot passenger, the best way to get to Belfast is to take the train from Larne harbour, which costs £3.90 for a one-way journey.

ON-BOARD FACILITIES

Generally, the bigger the ship, the better the facilities. All services have the minimum on-board amenities, such as a café or restaurant, toilets and a shop, while larger ferries may have cabins with private bathrooms, a cinema, a children's play area, video games, a choice of restaurants and a bureau de change. If you want to be sure what facilities and diversions are available on board, ask when you book or have a look at the ferry operator's website.

BY LONG-DISTANCE BUS AND FERRY

You can travel by long-distance bus and ferry to Ireland with Eurolines (www.eurolines.com). Inter-city bus services in Britain are operated by National Express (nationalexpress.com) and in Ireland by Bus Éireann (www.buseireann.ie), and you can travel from major UK cities, such as London, Birmingham, Oxford, Glasgow, Edinburgh, Bristol and Cardiff. The ferry routes that are used by these services are Holyhead to Dublin Port, Holyhead to Dun Laoghaire, Fishguard to Rosslare and Stranraer to Belfast.

TRAIN AND FERRY

It's possible to purchase one ticket (known as 'Rail and Sail') which includes a train journey to a ferryport in England and a sailing with Stena Line to a port in Ireland. For example, you can take a train from London (which stops en route at Birmingham, Leeds, Manchester, Liverpool and Chester) to Holyhead then sail to Dún Laoghaire on the Stena HSS. Alternatively, there's a service from London to the Welsh port of Fishguard (via Bristol, Cardiff and Swansea), from where you sail on the Stena *Europe* to Rosslare. For train information call National Rail Enquiries in England on 08457 484950 or see their website, www.nationalrail.co.uk To make a reservation call 08705 455455 and state that you are travelling by train.

Stena Line operate traditional and high-speed ferries between Rosslare and the Welsh coast

GETTING AROUND

BY ROAD

If you want to travel around the countryside, stopping in little villages, realistically you're going to need a car, as smaller places are not served by public transport. In both Northern Ireland and the Republic you drive on the left and speed limits (▷ 52) are observed and enforced. The main factor to consider, particularly when driving in the Republic, is time. On the map, distances may seem short, but a combination of country roads, less than comprehensive signage and some poorly maintained road surfaces can lead to journeys taking longer than you might anticipate. You can prepare for this by buying a detailed road map, allowing plenty of time to get to your destination and accepting the often slow speeds on Irish roads. Avoid taking a car into Dublin, particularly during the rush hour. For more information on driving and car rental, ▷ 51–54.

When several people are travelling together they may well find that taking a taxi is a sensible option for some shorter journeys. Taxis in Dublin, Belfast, Cork, Limerick and Galway have a meter. In other parts of the country you need to agree the fare with the driver in advance.

BY TRAIN

Getting around Ireland by train may not be as economical as using the bus, but it is fast—the maximum time for a long-distance journey will be less than 4 hours. There has been massive investment in improvements to major stations and in the railway network as a whole, although the network still does not cover the whole country. For example, there is no railway line which covers the west coast from north to south and no service at all in Donegal or the far southwest of the country. Getting from Dublin to Belfast is quick (2 hours) and easy, though, thanks to the excellent Enterprise service. See pages 55–57 for more detailed information.

Empty roads and wonderful scenery make driving a joy

BY BUS

Most of Ireland is covered by some sort of bus service, although the services can be somewhat haphazard, and on long journeys you will probably have to change buses at least once. However, buses are still the least expensive way of getting around and if time is not pressing, they are a good way to see the countryside. If it's your intention to travel around the island by public transport, consider investing in a special pass, such as the Irish Rover, which gives you unlimited travel on buses in the Republic and Northern Ireland, or the Emerald Card, which covers unlimited travel both on long-distance buses and on trains. See pages 46 and 56 for more information, including full details on the various bus passes that are available.

FLIGHTS WITHIN IRELAND

Taking internal flights in Ireland is not usually necessary, as it is not a large country and you may find that if you take into account check-in time and the journeys to and from the airport, that it does not save you much time. If you do prefer to fly, there are nine regional airports (including one on the Aran Islands), which operate domestic flights of no more than 45 minutes, at a cost of between €40 and €70 one way. See page 59 for information on routes, prices and airline contact details.

MAPS

Local Tourist Information Offices can supply you with a basic town map, although you will probably have to pay for a more detailed country map. Tourist Information Offices and book and magazine retailers such as Eason sell a wide variety of travel guides, street maps and road maps. If you are driving around the country, a map showing both major and minor roads is absolutely essential. See page 54 in the driving section for recommended maps.

Getting Around in Dublin

Dublin is a compact city, easily negotiated on foot and if you are visiting for a short time, you may find that you don't use public transport at all. However, if you do need to use transport, there's an extensive bus network, plenty of taxis, open-top bus tours, DART light railway and the new Luas light railway trams to get you about.

BUS

Buses in Dublin and its suburbs are operated by Bús Átha Cliath (Dublin Bus). Fares for adults within the city are between €0.85 and €1.75 (€0.55–€0.80 for children). If you plan to use the bus at least twice a day, a Rambler ticket covers unlimited city travel for varying periods: 1 day €5, 3 days €9.50, 5 days €14.50, 7 days €17.50. A family day ticket costs €7.50. Buy them from any newsagent displaying the sign *Dublin Bus Tickets*, from the Upper O'Connell Street office or on-line from www.dublinbus.ie or www.ticketmaster.ie

If you don't buy a prepaid ticket, you must pay the exact fare in coins (no notes) on the bus.

Contact details

Dublin Bus

59 Upper O'Connell Street

Tel 01 872 0000, passenger information 01 873 4222 (Mon–Sat 9–7); www.dublinbus.ie

Open: Mon 8.30–5.30, Tue–Fri 9–5.30, Sat 9–2.30, closed Sun and public holidays.

CITY BUS TOURS

The Dublin City Tour is an open-top bus tour, that takes in all the main attractions, with a lively commentary from the driver. The buses, operated by Dublin Bus, are beige and dark green. Tickets are valid for 24 hours from when they are stamped in the machine on board, and you can get on and off as many times as you wish during that period. Tickets are €12.50 for adults and €6 for children under 14. There are 19 stops around the city and buses run every 10 minutes from 9.30 to 5, and every 30 minutes from 5 until 6.30 April to September. The rest of the year buses run every 15 minutes from 9.30 to 4.30.

DART

The DART (Dublin Area Rapid Transit) is a light railway system which runs along the coast, from Howth, northeast of Dublin, to Arklow to the south. You are most likely to use the DART if your hotel is outside the city, if you arrive on foot at Dún Laoghaire port, or for day trips to one of the attractions en route. You can catch the bright green DART trains from Connolly, Tara Street or Pearse stations in the city; get tickets from the ticket desk or a vending machine (instructions in English, Irish, Spanish, German and French) which accepts cash, credit cards (Eurocard/MasterCard or Visa) and debit cards (Solo). As an example, an adult return from Pearse station to Dún Laoghaire costs €3.20 and the journey takes 20 minutes. You need to validate your ticket by stamping it in the machine before you get to the platform on outward and return journeys. The DART can get crowded during rush hour.

Contact details

www.irishrail.ie

LUAS

Opened in 2004, the Luas operates sleek modern trams on two city-to-suburbia routes. The Red Line runs from Dublin Connolly station (where it links to the DART) west to Heuston, then to Tallaght. The Green Line links St. Stephen's Green with Sandyford. Tickets range from a single journey to an annual pass, plus combined Luas–bus tickets. There are ticket machines, taking coins, notes and credit cards, at Luas stops, or you can buy from ticket agents, Luas or Dublin Bus (for combined Luas–bus tickets only). Prices range from €1.30 to €2 for an adult, €0.80 to €1 for a child. A one-day ticket costs €4.50 (child €2.50); a 7-day ticket costs €16 (child €7.50). There's park-and-ride parking at Sandyford, Stillorgan and Balally (€4 per day; €2.50 half day, free for disabled drivers); retain your Luas ticket for when you leave, or you'll pay an additional fee.

Contact details

Luas

Connex/Luas Depot, Red Cow Roundabout, Clondalkin, Dublin

Tel 1800 300 604 (Mon–Fri 9–5); www.luas.ie

DRIVING

Driving in Dublin is not fun, particularly during rush hour, and not necessary—the city is walkable, and there are plenty of buses to outlying attractions. In addition, city parking costs €2.50 an hour. For information on car rental, ▷ 51–52.

BICYCLING

Dublin is a relatively flat and compact city and many Dubliners cycle to work. The only place you can rent bicycles is outside the middle of the city—take bus number 46a to Belfield Bike Shop, University College, Dublin 4.

Contact details

Irish Cycling Safaris

Tel 01 260 0749; www.cyclingsafaris.com

TAXI

City taxis are metered and there are stands outside train and bus stations and at various points in the city. To call a taxi, try one of the companies listed below.

TAXIS	
COMPANY	**TELEPHONE**
Radio Cabs	01 677 2222
City Cabs	01 872 7272
Budget Cabs	01 459 9333
Pony Cabs	01 661 2233

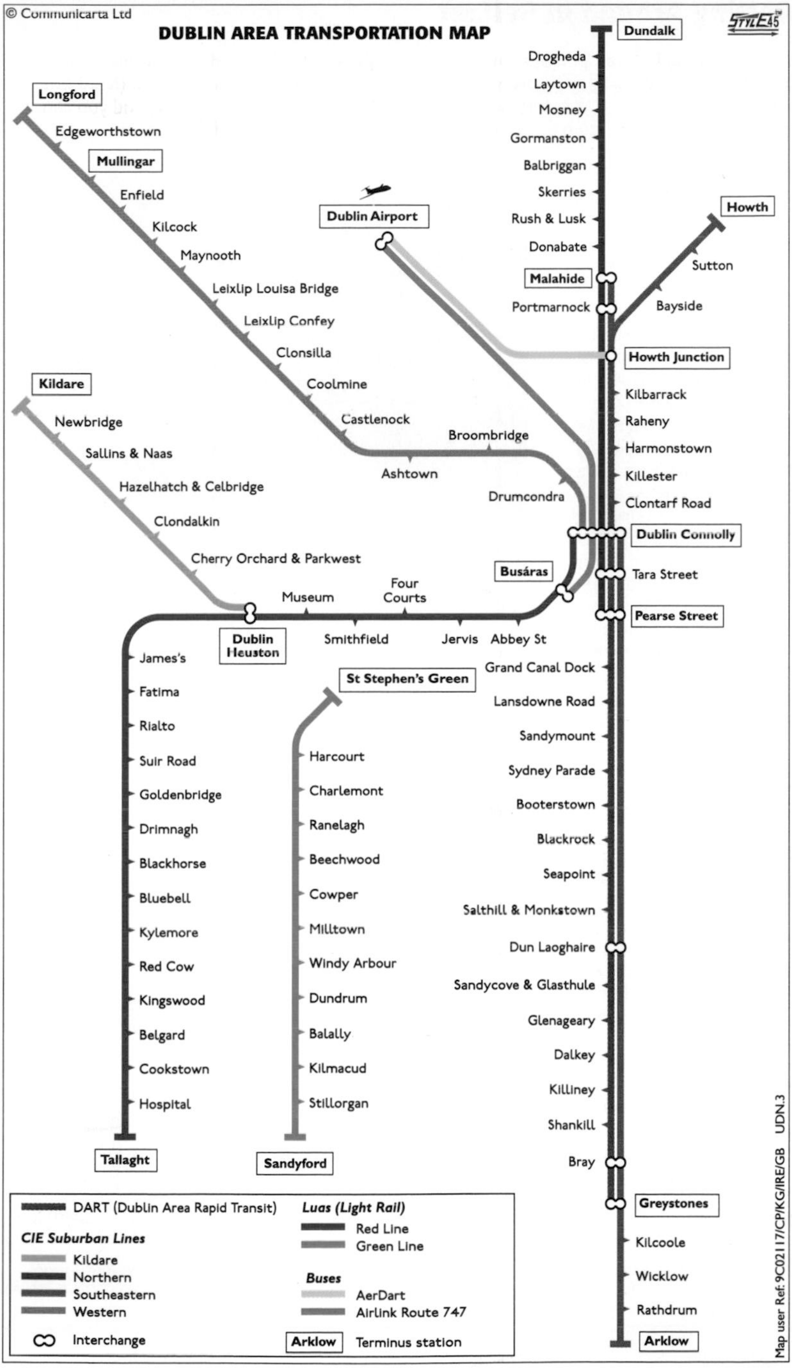

DUBLIN AREA TRANSPORTATION MAP

STYLE45

Dundalk
Drogheda
Laytown
Mosney
Gormanston
Balbriggan
Skerries
Rush & Lusk
Donabate
Malahide
Portmarnock
Howth Junction
Kilbarrack
Raheny
Harmonstown
Killester
Clontarf Road
Dublin Connolly
Tara Street
Pearse Street
Grand Canal Dock
Lansdowne Road
Sandymount
Sydney Parade
Booterstown
Blackrock
Seapoint
Salthill & Monkstown
Dun Laoghaire
Sandycove & Glasthule
Glenageary
Dalkey
Killiney
Shankill
Bray
Greystones
Kilcoole
Wicklow
Rathdrum
Arklow

Howth
Sutton
Bayside

Longford
Edgeworthstown
Mullingar
Enfield
Kilcock
Maynooth
Leixlip Louisa Bridge
Leixlip Confey
Clonsilla
Coolmine
Castleknock
Ashtown
Broombridge
Drumcondra

Dublin Airport

Kildare
Newbridge
Sallins & Naas
Hazelhatch & Celbridge
Clondalkin
Cherry Orchard & Parkwest

Dublin Heuston
Museum
Smithfield
Four Courts
Jervis
Abbey St
Busáras
James's
Fatima
Rialto
Suir Road
Goldenbridge
Drimnagh
Blackhorse
Bluebell
Kylemore
Red Cow
Kingswood
Belgard
Cookstown
Hospital
Tallaght

St Stephen's Green
Harcourt
Charlemont
Ranelagh
Beechwood
Cowper
Milltown
Windy Arbour
Dundrum
Balally
Kilmacud
Stillorgan
Sandyford

DART (Dublin Area Rapid Transit)

CIE Suburban Lines
Kildare
Northern
Southeastern
Western

Interchange

Luas (Light Rail)
Red Line
Green Line

Buses
AerDart
Airlink Route 747

Arklow Terminus station

Map user Ref: 9C02117/CP/KG/IRE/GB UDN.3

Getting Around in Belfast

The excellent public transport system in Northern Ireland, all controlled by Translink, consists of Belfast buses (Citybus), long-distance buses (Ulsterbus) and the train network (Northern Ireland Railways). Translink has worked hard to provide an integrated network, and you can get around the city and from the airports to the bus and train stations fairly simply.

BUS

Red buses operated by Citybus cover most of central Belfast, and blue buses operated by Ulsterbus cover the suburbs, with most buses leaving from Donegall Square in the heart of town. You can buy tickets in some newsagents and also at the Citybus kiosk on Donegall Square West, which is open Monday to Friday from 8am to 5.30pm. A ticket for a short distance (within Citybus's inner zone) costs 70p for an adult single and 35p for a child single. A single cross-city journey costs £1.10 for an adult and 55p for a child. A One Day Travel Card gives unlimited travel on Citybus and costs £3.20 for an adult and £1.60 for a child. You can buy all of these tickets on the bus from the driver.

- Timetables, tel 028 9066 6630, 7am–10pm; www.translink.co.uk
- For people who are hard of hearing or deaf, textphone 028 9038 7505.
- For Lost Property enquiries (Citybus), tel 028 9045 8345, Mon–Thu 8.45–5.30, Fri 8.45–2.

CENTRELINK

The Centrelink bus (service 100) goes between Donegall Square, Great Victoria Street station, Europa Buscentre, Laganside Buscentre and Central station every 12 minutes in peak periods. It's free if you have a valid train or bus ticket, otherwise it costs 70p for an adult single and 35p for a child single.

BUS TOURS

Citysightseeing (tel 028 9062 6888), charges £8 (child £3, family £20) and runs tours five times a day in summer; twice a day in winter, with commentary by guides who have been trained by the tourist board. Minicoach tours (£8; tel 02890 3324733; www.mimicoachni.co.uk), planned with the assistance of local historians tour the city's landmarks, leaving at 10.30am every day from the Belfast International Youth Hostel.

Not just for A-to-B journeys, some of Belfast's black taxis also provide tours with commentaries

TAXI

Taxis in Belfast are London-style black cabs, and you can find taxi stands at Central and Great Victoria Street train stations and in Donegall Square North. A reliable company is Value Cabs (tel 028 9080 9080).

DRIVING

As with many capital cities, a car is often more of a hindrance than a help in Belfast, as there are many one-way systems, you have to pay for all parking in the middle of the city (usually about £1–£1.20 per hour) and the local public transport system is efficient. There are several multi-level car parks in the city run by a company called NCP (National Car Parks), and the city has plans to build more. For information on where to rent a car, driving and parking, ▷ 51–54.

BICYCLING

You can rent bicycles at Life Cycles (opposite the rear entrance to Castle Court shopping mall), 36–37 Smithfield Market, Belfast, BT1 1JE; tel 028 9043 9959; www.lifecycles.co.uk

Get the useful brochure *Cycling in Northern Ireland* from the Belfast Welcome Centre. See page 61 for more information on bicycling in Northern Ireland.

Renting a bicycle is a great way to beat the city traffic jams

Driving in Ireland

Driving around Ireland is a good way to see the countryside and of getting to small villages that are not served by public transport. In recent years the volume of traffic on the roads has increased significantly and the peak visitor season of July and August sees a lot of traffic around the most popular places. The golden rule is always to leave yourself plenty of time, as your average speed is likely to be only 56–72kph (35–45 mph). This is because motorways often have only two lanes, many main roads have only one lane each way, and there are lots of box junctions and traffic lights instead of roundabouts (traffic circles).

SIGNPOSTS

In the Republic signage is erratic, which makes navigating tricky, even with a detailed road map. When there is a signpost, it may have up to eight arrow signs coming off it, so be prepared to read quickly! Older black and white signs give distances in miles, whereas new green and white signs use kilometres. In Northern Ireland signposts use miles.

BOX JUNCTIONS

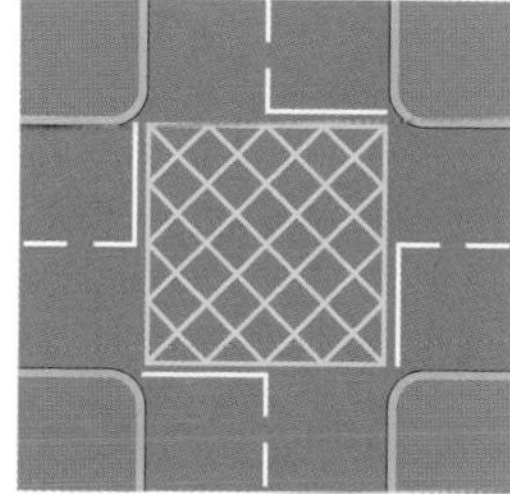

Where you see this yellow diamond pattern painted on the road surface, you should not enter the box unless it is clear that you can exit on the other side.

CAR RENTAL

You'll find the larger well-known car rental companies as well as smaller rental firms at airports, ferry ports and in towns. It is always best to book a car in advance, from home if possible. The Car Rental Council of Ireland's website www.carrentalcouncil.ie has information, although you can't actually reserve a car on this site.

- You must have a valid driver's licence, held for more than a year. An international licence is not acceptable.

MAIN ROADS

CAR RENTAL COMPANIES

The first telephone number is for the Republic, the second number is for Northern Ireland/UK.

NAME	TELEPHONE AND WEBSITE
Argus	01 4904444/0800 973490 www.argusrentals.com
Avis	1890 405 060/0870 6060100 www.avis.ie/www.avis.co.uk
Budget	1850 575767/0800 973159 www.budget.ie/www.budget.com
County	01 235 2030 www.countycar.com
Dan Dooley	01 677 2723/0800 282189 www.dan-dooley.ie
Europcar	01 614 2800/028 9031 3500 www.europcar.ie/www.europcar.com
Hertz	01 660 2255/08705 996699 www.hertz.com
National/Alamo	01 8444162/0800 212073 www.carhire.ie
Sixt/Irish Car Rentals	1850 206088/00800 47474227 www.irishcarrentals.com
Thrifty	1800 515800/0800 783 0405 www.thrifty.ie

- Many firms require a minimum age of 23, 24 or 25 and a maximum age of 70 so check when you book.
- Make sure you have personal insurance as well as Collision Damage Waiver (CDW).
- If you have any specific requirements such as an automatic transmission car, air-conditioning or a child seat, request these when you book. There is normally an extra fee.
- If you plan to rent in the Republic and drive into Northern Ireland, check that your insurance covers this. Most car rental firms in the Republic allow you to take rental cars into Northern Ireland.
- Most cars use unleaded fuel; make sure you know what your car takes before filling the tank.

RULES OF THE ROAD

- Drive on the left.
- You must wear seatbelts in the front and rear seats of the car at all times.
- Drivers and passengers on a motorcycle must wear a helmet.
- Speed limits, unless a sign indicates otherwise, are: Northern Ireland 30mph (48kph) in built-up areas, 60 mph (96kph) on the open road and 70mph (112kph) on motorways (expressways); Republic of Ireland: 50kph (31 mph) in built-up areas, 100kph (62mph) on the open road and 120kph (75mph) on motorways.
- Give way to the right at roundabouts (traffic circles) and always go left around them.
- There are tough laws against drinking alcohol and driving, and random breath-testing is carried out. Never drive under the influence of alcohol.
- In Northern Ireland, it is illegal to use a mobile (cellular) phone while driving. A similar ban is under consideration in the

DRIVING DISTANCES AND JOURNEY TIMES

This chart below gives the distances in kilometres (green) and duration in hours and minutes (blue; hours are given in the larger number) of a car journey between key towns. The times are based on average driving speeds using the fastest roads. They do not allow for delays or rest breaks.

(Below the diagonal: distances; above the diagonal: journey times.)

	Armagh	Athlone	Belfast	Cork	Derry/Londonderry	Donegal	Drogheda	Dublin	Dundalk	Dún Laoghaire	Galway	Kilkenny	Killarney	Larne	Limerick	Rosslare Harbour	Shannon Airport	Sligo	Waterford	Westport	Wexford
Armagh		222	049	516	142	202	112	150	047	205	333	329	542	117	409	407	415	210	357	334	354
Athlone	158		311	314	332	242	159	148	205	204	118	152	324	339	151	307	154	146	232	205	254
Belfast	66	224		539	136	232	135	213	110	228	423	351	618	030	444	429	504	240	420	405	416
Cork	395	218	425		643	548	408	338	429	348	302	207	119	606	134	256	153	451	152	416	244
Derry/Londonderry	114	233	115	449		107	247	325	223	340	400	501	652	142	517	542	507	200	530	324	529
Donegal	135	182	187	399	74		305	326	243	345	257	432	549	243	413	538	404	056	513	221	525
Drogheda	90	132	119	307	193	189		043	026	058	316	221	449	203	316	259	336	257	249	337	246
Dublin	139	125	168	261	242	219	50		104	019	305	151	420	241	246	218	306	302	220	338	205
Dundalk	53	150	83	342	159	179	36	85		118	322	242	508	137	335	320	354	240	310	341	307
Dún Laoghaire	149	140	178	266	252	229	60	10	95		320	200	428	255	255	205	315	317	223	353	152
Galway	241	91	307	206	278	205	226	219	244	233		232	304	451	128	402	118	200	312	118	350
Kilkenny	257	122	287	148	348	305	169	123	204	128	170		250	420	150	130	209	336	040	345	118
Killarney	385	228	436	90	459	408	354	309	353	314	216	195		646	136	351	155	453	247	418	339
Larne	100	259	36	460	120	182	154	203	117	212	341	327	471		512	457	532	308	447	433	444
Limerick	276	119	327	103	369	296	245	199	244	205	104	121	112	361		250	020	317	146	242	238
Rosslare Harbour	293	200	323	203	397	384	205	154	240	147	260	91	266	357	200		310	451	104	510	015
Shannon Airport	293	134	359	126	357	284	269	223	268	228	92	145	135	394	24	223		307	206	232	258
Sligo	147	118	202	335	137	64	200	214	169	228	141	241	344	236	232	320	220		416	124	438
Waterford	301	169	331	129	392	353	213	167	248	166	217	48	192	365	126	74	149	289		425	052
Westport	249	144	304	286	238	166	254	258	267	272	82	249	295	338	183	345	171	102	296		457
Wexford	279	186	308	189	382	370	190	140	225	132	247	78	253	343	186	16	210	305	61	331	

ROAD SIGNS

REPUBLIC OF IRELAND

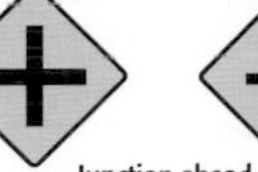

Series of dangerous bends ahead | Roundabout ahead | Junction ahead: with roads of equal importance | with roads of less importance | Road works ahead | Slippery stretch of road ahead

Unprotected quay, canal or river ahead | Unguarded level crossing ahead | Major road ahead, give way to traffic on it | Speed limit | End of speed limit

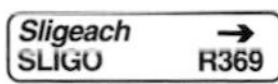

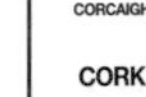

No entry | Clearway–stopping or parking prohibited | Direction sign–distances on green signs (as above) are generally in kilometres | Direction sign | City, town or village sign

NORTHERN IRELAND

Crossroads ahead | Roundabout ahead | Mini roundabout (roundabout circulation) | No through road | Double bend–first to left | Two-way traffic ahead

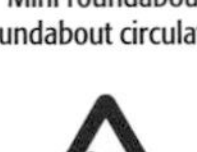
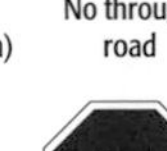

Cycle route ahead | Slippery road | Road works ahead | Stop and give way | Give way to traffic on major road | No stopping (clearway)

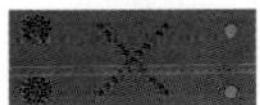

National speed limit applies | Maximum speed | No overtaking | No entry for vehicular traffic | One-way traffic | Do not proceed further in this lane

Republic, so check before you go. Currently, drivers are routinely prosecuted for dangerous driving brought about by using a mobile phone while driving.

- If you are involved in a collision, you must stop, give your name, the name and address of the car's owner and the car registration number to others involved. If you don't give your details at the time of the collision, you must immediately report the incident to the police.
- In the Republic, the Gardaí can issue on-the-spot fines for parking and speeding offences.
- For the rules of the road for Northern Ireland, look up the Highway Code online: www.highwaycode.gov.uk

BRINGING YOUR OWN CAR

Bringing your own car to Ireland from Europe is straightforward thanks to the car ferry services to Ireland from Britain and France. Contact your motor insurer at least a month before you travel to check that your car is covered in the Republic and/or Northern Ireland, or to arrange cover if it is not. As well as your passport, you'll need to bring a valid driving licence, International Driving Permit (where necessary) and your motor insurance and vehicle registration documents.

FUEL

There is a network of filling stations across Ireland, selling super unleaded, unleaded and diesel. Fuel is more expensive in the North than in the South—a litre of unleaded costs around €0.90 in the Republic and £0.80 in Northern Ireland.

PARKING

In Dublin and the Republic

Dublin is divided into five tariff zones, with the tariffs displayed on 'Pay & Display' machines. Zones are colour coded and you can tell the zone by the coloured strip on Pay & Display street signs and machines. The hourly rate varies from €0.63 in the blue zone to €1.90 in the yellow zone (heart of the city). The maximum parking time is 3 hours and fees apply from 7am to 7pm Monday to Saturday and 2pm to 6pm on Sundays, although in some streets you have to pay after 7pm and at weekends. Signs and the ticket machine will give information for that street. Parking in a Dublin car park costs €2.50 an hour.

In other parts of the country, there are car parks as well as disc parking schemes, where you buy a disc in a newsagents, scratch off the time, day, date and year and leave it on display inside your car. Discs are only valid in the area where they are bought.

In Belfast

- There are several NCP car parks in Belfast (Castle Court, Victoria Centre, Montgomery Street and Great Northern) that charge about £1.20 an hour.
- If you park in the street, you have to put money in a meter (£1 an hour), and the maximum stay is usually only an hour. Evenings and Sundays are usually free but there are exceptions, so check the signs.

WHERE NOT TO PARK

- Parking is restricted where there is a single yellow line painted by the roadside and prohibited on double yellow lines.
- Do not park at a bus stop, in a bus lane, on a pedestrian crossing or where there are school entrance markings.
- If you are illegally parked, you risk a fine, having wheels clamped or the car towed away. If your car is towed, there's a release fee of more than €125 (£280 in NI).

CAR BREAKDOWN AND ACCIDENTS

Emergency breakdown assistance is normally provided as part of a car rental, so check your documentation or the car key ring for the number to call. If you bring your own car to Ireland, check if membership of an automobile association in your home country entitles you to reciprocal assistance from a British or Irish organization.

TRAFFIC INFORMATION

- Phone: AA Roadwatch Traffic Information line, tel 1550 131811 (Republic) or 09003 401100 (Northern Ireland). Calls cost €0.79/£0.60 per minute, www.aaireland.ie
- Website: www.aaroadwatch.ie Updated every few minutes, this site gives latest road conditions, parking availability and local weather, and has a route planner for Ireland, the UK and Europe.
- Radio: You can hear traffic reports on RTE1, 2FM, Lyric FM and Today FM.

TIPS

- Avoid driving into or out of Dublin during the rush hour.
- Invest in a detailed road map, particularly for the Republic. The AA produces three detailed road maps—the Touring Map of Southern Ireland (scale 1:250,000), the Road Map Ireland (scale 1:300,000) and the Road Atlas Ireland (scale 1:200,000), all of which are very clear.
- Allow plenty of time for your journey and be patient. Country roads can be narrow and may have slow-moving agricultural vehicles.
- Don't overload your car. As well as being unsafe, it may invalidate your insurance.
- Ireland is generally safe but as always, do not leave valuables in your car.
- Dogs can be a small-town hazard—watch for them sleeping in the road.
- Sheep may stray onto the road on unfenced hills.

BREAKDOWN ORGANIZATIONS

ORGANIZATION	TELEPHONE NUMBERS	WEBSITE
The Automobile Association of Ireland (AA) Republic—23 Suffolk Street, Dublin 2	01 617 9950 (general enquiries), 01 617 9977 (to become a member), 1800 667788 (Republic) or 0800 667788 (Northern Ireland) for 24-hour rescue assistance service	www.aaireland.ie
The Automobile Association (AA) Northern Ireland	0870 600 0371 (general enquiries), 0800 667788 (breakdown assistance)	www.theAA.com
The Royal Automobile Club (RAC) Republic—RAC House, 232 Lower Rathmines Road, Dublin 6	1890 483483 or 01 412 5500 (to become a member)	www.rac.ie
The Royal Automobile Club (RAC) Northern Ireland	0870 572 2722 (general enquiries), 0800 828282 (breakdown assistance)	www.rac.co.uk

Trains

All train services in the Republic are run by Iarnród Éireann and by Northern Ireland Railways in Northern Ireland. The network does not cover the whole country. For example there is no railway line that covers the west coast, and no service at all in Donegal or the far southwest of the country, although the east coast of the island is well served. The good news is that journey times are short with almost all journeys less than 4 hours long.

REPUBLIC OF IRELAND

Over the last few years some €1.3 billion have been invested in the rail network in the Republic, which is operated by the national rail company Iarnród Éireann. This investment has resulted in the modernization of stations such as Heuston and Connolly in Dublin, which are now bright, airy and passenger-friendly. From Connolly station you can get trains to Belfast (▷ 56, The Enterprise Dublin–Belfast), Wexford, Rosslare Europort and Sligo and from Heuston there are services to such destinations as Galway, Limerick, Cork, Waterford and Westport.

JOURNEY TIMES FROM DUBLIN

The journey times below are approximate, and are for journeys from Dublin. All services are operated by Iarnród Éireann apart from the Dublin to Belfast route which is jointly run by Iarnród Éireann and Northern Ireland Railways. The telephone numbers have 24-hour recorded timetable information for that route.

TO	JOURNEY TIME	TIMETABLE INFORMATION
Ballina	3 hours 45 min	01 805 4299
Belfast	2 hours 5 min	01 805 4277
Cork	2 hours 40 min	01 805 4200
Galway	2 hours 40 min	01 805 4222
Killarney/Tralee	3 hours 50 min	01 805 4266
Limerick	2 hours 10 min	01 805 4211
Rosslare Europort	3 hours	01 805 4288
Sligo	3 hours 20 min	01 805 4255
Waterford	2 hours 40 min	01 805 4233
Westport	3 hours 35 min	01 805 4244

Buying a ticket

Tickets can be purchased from the ticket office in the station, online at www.irishrail.ie or from one of the automatic ticket vending machines at Connolly, Tara Street and Pearse stations in Dublin. These machines have instructions in English, Irish, Spanish, German and French and accept cash and credit cards (Eurocard/MasterCard, Laser and Visa). On most routes a day return costs the same amount as or only slightly more than a single, so avoid buying single tickets if you can. You can upgrade to first class on some services for an extra €10 for each journey.

Contact details

Timetables and fares
Tel 01 836 6222 (Mon–Sat 9–6, Sun and public holidays 10–6).
Travel Centre
35 Lower Abbey Street, Dublin; www.irishrail.ie

The revitalized rail network offers a comfortable, speedy service

NORTHERN IRELAND

Translink runs all of the public transport in Northern Ireland, including Northern Ireland Railways. There are four lines, all originating in Belfast, with services to Derry, Portadown (south of the capital), Bangor (east) and Larne harbour. All trains are totally non-smoking. The Belfast to Derry service takes about 2 hours and costs £8.20 for an adult single and £12 for a day return.

Buying a ticket

Tickets can be purchased from Great Victoria Street or Central stations, via the website www.translink.co.uk or by telephone 028 9089 9409.

Contact details

Translink timetable information
Tel 028 9066 6630;
www.translink.co.uk
Credit and debit card sales and reservations
Tel 028 9089 940 (Mon–Sat 9–5).

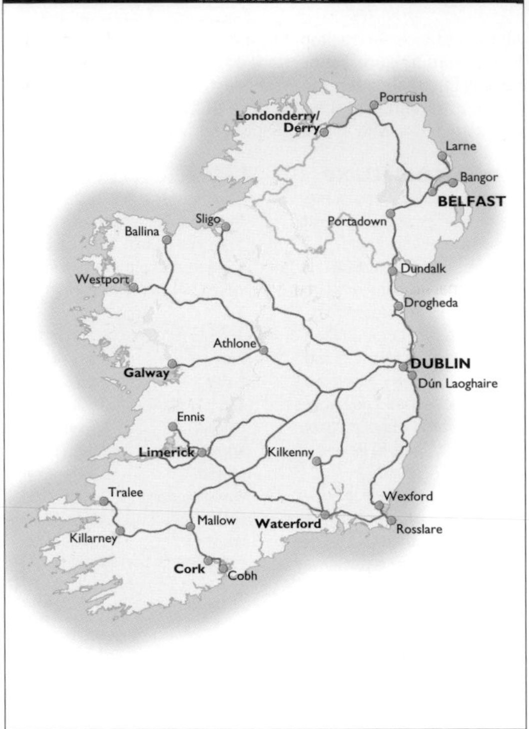

THE ENTERPRISE DUBLIN–BELFAST

The popular Dublin to Belfast route is jointly run by Iarnród Éireann and Northern Ireland's Translink. The service, known as the Enterprise, runs between Connolly station in Dublin and Central station in Belfast, and takes 2 hours and 5 minutes. From Dublin there are nine trains a day Monday to Thursday and Saturday, ten on Friday and five on Sunday. From Belfast there are eight trains a day Monday to Thursday and Saturday, nine on Friday and five on Sunday. Standard adult tickets cost €31/£22 for a single midweek, €32/£23 for a day return midweek and €46/£32 for an open return; you must use the return portion of your ticket within a month. You can pay a supplement of €27.50 or £20 to upgrade to first class (known as First Plus) on most trains. Tickets

RAIL NETWORK

RAIL AND BUS PASSES	
Irish Explorer Rail	Valid on trains only, for 5 days travel out of 15 consecutive days. Adult €115, child €58.50.
Irish Explorer Rail and Bus	8 days travel out of 15 consecutive days. Adult €176, child €88.
Irish Rover (bus only)	Unlimited travel for 5 days out of 15 consecutive days on Bus Éireann and Ulster Bus. Adult €152, child €84.
Emerald Card	Valid on Intercity, DART and suburban rail, Iarnród Éireann, Northern Ireland Railways, Ulsterbus and Bus Éireann. 8-day ticket adult €198, child €99; 15-day ticket adult €341, child €170.50.
Freedom of Northern Ireland	Unlimited travel on all scheduled bus and rail services in Northern Ireland operated by Citybus, Ulsterbus and Northern Ireland Railways. 1 day of unlimited travel £12, 3 days of unlimited travel out of 8 consecutive days £30, 7 days unlimited travel £45.
Eurail Pass	This pass is available to non-European residents and should be bought before arriving in Europe (where the cost is 20% higher). It provides unlimited rail travel in 17 European countries, including the Republic of Ireland. Passes are available for travel for 15 days, 21 days, one, two or three months.
Inter Rail Pass	Available to European residents only, this pass gives 50% off trains in Ireland, but is only worth buying if you plan to travel by train in several European countries, and not just around Ireland. You can buy the pass at train stations in participating European countries; www.interrailnet.com

are not available on the train, and must be bought in advance from the ticket counter at either station, or from one of the automatic vending machines at Connolly station, which accepts cash and credit cards. Your ticket also entitles you to travel on the DART in Dublin between Connolly and Tara Street or Pearse stations. The entire train is non-smoking, and on-board facilities include a trolley service of snacks, hot and cold drinks and a restaurant car. The train doors close up to 2 minutes before the train leaves, so allow enough time.

The Enterprise train service runs on the busy Dublin–Belfast route

RAIL JOURNEY TIMES

	Athlone	Belfast Central	Cork	Derry (Londonderry Waterside)	Drogheda	Dublin	Dundalk	Dún Laoghaire	Ennis	Galway	Kilkenny	Killarney	Larne Town	Limerick	Portadown	Portrush	Rosslare Strand	Sligo	Waterford Plunkett	Westport
Belfast Central	548																			
Cork	415	646																		
Derry (Londonderry Waterside)	801	158	1019																	
Drogheda	405	128	450	415																
Dublin	A130	B152	A233	B418	B033															
Dundalk	508	107	612	353	020	B052														
Dún Laoghaire	353	243	458	516	118	B023	139													
Ennis	418	745	226	948	543	A305	635	517												
Galway	102	643	431	1013	508	A223	533	445	541											
Kilkenny	257	549	405	917	417	A134	439	344	515	354										
Killarney	450	733	128	1038	553	A313	623	523	318	548	517									
Larne Town	651	053	854	258	235	B302	211	354	838	857	701	913								
Limerick	326	625	129	858	416	A205	518	417	045	450	421	248	745							
Portadown	517	027	654	242	103	B124	039	218	704	704	523	713	127	549						
Portrush	733	130	952	055	402	B347	252	439	920	945	736	1011	234	830	213					
Rosslare Strand	714	607	412	853	414	B257	439	249	542	812	220	431	654	332	458	826				
Sligo	704	608	838	834	423	B258	448	348	938	803	707	857	632	848	451	807	737			
Waterford Plunkett	341	702	303	924	508	A225	530	435	433	438	037	322	747	223	609	822	108	725		
Westport	155	826	531	958	638	A320	730	537	554	305	455	627	848	501	714	930	850	856	541	
Wexford	707	548	818	837	355	B238	420	230	741	806	1600	837	636	651	440	808	016	746	1108	654

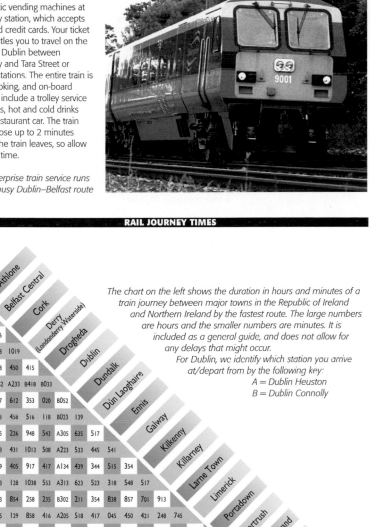

The chart on the left shows the duration in hours and minutes of a train journey between major towns in the Republic of Ireland and Northern Ireland by the fastest route. The large numbers are hours and the smaller numbers are minutes. It is included as a general guide, and does not allow for any delays that might occur.

For Dublin, we identify which station you arrive at/depart from by the following key:
A = Dublin Heuston
B = Dublin Connolly

Long-distance Buses

All buses in the Republic, apart from buses in Dublin, are run by Bus Éireann. In Northern Ireland, cross-country services are operated by Ulsterbus, which is owned by Translink. Despite the fact that Ireland is relatively small, some bus journeys can seem disproportionately long (for example the Cork to Sligo journey takes 7 hours), because you have to change once or even twice. For this reason, if you are going any distance, investigate all of your options; it will be faster to take a train, an internal flight, or rent a car, although it will almost certainly be cheaper to go by bus. If you are getting around the island by public transport, consider buying a pass such as the Emerald Card which gives you unlimited travel on buses and trains in the Republic and Northern Ireland (▷ 56). Students with an ISIC card can get a reduction.

Popular routes have several services a day: For example, there are 15 buses a day from Dublin to Galway and 13 from Dublin to Limerick; you can take a bicycle on many services for about €10.

MAIN BUS STATIONS

The bus stations listed below have a ticket office, bus information, at least one café, a newsagent, drinks machines, payphones, an ATM, toilets (at least one for people with disabilities) and a parent room. Busáras also has luggage lockers. Neither of the Belfast bus stations has luggage facilities, but you can leave bags safely at the Belfast Welcome Centre on Donegall Place.

Dublin

Busáras: Store Street, Dublin Tel 01 836 6111 (timetable); ticket office open Mon–Sat 8.30–7, Sun 9–7.

Belfast

Europa Buscentre: tel 028 9066 6630 (timetable); ticket office open Mon–Sat 7.30–6.30, Sun 12.30–5.30.

Laganside Buscentre: tel 028 9066 6630 (timetable); ticket office open Mon–Fri 8.30–5.45.

USEFUL CONTACTS

Bus Éireann: tel 01 836 6111; **www.**buseireann.ie

Ulster Bus (Translink): tel 028 9066 6630; **www.**translink.co.uk

BUS PASSES

- **Irish Rambler:** bus only (Republic) 3-day Rover adult €53, child €32; 8-day Rambler adult €116, child €74; 15-day Rambler adult €168, child €105.
- **Irish Rover:** bus only (all Ireland) 3-day Rover adult €68, child €38; 8-day Rover adult €152, child €84; 15-day Rover adult €226, child €124.
- **Irish Explorer:** rail and bus (Republic) 8-day Explorer adult €176, child €88.
- **Emerald Card:** rail and bus (all Ireland) 8-day Emerald Card adult €198, child €99; 15-day adult €341, child €170.50.
- **Freedom of Northern Ireland:** (NI) Travel on all Translink transport in Northern Ireland including city buses, long-distance buses and trains. Adult prices: 1 day £12, 3 out of 8 consecutive days £30, unlimited travel for 7 days £45.

BUSES TO BRITAIN

Bus Éireann operates some services to cities in Britain (Glasgow, Leeds, Manchester, Birmingham, London) in conjunction with the British long-distance bus company National Express (Eurolines). To book, contact Bus Éireann (tel 01 836 6111; www.buseireann.ie) or Eurolines (tel 08705 143219 or 01582 404511; www.eurolines.ie) An example is the 861 service which leaves Dublin Busáras at 10am, sails with Stena Line ferries at 11.10am and arrives at London's Victoria bus station at 8.45pm. An adult return at peak time is €59 (off-peak €49) and if you book a Euro Apex 15 days in advance, it costs €49 at peak time (€39 off-peak).

INTER-CITY ROUTES

FROM	TO	JOURNEY TIME	ADULT SINGLE	ADULT MONTHLY RETURN
Belfast	Derry	1 hour 40 min	£8.20	£10.00
Cork	Dublin	6 hours	€15.00	€24.00
Cork	Limerick	1 hour 50 min	€13.50	€22.00
Cork	Sligo	7 hours	€23.00	€37.00
Cork	Waterford	3 hours 10 min	€15.00	€22.00
Dublin	Belfast	3 hours	€19.00	€26.00
Dublin	Derry	4 hours 20 min	€18.50	€24.00
Dublin	Donegal	4 hours 15 min	€19.00	€24.00
Dublin	Limerick	3 hours 40 min	€15.00	€24.00
Galway	Belfast	6 hours 40 min	€27.00	€40.50
Galway	Sligo	2 hours 30 min	€12.50	€20.00
Limerick	Galway	2 hours 5 min	€13.90	€22.00
Waterford	Wexford	1 hour	€11.00	€17.50

Flights within the Island

Ireland's compact size means that taking flights within the Republic or between the Republic and Northern Ireland is not usually necessary; Irish people generally drive or take some form of surface public transport between towns. When deciding on your transport options between towns, you should take into consideration the time and cost of getting to and from the airports at each end, and how far in advance of the flight you need to check in. It's quite possible that the total time will not be much less than the journey time on the train. A one-way ticket from Dublin to Donegal (flight time 45 minutes) on Aer Arann costs €40 including taxes. A one-way ticket from Dublin to Galway (flight time 45 minutes) costs €70 including taxes.

FLIGHTS WITHIN THE ISLAND

FROM	TO	AIRLINE
Dublin	Cork	Aer Arann and Air Wales
Dublin	City of Derry	British Airways (Logan Air)
Dublin	Donegal	Aer Arann
Dublin	Kerry	Aer Arann
Dublin	Knock	Aer Arann
Dublin	Galway	Aer Arann
Dublin	Shannon	Aer Lingus
Dublin	Sligo	Aer Arann
Connemara	Aran Islands	Aer Arann Islands

REGIONAL AIRPORTS

AIRPORT	TELEPHONE	WEBSITE
Aran Islands	091 593034	www.aerarannislands.ie
Belfast City	028 9093 9093	www.belfastcityairport.com
City of Derry	028 7181 0784	www.cityofderryairport.com
Connemara	091 593034	www.aerarannislands.ie
Donegal	074 954 8284	www.donegalairport.ie
Galway	091 755 569	www.galwayairport.com
Kerry	066 976 4644	www.kerryairport.com
Knock	1850 672 222	www.knockairport.com
Sligo	071 683 96	www.sligoairport.com
Waterford	051 875589	www.flywaterford.com

AIRPORT FACILITIES

Facilities at regional airports are fairly limited, although usually include somewhere to eat, a taxi stand and an ATM. Regional airports benefit in particular from flights operated by budget airlines, and are increasing their facilities as passenger numbers grow. To find out more about the airports you are flying to and from, see the websites listed above right, or make enquiries when you make your booking. See also pages 42–44.

Aer Arann is an Irish domestic carrier, linking major destinations

AIRLINES OPERATING REGIONAL FLIGHTS

AIRLINE	TELEPHONE	WEBSITE
Aer Arann	00 353 1 814 1058 (International) 0800 587 2324 (UK)/0818 210 210 (Republic)	www.aerarann.ie
Aer Arann Islands	091 593 034 (Republic)	www.aerarannislands.ie
Aer Lingus	0845 084 4444 (UK)/0818 365 000 (Republic)	www.aerlingus.com
Logan Air	0870 850 9850 (UK)	www.ba.com
Air Wales	0870 777 3131 (UK)/1800 654 193 (Republic)	www.airwales.co.uk

Ferries

You can take ferries to many of the islands off the coast of Ireland, to cross a lough (lake) or simply to cross a narrow stretch of water, saving yourself a long drive. Some of these services only run in the summer and may be disrupted in bad weather. For most journeys it's not necessary to book as you buy your ticket on board or on the quay. Prices range from €4 to €20.

FERRIES ON LAKES

You can take a pleasure boat trip on one of Ireland's loughs:

- **Lough Derg:** Boats go from Mountshannon to Holy Island on Lough Derg; tel 061 921351.
- **Lough Erne:** Erne tours depart from Enniskillen at the south of Lower Lough Erne (May to September) and take in the monastic site on Devenish Island; tel 028 6632 2882; **www**.fermanaghlakelands.com
- **Lough Foyle:** Foyle Cruise Line runs day and evening tours on Lough Foyle; tel 028 7136 2857; **www**.foylecruiseline.com
- **Lough Neagh:** Lough Neagh tours (tel 028 8673 6813) and Master McGrá Cruises (tel 028 3832 7573; summer only) offer trips on Lough Neagh.

Car ferries provide some scenic shortcuts across estuaries and lakes

FERRY SERVICES

TO	FROM	CONTACT DETAILS
Republic of Ireland		
Aran Islands	Rossaveal	Aran Island Ferries, 091 568903/091 572273; www.aranislandferries.ie
Aran Islands	Galway	O'Brien Shipping, 091 567676 or 091 567283
Aran Islands	Doolin	Doolin Ferries, 065 707 4455; www.doolinferries.com
Arranmore Island	Burtonport	074 942 0532; www.arainnmhor.com/ferry
Ballyhack	Passage East	The Passage East Ferry Company, 051 382488 or 051 382480
Baltimore	Schull	Cary Craft, 028 28278
Bere Island	Castletownbere	Murphy's Ferry Service, 027 75014; www.murphysferry.com
Blasket Island	Dunquin, Dingle	066 915 6422
Cape Clear Island	Baltimore	Cape Clear Ferry, 028 39159 or 086 266 2197; www.capeclearferry.info
Cape Clear Island	Schull	028 28278
Clare Island	Westport	Clare Island Ferry, 098 25212; www.clareislandferry.com O'Malley Ferries, 098 25045
Garinish Island	Glengarriff	Blue Pool Ferry, 027 63333
Inishbofin Island	Cleggan	095 45903 or 095 44750; www.inishbofinferry.com
Sherkin Island	Schull	028 28278
Tarbert	Killimer	Shannon Ferries, 065 905 3124; www.shannonferries.com
Tory Island	Bunbeg	Donegal Coastal Cruisers, 074 953 1320
Valentia Island	Cahersiveen	The Skellig Experience, 066 947 6303; www.skelligexperience.com
Northern Ireland		
Island Magee	Larne	028 2827 4085; www.johnmcloughlinshipping.co.uk
Magilligan	Greencastle	074 938 1901; www.loughfoyleferry.com
Portaferry	Strangford	028 4488 1637; www.drdni.gov.uk/roads
Rathlin Island	Ballycastle	Caledonian MacBrayne, 028 2076 9299; www.calmac.co.uk

Horse-drawn Caravans and Bicycling

HORSE-DRAWN CARAVANS

For a holiday with a slower pace and a traditional feel, a horse-drawn caravan offers a wonderful way to see the countryside. The caravans, although small, have cooking facilities and most sleep up to four people, but check what you can expect before booking. There are four operators in the Republic (in Co. Laois, Co. Kerry, Co. Wicklow and Co. Mayo), but none in Northern Ireland. Visit www.horsedrawncaravans.com, ask in any Fáilte Ireland tourist information office or contact the Irish Horse-Drawn Caravan Federation (▷ below).

To rent a horse and caravan costs between €600 and €950 per week, the peak season being mid-July to the end of August. You will also have to pay a fee (approximately €12–€20 a night), to the owners of the place where you stop, which covers parking the caravan, grazing and use of shower facilities. Before setting off, you plan your route with the caravan provider, who instructs you on care of the horse.

Contact details

Irish Horse-Drawn Caravan Federation
Kilvahan Caravans, Kilvahan, Portlaoise, Co. Laois
Tel 0502 27048;
e-mail: kilvahan@eircom.net

Slattery's Horse-Drawn Caravans
1 Russell Street, Tralee, Co. Kerry
Tel 0667 126277;
email: david@slatterys.com;
www.slatterys.com

Clissmann's
Carrigmore Farm, Co. Wicklow
Tel 0404 48188;
www.clissmann.com/wicklow

Mayo Horse-Drawn Caravan Holidays
Belcarra, Castlebar, Co. Mayo
Tel 094 903 2054; www.irishhorsedrawncaravans.com

A fun way to experience rural Ireland's slow pace of life

BICYCLING

Bicycling is another great way to see the countryside as most of the country is relatively flat, the temperature is mild (if showery!) and there are plenty of quiet country roads. Tourist offices can give details on where to rent bicycles and have information about bicycle routes.

The Northern Ireland Tourist Board has an excellent free guide called *Cycling in Northern Ireland*, which lists routes, maps and details of nearby tourist information offices. It also publishes a *Walkers & Cyclists Accommodation Guide*, featuring places that provide extra services for walkers and bicyclists, such as secure, covered bicycle storage and a place to dry wet clothes. Tourism Ireland's *Cycling in Ireland* brochure has a useful directory at the back.

In Northern Ireland there are two mapped and signposted National Cycle Network routes that follow minor roads and often cut through parks and along river and canal paths. Route 95 is from Ballyshannon to Ballycastle (298km/186 miles) and Route 93 is from Belfast to Ballyshannon (368km/228 miles). You can buy route maps (£10.99 each) from bookshops or online at: www.sustrans.org.uk For an even longer cycleway, the Kingfisher Trail in Co. Fermanagh, which was the first long-distance cycle trail in Ireland, is 480km (300 miles) long.

Accompanied bicycle tours

Irish Cycling Safaris run week-long bicycling holidays all over Ireland from May to September where you cycle about 48km (30 miles) a day and your luggage is transported to your accommodation for you. The company is based in Dublin at Belfield Bike Shop, UCD, Dublin 4; tel 01 260 0749; www.cyclingsafaris.com

BICYCLING TIPS

- It is a legal requirement that you have a white or yellow front light and a red rear light on in darkness.
- Don't bicycle on footpaths.
- You must have a red reflector clearly visible on the back of your bicycle.
- Lock your bicycle if you leave it unattended.
- Be seen—wear bright reflective clothes.
- Unleashed dogs can be a small-town hazard to bicyclists.
- In unfenced areas, sheep may stray onto the road.
- Take waterproof clothing with you.
- Some roads in the Republic are in a poor state; potholes at the edge of the road mean that you have to bicycle in the middle, which has safety implications.

VISITORS WITH A DISABILITY

Ireland's facilities for visitors with disabilities are improving, and any new buildings and public transport must have disabled access. With some advance planning most forms of transport are accessible, although older city buses are not accessible to wheelchair users.

USEFUL ORGANIZATIONS

UK

The Royal Association for Disability and Rehabilitation (RADAR)
12 City Forum, 250 City Road, London, EC1V 8AF
tel 020 7250 3222; www.radar.org.uk

NORTHERN IRELAND

Disability Action
Portside Business Park, 189 Airport Road West, Belfast, BT3 9ED
tel 028 9029 7880; textphone 028 9029 7880; www.disabilityaction.org

REPUBLIC OF IRELAND

National Disability Authority
25 Clyde Road, Ballsbridge, Dublin 4
tel 01 608 0400; www.nda.ie

US

SATH
347 5th Avenue, Suite 610, New York City, NY 10016
tel +1 212/447-7284; www.sath.org

AIRPORT BUSES

Airlink Express buses (numbers 747 and 748) run by Dublin Bus are all fully wheelchair accessible. You can reserve wheelchair space on the Airbus service 300 from Belfast International Airport to the city (tel 028 9033 7011).

BUSES

Wheelchair access to buses in the Republic is not good. Newer buses in Northern Ireland (Citybus and Ulsterbus) have low floors for wheelchair access, but these are not in use everywhere. Belfast's Centrelink service, which connects the train and bus stations with the main shopping areas, is fully accessible to wheelchairs.

TRAINS/DART

Republic of Ireland

Iarnród Éireann prefers 24 hours notice from visitors with special needs so that they can arrange for assistance. Intercity and suburban trains are accessible only via a portable ramp. The DART is fully wheelchair accessible, with wide doors and a large open area on board. Guide dogs and hearing dogs are welcome, including in restaurant cars. To arrange assistance in advance, call the station (Connolly 01 703 2358, Heuston 01 703 3299, Pearse 01 888 0182, Tara Street 01 888 0132) or call the Access & Liaison Office (tel 01 703 2634).

Northern Ireland

Trains run by Northern Ireland Railways have space set aside for wheelchair users in each train carriage (car). To arrange assistance before you travel, call the station directly. Belfast Central station 028 9089 9400, Great Victoria Street station 028 9043 4424.

FERRIES AND AIR TRAVEL

Check with the ferry company before you book. For longer crossings, cabins adapted for passengers with limited mobility are available. If you are arriving by air, advise the airline when booking if you will need help. Larger airports such as Dublin, Belfast International and Shannon have suitable facilities, such as adapted toilets and wheelchairs to use; smaller airports have fewer facilities.

GETTING AROUND CITIES

In central Dublin, many pedestrian crossings have a beeping noise to indicate when it is safe to cross the road. Some also have a screen counting down the seconds to when pedestrians can cross. Some taxi firms have accessible taxis such as Radio Cabs in Dublin (tel 01 677 2222) and black cabs in Belfast.

HELPFUL GUIDES

- Iarnród Éireann's *Guide for Mobility Impaired Passengers,* with details of access and facilities in stations in the Republic, is available free at stations or by post from Access & Liaison Office, Room 213, Iarnród Éireann, Connolly Station, Dublin 1; tel 01 703 2634.
- *Belfast City Centre Access Guide* gives access information about public buildings, shops and banks for people with a disability. Pick up a copy at bus and train stations or the Belfast Welcome Centre.
- The National Trust's *Information for Visitors with Disabilities,* with details of facilities at their more accessible properties in England, Wales and Northern Ireland , is available from The National Trust 'Access for All' office, The National Trust, Kembrey Park, Swindon, SN2 8YL, UK; tel 020 7447 6742; accessforall@nationaltrust.org.uk
- The Royal Association for Disability and Rehabilitation (RADAR), which is based in England, publishes *Holidays in Britain and Ireland—A Guide for Disabled People*. Visit www.radarsearch.org
- There's an online guide to accessible transport in Northern Ireland: www.nitran.org.uk
- For large-print timetables of any bus or train service in Northern Ireland call Translink (Belfast) on 028 9066 6630.
- For information on accessible accommodation, see Fáilte Ireland's guide *Be Our Guest* available from tourist information offices. Disability Action (▷ above left) produces a guide for accommodation in Northern Ireland.

This chapter is divided into six regions, which are shown on the map on the inside front cover. Places of interest are listed alphabetically within each region. Major sights are listed at the start of each region.

The Sights

DUBLIN

The Republic of Ireland's booming capital has some of the country's finest attractions, from museums full of art and antiquities and priceless libraries to historic castles and cathedrals. Its handsome Georgian squares are meant for strolling, and it has good restaurants and a vibrant nightlife. The seaside towns in outer Dublin hold several attractions.

THE SIGHTS

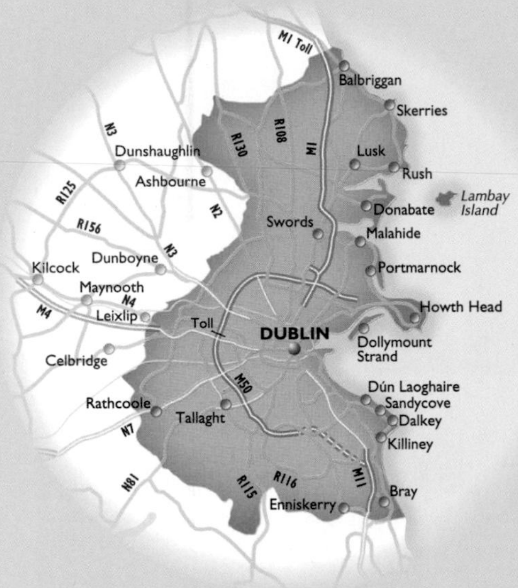

MAJOR SIGHTS

Dublin

St. Andrew's Church, Suffolk Street, Dublin 2 ☎ 1800 668668 (freephone) Jul, Aug Mon–Sat 9–7, Sun 10.30–3; Sep–end Jun Mon–Sat 9–5.30, public holidays 10.30–3
www.visitdublin.com • Excellent, informative English-language site

HOW TO GET THERE

Airport
Dublin International Airport, 11km (7 miles) north of city

Railway stations
Connolly Station, the main station, is in the middle of the city and is also on the DART line; **Heuston Station** is 3km (2 miles) west of the city, and linked to it by bus.

Inside the Oliver St. John Gogarty pub in Temple Bar (above). The Dublin City Arms (right). Ha'Penny Bridge (below)

TIPS

- Allow plenty of time at the Chester Beatty Library. Its unpromising name conceals one of the city's real hidden gems.
- The city's hop-on/hop-off tour buses are convenient for getting to the sights that are outside the main hub of the city.
- Summer weekends are a nightmare at Trinity College. If at all possible, visit on a weekday to avoid the crowds.
- Outside term time, Trinity College rents student rooms to visitors, providing a basic but inexpensive central base in a very special place.

SEEING DUBLIN

Dublin is a compact city, easy to walk around. Several of the main attractions, though, such as Kilmainham Gaol and the Irish Museum of Modern Art, will need taxis or public transport to reach them, the latter being generally good and inexpensive. Another option is to take one of the open-top bus tours, which link the attractions and allow you to get on and off as many times as you like. You should decide in advance which sights you want to see, and how many you can manage in a day. It's worth buying a Dublin Pass as it includes free entry to 30 attractions with the chance to jump the queues (lines), and transport from the airport into the city. It costs from €29 per day and is available from Dublin Tourism offices in the airport arrivals hall or in the city (main offices at Suffolk Street and O'Connell Street).

While you could cover the main sights on a weekend visit, there are so many attractions that a week would not be too long. Part of the city's charm is its people, and it would be a shame not to have a chance to relax in the bars and cafés and talk to people. Rushing round is not the best way to experience Dublin.

BACKGROUND

In recent years Dublin has become one of the hottest city destinations in Europe. But its roots go back to Viking times, and it celebrated a thousand years of history in 1988. Its location on the River Liffey was ideal for defence and for trade, and it is less than 112km (70 miles) from the British mainland. In the 12th century English invaders arrived, leading to several centuries of Anglo-Irish strife that is still unresolved in Northern Ireland.

The English presence did help the city to flourish, and left its mark in many of today's splendid houses, especially the Georgian areas around Merrion Square and other fine city squares. By the 18th century the independence movement was gaining ground, but it was not until the early 20th century that the final break from England was made. By 1972 Ireland was a member of the European Union, initiating the boom that really flourished in the 1990s, when not just the economy but fashion, the arts, food and Irish culture all blossomed and turned Dublin into the vibrant city that it is today.

DON'T MISS

TRINITY COLLEGE LIBRARY
The Library and the Book of Kells are essential (▷ 84–86)

CHESTER BEATTY LIBRARY
One of the best museums in Ireland (▷ 70–71)

KILMAINHAM GAOL
Powerful, moving and historically fascinating (▷ 76–77)

GUINNESS STOREHOUSE
Educational, entertaining, inventive, and one of the best views in Dublin (▷ 73)

NATIONAL MUSEUM
Unrivalled national collection of antiquities (▷ 80–81)

NATIONAL MUSEUM OF DECORATIVE ARTS AND HISTORY
Impressive branch of the National Museum, within Collins Barracks (▷ 80–81)

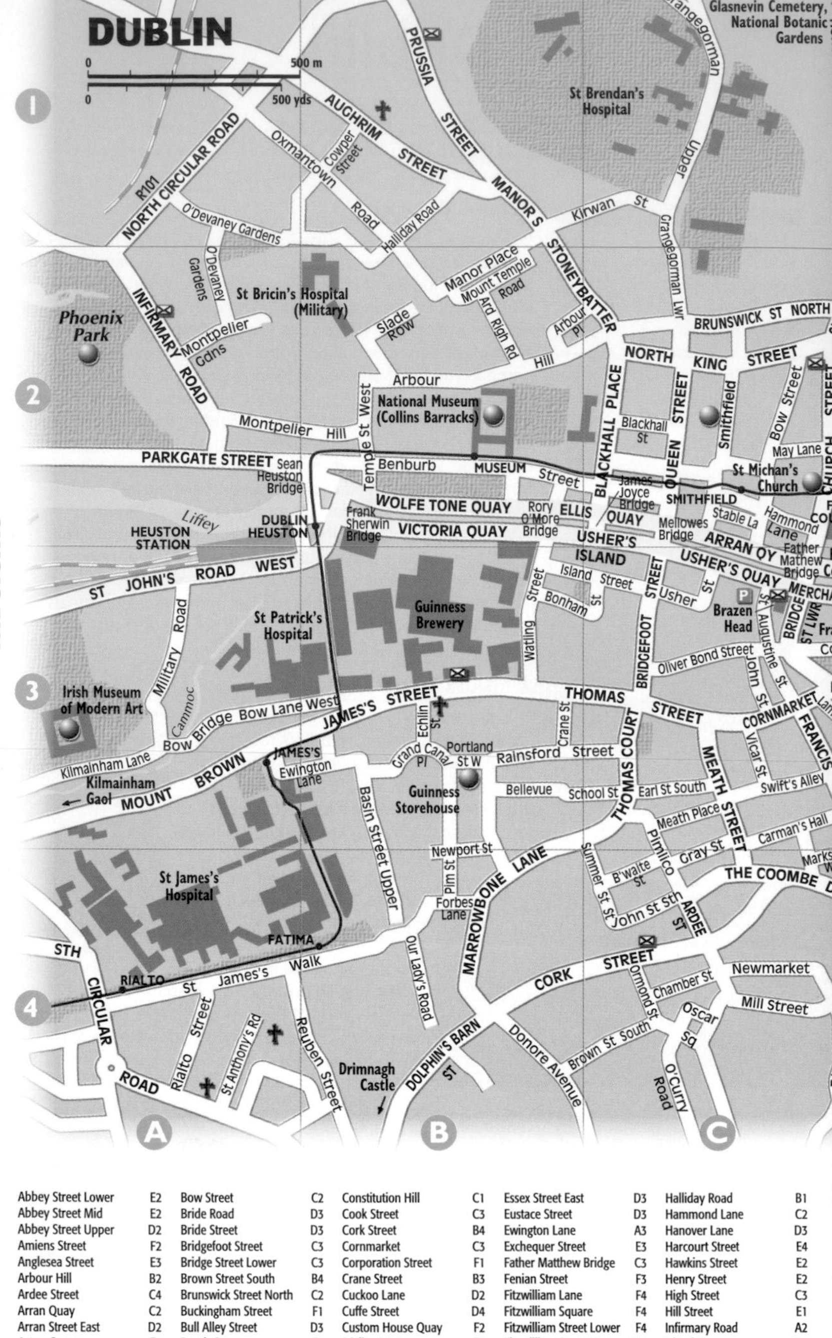

Abbey Street Lower E2
Abbey Street Mid E2
Abbey Street Upper D2
Amiens Street F2
Anglesea Street E3
Arbour Hill B2
Ardee Street C4
Arran Quay C2
Arran Street East D2
Aston Quay E2
Aughrim Street B1
Aungier Street D4
Bachelors Walk E2
Baggot Street Lower F4
Basin Street Upper B3
Bellevue B3
Benburb Street B2
Beresford Place F2
Bishop Street D4
Blackhall Place C2
Blackpitts C4
Blessington Street D1
Bolton Street D2
Bow Bridge A3
Bow Lane West A3
Bow Street C2
Bride Road D3
Bride Street D3
Bridgefoot Street C3
Bridge Street Lower C3
Brown Street South B4
Brunswick Street North C2
Buckingham Street F1
Bull Alley Street D3
Burgh Quay E2
Butt Bridge E2
Camden Row D4
Capel Street D2
Carman's Hall C3
Cathedral Street E2
Chamber Street C4
Chancery Place D2
Chancery Street D2
Church Street Upper C2
Church Street C2
City Quay F2
Clare Street F3
Clarendon Street E3
College Green E3
College Street E3
Constitution Hill C1
Cook Street C3
Cork Street B4
Cornmarket C3
Corporation Street F1
Crane Street B3
Cuckoo Lane D2
Cuffe Street D4
Custom House Quay F2
D'olier Street E2
Dame Street E3
Dawson Street E3
Dean Street C4
Dolphin's Barn Street B4
Dominick Street Lower D1
Dominick Street Upper D1
Donore Avenue B4
Dorset Street Upper D1
Drury Street E3
Earl Street North E2
Earl Street South C3
Echlin Street B3
Eden Quay E2
Ellis Quay B2
Essex Quay D3
Essex Street East D3
Eustace Street D3
Ewington Lane A3
Exchequer Street E3
Father Matthew Bridge C3
Fenian Street F3
Fitzwilliam Lane F4
Fitzwilliam Square F4
Fitzwilliam Street Lower F4
Fitzwilliam Street Upper F4
Fleet Street E3
Foley Street F1
Forbes Lane B4
Francis Street C3
Frank Sherwin Bridge B2
Frederick Street North D1
Gardiner Street Lower E1
Gardiner Street Mid E1
George's Quay F2
Golden Lane D3
Grafton Street E3
Grand Canal Place B3
Grangegorman Lower C1
Grangegorman Upper C1
Grattan Bridge D3
Halliday Road B1
Hammond Lane C2
Hanover Lane D3
Harcourt Street E4
Hawkins Street E2
Henry Street E2
High Street C3
Hill Street E1
Infirmary Road A2
Island Street B3
James Joyce Bridge C2
James's Street B3
Jervis Street D2
John Dillon Street D3
John Street C3
John Street South C4
Kevin Street Lower D4
Kevin Street Upper D4
Kildare Street E4
Killarney Street F1
Kilmainham Lane A3
King's Inns Street D2
King Street South E3
Kirwan Street B1
Lamb Alley C3

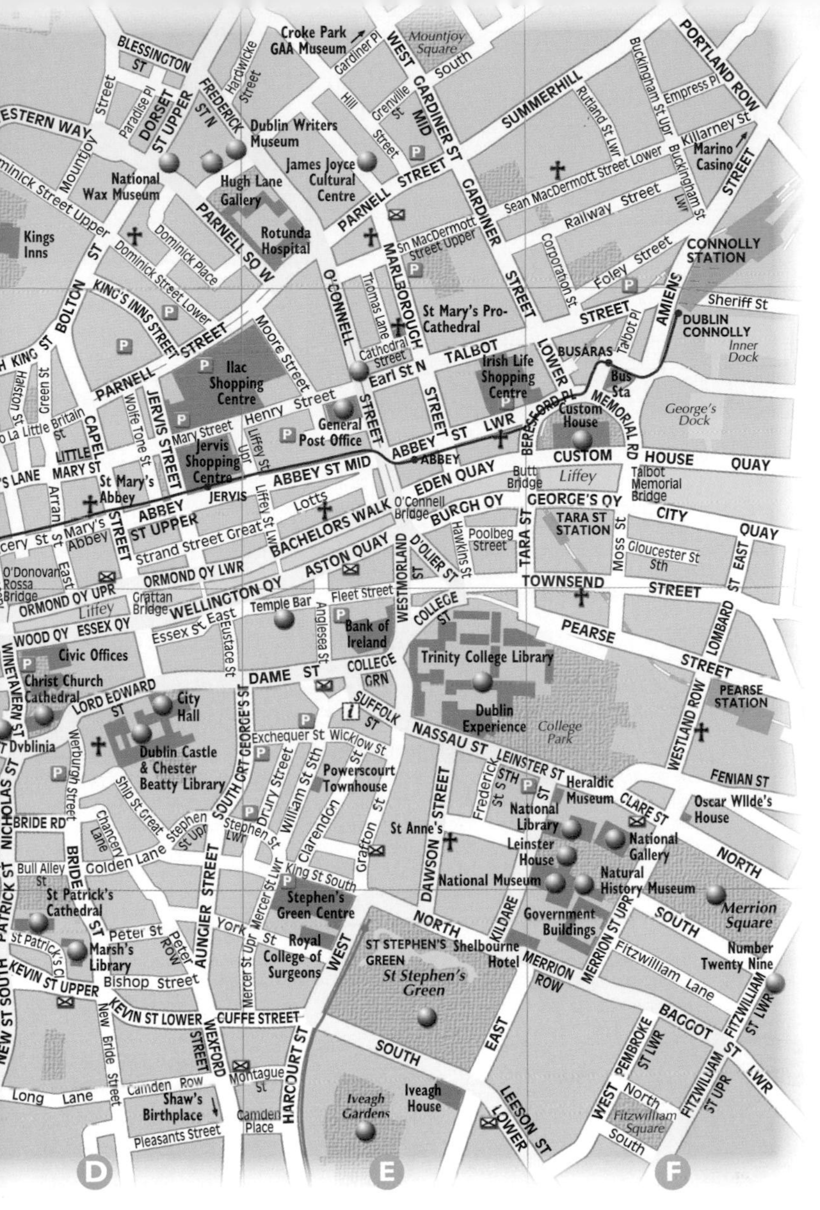
Croke Park GAA Museum
Mountjoy Square
Blessington St
Western Way
Dorset St Upper
Frederick St N
Hardwicke Street
Dublin Writers Museum
James Joyce Cultural Centre
Hugh Lane Gallery
National Wax Museum
Dominick Street Upper
Kings Inns
Rotunda Hospital
Parnell Sq W
Summerhill
Portland Row
Empress Pl
Killarney St
Marino Casino
Buckingham St Upr
Sean MacDermott Street Lower
Railway Street
Connolly Station
Gardiner Street
Parnell Street
Sn MacDermott Street Upper
Marlborough Street
St Mary's Pro-Cathedral
Talbot Street
Irish Life Shopping Centre
Busaras
Dublin Connolly
Inner Dock
Amiens Street
Sheriff St
Foley Street
Corporation St
Talbot Pl
Bus Sta
George's Dock
Custom House
Memorial Rd
Beresford Pl
Custom House Quay
Talbot Memorial Bridge
Butt Bridge
Liffey
George's Qy
City Quay
Tara St Station
Gloucester St Sth
Townsend Street
Pearse Street
Lombard St East
Pearse Station
Westland Row
Fenian St
Oscar Wilde's House
Bolton St
King's Inns Street
King St N
Ilac Shopping Centre
Moore Street
Henry Street
Earl St N
General Post Office
O'Connell Street
Abbey St Lwr
Jervis Street
Jervis Shopping Centre
Mary Street
Capel St
Little Mary St
Mary's Lane
St Mary's Abbey
Abbey St Upper
Abbey St Mid
Eden Quay
O'Connell Bridge
Bachelors Walk
Burgh Qy
Hawkins St
Poolbeg Street
Tara St
Strand Street Great
Ormond Qy Lwr
Aston Quay
D'Olier St
Westmorland St
O'Donovan Rossa Bridge
Ormond Qy Upr
Wellington Qy
Grattan Bridge
Temple Bar
Fleet Street
Bank of Ireland
College St
Wood Qy
Essex Qy
Essex St East
Eustace St
Anglesea St
Civic Offices
Christ Church Cathedral
Lord Edward St
Dame St
College Grn
Trinity College Library
Dublin Experience
College Park
City Hall
Dublinia
Dublin Castle & Chester Beatty Library
Exchequer St
Wicklow St
Suffolk St
Nassau St
Leinster St
Heraldic Museum
Clare St
Powerscourt Townhouse
South Great George's St
Drury Street
William St Sth
Dawson Street
Grafton St
St Anne's
Frederick St S
National Library
Leinster House
National Gallery
Merrion Square North
Natural History Museum
National Museum
Merrion Square
Government Buildings
Merrion St Upr
Nicholas St
Werburgh Street
Bride Rd
Bride St
Ship St Great
Chancery Lane
Golden Lane
Bull Alley St
St Patrick's Cathedral
Marsh's Library
Aungier Street
Stephen St Upr
Stephen St Lwr
King St South
Mercer St Lwr
Stephen's Green Centre
Royal College of Surgeons
Clarendon St
York St
Peter St
Peter Row
Kevin St Upper
Bishop Street
Kevin St Lower
Cuffe Street
New Bride Street
Wexford Street
Harcourt St
Montague St
Camden Row
Long Lane
Shaw's Birthplace
Camden Place
Pleasants Street
St Stephen's Green
Shelbourne Hotel
Merrion Row
Kildare
Fitzwilliam Lane
Number Twenty Nine
Baggot St Lwr
Fitzwilliam St Lwr
Fitzwilliam St Upr
Pembroke St Lwr
Fitzwilliam Square
Iveagh Gardens
Iveagh House
Leeson St Lower
D
E
F

The early Gothic nave dates from around 1226

CHRIST CHURCH CATHEDRAL

Dublin's second cathedral has a historical role as the seat of Irish bishops from the time of Viking Dublin. Next door, Dvblinia tells the history of the city.

67 D3 • Christchurch Place, Dublin 8 ☎ 01 677 8099 Mon–Fri 9.45–5, Sat, Sun 10–5. Check website for times of services Donation €5 waged, children (5–12; accompanied) free 49, 50, 51B, 54A, 56A, 65, 77A, 78A, 123, 90 from Tara Street DART station DART Tara Street, 25-min walk
www.cccdub.ie

RATINGS	
Cultural interest	●●●
Good for kids	●●●
Historic interest	●●●

TIP

- **You can access Christ Church Cathedral from Dvblinia across the bridge over St. Michael's Hill, but you are not allowed to go the other way, so visit Dvblinia first.**

DVBLINIA

67 D3 • St. Michael's Hill, Christchurch, Dublin 8 ☎ 01 679 4611 Apr–end Sep daily 10–5; Oct–end Mar Mon–Sat 11–4, Sun, public holidays 10–4.30 Adult €5.75, child (5–18) €4.25, family €15 Jun–end Aug
www.dublinia.ie

St. Laurence's heart is in this casket

This Gothic jumble of buttresses and spires has been a Protestant stronghold in Catholic southern Ireland since the Reformation and seat of Irish bishops for 1,000 years. Within its overtly Victorian walls lies a medieval core, and until 1871 it was the main church of the state. Strongbow (▷ 28) was responsible for turning the wooden Viking church to stone in 1172, and his tomb of 1176 is one of Christ Church's oldest remains. The Chapel of St. Laud holds the heart of St. Laurence O'Toole (died 1180), archbishop and patron saint of Dublin.

Much of the building collapsed in 1562 and had to be rebuilt, but the north wall, now disturbingly out of line with the rest of the building, is original. The transepts and part of the choir retain their Norman features, and there is an impressive eagle lectern dating from the 13th century. Don't miss the cathedral's crypt and its peculiar cornucopia of remnants.

DVBLINIA

Multimedia presentations of medieval Dublin here include the arrival of Strongbow, a merchant's house and the dockside at Wood Quay and a scale model of the city in 1500. There's a wonderful view over the city from St. Michael's Tower.

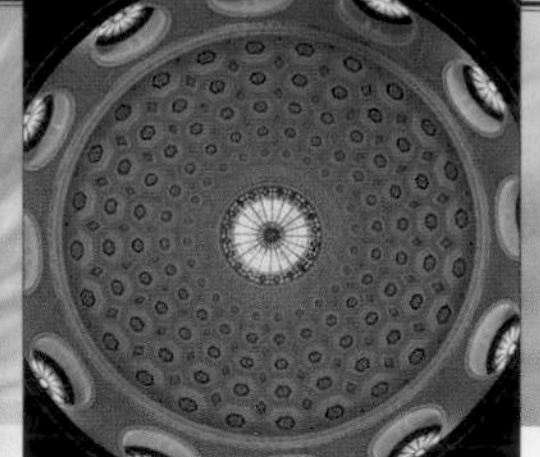

The dome of City Hall bathes the rotunda with natural light

CITY HALL

67 D3 • Cork Hill, Dame Street, Dublin 2 ☎ 01 672 2204 Mon–Sat 10–5.15, Sun, public holidays 2–5. Closed Good Fri, 24–26 Dec Adult €4, child €1.50 54 (from Burgh Quay), 50, 56A, 77A (from Eden Quay), 123, 150 On request Queen of Tarts restaurant
www.dublincity.ie/cityhall

The magnificent Corinthian portico of Thomas Cooley's Royal Exchange of 1779, in front of Dublin Castle on Lord Edward Street, has been the public face of the Dublin Corporation since 1852 and is still the City Hall, their principal meeting place. 'The Story of the Capital' exhibition on the ground floor relates the city's history, while the restored rotunda has statues of various Dublin worthies, and an Arts and Crafts mural depicting Dublin's past. Ireland's first President, Arthur Griffiths, lay in state here, as did Michael Collins after his assassination in 1922.

CROKE PARK GAA MUSEUM

Off map 67 E1 • Croke Park, St. Joseph's Avenue, Dublin 3 ☎ 01 819 2323 Mon–Sat 9.30–5, Sun, public holidays, 12–5 (on match days museum open only to Cusack Stand ticket holders. No stadium tours on match days) Museum: adult €5 (or €8.50 with stadium tour), child €3 (€5) 3, 11, 11A, 16, 16A, 123, 51A DART Connolly, 15-min walk Tour of stadium 30 min
www.gaa.ie

That Ireland's capital city should have the fourth largest sports stadium in Europe is no surprise in this sports-mad country. But the 85,000 capacity Croke Park does not host soccer or rugby games; in fact they are expressly forbidden. This is the home of the Gaelic Athletic Association (GAA), the governing body of

Dublin's Georgian Custom House was built on a bed of pine planks to prevent it from sinking into the marshy bank of the Liffey

Dalkey has the feel of a fishing village amid suburban Dublin

Gaelic games—Gaelic football, hurling, handball and rounders. It fills up every year for the dramatic All-Ireland finals, the excitement of which is portrayed in the film *A Day in September* shown in the stadium's museum. Croke Park plays an iconic part in modern Irish history, not least because of the notorious incident in November 1922, when British troops opened fire on the crowd and players, killing 12 people including Tipperary captain Michael Hogan. The museum explains the different codes (game rules), the political and historic context of the GAA, and enables you to catch up on games you may have missed through computer-accessed video highlights.

CUSTOM HOUSE

67 F2 • Custom House Quay, Dublin 1 01 888 2538 Mid-Mar to end Oct Mon–Fri 10–12.30, Sat, Sun, public holidays 2–5; Nov to mid-Mar Wed–Fri 10–12.30, Sun 2–5 Adult €1, family €3 Busáras, 5-min walk DART Tara Street Access to staff restaurant

One of the most prominent buildings on Dublin's waterfront, the Custom House was designed by James Gandon and completed in 1791. The classical façade, best seen from the opposite bank of the river downstream from O'Connell Bridge, is 114m (125 yards) long, and the huge green copper cupola is 38m (125ft) high. The building of the Custom House marked a high point in the development of the port of Dublin, but it was made virtually redundant only 10 years later when the Act of Union robbed Ireland of her income from duties. Today, it houses government offices and a small Visitor Centre explaining the work of the architect and the building's history and restoration.

DALKEY

353 G5 Dalkey Castle and Heritage Centre, Castle Street, Dalkey, Co. Dublin, tel 01 285 8366; Mon–Fri 9.30–5, Sat, Sun, public holidays 11–5 Heritage Centre: adult €6, child €4, family €16 59 from Dún Laoghaire DART Dalkey By arrangement, including visits to Dalkey Island www.dalkeycastle.com

Now a suburb of Dublin, Dalkey (pronounced 'Daw key') was once an important port in its own right. On its main street the fortified mansions of 15th-century trading families face each other. Of these, Archbold's Castle is little more than a three-floor shell, but Goat Castle contains a Heritage Centre with displays and reconstructions of the town's history, and you can take the 'warder's walk' around the castle's battlements. Above the harbour stands Bulloch Castle, built in the 12th century by monks from St. Mary's Abbey in Dublin to protect the harbour. Granite quarries on Dalkey Hill are popular with climbers and offer good views.

Don't miss There are boat trips to Dalkey Island, which has a Martello tower and monastic oratory; much of the island is now a bird reserve.

DOLLYMOUNT STRAND

353 G5 • Bull Island, Causeway Road, off James Larkin Road 130, 103, 104 (from Finglas) DART Clontarf Road, 20-min walk At Visitor Centre in season

A tidal lagoon separates this island beach, also called Bull Island, from Dollymount and Clontarf. Stretching 5km (3 miles) and now an important nature reserve, it was created by the construction of the North Bull sea wall, protruding 2.8km (1.75 miles) into Dublin Bay. Before the wall was completed in 1821, the maximum depth in Dublin's harbour at low tide was barely 2m (6ft), but the scouring effect of the River Liffey's waters rushing around the obstacle, has increased this to 5m (16ft) or more, allowing passage for much larger ships. You can drive onto the sand via a bridge at the west end and a causeway in the middle. There are fine views across the bay to the two Sugar Loaves and the Wicklow Mountains, and an interpretative centre (summer only) illustrates the island's wildlife.

DRIMNAGH CASTLE

Off map 66 B4 • Long Mile Road, Drimnagh, Dublin 12 01 450 2350 Apr–end Sep Wed, Sun 2–5 or by appointment; Oct–end Mar Wed 12–5, Sun 2–5 Adult €4, child (4–18) €2 77, 77A, 56, 18

Drimnagh Castle hides behind a school complex in the west Dublin industrial estates, but it's worth the search—a medieval, moated castle with a wonderfully restored 17th-century garden. The tower gateway leads into a walled courtyard, a world away from the surroundings. Inhabited for over 500 years, the castle was abandoned in the 1950s and slid into ruin.

Restoration began in the late 1980s, using traditional craft skills to bring the masonry and woodwork back to their former condition, and 5,500 tiles were specially made for the great hall in 1991. The fireplace is built of English sandstone, a striking effect against the white of the predominant local limestone. Outside, the moat once more flows with clear water. The castle is said to be haunted by Lady Eleanor Barnewell, who tragically died 500 years ago on the grave of her lover; he had been killed by her father because she was betrothed to someone else.

Dublin Castle and the Chester Beatty Library

The heart of historic Dublin, the castle now contains a superb gallery of religious art.

The interior was largely rebuilt in the 18th and 19th centuries

SEEING DUBLIN CASTLE AND THE CHESTER BEATTY LIBRARY

Long the symbol of Anglo-Norman power, the Dublin Castle complex is a mix of vice-regal classicism, medieval buildings, modern offices and a world-renowned museum. The Chester Beatty Library and Gallery of Oriental Art contains a collection of early religious manuscripts including fragments of second-century biblical tracts and ninth-century Koranic texts. On view at the castle itself are the fine State Apartments, its Undercroft, showing traces of the Viking fortress that was the earliest incarnation of the city of Dublin, and its Chapel Royal, a neo-Gothic gem of a church built in 1814.

RATINGS

Cultural interest	●●●●●
Good for kids	●●●
Historic interest	●●●●

BASICS

67 D3 • Dame Street, Dublin 2

01 677 7129

Mon–Fri 10–5, Sat, Sun 2–5. Closed during state business

State Apartments, Undercroft, Chapel Royal: adult €4.50, child (over 12) €2

50, 50A, 54, 56A, 77, 77A, 77B, 123

Access by 45-min guided tour only

Castle Vaults Bistro in Lower Yard

Castle foyer and Chester Beatty Library

www.dublincastle.ie
A very clever site that's easy to navigate.

TIPS

- **The State Apartments are often closed for security reasons ahead of important events and state occasions so call in advance to make sure you can join a tour.**
- **The best view of the Dubh Linn Garden is from the rooftop garden of the Chester Beatty Library; if this is closed, try the top floor of the Record Tower (Garda Museum).**

HIGHLIGHTS

STATE APARTMENTS

The State Apartments were designed to reflect the extravagant and fashionable lifestyle of the vice-regal court. Following a disastrous fire in 1684, they were remodelled by Sir William Robinson, who also designed the Royal Hospital at Kilmainham. He planned the Upper and Lower courtyards to complement the remaining buildings. From the entrance in the Upper Yard, a guided tour visits the Throne Room dating from 1740, where the throne is said to have been presented to William of Orange to commemorate his victory at the Battle of the Boyne. St. Patrick's Hall is hung with banners of the old order of the Knights of St. Patrick. Its ceiling, painted by Vincenzo Valdré in 1778, depicts links between Ireland and Britain. The apartments, with Killybegs carpets and Waterford crystal chandeliers, are used for presidential inaugurations and other ceremonial occasions.

The Undercroft was revealed when work was done on the Lower Yard in 1990. The city walls join the castle here and a small archway allowed boats to land provisions at the Postern Gate, also visible. In the base of the Norman Powder Tower, the original Viking defensive bank can be made out.

CHAPEL ROYAL

The Chapel Royal (officially the Church of the Most Holy Trinity) was designed by Francis Johnston and is best known for its ornate plaster decorations by George Stapleton and Richard Stewart's woodcarvings.

GARDA MUSEUM

The Garda (Police) Museum, Dublin Castle, Dublin 2 01 671 9597
Mon–Fri 9.30–4.30, Sat, Sun by appointment

The Garda Museum moved to the Record Tower in 1997. The museum displays uniforms and equipment charting policing in Ireland from the days of the Royal Irish Constabulary to the Civic Guard of 1922 (later renamed Garda Síochána na hÉireann). The top floor has the best view of the Dubh Linn Garden, and exhibits on the worldwide role of the Garda, working for the United Nations.

CHESTER BEATTY LIBRARY

✉ Chester Beatty Library and Gallery of Oriental Art, Dublin Castle, Dublin 2 ☎ 01 407 0750 🕐 May–end Sep Mon–Fri 10–5, Sat 11–5, Sun 1–5; Oct–end Apr Tue–Fri 10–5, Sat 11–5, Sun 1–5 Free

The Chester Beatty Library and Gallery of Oriental Art houses the collection of Sir Alfred Chester Beatty, a wealthy North American mining magnate of Irish descent, who died in 1968. Chief among the exhibits are the fragments of early religious texts. There are over 300 Korans, Babylonian tablets over 6,000 years old, Coptic Bibles, Jewish texts, Confucian scrolls and Buddhist literature, with explanations on these religions. The displays and exhibits are supported by touch-screen computers giving more information about the world's religions and the artwork inspired by them. Popular exhibits are the exquisite Burmese and Siamese *parabaiks* describing folk tales and drawn on paper made from mulberry leaves. There are also exhibition spaces here, housing collections of contemporary work. Don't miss the Pauline letters from AD180–200, and the gospels from AD250—the oldest full collections in the world; the delicate papyrus fragment of St. John's Gospel, taken from the Bodmer codex, the oldest New Testament scripture in existence; and the Chinese jade books, engraved then filled with gold.

BACKGROUND

Dublin takes its name from the 'Dubh Linn', the Black Pool at the confluence of the Liffey and Poddle rivers. The castle gardens now occupy that site and their Celtic-design parterre cleverly doubles as a helicopter pad for visiting dignitaries. The castle was built for King John in the 13th century and was renovated for use as a vice-regal palace in the 16th century. The oldest remaining part is the Record Tower, once used as a top-security prison. Red Hugh O'Donnell, son of a Donegal chieftain, was held here in 1592 for rebelling against the Crown. He escaped and, together with Hugh O'Neill, led the Nine Years War. Today the Record Tower houses a simple museum documenting the history of Ireland's police force.

Bermingham Hall and the Record Tower, seen from the Castle's Coach House (top left). Chinese ceiling of the Chester Beatty Library (top). Two examples of the Oriental art in the Chester Beatty Library (above)

The charming children's room in the Dublin Writers Museum

The Four Courts, seat of the High Court of Justice for Ireland (above). Statue of Cúchulainn in the GPO, O'Connell Street (below)

DUBLIN WRITERS MUSEUM

67 D1 • 18 Parnell Square North, Dublin 1 01 872 2077 Jun–end Aug Mon–Fri 10–6, Sep–end May Mon–Sat 10–5, Sun, public holidays 11–5 Adult €6.25, child €3.75, family €17.50 10, 11, 11A, 11B, 13, 13A, 16, 16A, 19, 19A DART Connolly, 20-min walk Self-guided audio tour about 30 min www.visitdublin.com

In a substantial northside Georgian town house, the Dublin Writers Museum reflects the important contribution the city has made to world literature. A portable audio commentary leads you round displays telling the story of Dublin's literary heritage, from the earliest times through to Patrick Kavanagh, Flann O'Brien and Roddy Doyle, taking in along the way Oscar Wilde, W. B. Yeats, Jonathan Swift, George Bernard Shaw and Samuel Beckett. With four Nobel laureates, it's an impressive record. Not so impressive, perhaps, is the collection of memorabilia, which is a little random beyond its literary basis. It includes the phone from Samuel Beckett's Paris apartment, Brendan Behan's typewriter and press pass, and Oliver St. John Gogarty's flying goggles. In the annexe there is a room devoted to children's literature, a café and a comprehensive bookshop. There are regular book readings and special exhibitions.

Don't miss Notable first editions on display include Joyce's *Ulysses* and *The Dubliners*, and Bram Stoker's *Dracula*.

DÚN LAOGHAIRE

353 G5 • Dún Laoghaire, Co. Dublin 7, 7A, 46A, 746 and local buses DART Dún Laoghaire

Part modern port facility and part seaside resort, Dún Laoghaire (pronounced 'Dun Leary'), 13km (8 miles) from central Dublin, is where the Holyhead car ferries have berthed since 1966. The massive stone piers of the harbour were built of Wicklow granite from the quarries on Dalkey Hill in the first half of the 19th century and enclose not only the ferry terminal but also the grand marinas of the Royal Irish Yacht Club. A walk along the piers is a popular seaside stroll of a couple of hours each, and affords splendid views back along the coast to Sandycove, Dalkey island and hill and across Dublin Bay. The spire of the former Mariners' Church dominates the town; it now contains the National Maritime Museum. Among its most popular exhibits are a longboat of 12m (39ft) seized from a French raiding party in Bantry Bay in 1796 (▷ 110) and the original optic, worked by clockwork and still functioning, from the Baily lighthouse on the Howth peninsula.

FOUR COURTS

66 C2 • Inns Quay, Dublin 7 01 872 5555 Mon–Fri 10–1, 2–4.30 when courts are in session 25A, 26, 37, 39A/B, 51, 66A/B, 67A, 68, 69, 70, 79, 83, 90, 172

Designed by Thomas Cooley and James Gandon, the architect of the Custom House farther downriver, the Four Courts was built between 1786 and 1802. A statue of Moses stands on the six-columned portico, flanked by Justice and Mercy in front of the great lantern tower. It takes its name from the old legal divisions: the courts of Common Pleas, Chancery, Exchequer and King's Bench. This is still Ireland's main criminal court, and public access is allowed when it is in session. What you see now was mostly restored in the 1930s after the building was gutted during the Civil War. It was held by anti-treaty forces and, when the government troops attacked, the resulting fires also destroyed many of Ireland's historic legal records dating back to the 12th century.

GENERAL POST OFFICE (GPO)

67 E2 • O'Connell Street, Dublin 1 01 705 7000 Mon–Sat 8–8 O'Connell Street buses DART Tara Street, 10-min walk www.anpost.ie

The General Post Office (GPO) building on O'Connell Street would attract little attention in a city of fine Georgian buildings, had it not been seized by Padraig Pearse and his rebel army in Easter 1916. From the steps outside he proclaimed the Irish Republic, then settled down to a week-long siege by the British Army. The building was destroyed, the rebels rounded up and their leaders executed, but the new Irish state adopted their struggle

A Celtic cross in Glasnevin Cemetery

and the GPO became something of a national icon. It was restored in 1929, but traces of bullet marks can still be identified on the outside. Inside, a bronze sculpture by Oliver Shepherd from 1935 depicts the death of the legendary Irish hero Cúchulainn, and is dedicated to the participants in the Easter Rising.

GLASNEVIN CEMETERY

Off map 66 C1 • Finglas Road, Glasnevin, Dublin 11 ☎ 01 830 1133 Mon–Sat 8.30–4.30, Sun 9–4.30 19, 40, 40A Wed, Fri 2.30, tel 01 830 1133
www.glasnevin-cemetery.ie

Established in 1832, when Catholics were finally allowed to conduct funerals, the list of occupants of Glasnevin Cemetery reads like a roll call of the key players in Ireland's story from the last 180 years. Daniel O'Connell is commemorated by a round tower standing 49m (160ft) high, Charles Stewart Parnell by a big lump of granite. Here, among the Victorian Gothic memorials, you will also find the last resting place of Eamonn de Valera, a leader in 1916 who went on to be Taoiseach (prime minister) seven times and President of Ireland twice. Michael Collins, Countess Markiewicz, Alfred Chester Beatty and Brendan Behan are among the other names familiar to any visitor to Dublin. There are sad reminders of famine and poverty in the many paupers' graves, and sections devoted to the Irish army and other services. Controversial sites include the grave of Roger Casement (there is some debate as to whether his real remains were returned by the British after his execution for treason), and a plot of more recent Republican activists. Pick up a plan (€1) from the cemetery office.

A mountain of barrels in this temple to the art of brewing

GUINNESS STOREHOUSE

See how the brewing giant turns water, barley, hops and yeast into Ireland's national drink.

66 B3 • St. James's Gate, Dublin 8 ☎ 01 408 4800, information line 01 453 8364 Jul, Aug daily 9.30–9; Sep–end Jun 9.30–5 Adult €13.50, child (6–12) €5, under 6 free 51B, 78A (from Aston Quay), 123 (from O'Connell Street) Self-guided Three bars and a restaurant
www.guinness-storehouse.com
Slick, nicely designed site, packed with information about Guinness.

RATINGS	
Cultural interest	●●●
Good for Guinness	●●●●●
Good for kids	●●●●

TIPS

- **Use public transport so you can enjoy the free Guinness.**
- **Make time to visit the excellent Guinness merchandise shop on the ground floor.**

The Gravity Bar atop the Storehouse has great views

For many people a trip to Dublin involves, in some way, a search for the mythical 'best pint of Guinness'. The Dublin brewer's status as a world brand ensures that a ready stream of visiting drinkers arrive to take up the challenge. The Guinness Storehouse off St. James's Gate is a good place to start. Here, an old warehouse next to the vast brewery has been transformed into a cathedral to the creation of this ale.

Seven floors of dramatic exhibits take you through the process from the water (it doesn't really come from the Liffey as the legends say), Irish barley, hops and yeast to the finished product. On the way you learn how the beer developed from a dark porter-style ale popular among Irish migrant workers in London to the distinctive global superbrand it is today. Escalators connect the floors in a pleasingly futuristic style redolent of Fritz Lang's classic 1920s film *Metropolis*. The labyrinthine displays include sections dedicated to the transport that has carried Guinness around world. You get a free pint in the seventh floor Gravity Bar, now reputed to be the best pint in Dublin. The views over the city to the docks and the mountains are impressive. Back on the ground floor, is a large, comprehensive Guinness merchandise shop.

Howth has a busy fishing fleet in addition to various boat trips

The cool and airy interior of the Hugh Lane Gallery

There are some striking works at the Irish Museum of Modern Art

HOWTH HEAD

353 G5 • Howth, Dublin 13 31, 31B DART Howth

The peninsula of Howth (rhymes with both) Head forms the northern arm of Dublin Bay, and is visible from many parts of the city. Although quite heavily developed, the shore itself is mostly cliff and has therefore escaped the middle-class housing that spreads around its central hill. A waymarked path stretches for 8km (5 miles) around the head itself, passing the Baily lighthouse, and makes an invigorating walk (you can catch a bus back).

On the northern side of the head, Howth town is a fishing port, its harbour facing the rocky islet of Ireland's Eye. Boat trips to view its puffin colony, Martello tower and sixth-century monastic ruins are available. The novelist Erskine Childers landed his yacht *Asgard* at Howth in 1914 with a huge consignment of German weapons, destined to be used in the Easter Rising of 1916. Little remains of St. Mary's Abbey except a shell rising above the steep streets of the town, but about 1km (half a mile) to the west, signs to the Deer Park Hotel also lead to the grounds of Howth Castle (not open) and the National Transport Museum. The gardens are famous for their azaleas and rhododendrons, and the transport museum contains some lovingly restored trams, buses, fire engines and other vehicles (Heritage Depot, Howth Castle Demesne, tel 01 848 0831, Jun–end Aug Mon–Sat 2–5; Sep–end May Sat, Sun, public holidays 2–5, Phone to confirm 01 832 0427; www.nationaltransportmuseum.org).

Don't miss The best views are from the 155m (510ft) Ben of Howth, near The Summit pub and the terminus of the tramway that once brought visitors up here.

HUGH LANE GALLERY

67 D1 • Dublin City Gallery, The Hugh Lane, Charlemont House, Parnell Square North, Dublin 1 01 222 5550 Closed for refurbishment, due to reopen late 2005 Free; Francis Bacon Studio: adult €7, under 18 free 3, 10, 11, 13, 16, 19, 46A DART Tara Street; Connolly, 10-min walk Guided tours by prior arrangement
www.hughlane.ie

This modern art gallery on the north side of Parnell Square may look inauspicious but it conceals some important works by Monet, Degas, Pissarro and Renoir, as well as extensive collections of 20th-century Irish artists such as Jack B. Yeats, Walter Osborne, Sarah Purser, Frank O'Meara and Norman Garstin. It is traditional in its layout, though the Henry Moore figure in the foyer and the bizarre man in a mangle (*The Wringer* by Patrick O'Reilly, 1996), add three-dimensional interest. Francis Bacon's London studio has been re-created, to illustrate the chaotic working lifestyle of this distinctive Irish artist. The house dates from 1762 and the core collection was bequeathed to the nation by Hugh Lane in 1908. Until the 1980s the Irish and British governments squabbled over precisely which nation he had meant, an issue now resolved.

IRISH MUSEUM OF MODERN ART

66 A3 • Royal Hospital, Military Road, Kilmainham, Dublin 8 01 612 9900 Tue–Sat 10–5.30, Sun, public holidays 12–5.30 Free 26, 51, 51B, 78A, 79, 90, 123 Heuston Station, 5 min-walk Tours of North Range May–end Sep, free
www.modernart.ie

Opposite the road to Kilmainham Gaol, a castellated gateway leads to a long drive up to the magnificent buildings of the old Royal Hospital. Based on Les Invalides in Paris this is one of the finest remaining 17th-century buildings in Ireland. A fine formal garden in the French style stretches away on its northern side, while to the west there are smooth lawns extending to the little graveyard of Bully's Acre, where there is a 10th-century cross shaft amid the graves of the hospital's military pensioners. Inside, a small exhibition explains the building's history and the main galleries display current works by leading contemporary artists. The museum's excellent website contains up-do-date information about what is being exhibited when you plan to visit.

IVEAGH GARDENS

67 E4 • Clonmel Street, Dublin 2 01 475 7816 Mar–end Oct Mon–Sat 8–6, Sun 10–6; Feb, Nov Mon–Sat 8–5, Sun 10–5; Dec, Jan Mon–Sat 8–4, Sun 10–4 14A, 15A/B/C, 44B/C, 48A, 86

This lovely secret park lies hidden behind the huge bulk of the National Concert Hall. To find it, you'll need to locate its only entrance, through a gateway at the end of an inconspicuous looking side street. The gardens were designed by Ninian Niven for the International Exhibition of Arts and Manufactures on Earlsfort Terrace in 1865, and are divided into three thematic sections. The central parterre, with its lawns, statues and fountains, is Italian in concept but also has echoes of the Bois de Boulougne in Paris. The southern end has a more naturalistic feel, with rocky outcrops reflecting North American landscapes. Beside this are a maze and archery lawn, both of which drew on Hampton Court in London for inspiration.

Mural based on Ulysses, in the James Joyce Cultural Centre

Picturesque Malahide Castle spans many centuries

The Casino at Marino is full of architectural curiosities

JAMES JOYCE CULTURAL CENTRE

67 E1 • 35 North Great George's Street, Dublin 1 01 878 8547 Mon–Sat 9.30–5, Sun, public holidays 12.30–5 Adult €5, family €15 3, 10, 11, 11A, 13, 16, 16A, 19, 19A, 22, 22A DART Connolly, 10-min walk Self guided, allow 30 min
www.jamesjoyce.ie

Joyce never lived in this restored Georgian terraced house just a few minutes from O'Connell Street but he did live nearby, in a succession of squalid houses in Dublin's north inner city, from 1893 to 1904. You can join a tour of Joyce's Dublin and see the exhibition of memorabilia upstairs, including the furniture from Paul Leon's apartment in Paris, where Joyce and Leon would discuss the progress of *Finnegans Wake* in the 1930s. If you are not familiar with Joyce's work, some of the references will seem obscure, but there is a good introductory video presentation, and a bookshop where you can buy almost everything he ever published.

James Joyce in casual pose—one of many memorials to the man

KILLINEY

353 G5 • Killiney, Co. Dublin 59 (from Dún Laoghaire) DART Killiney

This is an affluent suburb of exclusive villas and embassies, with exceptional views across the bay to Bray Head and the mountains, and north over Dublin Bay. The pebbly strand is reached through a dark tunnel beneath the DART railway line. From here a bracing seafront stroll stretches 6.4km (4 miles) to Bray, or you can climb for about 30 minutes through trees and formal gardens to the summit of Killiney Hill.

KILMAINHAM GAOL

See pages 76–77.

LEINSTER HOUSE

67 F3 • Kildare Street, Dublin 2 01 618 3166 Call for information 7, 7A, 8 (from Burgh Quay), 10, 11, 13A (from O'Connell Street) DART Pearse Admission by tour only, allow 1hr
www.irlgov.ie/oireachtas

Designed by Richard Cassels in 1745, Leinster House is the seat of the Oireachtas, the Irish parliament. The Dáil (lower house) meets in the former lecture theatre of the Royal Dublin Society. The Seanad (upper house) meets in the North Wing Saloon. Tours are available when parliament is not in session; book at least a week advance (tel 01 618 3000).

MALAHIDE CASTLE

349 G5 • Malahide, Co. Dublin 01 846 2184 Apr–end Oct Mon–Sat 10–5, Sun, public holidays 11–6; Nov–end Mar Mon–Sat 10–5, Sun 11–5. No tours 12.45–2 Adult €6.25, child (over 12) €3.75, family €17.50 42 DART Malahide Castle by tour only, allow 35 min
www.visitdublin.com

Malahide Castle, in 101ha (249 acres) of grounds, was home to the Talbot family from 1185 to 1976 and incorporates a mixture of styles, from its 12th-century core to the 18th-century embellishments. Family portraits are hung alongside works on loan from the National Gallery. In the stable block is Tara's Palace, a doll's house museum re-creating the 18th-century golden age of Irish great houses at one-twelfth scale (Apr–end Sep, Mon–Sat, 10–1, 2–5, Sun, public holidays 2–6; €2 charity donation). Next door the Fry Model Railway is a reconstruction of a transport system begun by engineer Cyril Fry in the 1930s (tel 01 846 3779, Apr–end Sep Mon–Sat 10–1, 2–5, Sun 2–6).

MARINO CASINO

Off map 67 F1 • Off Malahide Road, Marino, Dublin 3 01 833 1618 Jun–end Sep daily 10–6; May, Oct daily 10–5; Apr Sat, Sun 12–5; Jan–Mar, Nov–Dec Sat, Sun 12–4 Adult €2.75, child (3–18) €1.25, family €7 20A, 20B, 27, 27A, 27B, 42, 42C from middle of city; 123 Imp Bus from O'Connell Street DART Clontarf Road, 15-min walk Guided tour only, 45 min

Incongruous amid housing estates, the Casino is all that remains of the 18th-century neoclassical estate of the Earl of Charlemont. Nothing to do with gambling, it was an extravagant summerhouse to complement the now demolished Marino House. Despite its outward appearance, it has 16 rooms on three floors, and a host of architectural tricks retain the exterior integrity. Drainpipes are hidden in pillars, windows light more than one room, and doors are deceptively small, but in vast doorways.

Kilmainham Gaol

No other sight captures the iconography of the Irish struggle for independence quite like this well-preserved prison on a low hill in west Dublin.

Prison life was more comfortable for some

The main compound of the prison forms the heart of the museum (above). The gates are now open wide—for visitors (above right)

RATINGS

Cultural interest	●●●●
Historic interest	●●●●●
Photo stops	●●●

BASICS

Off map 66 A3 • Inchicore Road, Kilmainham, Dublin 8

01 453 5984

Apr–end Sep daily 9.30–5; Oct–end Mar Mon–Sat 9.30–4, Sun 10–5. Last tour 1hr before closing

Adult €5, child (4–16) €2, family €11

51B, 78A, 79

Heuston Station, 20-min walk

Access by guided tour only. Allow at least 1 hour plus 30 min to see exhibition

Tours by prior arrangement. Some older parts of the prison are difficult for wheelchair users

Tea room by exhibition

Beyond front desk

SEEING KILMAINHAM GAOL

This sinister place is where the leaders of the 1916 rising were executed. Its last prisoner, released in 1924, was Eamonn de Valera, who went on to become Taoiseach, and two-time president. Viewing is by guided tour only. After a video presentation in the basement you are led through the east wing, the chapel, the west wing, then the prison yards. A museum has some grim exhibits illustrating the lives and deaths of former inmates. The tours, accompanied by an enthusiastic and knowledgeable curator, last around 70 minutes and run every half hour. The gaol's history is put in context, not just as a place for political prisoners, but also for its role as a prison for common criminals.

HIGHLIGHTS

THE EAST WING

This is a painstakingly restored example of a 19th-century cell block. A three-floor shell, open to skylights in the roof, is ringed by tiny cells opening onto iron lattice landings. From the central ground floor, where the prisoners would eat, every cell door is visible and from the landings observation hatches allow warders to see inside every cell. Unlike older prisons, inmates here could not hide in the shadows; their behaviour was monitored 24 hours a day.

THE WEST WING

There's a stark contrast in the West Wing, with its labyrinth of dank, dilapidated corridors and tight, dimly lit cells. Recent graffiti in some corridors enhances the sense of squalor. Connecting the two is the prison chapel, where Joseph Plunkett married Grace Gifford the night before his execution in 1916. They spent 10 minutes together as a married couple before he was led away. Each cell is labelled with the names of the most significant occupants. With risings against British rule in 1798, 1803, 1848, 1867, 1883 and 1916, it is easy to understand the gaol's reputation as the place to hold political prisoners, and graffiti over one doorway threatens the gaolers with the 'vengeance of the risen people'. Charles Stewart Parnell was held here in 1883, in a pleasant suite of rooms that befitted his political standing. Other

prisoners were not so lucky and overcrowding was a significant problem. During the famine years, when thousands flocked to Dublin to find food, there were over 7,000 men and women, crammed into the cells.

ANSEO, TAR ÉIS SEACHTAIN NA CÁSCA, 1916,
BÁSAÍODH NA CINNIRÍ SEO A LEANAS
HERE, AFTER EASTER WEEK, 1916,
THE FOLLOWING LEADERS WERE EXECUTED
P.H. PEARSE
THOMAS J. CLARKE
THOMAS MACDONAGH
3 BEALTAINE, 1916
3 MAY, 1916
JOSEPH PLUNKETT
EDWARD DALY
MICHAEL O'HANRAHAN
WILLIAM PEARSE
4 BEALTAINE, 1916
4 MAY, 1916
JOHN MACBRIDE
5 BEALTAINE, 1916
5 MAY, 1916
CON COLBERT
ÉAMONN CEANNT
MICHAEL MALLIN
SEÁN HEUSTON
8 BEALTAINE, 1916
8 MAY, 1916
SEÁN MAC DIARMADA
JAMES CONNOLLY
12 BEALTAINE, 1916
12 MAY, 1916

THE YARDS

The exercise yards are where the 14 leaders of the Easter Rising were executed by firing squad and a cross marks the spot where the injured James Connolly was strapped to a chair so he could be upright when he was shot. However, the 1916 rising was not well-supported at the time, and its leaders were not portrayed as heroes until much later. In the civil war that followed independence, the Free State government dispatched a further 77 anti-treaty fighters against these grey walls.

THE MUSEUM

Among the grim items in the museum is a darkened room devoted to *memento mori* of each of the 1916 executed. You can also see the block of wood on which Robert Emmet's head was removed following his hanging in 1803. Emmet had hoped to bring Napoleonic firepower to the fight against the British, but it didn't materialize in the way he had planned. On a lighter note, there are many fine banners from the various Irish struggles; a charming home-made selection from the Irish Land League in 1879 declare 'the land for the people'.

BACKGROUND

The main body of the prison was built in 1789, and was restored by enthusiasts in the 1960s. It is the largest unused prison in Europe and has been in great demand as a film set since the 1960s. Bizarrely, the gaol scenes from that most English film *The Italian Job* (1966) were filmed here. More recently it reprized its real-life role in *Michael Collins* (1996), with Liam Neeson in the title role as the Irish military leader.

A prisoner's-eye view of the main compound through the bars of a sturdy cell door (top). Names that are now writ large in the history of Ireland feature on this plaque commemorating those executed after the Easter Rising (above)

TIPS

- **Wait for the rest of the tour group to leave before you take photos of the panoptican east wing, the effect is much greater.**
- **Avoid the busiest times; come early in summer, or later in winter after the school groups.**

Marsh's Library has a wonderful collection of important works

The glittering restored glass-houses at the Botanic Gardens

A statue of the founder proudly fronts the National Gallery

MARSH'S LIBRARY

67 D4 • St. Patrick's Close, Dublin 8 01 454 3511 Mon, Wed–Fri 10–1, 2–5, Sat 10.30–1 Adult €2.50, child free 50, 54A, 56A www.marshlibrary.ie

Behind St. Patrick's Cathedral stands the oldest public library in Ireland. Opened in 1707, and taking its name from Archbishop Narcissus Marsh (1638–1717), the Marsh Library has barely changed. The smell of the 25,000 ancient volumes hits you as you walk in. The farthest room contains the caged reading areas where scholars could view the most valuable of the library's books, but not go off with them. Among the prized volumes on display are Clarendon's *History of the Rebellion*, complete with anti-Scottish scrawlings in the margins by Jonathan Swift, and signed copies of works by Laud, Swift himself, John Donne and Hugh Latimer.

Don't miss The guest book includes the signatures of James Joyce and Daniel O'Connell.

MERRION SQUARE

67 F4 • Merrion Square, Dublin 2 Park open daylight hours 5, 7A, 13A, 45, 46B/C, 48A, 63, 86 DART Pearse

From a corner of Merrion Square Park, a reclining statue of Oscar Wilde (▷ right) gazes across the street to his former home at No. 1 Merrion Square. The gifted writer lived here from 1855 to 1878 in what is now the American College. The house, with its superb Georgian architraves and cornices, has been restored and can be seen on guided tours on Mondays, Wednesdays and Thursdays for a nominal charge. The square itself was laid out by John Ensor in the 1770s, with Leinster House and its attendant galleries on the western side. In the 1930s it passed from the family of the Earls of Pembroke to the Catholic Church, who planned to build a cathedral here. However the cost was prohibitive and the plan was dropped. Many of the fine Georgian buildings around the remaining three sides are still private houses. Daniel O'Connell once resided at No. 58, W. B. Yeats at No. 82, and the Duke of Wellington was born round the corner on Merrion Street Upper. The Georgian museum piece, No. 29 Fitzwilliam Street (▷ 79), is just off the square on the south side.

NATIONAL BOTANIC GARDENS

Off map 66 C1 • Glasnevin, Dublin 9 01 837 4388/01 804 0300 Mar–Oct Mon–Sat 9–6, Sun 10–6; Nov–Feb daily 9–4.30 19, 13 (O'Connell Street), 83 (Abbey Street) Tours by appointment, 1 hour, €2

A few kilometres north of the heart of the city, the National Botanic Gardens line the south bank of the Tolka River. They were founded by the Royal Dublin Society in 1795 and have benefited from extensive restoration work in recent years. The latest project was the Victorian Great Palm House, reopened in 2004. The impressive curvilinear range of glasshouses dates from the middle of the 19th century and was restored in the mid-1990s; they house orchids, ferns, succulents and tropical water plants. Outside there are 19.5ha (48 acres) of specimen trees, bedding plants and rockeries. The Burren Garden re-creates in miniature the limestone-loving flora of northwest County Clare (▷ 134–135). There is usually something worth seeing here, though spring and summer are the most striking periods.

NATIONAL GALLERY

67 F3 • Merrion Square and Clare Street, Dublin 2 01 661 5133 Mon–Sat 9.30–5.30, Thu 9.30–8.30, Sun 12–5.30 Free, except for special exhibitions in Millennium Wing 5, 7, 7A, 10, 13A, 44, 48A DART Pearse, 5-min walk From Shaw Room, Sat 3, Sun at 2, 3, 4; 1 hour Two restaurants in Millennium Wing www.nationalgallery.ie

Forming the western arm of the Leinster House complex, Ireland's National Gallery exhibits an important collection of European art from the 15th century to the present. Established by an Act of Parliament in 1854, it opened to the public 10 years later. With over 2,500 paintings and more than 10,000 works in other media, there is a great deal to see, though obviously not all on display at once.

The interior is confusing, but floor plans help you navigate. Everyone will find their own favourites among the works of Canaletto, Rembrandt, Caravaggio, Rubens and El Greco. There are huge collections of Irish works too, with an entire section devoted to the Yeats family: the work of Jack B. Yeats and

The magnificent reading room of the National Library

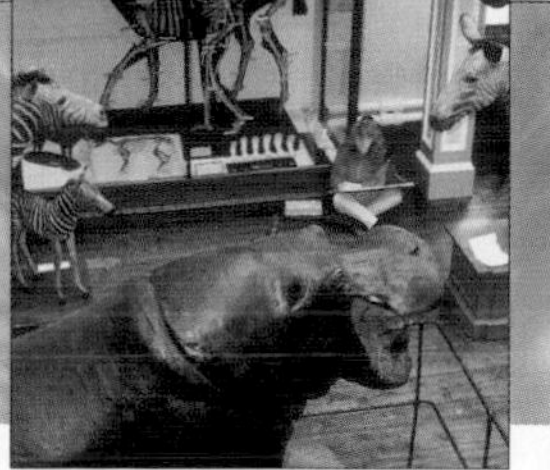
All manner of creatures in the Natural History Museum

Number Twenty Nine preserves an era of gracious living

his father John Butler Yeats. The Millennium Wing, specializing in 20th-century art and themed exhibitions, opens on to Clare Street and includes a restaurant and shop, contrasting markedly with the quiet Beit, Milltown and Dargan wings of the old Merrion Square side of the building.

NATIONAL LIBRARY

67 F3 • Kildare Street, Dublin 2 01 603 0200 Mon–Wed 10–9, Thu–Fri 10–5, Sat 10–1 10A, 11A/B, 13B, 14A, 15A/B/C, 20B, 46A/B, 84X, 116, 117, 118, 746 DART Pearse www.nli.ie

In a 19th-century Renaissance-style building on the northern flank of Leinster House, the National Library draws visitors mainly for its genealogical service, helping to trace visitors' Irish origins through the countless records and archives, and giving information about other research facilities across the country. It is the home of the Chief Herald, who can grant arms to those who fulfil the appropriate criteria. The impressive domed reading room counts James Joyce among its historic scholars, though you'll need a pass to see it (issued at the library for a fee; passport ID plus two passport-size photographs required). Exhibitions in the entrance hall reflect the library's huge collection. The library also runs the National Photographic Archive in Temple Bar.

NATIONAL MUSEUM

See pages 80–81.

NATIONAL WAX MUSEUM

67 D1 • Granby Row, Parnell Square, Dublin 1 01 872 6340 Mon–Sat 10–5.30, Sun 12–5.30 Adult €7, child (4–12) €5, family €20 11, 13, 16, 22, 22A DART Connolly, 20 min-walk

With serious displays on James Joyce and W. B. Yeats, as well as more recent Irish icons such as the Corrs and U2, the National Wax Museum offers entertainment with an educational twist. Audio descriptions give a narrative context, but you may feel none is necessary in the Hall of Megastars for the displays of Elvis Presley or Madonna. The Children's World of Fairytale and Fantasy includes a search for the Magic Lamp and there's an impressive three-dimensional re-creation of Leonardo da Vinci's *Last Supper*. Outside the foyer is being dismantled by a 6m tall (20ft) giant.

NATURAL HISTORY MUSEUM

67 F3 • Merrion Street, Dublin 2 01 677 7444 Tue–Sat 10–5, Sun 2–5 Free 7, 7A, 8 DART Pearse Guided tours, adult €2, child free
www.museum.ie

On the southern flank of Leinster House, the Natural History Museum contrasts markedly with the up-to-date museums that abound in modern Ireland. It is virtually unchanged since its opening in 1857 as the museum of the Royal Dublin Society. The first room you encounter is devoted to Irish animals, starting with the skeletons of huge Irish deer, now extinct. Around the walls, display cases are full of other stuffed Irish creatures, such as martens, otters and bats. There are birds and fish too, and, at the far end, insects and invertebrates. Upstairs, the emphasis is on creatures from the rest of the world. Here on the main floor are monkeys, bears, rhinos and marsupials. There are two gallery floors above this, the first devoted to vertebrates—the dodo is particularly popular—the second covers invertebrates: worms, insects, jellyfish, crabs and so on. A huge skeleton of a humpback whale is suspended from the ceiling, while the giraffe skeleton rises up from the floor below. Also featuring on the top floor are the delightful animal models in glass by Blaschka of Dresden, using refraction in light to re-create the shades of nature. The Natural History Museum, known irreverently as the 'dead zoo', is an excellent example of old-school museum values, showing the preserved bodies of animals with no real attempt at context.
Don't miss The Irish section includes the bizarre sunfish from Lough Swilly.

NUMBER TWENTY NINE

67 F4 • 29 Lower Fitzwilliam Street, Dublin 2 01 702 6165 Tue–Sat 10–5, Sun 2–5. Closed two weeks before Christmas Adult €3.50, child under 16 free 6, 7, 8, 10, 45 DART Pearse Access by guided tour only; 15-min video precedes 30-min tour Tea room next to gift shop

A visit to this well-preserved example of Dublin's elegant Georgian terraced houses gives a clear insight into the lives of the upper middle classes who lived in them. Every room is authentically furnished with items from 1790 to 1820. A short video presentation is followed by the tour, beginning with the kitchen and housekeeper's quarters then going upstairs to the dining room (set for dessert), the drawing room with its Dublin crystal chandeliers and huge windows overlooking the street, and the impressive marble-floored hallway. Upstairs again, you see the boudoir, the master bedroom, and the dressing room, then, on the top floor, the schoolroom and nursery, with their toys and educational games.

National Museum

The Kildare Street site houses such national treasures as the Ardagh Chalice and Tara Brooch. The Collins Barracks site is worth visiting for the building alone.

RATINGS

Cultural interest	●●●●●
Historic interest	●●●●
Specialist shopping	●●●

BASICS

NATIONAL MUSEUM OF ARCHAEOLOGY AND HISTORY

67 F3 • Kildare Street, Dublin 2
01 677 7444
Tue–Sat 10–5, Sun 2–5
Free
7, 7A, 10, 11, 13
DART Pearse
Tours last 40 min and depart from main entrance at regular intervals; adult €2, child (under 16) free
Museum café on ground floor
By back entrance

NATIONAL MUSEUM OF DECORATIVE ARTS AND HISTORY

66 B2 • Collins Barracks, Benburb Street, Dublin 7
Opening times as Kildare Street site
Free
25, 25A, 66, 67, 90
Tours available by advance reservation (tel 01 677 7444)

www.museum.ie
Excellent, easy to use website, covering all branches of the National Museum.

SEEING THE NATIONAL MUSEUM

The National Museum safeguards some of Ireland's most precious and important treasures—gold and silverware found in bogs, caves and burial mounds all across the country and memorabilia from the 20th-century struggle for independence. The Kildare Street site is based around a glorious marble-halled rotunda, the Benburb Street site is the old Collins Barracks, a fascinating building in its own right.

HIGHLIGHTS

PREHISTORIC IRELAND

The Prehistoric Ireland displays include tools and weaponry from the Stone Age and Bronze Age, with explanations of burial customs and reconstructed graves. One of the most impressive exhibits is the Lurgan Bog Boat, over 13m (43ft) long, pulled from a Galway bog in 1902 and dated to around 2500BC. There is a huge collection of Sheela na Gigs here too. These weird, often comically sexy, stone carvings of women date from a pre-Christian era.

ÓR—IRELAND'S GOLD

Bronze Age Ireland produced a wealth of gold jewellery and other items which may come as a surprise to anyone with preconceptions about this 'uncivilized' era. The collection includes gold lunulae dating back as far as 2000BC, and more sophisticated works such as the Gleninsheen Collar, which was made around 700BC.

THE TREASURY

The best known pieces of ancient Irish craftsmanship are preserved in the Treasury. The Tara Brooch, only 5cm (2in) across yet intricately patterned with Celtic motifs is believed to have been made in the eighth century AD, of white bronze, silver gilt, amber and glass, and symbolizes the inspirational early Christian design that flourished here while much of the British Isles languished in the Dark Ages. The superb Ardagh Chalice is also from that period—gilded and studded in multi-hued glass and decorated in gold filigree. The exquisite crozier from Clonmacnoise shows the wealth and power of the early church.

THE ROAD TO INDEPENDENCE–AR THOIRE NA SOAOIRSE
This part of the museum charts the rise of nationalism in the 19th century then concentrates on the first two decades of the 20th century. The 1916 Easter Rising is heavily represented with a collection of weapons that belonged to notable individuals.

OTHER EXHIBITS
Viking Ireland is explored upstairs, particularly the peaceful trading aspects of the Scandinavians who established their port at Dublin. The Medieval Ireland section feels a bit thin by comparison, perhaps reflecting the decline in indigenous culture during this period.

The impressive exterior of Collins Barracks (below left), housing the National Museum of Decorative Arts and History

The great hall of the National Museum of Archaeology and History (below middle), and its colonnaded exterior (below right)

NATIONAL MUSEUM OF DECORATIVE ARTS AND HISTORY
The layout at the Collins Barracks is a little more confusing, with 13 galleries on four floors around two sides of the central courtyard, but there's a leaflet to help you navigate, available from the reception desk. The section devoted to Irish Silver takes the silversmith's craft from the early 17th to the 20th century, and another section deals with coinage. It was the Vikings who first brought the concept of currency to Ireland's shores and this exhibition follows its history, from 10th-century hoards to the ATM. 'The Way We Wore' displays 250 years of Irish clothing, and the influence of European trends on local materials. Curator's Choice is an eclectic selection chosen for interesting stories or significance, and include a wedding gift from Oliver Cromwell to his daughter, King William's gauntlets from the day of the Battle of the Boyne in 1690, and a hurling ball love token.

The Ardagh Chalice (left), a wonder of early Celtic art, is in the museum's Treasury

BACKGROUND

The Kildare Street site, opened in 1896, was designed by Thomas Newenham and Thomas Manley Deane, in a style known as Victorian Palladian, with a dome that rises to 19m (62ft). The Collins Barracks, on the other hand, began life as the main barracks for the British garrison in Dublin and were built in 1700. The Irish Free State took them over in 1922 and they remained in military hands until the 1990s, renamed after Michael Collins. In the superb courtyard-cum-parade ground, you can still see 100 marching paces marked off against the wall.

TIPS

- Combine a trip out to the Collins Barracks with a visit to Kilmainham or the Museum of Modern Art.
- The Kildare Street museum isn't a large space, and can seem very congested, so try to avoid times when it is most likely to be crowded, for example weekend afternoons in summer.

Neon and car lights illuminate wide O'Connell Street

The Wellington Monument in Dublin's Phoenix Park

Naturally mummified remains open to view in St. Michan's crypt

O'CONNELL STREET

67 E2 • O'Connell Street, Dublin 1 Most central-city buses DART Tara Street, 5-min walk

A key thoroughfare in central Dublin, O'Connell Street leads down to the River Liffey and the always busy O'Connell Bridge. Two of Dublin's most famous department stores are here, Clery's and Easons, and there are busy shopping areas off Henry Street to the west. In the street opposite the GPO rises the Monument of Light, also called The Spire (▷ 18), a 120m (394ft) spike of stainless steel. The site was formerly occupied by Nelson's Pillar (demolished by a rogue IRA man in 1966), and then by a depiction of Anna Livia. The spire was raised in 2002 and despite problems with its lighting, has become a symbol of modern Dublin. Upper O'Connell Street was originally laid out in the 1740s and was connected to Lower O' Connell Street, then known as Sackville Street, in 1784. O'Connell Bridge, formerly known as Carlisle Bridge, was completed in 1790 and is overlooked by a grand statue of Daniel O'Connell, 'the Liberator', still bearing bullet marks from the fighting in 1916.

PHOENIX PARK

66 A2 • Visitor Centre, Phoenix Park, Dublin 8, tel 01 677 0095; Apr–end Sep daily 10–6; mid- to end Mar, Oct daily 10–5.30; Nov to mid-Mar Sat, Sun 10–5; adult €2.75, child €1.25, family €7 Daylight hours Free 10, 37, 38, 39 Heuston Station Free tickets for tours (Sat only) of Áras an Uachtaráin from Visitor Centre. No booking allowed Coffee shop and restaurant at Visitor Centre

Often claimed to be the largest city park in the world, Phoenix Park stretches west from Parkgate, near the Collins Barracks, for nearly 5km (3 miles). Within this huge open space, the most visible feature is the 62.5m (205ft) Wellington obelisk, commemorating the Battle of Waterloo in 1815. Nearby is Dublin Zoo, founded in 1830 and one of the oldest in the world (tel 01 474 8900; Mar–end Sep 9.30–6, Sun 10.30–6; Oct–end Feb Mon–Sat 9.30–dusk, Sun 10.30–dusk). On the northern side of the park, the stately home of the British Viceroys of Ireland became the Áras an Uachtaráin, official residence of the President of Ireland, in 1937. Guided tours are available every Saturday except at Christmas. The park passed into notoriety when the British chief secretary, Lord Frederick Cavendish, and his under secretary, T. H. Burke were assassinated here by a radical republican group known as the Invincibles in 1882. On the southern side, an area known as the Fifteen Acres is popular for Gaelic sports, and Pope John Paul II greeted over 1 million people here on his visit in 1979. To get the most from a visit to the park, head for the Visitor Centre, next to the restored Ashtown Castle, which traces the area's history from 3500BC through its time as a royal hunting ground to the present.

ST. MICHAN'S CHURCH

66 C2 • Church Street, Dublin 7 01 872 4154 Mid-Mar to end Oct Mon–Fri 10–12.45, 2–4.30, Sat 10–12.45; Nov to mid-Mar Mon–Fri 12.30–3.30, Sat 10–12.45 Tours: adult €3.50, child €2.50 83 Access to vaults by tour only

Unremarkable from the outside, St. Michan's secret lies in its crypt. Here in the dry atmosphere of its vaults, the assembled corpses became mummified rather than decomposing. Guided tours point out ancient remains and bodies of the 18th-century dead, including those of Henry and John Sheares, leaders of the rebellion in 1798. There is also a death mask of Wolfe Tone, and some believe Robert Emmet may have been buried in the churchyard. The church can trace its origins back to 1095 but the present structure is mostly from 1686.

ST. PATRICK'S CATHEDRAL

67 D4 • Patrick's Close, Dublin 8 01 475 4817 Mar–end Oct daily 9–6; Nov–end Feb Sat 9–5, Sun 9–2.30 Adult €4.20, family €9.50 50, 54A, 56A Beneath Minot's Tower opposite entrance www.stpatrickscathedral.ie

The Victorians restored the largest church in Ireland using money from the Guinness family to repoint and reinterpret the Gothic and Romanesque features it had acquired since its founding in 1191. At 91m (298ft) long, with a 43m (141ft) tower at its western end, it is not particularly big by European standards, and until the 1920s it stood amid slum housing, outside the old city walls. Today it overlooks a little park, and inside you will find the grave and some memorabilia of its most famous dean, Jonathan Swift. The author of *Gulliver's Travels* became dean of St. Patrick's in 1713. One notable curiosity is a wooden door, originally from the chapterhouse but now mounted at the junction of the north transept. Through a hole in this, the Earl of Kildare stretched out his hand to make peace with the Earl of Ormond (▷ 31), the supposed origins of the phrase 'chancing your arm'. Despite its pre-eminence in a predominantly Catholic city, the church belongs to the Protestant Church of Ireland.

The splendidly restored nave of St. Patrick's Cathedral

St. Stephen's Green is noted for its many statues and monuments

The modest, middle-class home where G. B. Shaw was born

ST. STEPHEN'S GREEN

67 E4 • Dublin 2 ☎ 01 475 7816 Mon–Sat 8–dusk; Sun, public holidays 10–dusk; Christmas Day 10–1 Inbound buses arrive on the west side of the square, outbound buses leave from the east side DART Pearse; Luas St. Stephen's Green

This public park of 9ha (22 acres) was originally a place of public executions and punishments. It was enclosed in 1669, and surrounding land was sold off to property developers. Trees and paths soon followed and Dubliners were charged for access. However, in 1877, Sir Arthur Guinness secured an Act of Parliament to make access free for all, and today it is a popular haven from the din of the surrounding traffic. It includes a sensory garden for the visually impaired. The main entrance is through Fusiliers' Gate on the corner facing Grafton Street. **Don't miss** St. Stephen's Green is full of monuments and statues that are worth seeking out.

SANDYCOVE

353 G5 • 13km (8 miles) south of Dublin 59 from Dún Laoghaire DART Sandycove

A tiny cove near Dún Laoghaire gives this affluent suburb its name. James Joyce lived briefly in the Martello tower overlooking a rocky peninsula. It features in the opening chapter of *Ulysses* and now houses a museum of Joycean memorabilia: his letters to Nora Barnacle, a 1935 edition of *Ulysses* illustrated by Matisse, a guitar and a waistcoat (vest) (Joyce Tower, Sandycove, tel 01 280 9265, Mar–end Oct. Mon–Sat 10–1, 2–5, Sun, public holidays 2–6). Nearby Forty Foot Pool is a sea-bathing facility, popular even in winter, with changing areas cut in the rock. Contrary to the old sign, mixed bathing is allowed.

SHAW'S BIRTHPLACE

Off map 67 D4 • 33 Synge Street, Dublin 8 ☎ 01 872 2077 May–end Sep Mon–Sat 10–5, Sun, public holidays 2–6 Adult €6, child (over 12) €3.50, family €16 16, 19, 122 DART Grand Canal Dock, 15-min walk www.visitdublin.com

The plaque on 33 Synge Street records George Bernard Shaw as the 'author of many plays', which is how the Nobel Laureate wanted his birthplace to be commemorated. He was born in this terraced house in 1856 and left to go to London in 1876. Inside there isn't a great deal about Shaw himself, but the house has been restored to reflect the life of a middle-class family in Victorian Dublin. Shaw didn't write any of his works (*Pygmalion, Arms and the Man, Man and Superman* to name a few) in Dublin, but like Joyce he drew heavily on his experiences of the city and its characters.

SMITHFIELD

66 C2 • Smithfield Village, Dublin 7 25, 25A, 67, 67A (from Middle Abbey Street); 68, 69, 79 (from Aston Quay), 90 (from Connolly, Tara and Heuston stations) www.smithfieldvillage.com

Once notoriously run down, this corner of Dublin is reinventing itself since its initial redevelopment in the 1990s. You can still find traces of the old Smithfield. The Jameson Distillery is in Bow Street, no longer in production, but tours show how whiskey was made from the sixth century onward and end with a tasting session (daily 9.30–6). The old distillery chimney has a viewing platform on top, 41m (135ft) above the street, via an external glass lift, offering a 360-degree view of the city (tel 01 817 3800, Mon–Sat 10–5, Sun 11–5). Next door the Chief O'Neill's Hotel complex takes its name from the Chicago policeman who compiled a famous collection of Irish tunes, and specializes in traditional Irish food and music. Smithfield Square is lit at night by 12 brazier lanterns, each 26m (85ft) high.

TEMPLE BAR

67 E3 Temple Bar Information Centre, 12 East Essex Street, Temple Bar, Dublin 2, tel 01 677 2255 All central city buses pass Temple Bar DART Tara Street, 10-min walk www.templebar.ie

Promoted as 'Dublin's Cultural Quarter' Temple Bar takes its name from the Anglo-Irish aristocrat Sir William Temple, who owned much of the land in the 17th century. Within this block of narrow streets you'll find countless pubs popular with drinking parties, traditional music, cafés and nightclubs. You'll also find the National Photographic Archive (Meeting House Square, tel 01 603 0370, Mon–Fri 10–5, gallery also Sat 10–2), with regular exhibitions; the Irish Film Centre, showing art house movies; the Ark, a cultural facility for four- to14-year-olds; and Project, a venerable artist-based venue with a pedigree stretching back to the 1960s, when Temple Bar was a rundown wasteland. By the 1970s the site was earmarked for a bus station, and the bus company began letting out the buildings cheaply to artists and musicians. Temple Bar established a bohemian reputation for its buzzing nightlife, and in doing so won a reprieve from the wrecking ball. The most evocative entrance is over the Ha'penny Bridge (there used to be a toll), and through the Merchants Arch. Open-air performances often take place in nearby Meeting House Square.

Trinity College Library

The iconic intricacy of the Book of Kells draws visitors to Trinity College, Ireland's premier seat of learning. A fascinating exhibition puts the art of the ninth-century scribe in perspective.

Trinity's busy main entrance (above). Sphere Within a Sphere *(right) by Arnaldo Pomodoro, outside the Berkeley Library*

The spacious campus (above). The Long Room *(right) is an atmospheric place with a magnificent collection of books*

RATINGS

Cultural interest	●●●●
Historic interest	●●●●
Specialist shopping	●●●
Walkability	●●●

BASICS

67 E3 • College Street, Dublin 2
01 608 2320
Jun–end Sep Mon–Sat 9.30–5, Sun 9.30–4.30; Oct–end May Mon–Sat 9.30–5, Sun 12–4.30. Closed 10 days over Christmas and New Year
Adult €7.50, family €15
All cross city buses
DART Tara Street

www.tcd.ie/library/
Comprehensive information about the college.

TIPS

- **Visit on a Sunday morning in June for the best view of the campus with the fewest students and other visitors.**
- **You can wander around the main courtyards and admire the historic buildings for free, but remember it's a working university and private property.**
- **Take your time at the Book of Kells; its intricacy is scarcely credible at first glance.**

SEEING TRINITY COLLEGE LIBRARY

No visit to Dublin is complete without seeing one of the most famous illuminated manuscripts in the world. The intricate beauty of the Book of Kells has been imitated countless times, but to see the pages themselves, and those of the similarly ornate books of Durrow and Armagh, is really memorable. There is more here than just these revered texts though. The exhibition 'Turning Darkness into Light' brings a context to the works, and upstairs, the barrel-ceilinged Long Room is filled with the intoxicating musk of over 200,000 ancient leather-bound books.

The entrance to the Old Library is through the gap in the square on the right-hand side. It faces a group of modern buildings including the Berkeley Library, which was designed by Paul Koralek in 1967. The exhibition is reached through the shop at street level.

HIGHLIGHTS

EXHIBITION

'Turning Darkness into Light' is the name of the exhibition in the Old Library that leads you up to the displayed pages of the Book of Kells. It explains the context of the book, follows the development of writing and illuminating manuscripts and has examples of Ogham and Ethiopian scripts. Pages, and individual illustrations, have been enlarged to the size of a person, so you can stand back and identify the truly stunning detail of the monastic scribe's art.

THE BOOK OF KELLS

The Book of Kells itself is displayed in a darkened room known as the Treasury. The book is bound in four volumes, two of which are always on display, so you are able to see two double page spreads at a time, and these are turned every three months. It was written, if that is the right word for its spectacularly ornate pages, in the ninth century AD by monks at St. Columba's monastery at Iona on the west coast of Scotland. It was transferred to the monastery at Kells in County Meath

for safekeeping during the Viking raids and then its history is less certain. It arrived in Dublin in 1653, during the Cromwellian upheavals, and was acquired by Trinity College in 1661. Its brilliantly elaborate pages reveal both the craft and the wit of its scribes. The text is the four Christian gospels, written in Latin. Each evangelist is portrayed in minute detail and each gospel begins with just a few words on a magnificently decorated page. Some of the pages, known as 'carpet pages', have no words at all, just the swirling abstract ornamentation which has become the hallmark of this incredible era of Celtic art. Also on display in the Treasury are the equally fabulous, but less well-known books of Durrow and Armagh, which may originate from the seventh century AD. They too demonstrate the tremendous scope and vision of the monastic scribes, again displaying an intricacy of penmanship that could scarcely have been visible in that distant age before electric lighting and artificial magnification.

Intricate Celtic art frames a portrait of St. John in the Book of Kells (above)

THE LONG ROOM

The Long Room is up the stairs from the Treasury. As in Marsh's Library at St. Patrick's Cathedral, the smell of old books hits you as you walk in. They are piled high to the ceiling, which was extended in 1860 to fit more in. The gallery bookcases were added at this point. The central aisle is lined with busts of scholars and there is also a harp on display, believed to be the oldest in existence, though its 15th-century provenance means it can't be the legendary harp of Brian Boru, the 11th-century High King of Ireland, as one story claims. Another display has a rare copy of the Proclamation of the Irish Republic, as read out by Padraig Pearse from the steps of the GPO in 1916, Robert Emmet's arrest warrant and other papers from the struggle for independence.

Oliver Goldsmith (below) was one of many illustrious students

BACKGROUND

Trinity College is a modern working university and so, unless you visit on Sunday morning or in high summer, its courtyards are usually teeming with students and their bicycles. Founded by Queen Elizabeth I in 1592, it is Ireland's oldest university. Although this Georgian building (1759) is grand in its own right, its impact is lessened by the proximity of the traffic and the more overt classicism of James Gandon's east front of the Bank of Ireland across the road. This dates from 1785 and was added to an older building, which once housed the Irish parliament.

Past the Porter's Lodge you come out into Parliament Square, with the chapel, built in 1798, to the left and the Examination Room, of 1791, to the right. Ahead of you is the Campanile, a bell tower 30m (98ft) high added to the square in 1853. Beyond it, the red-brick building is known as the Rubrics. With its origins around 1700, this is the oldest surviving building on the campus. The playwright Oliver Goldsmith had chambers on the top right-hand side next to the Old Library. Before the rebuilding work of the 1980s, the Book of Kells was kept upstairs in the Long Room, and the area known as the Colonnades below, where the shop, exhibition and Treasury are now, was a crowded storage area for the library's overflowing book collection. When the building was originally built, this area had been left open to prevent damp rising into the library. It was filled in to house more books in the 1860s.

THE EAST

The East has something for everyone: quiet lakes, lush gardens, the Wicklow Mountains and the rolling pastures of The Curragh. There are prehistoric and monastic sites in the Boyne Valley, medieval streets, monuments and abbeys in Kilkenny, while Wexford's sandy beaches give way to river estuaries—havens for wildlife.

MAJOR SIGHTS

Dating from the 15th century, the evocative ruins of the Cistercian Bective Abbey stand among peaceful meadows by the River Boyne

Looking out from Bray towards the steep slope of Bray Head

AVOCA HANDWEAVERS

353 G6 • Old Mill, Avoca, Co. Wicklow 0402 35105 Daily 9–6 (5.30 Oct–May) On Bus Éireann service Dublin–Arklow Rathdrum Station 9km (5.5 miles) Available on request By shop
www.avoca.ie

It's hard to escape the Avoca brand in Ireland. Whether you're shopping on Grafton Street or browsing in craft outlets , you'll see the name of this little Wicklow Mountains village on high-quality mohair and cashmere garments, manufactured in the tiny weaving shed at the Old Mill on the edge of the village. Established in 1723, it is one of the oldest factories in continuous use in Ireland. Visitors can get a feel for the clatter of the weaving shed, with its array of working handlooms and machine looms, before visiting the factory shop. The rest of the village is hardly exciting but is neatly painted, thanks mostly to its starring role in the BBC comedy drama *Ballykissangel*.

BECTIVE ABBEY

349 G4 • Bective, Navan, Co. Meath 046 943 7111 Daily, daylight hours Free Bus Éireann service Navan to Scurloughstown stops at Bective Cross
www.meathtourism.ie

Founded in 1147 as a daughter abbey to Mellifont (▷ 102), Bective was an Anglo-Norman, Cistercian foundation, but little survives from that period. What you see today, in a field by the River Boyne, is largely the 15th-century defensive additions. A square tower rises above the remaining walls of the cloister, nave and chapterhouse. Also discernible are the fireplaces, chimneys and windows of the fortified mansion that the site became after the monastery's dissolution in 1543. A medieval bridge across the river indicates the abbey's former importance—its abbot once even held a seat in the English parliament.

BRAY

353 G5 Tourist Information Office, Bray, Co. Wicklow, 01 286 7128 45, 84 (from Eden Quay, Dublin) DART Bray
www.bray.ie

Bray sits on a long sweep of shingle beach at the south end of Killiney Bay. Once promoted as a resort for wealthy Dubliners, it is now a desirable commuter town, backed by Bray Head and the distinctive cones of the Great and Little Sugar Loaf hills, and home to the National Sea Life Centre (tel 01 286 6939). On the slopes of the Little Sugar Loaf, holding out against the relentless advances of new housing, Killruddery House and Gardens have been in the Brabazon family since 1618. The gardens were designed in French classical style in the 1680s by Bonet, who also worked on Versailles. The 17th-century house, redesigned in Elizabethan style in 1820, contains a mantelpiece by Grinling Gibbons and bookcases by Chippendale (tel 01 286 3405, gardens: Apr–end Sep daily 1–5; house: May, Jun, Sep daily 1–5).

BRÚ NA BÓINNE

See pages 90–93.

CASTLETOWN HOUSE

353 G5 • Celbridge, Co. Kildare 01 628 8252 Mid-Apr to end Sep Mon–Fri 10–6, Sat, Sun, public holidays 1–6; Oct Mon–Fri 10–5, Sun, public holidays 1–5; Nov Sun 1–5 Adult €3.50, child (4–15) €1.25 67, 67A from Dublin Guided tour only, 1 hour Hazelhatch & Celbridge

An avenue of lime trees 1km (half a mile) long leads up to this grey stone country house, designed for the Irish politician William Conolly in 1722, with a view over meadows to the River Liffey and the mountains. The main hall has stucco work by the Lafrancini brothers and an enormous painting, *The Boar Hunt* by Paul de Vos (1596–1679). Conolly made his fortune buying and selling forfeited property after the Battle of the Boyne, but never lived to see his great house completed, a task left to Lady Louisa Conolly, the wife of his great nephew, who moved there in 1759. The interiors have been left virtually untouched since her death in 1821. One room, known as the Print Room, is lined with paper taken from 18th-century magazines. The house was acquired by the Irish state in 1994.

CARLOW

352 F6 Tourist Information Office, Tullow Street, Carlow, Co. Carlow, tel 059 913 0411; Jun–end Aug Mon–Fri 9–1, 2–5.30, Sat 10–1, 2–5.30; Sep–end May Mon–Fri 9–1, 2–5 Bus Éireann service from Dublin Carlow
www.southeastireland.com

Carlow is a somewhat unremarkable place, although there is good shopping off its wide open square. Away from the heart of town a pleasing tangle of early 19th-century streets suggests future potential, but Carlow's most impressive feature, its castle (open daylight hours), lies stranded in wasteland by the Barrow River amid modern housing schemes. The two remaining round towers and a section of curtain wall date from the 13th century. The rest was bizarrely destroyed in 1814 by a local doctor trying to convert the site into a mental hospital with the aid of high explosives.

The early 19th-century Gothic Cathedral of the Assumption,

The enormous granite capstone on the dolmen at Browneshill

A fishermen's guild banner in Drogheda's Millmount Museum

The imposing modern façade of St. Peter's Church in Drogheda

one of the first Catholic churches built after the Emancipation Act, was designed by Thomas Cobden and is topped by an impressive lantern tower. The courthouse building, somewhat marred by the heavy traffic, is a striking replica of the Parthenon, and was supposedly intended for Cork City until a mix-up of documents gave Carlow one of its grandest buildings. About 3km (2 miles) out of town on the R726 the Browneshill Dolmen (open daylight hours) stands in a field opposite a car showroom. A surfaced track leads from a little parking area to the array of stones which date from 2500BC, and would originally have been covered in earth. The precarious capstone is believed to be one of the largest in Europe.

CAVAN

348 F4 Tourist Information Office, 7 Farnham Street, Cavan Town, Co. Cavan, tel 049 433 1942 Bus Éireann service from Dublin
www.cavantourism.ie

Cavan is bypassed by the busy N3 Dublin–Donegal road, so its narrow main shopping street (Farnham Street) is a pleasant place to linger. The shops are mostly independently owned, their bright frontages harking back to an older Ireland, all but vanished this far east. Of the 14th-century Franciscan friary, to which the town owes its origin, the belfry tower remains, in a run-down churchyard near the bus station. The huge green rotunda and neoclassical façade of St. Patrick's Roman Catholic Cathedral, built in 1942, stand out in the north of the town. The nearby courthouse is also in an imposing Classical style, but there is little else to detain you here.
Don't miss Just 3km (2 miles) outside town, Cavan Crystal produces fine lead crystal.

DROGHEDA

349 G4 Tourist Information Office, Mayoralty Street, Drogheda, Co. Louth, tel 041 983 7070 Bus Éireann from Dublin Drogheda

Viking traders established this port town spanning both banks of the River Boyne in AD911. Its name 'Droichead Atha' means 'bridge by the ford', though the river was not bridged until the Normans came in the 12th century. The industrial heart of the town is undergoing a renaissance today and modern Drogheda has been immeasurably improved since the M1 toll bridge to the west diverted Dublin–Belfast traffic out of the town. The northern side of the river has the main shopping area and medieval remains such as St. Lawrence's Gate, a four-floor barbican, and Magdalene Tower, a remnant of a once-important Dominican friary from 1224. On the south side of the river and accessed from the riverside by steep steps is the Millmount fortification. A Martello tower crowns an Anglo-Norman motte from the 12th century (guided tour only). A museum, a craft centre and restaurant are housed in the next door barracks, and there are splendid views (Millmount Museum, tel 041 983 3097, Mon–Sat 10–6, Sun, public holidays 2.30–6). There's a Heritage Centre and more medieval defences near Millmount.

DUNMORE CAVE

352 F6 • Ballyfoyle, Kilkenny, Co. Kilkenny 056 776 7726 Mid-Jun to mid-Sep daily 9.30–6.30; mid-Mar to mid-Jun, mid-Sep to end Oct daily 10–5; Nov to mid-Mar Sat, Sun, public holidays 10–5 Adult €2.75, child (6–17) €1.25, family €7 Kilkenny Kilkenny Station Access by guided tour only, 45 min Café in Visitor Centre In Visitor Centre

This impressive cave lies on a gentle rise in the limestone hills south of Kilkenny. An interpretative area guards the entrance and visits to the fantastical arrays of stalactites and stalagmites below ground are by guided tour. A steep series of 706 steps leads into the cave, which has three main chambers and contains traces of occupation stretching back over 3,500 years. The 7m-high (23ft) Market Cross is just one of the huge stalagmites in chasms known as the 'cathedral' and the 'town hall'. Back in the interpretative area you can see interactive displays of remains and treasures found in the cave. The most macabre remains are those of the 44 woman and children who possibly suffocated during a Viking raid in AD928. In 1999 Viking coins and silver jewellery were discovered here dating from a similar time.

Magdalene Tower: the last remnant of a friary

Brú na Bóinne

Older than the pyramids of Egypt and Stonehenge in England, Brú na Bóinne is one of the most important prehistoric monuments in Europe and is eastern Ireland's most visited historic site.

Fronted by quartzite, the Newgrange tomb (above) is the most familiar and stunning of the monuments. Detail on the inscribed stones at Newgrange (right). Characteristic whorl motifs in the rocks (far right)

RATINGS	
Cultural interest	●●●●
Good for kids	●●●
Historic interest	●●●●●

BASICS

349 G4

Brú na Bóinne Visitor Centre, Donore, Co. Meath, tel 041 988 0300

Nov–end Feb daily 9.30–5; Mar, Apr daily 9.30–5.30; May daily 9–6.30; Jun to mid-Sep daily 9–7; mid-Sep to end Sep daily 9–6.30; Oct daily 9.30–5.30. Knowth open May–end Oct only

Exhibition only: adult €2.75, child (under 16) €1.50, family €7; exhibition and Newgrange: adult €5.50, child (under 16) €2.75, family €13.75; exhibition and Knowth: adult €4.25, child (under 16) €1.50, family €10.50; exhibition, Newgrange and Knowth: adult €9.75, child (under 16) €4.25, family €24.25

Bus Éireann service to/from Drogheda to Donore village (10-min walk)

Drogheda Station 8km (5 miles)

Access by tour only, each lasting 1 hour 15 min

Café at Visitor Centre

At Visitor Centre

www.meathtourism.ie
Enthusiastic overview of whole county.

SEEING BRÚ NA BÓINNE

Brú na Bóinne, the 'palace of the Boyne', is the name given to a large group of neolithic remains in the central Boyne Valley 11km (7 miles) west of Drogheda. The huge, white-fronted passage tomb of Newgrange is the best known, but the nearby mounds of Knowth and Dowth were probably of equal importance historically. These great tombs are over 5,000 years old. We can only guess at the significance of their swirling rock art but the impact of the winter solstice sun, which stunningly lights up the tombs' darkest recesses, was clearly important. You can only visit the main site with an organized tour from the Visitor Centre, but it is worth spending time in the centre itself, learning about the culture that gave rise to these extraordinary monuments.

There are over 50 lumps and bumps with ritual significance around Brú na Bóinne. Of the three major tombs, you can visit the interiors of Knowth and Newgrange on organized tours, but visitor numbers are restricted to 700 a day. Your ticket buys you a seat on an allotted minibus, which leaves from beneath the Visitor Centre. Some of the stops on these tours are assigned to tour operators coming from Dublin, so if you want to guarantee a visit to the tombs themselves you may be better joining one of those. Otherwise, arrive early and be prepared to wait. Once you have bought your ticket you can explore the surrounding countryside until your tour is due to leave.

HIGHLIGHTS

KNOWTH

Knowth is the most westerly of the great tombs, and is only accessible by tour, although it can be seen from the nearby road. The mound is outlined by 127 huge edging stones. Surrounding the main tomb are at least 18 smaller tombs, some of which predate the larger tomb. There has been human activity here from far back in prehistory through to the early Christian period and understanding the complex story of the site's development has not been easy. Inside the tomb are two passages, both lined with upright stones. Their faces are

adorned with swirling patterns and lines. The eastern passage contains a large ditch. This was added in the early Christian era and demonstrates the mound's lasting spiritual importance across the millennia. Knowth tends to attract fewer visitors than Newgrange, so you may well find it easier to get a ticket for this site than for the better known tomb.

NEWGRANGE

This mound, fronted by white quartzite, is the most familiar of all the Brú na Bóinne monuments. Actually the frontage is the result of restoration work carried out in the 1960s, but the effect is truly stunning. The nearest source for quartzite is 64km (40 miles) away, beyond Dublin in the Wicklow Mountains, so whoever built this tomb had the ability to transport materials to the site over long distances. The whole mound is 100m (330ft) across and about 10m (33ft) high. There are 97 boulders forming an edging ring and until the 17th century there was a large standing stone positioned at the summit. At the entrance, one of these edging stones is adorned with the distinctive spiral and line motifs that characterize the rock art that has been found in the surrounding area. Above it stands the rectangular opening known as the roof box. Studying the site between 1962 and 1975, Professor M. J. O'Kelly made the remarkable discovery that the midwinter sun penetrates a slit in this chamber, sending a narrow shaft of light up the main passageway to illuminate the recess at the back of the north chamber. To be among the lucky few to witness the magic of this moment on the morning of the winter solstice, you must win a lottery draw which you can enter at the Visitor Centre, but you'll be among more than 20,000 hopefuls who apply each year. For the rest of us, the experience is reconstructed using an accurately positioned electric light. Astronomical calculations reveal that this effect would have been even more dramatic 5,000 years ago. Subtle shifts in the earth's axis and orbits have left the light falling slightly short of illuminating the whole chamber; when it was constructed the dawn light would have filled the whole of the back wall during the winter solstice. Another particularly remarkable feature of the Newgrange tomb is the construction of its roof. The massive stones above the chambers have been interlaced in such a way as to render them completely watertight, even after 5,000 years. The best examples of rock carving are to be found on the roof and walls of the right-hand chamber as you go in.

Quartzite used to face the tomb was dragged over huge distances

TIPS

- **Visit the Knowth and Newgrange monuments for a proper appreciation of the scale of the site and the quality of neolithic carving.**
- **Don't leave Brú na Bóinne until last on a day trip. Go there first, buy your ticket, then explore the rest of the Boyne Valley.**
- **Many good Boyne Valley tours from Dublin will include a ticket for the Newgrange monuments.**
- **If you can't get on a tour of the monuments, explore the Visitor Centre, visit the Dowth mound for free then head west for Loughcrew (▷ 102), where you can have a passage tomb to yourself.**

DOWTH

Dowth is the least known of the three great tombs, and though it contains some of the finest rock art to be seen anywhere in Ireland, its interior is out of bounds to visitors. However, you are free to roam about its grassy site, a freedom which is not allowed at Newgrange or Knowth. The mound is over 61m (200ft) across and about 14m (46ft) tall; the crater on its summit is the result of enthusiastic Victorian excavations. Some early Christian remains were found within

NEWGRANGE TOMB

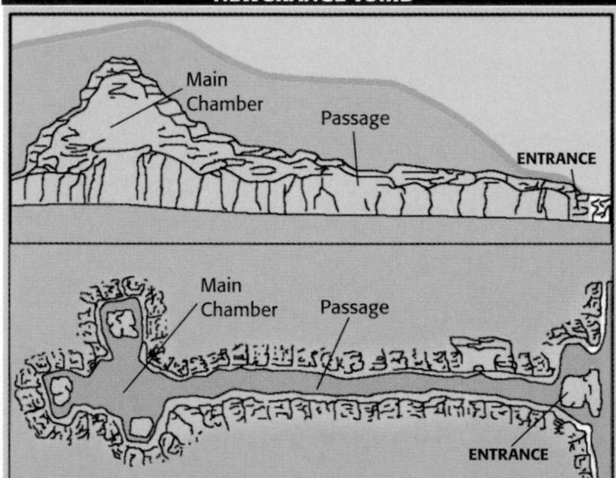

The diagrams on the right show a cross-section (top) and plan (bottom) view of the Newgrange tomb. The sun shines directly into the chamber on the winter solstice

and one of the passages connects to an early Christian *souterrain* (underground chamber). There are two principal neolithic tombs inside and the mound is outlined by 115 edging stones.

THE BRÚ NA BÓINNE VISITOR CENTRE

The Visitor Centre is more than just a conduit to the tomb visits—it deserves at least half an hour's attention in its own right. There are detailed touch-screen explanations of how the site evolved, who built it and how it was discovered. Among the life-size reconstructions are a cross-section of an archaeological survey, showing the painstaking methods used by the researchers investigating the site, and a re-creation of the main passage inside the Newgrange tomb, crucially widened so that wheelchairs can fit all the way in (the actual site is not accessible to wheelchair users because the passages are too narrow). A 7-minute audio-visual presentation shows you what the solstice light looks like and there are even hands-on demonstrations of carbon-dating. In addition to viewing the cabinets displaying finds from the sites, you are invited to share your theories on the meanings behind the swirling artforms. The viewing area includes the free use of telescopes and there is a good bookshop, café and tourist information desk.

Rich in spiral carvings, Knowth had great spiritual significance

Inscribed decoration on a stone found at the Newgrange tomb

There is also a passage tomb in the nearby Knowth mound

BACKGROUND

The whole Brú na Bóinne area is designated a World Heritage Site by UNESCO, putting it on equal footing with Stonehenge (1,000 years younger) and the pyramids of Giza (100 years younger). The antiquity of the site means it is difficult to know who began the structures and what their cultural significance was. The pre-Celtic founders may have come from the Iberian Peninsula, as some experts have suggested their swirling art-work indicates. But other authorities claim this is a specifically Irish phenomenon. Knowth was certainly already built when the 'beaker people' (named for their characteristic pottery) arrived from mainland Europe and occupied the site around 1800BC. It featured heavily in the lives of the Iron Age Celts from around 500BC, and plays a part in the dazzling array of legends that were passed down in the Irish language from these people. Newgrange was supposedly the home of Tuátha dé Danann, troglodytic followers of the goddess Danu. Warrior hero Cúchulainn was conceived here, the kings of Tara were said to have been buried here and Diarmuid, the wounded lover of Finn McCool's wife Gráinne was carried here to be brought back to life. All these stories made Brú na Bóinne a powerful symbol, so it is no surprise that the early Christians also occupied the site, adding their dead to the prehistoric tombs. By the ninth century this was an important stronghold of the Uí Néill clan, but the Middle Ages saw its decline and eventual abandonment. The tombs remained untouched until 1699, when renewed interest in antiquities brought them back into public knowledge.

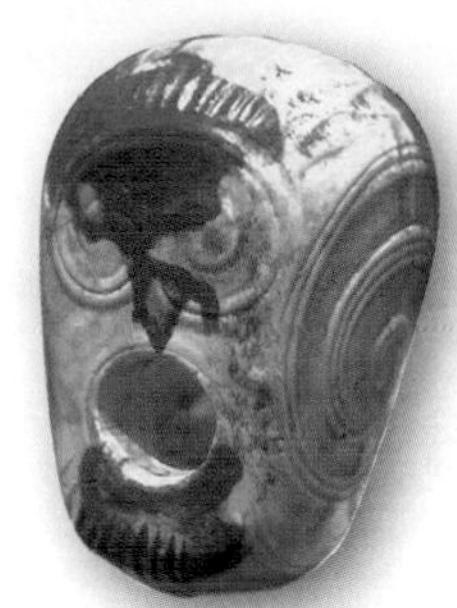

An insight into past civilizations: This carved mace head (above) was found at Knowth

Glendalough

The well-preserved monastic settlement of Glendalough lies in a beautiful upland valley. Lakes and woodland trails add to the charm of this part of the Wicklow Mountains.

There are good woodland strolls to enjoy around Glendalough

SEEING GLENDALOUGH

The remarkable combination of a well-preserved monastic settlement with a beautiful lake and mountain setting makes Glendalough one of eastern Ireland's premier attractions. The excellent modern Visitor Centre helps you to understand, not just what you can see on the ground, but also its place in Irish history. The two lakes and the mountains that surround it are superb walking territory, whether you're looking for a woodland stroll or a more challenging upland circuit. There are clearly waymarked paths between the principal sites, and for the most part these are even, with few steps or gradients. The free Visitor Centre parking area is the best spot to start from if you want to see all the sites on foot.

RATINGS

Historic interest	●●●●●
Outdoor pursuits	●●●
Photo stops	●●●●

BASICS

353 G6 • Glendalough, Bray, Co. Wicklow

0404 45325/45352

Visitor Centre: mid-Mar to mid-Oct daily 9.15–5.15; mid-Oct to mid-Mar daily 9.15–4.15

Visitor Centre: adult €2.75, child (6–16) €1.25, family €7

St. Kevin's Bus Service twice daily from Bray and Dublin

Rathdrum 11km (7 miles)

Available on request, allow 50 min

At back of Visitor Centre

TIPS

- **Access to the site in the valley is free. You only pay if you want to park by the Upper Lake or go to the Visitor Centre.**
- **A walk on one of the marked trails around the glen will give you a better perspective than just wandering round the ruins and will also get you away from the crowds. Pick up a free leaflet from the Visitor Centre.**

HIGHLIGHTS

MAIN SITE

Glendalough means the 'valley of the two loughs' although the principal site is below the Lower Lough on slightly raised land by the confluence of the Gledasan and Glenalo rivers. Here you'll find the ruins of St. Ciaran's Church, and those of St. Kevin's Church, often called St. Kevin's Kitchen because its tower resembles the chimney stack of a bakehouse. The body of this barrel-vaulted oratory is made from hard mica schist and dates from the 12th century. A double arch by the Glendalough Hotel leads you into the churchyard where the remains of the cathedral stand, its ninth-century nave and chancel now roofless. The Priest's House contains carvings of St. Kevin and dates from the 12th century. The 30m (100ft) round tower would have served as a belfry, lookout tower and treasury. Although the conical roof has been restored, the rest of the tower is in its original condition, an indication of how well this site has been preserved over the centuries. There's a high cross here, though its impact is lessened by the proliferation of wheelhead motifs on the surrounding graves—this is still a working cemetery for the residents of the glen and the nearby village of Laragh. On the far side of the churchyard, the 10th-century St. Mary's Church may have housed St. Kevin's tomb.

UPPER LOUGH SITES

Between the Visitor Centre and the bridge stands the Deerstone, which despite its spurious legend of does squirting milk into its hollow to feed Kevin's disciples, is actually a much older grinding stone from the glen's prehistoric inhabitants. Beyond the Lower Lough, another group of important sites includes the 10th-century Reefert Church, with its tombs of local chiefs, and St. Kevin's Cell, the beehive-style hut where the settlement began. Above here, you can walk up past the Poulanass Waterfall into the surrounding mountains, or follow the old miners' road up the northern shore of the Upper Lough to see the remains of the lead and silver mines that were established in the rocky outcrops at the head of the valley. These were part of a larger mining operation in the next glen, and were worked between 1850 and 1875. On the cliffs on the south side of the lough, the peculiar Teampull na Skellig is a platform cut into the rock, the site of the very early 'Church of the Rock'. Nearby St. Kevin's Bed is a Bronze Age burial site, later associated with Kevin's escape from Kathleen, a temptress whom he eventually threw in the lough to drown.

VISITOR CENTRE

The Visitor Centre also acts as an information outlet for the Wicklow Mountains National Park. It's at the entrance to the glen, just beyond the site of the Trinity Chapel. The main audio-visual presentation lasts 17 minutes and concentrates on Glendalough's Christian heritage. The interactive displays are more balanced, putting the remains in the wider context and explaining the key features: the high cross, the carvings, the round tower. A scale model shows what the monastic settlement might have looked like in the 12th century.

BACKGROUND

The reclusive St. Kevin first established a monastic presence in this U-shaped glacial valley in AD570. The remote location was ideal for his hermitic tendencies, but he emphasized them still further by spending time in a cave (St. Kevin's Bed), accessible only by boat, on the cliffs above the Upper Lough. St. Kevin came from one of Leinster's ruling families and was abbot here until his death in AD618. He encouraged Glendalough's reputation for learning and its renown spread across Europe. This was a place of pilgrimage too, seven trips here were equivalent to one trip to Rome even as late as 1862. Though it survived Viking and Norman raids, as well as those of indigenous bandits, the settlement began to decline in importance with the wave of French monastic foundations that followed the Anglo-Norman occupation of Ireland. But there were still monks resident here when the monastery was dissolved in the 16th century. St. Kevin's feast day (3 June) continued to draw visitors to Glendalough into the 19th century, by which time they had acquired a rather bawdy reputation. The middle of that century saw an increased interest in archaeology and the site was taken over by the Commissioners of Public Works in 1869.

The well-preserved round tower at Glendalough is one of Ireland's most famous (above)

St. Kevin's Church (top left), seen through the headstones of the graves around it

Glendalough's monastic remains have a beautiful and peaceful lakeside setting (top middle)

The stone exterior of St. Kevin's Church (top right), which is often called St. Kevin's Kitchen

Craggy rocks punctuate the low-lying coastline at Hook Head

The zebra-striped lighthouse on Hook Head is Ireland's oldest

The Irish National Heritage Park re-creates 9,000 years of history

ENNISCORTHY 1798 CENTRE

353 G7 • National 1798 Visitor Centre, Mill Park Road, Enniscorthy, Co. Wexford, tel 054 37596; Mon–Fri 9.30–6, Sat–Sun 11–6; adult €6, child (4–16) €3.50, family €16 • Bus Éireann service from Dublin • Enniscorthy • Allow at least an hour • In foyer
www.1798centre.com

If you are a bit unsure of the details of the 1798 rebellion in the south of Ireland, this superb visitor attraction, built to mark the rising's bicentenary, puts the whole period in perspective. Using a mix of audio-visuals and informative displays you are taken through the economic and political conditions that led up to the conflict. The culmination is a reconstruction of the eventual showdown on Vinegar Hill, where the crown's forces under General Lake stormed the rebels' headquarters, defended by 20,000 pikemen. In the confusion the rebel army was able to slip away with barely 500 dead. The hill rises up on the far side of the Slaney River, while the town itself climbs up the western bank of the river; there is a more traditional museum in the Norman Castle close to the pedestrian-only middle of town.

GLENDALOUGH

See pages 94–95.

HOOK HEAD PENINSULA

352 F8 • Hook Head, Fethard-on-Sea, Co. Wexford • Hook Lighthouse Centre, tel 051 397055 • Guided tours Mar–end Oct daily 9.30–5.30 • Visitor Centre free; lighthouse tour adult €4.75, child (5–16) €2.75, family €14
• Access to lighthouse is by tour only (30 min) • In former keepers' cottages
www.thehook-wexford.com

County Wexford points a finger into the crashing waters of the Atlantic Ocean at Hook Head. The lighthouse at the end of the peninsula is one of the oldest working lighthouses in the world. Records show its origins to be in the fifth century AD and its red sandstone base dates from 1172. There is a small cafe and Visitor Centre.

The Head is a strange place. A walk along the water's edge reveals blow holes–best seen on a blustery day as long as you exercise caution–and dangerous rocky ledges. It's no place for a swim: Even on calm days there can be freakishly large waves.

Two abbeys were founded at the base of the peninsula. Dunbrody, dating from 1182 (tel 051 388603, Jul, Aug 10–7; May, Jun, Sep daily 10–6), lies in open meadows by a tributary of the Barrow River and its Visitor Centre, in the courtyard of a ruined castle, doubles as a cookery school. Tintern (tel 051 562650, mid-Jun to late Sep daily 9.30–6.30), founded in 1200 by Cistercians from the abbey of the same name in south Wales, is more impressive. At the head of a tidal creek on Bannow Bay, it is reached down a gravel road and retains its nave, chancel chapel, cloister and tower.

A tour of Hook Head should also include Duncannon, a seaside resort with a huge sandy beach and an excellent star-shaped fort from the 16th century, and Slade, where the ruins of a 15th-century castle guard a tiny fishing harbour.
Don't miss In season there are guided tours round the Hook Head lighthouse, which was only fully automated in 1996.

IRISH NATIONAL HERITAGE PARK

353 G7 • Ferrycarrig, Wexford, Co. Wexford • 053 20733 • Daily 9.30–6.30 (to 9.30pm Oct) • Adult €7, child (4–12) €3.50, child (13–18) €4, family €17.50 • 10-min audio-visual presentation followed by 70- to 90-min tour • Wexford • Fulacht Fiadh Restaurant
www.inhp.com

On the edge of Wexford, just off the northern bypass, the Irish National Heritage Park is a good place to stop if you have just entered the country from the Rosslare ferry. In 14ha (35 acres) of reclaimed marsh and swamp, 9,000 years of Irish history have been re-created through a series of full-scale models. There's a mesolithic site with its dolmen and camp, a Bronze Age area, showing how a cist burial would have looked, and a ring fort, a common feature of the Irish landscape, complete with its wooden stockade. You can see how a monastic settlement would have looked, with its high cross, oratory and water mill, visit a *crannóg*, reconstructed on an island in the marsh, and appreciate the craft of the Viking shipbuilders who settled this area. Against the criticism that this is theme park Ireland (in summer there are actors in costume around the site), the reconstructions can prove invaluable when you are trying to interpret many of the sites you will see in the rest of the country, putting the early Christian era in perspective and helping you understand less obvious remains such as those at Tara or Kells.

JERPOINT ABBEY

352 F7 • Thomastown, Co. Kilkenny • 056 772 4623 • Jun–13 Sep daily 9.30–6; Mar–end May, 14 Sep–end Oct daily 10–5; Nov daily 10–4 • Adult €2.75, child (6–18) €1.25, family €7 • Bus Éireann service from Kilkenny to Thomastown • Thomastown • Tour available on request, 45 min

The highlights of this 12th-century Cistercian ruin in the

Stone tomb decoration at the 12th-century Jerpoint Abbey

Old-fashioned mangles are among the exhibits at Johnstown

St. Columba's ancient stonerooted oratory tucked away in Kells

Nore Valley are the Romanesque carved figures to be found in the chapels of the north and south transepts. Their surprisingly cartoon-like qualities give a warm, human feel to what would otherwise be another set of cold monastic remains. There are smiling and weeping bishops, monks and knights, and a distinctive woman in a long pleated skirt. The Gothic tower, cloister and roofless nave date from the 14th and 15th centuries. A little Visitor Centre explains the significance of the carvings and traces the history of high crosses in the area.

JOHNSTOWN CASTLE

353 G7 • Johnstown Castle Estate, 6.4km (4 miles) from Wexford, Co. Wexford 053 42888 Gardens: 9–5.30 (may alter in winter). Museum: Jun–end Aug Mon–Fri 9–5, Sat, Sun and public holidays 11–5; Apr, May, Sep–early Nov Mon–Fri 9–12.30, 1.30–5, Sat, Sun and public holidays 2–5 Gardens: May–end Sep, car €5, pedestrian/bicyclist €2, Oct–end Apr free. Museum: adult €5, child (5–16) €3, family €15. Note: May–end Sep museum visitors must also pay garden fee In July and August By museum

Close to the route from the Rosslare ferry port, Johnstown Castle is well signposted off the N25, just south of the Duncannon intersection. The site is a little confusing, being also the home of an agricultural college and an array of government departments relating to countryside matters, but at its heart lies the fabulously Gothicized castle, and the agricultural and famine museums, established in the castle's stable block. The foyer, where there is a display, is as close inside the castle as visitors can get, but you can wander in its 20ha (50 acres) of gardens, see the peacocks, walled garden and ornamental lakes. The agricultural museum re-creates country trades and scenes from the last 200 years. Displays explain transport and farming and show a large collection of furniture and implements. The famine exhibition, within the museum, attempts to put this national tragedy of the 1840s in perspective, explaining the role of the potato and the changes that followed in the wake of the disastrous blight.

Don't miss A fascinating series of farmhouse kitchens in the agricultural museum compares the domestic lifestyles of 1800, 1900 and 1950.

KELLS

349 F4 Kells Heritage Centre, The Courthouse, Headfort Place, Kells, Co. Meath, tel 046 924 7840; May–end Sep Mon–Sat 10–5.30, Sun and public holidays 2–6; Oct–end Apr Tue–Sat 10–5; adult €4, child (4–16) €3, family €12 Bus Éireann from Dublin www.meathtourism.ie

Straddling the lumbering traffic queues of the N3, Kells (Ceanannas Mor) wouldn't get much attention were it not for its connections with the famous book, now in Trinity College, Dublin. St. Columcille (also known as St. Columba) established a monastic settlement here in AD550. Of this settlement only a well-preserved oratory building (St. Columcille's House) remains. It's tucked away beyond the church near a handball club and you'll need to get the keys, as a sign instructs, before you can visit. The churchyard also contains some good high crosses and an impressive round tower, but the best high cross, the Market Cross, with its graphic depictions of biblical stories, stands under a shelter outside the Old Courthouse. It has moved around a little since its origins in the 10th century: Cromwell's troops used it as a gallows and in the 1990s it was knocked over by a car.

In its present site, the Market Cross draws you into the Heritage Centre, which occupies the delightful Georgian Old Courthouse. Here a 17-minute audio-visual explains how the famous book came to Kells. In AD807 Viking raiders forced the monks on Iona, Scotland (▷ 84) to flee. They came to this older Columban site and brought their beautiful manuscript with them to complete. It is thought that it was stolen for its gold case 200 years later, then buried in a bog before being rediscovered and making its way to Dublin. Touch screen computers allow you to view pages of a virtual Book of Kells and there are replicas of other valuables to be found in the National Museum. A scale model shows how the monastic town would have looked in its heyday, but it isn't easy to relate this to the trundling lines of cars and trucks you see today. In the nearby village of Crossnakeel is a memorial to Jim Connell, the union organizer who wrote the socialist anthem *The Red Flag.*

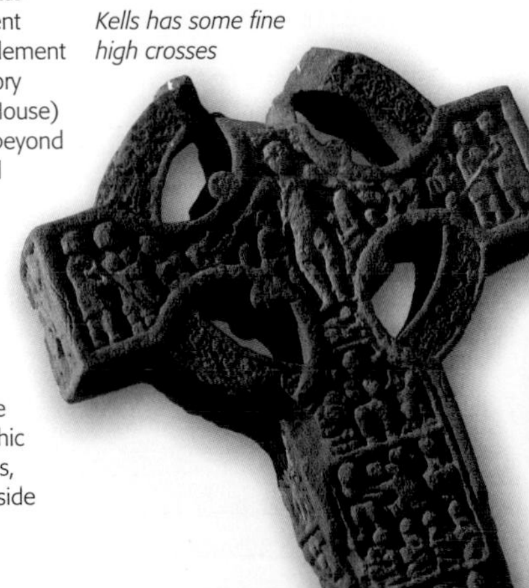
Kells has some fine high crosses

Kildare

Synonymous with horse racing—a particular passion in Ireland—Kildare not only has the foremost racetrack in the country (The Curragh), it's also the location of the National Stud, home to some of the world's most valuable bloodstock.

A stone carving of men on horseback in the Stud museum

SEEING KILDARE

The low-lying county of Kildare is barely half an hour's drive from Dublin on the M7. This is racing territory: More than 140 registered stud farms breed world-class flat-racing horses and in Punchestown and The Curragh County Kildare has two of the country's leading racecourses. For this reason, Kildare town's principal attractions are related to the National Stud, a state-owned venture breeding some of the most famous horses in the world. Next to the Stud a pair of renowned gardens have been planted. The Japanese Garden reflects the passion of the Edwardian era for Eastern religious design. The more recent St. Fiachra's Garden follows modern concepts, allowing a habitat to develop without heavy-handed interference.

RATINGS	
Cultural interest	●●●
Photo stops	●●●
Walkability	●●●

BASICS

352 F5

Kildare Tourist Information Office, Market House, Kildare, Co. Kildare, tel 045 521240; May–end Sep Mon–Sat 9.30–1, 2–5; Oct–end Apr Mon–Fri 10–1, 2–5

Bus Éireann service from Dublin

Kildare

www.kildare.ie/tourism
Comprehensive county guide, few pictures but good links.

TIP

- Visit the National Stud between February and June to see the foals in the paddocks off Tully Walk.

HIGHLIGHTS

THE NATIONAL STUD

Irish National Stud, Tully, Kildare, Co. Kildare 045 521617 Mid-Feb to mid-Nov daily 9.30–6 Both gardens and Irish National Stud: adult €8.50, child (under 12) €4.50, family €18 Tours of National Stud every hour, allow an hour Wavertree Restaurant In foyer
www.irish-national-stud.ie

The National Stud was founded at Tully on the edge of Kildare town by Colonel William Hall-Walker in 1900. This was once the site of the 12th-century Black Abbey and its scant remains can still be seen. Hall-Walker was the heir to a Scottish brewing family and had theories about the astrological influences on stock breeding. The stable buildings have lantern roofs designed to ensure the correct parts of the night sky would illuminate the stallions. He gave the whole complex to the British government and was rewarded with a title, Lord Wavertree. In the 1940s it was transferred to the Irish state. Today there are up to seven stallions at work per season, with each one able to service over 100 mares at around €85,000 each. The best time to visit is between February and June when there may be as many as 300 foals in the stables and paddocks. As well as guided tours of the paddocks and stable blocks, you can visit the Horse Museum, which contains racing memorabilia and the skeleton of Arkle, one of the stud's most famous racehorses.

THE JAPANESE GARDENS

Colonel Hall-Walker established the Japanese Gardens on reclaimed bogland between 1906 and 1910. They were designed by Tassa Eida, a renowned Japanese gardener, and his son Minoru. Their significance is not purely horticultural, they also portray the journey of a man through life, from his birth to the afterlife. The set pieces have names such as the Hill of Ambition, the Marriage Bridge, the Hill of Learning, the Island of Joy and Wonder, and the Tunnel of Ignorance. As you might expect, there are pagodas and little red bridges alongside some important specimen trees and bushes.

ST. FIACHRA'S GARDEN

St. Fiachra's Garden was constructed to commemorate the millennium—the sixth-century Irish cleric St. Fiachra is the patron saint of gardeners. Designed by Martin Hallinan, it uses limestone and water to create an island hermitage. Its woodland, wetland and rock gives it a much more natural feel than the otherworldly atmosphere of the Japanese Gardens. An inner subterranean garden is decorated with Waterford crystal, lighting the darkness of the hermit's cave. A statue of St. Fiachra himself, holding a symbolic seed of creation, sits on a rock that juts out into the lake.

A statue of St. Fiachra (top) in his naturally evolving garden. Little red bridges lead the way in the Japanese Gardens (above)

BACKGROUND

Kildare's central square is pleasantly quiet, with a heritage and information centre in the old Market House. Here you can watch a 12-minute video explaining the area's history and read about the significance of the Curragh for horse racing and the military. In the early Christian period there was a monastic settlement in Kildare, dedicated to St. Brigid. It was badly damaged in a Viking raid in AD835, but its surviving round tower, on the far side of the cathedral, is the second tallest in Ireland. The cathedral itself has had a chequered past. Its Gothic predecessor was destroyed by Cromwell's troops in 1641 and it wasn't until 1896 that its restoration was completed. You can see the last vestiges of Kildare Castle behind the Silken Thomas restaurant.

For centuries this was a frontier town on the edge of the English Pale. At times its position was so precarious that it almost vanished completely as a settlement. However with the development of The Curragh, and the construction of the turnpike road from Dublin to southwest Ireland in the middle of the 17th century, the town's fortunes revived.

Although a motorway cuts across its heart, the area known as The Curragh, which begins on the eastern edge of town, is still the largest tract of semi-natural grassland in Europe. The space and grass attracted the attentions of horse breeders in the 13th century and racing enthusiasts from the 18th century. The racecourse is now the headquarters of flat racing in Ireland and stages up to 20 meetings a year. The wide open space of The Curragh has also always appealed to soldiers. The British established military bases here, which are still in use by the modern Irish army; Kildare town's artillery barracks were only recently vacated. The main hub of military life is now at the Curragh Camp 8km (5 miles) or so to the east.

There are wonderful views from St. Brigid's cathedral round tower (above). Exercising on The Curragh, the venue for many classic races (below)

Kilkenny

Ireland's biggest and most attractive inland city, Kilkenny has an historic castle, a fine cathedral and some ancient buildings. The compact medieval core means everything is within walking distance.

The library of Kilkenny Castle, which dates back to 1172

RATINGS

Historic interest	●●●●
Specialist shopping	●●●●
Walkability	●●●

BASICS

352 F7

Tourist Information Office, Shee Alms House, Rose Inn Street, Kilkenny, Co. Kilkenny, tel 056 77 51500

Bus Éireann services from Dublin

Kilkenny

www.southeastireland.com
Good portal to the whole region.

TIPS

- If you don't have time for the castle tour, you can enjoy the gardens for free and also see the servants' areas and kitchens by visiting the bookshop and art gallery.
- If the round tower at the cathedral is closed, you can still get a reasonably elevated view of the town from the top deck of the Market Cross Shopping Centre parking.

SEEING KILKENNY

Kilkenny rose to prominence in the 13th century with the powerful Anglo-Norman Butler family, the Earls of Ormond. Their castle rises above a bend in the River Nore, looking out over a modern urban core with plenty of historic nooks. The local limestone produces a black stone known as Kilkenny marble, and you can see it deployed to good effect on many of the city's public buildings.

HIGHLIGHTS

KILKENNY CASTLE

Kilkenny Castle, The Parade, Kilkenny 056 77 21450 Jun–end Aug daily 9.30–7; Apr, May daily 10.30–5; Sep daily 10–6.30; Oct–end Mar daily 10.30–12.45, 2–5 Adult €5, child €2, family €11 Guided tour only, a 15-min audio-visual presentation followed by 45-min tour

The Anglo-Norman Strongbow (▷ 28) first built a wooden castle on the rocky bend above the river in 1172. His son-in-law William Marshall, Earl of Pembroke, strengthened it with local stone and created the medieval stronghold that remains today. James Butler, Third Earl of Ormond, bought the castle in 1391, and his family stayed until 1935, when the castle was acquired by the Irish state. In the late 17th and early 18th century, the Butler family's wealth grew and they improved their castle by adding a classical gateway and removing the war-damaged east wall. In the late 18th century came the gardens and stables (now the National Design Centre and National Craft Gallery). The 19th century saw the creation of the Long Gallery to house the family's considerable art collection, and the addition of the south curtain wall created extra bedrooms.

The castle visitors now see displays this Victorian elegance. As well as the impressive Long Gallery, with its portraits and hammer-beam roof, you see the Chinese bedroom, reflecting the Victorian's Oriental obsession, the Drawing Room, Library and Ante Room, all exquisitely furnished. The parkland extends to 20ha (50 acres) and includes a formal rose garden as well as mature woodland and a children's playground. Off the servants' corridor, by the old kitchen (now a bookshop), is the Butler Gallery of Contemporary Art (free) housing exhibitions by international artists and sculptors.

ST. CANICE'S CATHEDRAL

Irishtown, Kilkenny 056 776 4971 Mar–end May Mon–Sat 9–1, 2–6, Sun 2–6; Jun–end Sep Mon–Sat 9–6, Sun 2–6; Oct–end Feb Mon–Sat 10–4 Adult €3, child (under 12) €1.50. Round tower: adult €2, child €1; restricted opening in winter

The present cathedral was built in the 13th century in the early English Gothic style, but suffered in 1332 when its tower collapsed under the weight of lead on its roof. This over-zealous application was a penance imposed on William Outlaw, for consorting with Dame Alice Kyteler, who had been accused of witchcraft. The Kyteler family slab is the oldest memorial in the cathedral. The round tower, to the east of the building, has lost its cone, but still commands impressive views of the town and countryside. It is 30m (100ft) high and dates from AD849, when the cathedral was at the core of a monastic settlement. You can see traces of this Romanesque structure in the arches of the choir's north wall and in the north transept door. Cromwell's troops stabled their horses inside, smashed all the windows and threw out the monuments. When they were put back no one could remember their original places, so they now stand in orderly lines.

KILKENNY CITY

A walk around Kilkenny reveals some interesting buildings. The Tourist Information Office is in the Tudor Shee Alms Houses. On Parliament Street, the Courthouse has a 19th-century classical frontage on a fortified medieval house, which once served as a prison. Across the road, Rothe House was built in 1594 around a cobbled courtyard and is now home to a small museum (tel 056 77 22893, Jul, Aug Mon–Sat 10–6, Sun 3–5; Apr–end Jun, Sep–Oct Mon–Sat 10–5, Sun 3–5; Nov–end Mar Mon–Sat 1–5).

BACKGROUND

St. Canice founded the monastic settlement here in the sixth century and by the 13th century the adjacent town had become an important base for Norman rule in Leinster. Parliaments were held here from the 13th to the 15th centuries. In 1366, the notorious Statute of Kilkenny was passed, forbidding English settlers from speaking Irish, wearing Irish clothes or marrying Irish women. The natives were excluded from the city and to this day the area around St. Canice's, which lay beyond the city wall, is known as Irishtown. By the 17th century, however, the city had become a focal point of Catholic resistance. A confederate parliament was established in 1642, with money and arms from the Vatican. It dissolved acrimoniously in 1648, and by 1650 Cromwell arrived at the city gates with a considerable army. The siege lasted five days, but was ended without the bloodletting that characterized his occupation of Wexford or Drogheda. Today the city is best known for its beer—Smithwick's brewery occupies the site of the old Franciscan friary.

One of the highly decorated ceilings in elegant Kilkenny Castle (above main).
The castle's Long Gallery (above top), which boasts portraits by Van Dyck and Lely.
The remodelled castle (above middle) overlooking the Nore.
Kilkenny is well stocked with good shops and pubs (above)

Entrance to one of the burial chambers at Loughcrew Cairns

The art of lace-making is still practised in County Monaghan

Impressive carved high cross and round tower at Monasterboice

LOUGHCREW CAIRNS

348 F4 • Loughcrew Hills, Oldcastle, Co. Meath 049 854 2009
Daily all year, daylight hours
Free (deposit for keys to Cairn T)
Bus Éireann service to Oldcastle
At Loughcrew Historic Gardens
On ridge between Cairnbawn East and Cairnbawn West
www.meathtourism.ie

In west County Meath, far from the bustle of Brú na Bóinne, the Loughcrew Hills hold a remarkable series of 5,000-year-old passage graves. On these grassy hilltops, there are no interpretative displays or audio-visual tour. You may even have them to yourself. It's 400m (quarter of a mile) or so from the road up to the eastern summit where Cairn T is the most dramatic feature, 35m (115ft) across, with 37 edging stones. Inside, a cross chamber is lined with inscribed stones. The western summit is about twice as far from the road and has more impressive cairns. The Patrickstown cairns are the most easterly group. Sadly they were virtually destroyed by 19th-century enthusiasts, but were found to contain important neolithic artwork. You can get a key to Cairn T from Loughcrew Historic Gardens about 3km (2 miles) away. It is also worth visiting, to see how generations of the Naper family have fashioned a landscape blending nature and fantasy (tel 049 854 1356, summer: daily 12.30–4; winter: Sun, public holidays 1–3).

MELLIFONT ABBEY

349 G4 • Tullyallen, Drogheda, Co. Louth 041 982 6459 (1 Nov–30 Apr 041 988 0300) May–end Sep daily 10–6 Adult €2, child (6–18) €1, family €5.5 Bus Éireann service from Drogheda to Tullyallen Cross (5km/3 miles) Drogheda (8km/5 miles) 40-min tour on request

Sadly, only a gatehouse and an octagonal lavabo (washhouse) remain above head height at this important medieval abbey in a quiet valley on the banks of the Mattock River. The motherhouse of all Cistercian establishments in Ireland, it was founded in 1142 by monks from Clairvaux, France. Over 150 monks fled from here at the time of its suppression in 1536. In the 17th century the abbey became the country mansion of Edward Moore, saw the surrender of Hugh O'Neil in 1607, suffered a Cromwellian siege, and became headquarters for William of Orange during the Battle of the Boyne in 1689. By 1723, however, it was abandoned, and by the middle of the 19th century its ornate ruins were doubling as a pigsty. Four sides of the Romanesque lavabo remain from 1200 and the 14th-century chapterhouse has been re-roofed and contains a collection of glazed tiles. On a bank above the Visitor Centre stands the roofless shell of a Protestant church dating from 1542.

MONAGHAN

348 F3 Tourist Information Office, Dublin Road, Monaghan, Co. Monaghan, tel 047 81122; Apr–end Oct Mon–Fri 9–1, 2–5. Closed Nov–end Mar Bus Éireann service from Dublin
www.irelandnorthwest.ie

One of the three Ulster counties that became part of the Republic after 1922, Monaghan has a landscape of glacial drumlins, the low 'basket of eggs' topography caused by the passage of great ice sheets. Amid these countless ridges of boulder clay lie dozens of lakes, making this a popular county with anglers, though few other visitors linger. The small county town has a neat shopping street and a good local museum in a Victorian town house. The nearby Market House is a surprisingly elegant Georgian affair from 1792. Grander in scale is the enormous Gothic Revival Roman Catholic Cathedral of St. Macartan, standing high on the east side of town. Elsewhere, the towns and villages of County Monaghan are largely the creation of 17th-century plantations (▷ 30), with perhaps Clones being the most appealing.

MONASTERBOICE

349 G4 • Monasterboice, Drogheda, Co. Louth Daylight hours Bus Éireann service from Drogheda to Monasterboice Inn

This much pictured monastic site is probably a little smaller than you might imagine from the coverage it receives. What you'll find, 1.6km (1 mile) from the intersection with the new M1, is a neat, working cemetery, a splendid 34m (110ft) round tower, without its cone, and a set of truly magnificent high crosses. Little remains of the rest of the monastic settlement first established by St. Buithe in the fifth century. There are some extant walls from a large church building, probably originating in the eighth or ninth century. Also visible, but not very exciting, are the remains of a smaller 13th-century church. It is the crosses that draw people, and these are among the best in Ireland. The Cross of Muiredach is a ridiculously elaborate wheel head cross from the 10th century. On its base the inscription translates as 'A prayer for Muiredach by whom was made this cross'. Standing 5m (16ft) tall, its panels are carved with almost cartoonish detail: The miserable damned are dispatched to hell by a swift kick from Satan, the joyous saved ascend with Jesus, who stands judgmentally over the east face. His Crucifixion is portrayed on the head of the cross.

Relive the harsh voyages to the New World on the Dunbrody

Autumn leaves on the waterfall in the gardens at Mount Usher

The remains of Slane's friary church have wonderful views

MOUNT USHER GARDENS

353 G6 • Ashford, Co. Wicklow 0404 40116 Mar–end Oct daily 10.30–6 Adult €6 Bus Éireann service from Dublin Wicklow Station 8km (5 miles) In courtyard
www.mount-usher-gardens.com

There is a deliberately natural style to these gardens, which line the banks of the Vartry River on the southern edge of Ashford. They were begun in 1868 by Edward Walpole, a Dublin businessman, who used Mount Usher as a base for walking in the Wicklow Mountains. There are over 5,000 specimens across the estate's 8ha (19 acres), including azaleas, Chinese conifers, bamboos, Mexican pines and pampas grasses. The maples are particularly fine in autumn and the river acts as a unifying feature.

NEW ROSS

352 F7 Dunbrody Visitor Centre, The Quay, New Ross, Co. Wexford, tel 051 421857; May–end Aug daily 9–6; Apr, Sep daily 10–6.30; Oct–end Mar daily 10–5 Bus Éireann service from Dublin At Dunbrody Visitor Centre
www.dunbrody.com

This old inland port on the Barrow River has started to feel the wealth of the euro boom, and its wharfside warehouses are being redeveloped. The narrow streets wind up the steep riverbank to the Three Bullet Gate, a remnant of a once extensive town wall. Cromwellian destruction might have seen the end of the town were it not for the proximity of the Kennedys' ancestral home. Since the 1960s, this has ensured a steady stream of visitors. The John F. Kennedy Memorial Park, opened in 1968, 12km (7.5 miles) south of town, is a 252ha (622-acre) arboretum that's best in spring and autumn (tel 051 388 171, May–end Aug daily 10–8; Apr, Sep daily 10–6.30; Oct–Mar daily 10–5). The impressive *Dunbrody Heritage Ship*, a full scale reproduction of a New Ross emigrant vessel of the 19th century, has guides in period costume explaining the harsh conditions experienced by the passengers. There's a full database of those who made the journey to the USA between 1820 and 1920. The 40-minute tour is preceded by a video about its construction.

A costumed guide on the Dunbrody *(above)*

POWERSCOURT

See pages 104–105.

SLANE

349 G4 Tourist Information Office, Janesville Cottages, Slane, Co. Meath, tel 041 988 4055 Bus Éireann service from Dublin
www.meathtourism.ie

Perhaps better known these days for the huge rock concerts that take place in front of the castle, Slane is a tidy estate village, marred by the major road intersection at its heart. Through the traffic you may discern the four identical Georgian houses that face each other over the crossroads, but it's satisfying to take the winding lane off the N2 in the north of the town, up to the Hill of Slane. From here St. Patrick is said to have lit a Paschal (Easter) fire in AD433, in defiance of the pagan King of Tara, announcing the arrival of Christianity in Ireland. There's a fine view up here, and remains of a friary church and college established in 1512. The castle (tel 041 988 4400, mid-May to mid-Aug, end Aug–early Sep Mon–Thu 12–5), west of the village, is the ancestral home of the Conynghams, offering guided tours. U2 recorded their 1984 *Joshua Tree* album here.

TARA

349 G5 • Hill of Tara, near Navan, Co. Meath 046 902 5903 (Nov–Apr call 041 988 0300) Main site: open daylight hours. Visitor Centre in St. Patrick's Church: mid-May to mid-Sep daily 10–6 Main site: free. Visitor Centre: adult €2, child €1, family €5.50 35 min, available from Visitor Centre in summer South of Navan off N3
www.meathtourism.ie
www.heritageireland.ie

Tara has played a central role in early Irish history and has over 30 visible monuments, part of a ritual landscape with an unbroken history of 4,000 years up to the sixth century AD. Among the more impressive remains is the Mound of the Hostages, a passage grave which contained 40 Bronze Age cremations. Tours and an audio-visual display are available in summer from the Visitor Centre in St. Patrick's Church on the site. If it's closed, a little tea and gift shop sells books with explanations of the monuments, from the scientific to the silly. Names recall the site's former importance as home of the High Kings of Ireland—the Royal Enclosure, Rath of the Synods, Banquet Hall.

Don't miss In a ring feature known as Cormac's House, the Lia Fáil is the stone on which the High Kings were crowned.

Powerscourt

The magnificent series of gardens, both formal and semi-natural, of Powerscourt House have the shapely Great Sugar Loaf as a backdrop.

RATINGS	
Cultural interest	●●●●
Photo stops	●●●●
Specialist shopping	●●●

Statue of a gilded winged horse in the Italian garden (above)

Powerscourt gardens boast superb vistas across to the peak of the Great Sugar Loaf (top)

The most memorable feature of Powerscourt is the view from the terrace, over a broad sweep of wooded garden to the graceful peak of the Great Sugar Loaf on the horizon. This superb vista is the set piece of a house and garden originally designed by Richard Cassels for the First Viscount Powerscourt in 1731. Subsequent additions included the Italian garden, which drops away from the terrace on a grand staircase, lined by winged horses, leading to the circular Triton Lake and a 30m (100ft) fountain. Looking back from here, your eye is carried up to the grey stone Palladian façade with its twin copper domes. This exquisite scene took over 100 labourers 12 years to create in the middle of the 19th century. On the same level as the house, and dating back to the 1740s, lie the walled gardens. More formal than the rest of the estate but not as severe as some in the French style, they include vivid rose beds and fragrant borders. One entrance is through the Bamberg Gate, an intricate piece of wrought ironwork from Bavaria.

TIPS

- It's free to enter the estate. You only pay if you're visiting the house exhibition or the gardens.
- Christmas holidays are very hectic in the house, with Santa Claus and the usual shopping frenzy, but the gardens are much quieter, though, obviously, there is less to see than there is in spring or summer.

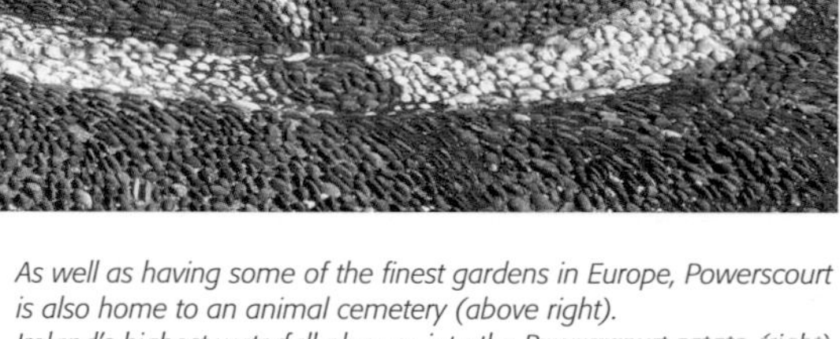

As well as having some of the finest gardens in Europe, Powerscourt is also home to an animal cemetery (above right). Ireland's highest waterfall plunges into the Powerscourt estate (right)

A leaflet guides you round a 40-minute or a one-hour tour of the estate and efforts have been made to allow for wheelchair access where possible.

POWERSCOURT HOUSE AND WATERFALL

The house itself was gutted by fire in 1974 and stood virtually derelict until 1996, when a clever regeneration was devised. The roof was restored, but most of the interior was left empty. An exhibition space was created and the ballroom restored, using traditional craft methods, to act as a function room. Today, a visit to the house exhibition is a peculiar mix of building history and stately home, but the house is greatly overshadowed by the gardens. Elsewhere the estate has turned its attentions to retail outlets, and these occupy the west wing along with a restaurant, cafés and gift shops. The estate glasshouses now house the Powerscourt Garden Centre, selling plants and gardening equipment, and much of the land to the north front of the house is given over to golf courses. Also part of the estate, but 5km (3 miles) away is the Powerscourt Waterfall, Ireland's highest at 121m (398ft). This is surrounded by specimen trees and is popular with wedding photographers (summer 9.30–dusk; winter 10.30–dusk).

BASICS

353 G5 • Powerscourt Estate, Enniskerry, Co. Wicklow

01 204 6000

Daily 9.30–5.30

Adult €6.50, child (5–16) €4.50

44 (from Dublin), 185 from Bray DART

DART Bray then bus

40 min or 1 hour

Restaurant and café in main house foyer

In main foyer

www.powerscourt.ie
Basic site for the estate with some nice pictures.

Trim's gaunt and dramatic 14th-century Yellow Steeple

The brightly painted town of Wexford is built on three levels

Granite moorland and peaks of the Wicklow Mountains

TRIM

349 F5 Trim Visitor Centre, Castle Street, Trim, Co. Meath, tel 046 94 37227; Apr–end Oct Mon–Sat 9.30–5.30, Sun 12–5.30; Nov–end Mar Mon–Wed, Fri–Sat 10–12.30, 1.30–5, Sun, public holidays 12–5.30 Visitor Centre: adult €3.20, child €1.90 Bus Éireann from Dublin **www**.meathtourism.ie

This small town on the banks of the River Boyne is home to the largest Anglo-Norman castle in Ireland (tel 046 38619, Easter–end Oct daily 10–6; winter Sat, Sun 10–5. Access to the keep by guided tour only). Its curtain wall is over 400m (quarter of a mile) long and encloses a site of 1.2ha (3 acres). The central keep is 21m (70ft) high and the walls are 3.3m (11ft) thick. Together with the 10 D-shaped towers in the surrounding walls, it has barely been altered since the 13th century, though it does bear the scars one would expect from a fortification so close to the edge of the English Pale (▷ 31). Many of the castle scenes in *Braveheart* (1995) were filmed here. Across the river, the Sheep's Gate and the Yellow Steeple, the belfry tower of an Augustinian abbey, rise from a meadow, left undeveloped on their medieval sites when the town's focus shifted towards the opposite bank in the 18th century. Downstream of the castle, on the edge of new housing developments, the ruins of the 13th-century cathedral of SS. Peter and Paul is connected to the Hospital of St. John the Baptist by an ancient bridge, on the north side of which is one of Ireland's oldest pubs. You can get a feel for how these fine medieval remains are related to each other in the Visitor Centre near the castle where 'The Power and the Glory', a multimedia presentation, documents the impact of the arrival of the Normans.

WEXFORD

353 G7 Tourist Information Office, Crescent Quay, Wexford, Co. Wexford, tel 053 23111; Apr–end Oct Mon–Sat 9–6; Nov–end Mar Mon–Fri 9–5 (due to move during lifetime of this guide) Bus Éireann service from Dublin Wexford **www**.southeastireland.com

The Vikings established Wexford as a port and shipbuilding town in the eighth century. In the Middle Ages it was an important English garrison town, but when Cromwell arrived in 1649 the rebellious spirit of the townspeople cost them dearly and several hundred were executed on the Bullring. Rebelliousness continued, however, and in 1798 a republic was declared here. The long, narrow main street runs parallel with the quay, only lightly used today. Little obvious remains of the old town, the Westgate tower being the sole survivor of the 14th-century walls. Nearby are the ruins of Selskar Abbey, built by Henry II in penitence for the murder of Thomas à Becket. The opera festival every October (▷ 212), attracts performers and devotees from all over the world.

Don't miss A statue of a pikeman on the Bullring is a memorial to the town's role in the 1798 rebellion.

WEXFORD WILDFOWL RESERVE

353 G7 • North Slobs, Wexford, Co. Wexford 053 23129 Easter–end Sep daily 9–6; Oct–Easter daily 9–5. Closed occasionally: notice on gate Free 1 hour, available on request In Exhibition Centre Wexford

Behind the sea wall on the north side of Wexford Harbour lies the North Slobs, 3m (10ft) below high tide level. This wetland area was drained from marshland in the 19th century to form a farming landscape, but its meadows and drainage channels also provided an ideal habitat for birdlife. In winter you might see 29 different species of duck and 42 types of wader. The 10,000 Greenland white-fronted geese form as much as half of the world's total population and the pale-bellied Brents also arrive on a globally significant scale. The Reserve's 100ha (247 acres) include a series of accessible hides for visitors to observe the birds. One is next to the Victorian pumping station—its chimney is a landmark, though its steam pump has long since been replaced by an electric version putting 4 tons of water back into the sea every minute.

WICKLOW MOUNTAINS NATIONAL PARK

353 G6 • Information Point, Upper Lough, Glendalough, Co. Wicklow 0404 45425 May–end Sep daily 10–6; Nov–end Apr weekends only 10–dusk Glendaloughbus twice daily from Dublin and Bray At Upper Lough parking place

The Wicklow Mountains National Park rises from the suburbs of south Dublin and covers some 17,000ha (42,000 acres) of high granite moors, wooded valleys and lakes. The highest point is Lugnaquilla, at 925m (3,035ft), a rounded peak rising above Glenmalur. The mountains are traversed by the spectacular military road from Dublin to Laragh, and crossed by the high passes of the Wicklow Gap and the Sally Gap. In the western foothills, several valleys have been flooded to form the beautiful Blessington Lake, sometimes called Pollaphuca Reservoir. At the core of the park lies Glendalough (▷ 94–95) where, appropriately, the Visitor Centre for the monastic settlement doubles as a national park information office.

THE SOUTH

The dramatic coastline of the South, with its long, rocky peninsulas, often overshadows the delightful river valleys inland. Charming coastal villages and harbours contrast with three of Ireland's busiest cities: Cork, Limerick and Waterford. The Dingle Peninsula and the Ring of Kerry are rich in spectacular scenery, pleasant towns and ancient sites.

MAJOR SIGHTS

Adare Manor sits in lovely grounds bordering the River Maigue

ADARE

Unusual architecture and a massive ruined castle mark out this prosperous little town.

351 D7 Heritage Centre, Main Street, Adare, Co. Limerick, tel 061 396255; daily 9.30–5 (exhibition closed Jan, Feb) Adare

RATINGS	
Cultural interest	●●●
Historic interest	●●●●
Photo stops	●●●●

TIP

- **There is an extensive free car parking area signposted behind the Heritage Centre.**

Adare has a reputation for wealth and prettiness, displayed in its green park, brick houses and thatched cottages that have more the feel of a smart English commuter village than an Irish one. Much of the town's charm is the result of remodelling by the Earls of Dunraven at the end of the 19th century.

Adare's history goes much further back than that, however, and evidence of its status in medieval times can be seen in the several ruined abbeys within it. Holy Trinity Abbey was founded in 1230 for monks of the Trinitarian Order, which had been set up to rescue hostages seized during the Crusades. It was known as the White Abbey, for the colour of the monk's habits, and its low square tower, restored and battlemented in 1852, dominates the high street. Tucked behind is the circular dovecot, unusual in Ireland, which would have provided a useful additional food source for the monks.

The Augustinians built a friary on the riverbank opposite the castle around 1314, and the elegant church was restored and reopened as the parish church in 1937. The extensive ruins of a Franciscan friary, dating to 1464, lie in the parkland of Adare Manor, south of the river. This 19th-century mansion was the seat of the Earls of Dunraven and is now a hotel.

The massive remains of the castle lie on the north bank of the River Maigue, a short walk from the middle of the town, and are currently closed for structural work. Known as Desmond Castle, it dates back to 1326 and the Second Earl of Kildare, though there was an earlier O'Donovan structure on the same site. The castle withstood several sieges, but was finally demolished by Cromwell's men in 1657.

The Heritage Centre on Main Street describes the town's early history, in several languages, and a 20-minute film depicts the town today. You can also take a guided half-hour walk of the town's highlights from here (advance booking required, tel 061 396666).

Ahenny's crosses still celebrate the art of their ancient carvers

AHENNY HIGH CROSSES

352 F7 Heritage Centre, Main Street, Carrick-on-Suir, Co. Tipperaray, tel 051 640200; Mon–Fri 10–5, Sat 10–1 Donation box for upkeep of churchyard 8km (5 miles) north of Carrick-on-Suir

There is a remarkable dignity and remoteness about this pair of wheel crosses standing 2.5m (8ft) high in a graveyard on a green hillside. Perhaps it's the conical capstones which bring to mind the statues of Easter Island, or the dominance of the high central spoke. The resemblance ends there, however, for the pinkish sandstone of these monuments was carved by unknown hands in the eighth century AD. Moss and lichen mellow the effect of the intricate Celtic motifs, spirals and geometric designs carved onto every surface; human figures can be made out on the bases.

The crosses are signed off the R697 Kilmaganny road, north of Carrick-on-Suir. From any other direction, signposting is poor.

ARDFERT CATHEDRAL

350 B7 • Ardfert, Co. Kerry 066 713 4711 Visitor Centre: May–late Sep daily 9.30–6. Site: open access at other times Adult €2, child €1, family €5.50 Tralee, 10km (6 miles) www.heritageireland.ie

In the low-lying coastal landscape north of Tralee, locally born St. Brendan (AD484–577) founded a monastery in the sixth century. Nothing remains, but the importance of this ecclesiastical site can be gauged by the three medieval churches here, and the 13th-century friary to the east. The main structure, just north of Ardfert village, is the battlemented and roofless cathedral, which dates from the 13th to the 17th centuries. Note the fine lancet windows, Romanesque

The ancient walls of Ardfert Cathedral, with a Celtic cross

There are magnificent views from the Beacon at Baltimore

The Spinning Wheel pub at Castletownroche on the Beara

sawtooth carvings around the arched doorways, and the blind staircase that would have led to a gallery. There are remains of two other churches in the churchyard. Restoration continues to stabilize these structures, worn away by sandblast from the sea.

Don't miss In a small chapel at one end of the cathedral is the inscribed family tomb of Honora, Lady Dowager of Kerry (*d*1668).

ARDMORE

352 E8 Seafront car parking area, Ardmore, Co. Waterford, tel 024 94444; seasonal opening
www.waterfordtourism.org

Golden sands and a stone pencil-tower, 29m (95ft) tall, mark this coastal village at the western end of the scenic South Coast Drive, and the start of St. Declan's Way, stretching for 94km (59 miles) to Cashel on an old pilgrimage route. St. Declan, an early Christian bishop, chose Ardmore for a church in the fifth or sixth century, and is believed to have been buried in the small oratory in the churchyard. The round stone tower is a superb example of its kind, built as a retreat for the monks and their treasures in a time of Viking raids. The biggest remains are those of the 12th-century cathedral.

ATHASSEL PRIORY

352 E7 Town Hall, Main Street, Cashel, Co. Tipperary, tel 062 61333; May–end Sep
www.cashel-emly.ie

The broken remains of abbeys are scattered throughout this rich farmland, and Athassel is a stony ghost of one of the biggest and best. Driving south from Golden (6.4km/4 miles west of Cashel), you get a fabulous view over the riverside site, accessed over a stile. Founded in the late 12th century by William FitzAdelm de Burgo (*d*1205), this was one of the wealthiest monasteries in Ireland until its destruction in 1447. A town grew around it, but was burned down and vanished. The walls are remarkably high and ruins are not fenced; you go among them at your own risk.

Don't miss The primitive carvings of a man and woman in medieval dress are set in a wall.

BALTIMORE

350 C9 Tourist Information Office, Town Hall, Skibbereen, Co. Cork, tel 028 21766; Jul, Aug Mon–Sat 9–7, Sun 10–5; Jun, Sep Mon–Sat 9–6; Oct–end Mar Mon–Fri 9.15–1, 2–5.15; Apr, May Mon–Sat 9.15–1, 2–5.15

This once wealthy fishing village, sheltered from the Atlantic by a rocky headland, has had bad luck: In 1537 fishermen from rival Waterford burned it down after one of their boats was seized in the harbour, and in 1631 Algerian pirates pounced, killing dozens and kidnapping hundreds to sell as slaves in North Africa. After the second outrage many inhabitants moved upriver to the relative safety of Skibbereen, which suffered worse than most in the famines. Today, visitors come for the rocky bays and seabirds, for access to the islands of Roaringwater Bay (▷ 124) and to take the winding road up the headland for extensive views.

BANTRY HOUSE

See page 110.

BEARA PENINSULA

350 B8 St. Peter's Grounds, Castletown Bearhaven, Co. Cork, tel 027 70054; summer Mon–Fri 9–4
www.bearatourism.com

The rugged massif of the Caha Mountains forms the spine of this large peninsula, with Hungry Hill (685m/2247ft) its highest point. It is crossed by the scenic Healy Pass (330m/1082ft), a famine road completed by Bantry-born Timothy Healy and encircled by the Beara Ring Drive. You can walk the Beara Way (197km/123 miles) or follow a 171km (107-mile) bicycle route. Castletown Bearhaven is the main town, a fishing port on the south side sheltered by the hills of Bear Island. The Call of the Sea Visitor Centre, on the north edge of the town, is particularly good for children. Eyeries, on the northern shore, is the home of Milleen cheese. Allihies is known as an artists' town, and its beach of crushed quartz is the spoil from the old copper mines. Dursey Island, populated by choughs, gannets and skuas, lies just off the western tip, linked to the mainland by a cable car.

BLARNEY CASTLE

See page 111.

CAHER

352 E7 Castle Car Park, Caher, Co. Tipperary, tel 052 41453; Apr–Oct daily 10–5 Caher

This busy little 18th-century town has two main attractions. The first, Caher Castle, stands on a crag beside the River Suir (mid-Jun to mid-Sep daily 9–7.30; mid-Oct to mid-Jun daily 9.30–4.30 or 5.30). It is one of the best preserved Norman castles in Ireland, with keep, tower and outer wall largely intact.

The Swiss Cottage is a great contrast—a thatched rustic building with stickwork verandahs, set in parkland. It was built in 1810 to designs by John Nash, and reflects a vogue for the *cottage orné*. Admission is by guided tour (mid-Apr to mid-Oct daily 10–6; mid-Mar to mid-Apr Tue–Sun 10–1, 2–6; mid-Oct to mid-Nov Tue–Sun 10–1, 2–4.30).

BANTRY HOUSE

One of Ireland's best Georgian mansions, Bantry House is surrounded by 18ha (45 acres) of terraced gardens.

350 C8 • Bantry, Co. Cork 027 50047 Mid-Mar to end Oct daily 9–6 Adult €10, child (under 14) free Tea room Crafts shop Self-guided audio tour of Armada Exhibition available in six languages
www.bantryhouse.ie

RATINGS	
Good for kids	●●●
Historic interest	●●●●
Photo stops	●●●●●

On the southwestern edge of bustling Bantry town, just off the N71, this pink and white house makes the very best of its views over the wooded islands of Bantry Bay. The mansion dates from 1700, and is still owned by the White family, who acquired it in 1739. In 1945 it became the first great house in Ireland to open its door regularly to the public, who have flocked here ever since to admire the treasures amassed by the Earls of Bantry. Richard White, the second earl, was the chief collector, who brought back much of what is on show today from his wide travels in Europe. Look for the Aubusson tapestries in the Rose Drawing Room, reputedly made for French queen Marie Antoinette, and the portraits of George III and Queen Charlotte by Allan Ramsey in the Blue Dining Room.

The house stands on the third of seven terraces, a feature of the extensive formal gardens also created by the second earl. Highlights include the Italianate garden, and the glorious Wisteria Circle. Walk up the Stairway to the Sky, 100 restored stone steps, for the best views over the house to Bantry Bay.

In the courtyard of the house, the Armada Exhibition Centre tells of the attempted French invasion of December 1796, in support of the United Irishmen. The 48 ships made it from Brest, but were prevented from landing in the bay by stormy weather and forced back. It was Richard White (1765–1851) who raised the alarm, and was made an earl for his pains. Nationalist Wolfe Tone (1763–98) was one of those on board the failed fleet, and a statue of him stands in Bantry town's square, which is also named after him.

Cross-section of a Spanish vessel in the Armada Centre (right).
Bantry House has a superb setting on the bay (below)

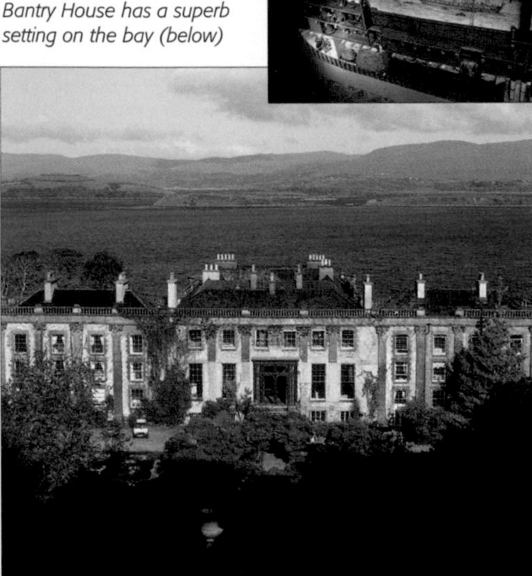

Clonakilty's main street is lined with brightly painted buildings

CLONAKILTY

351 C9 25 Ashe Street, Clonakilty, Co. Cork, tel 023 33226; Mon–Sat 9–6 30km (18 miles) west of Kinsale
www.corkkerry.ie

This lively little market town was once known for linen manufacture but is now best remembered for its associations with patriot Michael Collins (1890–1922), whose statue stands on Emmet Square. Collins was born 8km (5 miles) west at Sam's Cross, and you can learn more on the 1921 Trail at the Arigideen Valley Heritage Park, at Castleview (Jun–Sep daily, slide show and talk Thu 7.45pm). Just east of the town are the attractive Lisselan Estate Gardens (Jul, Aug daily 8–8; May, Jun, Sep 8–7; Apr, Oct 8–5; rest of year 8–4).

Don't miss There is a sandy beach at nearby Inchydoney Island.

CLONMEL

352 E7 Sarsfield Street, Clonmel, Co. Tipperaray, tel 052 22960; Mon–Fri 9.30–1, 2–5 Clonmel
www.visitclonmel.com

Clonmel dates back to the 12th century, and the best way to see its historic buildings is via the Heritage Trail (leaflet from the tourist office). Highlights include the arcaded Main Guard of 1684 and the blue-painted Town Hall on Parnell Street. Hearns Hotel is where Italian Charles Bianconi (1786–1875) established what would become the most famous bus company in Ireland in 1815. Around 20 gleaming antique cars are on display at the Museum of Transport on Emmet Street (tel 052 29727; Jun–end Aug Mon–Sat 10–6, Sun 2.30–6). A literary festival in September recalls a number of famous local authors.

COBH

See page 114.

Famous for the Blarney stone (above), the castle is a wonderful old ruin (right), set amid beautiful gardens (below right)

BLARNEY CASTLE

If you kiss the Blarney stone at Ireland's most famous castle, 8km (5 miles) northwest of Cork, it's said you'll pick up the 'gift of the gab'.

Blarney Castle is a romantic 15th-century ruin beside a pretty village, set in landscaped gardens with 18th-century grottoes. In high summer the parking area fills to bursting point, and tour parties from every nation thread their way around the tower and through the park. Out of season, or early in the morning, it has a magical peace about it.

A square stone tower, the castle is perched on a rocky hillock framed by trees, with broken battlements and two separate watchtowers. As you enter, above your head is the good-natured banter surrounding the ultimate Irish cliché, the kissing of the Blarney Stone.

Entry through the thick stone walls is via a double outer door, complete with murder hole and right-handed spiral staircase to confound attackers. Follow the red arrows and keep to the one-way system, vital when so many narrow winding stairs and awkward doorways are involved. You'll pass chambers described as the great hall, bedrooms, kitchen and so on. They are mostly damp-looking and crumbling, with little to distinguish one from another, but the countryside views from the windows as you climb higher somehow make it all worth while.

KISSING THE STONE

'Blarney' means eloquent nonsense, a term said to have been coined by Elizabeth I, who wearied of the successful stalling tactics of owner Cormac McCarthy when she tried to take over his castle. Kissing the stone—allegedly half of the Stone of Scone, presented to McCarthy by Robert the Bruce after his support at Bannockburn in 1314—involves lying down and leaning backwards over a parapet. A photo is taken, and you'll be given a ticket to collect your picture later (it costs €9; there are no previews and it's not a flattering pose).

In the 18th century the castle came into the hands of the Jeffereys, who made the gardens. Follow the path south from the tower, passing through a narrow stone tunnel, to explore the gardens. A network of paths leads through carefully crafted woodland ornamented with lumps of naturally sculpted limestone. A grotto, artfully constructed beneath a giant yew, is named the Witches' Kitchen. Nearby the Wishing Steps lead down to a murky pool (another 'tradition': Walk down and up backwards and your wish will come true). Rock outcrops have such fanciful names as Druids' Circle and Sacrificial Altar.

RATINGS	
Good for kids	●●●●
Historic interest	●●●
Photo stops	●●●●●

BASICS

351 D8 • Blarney, Co. Cork

021 438 5252

Jun–end Aug Mon–Sat 9–7, Sun 9.30–5.30; May, Sep Mon–Sat 9–6.30, Sun 9.30–5.30; Oct–end Apr Mon–Sat 9–sundown, Sun 9.30–sundown

Adult €7, child (8–14) €2.50, family €16

Guide book, in English, French and German, €5

Gift shop and bureau de change

By gate and by castle

www.blarneycastle.ie
Easy to use site with photos and good practical and historical information.

Cork

The second city of the Republic, and a European Capital of Culture in 2005, Cork is a community with top-class shopping and a buzzing cultural life.

Footbridge over the River Lee

RATINGS	
Chain store shopping	●●●●●
Cultural interest	●●●●
Good for food	●●●●
Specialist shopping	●●●●●

Cork has a good blend of big stores, individual shops and market traders

SEEING CORK

Cork is a vibrant, modern industrial and university city. Its status as a European Capital of Culture for 2005 has resulted in major refurbishment, visible in the improvements along Patrick Street (a main artery of the shopping district) and increased pedestrianization. The level heart of the city lies between the North and South Channels of the River Lee, and waterways and bridges have given it the soubriquet of Ireland's Venice. Three-spired St. Fin Barre's Cathedral (1870) lies to the south.

HIGHLIGHTS

PATRICK STREET

Cork is second only to Dublin for the quality and variety of its shopping, and exploring is easy in such a compact district. Patrick Street is the hub, curving south from the North Channel, and you'll find all the big name shops and department stores here including Roches (which started out in Cork), Dunnes, Penneys and Brown Thomas, and all the chain stores. Step off the main drag and pedestrianized lanes branching north to Paul Street and south to Oliver Plunkett Street (named after a 17th-century martyr) are lined with classy independent retailers and appealing eateries.

ENGLISH MARKET

For the very essence of the city, visit this covered food emporium, in a building designed by Sir John Benson in 1881, and restored after a fire in 1980 (access is from Grand Parade, St. Patrick's Street, Princes Street and Oliver Plunkett Street; Mon–Sat 8–6). In the early morning you'll see top local restaurateurs in here, picking out the best of the meat, vegetables and fabulous fresh fish: flatfish, langoustines and conger eels, as well as salt cod, mackerel and smoked salmon.

Buy your black or white puddings from the array of butchers' stalls, or be brave and go for the traditional Cork dish of tripe and drisheen (cow's stomach lining). Iago sells the best Irish cheeses, including delicately smoked Gubbeen (West Cork), Benoskee (Dingle), Cashel Blue and Brie-like Maighen (both from Tipperary)—taste before you buy. Odd corners hold unexpected delights, such as the tiny Good Yarns bookshop, packed from floor to ceiling; and the barber shop (hot towel, shave and massage €19). Sit in the upstairs café and watch Cork life passing below.

TIP

• The Visitor Centre is at the eastern end of Grand Parade beside the Grafton multi-level parking; you can buy disks for on-street parking here, and also get tickets for the open-top bus tours which take around 1 hour.

CRAWFORD ART GALLERY

✉ Emmet Place ☎ 021 427 3377 🕑 Mon–Sat 10–5

This outstanding municipal collection is housed in a redbrick building, erected in 1724 as the custom house, when Emmet Street was the King's Dock. As well as rotating exhibitions from the permanent collection of paintings, and the Sculpture Room, there is a modern space for temporary shows which may include video and photography. Up the big staircase (with brilliant stained glass by James Scanlon, 1993) the displays on the upper floor include

depictions of Aran islanders by Charles Lamb RHA (1893–1964), and a portrait of actress Fiona Shaw by Victoria Russell (1964–). There's a historical image of the local sport of road bowls by Daniel MacDonald (1821–53), and James Humbert Craig's Lowryesque figures huddled against the rain in *Going to Mass* (c1935). Séan Keating's icon of Irish nationalism, *Men of the South* (1921) is here, as are impressionistic landscapes by Jack B. Yeats (1871–1957).

Well-worn stone of Parliament Bridge, over the Lee (above). A tribute to rock legend Rory Gallagher, on Rory Gallagher Square (right)

CORK CITY GAOL HERITAGE CENTRE

✉ Sunday's Well ☎ 021 430 5022 ⓘ Mar–end Oct daily 9.30–5, Nov–end Feb daily 10–4; www.corkcitygaol.com

Whatever time of year you visit, it's always bone-cold inside the walls of this grim, castle-like structure on a steep hillside to the northwest of the city. Inside, the cells and corridors resonate with the unhappiness of the men and women incarcerated here between 1824 and 1928. Cells are furnished in 19th- to early 20th-century style, and the audio tour and audio-visual presentation bring it all to life with the stories of individual prisoners. In the early days felons were isolated in single cells to avoid further corruption, and left in silence (even the warders' boots were muffled) to contemplate their crimes. In reality, such treatment often led to madness. Dusty dummies give an accurate sense of waste and decay, and picnic tables seem incongruous beside the entrance arch where prisoners were hanged.

In the 1950s the empty buildings became the unlikely headquarters of the budding Radio Éireann, which could get a good signal this high above the city. A separate radio museum is housed upstairs.

BACKGROUND

Cork's history dates back to the founding of a monastery on marshland here by St. Finbarr in the mid-seventh century. The Vikings built a town, and walls were constructed around the core; these were demolished in the 17th century, after a siege by William of Orange's men. Cork's 19th-century prosperity was founded on sea trade, notably shipping butter to Australia and South America. Part of the city was burned in 1921 by the English during the nationalist uprisings. You can learn more at the Cork Vision Centre on North Main Street (Tue–Sat 10–5) and the Public Museum in Fitzgerald Park (Mon–Fri 11–1, 2.15–5, Sun 3–5).

BASICS

351 D8

Áras Fáilte, Grand Parade, Cork, Co. Cork, tel 021 4255100; Jul, Aug Mon–Fri 9–6, Sat, Sun 9.30–4.30; Sep–end Jun Mon–Fri 9–5, Sat 9.30–4.30

Cork

Ferries from Roscoff and Swansea; ferry port at Ringaskiddy, tel 021 455 1119, 16km (10 miles) southeast

www.cork-guide.ie

www.corkkerry.ie

Useful site covering the whole Cork region, with listings of accommodation, nightclubs, attractions and more.

A historically important harbour is overlooked by the cathedral

COBH

An attractive Georgian harbour town, Cobh was the last port of call in 1912 for the *Titanic*.

RATINGS

Cultural interest	●●●●
Good for kids	●●●
Historic interest	●●●●●

BASICS

351 D8

Old Yacht Club, Westbourne Place, Cobh, Co. Cork, tel 021 481 3301; Mon–Fri 9.30–5.30, Sat, Sun 1.30–5

Cobh, from Cork

Vehicle ferry from Glenbrook, Co. Cork, 5-minute crossing, daily 7am–12.15am, tel 021 481 1223

TIP

- **Approaching Cobh by road, turn left at ruined Bellvelly Tower and take the shorter route through rolling farmland and over the crest of the ridge to emerge directly behind St. Colman's Cathedral.**

The Navigator, *by M Gregory, on the Promenade*

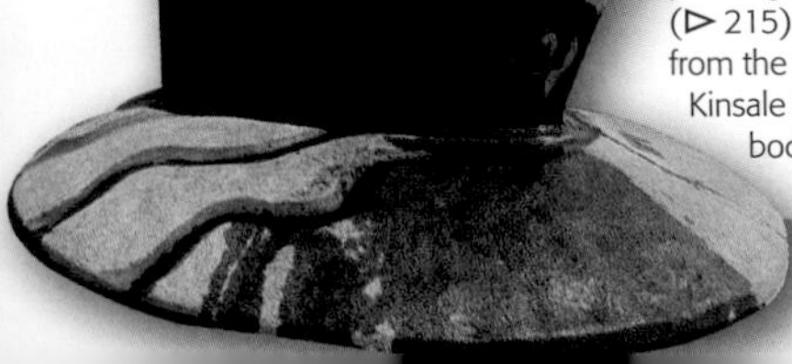

The town of Cobh (pronounced Cove), on the south side of Great Island east of Cork city, is a naturally sheltered harbour, which made it a significant embarkation point for naval fleets during the Napoleonic Wars of the 18th century, for emigration and prison ships in the 19th, and for the glamorous trans-Atlantic liners of the 20th. Today it is a seaside resort, with brightly painted Regency frontages above little shops and restaurants. Popular with sailors, Cobh is also Ireland's leading venue for windsurfing, with races every Sunday, and also on Tuesdays in summer (tel 021 481 1237 for information).

St. Colman's Cathedral, by architects Pugin, Ashlin and Coleman, was completed in 1915 and stands high above the town. The graceful spire, 91.5m (300ft) tall, conceals a carillon of 51 bells, which ring out tunes on summer Sunday afternoons. Inside, note the rose window framed by dummy organ pipes, and the mosaic floors. (Mass: Mon–Fri 8 and 10am; Sat 6pm Sun 8, 10, 12, 7pm.)

ARRIVALS AND DEPARTURES

Between 1791 and 1853 almost 40,000 convicts passed through Cobh on their way to Australia and other distant penal colonies, banished for crimes that ranged from petty theft to murder. And in the 1820s prison hulks were moored here, dealing with overspill from the crowded land jails. Between 1815 and 1970 more than 3 million people took their last view of Ireland here, as they emigrated to the US, Canada and other places. These stories are well told at the Queenstown Story Heritage Centre at the western end of the seafront (May–end Oct Mon–Sat 10–6; 10–5 rest of year). The town was renamed 'Queenstown' in honour of Queen Victoria who visited in 1849, but reverted to Cobh in 1920.

A statue on the quay by sculptor Jeanne Rynhart depicts three children who left here on the SS *Nevada*. The girl, Annie Moore, was the first to enter the US through Ellis Island, on 1 January 1892. The *Titanic* called into Cobh on 11 April 1912, taking on a final 123 passengers before heading west. The daily Titanic Trail walking tour (▷ 215) highlights the town's links with the notorious liner. Survivors from the *Lusitania*, sunk by a German submarine off the Old Head of Kinsale in May 1915, were brought ashore here, and around 150 bodies lie in the old cemetery, 3km (2 miles) north of town.

Excavations at Drombeg revealed a ceremonial burial

Exotic creatures graze happily at the Fota Wildlife Park

A little piece of Italy seemingly dropped into Garinish Island

DINGLE PENINSULA

See pages 116–119.

DROMBEG STONE CIRCLE

351 C9 • Town Hall, Skibereen, Co. Cork, tel 028 21766; Jul, Aug Mon–Sat 9–7, Sun 10–5; Jun, Sep Mon–Sat 9–6; Oct–end Mar Mon–Fri 9.15–1, 2–5.15; Apr, May Mon–Sat 9.15–1, 2–5.15

At this Bronze Age site east of the coastal village of Glandore, 17 stones form one of the best prehistoric circles in the country. During excavations in the 1950s the cremated remains of a body were found buried in an urn in the middle of the circle. The remnants of two round huts stand to the west of the circle, with a lined pit from around AD368, where fire-baked stones were used to heat water for cooking.

FOTA WILDLIFE PARK

351 D8 • Carrigtwohill, Co. Cork 021 481 2678 Mid-Mar to end Oct Mon–Sat 10–6, Sun 11–6; Jan to mid-Mar Sat 10–4.30, Sun 11–4.30. Closed Nov–end Dec Adult €9.50, child (3–16) €6, under 3 free, family €29 Fota Wildlife Park station on Cork–Cobh route
www.fotawildlife.ie

More than 90 species of exotic animals live in this wildlife park, 10km (6 miles) east of Cork city. It was established in 1983 to breed endangered species, and the cheetahs are a particular success story, with more than 150 cubs born here. Ostriches, giraffes, zebras, kangaroos and ring-tailed lemurs are just some of the animals to see in the 28ha (70 acres) of lush countryside.

Opulent Fota House, with famous gardens and arboretum (Mon–Sat 10–6, Sun 11–6), is a neoclassical mansion dating from 1825. Stories of its residents, including servants, are brought to life with videos in each room.

GARINISH ISLAND/ILNACULLIN

350 C8 • Garinish Island, Bantry Bay, Co. Cork 027 63040 Jul–end Aug Mon–Sat 9.30–6.30, Sun 11–6.30; May–end Jun, Sep Mon–Sat 10–6.30, Sun 11–6.30; Apr Mon–Sat 10–6.30, Sun 1–6.30; Mar, Oct Mon–Sat 10–4.30, Sun 1–5 Adult €3.50, child €1.25, family €8.25 Ferry from opposite Eccles Hotel, Glengariff, tel 027 63116

Of all the islands in Bantry Bay, Garinish, or Ilnacullin, is the most intriguing, for it is the site of a wondrous Italianate garden. The island covers just 15ha (37 acres) and was a barren rock until 1910, when Annan Bryce bought it from the British War Office and engaged the services of garden designer and architect Harold Peto. Bryce's planned house was never started, but his semi-tropical gardens survive, and were gifted to the nation in 1953. Camellias, magnolias and rhododendrons thrive in the mild climate. Ferries leave from Glengariff, a small leafy town with a nature reserve to the north, sheltering ancient woodland. The Glengarriff Bamboo Park (daily 9.30–7) on the eastern edge has 30 species of bamboo, plus 12 types of palm trees and tree ferns.

HOLY CROSS ABBEY

352 E7 • Holy Cross, Co. Tipperary 0504 43173 Abbey church: daily all year; interpretative centre daily May–end Sep; Apr, Oct Sat, Sun. Services daily Donations welcomed Guided tours, summer only

In a landscape dotted with ruined abbeys, Holy Cross is a surprise—restored and very much alive. It was founded as a Cistercian house in 1180 by Donal Mór O'Brien, and extensively rebuilt in the mid-15th century by the wealthy James Butler, fourth Earl of Ormond. Its fragment of the True Cross made it Ireland's top pilgrimage site, until the effects of the Dissolution took their toll in the 16th century and it was abandoned. An Act of Parliament in 1969 enabled its reconstruction, and it reopened in 1975.

Functional buildings form two sides of the cloister, with the mighty limestone church on the north side. Inside, the church feels cool and modern, with its whitewashed walls, vaulted roof of grey stone, plain glass windows, modern altar and raked floor. Look for faint traces of a medieval mural on the west wall, and the Gothic stone sedilia (canopied seats) in the chancel. **Don't miss** The modern Padre Pio gardens, beside the River Suir, have bronze Stations of the Cross by Enrico Manfrini.

JAMESON'S OLD MIDLETON DISTILLERY

351 D8 • Midleton, Co. Cork 021 461 3594 Mar–end Oct frequent tours daily 10–6, last tour 4.30; Nov–end Feb tours daily at 11.30, 2.30 and 4 Adult €7.95, child €3.50, family €19.50 Tours and leaflet available in seven languages, also Braille
www.whiskeytours.ie

Midleton is a small town dominated by the silver-grey spire of its cathedral and the massive bulk of the distillery, which took over whiskey production in 1975. The original 1825 distillery has been restored. A gleaming copper still stands before the Visitor Centre and a 10-minute film, followed by a 50-minute guided tour (largely out of doors), give an insight into the history and skills of whiskey manufacture. You see the progress of the grain through malting, fermenting and blending, and the world's biggest pot still (capacity 144,000 litres/32,000 gallons). The tour ends with a whiskey tasting.

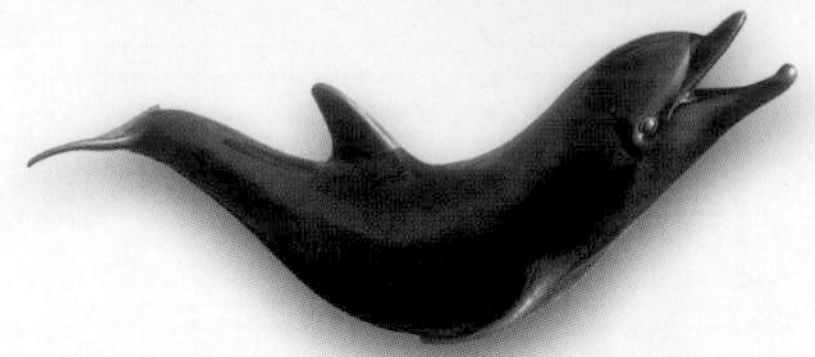

Dingle Peninsula

The Dingle Peninsula, 46km (28 miles) long, with big mountains, sweeping green valleys, sandy bays and sparkling waters, is rich with the historical echoes of ancient cultures, St. Brendan and the now-deserted Blasket Islands.

Sunset over the Blaskets, former beacon of west-coast literature

One of southeast Ireland's most famous pubs

Dingle harbour, home to fishing boats and dolphin-watching trips

RATINGS

Cultural interest	●●●●
Historic interest	●●●●●
Outdoor pursuits	●●●●●
Photo stops	●●●●

BASICS

350 B7

The Quay, Dingle, Co. Kerry, tel 066 915 1188; May–end Sep Mon–Sat 9–7, Sun 10–1, 2–5; Oct–end Apr Mon–Sat 9–5

Ferry to Great Blasket from Dunquin, tel 066 915 6422; from Dingle, tel 066 915 1344

www.dingle-peninsula.ie
Detailed tourist site with information on everything from folklore, music and history to accommodation, attractions and events.

TIPS

- **Follow the Slea Head Drive clockwise for the best views.**
- **Dingle is an area where Gaelic is still widely spoken, so road signs are likely to be in Irish.**

The mystical Blasket Islands beckon from beyond the tip of the Dingle Peninsula (opposite)

SEEING THE DINGLE PENINSULA

Seen from anywhere along this coast, it is the mountains which first define the Dingle Peninsula: the Slieve Mish mountains to the east reaching to 851m (2,791ft), and the high peaks of Mount Eagle (516m/1,692ft) and Mount Brandon (952m/3,122ft) to the west. In the middle are green valleys becoming steadily more stony towards the western tip and Dunquin.

There are rocky cliffs at Slea Head and Brandon, and superb sandy bays on the north shore around Castlegregory, and on the northwest tip around Ballyferriter. One of the best viewpoints is at the top of the Connor Pass (456m/1,496ft), reached by a hair-raising narrow and winding road. The N86 is a more direct route between Tralee and Dingle. The Slea Head Drive is a scenic loop from Dingle; follow it clockwise for the best views. The Dingle Way long-distance path goes from Tralee for 179km (111 miles) round the peninsula. Settlements tend to be scattered, and Dingle, on the southern shore, is the only significant town.

HIGHLIGHTS

BLASKET ISLANDS

Blasket Centre, Dunquin 066 915 6444/915 6371 Jul–end Aug 10–7; Easter–end Jun, Sep–end Oct daily 10–6. Closed Nov–Easter Adult €3.50, child (under 16) €1.25, family €8.25 Audio-visual presentation; leaflet in six languages Good bookshop

The green humps of the Blasket Islands lie off the western end of the Dingle. They have captured a very special place in Irish consciousness for their remarkable literary heritage depicting their world apart. The village on An Blascaod Mór (Great Blasket) was abandoned in 1953, but in summer you can visit by ferry from Dunquin or Dingle town, and even stay overnight: there's a café and weaver's workshop, the sandy beach of Trágh Bhán and colonies of seals. Manx shearwaters and storm petrels occupy Tearacht, to the west; Inishvickillane, to the south, is owned by former Taoiseach Charles Haughey.

The struggle for, and celebration of, life on these isolated islands is revealed in the modern Blasket Centre, built in 1993. With framed views of the Blaskets, stained glass by Róisín de Buitléar and

sculptures, the building itself is a work of art. Exhibitions tell of island life in this remarkable community, focusing on the autobiographies written by three people who lived there: Tomás Ó Criomhthainn (1855–1937, *The Islandman*), Peig Sayers (1873–1958, *Peig*) and Muiris Ó Súileabháin (1904–50, *Twenty Years A-Growing*).

CELTIC AND PREHISTORIC MUSEUM

Kilvicadowning, Ventry 066 915 9191 May–end Oct daily 10–5; Nov–end Apr call for hours Adult €5, child (4–12) €3 Small area for sale of antiques **www.**kerryweb.ie

Just west of Ventry Strand, this traditional-looking building on the left holds a few surprises. The first is its bright, modern interior and relaxed mood with music playing, and the next is the guidebook that comes on loan with your ticket—a huge spiral-bound affair, mixing *Far Side* cartoon humour with detailed and knowledgeable information about the exhibits. What you go on to see, simply displayed in just six small rooms, is a fabulous collection of antiquities from across the globe. They include a nest of fossilized dinosaur eggs, a genuine mammoth skull with tusks 3m (10ft) long, fished from the North Sea, Stone-Age hand-tools of chipped flint and neatly coiled Bronze-Age brooches. Through it you get a real sense of the development of man's skills in making tools and more decorative items, and an insight into the sort of people who were the early settlers on the Dingle.

GALLARUS ORATORY

Visitor Centre, tel 066 915 5333; Apr–end Sep daily 9–9 Adult €3, child (under 16) free

Apart from a minor sag in the roofline, this deceptively simple stone church looks much as it did when it was first built, some time between the seventh and twelfth centuries, and it is outstanding among the ancient sites of Ireland. The walls are of pinkish sandstone, as thick as your arm and chest together, and constructed entirely without mortar. Its form resembles the keel of an upturned boat and echoes the shapes and hues of the hills around. The Visitor Centre below offers a video interpretation, a restaurant and gift shop and an ugly white path up to the Oratory. Somehow, all this detracts from a serene and beautiful structure which speaks for itself. To avoid these distractions, park by the gate up the side road, and walk the shorter route across.

INCH STRAND

Inch, the most famous beach in Ireland, stretches 5km (3 miles) south of Dingle. To the east, a ridge covered with marram grass shelters the marshy shallows of Castlemaine Harbour, beloved of oystercatchers, ringed plovers and other waders. To the west, there seems to be a permanent mist of spray from the waves, softening a view punctuated by people fishing, flying kites and picnicking. A lifeguard is on duty in summer. For some, the golden sands are synonymous with the 1972 movie *Ryan's Daughter*. Credited with putting Dingle on the world map, the movie has its own memorial stone at a windswept picnic spot above a tiny harbour west of Slea Head.

Top to bottom:
The Slieve Mish Mountains

Beautiful Coumenole Beach, on the Dingle Peninsula

Gallerus Oratory occupies a lonely hillside

Drombeg Fort sits on a high promontory on the coast

ANASCAUL

This little village is set amid green hills, halfway between Inch and Dingle. Among several pubs on the broad main street, you might recognize the traditional pink-painted Dan Foley's from many a postcard. A more surprising find is the South Pole pub, by the bridge. It was bought and named by sailor Tom Crean (1877–1938), a remarkable and modest man who took part in three of the most famous voyages of Antarctic discovery with Robert Falcon Scott and Ernest Shackleton. In the early 1920s he retired here and opened the pub, with his wife, Nell. Today it is full of photographs and other memorabilia, a popular haunt of modern explorers for whom the ice presents the ultimate challenge—and the Guinness is good, too. A statue of Crean with two husky pups was unveiled in 2003 in the little park opposite, and a 13km (8-mile) walk in the area is named after him.

DINGLE TOWN

Dingle started out as the site of a fort and trading port, developed into a fishing town, and is now the main tourist hub for visitors to the peninsula. Its narrow streets clog up quickly with traffic in summer, but there are good pubs, craft and antiques shops, and diving, sea-angling, sailing and dolphin watching to enjoy.

Separated from Dingle Bay by a long, hilly spit of land, the town has a sheltered harbour. Waterborne tours leave from the western quay, near the tourist office. The most popular are those that include a visit with Fungi, a wild Atlantic bottlenose dolphin who has made the area his home since 1983, and who seems to love the company of visitors. Also along the seafront here, the Dingle Oceanworld Aquarium (tel 086 915 2111; Jul, Aug daily 10–8.30; May, Jun, Sep 10–6.30; Oct–end Apr 10–5) celebrates local marine life, with a touch pool, sharks, spider crabs and lumpsuckers, and a tunnel that goes 9m (29.5ft) through the middle of the ocean tank.

BACKGROUND

The earliest inhabitants of this area left plenty of signs of their habitation, from stone circles, cup-marked boulders, Iron-Age forts and Ogham-inscribed stones to the distinctive drystone cells (beehive huts) of the early Christians who, from the fifth century on, sought refuge here. The nature of the ground makes it hard to tell remains of an ancient dwelling from a pile of stones: Louis Mulcahy's free map is helpful for identifying the best sites (▷ 216). In the sixth century St. Brendan (AD484–577) sailed from Brandon Creek, on the northern coast, at the start of his epic voyage. In 1579 a Spanish army of supporters of the Desmonds built a fort, Dún an Óir, at Ferriter, to be wiped out the following year by the English under Lord Grey.

The Connor Pass is a spectacular drive (above main)

Famous Inch Strand (top)

Traditional buildings on Dingle's Dykegate Street (above middle)

Dingle clusters around its busy harbour (above)

Killarney and Killarney National Park

This stunning national park of lakes and mountains is bordered by a lively tourist town.

Killarney National Park's lakes and hills, from Ladies' View

SEEING KILLARNEY NATIONAL PARK

The park encompasses three island-spotted lakes: Lough Leane, or Lower Lake, Muckross or Middle Lake, and Upper Lake. For a breathtaking overview, visit Ladies' View to the south. Macgillycuddy's Reeks, rising to 1,039m (3,408ft), loom to the west. Killarney town, on the eastern edge of the park, is the main hub for accommodation, shopping, pubs and restaurants.

There are lots of ways to explore, including bicycle routes and signposted nature trails. Make the classic round trip from Kate Kearney's Cottage by horse-drawn jaunting car, on horseback or by bicycle, cross over the high pass called the Gap of Dunloe, and return to Killarney by cruise boat. The tourist office in Killarney has maps, information and more to help you decide, and there is information about the park itself at Muckross House.

RATINGS

Good for kids	●●●●
Historic interest	●●●
Outdoor pursuits	●●●●●
Photo stops	●●●●●

BASICS

350 C8

Beech Road, Killarney, Co. Kerry, tel 064 31633; daily 9.15–5.15. Closed Sun Oct–end May

Killarney

www.killarney.ie
Practical site with good information including entertainment, cinema listings, weather and town map.

TIP

- **Horse-drawn jaunting cars are a great way to travel between Killarney town and Muckross, and the jarvies (drivers) have a fund of local knowledge and stories.**

HIGHLIGHTS

KILLARNEY

Killarney is a seasoned vacation town that fills to bursting point in summer, and has done so since the Victorians started flocking here to admire the romantic scenery. A poorly signed one-way system makes driving through the middle of the town bewildering, but once you have parked your car, you'll find it's quite compact. The stately Catholic cathedral, St. Mary's, is on the western edge. It was designed by A. W. N. Pugin and dates from 1842, but underwent restoration in the 1970s, and again in recent years.

Scenic walks lead from the western end of New Street to Lough Leane and the lakeside tower of Ross Castle (Jun–end Aug 9–6.30; mid-Mar to end May, Sep to mid-Oct 9.30–5.30; mid-Oct to mid-Nov 9.30–4.30). A square stone keep, surrounded by the remains of curtain walls, the castle dates from the late 15th century and was a residence of the O'Donoghues. It is famed as the last castle to stand out against Cromwell's English armies, falling at last in 1652, and guided tours show it furnished to reflect that period. Nearby, you can rent a boat and row to Inisfallen Island, with its monastic remains.

GAP OF DUNLOE

The Gap is a deep cleft in the mountains to the west of the park, splitting Purple Mountain (832m/2,729ft) from the long range of Macgillycuddy's Reeks. A rough road winds through the ravine and over the pass between the mountains, through the park's most wild and romantic scenery, and it's not hard to believe that the last wolf in Ireland was killed up here in 1700. You can drive only as far as Kate Kearney's Cottage (pub, restaurant and souvenirs); after that, it's a walk of 11km (7 miles) to the other side, but in summer most people go by jaunting car or on the back of the somewhat jaded horses, who know the route only too well. On the way there are stone bridges dwarfed by sweeping mountains, thrilling dark pools (including the Black Lough, where St. Patrick is said to have drowned

O'Connor's pub in Killarney (opposite top)

Enjoying the scenery and the banter on a jaunting-car trip through the Gap of Dunloe (opposite below)

the last Irish serpent), and magnificent views to the north and south. The road brings you down to the shores of the Upper Lake and Lord Brandon's Cottage café, from where you can catch a boat through the lakes to Ross Castle.

MUCKROSS ESTATE

☎ 064 31440 ⏰ House, gardens and craft centre: all year daily 9–5 (to 7pm Jul, Aug); Farms: Mar–end Oct daily 10–5 Estate: free. House or farms: adult €5.50, child (under 18) €2.25, family €13.75; joint ticket adult €8.25, child (under 18) €3.75, family €21 Garden Restaurant
www.muckross-house.ie

The Muckross estate, properly called Bourn-Vincent Memorial Park, lies within the national park 6.5km (4 miles) south of Killarney. At its heart is the Victorian mansion of Muckross House, with its extensive gardens, a crafts centre and the Traditional Farms—three working farms, dating from the 1930s, complete with animals. The house was designed in 1843 by Edinburgh architect William Burns, and its interior is comfortably and richly furnished. Highlights include the room where Queen Victoria stayed in 1861, items of Killarney inlaid furniture in the library, and watercolours of local views by Mary Herbert, wife of Henry Herbert, who built the house.

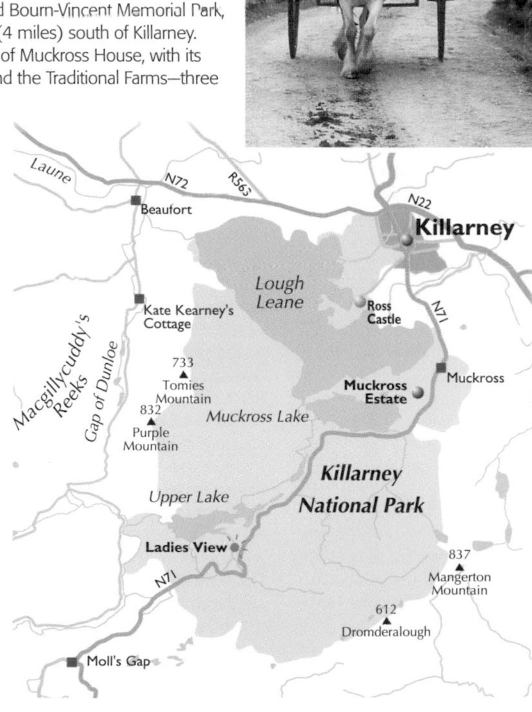

BACKGROUND

Killarney has been called upon to cater to large numbers of tourists since the Victorian era. For the national park, we have to thank Californian William Bowers Bourn, who bought the Muckross estate in 1911 and, with his son-in-law Arthur Rose Vincent, presented it to the nation in 1932. It was Ireland's first national park, later extended to protect a larger area.

Shoppers in a pretty, brightly painted Kinsale street

Romantic Lismore Castle sits on a wooded hilltop

Lough Gur Stone Age Centre re-creates a neolithic homestead

KINSALE

351 D8 Pier Road, Kinsale, Co. Cork, tel 021 477 2234; Jul, Aug Mon–Sat 9–7, Sun 10–5; Sep–end Jun Mon–Sat 9–6
www.kinsale.ie

The smart little town of Kinsale, south of Cork, has become known as a culinary oasis, bolstered by the prestigious annual Gourmet Festival. It has a mixture of interesting little shops and elegant small hotels, including the famous Blue Haven on the site of the old fish market of 1784. The back streets are stuffed with restaurants to suit all tastes and budgets.

A huge rusted iron buoy and anchors outside Kinsale Regional Museum in Market Square (Wed–Sat 10.30–5.30, Sun 2–5.15) reflect the town's fishing heritage. In fact, many streets are on land reclaimed from the sea during the 13th century. The modern harbour, bristling with sailing masts, is popular for diving and fishing, including deep-sea angling and blue shark fishing. Wading birds occupy the mudflats, and swans complete the idyllic scene. Desmond Castle, on Cork Street, dates from 1500 and served as a prison in times of war; it now houses the International Museum of Wine (mid-Apr to end Oct daily 10–6). **Don't miss** Charles Fort, a 17th-century fortress, lies on the east side of the bay in Summer Cove (mid-Mar to end Oct daily 10–6; Nov–end Feb Sat, Sun 10–5).

LISMORE

352 E8 Lismore Heritage Centre, Lismore, Co. Waterford, tel 058 54975; Jan–end Oct Mon–Fri 9.30–6, Sat 10–5.30, Sun 12–5.30. Closed Nov–end Dec
www.lismoreheritage.com

Dancer Fred Astaire (1899–1987) was just one celebrity who succumbed to the charms of this pretty Georgian town, as a blue plaque on Maddens Bar on Main Street testifies. He came initially to visit his sister Adèle, who lived in the splendid Lismore Castle, its square towers visible from the north bank of the River Blackwater. It had previously passed through the hands of Sir Walter Raleigh and Richard Boyle (▷ 32), father of the famous physicist Robert (1627–91), whose story is depicted at the Heritage Centre. The castle is now the Irish home of the Dukes of Devonshire and not open, but visitors can explore the magnificent gardens (mid-Apr to end Sep, daily 1.45–4.45). Edmund Spenser, a friend of Raleigh, composed his epic poem *The Faerie Queen* (1590) while staying here.

North Mall, bedecked with hanging baskets, leads to the cathedral, named in honour of St. Carthagh, who founded a monastic school of international importance here in AD633. The present building mostly dates from the 17th and 18th centuries. Highlights include a window in the south transept by English Pre-Raphaelite artist Edward Burne-Jones (1833–98), the splendidly carved 16th-century McGrath tomb, and the carved stones from earlier churches on the site, dating back to the ninth century, now set into the end wall. A forlorn, unmarked spot in the northeast corner of the churchyard is the site of a famine grave. Elsewhere, elegantly scripted slab tombstones are overgrown with moss and ivy, and surrounded by spring bulbs. **Don't miss** The 40-minute circular walk through the woods to the 19th-century folly towers of Ballysaggartmore, signposted from the road about 1.6km (1 mile) west of the town—anti-(counter-) clockwise is best.

LISTOWEL

350 C7 St. John's, The Square, Listowel, Co. Kerry, tel 068 22590; Jun to mid-Sep Mon–Sat 10–6
www.kerrywritersmuseum.com

Listowel has two main claims to its place on the visitors' map: an imaginative literary museum and an antique monorail. Seanchaí (pronounced Shanakey), meaning storyteller, is the name of the former, in a fine Georgian house on the town square (Apr–end Sep daily 10–6; Oct–end Mar Mon–Fri 10–5). It celebrates the works of John B. Keane, Bryan MacMahon, Brendan Kennelly, Maurice Walsh and others, with an inspirational audio-visual experience. In contrast, there is little spiritual about the Lartigue Monorail of 1888, which runs on the coast between Listowel and Ballybunion (tel 068 22212). Unusually, the single rail runs mid-carriage rather than under the wheels.

LOUGH GUR STONE AGE CENTRE

351 D7 • Ballyneety, Co. Limerick 061 385186 Site: open access. Visitor Centre May–end Sep daily 10–5.30 Adult €4.50, child (4–12) €2.50, family €12.95
www.shannonheritage.com

Some 3,000 years ago neolithic farmers picked out the prettiest spot in County Limerick for their settlement: crescent-shaped Lough Gur. The site has been thoroughly excavated, and its story is told in the snug thatched replica longhouse and roundhouse above the lake. The ruined castle visible from the parking area dates from 1500, and is private, but adds to the picture, with cattle across the water and swans surveying picnickers. Nearby are a wedge tomb and the Grange stone circle. More antique sites can be seen from the lakeside.

LIMERICK

A busy industrial city at the head of the Shannon estuary, Limerick has a medieval heart and a world-class arts museum.

You won't go far in Limerick today without seeing references to *Angela's Ashes*, Frank McCourt's grim 20th-century memoir of childhood poverty. You can take a tour based on the book (▷ 218) and visit the Ashes Exhibition on Pery Square (Mon–Fri 10–4.30), but there's a great deal more to discover in this intriguing city.

Limerick was founded by Vikings around AD922 as a trading port and the town prospered. In the 12th century the settlement on King John's Island (between the Shannon and Abbey rivers) was fortified by a wall, and became known as English Town, with Irish Town on the opposite bank. In Georgian times it spread south, with the best developments around the People's Park. Today the two areas are linked by ruler-straight O'Connell Street, parallel to the river and the main shopping street of the city, usually choked by traffic.

MAIN ATTRACTIONS

There are two medieval highlights to explore. The first is King John's Castle, dating from 1200, whose great drum towers loom above the river (mid-May to end Aug daily 9.30–5.30; Apr to mid-May, Sep, Oct daily 10–5; Oct–end Mar daily 10.30–4.30). Inside, animated and interactive exhibits bring the story of the castle to life

The second medieval treasure is square-towered St. Mary's Cathedral, parts of which date back to 1168. It was founded by King Donal Mór O'Brien (also responsible for Cashel and Holy Cross), and restoration in the 1990s removed the interior plaster for greater authenticity. A new place has yet to be found for the oak misericords of 1480–1500, superbly carved with griffons, swans, other beasts and angels, that lie propped up in a side chapel. A single limestone slab, over 4m (13ft) long, forms the altar, and the cannon balls date from 1691, when William of Orange's troops besieged the city.

The Hunt Museum, in a modest grey-fronted Georgian customs house of 1765, has a wondrously eclectic collection spanning 9,000 years, amassed by John and Gertrude Hunt (Mon–Sat 10–5, Sun 2–5). They include a virtually intact disk shield of c750BC, found in County Antrim; a Roman pierced bronze cooking strainer from the 2nd century; a small bronze horse believed to be by Leonardo da Vinci; an emerald seal that belonged to Charles I; a delicate 17th-century German dish made of lapis lazuli; sketches by Henry Moore and paintings by Jack B. Yeats; and a menu card by Picasso. Exhibits are well labelled and beautifully displayed.

RATINGS	
Chain store shopping	●●●●
Historic interest	●●●
Photo stops	●●●

BASICS

351 D6

Arthur's Quay, Limerick, Co. Limerick, tel 061 317522; Mon–Fri 9.30–5.30 (also weekends Jul, Aug)

Limerick

www.limerick.com
Up-to-date information about what's going on in the city, for residents and visitors, including news, sport and history.

The great polygonal towers and ramparts of King John's Castle dominate the town (top).
A Georgian doorfront (above).
The Treaty Stone, where the Treaty of Limerick was signed (below)

Fantastic limestone formations in Mitchelstown Cave

White buildings of the former signal station top Mizen Head

The Sheep's Head lighthouse is a beacon on this turbulent coast

MITCHELSTOWN CAVE

351 E7 • Burncourt, Caher, Co. Tipperary 052 67246 Daily 10–6 Adult €4.50, child €2, family €12.50 45-min tour, according to demand 12km (7.5 miles) east of Mitchelstown signed on country roads from the N8 www.mitchelstowncave.com

The entrance to this spectacular natural wonder is about as low key as you can get. If it weren't for the flagstaff outside the farmhouse, it would be easy to miss. An unpromising grey metal door in the rock leads to the 88 concrete steps that descend into a wonderland of limestone, created over millions of years by dripping water depositing limestone to form the translucent stone curtains, stalactites, stalagmites and even sideways-growing halectites. The temperature is a steady 12°C (54°F), and the air feels dry and fresh. For 1km (half a mile), successive caverns open out, revealing ever more fantastic formations, and culminating in the Tower of Babel. The rich hues are natural, not a trick of artificial light.

Nearby Ballyporeen celebrates its links with former US president Ronald Reagan, with a pub and Visitor Centre named after him.

MIZEN PENINSULA

350 B9 North Street, Skibereen, Co. Cork, tel 028 21766; Jun–end Aug Mon–Sat 9–7, Sun 9–5; Sep–end May Mon–Fri 9–5 Summer sailings to Baltimore and Clear Island www.mizenhead.net

This rugged peninsula stretches southwest between Dunmanus and Roaringwater bays, with the high point of 407m (1,334ft) Mount Gabriel at its landward end, and 23m (75ft) high cliffs at its seaward end. Ballydehob has a statue of local wrestling hero Dan O'Mahony on the main street and a disused 12-arch tramway viaduct. Skull is an amiable fishing village, with Eire's only planetarium (Mar–end Sep). At the tip of the peninsula, beyond Goleen and the beaches of Barley Cove, lies Cloghane Island, linked to the mainland by a bridge, and site of the Mizen Head Visitor Centre (Jun–end Sep daily 10–6; mid-Mar to end May, Oct daily 10.30–5; Nov to mid-Mar Sat, Sun 11–4).

ROARINGWATER BAY

350 C9 Town Hall, Skibbereen, Co. Cork, tel 028 21766; Jul, Aug Mon–Sat 9–7, Sun 10–5; Jun, Sep Mon–Sat 9–6; Oct–end Mar Mon–Fri 9.15–1, 2–5.15; Apr, May Mon–Sat 9.15–1, 2–5.15 To Sherkin Island from Baltimore (tel 028 20218) and Skull (028 28138), May–end Sep. To Clear Island from Baltimore (tel 028 39135), and Skull in summer only (028 28278) www.oilean-chleire.ie (Clear Island)

In the far southwest corner of Ireland, Roaringwater Bay is around 12km (7.5 miles) long and up to 8km (5 miles) wide. Of the 15 islands within the bay, Sherkin and Cape Clear are the largest. Sherkin, a 10-minute boat ride from Baltimore, has a 15th-century abbey, a ruined castle, good beaches and rare plants. Cape Clear is a stop-off point for migratory birds, and its observatory is well established (tel 028 39181).

Distinctive modern features of the bay are the buoys and snaking black lines of the mussel- and oyster-culture industries. Both species thrive in the plankton-rich, clear waters. The Fastnet Lighthouse lies 6km (3.5 miles) southwest of Cape Clear Island.

ROSCREA

352 E6 Roscrea Castle Complex Heritage Centre, Roscrea, Co. Tipperary, tel 090 921850; Mar–end Oct daily 10-6; Nov–end Feb Sat, Sun 10–4.30 Roscrea

Noted for its medieval architecture, Roscrea is dubbed Ely O'Carroll Country, after the two ancient Irish families who dominated its history until their lands were seized by the English in the 17th century. In the middle of town stands a huge 13th-century golden-towered castle, with a Queen Anne mansion and formal walled garden within the high curtain wall. The Roscrea Castle Complex Heritage Centre and Damer House (Apr–end Oct daily 10–6; Nov–end Mar Fri–Sun 9.30–4.30) has exhibitions about the town's history and there's a heritage walk taking in the weathered 12th-century wheel cross and round tower of St. Cronin's, and the tower of a 15th-century Franciscan friary.

Don't miss A comically incongruous fountain in the town square has four cherubs pouring water.

SHEEP'S HEAD PENINSULA

350 B9 The Courthouse, The Square, Bantry, Co. Cork, tel 021 438 1624; seasonal opening

This fertile peninsula lies between Dunmanus and Bantry bays and its main town, Durrus, gives its name to a distinctive local cheese. Low rocky hills in the east give way to a rugged shoreline, and there are great views to the north and south from the Seefin pass above Kilcrohane (346m/1,136ft). The climate is mild, encouraging exotic growth at Kilravock Garden (summer weekends, tel 027 61111). Yachts moor in Ahakista Bay, and it feels like a prosperous, tranquil backwater. A memorial garden on the shore just east of the bay, however, shows that it is touched by tragedy: The garden honours the 329 people who died on 23 June 1985, when Air India flight 182 from Montréal to Bombay exploded off the coast here.

ROCK OF CASHEL

A tightly clustered round tower, medieval chapel, Gothic cathedral and 15th-century castle loom 61m (200ft) above the plain on a dramatic limestone outcrop.

In an area of rich farmland scattered with ruined monastic sites, this is the best of all, visible for miles, and a microcosm of an age when archbishops behaved like kings. The rock was actually the seat of Munster kings from the fourth century, including Brian Boru, who later became king of all Ireland. In 1101 King Muircheartach Ua Briain presented the site to the Church, and it remained in use until the mid-18th century, when its decaying buildings, costly to maintain, were abandoned in favour of St. John's Church, in the town below.

EXPLORING THE ROCK

The steep climb to the main door gives a sense of the majesty and impregnability of the site, and leaves you breathless in all respects. Above is the outer wall of the Hall of the Vicars Choral, constructed for the medieval choir and restored inside. Beyond the stairs of the gatehouse is a replica of the 12th-century St. Patrick's Cross, then the first building you see is the cathedral, a vast cruciform dating from 1230, and roofless since 1848. Look up at the gargoyles around the Gothic windows. The squat, brooding tower was added in the 15th century, when the archbishops were at the height of their power, and this end of the church was rebuilt as a fortified tower house. Its appearance today is grim and forbidding. In contrast, the older Cormac's Chapel, wedged uncomfortably between the choir and the south transept of the cathedral, seems positively light-hearted, with its twin square towers and Romanesque arches. It was built by Bishop Cormac MacCarthy in 1127, and traces of wall paintings in blue, red and gold can be seen in the chancel. The carving around the doorways is particularly good, with faces around the chancel arch. The deeply carved tomb is probably Viking, and was moved here from the cathedral for shelter.

The oldest building of the Rock is a round tower of 1101, 28m (92ft) high, on the far side of the cathedral.

CASHEL TOWN

In the town, seek out one of Ireland's most prized cheeses, creamy Cashel Blue. The Heritage Centre (tel 062 82511; mid-Mar to end Sep daily 9.30–5.30; Oct to mid-Mar Mon–Fri 9.30–5.30) portrays the history of the town. At the Bolton Library on John Street you can see a monk's encyclopaedia of 1168 and the smallest book in the world (Mon–Fri 10–4.30). The Folk Village, in a row of thatched cottages on Dominic Street, re-creates 18th-century rural life and has displays on Republican history (daily 9.30–7.30). The handsome Cashel Palace Hotel was originally the archbishops' palace of 1732.

RATINGS	
Cultural interest	●●●●
Good for kids	●●●
Historic interest	●●●●●
Photo stops	●●●●

BASICS

352 E7 • Cashel, Co. Tipperary

062 61437

Mid-Jun to mid-Sep 9–7; mid-Mar to mid-Jun, mid-Sep to mid-Oct 9–5.30; mid-Oct to mid-Mar 9–4.30

Adult €5, child (6–18) €2, family €11

On Dublin–Cork route

20-min video, in restored choir buildings, sets the scene

TIP

- There are no toilet facilities on the Rock.

Majestic ruins atop the Rock of Cashel stand out in romantic silhouette against the surrounding flat land (top)

Finely carved stonework gives a hint of the former splendour of the ecclesiastical buildings on the Rock (above)

Waterford

A commercial fishing port founded by Vikings and once Ireland's second city, Waterford has the fifth most popular attraction in the country—its world-famous glass factory.

Admiring the merchandise in the Waterford Crystal Visitor Centre

Reginald's Tower—one of many medieval relics in Waterford

A stained-glass window in the Cathedral of the Most Holy Trinity

RATINGS	
Good for kids	●●●
Historic interest	●●●●
Specialist shopping	●●●●

BASICS

352 F7

The Quay, Waterford, Co. Waterford, tel 051 875 823; May–end Oct Mon–Fri 9–6, Sat 10–6. Also at Waterford Crystal, tel 051 358397; Mar–Oct daily 8.30–6; Nov daily 9–5

Waterford

www.waterfordtourism.org
Good site for getting a first picture of the city.

www.waterfordvisitorcentre.com
Waterford Crystal factory's website gives a virtual tour of the factory, and information on shopping at the Visitor Centre. For on-line shopping: www.waterford.com

SEEING WATERFORD

The city spreads along the south bank of the River Suir. Broad Merchant's Quay runs beside the river, with a variety of shops, hotels and other buildings facing the water. These include the handsome old Granary of 1872 housing the tourist office and Treasures Exhibition at the western end, and the circular medieval Reginald's Tower at the eastern end.

The main shopping area lies in the rabbit warren of small streets behind Merchant's Quay. The Georgian elegance of the city is epitomized by the Port of Waterford Company building, at the top of Gladstone Street, with its imposing blue door topped by the city crest and a magnificent fanlight. Architect John Roberts' Catholic Cathedral of the Most Holy Trinity of 1793, lit inside by 10 exquisite crystal chandeliers, is equally elegant.

HIGHLIGHTS

TREASURES EXHIBITION

The Granary, Merchants Quay, Waterford 051 304 500 Apr–end Sep Mon–Sat 9.30–6, Sun 11–6; Oct–end Mar Mon–Fri 10–5, Sun 11–5 Adult €6, child (9–18) €3.20, family €12

Waterford's Heritage Centre tells the story of the city's development in the context of the history of Ireland. A glass lift rises to the third floor for a tour of the Viking, Anglo-Norman and medieval city, then you proceed to the 18th century on the second floor, where a 12-minute audio-visual show brings you into the 19th century and beyond.

Look for a curved Viking flute of *c*1150, made from a swan or goose bone; a gold kite-shaped brooch of the same era; the medieval Great Charter Roll, depicting all the lord mayors of Waterford; and a red velvet hat given by Henry VIII to the mayor in 1536. There's also the tale of local boy Thomas Francis Meagher, convicted of treason after the Young Ireland Rebellion of 1848. He escaped being sent to Australia and fled to New York, where he became a Civil War hero and founded the *Irish News*; he is also credited with introducing the Irish flag. Other famous sons of Waterford featured include Shakespearean actor Charles Kean (1811–68) and opera composer William Vincent Wallace (1812–65), both, coincidentally, born in the same house.

WATERFORD CRYSTAL

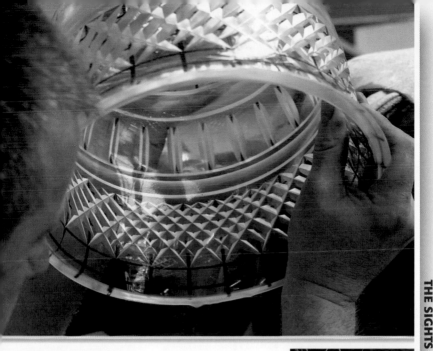

Off N25 Dungarvan road 051 332 500 Gallery: daily Mar–end Oct 8.30–6; Nov–end Feb 9–5 Gallery: free. Tours: adult €8, child under 12 free 45 min, Mar–end Oct daily 8.30–4.15; Nov–end Feb Mon–Fri 9–3.15

It is easy to take for granted the sparkling chandeliers made of hand-cut crystal that adorn the public and private buildings of Waterford and, indeed, the rest of the world. But visit the factory where that crystal is made, and you realise how much skill and time goes into every piece of glass. The skills required to blow, cut and polish the glassware, from a tumbler to a trophy, are a revelation.

Glassmaking became an industry here in 1783 and thrived until 1851, when heavy taxation and a lack of funds stopped production. Waterford Crystal was revived in 1947, and now dominates the top end of the market in much of Europe and America. It has an excellent Visitor Centre, the fifth most popular attraction in Ireland.

The factory is modern, covers 16ha (40 acres) and employs around 1,600 workers, and though working conditions have upgraded since the early days, the skills are much the same, and an apprenticeship still takes about eight years. During the factory tour, with the roaring furnace ever present, you'll see the whole process, from blowing molten glass at 932°C (1,710°F) to wedge-cutting the finished piece on a diamond wheel. Waterford crystal is distinctive for its clarity, sparkle and weight—the thicker glass allows for deeper facets to be cut. Afterwards, visit the gallery and shop with new appreciation.

Hard at work—a cutter (top) and a glass blower (above) creating exquisite Waterford Crystal

BACKGROUND

Waterford dates back to 7000BC, when Stone-Age hunter-gatherers congregated on the banks of the Suir. By 2000BC settlers were mining copper all along this coast. Viking raids in AD795 turned to settlement after 914, with a fort called Dundory built on the triangle of high ground between two rivers, and the establishment of a town they called Vadrafjordr. The Anglo-Normans gained power here in the 12th century, and largely held on to it until the religious and political upheavals of the mid-17th century, when the city walls failed to repel Cromwell's army. Despite this, the town has the largest collection of medieval walls and towers still standing in Ireland. In the 18th and 19th centuries Waterford prospered, and much of the town dates from this era.

The ruins of Timoleague Abbey include this open arcade

A common scene in Irish pubs—laughter, music and Guinness

The St. Brendan Voyage legend, depicted on a Tralee gable

TIMOLEAGUE ABBEY

351 D9 • Timoleague, Co. Cork
Open access

The monks who selected this site for their abbey in the sixth century chose well. It's on a bend of the Argideen, renowned for its fish and birdlife, where it runs into Courtmacsherry Bay, backed by a wooded hill. For the best views, approach from the south. The substantial ruin dates from 1312, when Franciscans moved in at the behest of Donal Glas MacCarthy. Forced out at the Reformation, the monks returned in 1604, but were burned out again in 1642 by Cromwell's men, who discovered thousands of barrels of wine in the vaults.

Of the two later churches in the village, the Church of the Ascension reflects in miniature the square tower of the abbey; the Catholic church has a window dating to 1929 by artist Harry Clarke, whose work is prominently displayed in Cork's Crawford Art Gallery (▷ 112). The formal castle gardens, with terraces and herbaceous borders date from the 1820s (Jun–end Aug Mon–Sat 11–5.30, Sun 2–5).

TRALEE

350 B7 Ashe Memorial Hall, Tralee, Co. Kerry, tel 066 712 1288; Jul, Aug Mon–Sat 9–7, Sun 9–6; Apr–end Jun, Sep, Oct Mon–Sat 9–6; Nov–end Mar Mon–Sat 9–5 Tralee
www.discoverkerry.com

This is the county town of Kerry, the northeast gateway to the Dingle Peninsula (▷ 116–119) and known for its Rose of Tralee International Festival—a week-long party and beauty pageant that brings over 200,000 visitors into town in August (▷ 219). The town sprawls on the flatlands east of Tralee Bay and is very much a functional hub, with plenty of accommodation and excellent sandy beaches nearby at Banna and Derrymore. The town was founded in the 13th century by the powerful Earls of Desmond. Its chequered medieval history is well told in the time-journey style 'Kerry the Kingdom', at the Kerry County Museum at the head of Denny Street (Mar–end Dec daily).

VALENCIA ISLAND & SKELLIGS

350 A8 Beech Road, Killarney, Co. Kerry, tel 064 31633; Mon–Sat 9.15–5.15

Valencia, just off the northwest tip of the Iveragh Peninsula, makes an interesting detour from the Ring of Kerry (▷ 260–261). It is 11km (7 miles) long and boasts its own signposted Ring drive and a coastal walk, both of which offer great views from the spinal ridge. Shortly after the bridge crossing from Portmagee, look for the cliff-top memorial marking the spot where the first transatlantic telegraph message was sent in 1866.

The slate slabs used in the walls of some field boundaries came from the old quarry, signposted north of Knightstown, which has a grotto to Our Lady and St. Bernadette. Its slates also adorn roofs from the Paris Opera House to the Houses of Parliament in London. On the eastern end of the island is the Georgian village of Knightstown, with a red clock tower on its harbour dating from the late 1800s. Glanleam Sub-Tropical Gardens, west of here were created in the mid-19th century by the Knight of Kerry, a title held by the foremost local landowner.

The jagged islands off the end of the peninsula are Great Skellig, or Skellig Michael, and Little Skellig, where 20,000 pairs of gannets nest, making it the second largest gannetry in the world. Skellig Michael is the more distant of the pair, 13km (8 miles) offshore and up to 217m (712ft) high, and has a lighthouse from 1820. Christian monks sought refuge here in the sixth century, surviving on trade with passing ships before abandoning it in the 11th century. Hundreds of precipitous steps lead up to their beehive huts. Visit on a cruise from the excellent Skellig Experience Visitor Centre on Valencia Island, just over the bridge from Portmagee (Mar–end Nov daily 10–6).

WATERFORD

See pages 126–127.

YOUGHAL

352 E8 Market Square, Youghal, Co. Cork, tel 024 20170; Mon–Fri 9–5.30, Sat, Sun 9.30–5 Youghal
www.youghal.ie

This venerable harbour and market town (pronounced Yawl) is at the mouth of the Blackwater River on a broad, sandy bay. In the 16th century it was plagued by pirates, and when the rebel Earl of Desmond landed here in 1579 he found the town walls easy to break through. For helping to suppress the Desmond rebellion, English adventurer Sir Walter Raleigh was rewarded with extensive lands in the area. One of the most notable buildings in town is the Clock Gate of 1777, straddling the long, narrow Main Street. In 1954 the old harbour area became a film set for John Houston's *Moby Dick*. Guided walks from the Heritage Centre (Mon–Fri 9–5.30, Sat, Sun 9.30–5) explore many fascinating facets of the town. Fox's Lane Folk Museum is dedicated to 1850–1950 domestic gadgets, centred on a fully equipped 19th-century Irish country kitchen (summer, Tue–Sat 10–1, 2–6).

THE WEST

Expansive and remote, the landscapes of the West are stunning in their beauty: towering sea cliffs, lonely beaches, rugged mountains, vast stretches of stark bogland and the limestone plateau of The Burren. Irish language and music are prominent here. Lively Galway City is the regional capital, while County Sligo is full of prehistoric remains.

MAJOR SIGHTS

A sandy beach, dominated by the rugged cliffs of Achill Island

ACHILL ISLAND

Gloriously rugged cliffs, bays and mountains make Achill Island, County Mayo's Atlantic outpost, an exhilarating place to visit.

346 B4 Achill Tourism, Cashel, Achill Island, tel 098 47353; Jul, Aug Mon–Fri 9.30–5, Sat 11–3; Sep–end Jun Mon–Fri 10–4
www.achilltourism.com

RATINGS	
Historic interest	●●●
Outdoor pursuits	●●●
Photo stops	●●●●●

Achill is Ireland's largest island, an irregular chunk of mountainous land some 22km (14 miles) wide and 19km (12 miles) from north to south. The mountains of Knockmore (340m/1,115ft) and Minaun (403m/1,322ft) dominate the southern half, while the peaks of Croaghaun (668m/2,191ft) and Slievemore (672m/2,204ft) rise in the north. Around 2,500 people live here.

Achill Island is connected to the mainland by Michael Davitt Bridge. The narrow coast road signposted 'Atlantic Drive', which runs south along the sound, is the best introduction to the island. It passes austere 15th-century Carrickildavnet Castle, one of the strongholds of County Mayo's famed and feared pirate queen Grace O'Malley (*c*1530–1600), also known as Granuaile, whose family motto was 'Invincible on land and sea'. Granuaile harassed the English by land and sea in Tudor times, and few, if any, got the better of her. Fearing that enemies would steal her ships by night, she slept with one end of a silk thread tied to her toe and the other running through the window out to hawsers of her fleet. Next to the castle stands the ruin of Kildownet church. A location map of the graveyard on the wall of the church locates several poignant sites that reflect hard times on Achill.

The 'Atlantic Drive' turns north for a beautiful run up the wild west coast. Towards the top of the island you reach the village of Keel, with its long beach and spectacular view of the lofty Cliffs of Minaun. Just beyond lies Dooagh, where on 4 September 1987 Don Allum, the first man to row the Atlantic both ways, came ashore after 77 days at sea. The village pub has photographs of the event. The road ends 5km (3 miles) beyond Dooagh at Keem Strand, a lovely unspoiled beach in a deep bay with a memorable cliff walk (▷ 248).

Another of Achill Island's remarkable sites is the deserted village of 74 roofless houses on the southern slope of Slievemore. The village was abandoned during the Great Famine, but was used as a 'booley' village—a summer grazing and milking settlement—until the 1940s.

Arranmore has a rugged coastline with tiny islets offshore

ARRANMORE

347 D1 Donegal Tourist Information Office, The Quay, Donegal, Co. Donegal, tel 074 972 1148; Jun–end Aug 9–6, Sun 10–4; Sep–end May Mon–Fri 9–6, Sun 10–6 From Burtonport, tel 074 952 0532

Arranmore is also called Aran Island, but is generally referred to as Arranmore to prevent confusion with the better-known Aran Islands in Galway Bay (▷ 131). The Arranmore ferry from Burtonport takes just 20 minutes, and this ease of access means that the attractively hilly island sees plenty of visitors. Most come for the day, but to get a real taste of the island it's best to stay overnight—especially in August, during Arranmore's annual festival. Most of the action takes place on the cultivated eastern side, in the bars and shops of the little fishing and ferry-port village of Leabgarrow. From here you can wander narrow lanes towards the rugged west coast, or turn aside to climb one of the three modest peaks for the view from 227m (745ft).

BLOODY FORELAND

347 E1 Dungloe Tourist Information Office, The Quay, Dungloe, Co. Donegal, tel 074 952 1297; Jun–end Sep, or Donegal Tourist Information Office (▷ Arranmore)

The best time to be at Bloody Foreland is an hour before sunset, when the sun tips the red cliffs around Altawinny Bay and makes them glow blood-red to dramatic effect. With the cone of Bloody Foreland rising 314m (1,030ft) behind, you look out over sloping fields of heather and gorse, across 11km (7 miles) of sea towards the long, low bar of Tory Island (▷ 148) on the northern horizon. The headland is signposted off R257 between Bunbeg and Gortahork.

ARAN ISLANDS

The bleakly beautiful landscape of these islands reveals extraordinary stone walls and ancient forts. The islands are one of the last bastions of traditional language and lifestyle.

The three Aran Islands lie in line across the mouth of Galway Bay. The largest and most seaward of the group is Inishmore, 14.5km (9 miles) long. In the middle lies Inishmaan (5km/3 miles long), while the smallest and roundest island, Inisheer (3km/2 miles wide) is the most easterly. All three islands share the same distinctive landscape of bleak grey limestone, void of grass in most parts but supporting sheets of wild flowers. Narrow *boreens,* or lanes, thread through the islands, and like the small rocky fields, are bounded by stone walls that are sturdy, but so loosely constructed that you can see blue sky or green sea between each individual stone.

Irish is spoken throughout the islands, but principally on Inishmaan, the most isolated of the three. Here you'll find plenty to photograph.

INISHMORE

Inishmore has the most striking archaeological remains, the largest village, Kilronan, and more visitors than the other two islands put together. There's an excellent Heritage Centre and island museum in Kilronan, and you can buy genuine hand-knitted Aran sweaters in An Púcán Craft Shop before taking a pony-and-trap or minibus tour of the island. The main attraction is Dún Aengus, a large Iron Age stone fort perched on the edge of a 90m (295ft) cliff. Its sister stronghold of Dún Dúchathair, the Black Fort, is on its own lonely cliff top.

INISHMAAN AND INISHEER

Of the three islands Inishmaan is farthest from a mainland harbour, and is the least affected by tourism. The playwright J. M. Synge stayed here each year between 1898 and 1902, researching his definitive book *The Aran Islanders*; you can visit Teach Synge (tel 091 537700; May–end Sep Mon–Sat 10–6, other times by appointment), the cottage where he lodged and which is now restored. You may see island men in homespun suits and women wearing traditional shawls and full skirts. The island co-operative works hard to maintain employment and to encourage a sympathetic understanding of Inishmaan among visitors.

Inisheer, easily reached from Doolin, is small enough to walk in a morning, and there's a cheerful pub with frequent music sessions.

RATINGS

Cultural interest	●●●●●
Historic interest	●●●
Photo stops	●●●●●
Specialist shopping	●●●●

BASICS

350 C5

Tourist Information: Inishmore, tel 099 61263; Inishmaan, tel 099 73010; Inisheer, tel 099 75008/75022; www.iol.ie/~discover/islands.htm

Island Ferries, tel 091 561767. Departs from Rossaveal several times a day

Aer Arann, tel 091 593034; www.aerarannislands.ie Flights depart from Connemara Regional Airport, hourly during peak season

Aran Heritage Centre, Kilronan, Inishmore, tel 099 61355; open Jun–end Aug daily 10–7; Apr–end May, Sep–end Oct daily 11–5

www.visitaranislands.com
Gives an overview of Aran's attractions and wildlife, with an interactive map and useful links.

The remains of Dún Aengus fort blend with the rocky landscape of Inishmore (top)

The purple hues of dawn light up a cluster of gravestones on Inishmore (above)

BUNRATTY CASTLE AND FOLK PARK

With one of Ireland's best preserved castles, Bunratty is the lead player in a full-scale tourist attraction, with a folk park offering a glimpse of 'old Ireland'.

RATINGS	
Good for kids	●●●●●
Historic interest	●●●●
Photo stops	●●●●
Walkability	●●●●

BASICS

351 D6 • Bunratty Castle and Folk Park, Bunratty, Co. Clare

061 360788

Jun–end Aug daily 9–6 (Folk Park closes 6.30); Apr–end May, Sep–end Oct 9–5.30; Nov–end Mar 9.30–5.30. Last admission to castle 4pm all year

Adult €11, child (under 12) €6.25

www.shannonheritage.com
Informative site for Bunratty, and other Shannon area attractions.

TIP

- Visit early in the day to avoid the main influx of tour buses (in peak season) and school parties (term-time weekdays).

Bunratty's Tower House (top). Old signage forms an evocative display in the Folk Park (above)

Visitors landing at Shannon Airport don't have far to go for a taste of 'Ould Ireland', because Bunratty Castle and Folk Park are set up to present an agreeably nostalgic version of Irish history. The Folk Park re-creates a corner of 19th-century Ireland with a large number of carefully reconstructed buildings and workplaces, some incorporated into a 'village street'. These include cottages and farmhouses into which visitors are welcomed by guides in period costume; and, at the other end of the social scale, the fine Georgian country residence of Bunratty House into which the last resident owners of Bunratty Castle moved in 1804. The Folk Park has a working watermill producing flour for sale, and a forge at which the blacksmith makes the sparks fly. There's a church, a pub for relaxing over a Guinness or two, and a teashop/bakery where you can buy or eat scones and bread. Garden-lovers will be delighted by the restored walled garden of Bunratty House, and also by the other gardens which have been laid out in the authentic vernacular style appropriate to their parent dwelling: cottage garden, farmhouse garden and so on. There are plenty of domestic and farm animals in the 10ha (25 acres) of the Folk Park, along with working thatchers, weavers, churners of fresh butter, and other costumed guides. All this makes the Folk Park a very child-friendly attraction, and you may find yourself competing for space and the guides' attention with some of the school parties that frequent Bunratty. Coach parties are another common cause of congestion.

BUNRATTY CASTLE

A tall tower house, Bunratty Castle was built around 1425 on the site of a former castle by the MacNamara clan, before passing into the hands of the O'Briens, who later became Earls of Thomond. The castle has been very thoroughly and expertly restored, and fitted out with rare and appropriate furniture, paintings and tapestries from the 15th and 16th centuries. The Main Guard, a splendid vaulted feasting hall with a minstrels' gallery, nowadays hosts 'medieval banquets' twice an evening (reservations required). Guests eat with their fingers, drink copious quantities of mead poured by serving wenches in low-cut gowns, and sing along with the robed and caped Bunratty Singers. This is not for everyone; your enjoyment level will depend on your mood and companions—the bigger and jollier your party, the better.

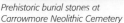

Prehistoric burial stones at Carrowmore Neolithic Cemetery

The Cliffs of Moher rise sheer out of the water on Ireland's rocky west coast, with nothing but ocean between here and America

THE BURREN

See pages 134–135.

CARRICK-ON-SHANNON

348 E4 The Marina, Carrick-on-Shannon, Co. Leitrim tel 071 962 0170; Apr–end Oct, Tue–Sat 9.30–1, 2–5.30 Carrick-on-Shannon www.carrickonshannon.ie

Carrick-on-Shannon, a pleasant, easy-paced town on a fine fishing and boating river, has thrived since the reopening of the Ballyconnell and Ballinamore Canal as the Shannon–Erne Waterway in 1994. It provides the missing link between Upper Lough Erne and the Shannon, opening up a boating route from Belleek though the heart of Ireland to Limerick and the Shannon Estuary, a distance of 380km (236 miles).

Don't miss You can rent boats of all sizes at Carrick, and get fishing permits, tackle and advice.

CARROWMORE NEOLITHIC CEMETERY

347 D3 Tourist Information Office, Aras Reddan, Temple Street, Sligo, Co. Sligo, tel 071 916 1201 Open access www.irelandnorthwest.ie

Out in low-lying country west of Sligo town, off the Strandhill road (look for brown 'heritage' road signs), are scattered burial sites known as the Carrowmore Megalithic Cemetery. The oldest of these tombs may date back more than 7,000 years to early Stone Age times, making this the oldest and largest prehistoric burial site in Ireland. Over centuries many of the tombs have been robbed of their stone; others were dug into out of curiosity or in hopes of unearthing buried treasure, but around 30 are still easily identifiable. Some are not much more than a pile of stones, but others retain their doorways and side walling, and are complete enough to crawl inside. The dates of burial items recovered from the graves span 3,000 years and include flint arrowheads, stone tools, ornaments of bone and the remains of human bones burned in cremation. A little way to the north Creevykeel court tomb is signposted off the N15 at Cliffony, 22km (14 miles) north of Sligo. In contrast to the older and cruder Carrowmore tombs, this structure of 3,000–2,000BC is a sophisticated mound with several chambers.

CÉIDE FIELDS

347 C3 Visitor Centre, off R314 east of Ballycastle, Co. Mayo, tel 096 43325; mid-Mar to end Nov €3.50

Céide Fields Visitor Centre has been carefully designed in a pleasing pyramid shape to blend with the landscape. An excellent display explains how climate change and forest clearance around 3,000–2,000BC allowed blanket bog to creep in and smother a Stone Age agricultural landscape. A guided tour across the bog shows the excavations, which have revealed walls of massive stones built in straight lines by those primitive farmers.

CLARE ISLAND

346 B4 Tourist Information Office, James Street, Westport, Co. Mayo, tel 098 25711; Jul–end Oct daily 9–6; Nov–end Jun Mon–Fri 9–6, Sat 10–2 Ferry (tel 098 26307 or 25045) from Roonagh Pier, 11km (7 miles) west of Westport, Co. Mayo www.anu.ie/clareisland

Clare Island's humped green shape lies at the mouth of Clew Bay. The gaunt old castle at the harbour was the chief stronghold of the 16th-century pirate queen Grace O'Malley or Granuaile—who probably lies buried in the ruined abbey on the island's south coast road. The climb to the Knockmore summit (461m/1,512ft) is rewarded by the view over Clew Bay. If you stay overnight in summer, be warned that the island's farmers and fishermen work till the light fades, so the pub often doesn't open until midnight.

CLIFFS OF MOHER

350 C6 Cliffs of Moher Tourist Information Office, Liscannor, Co. Clare, tel 065 708 1171; Jun–end Sep Bus from Lahinch

A towering layer-cake of shale, sandstone and silt form a great rampart 208m (682ft) high, facing Galway Bay. In summer they are generally crowded with visitors, here for the superb views of the Aran Islands and along the Clare coastline for 48km (30 miles) southwest to Loop Head. A word of warning: The cliff edge is unguarded, so take great care, especially in windy weather.

In 1835 Sir Cornelius O'Brien, the local member of parliament, built the tower that stands on the cliffs. On a clear day, you may see the mountains of County Kerry to the southwest and Connemara's Twelve Bens to the northeast from the roof of O'Brien's Tower.

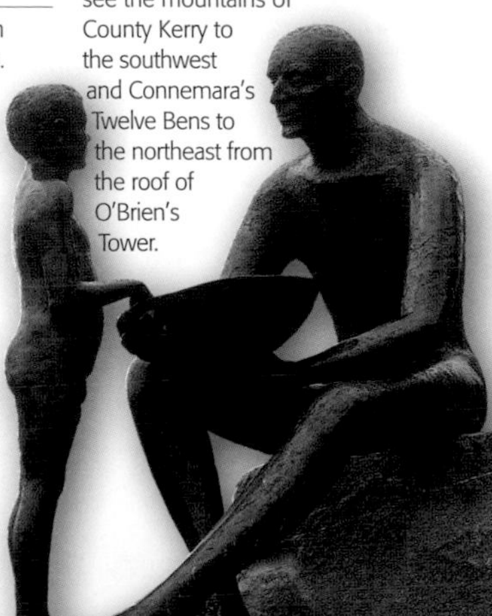

Father and son statue in Carrick-on-Shannon

The Burren

This extraordinary landscape of naked limestone domes has the finest display of spring and summer wild flowers in Ireland. Ancient churches and castles stand alongside friendly pubs given to superb sessions of traditional music.

SEEING THE BURREN

The Burren rises as a cluster of grey domed hills in the northwest corner of County Clare with terraced sides whose western feet slope to the sea at Galway Bay. Villages are scattered round the fringes: Ballyvaughan on the north coast, Doolin and Lisdoonvarna to the west, Kilfenora with its Burren Visitor Centre in the south, connected by the R477 coast road and the R476 and R480. One main road, the N67, crosses the interior from Ballyvaughan to Lisdoonvarna. There are no settlements here, but this is where many of the most interesting historical sites are found. The 'Folding Landscape' map of The Burren, available locally, is invaluable.

RATINGS	
Cultural interest	●●●●
Outdoor pursuits	●●●
Photo stops	●●●●

BASICS

351 C6

Burren Centre, Kilfenora, Co. Clare, tel 065 708 8030; Jun–end Aug daily 9.30–6; Mar–end May, Sep–end Oct 10–5; Nov–end Apr by appointment

www.theburrencentre.ie
A stylish, easy-to-navigate site, with good information about The Burren Centre and the area's unusual plant life.

The seemingly bleak Burren is incredibly rich in plant life (top)

Prehistoric dolmens are scattered across The Burren (above)

HIGHLIGHTS

WILD FLOWERS

The Burren supports Ireland's richest flora. In spring you'll find the royal blue trumpets of spring gentians and the sulphur-yellow of primroses; in summer the hills flush crimson with bloody cranesbill and are spotted white with eyebright. Orchids of many kinds grow here: spotted, early purple, marsh, bee, butterfly and frog orchids.

Plants that wouldn't normally be found within a thousand miles of each other grow contentedly in neighbouring cracks and hollows in the limestone pavements and on the hill slopes: northern species such as mountain avens, southerners such as the bright yellow hoary rockrose; alpine saxifrages flourish down at sea level; woodland ivies and violets thrive in this treeless place.

VILLAGES AND MUSIC

The Burren villages are great places for traditional music, for which County Clare is famous. Ballyvaughan on Galway Bay is the 'capital' of the north Burren, and Monk's Bar (tel 065 707 7059) is the place for music here (traditional Thursday, pop Saturday). South across the hills lies Kilfenora where you can get an overview of the flora, geology and history of the region in the Burren Centre, and find great music in Linnane's (tel 065 708 8157) and Vaughan's (tel 065 708 8004). On the coast to the west, Doolin is the best-known village for music in Ireland; you'll find tunes in McDermott's (tel 065 707 4700) and McGann's (tel 065 707 4133) by the bridge, and lively songs in O'Connor's (tel 065 707 4168) down the lane. Near Doolin, Lisdoonvarna is Ireland's only spa whose waters are still drunk for medicinal purposes. Nowadays the village is known for its Matchmaking Festival each September (tel 065 707 4005 or 065 707 40442), when lonely and not so lonely hearts get together. Try the Roadside Tavern (tel 065 707 4084) for live music.

ARCHAEOLOGICAL AND HISTORICAL SITES

The middle of The Burren is deserted today, but evidence of former human settlement is plentiful. Two impressive Stone Age tombs stand beside the R480 Ballyvaughan to Corofin road: Poulnabrone portal dolmen (c4,000BC), a square stone chamber topped by a huge capstone, and the nearby Gleninsheen wedge tomb (c2,500BC). Later Burren settlers built stone ring forts: Two excellent examples are Caherballykinvarga just east of Kilfenora, still standing up to 4.5m (15ft) high in places, and the poignant ruin of Cahermacnaghten, beside the Ballyvaughan to Kilfenora road.

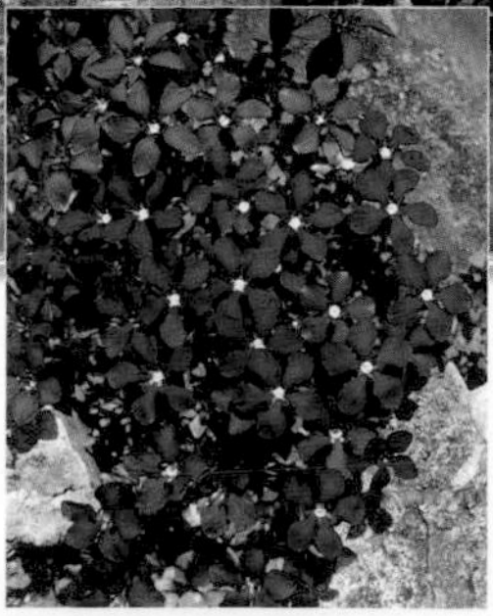

The Burren is rich in ruins: There is fine stonework at Corcomroe Abbey to the east of Ballyvaughan; four heavily carved 12th-century High Crosses stand outside the roofless Kilfenora Cathedral; and there is another further south near Dysert O'Dea church. Towers and fortified houses of note include Newtown Castle (just southwest of Ballyvaughan; tel 065 707 7200; open daily 9–5, call to check Nov–end Dec), and Leamaneh Castle east of Kilfenora (not open to public, but visible from the road).

AILLWEE CAVE

South of Ballyvaughan off R480 · 065 707 7036 · Jul, Aug daily 10–6.30, Jan–end Jun, Sep–end Nov 10–5.30; Dec by appointment · Adult €8.50, child €4.50

This show cave leads you into the subterranean world of The Burren, a honeycomb of caverns and passages eaten out of the rock by the chemical action and the friction of rainwater on limestone. You'll see stalactites and stalagmites, sheets of glittering calcite, open caverns of church-like size, and a rushing underground waterfall.

THE BURREN WAY

This is one of Ireland's official 'Waymarked Ways', a walk that runs for 35km (22 miles) from Ballyvaughan southwest through the heart of The Burren. Old country roads, tracks and walled *boreens* take you across the hills and valleys to Doolin. From here a delightful coastal path leads to the Cliffs of Moher (▷ 133). A map guide based on the 'Folding Landscape' of The Burren is available locally.

BACKGROUND

The porous, almost waterless limestone of The Burren, scraped smooth by glaciers, has never provided easy living conditions for humans, although it makes an ideal bedrock for plant life. By the mid-17th century General Ludlow was reporting to Oliver Cromwell that The Burren possessed 'not any tree to hang a man, nor enough water to drown him, nor enough earth to bury him.' Cattle herding still takes place, though, keeping the scrub down and aiding growth of wild flowers. Tourism is an ever stronger factor in the local economy, as more people discover the flowers, the music and the lonely beauty of these hills.

TIPS

- **A flower book and a small hand lens will increase your enjoyment of the wild flowers.**
- **Wear walking shoes and watch your step when exploring The Burren's limestone pavement—loose chunks can be ankle-breakingly wobbly underfoot.**
- **Traditional music sessions tend to start around 9.30pm. In summer get to the pub at least an hour beforehand if you want a seat anywhere near the musicians. If you want to join in, just ask—but be sure you can play to a high enough standard not to spoil the tune.**

Walking the limestone plateau (top).
Spring gentian (middle).
A traditional pub music session (bottom)

The ornate doorway of the ancient abbey of Cong

Main Street, Cong, and the Quiet Man coffee shop

CLONFERT CATHEDRAL

352 E5 • Clonfert, Co. Galway Tourist Information Office, Keller Travel, Bridge Street, Ballinasloe, Co. Galway, tel 0909 642604; Jun–end Oct Tue–Sat 10–5.30, but call to confirm Signposted off R356 Banagher–Eyrecourt road

The first impression of Clonfert Cathedral is that it is small, but it is an architectural gem with some masterful stonework. The site was originally occupied by a monastery founded in AD563 by St. Brendan the Navigator, the putative discoverer of America. The Cathedral of St. Brendan was built around 1160 and later additions include a 13th-century chancel with delicate lancet windows, and a 15th-century tower.

St. Brendan's monastery was burned by Vikings three times during the 12th century and rebuilt by the monks, but was finally destroyed in 1541. A 1900s restoration accounts for its excellent state of repair and continued use for worship. **Don't miss** The frame of the west door is a riot of staring heads, animal grotesques, floral and geometric carving.

CONG

347 C4 Tourist Information Office, Abbey Street, Cong, Co. Mayo, tel 0949 546542; Jul, Aug daily 9.30–7; mid-Mar to end Jun, Sep–end Nov daily 10–6. Closed Dec to mid-Mar On R345 Clonbur–Headford road

Most visitors come to Cong to see the famous abbey, but the village of stone houses and waterways, between loughs Corrib and Mask, is a delightful place—so much so that this is where John Ford shot most of his celebrated 1952 film *The Quiet Man*, with John Wayne and flame-haired Maureen O'Hara. The thatched Quiet Man Heritage Cottage on Circular Road (tel 092 46089; open Jun–end Oct daily) has a display on the archaeology and history of the area. You can also follow a dry canal dug as a relief project during the Great Famine of 1845–49. It was intended to connect the two lakes, but the limestone is so porous that it never held water.

Cong Abbey (open daily) consists of a range of 12th-century grey limestone buildings with elaborately carved pillars. Beside the river is the monks' fishing house—when a fish entered the net, it would cause a bell to ring in the monastery kitchen.

CONNEMARA

See pages 138–141.

COOLE PARK

351 D5 • Co. Galway 091 631804 Visitor Centre Jun–end Aug daily 10–6; Apr–end May, Sep 10–5 Adult €2.75 child (6–18) €1.25, family €7 Signposted off N18, 2km (1.2 miles) northeast of Gort

Lady Augusta Gregory (1852–1932), patron of the Irish literary revival of the late 19th and early 20th centuries, entertained writers and artists at Coole. The house was demolished in 1941, but the wooded grounds and 'glittering reaches of the flooded lake'—as W. B. Yeats wrote in *Coole Park and Ballylee* (1931) —now form a forest park. **Don't miss** The Autograph Tree (a lovely copper beech) bears the signatures of many literary and artistic lions of the past.

CRAGGAUNOWEN PROJECT

351 D6 • Quin, Co. Clare 061 360788 Apr–end Sep daily 10–6 Adult €7.50, child (under 12) €4.50 6km (4 miles) southeast of Quin

Craggaunowen is one of the best 'step-into-the-past' open-air sites in Ireland. It's all too easy to gain a mistily romantic notion of life in pre-Christian Celtic Ireland, but at Craggaunowen, costumed guides interpret the realities of the fifth and sixth centuries in the re-created buildings here. Exhibits include a fenced dwelling built on a *crannóg* or artificial island in a lake, a ringfort with a round rampart of earth protecting a huddle of cylindrical thatched huts, a *fulacht fiadh* or cooking pit for boiling meat over fire-heated stones, and a length of planking road that crossed the bog some 2,000 years ago. You can also see the leather-hulled currach *Brendan*, which explorer Tim Severin built and sailed to Newfoundland in 1976–77 to substantiate the claim that St. Brendan once made the journey. Look for the patched-up hole that an iceberg tore in her side.

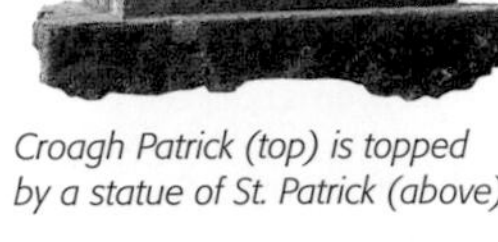
Croagh Patrick (top) is topped by a statue of St. Patrick (above)

CROAGH PATRICK

346 C4 Tourist Information Office, James Street, Westport, Co. Mayo tel 098 25711; Jul, Aug daily 9–6; May–end Jun, Sep–end Oct Mon–Sat 9–5.45; Nov–end Apr Mon–Fri 9–5.45, Sat 10–1 Off R335 at Murrisk, 8km (5 miles) west of Westport

In AD432 St. Patrick preached at the summit of Croagh Patrick and

The simple gravestone of W. B. Yeats in Drumcliff churchyard

banished all the snakes from Ireland. The cone-shaped peak that overlooks Clew Bay is Ireland's holy mountain (▷ 342), with a steepish path up from Campbell's Bar in Murrisk to a saddle at 450m (1,475ft), then a knee-cracking scramble up a very steep boulder slide to the summit chapel at 762m (2,500ft). The reward is a superb view.

DRUMCLIFF

347 D3 Tourist Information Office, Aras Reddan, Temple Street, Sligo, Co. Sligo, tel 071 916 1201; Mon–Fri 9–5, Sat 10–2

It was near Drumcliff in AD561 that St. Columba's kinsmen killed 3,000 followers of St. Finian in the notorious 'Battle of the Book'. The grey Protestant church of Drumcliff is dedicated to St. Columba, who founded a monastery here. The main attraction at Drumcliff, though, is the grave of W. B. Yeats in the churchyard, with a plain limestone headstone bearing his self-penned epitaph:

Cast a cold Eye
On Life, on Death.
Horseman, pass by!

ENNIS

351 C6 Arthur's Row, Ennis, Co. Clare, tel 065 682 8366; Jun–end Sep daily 9.30–5.30; Apr, May, Oct–end Dec Mon–Sat 9.30–5.30; Jan–end Mar Mon–Fri 9.30–5.30 Ennis www.shannonregiontourism.ie

Ennis, county town of Clare, is the bustling heart of commercial and social life for a wide rural region, with old-fashioned shop-fronts lining the streets. In the town, a column remembers Daniel O'Connell (1775–1847), who swept to Parliament in 1828 after a mass meeting in Ennis. The ruined Franciscan friary on Clare Road (tel 065 28366; May–end Sep) contains the Creagh tomb.

Donegal Craft Village is home to a number of talented artisans

DONEGAL

A fine castle looms over the small town of Donegal, known also for great music and a good railway museum.

348 E2 Donegal Tourist Information Office, The Quay, Donegal, Co. Donegal, tel 074 972 1148; Jul, Aug Mon–Sat 9–6, Sun 9–2; Sep–end Jun Mon–Fri 9–5 www.irelandnorthwest.ie

RATINGS	
Cultural interest	●●●
Historic interest	●●●
Specialist shopping	●●●
Walkability	●●●

TIP

- **After your walk, try a little retail therapy on The Diamond: Magee's (tel 074 972 2660) and The Sweater Shop (tel 074 972 2777) both specialize in Donegal handmade tweeds and woollens.**

Although it's the county town, Donegal is a modest little place with attractively small-scale streets overshadowed by the gabled walls and turrets of Donegal Castle. The town in its present form was laid out in the early 17th century around a central square known, as in many of the northerly Irish towns, as 'The Diamond'. Looming up on its rocky knoll behind The Diamond is Donegal Castle, a great Jacobean mansion. It was built in 1623 on what remained of a 15th-century fortress of the O'Donnell clan, who demolished it late in the 16th century rather than let it fall into the hands of the English. In 1601 'Red Hugh' O'Donnell also caused the ruin of Donegal Friary while besieging his cousin Niall Garbh, who was holed up inside with some English allies. The bombardment ignited barrels of English gunpowder.

A STROLL THROUGH TOWN

The best way to enjoy Donegal town is to stroll around with a copy of the Town Trail from the Tourist Office. You can tour the castle (Tirchonaill Street; tel 074 22405; Mar–end Oct daily), which is furnished in mid-17th-century style. Wandering through the ruins of the friary, 1.5km (1 mile) south by the River Eske, try to picture the learned Michael O'Clery and his assistants Peregrine O'Clery, Peregrine O'Duignean and Fearfeasa O'Maolconry laboriously compiling their 'Annals of the Four Masters'. This wonderful document (copies can be seen in the National Library in Dublin) is a vivid history of the island from 2958BC (40 years before Noah's Flood) until AD1616. The Donegal Railway Heritage Centre (Tirchonaill Street, tel 074 972 2655; daily 9–5) recalls a now defunct scenic local line, with a simulator and rail exhibits.

Memorial to the four writers of the Annals

Connemara

Connemara has some of the finest, wildest scenery in the west of Ireland and wonderful white sand beaches. Sturdy Connemara ponies roam the moorland and there's exciting but easily managed mountain walking in the Twelve Bens.

A typical Connemara scene, near Roundstone, with Mount Errisbeg as a distant backdrop

SEEING CONNEMARA

Connemara is the westernmost part of County Galway, between the great Lough Corrib in the east and the ragged, wild Atlantic on the west. In the north, it slopes to the narrow fiord of Killary Harbour, while the southern border is formed by Galway Bay. The heart of Connemara is a vast stretch of lonely bog, broken by the dramatic rise of twin mountain ranges—the Maumturks to the east, and the Twelve Bens farther west. The N59 runs west from Galway City through the Connemara heartland, bordering the wild, lonely and beautiful area known as Iar-Connacht, the 'back of Connacht' on its way to Clifden, the region's 'capital' and sole town of any size. Then it bends back through northern Connemara. Buses are few, trains non-existent. The narrow winding roads are good for slow drivers, excellent for bicyclists, and best of all for walkers.

RATINGS

Good for kids	●●●●
Historic interest	●●●
Outdoor pursuits	●●●●●
Photo stops	●●●●●

BASICS

346 B5/C5

Connemara Tourism, The Square, Clifden, Co. Galway, tel 095 22622, Jul–end Sep daily 9–6; Oct–end May Mon–Fri 9–5.45, Sat 9–12.45

www.connamara-tourism.org
Good information on the whole area.

TIPS

- Book early if you want to stay in Clifden when the Connemara Pony Show is on (mid-Aug), as the event attracts big crowds.
- The south coast route from Galway to Clifden is slower but far more scenic than the fast N59.

HIGHLIGHTS

CLIFDEN

346 B4 Clifden Tourist Information Office, Galway Road, Clifden, Co. Galway, tel 095 21163; Jul, Aug Mon–Fri 9.30–6, Sat–Sun 10–5.45; Sep–end Jun Mon–Fri 10–6, Sat 10–5.30; www.westireland.travel.ie

The only town in Connemara, Clifden has everything you could want from banks, supermarkets and music pubs to the excellent Connemara Walking Centre (Island House, Market Street, Clifden; tel 095 21379) which will help with guided and solo walks. Its focus is the town square and twin thoroughfares of Main and Market streets, teeming with visitors in summer. The town comes fully alive in mid-August when it hosts the Connemara Pony Show (▷ Tips).

KYLEMORE ABBEY

Kylemore Abbey Visitor Centre and Walled Garden, Kylemore, Connemara, Co Galway, tel 095 41146 Adult €10, child (12–16) €6.50; www.kylemoreabbey.com

Kylemore Abbey, grey and impressive, dominates Pollacappul Lough just east of Letterfrack. The house was built as a grand Gothic country seat in the 1860s by Manchester businessman Mitchell Henry, and in the late 19th century was the heart of a 5,600ha (13,850-acre) estate. After World War I it became a convent of Belgian nuns whose own convent was destroyed during the first Battle of Ypres. They run a school here now, so it's not open to the public, but the beautiful Walled Garden is a major attraction.

ROUNDSTONE

346 B5 Clifden Tourist Information Office (▷ above); www.westireland.travel.ie

On the shores of Bertraghboy Bay, Roundstone has a diminutive harbour and a scatter of pubs and small shops.

Robust little Connemara ponies (left). Clifden, the capital of Connemara, with the Twelve Bens beyond (opposite, main). Ballyconneely beach (inset left). Live music in E. J. King's, Clifden (inset middle). Kylemore Abbey (inset right)

ROMANTIC ROADS

The beautiful switchback road that runs west out of Clifden to encircle the Kingstown Peninsula is called the Sky Road, while the drunkenly twisting and bumping road between Ballyconneely and Roundstone is known as the Brandy and Soda Road. Another, built between Cashel and Rosmuck as a famine relief measure using turf and grass, is *Bóthar na Scrathóg*, the road of the top-sods.

Peat cutter at work near Costelloe, in Connemara (above). Cross-leaved heath is a typical bogland plant (right)

MORE TO SEE

PADRAIG PEARSE'S COTTAGE

✉ Turlough, Gortmore, Rosmuck, Co. Galway, signposted from R340 ☎ 091 574 4292 🕒 End May–end Sep daily 10–6 💰 Adult €1.50, child 75 cents, family €4.25

On the shores of Lough Oiriúlach near Gortmore stands the thatched, whitewashed cottage built by poet, teacher and ardent nationalist Padraig Pearse in 1903–04, now a national monument. In these small, simply furnished rooms, and out in the rocky countryside round about, Pearse perfected his Gaelic, taught students from Dublin, and formulated his ideas for Irish national independence. It was he who proclaimed the infant Irish Republic from the steps of Dublin's GPO (▷ 72–73) on Easter Monday 1916. A few days later Pearse was shot as a traitor in Kilmainham Gaol (▷ 76–77).

Beside O'Dowd's bar a track leads to the summit of Errisbeg, the hill that rises 300m (985ft) behind the village.

Roundstone Musical Instruments (IDA Craft Centre, Roundstone, tel 095-35875, Jul, Aug daily 9–7, May, Jun, Sep, Oct daily 9.30–6, Nov–end Apr Mon–Sat 9.30–6) is based on the workshop of Malachy Kearns, Ireland's master maker of *bodhrán*, the drums that power Irish traditional music.

TWELVE BENS, THE MAUMTURKS AND THE INAGH VALLEY

Much of the drama and beauty of Connemara derives from the mountain ranges that rise from the central bogs of the region: the amorphous mass of the Maumturks, and on their western flank the more shapely peaks of the Twelve Bens. Guided walks in the mountains, including the ascent of Benbaun (at 729m/2,392ft the highest of the Twelve Bens), are offered by Connemara Walking Centre (▷ 138, Clifden) and the Connemara National Park Visitor Centre (▷ 141); you can also climb 438m (1,437ft) Diamond Hill by a waymarked track. Bisecting the Twelve Bens/Maumturks massif is the outstandingly beautiful Inagh Valley with its long lake. The N59 road encircles the mountains, while the R344 runs through the Inagh Valley.

CAUSEWAY ISLANDS

ℹ Galway Tourist Information Office, Aras Fáilte, Forster Street, Galway, Co. Galway, tel 091 537700; Jun–end Sep daily 9–5.45; Apr–end May Mon–Sat 9–5.45; Jan–end Mar, Oct–end Dec Mon–Fri 9–5.45, Sat 9–12.45; **www.irelandwest.ie**

At Costelloe (Casla) on the R336 Galway City–Maam Cross road, a left turn goes west across the islands of Lettermore, Gorumna and Lettermullan. They are linked by causeways that were built as part of a famine relief scheme. Well off the beaten tourist track, these Irish-speaking islands have thatched cottages, sprawling villages and tiny stone-walled fields in a windswept, weatherbeaten landscape scabbed with huge granite outcrops.

NORTHERN CONNEMARA

ℹ Clifden Tourist Information Office (▷ 138)

The N59 runs from Clifden to Leenane through northern Connemara, with side roads leading north to a beautiful coast of deeply indented bays. Letterfrack, a neat little 19th-century village built by Quakers, is home to the Connemara National Park Visitor Centre (▷ 141). North of Letterfrack there are some superb white sand beaches, Rusheenduff and Glassillaun being especially striking. Out at Renvyle Point, the Renvyle House Hotel was formerly the country retreat of Dublin surgeon and man of letters Oliver St. John Gogarty ('Buck Mulligan' in James Joyce's *Ulysses*) who entertained W. B. Yeats, George Bernard Shaw and other luminaries of the Irish literary revival in the late 19th century.

INISHBOFIN

ℹ Clifden Tourist Information Office (▷ 138) ⛴ Inishbofin Ferry Service from Cleggan, tel 095 45903/44750 💰 Adult €15 return, child (5–12) €8 www.inishbofin.com

Inishbofin lies some 5km (3 miles) north of Aughrus Point, some 45 minutes by ferry from the fishing village of Cleggan, and has a population of just 200. The islanders are very welcoming, and the pace of life here is easy. Inishbofin is ideal for exploring on foot, and is particularly attractive to birdwatchers for its huge population of seabirds. The best guidebook is *Inis Bó Finne/Inishbofin, A Guide to the National History and Archaeology* by David Hogan and Michael Gibbons (available on the island or from Connemara Walking Centre at Clifden, ▷ 138). Sites include a Heritage Centre at the pier, a star-shaped Cromwellian fort built in 1656 to house Catholic gentry condemned to transportation, and the ruins of a 14th-century church on the site of the seventh-century monastery of the hermit St. Colman.

Dawn breaks over Lough Corrib, near Oughterard

CONNEMARA NATIONAL PARK

346 B4 Connemara National Park Visitor Centre, Letterfrack, Co. Galway, tel 095 41054; Jun–end Aug daily 9.30–6.30, Mar–end May, Sep–end Oct 10–5.30 Adult €3, child €1.30, family €5

Around 3,000ha (7,400 acres) of blanket bog and four of the Twelve Ben peaks are protected as the Connemara National Park. Bird life and flora are rich and varied, red deer have been reintroduced and a herd of wild Connemara ponies established. The Visitor Centre in Letterfrack offers an audio-visual display introducing the Connemara National Park, and gives information about guided walks, self-guided nature trails, pony trekking and other activities.

ALCOCK AND BROWN MONUMENT

Ballinaboy, signposted from R341, 3.5km (2 miles) south of Clifden
Open access

Two signposted routes lead from the crossroads on the R341. A right turn brings you to the Alcock and Brown monument, a tall splinter of dark stone silhouetted on a hillside between Mannin Bay and Ardbear Bay, with wonderful views over west Connemara. The memorial commemorates Sir John Alcock and Sir Arthur Whitten Brown, who accomplished the first non-stop transatlantic flight in June 1919. The rough road on the left from the crossroads (better walked than driven) leads in 1.5km (1 mile) to the site where they landed their Vickers Vimy bomber plane nose-down in Derrygimlagh bog.

BACKGROUND

Connemara is the most romantic place-name in Ireland, one that evokes images of steep mountains, ragged coasts, turf cutters, horse and donkey carts, fishermen in black curragh canoes—a landscape for poets, artists and dreamers that's wildly, extravagantly beautiful. But the poor soil, stony bogs, harsh mountains and rocky coasts reveal that this has always been a poor region. Many of the long, straight bog roads, the lonely jetties and causeways were built as famine relief works in the 19th and early 20th centuries. As a result of geographical and cultural isolation in the past, much of Connemara is a Gaeltacht or Irish-speaking region. People still struggle to make a living, and tourism (of a more or less 'green' variety) is a cornerstone of the local economy.

MORE TO SEE

BEACHES OF THE WEST

Western Connemara is famed for its wonderful white sand beaches. Among the best are those at Ardmore (R340 between Kilkieran and Carna); Gorteen Bay and Dog's Bay (R341 just west of Roundstone); around Ballyconneely at Creggoduff (Connemara Golf Club) and Mannin; between Claddaghduff and Omey Island; and northern Connemara (Renvyle Point, Rusheenduff and Glassillaun).

OMEY ISLAND

Opposite Claddaghduff, 3km (2 miles) southwest of Cleggan
Clifden (▷ 138)

Around 20 people live on Omey, accessible by a 1km (0.5-mile) causeway at low tide (tide information is available from the Connemara Walking Centre in Clifden or ask at Sweeney's pub, Claddaghduff, tel 095 44345). You can walk a circuit of 8km (5 miles) around the island, or just explore at will. Mainlanders have been buried here since pre-Christian times and there's a large graveyard where the causeway reaches the island. There are also remains of a medieval church and a holy well.

GALWAY

The liveliest city in the west of Ireland, Galway has a galaxy of historic buildings with elaborate stone-carved embellishments, and claims the famous Claddagh Ring, a must-have for all true lovers.

Galway is a great city to explore on foot. Kennedy Park with its benches, flower-beds and shrubberies is at the heart of Eyre Square, and from here Galway's chief thoroughfare runs south through the middle of the city.

Medieval Galway enjoyed great prosperity through trade, not only with the rest of Ireland, but also with Spain and with other continental countries. It all came to an end after the city was attacked by Oliver Cromwell in 1652, and again by King William III in 1691, but you can see evidence of this former wealth in embellishments to ancient doorways, window frames and walls. Rich merchants would employ the best stone-carvers to adorn their town houses with their coats of arms, and with grotesque sculptures and heraldic beasts. Lynch's Castle, an impressive 15th-century tower house (now a bank; ground-level display open during business hours) at the junction known as the Four Corners where William Street becomes Shop Street, is especially well provided with sculptures, as is the Collegiate Church of St. Nicholas in Church Lane (always open) with its graveslabs adorned with bas-reliefs showing the tools of the trade followed by the departed.

MEMORIALS AND MUSEUMS

Behind Lynch's Castle on Market Street, a 17th-century window is preserved to mark the spot where in 1493 Mayor James Lynch Fitzstephen personally hanged his own son Walter for murdering a visiting Spaniard. Across the street you'll find No. 8 Bowling Green, the home of Nora Barnacle before she eloped with James Joyce in 1904. It is now the Nora Barnacle House Museum (tel 091 564743; mid-May to mid-Sep Mon–Sat 10–5).

On Quay Street nearer the River Corrib you'll find Thomas Dillon's Claddagh Gold jewellery shop (tel 091 566365) where you can browse through a small museum and learn the story of the Claddagh Ring, Galway's world-famous love token. Just round the corner in the Tudor-era Spanish Arch is Galway City Museum (tel 091 567641; Apr–end Oct), a fascinatingly unfocused collection of mementoes from ancient fishing tools and traps for badgers to the orations of heroes and the pikestaffs of rebels.

RATINGS

Historic interest	●●●
Specialist shopping	●●●
Walkability	●●●

BASICS

351 C5

Tourist Information Office, Aras Fáilte, Forster Street, Galway, Co. Galway, tel 091 537700; Jul–end Sep daily 9–6; Oct–end May Mon–Fri 9–5.45, Sat 9–12.45

Galway

www.irelandwest.ie
Full details of everything you need to know about Galway and the region.

TIPS

- If you're going to be in the city in the last two weeks of July (Arts Festival) or the first week in August (Galway Races), reserve accommodation well in advance.
- For traditional music, try Taaffes in Shop Street, Roisin Dubh in Upper Dominick Street or The Crane, across the river in Sea Road, where they often have Irish set dancing in the upstairs room (visitors are welcome to join in).

Every September Galway plays host to an Oyster Festival (top). Galway's streets are lined by bright frontages (above)

The Slieve League cliffs are simply breathtaking

Rocky Malin Head is the most northerly point in Ireland

The lush pastures of Leenane as seen in the movie The Field

GLENCOLUMBKILLE AND SLIEVE LEAGUE

347 D2 Donegal Tourist Information Office, Quay Street, Donegal, Co. Donegal, tel 074 972 1148; Jun–end Sep Mon–Sat 9–6; Oct–end May Mon–Fri 10–6 or 9–5 (closed for lunch) On R263, west of Killybegs. Slieve League signposted 'Teelin Pier' from Carrick, then 'Bunglass: The Cliffs'

Seen from the little parking bay high on a windy ledge at Bunglass, the Slieve League cliffs are hugely impressive—a great wall of multihued rock that plunges 595m (1,952ft) into the sea below, claiming the title of 'highest sea cliffs in Europe'. Walkers with a good head for heights can teeter along the very narrow 'One Man's Path' to the summit of Slieve League, but definitely not in windy conditions or when the ground is slippery.

There's something special about the atmosphere in Glencolumbkille, tucked away in a hidden cleft among these remote seaward mountains 10km (6 miles) along the R263 from Carrick. This peaceful green valley is where St. Columba (born in Donegal in AD521) established a monastery. There's a Folk Village Museum with traditionally built and furnished thatched homes (tel 074 973 0017; Easter–end Sep daily, Oct Mon–Fri). Walkers can follow *An Turas Cholmcille*, Columba's Journey, for 5km (3 miles) round 15 stations or sacred sites composed of standing stones, prehistoric tombs and incised crosses, to reach St. Columba's Chapel, Bed and Well.

GLENVEAGH NATIONAL PARK

348 E1 • Glenveagh National Park Visitor Centre, Co. Donegal, tel 074 913 7090; mid-Mar to mid-Nov, daily; Glenveagh Castle and gardens, tel 074 913 7262; mid-Mar to early Nov, daily 10–6; castle interior by tour only Adult €4.75, child (6–18) €2.25 Signposted on the R251 Gweedore–Letterkenny road, 16km (10 miles) east of Dunlewy

Queen Victoria had popularized 'Scottish Baronial' style when John George Adair built Glenveagh Castle in 1870–73. Adair, a harsh, evicting landlord, bought a vast area of Donegal and chose the most scenic spot for his granite castle and its gardens and grounds, looking across Lough Beagh to the rugged backbone of the Derryveagh Mountains. Adair's American wife Cornelia introduced the rhododendrons that now flower so vividly here in early summer. Later owner Henry McIlhenny improved and landscaped the gardens, so that today's visitor, after a tour of the smart but comfortable rooms of the castle, can stroll through a judicious blend of native and exotic plants and trees. **Don't miss** Out in the wider National Park there are superb walks (▷ 250–251); family-friendly and more demanding. Keep binoculars handy in case you spot one of the large herd of red deer that roam through the 9,600ha (23,720 acres).

INISHOWEN

348 F1 Letterkenny Tourist Information, Blaney Road, Letterkenny, Co. Donegal, tel 074 912 1160; Jul, Aug Mon–Fri 9–6, weekends variable hours; Sep–end Jun Mon–Fri 9–5

The diamond-shaped Inishowen Peninsula stretches north from Derry city, flanked on the east by Lough Foyle and on the west by Lough Swilly. Many visitors make the long journey up through Inishowen for the sake of standing on Malin Head, the most northerly point of Ireland and a place that sets the tone of wildness and the prevailing view of mountain, moor and rugged coastline. Inishowen is a remote and underpopulated region of Donegal, and once you get down to west-facing beaches such as White Strand Bay (Malin Head), Pollan Bay (Doagh Isle), Tullagh Bay (Clonmany) and Crummie's Bay (Dunree Head) you're likely to have them to yourself. The tremendous White Strand, which runs for 5km (3 miles) south from Buncrana, is better-known and more frequented. Doagh Island, in reality a peninsula to the south of Malin Head, is rich in sand dunes covered in wonderful wild flowers in summer, and has the ruin of 16th-century Carnickabraghy Castle at its edge. Birdwatchers may spot waders at Trawbreaga Bay and on the mudflats around Inch Island.

The 3,700-year-old circular stone fort of Grianan of Aileach (off N13, 5km/3 miles west of Derry) was a stronghold of the O'Neill Kings of Ulster. Stone steps climb to the top of the 5.5m (18ft) walls for a fabulous view over loughs Swilly and Foyle.

KILLARY HARBOUR

346 B4 Tourist Information Office, Galway (▷ 142) www.irelandwest.ie

Killary Harbour, lying between counties Galway and Mayo, forms the northern boundary of Connemara. The fiord-like inlet is 45m (150ft) deep, and mountains rise dramatically on both sides—south the 550m (1,800ft) bulk of the Maumturks; north the flanks of Mweelrea (819m/2,687ft) and Ben Gorm (750m/2,460ft). At the eastern or inland end lies Leenane, huddled under the mountains; here the Leenane Sheep and Wool Museum (tel 095 2323/42231; Apr–end Oct daily 9.30–6) displays spinning and dyeing techniques and provides information on rare breeds.

Amid the ruins, the round tower at Kilmacduagh points skyward

A fishing boat pulled up on the shore of Lough Gill, where larger craft take visitors to see Yeats's Lake Isle of Innisfree

KILMACDUAGH MONASTIC SITE

351 D6 • Co. Clare Aras Fáilte, Forster Street, Galway, Co. Galway, tel 091-537700 (▷ 142) On the R460 Gort–Corofin road, 5km (3 miles) southwest of Gort
www.irelandwest.ie

Kilmacduagh monastic site, founded around AD610 by St. Colman MacDuagh, stands against a backdrop of the domed limestone hills of The Burren across the border in County Clare. The impression is of a close-knit community of buildings, which reflect a thousand years of Christian occupation of Kilmacduagh, despite Viking attacks in the ninth and tenth centuries. The most striking feature today is the 11th-century round tower, 34m (111ft) tall, which leans noticeably out of true. The roofless cathedral nearby predates the coming of the Normans to Ireland, though it was rebuilt in graceful Gothic style in the 14th century. Nearby is the Abbot's House or Bishop's Castle, a two-floor, square block of a fortified tower house. Also on the site are O'Hyne's Abbey, founded in the 10th century, and St. John's Oratory, a lovely little building that might date back to St. Colman's time.

KILRUSH

350 C6 Kilrush Tourist Information Office, Francis Street, The Square, Kilrush, Co. Clare, tel 065 905 1577; Jun–end Sep daily 10–1, 2–6
www.shannonregiontourism.ie

There's an attractive Georgian air to Kilrush, a laid-back little town near the mouth of the Shannon Estuary. Kilrush looks seaward for its livelihood and entertainment: The marina contains 120 berths. On Merchant's Quay you'll find the Scattery Island Centre (tel 065 905 2139; mid-Jun to mid-Sep daily 10–6) with an exhibition about the monastic site on Scattery Island 1.5km (1 mile) from Kilrush. At the centre you can book a boat ride to the island, where a fine round tower stands 33m (108ft) high and the remains of several medieval churches mark the site of St. Senan's monastery. Other attractions of Kilrush are its horse fairs in June, October and November, and the beautiful Vandeleur Walled Garden (tel 065 905 1760/1047) which is being restored.

Don't miss Dolphin-watching trips run regularly from the town, and there's a lively Dolphin Festival in July to view and celebrate these appealing creatures.

LISSADELL HOUSE

347 D3 • Drumcliff, Co. Sligo 071 916 3150 May–end Sep daily 11–6 Adult €6, child (under 16) €3 13km (8 miles) northwest of Sligo; signed off N15 Sligo–Bundoran road

Lissadell House, though somewhat grim and grey from the outside, is one of the most romantic Great Houses in Ireland, thanks to its associations with Ireland's 'national poet' W. B. Yeats and with the celebrated nationalist leader Constance Gore-Booth, Countess Markievicz. The Gore-Booth family had lived at Lissadell on the northern shore of Drumcliff Bay since 1604, and Sir Robert Gore-Booth built the present neoclassical house there in 1832. Yeats first visited in 1894 at the height of his romantic nationalist 'Gaelic Revival' phase, and became firm friends—and maybe fell in love with—the two Gore-Booth sisters, Constance and Eva:

'Two girls in silk kimonos, both Beautiful, one a gazelle.'

Constance, who married Count Casimir Markievicz, became an ardent nationalist, and took a leading part in the Irish independence movement. She was condemned to death (a sentence later commuted) for her part in the Easter Rising of 1916.

The house and grounds saw decades of neglect during the 20th century. The grounds are still in a bit of a tangle, but on a tour of the restored rooms of the house you can see caricatures of the Gore-Booth family, servants and pets painted on the dining room walls by Count Markievicz. Photographs and portraits of the Gore-Booth sisters help to bring their story to life, while the billiard room is devoted to an exhibition of the 19th-century Arctic explorations of Sir Henry Gore-Booth, father of Constance and Eva.

LOUGH GILL

347 D3 Tourist Information Office, Aras Reddan, Temple Street, Sligo, Co. Sligo, tel 071 916 1201; Mon–Fri 9–5, Sat 10–2
www.irelandnorthwest.ie

Lough Gill straddles the Sligo–Leitrim border. There are plenty of W. B. Yeats-related sites around the western or Sligo end of this beautiful lake, which both the Yeats brothers—poet William and painter Jack—knew and loved from early boyhood. The R286, 287 and 288 roads form a circuit of Lough Gill, a lovely half-day excursion. On the southern shore the R287 leads past the signposted Dooney Rock beauty spot, a cliff-top viewpoint over the lake, and Slish Wood where young William once camped out alone overnight.

On the north shore the R286 makes a delightful lakeside run east over the Leitrim border to Parke's Castle (near Dromahair; tel 071 64149; Mar–end Oct daily 10–6), a strikingly impressive and complete-looking fortified house with a turreted

The conical outline of Mount Errigal, east of Gweedore, not snow-capped as it may appear, but topped with pale rock

A stark white statue of the Virgin on the roadside at Nephin Beg

bawn or enclosed courtyard. It was built on the site of an O'Rourke tower in 1609 by Captain Robert Parke, and after centuries of dereliction has been superbly restored with Irish oak roofs pegged in traditional style. From the shore there's a good view of tiny, thickly wooded Innisfree, subject of Yeats's best-known poem, *The Lake Isle of Innisfree*. You can rent a boat at the castle jetty and row out to where Yeats dreamed of living:

'I will arise and go now, and go to Innisfree,
And a small cabin build there, of clay and wattles made.'

MOUNT ERRIGAL

348 E1 · Dunlewy Lakeside Centre, Dunlewy, Co. Donegal, tel 074 953 1699; Easter–end Oct Mon–Sat 10.30–6, Sun 11–7; Tourist Information Offices at The Quay, Dungloe, Co. Donegal, tel 074 952 1297; seasonal opening or Blaney Street, Letterkenny, Co. Donegal, tel 074 912 1160

The quartzite cone of Mount Errigal is a landmark for many miles in northwest County Donegal. At 752m (2,468ft) Errigal is the highest of Donegal's many mountains, and its peak catches the eye because of the way the naked quartzite gleams like snow. Approaching along the R251 from Bunbeg you see the rugged screes, corries and cliffs of the mountain's west face at their most formidable. But once you have passed the bulk of Errigal it seems less daunting.

Errigal is in fact an easy mountain to climb if you are sensibly shod, reasonably fit and prepared for a sudden change in the weather. The path up the eastern ridge leaves a pull-off on the R251 at a 'walking man' waymark and makes a steady ascent of around 530m (1738ft), following a clear track over heather and then broken quartzite.

There's a surprise at the top—the mountain has a twin summit, with the two peaks linked by a very narrow ridge. Wonderful views over the lakes and mountains of Donegal reward the effort of the climb; it is said that a person with exceptionally good eyesight on an exceptionally clear day can see Scotland, 320km (200 miles) away.

MULLET PENINSULA AND NEPHIN BEG MOUNTAINS

346 B3/C3 · Tourist Information Office, James Street, Westport, Co. Mayo, tel 098 25711; Jul, Aug Mon–Sat 9–6, Sun 10–6; Sep, Oct Mon–Sat 9–5.45; Nov–end Feb Mon–Fri 9–5.45, Sat 10–1; Mar–end Jun Mon–Sat 9–5.45

The Mullet Peninsula hangs like a ragged arm from the rounded shoulder of northwest County Mayo, one of the wildest and least-populated corners of Ireland. The low-lying, isolated Mullet, composed mostly of mountain and bog, is a Gaeltacht area, so you will hear only Irish spoken in the peninsula's sole village of Binghamstown. The eastern or landward side of the Mullet cradles Blacksod Bay and is sandy in parts, but also spread with mud flats.

Birdwatching is sensational here, as it is by Termoncarragh Lake at the head of the peninsula, where you may with luck spot the rare red-necked phalarope. The western or Atlantic coast of the peninsula has a succession of beautiful sandy (and seaweedy) strands. From the beaches of Belderra and Cross there are good views of the tiny island of Inisglora 1.5km (1 mile) out to sea, where—according to legend—the four children of Lir spent 300 years in exile in the shape of swans, thanks to the evil magic of their jealous stepmother.

Inland of the Mullet, the Nephin Beg Mountains are the loneliest in Mayo if not in the whole of Ireland. In these 130sq km (50sq miles) of unpopulated, roadless mountains you can leave busy urban life behind and feel truly alone. The waymarked Bangor Trail, a long-distance path that runs for 45km (28 miles) from Bangor Erris south to Newport through the heart of the range is a true challenge for strong and determined walkers.

SKREEN CHURCHYARD

347 D3 • Skreen, Co. Sligo · Tourist Information Office, Aras Reddan, Temple Street, Sligo, Co. Sligo, tel 071 916 1201; ▷ 146 On N59 Sligo–Ballina road, between Dromard and Templeboy
www.irelandnorthwest.ie

At first glance there's nothing very special about the tombs scattered in the tangle of undergrowth in Skreen churchyard. But take your time here and you'll discover some fine pieces of stone carving. Many of the stone graveslabs and tomb chests are heavily carved with cherubim, seraphim, skulls, crossbones and other *mementi mori*. Most are the work of the Diamond family, a dynasty of stonemasons who have been living and working locally for more than 200 years. Pride of the place is the tomb-chest that Andrew Black commissioned in 1825 in memory of his father Alexander (*d*1810), a prosperous farmer. The carving shows Mr. Black Senior dressed dapperly in tall hat, waistcoat, many-buttoned tail coat, breeches, stockings and buckled shoes, ploughing a field with a prancing pair of what appear to be racehorses. In the air before the ploughman hang the implements of his calling: hay fork and rake, flail, spade and broad-bladed shovel.

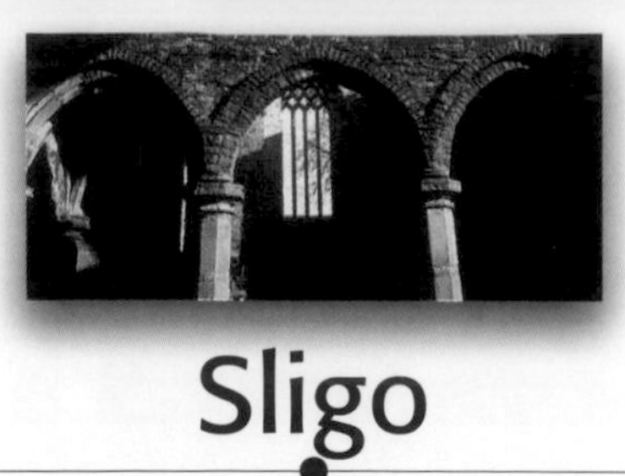

Sligo

Sligo is the heart of 'Yeats Country', where Ireland's national poet William B. and his painter brother Jack are commemorated and celebrated. Victorian shop-fronts line the narrow streets yet it has all the amenities of a modern town.

Sligo Abbey dates from the 13th century (above left). Traditional band Dervish playing in Furey's Bar (above middle). Strolling across a bridge in Sligo town (above right)

RATINGS	
Cultural interest	●●●●●
Historic interest	●●●
Walkability	●●●●

BASICS

347 D3

Tourist Information Office, Aras Reddan, Temple Street, Sligo, Co. Sligo, tel 071 91 61201; Apr–end Sep daily 9–5.30; Oct–end Mar Mon–Thu 9.30–5.30, Fri 9.30–5 (times may vary)

Sligo

www.irelandnorthwest.ie
The excellent official website of the regional tourist board.

TIP

- **Wednesdays are a good bet for extra-special music sessions at Furey's/Sheela-na-gig (▷ 147). Brian McDonagh, a member of the band Dervish, is the licensee, and when not away touring he'll often sit down on a Wednesday evening to trade tunes with any musicians there. Other members of Dervish are often around, too, for the *craic* and a few tunes.**

SEEING SLIGO

Sligo is extremely walkable, with a tight grid of central streets containing most of the attractions. The Garravogue River bisecting the town is spanned by Hyde Bridge and New Bridge and one block to the south, running parallel to the river, is the main shopping thoroughfare of Castle Street.

HIGHLIGHTS

YEATS MEMORIAL BUILDING

Hyde Bridge 071 914 2693; www.yeats-sligo.com

The handsome redbrick building at the west end of Hyde Bridge is the headquarters of the Yeats Society. Dedicated to promoting the work and reputation of Ireland's national poet, William Butler Yeats (1865–1939), the Society hosts an annual Yeats Summer School in the first two weeks of August, with talks, readings and excursions to Yeats' sites attracting thousands. Whatever your question about W. B. Yeats, you'll find your answer here, and there's also a permanent photographic exhibition. Sligo Art Gallery (tel 071 914 5847), on the upper floors, mounts 15–20 exhibitions a year.

YEATS STATUE

Rowan Gillespie's bronze sculpture of W. B. Yeats was erected on Stephen Street, at the east end of Hyde Bridge, by the people of Sligo in 1989 to commemorate the 50th anniversary of the poet's death. Yeats is shown in archetypal poetic stance, luxuriant locks streaming, one hand artistically poised, staring into space with an absent expression on his bespectacled face. His billowing cloak is overprinted with a jumbled mass of lines from his poems.

SLIGO COUNTY MUSEUM AND YEATS MEMORIAL ROOM

Stephen Street 071 914 1623 Jun–end Oct Tue–Sat 10–12, 2–4.30; Nov–end May Tue–Sat 2–4.30 Free

A former presbytery is home to Sligo County Museum which gives an enjoyable run-through of local history via photographs and objects, including a fiddle that belonged to Michael Coleman, one of the brightest stars in Ireland's traditional music firmament. The main attraction is the Yeats Memorial Room, a small room with formal and informal photographs (including images of his funeral), as well as letters and his 1923 Nobel Prize for literature.

MODEL ARTS AND NILAND GALLERY

✉ The Mall, Sligo, Co. Sligo ☎ 071 914 1405
🕐 Tue–Sat 10–5.30, Sun 11–4 ✋ Free

Model Arts puts on concerts of jazz, contemporary and classical music, and runs literary and music festivals. The Niland Gallery, based on a collection started by Sligo's late county librarian Nora Niland, has a dazzling range of art, with Irish artists predominating. Pride of the gallery is its definitive collection of paintings, watercolours and drawings by Jack B. Yeats (1871–1957), brother of poet William. Yeats's mystic and elliptical Sligo

landscapes-with-figures such as *The Graveyard Wall, The Sea and The Lighthouse* and especially the haunting, ghostly late work *Leaving The Far Point* are wonderful to linger over. Among the other works you'll find landscapes by Paul Henry and Sean Keating, and the subtle portraits of Estella Solomons.

Sunset over Sligo Bay (above)

The dramatic monument to W. B. Yeats in Sligo town (left)

SLIGO ABBEY

✉ Abbey Street ☎ 071 914 6406 🕐 Mid-Mar to end Oct daily 10–6; Nov–1 Jan Fri–Sun 9.30–4.30 ✋ Adult €2, child (5–16) €1

The 13th-century Dominican friary, under an arched tower, is in a remarkably good state of preservation, considering its history of fires and vandalism. It has a beautiful medieval rood screen, elaborate carving on the high altar and the tomb of Cormac O'Crean (*d*1506), a graceful east window and retains cloister arches and a chapter house.

HARGADON'S AND FUREY'S/SHEELA-NA-GIG

As in most other Irish towns, social life is at its liveliest in the pubs, and there are two superb examples here. Hargadon's (O'Connell Street; tel 071 917 0933) has no music—it's a talking pub, with a wonderful old-fashioned front bar complete with apothecary's drawers and little walled-off snugs. Furey's (Bridge Street; tel 071 914 3825), is another matter; it's owned by the well-known Sligo traditional band Dervish, and a tremendous session may burst out at any moment. In fact, Furey's is so good they named it twice: It's also known as the Sheela-na-gig, after a fertility symbol.

BACKGROUND

On the main route between the ancient provinces of Ulster and Connacht, Sligo was always an important town. Georgian and Victorian houses, churches and commercial premises survive in large numbers, giving it an appealingly settled and old-fashioned air. It's the Yeats connection, however, that fixes Sligo on the tourist map. The long holidays that William and Jack spent here with their Pollexfen cousins in the 1870s and '80s installed Sligo deep in the affections of both brothers, and Yeats' aficionados come from all over the world to see the place that inspired so many memorable poems and paintings.

Natural light pours in over Yeats's desk at Thoor Ballylee

A whole spectrum of colours accompanies the sunset over Clew Bay, less peaceful by far when pirates ruled the waves here

THOOR BALLYLEE

351 D5 • Gort, Co. Galway 091 631436 Jun–end Sep Mon–Sat 10–6 Adult €6, child (under 12) €1.50 Signposted off N66, 5km (3 miles) northeast of Gort

I the poet William Yeats…
Restored this tower for my wife George.

William Butler Yeats characteristically celebrated in verse his restoration of the 16th-century tower house that became his country retreat and preferred writing spot. You can wander through the four floors, viewing Yeats' first editions and memorabilia, while listening to recordings of the man reading his own works, including extracts from his 1928 collection *The Tower*, inspired by Thoor Ballylee.

TORY ISLAND

348 E1 • 11km (7 miles) north of Bloody Foreland 1 to 2 hours, depending on weather, from Bunbeg, tel 074 953 1991, or 45 min to 1 hour from Magheroarty, tel 075 35061 Visitor Information: tel 075 35502, or Donegal Tourist Information Office, Quay Street, Donegal, Co. Donegal, tel 074 972 1148
www.irelandnorthwest.ie

The crossing to Tory Island can be a corkscrew affair. All the more pleasant, then, to be welcomed with a handshake or a kiss by the King of Tory, a post first created by St. Columba in the sixth century AD, and still filled by a resident Tory islander. The 'walls' of Tory are formidable cliffs, topped by a flat, treeless and windswept plateau.

Around 150 Irish-speaking people live on Tory Island, and they are often cut off for weeks at a time in winter; they are correspondingly hospitable and pleased to see visitors.

If the weather allows, birdwatching and walking are superb here, and there is a tremendous atmosphere in the pubs when musicians are on the island, especially during the Tory Island Festival in July. Some members of the community have created a 'naïve' school of art, and you can enjoy these spirited landscapes and portraits at the Dixon Gallery (West Town; tel 074 913 5011; May–end Sep daily 9–5), which occupies the former cottage of James Dixon, the island's pioneer fisherman-painter.

WESTPORT AND CLEW BAY

346 C4 Tourist Information Office, James Street, Westport, Co. Mayo, tel 098 25711; Jul–end Oct daily 9–6; Nov–end Jun Mon–Fri 9–6, Sat 10–2 Westport

Westport is a delightful town, both for its character and its looks. Before good roads were built into western Mayo during the 19th century, it was an isolated place, and still retains that sense of self-sufficiency. Westport was laid out for the Marquess of Sligo in the 1780s by James Wyatt, one of the supreme architects of the Georgian era. His grid pattern, with the parallel thoroughfares of Bridge Street and James Street running uphill from The Mall beside the Carrowbeg River, still survives, and gives the town an orderly, manageable air. At the top of Bridge Street there's a tall clock tower; on the Octagon, at the top of James Street, a column supports a statue of St. Patrick, whose holy mountain of Croagh Patrick (▷ 136) is visible from the outskirts of town.

Westport has enjoyed an influx of artistic settlers from all over the world, attracted by the town's pleasant atmosphere. The Westport Arts Festival in the second half of September brings music, plays, painting, poetry, street theatre and other events to the town. Westport is also one of the best towns in Ireland for traditional music session pubs. The best-known of these is the bar on Bridge Street that's named after its owner, Matt Molloy, who plays flute with Ireland's most famous traditional music band, The Chieftains. When world tours and other commitments allow, he's there to join in the sessions. Other great venues include Hoban's at the Octagon, and McHale's on Lower Peter Street.

Westport House (signposted on the road to Westport Quay; tel 098 27766/25430, Apr–end Sep daily) was completed in 1779 by Wyatt, and contains beautiful ceilings and a collection of furniture, silver, glass and pictures that reflects the taste of the Browne family, Marquesses of Sligo, through the centuries. The grounds are a great place for children, with a log flume, miniature train, bouncy castle and pedal-yourself boats on the lake.

Westport Quay is lined with restored stone warehouses converted to restaurants, a hotel and shops. Here you'll find the Clew Bay Heritage Centre (The Quay; tel 098 26852; Apr–end Oct Mon–Fri 10–2), with a small museum of local interest and an introduction to Clew Bay, which opens from Westport Bay to the west of the town.

There may not be 365 islands in Clew Bay, as locals claim, but there are certainly a lot of them. Clew Bay is a beautiful wide bay some 13km (8 miles) wide and 21km (13 miles) long, lined with sandy beaches at Mulrany on the north and between Louisburgh and Murrisk on the south. If you want to get active, contact Mayo Sailing Club at Rosmoney Quay (tel 098 26160) and the tourist information office for details of sporting activities.

THE MIDLANDS

The flat landscape of the Midlands features wide areas of raised bog, and is dotted with lakes and the gentle Slieve Bloom Mountains. It contains several important sights: the Georgian town of Birr with its magnificent castle gardens, the Famine Museum at Strokestown Park and the exquisite high crosses and round towers of Clonmacnoise.

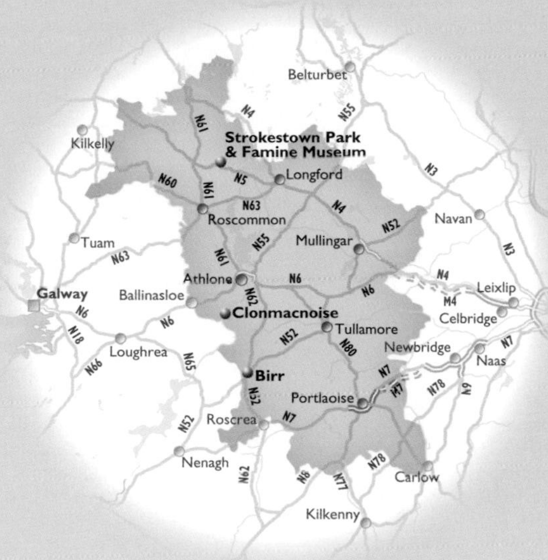

MAJOR SIGHTS

Perfectly proportioned Abbeyleix House was once a boys' school

Athlone Castle is still an imposing place

Exquisite woodcarving on the fireplace at Belvedere House

ABBEYLEIX

352 F6 · Tourist Information Office, Lawlor Avenue, Portlaoise, Co. Laois, tel 0502 21178; Jun to mid-Sep Mon–Fri 9.30–5.30
www.eastcoastmidlandsireland.com

Abbeyleix is a handsome Georgian town that was laid out at the gates of his park by Viscount de Vesci, the 18th-century Lord of Abbeyleix House. At Abbeyleix Heritage House (tel 0502 31653, Mon–Fri 9–5, Sat, Sun 1–5), in the former boy's school, you can learn about the town's development from its origins as a huddle of houses around a 12th-century Cistercian monastery. There's also a display on the town's long-defunct carpet industry; when the ill-fated *Titanic* set sail on her disastrous maiden voyage in 1912, her stateroom floors were covered with Abbeyleix carpets.

In the old walled garden of Abbeyleix's former convent is the Abbey Sense Garden (tel 0502 31325/31636; Mon–Fri 10–4, also May–end Sep Sat, Sun 2–6), designed for touching, seeing, hearing, smelling and tasting.

Morrissey's pub (tel 0502 31233) on Main Street is a real old-fashioned bar/grocer where only the prices seem to have changed since the 19th century.

ATHLONE

348 E5 · Athlone Castle, Co. Westmeath, tel 0906 494630; Jul, Aug Mon–Sat 9–6; Apr–end Jun, Sep–end Nov Mon–Fri 9.30–1, 2–5.30 · Athlone
www.athlone.ie

As the county town and the commercial and social hub for a wide rural area, Athlone is a lively base for boating and fishing on the River Shannon. The best place for a pint, a tune and all the local information, is Sean's Bar on Main Street (tel 0902 92358), an establishment of great character that has been a pub for at least 400 years.

The world-renowned tenor John McCormack (1884–1945) was born in The Bawn at the heart of Athlone. In the excellent Castle Museum and Visitor Centre in the keep of Athlone Castle (tel 0906 492912/472107; Apr–end Sep daily 10–5.30), you can choose one of McCormack's songs from a selection of 78rpm records, and have it played on the great man's portable gramophone. Upstairs there's an eclectic display of bygone implements of rural life and agriculture. From the battlements there's a good view of the town and the River Shannon towards Lough Ree.

BELVEDERE HOUSE

348 F5 • Mullingar, Co. Westmeath · 044 49060 · May–end Aug Mon–Fri 9.30–6, Sat, Sun 9.30–8; Nov–end Dec, Jan–end Apr daily 10.30–4.30 · Adult €6, child (3–16) €4 · On N52, 5.5km (3.5 miles) south of Mullingar

With its fine plasterwork ceilings and decoratively carved woodwork, this 18th-century fishing and hunting lodge and gardens make an enjoyable excursion. Pride of place among the many follies in the grounds goes to the Jealous Wall, a large sham castle frontage, complete with turrets, Gothic arches and 'shattered' windows. It was built in 1760 on the orders of the 'Wicked Earl', Robert Rochfort, First Earl of Belvedere, to block his view of Tudenham Park, the home of his younger brother, with whom he had quarrelled. The Wicked Earl also suspected his other brother, Arthur, of having an affair with his young wife, Mary, in 1743. Lord Belvedere sued Arthur for £20,000, and at length had him imprisoned, where he eventually died. Mary, was shut away in another of the earl's houses, where she remained under lock and key for more than 30 years.

After the earl's death in 1774, one of her sons released her, still clad in a dress she had worn before her incarceration and still protesting her innocence.

BLACKWATER BOG

352 E5 · 0909 674114 · Tours every hour, Apr–end Oct daily 10–5 · Train ride adult €6, child (12–16) €5.10, under 12 €4.10, family €19 · Signed off R357 Cloghan road, 1.5km (1 mile) southeast of Shannonbridge
www.bnm.ie

The Blackwater Bog covers some 8,000ha (19,770 acres) of counties Offaly, Westmeath, Roscommon and Galway, some untouched, other parts exploited for fuel and fertilizer. Destruction of the bogs over the past 50 years has been on such a massive scale that an international outcry by conservationists ensued, and exploitation is due to cease by 2030. In the meantime, the 'Clonmacnoise & West Offaly Railway' will take you for 8km (5 miles) round the bog and you can see how it has been turned into a desolate quagmire and how it will be developed for eco-recreation in the future.

Intriguing face sculptures in the castle grounds (above). Outside the castle you can see the restored old telescope (right)

BIRR

Birr has wide streets of Georgian houses but its greatest attraction is the Birr Castle Demesne, its Science Centre and the Giant Leviathan telescope.

The Parsons family settled at Birr in 1620, and as the Earls of Rosse they directed the fortunes of the area from then on. During the 18th century they laid out a model Georgian town with a central square and wide tree-lined streets or 'malls' flanked with well-built houses and neat gardens. The Birr Town Trail, set out in a little leaflet obtainable from the Tourist Information Office, takes you around the best parts. Notice the carved surrounds of the shop-fronts here.

BIRR CASTLE DEMESNE

The chief attraction of the town is undoubtedly Birr Castle Demesne (tel 0509 20340/20336, mid-Mar to end Oct daily 9–6, Nov to mid-Mar 10–4). The castle itself, founded in 1170 and altered in the succeeding centuries, is still the private residence of the Earl and Countess of Rosse, and is not open to the public. But the family have tastefully developed the demesne (grounds) as a public attraction, with woodland walks, formal and informal gardens and water features. There are rose gardens and a very fine collection of magnolias, and a path between gigantic hedges of box that date back to the 17th century. The demesne is also home to the National Birds of Prey Centre where you can admire eagles, hawks, owls and falcons.

Plenty of experimental plant work has been carried out at Birr Castle Demesne, and the Birds of Prey Centre is actively involved with schemes to reintroduce birds into the wild. The earls and countesses of Rosse seem always to have had enquiring, scientific minds. The Science Centre in the castle stables gives a very accessible account of the family's various achievements in science, including the development by the third earl, William Parsons (1800–67), of the huge telescope named Leviathan which is still kept in the grounds and is demonstrated three times a day. This telescope, 21m (70ft) long, contains the largest cast metal mirror ever made. Gazing through it in April 1845, the Third Earl was the first man to see a whirlpool nebula, the spiral glow of another galaxy 40 million light years away. The photographs taken of the newly installed telescope by the earl's wife, Mary, a noted pioneer of photography, are remarkable.

RATINGS

Good for kids	●●●●
Historic interest	●●●●
Photo stops	●●●
Walkability	●●●

BASICS

352 E6

Birr Tourist Information Office, Castle Street, Birr, Co. Offaly, tel 0509 20110; May–end Sep

TIPS

- **To avoid disappointment, telephone Birr Castle Demesne in advance for telescope demonstration times.**
- **Children might enjoy searching for Sweeney, a legendary Irish king driven mad and forced to live as a bird after being cursed by St. Ronan. They'll find his gradually dissolving wickerwork figure perched in a holly tree, hidden in the undergrowth near Lover's Walk.**

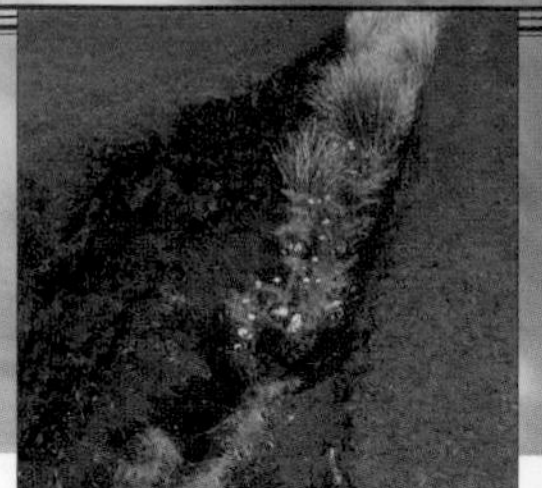

Peat in the Bog of Allen is cut by machine these days

Extensive remains of the 12th-century Boyle Abbey

Charleville Forest Castle is richly ornamented (above and below)

THE SIGHTS

BOG OF ALLEN

352 F5 · Lough Boora Parklands on the R357 near Kilcormac, off N52 between Birr and Tullamore, Co. Offaly; Bog of Allen Nature Centre, Lullymore, Rathangan, Co. Kildare, tel 045 860133; Mon–Fri 9.30–5 · Adult €5
www.loughbooraparklands.com

The great Bog of Allen stretches some 100km (62 miles) from County Kildare through County Offaly to the River Shannon. This is a 'raised bog', formed when water trickles down from higher ground and collects on an impermeable base which, in this case, is a thick sheet of clay spread by the retreating glaciers of the last Ice Age. The bog holds up to 20 times its own weight of water and the peat can be 10m (32ft) or more in depth. At first glance it appears lifeless, but closer inspection reveals abundant plant life, including many kinds of sedges, sundews and the brilliant orange stars of bog asphodel.

The practice of cutting peat (turf) for domestic fuel makes little impression on the bog, but commercial exploitation for industrial fuel and gardening since World War II by the Irish Peat Board, has seen destruction on a vast scale. You can learn all about the protection and conversion of the bog into wildlife and amenity parks at Lough Boora Parklands near Kilcormac.

BOYLE

347 D4 · Boyle Tourist Information Office, The Courthouse, Market Street, Boyle, Co. Roscommon, tel 071 966 2145; Easter, then mid-May to mid-Sep Mon–Sat 10–5.30

Boyle is a handsome town with a pleasing mixture of Georgian and Victorian architecture. By far the most important and striking building is Boyle Abbey (tel 079 62604; Easter–end Nov daily), standing magnificently beside the River Boyle on the eastern edge of town. Founded in 1161 by the Cistercian community, the remains of the old monastery cloister garden, kitchens, refectory and so on are in a very good state of preservation, as is the abbey church itself.

There's an exhibition in the gatehouse, where jambs are scored with sword cuts and ancient graffiti from the garrison that occupied the abbey from 1603 until 1788. In that year the Connaught Rangers, or 'The Devil's Own' as the roughneck militia were called, moved to King House at the east end of Main Street (tel 079 63242; May–end Sep daily 10–6; Apr, Oct Sat, Sun). This lovely early Georgian mansion had just been vacated by the King family in favour of their grand Rockingham estate (now Lough Key Forest Park, ▷ 160). King House is a wonderful place for children, with storytelling, activities and dressing-up to help bring history to life; adults can watch audio-visual displays on the history of the King family and the area, and also on the Great Famine. Frybrook House (tel 079 62170; Jun–end Sep daily 2–6), a well preserved Quaker house, dates from the mid-18th century.

Don't miss The grotesque and humorous carvings, floral capitals and decorative pillars are rare for the austere Cistercian order.

CHARLEVILLE FOREST CASTLE

352 E5 • Tullamore, Co. Offaly · 0506 21279 · Jun–end Aug daily 10–5; Sep–end May by appointment · On N52 Birr road south of Tullamore
www.charlevillecastle.com

Five beautiful avenues of Irish yew radiate from the castle, an imposing neo-Gothic country house built with grand spires, turrets and pinnacles in 1798, and walled as if to shut out the world. There is elaborate stucco in the gallery which runs the whole width of the house; here the Bury family could promenade and admire the gardens in inclement weather. Thickly tangled oak woods and an eerie atmosphere surround 'the most haunted house in Ireland'.

CLONALIS HOUSE

347 D4 • Castlerea, Co. Roscommon · 094 962 0 014 · Jun–end Aug Mon–Sat 11–5 · Adult €7, child €5 · Castlerea · On N60, just west of Castlerea
www.clonalis.com

Clonalis House is a late Victorian Italianate country house. Its interest lies in the antiquity of its owners, the O'Conors, once the Kings of Connacht. One Ruaidri Ua Conchobair (Rory O'Conor) reigned from 1166–86 as the last High King of Ireland. The O'Conors preserve an enormous archive of family papers and historical documents. You can also see the great Stone on which the O'Conor chiefs have been inaugurated since pre-Christian times, and the harp that belonged to Turlough O'Carolan (1670–1738), the blind harpist, composer and poet known as the last of the traditional court bards. The O'Conor Don (clan chief) of the day was a keen patron of O'Carolan.

CLONMACNOISE

See pages 154–157.

Clonalis House, ancestral seat of the O'Conor family

The ruins of Fore Abbey, framed by an ancient archway (above) A brightly painted water pump in the grounds at Clonalis (below)

EMO COURT

352 F6 • Emo village, Co. Laois 0502 26573 House: mid-Jun to mid-Sep Tue–Sun 11–6.30; gardens: daily Adult €2.75, child (5–18) €1.25, family €7 Signposted from N7 Kildare–Portlaoise road

Architect James Gandon, who is best known for great public building works such as Dublin's Custom House, the Four Courts and O'Connell Bridge, designed the Earl of Portarlington's grand neoclassical mansion of Emo Court in 1792. The family was in residence here until 1920, when it became a Jesuit seminary. The house was restored during the 1970s, and it was acquired by the Irish nation in 1996.

The focal points as you approach the mansion are the great green dome that tops the building and the imposing colonnaded portico through which you enter. The inside is full of fine plasterwork and *trompe l'oeil* decoration.

The gardens are divided into two principal parts—the Grapery, which has a path leading through the shrubberies down to the lakeshore, and the Clucker—so called because it was laid out on the site of a former nunnery—where rhododendrons and azaleas bring a riot of early summer hues among the cedars, pines and maples.

FORE

348 F4 Mullingar Tourist Information Office, Market House, Mullingar, tel 044 48650; Mon–Fri 9.30–5.30 Signposted off the R195 near Castlepollard (on R394, 21km/13 miles north of Mullingar)

The village of Fore is famous for the legendary Seven Wonders of Fore, evidence of which lie in the fields on the outskirts. Pilgrims visit regularly, and though the Wonders may look rather unremarkable to sceptics, local belief is strong.

The first of them is 'the monastery in the quaking scraw', a fine range of monastic buildings, complete with gatehouse and dovecot, which were built on a rock that's surrounded by a quaking bog). Then comes the 'water that flows uphill' and the 'mill without a race'—the ruin of a mill that is said to have been founded here by St. Fechin in a then waterless place; the stream, apparently defying gravity by flowing uphill, appeared with a stroke of his staff. 'The tree that won't burn' is next—a stump that has been poisoned by the thousands of copper coins pushed into its trunk as offerings by miracle-seekers. Then there's the 'water that won't boil'—but who's going to try, when legend has it that the water of the muddy remnants of St. Fechin's holy well brings bad luck to anyone even attempting to boil it.

On the other side of the road you'll find 'the stone raised by St. Fechin's prayers'. The massive lintel of a 12th-century church, carved with a Greek cross in a circle, reputedly rose into place on the saint's prayers. Lastly, there's the 'anchorite in a stone', which is actually the cell of 17th-century hermit Patrick Begley, within what looks like a church but is in fact the mausoleum of the Greville Nugent family. Should the mausoleum be locked when you arrive, then you can collect the key for it from the Seven Wonders pub in the village.

HEYWOOD HOUSE GARDENS

352 F6 • Ballinakill, Co. Laois 0502 33334 May–end Aug daily, dawn to dusk Free Off R432 outside Ballinakill, 7km (4 miles) from Abbeyleix

Nothing remains of Heywood House—the 18th-century mansion was burned to the ground in 1950—but it's worth coming here to wander among the remarkable gardens. They were designed in 1909 by celebrated architect Sir Edwin Lutyens and planted in the subsequent three years by his frequent collaborater, garden designer and plantswoman supreme, Gertrude Jekyll. The well-tended landscape includes fine terraces and garden 'rooms'—themed areas enclosed within 'walls' of neatly clipped hedges—and there's a lovely lime walk and a scatter of pavilions.

KILBEGGAN

352 E5 Mullingar Tourist Information Office, Market House, Mullingar, Co. Westmeath, tel 044 48650; Mon–Fri 9.30–5.30

Kilbeggan is a good example of the kind of wayside settlement that grew into a flourishing town by virtue of its position on the Grand Canal. The main feature of the town is Locke's Distillery on Main Street (tel 0506 32134; Apr–end Oct daily 9–6; Nov–end Apr 10–4). It was in production for a full 200 years, until 1957, and is now a fine museum of whiskey. Exhibits include an old steam engine and a working mill-wheel. You can still buy Locke's whiskey—among the range sold here, are bottles of Locke's single malt, which nowadays is made at Cooley's Distillery in Co. Louth. Devotees say it's one of the smoothest whiskeys in Ireland.

Clonmacnoise

The best-preserved of Ireland's remarkable monastic sites, Clonmacnoise was the most important Irish monastery of the Golden Age. Approach by water for an unforgettable view of Clonmacnoise overlooking the River Shannon.

Looking out over the river at Clonmacnoise as the sun sets

The round tower and Celtic crosses

Clonmacnoise was one of Ireland's foremost early churches

SEEING CLONMACNOISE

Clonmacnoise lies on a great bend of the River Shannon, some 11km (7 miles) downstream of Athlone, near the meeting point of three counties: Offaly, Westmeath and Roscommon. The site, one of Ireland's most popular tourist destinations, is well signposted from all roads in the region. It also has its own jetties on the river bank for foot-passengers arriving by water.

Whether you arrive by road or by boat, you'll enter through the Visitor Centre, essential to your appreciation of Clonmacnoise. The monastic site lies immediately east of the Visitor Centre, with the Round Tower and churches huddled compactly together inside their surrounding wall. As you enter the site, O'Rourke's Tower lies to the left beyond the copy of the Cross of the Scriptures. Ahead is the copy of the South Cross, with the cathedral just beyond it. At the far side of the site you can follow a marked path for 450m (490 yards) to the isolated Nuns' Church.

HIGHLIGHTS

CLONMACNOISE FROM THE RIVER SHANNON

By far the most enjoyable way to arrive is to rent a boat at Athlone and cruise here. The view is of towers, churches and a snowdrift of gravestones, enclosed within a protective wall on a green bank and reflected in the river. Altogether this aspect of Clonmacnoise forms an unforgettable ensemble and a perfect photograph.

CROSS OF THE SCRIPTURES

The High Crosses facing wind and weather on the monastic site are copies; the originals, too precious to be exposed to the elements, are on display in the Visitor Centre. The best preserved, the Cross of the Scriptures, stands 4.5m (15ft) high. It is sometimes called Flann's Cross—an inscription on the base attributes it to King Flann, High King of Ireland at the turn of the 10th century when the cross was carved. Abbot Colman Conailleach probably erected the cross CAD910. It is richly carved with biblical scenes: St. Anthony besting the Devil, the Saved called to eternal life, and Christ in his tomb being awoken by a peck on the lips from a bird that might be the Holy Dove.

RATINGS	
Historic interest	●●●●●
Cultural interest	●●●●●
Photo stops	●●●●●
Walkability	●●●●

BASICS

352 E5 • Co. Offaly

Visitor Centre, tel 090 967 4195; mid-May to early Sep daily 9–7; mid-Mar to mid-May, early Sep–end Oct 10–6, Nov to mid-Mar 10–5.30

Adult €5, child (under 18) €2, family €11

Signposted from N62, 21km (13 miles) south of Athlone, or from Shannonbridge on R357, 13km (8 miles) southeast of Ballinasloe

TIPS

- If you visit in the summer, try to be there by 9am. The site gets very crowded, especially at weekends.
- Purely for fun: why not join a cruise to Clonmacnoise from Athlone aboard a replica Viking ship? The crew of the *Viking* (tel 0906 473383/473392) will be dressed as Vikings, and you can borrow a costume to make your arrival at the monastery exciting for all concerned!

Detail of a Celtic cross (opposite)

MORE TO SEE

OTHER CHURCHES

Clonmacnoise contains five other churches in various states of repair: The 11th-century O'Connor's Church (Temple Connor, between O'Rourke's Tower and MacCarthy's Church), still used for services; the remains of 12th-century Temple Kelly, consisting of a few broken walls near St. Ciarán's Church; Melaghlin's Chapel (Temple Melaghlin, just south of St. Ciarán's Church), a simple church *c*1200 with a delicately sculpted double window; the 12th-century Dowling's Church (Temple Dowling, next to the South Cross replica)—the inscription over the door reads: 'Mr Edmund Dowling of Clondalare W. built this chapel to the greater glory of God & use of his posterity'; Temple Hurpan, added to the east end of Dowling's Church in the early 18th century, so that both share the round-headed east window of Dowling's.

SOUTH CROSS AND NORTH CROSS, VISITOR CENTRE EXHIBITION

The Cross of the Scriptures may be the most striking of the Clonmacnoise High Crosses, but don't ignore the other two great crosses on display. The ninth-century South Cross, badly weathered, shows a Crucifixion with the identifiable figures of Longinus the lance-bearer and Stephaton the sponge-bearer; while the North Cross, perhaps dating back as far as AD800, has stiffly posed lions and a motif of spiralling foliage. The cross-legged figure here might be Cernunnos, the horned god of the woods and of virility, revered in Celtic pagan mythology.

GREEN MEN, NUNS' CHURCH

The Cernunnos figure on the North Cross is not the only pagan symbol at this most Christian of sites. Among the carvings around the west door and the chancel arch of the Nuns' Church you can pick out a couple of Green Men. These enigmatic figures are always shown with tendrils of foliage emerging from one or more of their facial orifices. They seem pagan in character, yet they are found in medieval church decoration all over Europe and beyond.

GRAVE SLABS

Also in the Visitor Centre exhibition is a unique collection of grave slabs. Dating from the eighth century to the twelfth, they represent Europe's largest collection of early Christian burial markers. Some are decorated with interlace carving and incised crosses of various shapes. One of the slabs is clearly marked 'Colman', another implores, '*Ior do thuathal saer*, a prayer for Thuathal the Craftsman'.

O'ROURKE'S TOWER (ROUND TOWER)

Once out of the Visitor Centre and into the roughly circular walled site of the monastery, most visitors turn left past the copy of the Cross of the Scriptures and head for the most obvious landmark, O'Rourke's Tower. The O'Rourke in question was probably Fergal O'Rourke, King of Connacht, who died in AD964, roughly the same time the tower was built for protection against the frequent attacks of the Danes. The tower, 20m (65ft) high, is built of beautifully shaped, slightly curved stones. But the top is incomplete; the cap was blasted off by a lightning strike in 1135, as meticulously recorded by the monks.

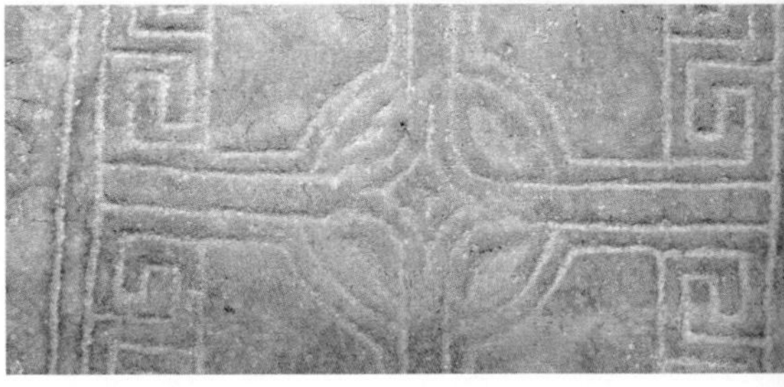

Detail of the ancient carvings on a Celtic cross

THE CATHEDRAL OR MACDERMOT'S CHURCH

East of O'Rourke's Tower is Clonmacnoise Cathedral, a neat incorporation of the original church built in AD904 by Abbot Colman and High King Flann Sinna (▷ 155, Cross of the Scriptures) within a 12th-century rebuilding. Many ancient fragments of carved stones lie in a side chapel. The Gothic arch of the north door is made up of a whole nest of recessed courses carved with barley-sugar fluting and foliage, in which the sculptor has set the dragons of sin to writhe helplessly. This door has a special property—if you bring your mouth close to the stonework on one side and whisper, the sound will be carried around the top of the arch and down to a listener's ear pressed against the opposite jamb. In medieval times, priests could hear the confession of a leper in this way without risk of contamination. Nowadays it's children who rejoice in the secret of the Whispering Door.

ST. CIARÁN'S CHURCH (TEMPLE CIARÁN)

Immediately east of the Cathedral lies the diminutive St. Ciarán's Church, *c*AD800. The founder of Clonmacnoise is said to be buried at the far end. For centuries farmers would anoint the corners of their fields with earth scraped from the floor of St. Ciarán's Church to protect their corn and cattle. Eventually the floor became so hollowed that stone slabs were laid. But old beliefs die hard, and you may still see pilgrims furtively collecting a handkerchief full of earth from just outside the church. Sufferers from warts anoint them with rainwater from the hollow of the *bullaun* or ancient quernstone inside St. Ciarán's Church, a very old practice that persists in rural Ireland.

MACCARTHY'S CHURCH (TEMPLE FINGHIN)

Against the monastery's surrounding wall due north of St. Ciarán's Church stands the 12th-century MacCarthy's Church, unmistakable because of the miniature round tower with its herringbone cap of stone tiles that rises from the south wall of the church. The tower, probably a belfry rather than a defensive stronghold as its door is vulnerably placed at ground level, was built in 1124, some say by Big Finian MacCarthy. The Romanesque chancel arch is decorated with weathered but still beautiful chevron carving.

THE NUNS' CHURCH

Many visitors miss this exquisite little church, because it lies a short walk east of the main site. The carvings are superb, far richer than in any of the other Clonmacnoise churches, with Romanesque chevrons, faces, beaked beasts and other grotesques. The church was built in 1167 as an act of penance by Dervorgilla O'Rourke, whose act of folly (▷ 266) led indirectly to the end of the Golden Age of Celtic Ireland.

CLONMACNOISE CASTLE

Opposite the entrance to the Visitor Centre the substantial ruins of a Norman castle lean from their grassy mound. It was built *c*1203 by Norman baron Sir William de Burgo in a very advantageous site, both on the river and on the Esker Riada (▷ Background). The English destroyed most of it in 1650, just before the Cromwellian invasion. The remaining two-floor keep leans at a crazy angle above its deep ditch.

MacCarthy's Church and its round tower

Among the ruins of the Nuns' Church

BACKGROUND

When he founded the monastery of Clonmacnoise around cAD548, St. Ciarán chose the site extremely well. The monastery stood not only on Ireland's largest navigable river, but also on the glacial ridge called Esker Riada, the King's Highway, the main east–west high road of the kingdoms of Connacht and Leinster. Clonmacnoise enjoyed more than six centuries of prosperity and pre-eminence as Ireland's chief religious and educational centre. Monks from all over Europe came and Kings of Ireland were buried here. Yet those were tough times. The Vikings attacked at least eight times; the locals outdid them, attacking on nearly 30 occasions and setting the monastery on fire a dozen times. After the arrival of the Normans in 1180, Clonmacnoise began to decline, and in 1552 English soldiers stole every treasure, and smashed what they could not carry away.

The fine craftsmanship that created these wonderful crosses—and their survival down the centuries—is quite remarkable (below)

GUIDE TO CLONMACNOISE

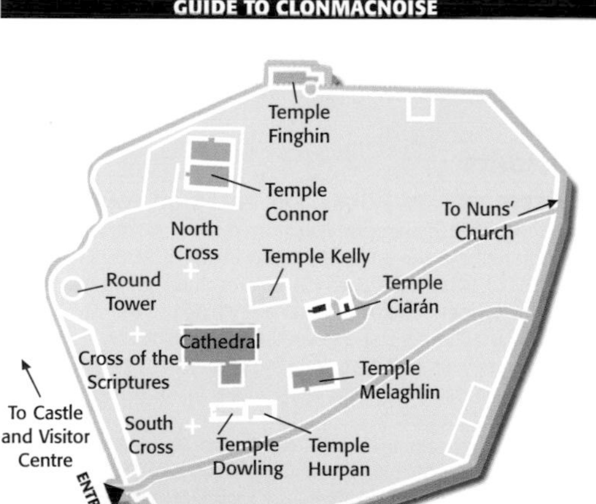

The plan on the left shows the layout of Clonmacnoise. There are also numerous gravestones scattered across the site that are not shown separately on the plan

Strokestown Park and Famine Museum

Ireland's best museum on the Great Famine, and three centuries of one family's possessions.

The intricately worked wrought-iron gates of Strokestown Park

Neat box hedges enclose bright formal plantings

The Famine Museum displays many poignant exhibits

RATINGS	
Cultural interest	●●●●●
Historic interest	●●●●●
Walkability	●●●

BASICS

348 E4 • Strokestown, Co. Longford

071 963 3013

Mid-Mar to end Oct daily 10–5.30

House, Famine Museum and Gardens individually: adult €5.50, child (under 13) €2.20; combined ticket for all three: adult €13.50, child (under 13) €5.70, family €28

Signposted in Strokestown on N5 between Scramoge and Tulsk, 21km (13 miles) west of Longford

www.strokestownpark.ie
A good introduction to the Park and Famine Museum.

SEEING STROKESTOWN PARK AND FAMINE MUSEUM

Strokestown Park is a fine, predominantly 18th-century Palladian building, where a conducted tour starts in the entrance hall and continues by way of the Drawing Room and Library. On the upper floor you view the Lady's and Gentleman's Bedrooms, the Schoolroom and Nursery, before descending to the Dining Room and discovering the world of the family's servants in the Kitchen.

The Famine Museum that now occupies the old stable block is arranged in a series of rooms. Room 1 sets the Ascendancy scene, Room 2 shows the growth of destitution among the Irish poor. Room 3 examines the role of the potato in 19th-century Ireland and the beginning of the catastrophic potato blight, while Rooms 4 and 5 look at the relief efforts that were employed during the Great Famine. There's also a display on eviction and emigration, and some images and discussion of famines across the world today.

The Walled Garden provides a quiet place to process these stark, terrible images.

HIGHLIGHTS

STROKESTOWN PARK HOUSE: THE PERSONAL TOUCH

What distinguishes Strokestown Park from most of the other mansions open to the public is the very strong image of successive generations of its owners that visitors receive. This highly personal atmosphere springs from the fact that everything you see was chosen and used by the owners over their three centuries of incumbency, right up until the sale of the property in 1979 by Olive Pakenham-Mahon, the last of the family to live here, in a poignant genteel poverty.

Upstairs, the Schoolroom (1930s copybooks 'Please rule your margins all the same width' neatly laid out on tiny desks) and Playroom (miniature Baby Austin car, doll's house, rocking horse, dressing-up clothes) mirror the privileged yet highly regulated life of an Ascendancy child.

FAMINE MUSEUM

As with the house, the impact of the Famine Museum comes from the interplay between the intimate details of the Mahon family's attitudes and behaviour during the Famine, and the wider picture in Ireland and in mainland Britain (▷ 36–37).

The exhibition describes how incoming 17th-century Anglo Protestants took over most of Ireland. In the 1620s Irish Catholics owned two-thirds of the land, but after the Cromwellian suppressions of the 1650s, only 30 years later, they held less than one-tenth. In those decades one in three of the Catholic population died of famine, disease or massacre, a far higher proportion than died during the Great Famine, and the system of land tenure kept the poor in abject poverty. British political cartoons depicted the Irish tenantry as 'indolent, idle, inclined to do evil, and beyond the pale of civilization', and

the Anglo-Irish landlords as feckless drunkards. Such contemptuous attitudes contributed to the disaster of the Great Famine of 1845–49, when the *Phytophthora infestans* fungus wiped out the potato crops on which the people were utterly dependent. The British Government fumbled its relief efforts with a mixture of clumsiness and callousness, and mass evictions and emigration added to the misery.

Against this background moves the story of the Mahons on their estate that stretched for 2,400ha (5,930 acres), and of the evictions carried out by Major Denis Mahon during the Famine. Family papers exhibited include a letter of 7 November 1847 from Mahon's agent proposing the eviction and enforced emigration to America of two-thirds of the local population, and a pathetic letter to the Major from his tenants which asks, 'What must we do?—our families really and truly suffering at present, and we cannot much longer withstand their cries for food.' The letter makes veiled threats of action unless relief is forthcoming; and such action did follow, later that year, when the Major was shot dead. This picture of seigneurial hard-heartedness is balanced by a thoughtful coda by the Major's great-great-grandson, pointing out that landlords like Denis Mahon had insufficient personal resources and no government grants to help their tenants, and that paying for them to emigrate was preferable to letting them starve.

In spite of its size, Strokestown retains a very personal air

WALLED GARDENS

In 1997 the refurbished Walled Gardens were opened to the public after years of neglect. You can enjoy roses, wild flowers and the longest herbaceous border in the British Isles, as well as the neat green swards of the lawn tennis court and the croquet lawn, a magnificent lily pond and shady walkways under the trees.

TIPS

- Leave plenty of time for the Famine Museum. Once you start reading the contemporary letters and inspecting the cartoons, you'll want at least an hour for this part of the tour.
- In Rooms 4 and 5 of the Famine Museum, don't miss the grim model of Strokestown Workhouse with its black walls. The cutaway section of the roof lets you look into the cheerless, crowded dormitories where children were separated from their parents and husbands from wives.

BACKGROUND

The story of the Mahons is that of many other Anglo-Irish families: a huge 17th-century grant of land by the English crown, the laying out and working of a vast estate, the building and improvement of the fine mansion, three centuries of ease and prosperity as bastions of the Ascendancy, followed by a gradual decline during the 20th century and the eventual sale of house and lands. The difference here is that the family's attitudes to its tenants are explored with insight and honesty in the remarkable museum dedicated to the Great Famine.

Serene Lough Key, scenically dotted with wooded islands

The castle on the Rock of Dunamase, razed by Cromwell

A misty, distant view of the Slieve Bloom Mountains

LOUGH KEY FOREST PARK

347 E4 • Boyle, Co. Roscommon 071 966 2363 Apr–end Oct daily 10–6 €5 per car Boyle Signposted on N4 Carrick-on-Shannon road, 3.2km (2 miles) east of Boyle

Lough Key Forest Park comprises 350ha (870 acres) of beautiful woodlands with footpaths, and the island-dotted Lough Key. It forms part of the once-mighty Rockingham Estate, which was based on the classical-style Rockingham House, to which the King family moved from Boyle in 1788 (▷ 152). In 1957 the great house burned down and the estate was sold to the nation.

Water taxis run from the lake jetty to the islands, or you can rent a rowing boat and scull out to Castle Island with its 19th-century folly, or to Trinity Island where you can see the ruins of the 12th-century Trinity Abbey. Lough Key is also very well-known for coarse fishing.

LOUGH REE

348 E5 • North of Athlone Tourist Information Office, Athlone Castle, Athlone, Co. Westmeath tel 0906 494630; for hours ▷ 150 www.athlone.ie

Lough Ree, formed by a great widening of the River Shannon where counties Westmeath, Roscommon and Longford meet, is a ragged, fishtail-shaped lake 25.5km (16 miles) long. Islands dot this mighty stretch of water, superb for both boating and fishing. You can rent boats and fishing tackle at various places around the lake. Athlone has several tackle shops, such as Strand Fishing Tackle (The Strand, tel 0902 79277), and day-boat and cruiser rental companies include Inner Lakes Marina (tel 0902 85424) and Waveline Cruisers of Quigley's Marina (tel 0902 485711), both at Killinure near Glasson, 6.5km (4 miles) north of Athlone; and Athlone Cruisers at Jolly Mariner Marina, Coosan (tel 0902 72892 or 72113). Check at the marina which islands you can land on (your craft will need an anchor, and a rowing dinghy). The most rewarding island is Inchcleraun or Quaker's Island towards the north end of Lough Ree (anchor near red lake navigation marker No. 7). You can explore the ancient churches of Teampull Diarmuid and Teampull Mor, the tiny 12th-century Chancel Church and the Church of the Dead near the shore, and near the middle of Inchcleraun the 12th-century Clogás Oratory with its bell tower.

ROCK OF DUNAMASE

352 F6 Tourist Information Office, Lawlor Avenue, Portlaoise, Co. Laois, tel 0502 21178; for hours ▷ 150 www.eastcoastmidlandsireland.com

Rising dramatically from the flattish County Laois countryside, the Rock of Dunamase is covered in the broken walls and towers of a castle. It was built during the mid-12th century by Dermot MacMurrough, King of Leinster, who famously eloped with Dervorgilla, wife of Tiernan O'Rourke (▷ 157, 266) and later invited the Normans to Ireland. The alliance was cemented when his daughter Aoife married their leader Richard de Clare ('Strongbow'), who turned the fort into a massive stronghold. It lasted nearly 500 years, until Cromwell's men blew it up in 1650.

You can climb the three steeply sloping wards to reach the broken but sturdy keep, from where there are stunning, far-reaching views, from the Slieve Bloom Mountains to the Wicklow Hills.

SLIEVE BLOOM MOUNTAINS

352 E6 Tourist Information Office, Lawlor Avenue, Portlaoise, Co. Laois, tel 0502 21178; for hours ▷ 150 www.eastcoastmidlandsireland.com; Tourism Office, Bury Quay, Tullamore, Co. Offaly, tel 0506 25015; May–end Sep Mon–Sat 9–6, Sun 12–5; Oct–end Apr Mon–Sat 10–5, Sun 12–5 www.kinnitty.net

Journeying across the waist of Ireland, the gently domed ridges of the Slieve Bloom Mountains will be in view for much of the way. Really too low to be mountains, they are a shapely range of hills that assume mountainous proportions amid the low landscape. They are surprisingly wild, given their small compass, with swathes of upland moor, hidden waterfalls and deep forested valleys. The Slieve Bloom Way loops round their heights.

STROKESTOWN PARK AND FAMINE MUSEUM

See pages 158–159.

TULLYNALLY CASTLE AND GARDENS

348 F4 • Castlepollard, Co. Westmeath 044 61159 Gardens: Jun–end Aug daily 2–6; May, weekends and public holidays only; castle: by appointment for groups only Gardens: adult €5, child (6–16) €2.50 Signposted off R394, 21km (13 miles) north of Mullingar www.tullynallycastle.com

Tullynally Castle has been the seat of the Pakenham family (now Earls of Longford) since 1655, and they still live in the house that was rebuilt during the 19th century into a full scale Gothic castle. The tour takes in the Great Hall, library, dining room and domestic rooms such as the Victorian kitchen, laundry and drying room. Outside are lovely gardens and grounds.

NORTHERN IRELAND

The provincial capital of Belfast and the lovely walled city of Derry compete for attention with the spectacular Antrim Coast and the Giant's Causeway—the most visited sight in Northern Ireland. The Mountains of Mourne and Lough Erne are scenic beauty spots, while the Ulster American Folk Park is a poignant look at Irish emigration.

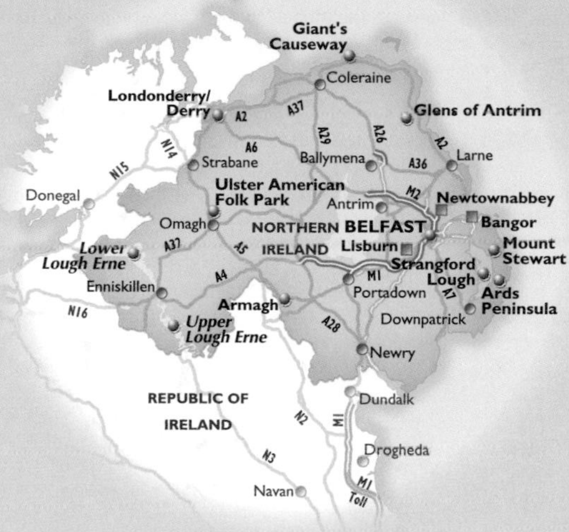

MAJOR SIGHTS

Ards Peninsula and Strangford Lough

Long sandy beaches and an island-dotted lough, with superb birdwatching and other activities.

RATINGS

Good for kids	●●●●
Outdoor pursuits	●●●●
Photo stops	●●●

BASICS

349 H3

Bangor Tourist Information Office: 34 Quay Street, Bangor, Co. Down, tel 028 9127 0069; Jul, Aug Mon–Fri 9–6 (opens 10am on Tue), Sat 10–5, Sun 1–5; Sep–end Jun Mon–Fri 9–5 (opens 10am on Tue) Sat 10–4, closed Sun

Downpatrick Tourist Information Office: St. Patrick's Centre, 53a Market Street, Downpatrick, Co. Down, BT30 6LZ, tel 028 4461 2233; Jul, Aug Mon–Sat 9.30–6, Sun 2–6; Sep–end Jun Mon–Sat 9.30–5

www.northdown.gov.uk
Borough council site, with a good, informative section for tourists.

A brightly painted fishing boat in Strangford Harbour (top).
A cormorant in flight (above).
The car ferry crossing the lough (opposite top).
Scrabo Tower is silhouetted by the setting sun (opposite inset)

SEEING THE ARDS PENINSULA AND STRANGFORD LOUGH

The Ards Peninsula and Strangford Lough are just to the east of Belfast, and are easily reached from the city. The A2 road runs east from Belfast through Bangor before turning south along the outer Ards coast through a string of east-facing seaside villages, down to Portaferry at the southern tip. Here it meets the A20, which has come from Belfast through Newtownards, and then goes south along the inner, or Strangford Lough, shore of the Ards Peninsula by way of Mount Stewart and Grey Abbey.

The A22 Downpatrick–Belfast road follows the landward or western shore of Strangford Lough. The A25 from Downpatrick links to the A2/A20 at the southern tip of the Ards Peninsula by way of the Portaferry–Strangford ferry.

HIGHLIGHTS

COAST AND VILLAGES OF THE ARDS PENINSULA

East of Belfast, the Ards Peninsula hangs off the shoulder of County Down like a long, outward-crooked arm. The peninsula stretches south for some 40km (25 miles) and is edged with a fine sweep of coastline. From the seaside resort of Bangor you follow the A2 to Donaghadee, Ulster's chief passenger port from the 16th to the 19th centuries. Boats ran from Portpatrick in Scotland, and the big harbour with its lighthouse and Georgian houses speak of its past importance. But competition with the Stranraer–Larne ferry route overcame the Portpatrick–Donaghadee service, and it stopped in 1849.

The switchback coast road runs beside a shoreline of wonderful sandy beaches, passing through Ballywalter and Ballyhalbert and the fishing village of Portavogie. Stop here to sample some Portavogie prawns, straight out of the sea, before continuing to Cloughey, where you turn off to Kearney, a former fishing village that has been restored to an unlikely but beautiful neatness by the National Trust.

GREY ABBEY

349 H3 • Church Street, Greyabbey, Co. Down 028 9054 6552/3033
Apr–end Sep Tue–Sat 10–7, Sun 2–7; Oct–end Mar Sat 10–4, Sun 2–4 Free

Grey Abbey was founded in 1193 by Affreca, wife of the Norman Lord of Ards, Sir John de Courcy. In those uncertain times, only 20 years after the Norman invasion, Irish-born monks were thought to be too sympathetic to local warlords, so Grey Abbey's first monks were imported from Cumbria in northwest England.

The imposing ruins by the shore, with their Gothic doorways and windows, incorporate a re-created herb garden.

STRANGFORD LOUGH

Strangford Lough is a giant tidal inlet, 30km (19 miles) long, between the Ards Peninsula and the mainland. A twice-daily flush of tides pours through a tiny gap only 458m (500 yards) wide at Portaferry. Strangford Lough contains 70 islands and vast mudflats and sandbanks, exposed at low tide. Birdwatching is first class. A haven for wildlife, it is protected by designations that include Site of Special Scientific Interest, Marine Nature Reserve and National Nature Reserve. The lough is managed by the National Trust (Visitor Centre at Castle Ward, tel 028 4488 1411, ▷ 175). At Portaferry, the Exploris aquarium in the Rope Walk, Castle Street, with its 'Touch Tank', and the seal sanctuary (Apr–end Sep Mon–Fri 10–6, Sat 11–6, Sun 12–6; Oct–end Mar Mon–Fri 10–5, Sat 11–5, Sun 1–5) are popular attractions.

SCRABO TOWER

For a memorable view, climb the 122 steps to the top of Scrabo Tower at the summit of Scrabo Hill Country Park, off the A21 south-east of Newtownards (tel 028 9181 1491; Jun–end Sep Sat–Thu 10.30–6). The tower was erected in 1857 by the tenants of Charles Stewart, third Marquis of Londonderry (▷ 184, Mount Stewart), to commemorate his charity during the Great Famine. From the viewing platform 41m (135ft) high, you enjoy a fabulous panorama over the Ards Peninsula and Strangford Lough, south to the Mountains of Mourne and east across the sea to the Scottish hills.

Scrabo Tower (above)

BIRDWATCHING

The birdwatching on Strangford Lough is among the best in the British Isles. The varied habitats of the lough give food and shelter to birds all year round. Especially spectacular are the winter gatherings of up to 40,000 waders (oystercatcher, lapwing, curlew, knot, redshank) and 20,000 waterfowl (gadwall, pintail, wigeon, goldeneye, red-breasted merganser, Slavonian grebe), as well as up to 15,000 pale-bellied Brent geese. In spring/summer breeding species include heron, cormorant, great crested grebe, eider and black guillemot, along with gulls and terns. There's excellent birdwatching at Castle Espie Wildfowl and Wetlands Centre, signposted off the A22, 5km (3 miles) south of Comber (tel 028 9187 4146; Mar–end Sep Mon–Sat 10.30–5, Sun 11.30–5.30; Oct–end Feb Mon–Sat 11.30–4, Sun 11.30–5) and Quoile Pondage Countryside Centre, signposted off the A25 at Downpatrick (tel 028 4461 5520; Apr–end Aug daily 11–5, Mar, Sep Sat, Sun 1–5). Visit www.birdwatch-ni.co.uk for more information.

BACKGROUND

The Ards Peninsula has always been a place apart from the mainstream, full of small farms and fishing villages, and Strangford Lough shares its feeling of isolation. The scatter of little islands in the lough, some accessible by causeways known only to locals, made ideal defensive positions for early settlers, and the pioneer Christians also found them safe havens. The Ards was a busy place, and Donaghadee served as Ulster's main entry port from mainland Britain, but now the area is one of the most peaceful spots in Northern Ireland.

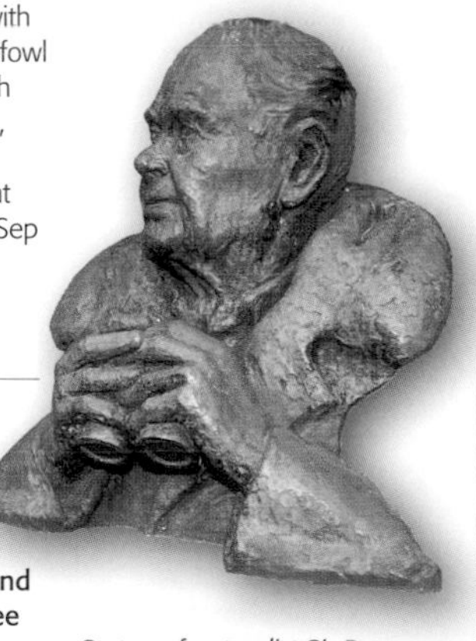
Statue of naturalist Sir Peter Scott at Castle Espie

Superb stone carving on Ardboe High Cross

Ardress House overlooks its beautiful rose garden

The Argory, topped by a weather vane, and its sundial garden

ARDBOE HIGH CROSS

349 G2 • Open access • Free
Tourist Information Office, The Burnavon, Burn Road, Cookstown, Co. Tyrone, BT80 8DN, tel 028 8676 6727; Jul–end Sep Mon–Sat 9–5, Sun 10–4
Signposted from Newport Trench on B73, 16km (10 miles) east of Cookstown
www.cookstown.gov.uk

On the flat western shore of Lough Neagh (▷ 181), the magnificent Ardboe High Cross, carved in the ninth or tenth century, stands 5.5m (18.5ft) tall. The shaft and head are heavily carved with biblical scenes, but weathering has blurred the finer details. The cross suffered at the hands of pilgrims, too, especially those making their final prayers before emigrating, who would take a fragment for good luck.

The carvings on the east and south faces are of Old Testament scenes, while the west face deals with New Testament themes. Look on the east side for Adam and Eve under a spreading Tree of Knowledge, Abraham about to sacrifice Isaac and Shadrach, Meshach and Abednego in the Fiery Furnace. On the south is Cain dealing brother Abel a thump with a flail, Samson and his lion and a cramped David and Goliath. The west has the Adoration, the miracles of the wine and water at Cana and the loaves and fishes at Galilee, and Christ's entry into Jerusalem on a smartly stepping donkey. The Passion occupies the west face of the cross head, while the east depicts the Last Judgement.

Behind the cross stands a beech tree, pierced by thousands of coins pushed into its trunk by supplicants hoping to leave their troubles behind—or transfer them to anyone who would steal the coin. Sadly, the metal of the coins has gradually poisoned the tree. Beyond the tree is the ruin of a 17th-century church, on the site of a monastery established in the sixth century by St. Colman Muchaidhe. Legend has it that when the workers building it became faint from lack of food, the saint sent his cow to walk across the lake and bring them milk. It is also said, somewhat at odds with chronology, that the left-over milk was mixed with the mortar used to build the High Cross, ensuring its survival over the centuries and naming it: *Ard Bo* means 'the hill of the cow'.

ARDRESS HOUSE

349 G3 • 64 Ardress Road, Portadown, Co. Armagh, BT62 1SQ
028 3885 1236 • Jun–end Aug Wed–Mon 2–6; mid-Mar to end May, Sep Sat, Sun 2–6 • Adult £3, child (under 12) £1.50 (NT members free)
Signposted on B28 between Portadown and Charlemont
www.nationaltrust.org.uk

When Dublin architect George Ensor acquired Ardress by marriage in 1760 he embarked on an ambitious project to transform the 17th-century farmhouse into a neoclassical country house. Ensor added a new wing to one side, a matching mock wing (complete with false windows) on the other side for balance, and an imposingly broad frontage entered through a pedimented porch. Yet you can still see the original farmhouse roof, peeping over the curly gables and urns of the Georgian extension.

Inside, there's wonderful stucco work in the drawing room, notably the panels depicting the Four Seasons, and some fine Chippendale furniture and Waterford crystal. Outside, it's all geared towards family fun. The cobbled 18th-century farmyard attached to the house has a collection of agricultural tools and a variety of farm animals—goats, ducks, hens, pigs and ponies—and there's a children's play area. **Don't miss** The walled garden has a beautiful display of old Irish roses, and the orchard has old Irish varieties of apple trees. Further afield, footpaths lead through the woods and along the Tall River.

ARDS PENINSULA

See pages 162–163.

THE ARGORY

349 G3 • 144 Derrycaw Road, Moy, Dungannon, Co. Tyrone • 028 8778 4753 • House: Jun–end Aug daily 1–6; mid-Mar to end May, Sep Sat, Sun 1–6. Grounds: May–end Sep daily 10–8; Oct–end Apr 10–4 • Adult £4.50, child (4–18) £2.40 (NT members free)
Signposted off M1 at Junction 14
www.nationaltrust.org.uk

Time at The Argory is frozen in the year 1906. This handsome country house in its 130ha (320 acres) of well-wooded grounds by the River Blackwater presents a picture of a well-to-do Anglo-Irish home immediately before Independence. Built in 1824 by Walter McGeogh, it is entered through a fine wide portico, into the hall with its massive cast-iron stove, and visitors are plunged into the Edwardian era and world of the McGeogh-Bond family. Photographs and portraits hang on the walls of the study, dining room and billiard room. The Steinway grand piano stands in the drawing room. Up the curved staircase is a barrel organ that was an original fixture of the house. It is played once a month (telephone for dates). There is no electricity, and lamps diffuse the soft yellow light of acetylene gas from the plant installed in the stables in 1906. You can inspect the gas plant and the horse carriages in the stable yard, and then go on through the formal gardens and along the riverbank footpaths.

ARMAGH

Two splendid cathedrals and handsome Georgian buildings greet visitors to Armagh. One of the oldest cities in Ireland, this little grey-roofed city was the ancient capital of Ulster, and the seat of both Catholic and Anglican Bishops of Ireland.

RATINGS	
Historic interest	● ● ● ●
Photo stops	● ● ●
Walkability	● ● ●

BASICS

349 G3

Tourist Information Office, Old Bank Building, 40 English Street, Armagh, Co. Armagh, BT61 7BA, tel 028 3752 8329; Mon–Sat 9–5, Sun 2–5

www.armagh.gov.uk
Well-designed site with a great interactive tourist map

TIPS

- **If you happen to be in Armagh on or around 12 July, the day of Orange Order parades all across Northern Ireland, don't be surprised if you find all public attractions have been closed for the day. Best to telephone and check.**
- **There are several saucy medieval carvings, including a donkey-eared Sheela-na-gig, in the Chapter House of the Anglican Cathedral.**

THE CATHEDRALS

Exploring Armagh, you can hardly help but start with its two great cathedrals—they are by far the most eye-catching and significant buildings in town. The Anglican Cathedral of St. Patrick (Apr–end Oct 10–5; Nov–end Mar 10–4) is the smaller and by far the older of the two. Its largely 19th-century exterior of pink sandstone conceals parts of a mid-13th-century cathedral, which itself was preceded by other churches going back in time to AD444 when St. Patrick himself built the first church on this site. Enjoyable highlights of the present cathedral include the various gargoyles and stone-carved grotesques high on the walls both inside and out. The Chapter House contains the fiendishly grinning Iron Age effigy called the Tandragee Idol. Brian Boru, the High King of Ireland, killed in 1014 as his army defeated the Vikings at the Battle of Clontarf, lies buried somewhere inside the hill.

Across the valley on Cathedral Road are the two huge rocket-like towers of the Roman Catholic Cathedral of St. Patrick (Mon–Sat 10–5). The interior is an unrestrained Gothic burst of mosaic, marble and golden angels on the wing. Construction of the cathedral, funded chiefly through public subscription, bazaars and raffles, started in 1838, but was halted during the Great Famine of the 1840s. It was finally completed in 1873.

AROUND THE CITY

There are several other enjoyable attractions in Armagh. On English Street near the neat Georgian Mall, St. Patrick's Trian (tel 028 3752 1801; Mon–Sat 10–5, Sun 2–5) has displays covering the city's links with the saint, the story of the city itself and *Gulliver's Travels* (the author Johathan Swift spent a lot of time in Armagh). Life in Armagh in the 18th century is entertainingly re-created at the Palace Demesne (tel 028 3752 9629; Mon–Sat 10–5, Sun 2–5). Armagh's old-fashioned Robinson's Library (Abbey Street; tel 028 3752 3142; Mon–Fri 10–1, 2–4) has, among its ancient leather-bound tomes, a first-edition *Gulliver's Travels* marked up by Swift himself. Due to reopen in late 2005, the Planetarium is a popular attraction.

Don't miss The long-case clock in the Catholic cathedral was first prize in one of the raffles held to raise money for building works, and is still waiting to be claimed by the person who won it—in 1865.

The splendid view from atop the Catholic cathedral (main, left)

St. Patrick's Catholic Cathedral sits at the top of a long flight of steps (top right)

The Anglican Cathedral of St. Patrick (above)

Belfast

Northern Ireland's biggest, most important and lively city has a fascinating, sometimes grim, history. The capital offers vibrant nightlife and Belfast people enjoy a great line in black humour.

City Hall (above left). A Shankill Road mural (middle). The Botanic Garden (above right). Big Fish *at Laganside (opposite)*

RATINGS	
Cultural interest	●●●●●
Good for kids	●●●●
Historic interest	●●●
Photo stops	●●●

BASICS

349 H2

Belfast Welcome Centre, 47 Donegall Place, Belfast, BT1 5AD, tel 028 9024 6609; Jun–end Sep Mon 9.30–7, Tue–Sat 9–7, Sun 12–5; Oct–end May Mon–Sat 9–5.30

Belfast

www.gotobelfast.com
Full information; good events section.

A festival character in front of the Albert Clock (below)

SEEING BELFAST

The River Lagan flows north through Belfast into Belfast Lough, cutting the city in two; just about everything that a visitor would want to see or do is west of the river. Most of the grand public buildings, such as St. Anne's Cathedral and the Town Hall, are in the middle of the city, while along the river are the Lagan Lookout, Sinclair Seamen's Church, Waterfront Hall and the other riverside attractions. Just to the west are the Falls and Shankill roads with their vivid murals—black taxi tour territory (▷ 171). About 1.5km (1 mile) to the south of the city lies Belfast's university quarter with Queen's University, the Botanic Gardens, the Ulster Museum and some fine parks.

Belfast is very easy to negotiate—most of the main attractions are within a few minutes' walk of each other—and there are a number of green and pleasant ways to get around: on foot or by bicycle, on one of the frequent city buses or cruising along the River Lagan by boat (or walking along its towpath).

HIGHLIGHTS

DONEGALL SQUARE

172 B3

The heart of Belfast is Donegall Square, whose broad pavements and flowerbeds surround the giant City Hall (▷ below). Buildings to admire around Donegall Square include the Italianate sandstone Marks & Spencer, the Scottish Provident Building with its cavorting dolphins and guardian lions, and the Linenhall Library (tel 028 9032 1707, Mon–Fri 9.30–5.30 Sat 9.30–1), a wonderful, hushed, old-fashioned library (with a tea room that's a Belfast institution) whose Political Collection offers an overview of the recent Troubles.

CITY HALL

172 B3 • Donegall Square, Belfast, BT1 5GS ☎ 028 9027 0456 Tours Jun–end Sep Mon–Fri at 11, 2, 3, Sun 2.30; Oct–end May Mon–Fri 11, 2.30, Sat 2.30 Free

The great green dome of the City Hall (opened in 1906) rises 53m (173ft) into the sky and is a prime Belfast landmark. Patterned Italian marble and elaborate stucco greet you in the hall, from where tours of the building ascend beneath the dome to the oak-panelled Council

The Belfast
Together with
The Unco Laddie.

MORE TO SEE

STORMONT CASTLE

Off map 173 D3

Seat of the on–off Northern Ireland Assembly, Stormont Castle lies 8km (5 miles) east of the city, and is easily accessible by City bus 16, 17 or 20. The very imposing castle at the end of its mile-long drive is only open to the public by appointment, but there are great walks in the woods and across the open parkland that surround Stormont.

Waterfront Hall (above)

The Crown Liquor Saloon (right)

THE PEOPLE'S MUSEUM

Off map 172 A2 • Fernhill House, Glencairn Road, Belfast, BT13 3PT 028 9071 5599 Mon–Sat 10–4, Sun 1–4

A re-created 1930s working-class house telling the story of life in the Shankill area and also of Unionism in Northern Ireland.

AN CULTÚRLANN MACADAM O'FIAICH

Off map 172 A3 • 216 Falls Road, Belfast, BT12 6AH 028 9023 9303 Sun–Wed 9–9, Thu–Sat 9–10

Here exhibitions, music concerts and a bookshop promote the Irish language and culture.

ST. MALACHY'S CHURCH

172 C4 • Alfred Street, Belfast, BT2 8EN 028 9032 1713 Daily 8–5.45

The church may look unprepossessing from the outside with its dingy red brick and lurid pink paintwork, but it shouldn't be judged by its cover. Inside you'll find an early Victorian extravaganza of elaborate stucco, fan-vaulting that's said to be a tribute to King Henry VII's chapel in Westminster Abbey, a fine altarpiece carved by the Piccioni family (from the Tirol), and later window glass with purple art nouveau lilies.

Chamber. This splendid civic apartment contains two tellingly contrasted items. One is the Lord Mayor's handsomely carved throne. The other is an icon for all Orangemen: the plain and simple round wooden table at which the Unionist leader, Sir Edward Carson, signed the Solemn League and Covenant of Resistance against Home Rule on 28 September 1912. Over 400,000 Ulster Protestants were to follow him as signatories, some in their own blood.

GRAND OPERA HOUSE

172 A4 • 2–4 Great Victoria Street, Belfast, BT2 7BA 028 9024 1919/3411 By arrangement

www.goh.co.uk

The Grand Opera House is a splendid example of a late Victorian music hall. Ornate outside and all overblown opulence within, it has suffered various vicissitudes down the years, from relegation to a second-class cinema in the 1950s to a brace of IRA bombs in 1991 and 1993, which damaged but failed to destroy it. Yet one look at the giant gilt elephants, the cherubs and swags of golden fruit and flowers tells you of its aspirations when it was opened in 1895. Nowadays restored and refurbished, the Grand Opera House puts on a wide variety of entertainment that includes live music, comedies, dramas, musicals, pantomime, Shakespeare, ballet...and, of course, opera productions.

CROWN LIQUOR SALOON

172 A4 • 48 Great Victoria Street, Belfast, BT2 7BA ☎ 028 9027 9901
Mon–Sat 11.30am–midnight, Sun 12.30–11pm

This Victorian 'temple of intemperance' is, as its owners the National Trust proudly claim, 'the most famous pub in Belfast'. The Trust bought the pub in 1978 and spent £400,000 restoring it because they recognized it for what it was: a supreme example of the Golden Age of public house design. From the colonnaded gilt and marble frontage to the interior with its curved bar, embossed ceiling and ornate wood snugs, with frosted glass and service bells, the Crown Liquor Saloon is gloriously, frothily over the top. Note the inlaid crown on the floor at the entrance. It was installed there in 1895 by the nationalist owner Patrick Flanagan, so that all his customers could tread it underfoot.

ST. GEORGE'S MARKET

172 C4

This handsome 1896 red-brick and stone building at the junction of May and Oxford streets is Belfast's only surviving Victorian market hall. Organic produce, flowers, knick-knacks and a lively fish market, under a restored roof of glass and cast iron, are the focus for shoppers on Tuesdays and Fridays. The hall is also used for exhibitions, art and craft shows and a New Year party.

The Crown Liquor Saloon's interior is pure Victoriana

The Harland & Wolff shipyard cranes are a city landmark

A maritime theme pervades the Sinclair Seamen's Church

PUBS

A good way to sample the best of Belfast pubs is to join the Historical Pub Tour of Belfast (tel 028 9268 3665; May–end Oct Thu 7, Sat 4) that starts at Flannigan's (upstairs at the Crown Liquor Saloon, ▷ above). Belfast's most characterful pubs include White's (tel 028 9024 3080)—Belfast's oldest pub (so it claims)—in Winecellar Entry, and the Morning Star (tel 028 9032 3976) in Pottinger's Entry, a pub with a superb semi-elliptical bar and a menu that can include emu, kangaroo and crocodile. Guess the nationality of the licensee! Bittles Bar (tel 028 9031 1088) in Victoria Street is a wedge-shaped corner pub with some splendid paintings of Irish literary figures; the Kitchen Bar (tel 028 9032 4901) on Victoria Square offers local real ales and traditional music; Kelly's Cellars (tel 028 9032 4835) in Bank Street is a dark, delightful old place.

SINCLAIR SEAMEN'S CHURCH

172 C1 • Corporation Square, Belfast, BT1 3AJ ☎ 028 9071 5997 Wed 2–5, Sun for services at 11.30 and 7 Free

This is an L-shaped Presbyterian church of 1857, furnished in a nautical style to attract visiting sailors. The font is a ship's binnacle; the pulpit resembles the prow of a ship; nautical themes feature in the stained-glass windows; the mast of a Guinness barge and ships' riding lights decorate the walls. Services commence with the ringing of HMS *Hood*'s brass ship's bell. Even the welcome sign by the door conveys its message by semaphore flags. Seafaring worshippers will never be turned away—50 seats are reserved for them.

BOTANIC GARDENS

Off map 172 B5 • Stranmillis Road, Belfast, BT7 1LP
☎ 028 9032 4902 Gardens: daily until dusk; Greenhouse and Tropical Ravine: Mon–Fri 10–12, 1–5, Sat, Sun 2–5 (Oct–end Mar until 4) Free

These classic 19th-century gardens beside the river contain two pieces of High Victorian glass-and-cast-iron architecture: the great Glasshouse of 1839–40 with its Cool Wing full of bright plants and

THE HARBOUR COMMISSIONER'S OFFICE

172 C1 • Corporation Square, Belfast, BT1 3AL, off Donegall Quay near Lagan Lookout ☎ 028 9055 4422
Tours for booked parties only

The city has few grander buildings than this one, built in 1854 to reflect Belfast's Victorian prosperity. The interior has wonderful floors of mosaic and inlaid marble, heavy plaster mouldings and stained-glass windows. Upstairs there are maritime paintings, and in the barrel-roofed Barnet Room the stained-glass windows depict the arms of old colonial partners in trade such as Canada, Australia, India and the United States.

The Barrel Man *sculpture on Portside*

An exhibition at the Ormeau Baths Gallery (inset). Exhibits from Irish history in the Ulster Museum (above)

its steamy Stove Wing and mighty central dome. There's more steam in the nearby Tropical Ravine, where you stroll round a gallery looking down through the canopy of a miniature tropical rain forest. The wide lawns of the Botanic Gardens provide a place to relax for students from nearby Queen's University.

MORE TO SEE

ORMEAU BATHS GALLERY

172 B4 • 18a Ormeau Road, Belfast, BT2 8HS 028 9032 1402
Tue–Sat 10–6
Frequently changing exhibitions of contemporary art from Ireland and elsewhere are displayed on two floors of an imaginatively converted old public baths.

ULSTER MUSEUM

Off map 172 B5 • Botanic Gardens, Stranmillis Road, Belfast, BT9 5AB
028 9038 3000 Mon–Fri 10–5, Sat 1–5, Sun 2–5 Free
www.ulstermuseum.org.uk
Displays in the Ulster Museum include Stone and Bronze Age implements, jewellery and religious icons of the Dark Ages and medieval Ireland, and machines and mementoes of Ulster's great industrial heritage of shipbuilding, textiles and heavy industry. The history of the Troubles is not neglected. There's also an absorbing display of the treasures dredged up from the 1588 wreck of the Spanish warship *Girona*—everything from clothing to gold trinkets—and a fine art collection that includes Turner and Stubbs, a selection of Impressionists and modernists, and works by Belfast-born Sir John Lavery.

ST. ANNE'S CATHEDRAL

172 B2 • Donegall Street, Belfast, BT1 2HB 028 9032 8332 Mon–Sat 10–6 Free
www.belfastcathedral.org
Consecrated in 1904, St. Anne's Cathedral is an impressive church built of stone from all 32 counties of Ireland. Highlights include the 'Occupations of Mankind' carvings on the capitals of the nave pillars, the glorious modern stained glass of the east window, and the maple and marble of the nave floor. Don't miss the 1920s mosaics by the Martin sisters, or the prayer book written out by hand on cigarette paper by a World War II captive in a Japanese prisoner-of-war camp.

RIVER LAGAN EXPLORATIONS

172 C2 The Lagan Lookout Visitor Centre, Donegall Quay, Belfast, BT1 3EA tel 028 9031 5444; Apr–end Sep Mon–Fri 11–5, Sat 12–5, Sun 2–5; Oct–end Mar Tue–Fri 11–3.30, Sat 1–4.30, Sun 2–4.30
The Lagan Lookout Visitor Centre has displays on Belfast shipbuilding and the story of the River Lagan. The Lagan Boat Company (tel 028

BELFAST TALES

LIGHT THAT LASTED

While exploring Sinclair Seamen's Church, look for the silver torch displayed next to the big brass bell of HMS *Hood*. Some survivors of a shipwreck were left clinging to a rock with only this torch as a resource. Its light lasted just long enough for them to be spotted and rescued.

BELLS AFORE YE GO

Messrs Dunville's, whiskey distillers, conducted their craft next door to St. Malachy's Church on Alfred Street. Judging that the vibrations caused by the tolling of the church bell were spoiling their product, Dunville's complained—and the bell was taken down.

9033 0844) runs trips from Donegall Quay: upriver past the fine new developments and out into green countryside; downriver to view the shipyards of Harland & Wolff where *Titanic* was built and where the twin giant yellow cranes called Samson and Goliath are familiar Belfast landmarks. You can walk or bicycle along the Lagan's towpath, which runs south for several miles to Lisburn. Leaflet guides are available from the Belfast Welcome Centre (▷ 166).

BLACK TAXI TOURS

☎ 028 9064 2264 or 0800 052 3914 ⌚ Depart Belfast City Centre daily, 10, 12, 2, 4, 6, also 8 in summer ✋ £25 for up to 3 people, £8 per person for 4+

Black Taxi tours let you see West Belfast, the area where the Troubles were focused, from an insider's viewpoint, thanks to the local knowledge of the drivers. They will show you the loyalist Shankill Road and nationalist Falls Road (astonishingly close together), the battered, graffiti'd Peace Line that separates the two opposed communities, and the vivid, sectarian gable-end murals for which Belfast is famous.

Murals on Shankill Road gables reflect sectarian passions

The Halloween Parade (left). The stately Stormont, seat of the Northern Ireland Assembly (above)

NORTH BELFAST

To the north, the city rises up to Cave Hill, 367m (1,204ft). City buses 8, 9, 10 and 45–51 from Donegall Square will take you up to Belfast Castle on its lower slopes. This splendid Victorian 'Scottish Baronial' edifice, built for the third Marquess of Donegall in 1870, contains a small Heritage Centre on its top floor. Close by is Belfast Zoological Gardens (tel 028 9077 277; Apr–end Sep daily 10–5; Oct–end Mar daily 10–4.30), where animals of Africa, Asia and South America live in the relative freedom of large, grassy enclosures.

Try the Cave Hill walk if you need a breath of air outside the city. You can get a free trail map, literature and information from Cave Hill Heritage Centre (Belfast Castle, Antrim Road, Belfast, BT15 5GR, tel 028 9077 6925). The waymarked trail leads up through woods, then by the neolithic caves in the great basalt cliff of Napoleon's Nose, to a mountain path leading to the old earthwork called McArt's Fort at the summit of Cave Hill. From here the view over Belfast, the Ards Peninsula and Belfast Lough is superb.

BACKGROUND

Belfast is a solid Victorian city built largely on the sea trading, shipbuilding and textile trades, with large public buildings that sit grandly amid fading red-brick terraces and commercial premises. Parts of Belfast are a bit shabby, but down along the River Lagan and around the heart of the city the old place is smartening and modernizing itself at a great rate.

It is a city packed with attractions, most of them uncrowded. And, contrary to many first-time visitors' expectations, it is a very friendly city. Belfast people are generous with their time and help; they often speak with black and mordant humour; and they don't usually hold back from conversation.

LEANING TOWER OF BELFAST

Some will tell you that W. J. Barre was drunk when he designed the Albert Memorial Clock Tower in 1865, and it certainly inclines perceptibly—1.25m (4ft) out of true, in fact. The truth is more prosaic. The wooden foundations have warped and shifted over the years. Still, it's given the locals the opportunity to joke: 'Albert's got the time, and he's got the inclination too.'

TIPS

- **Getting around the city without a car is easy. Guided bicycling tours are offered by City Cycle Tours and Lifecycles (Smithfield Market, tel 028 9043 9959; www.lifecycles.co.uk). For guided walking tours of Belfast Old Town telephone 028 9023 8437; for the middle of the city it's 028 9024 6609, and for a Titanic Trail 028 9024 6609. Independent city walkers will find the 'On the Hoof' map and guide useful, available from the Belfast Welcome Centre (▷ 166, Basics).**
- **If you want to appreciate the architecture of St. George's Market as a building, try to arrive there after 4pm when the stalls are packing up and the crowds have thinned out.**

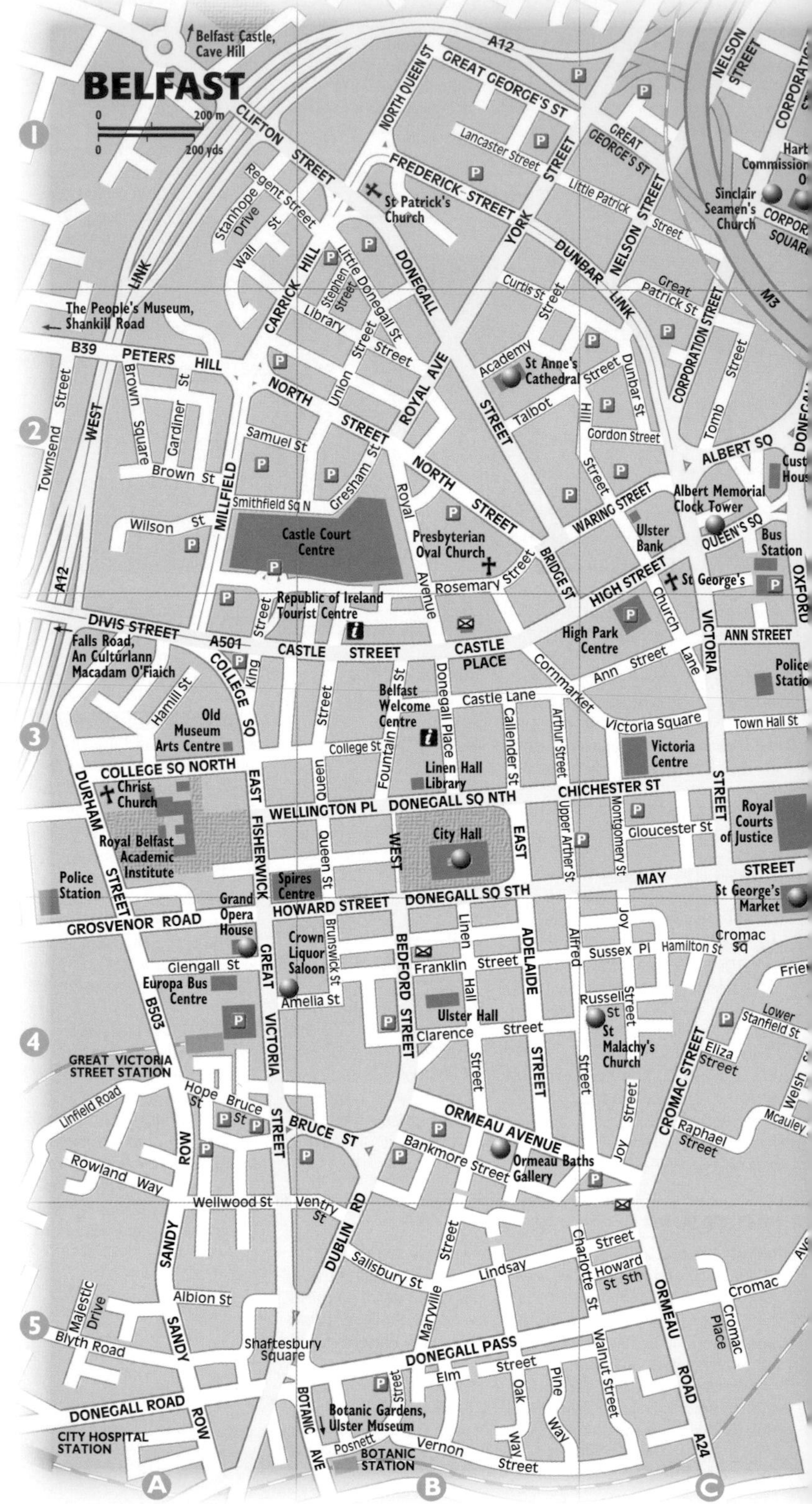
BELFAST
Belfast Castle, Cave Hill
The People's Museum, Shankill Road
Falls Road, An Cultúrlann Macadam O'Fiaich
Castle Court Centre
Republic of Ireland Tourist Centre
Belfast Welcome Centre
Linen Hall Library
City Hall
Old Museum Arts Centre
Christ Church
Royal Belfast Academic Institute
Spires Centre
Grand Opera House
Crown Liquor Saloon
Europa Bus Centre
Great Victoria Street Station
Ulster Hall
St Patrick's Church
St Anne's Cathedral
Presbyterian Oval Church
High Park Centre
Albert Memorial Clock Tower
Ulster Bank
St George's
Bus Station
Victoria Centre
Royal Courts of Justice
St George's Market
St Malachy's Church
Ormeau Baths Gallery
Sinclair Seamen's Church
Botanic Gardens, Ulster Museum
Botanic Station
City Hospital Station
Police Station

THE SIGHTS

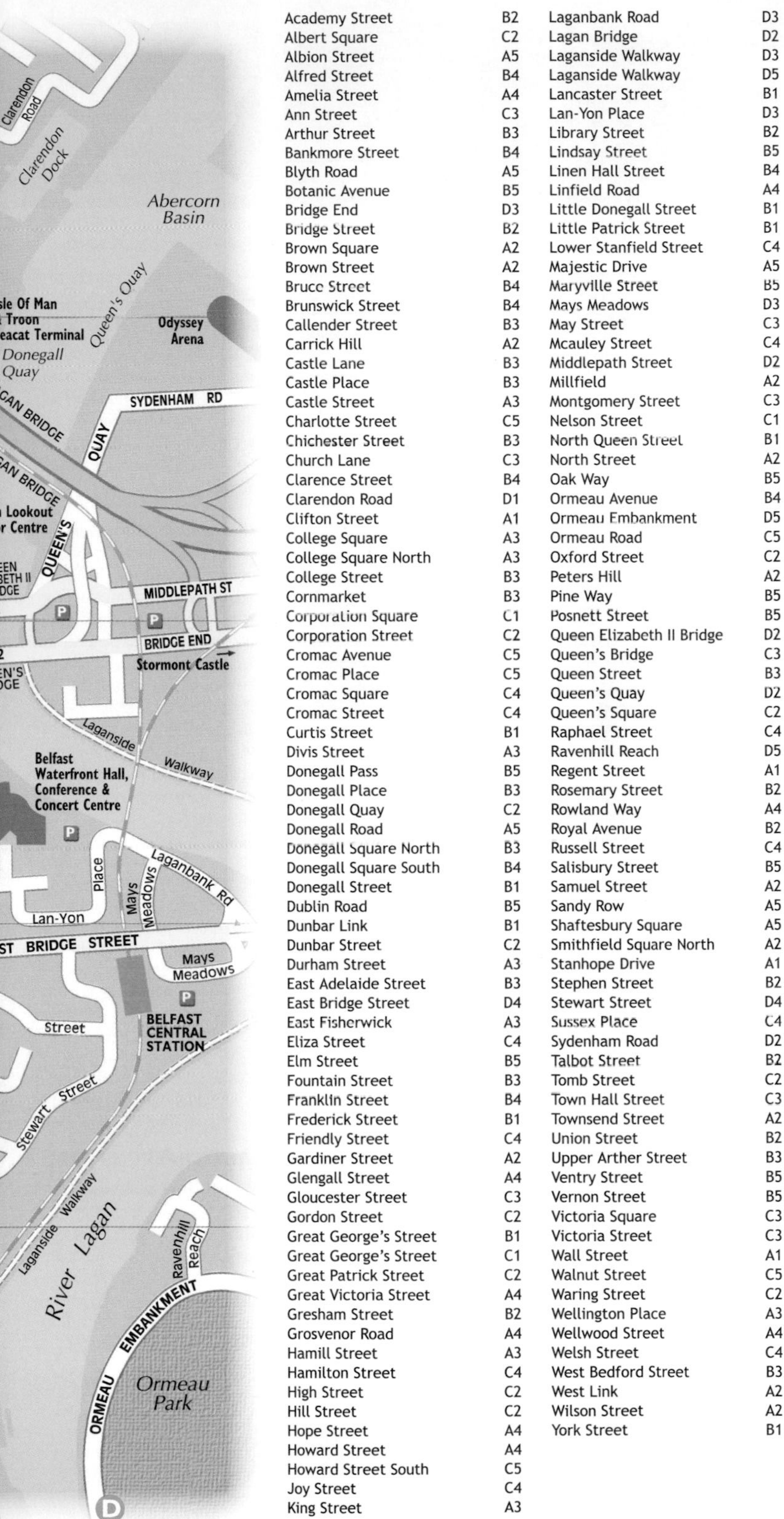
Clarendon Road
Clarendon Dock
Abercorn Basin
Queen's Quay
Odyssey Arena
Donegall Quay
SYDENHAM RD
QUAY
QUEEN'S
MIDDLEPATH ST
BRIDGE END
Stormont Castle
Laganside Walkway
Belfast Waterfront Hall, Conference & Concert Centre
Laganbank Rd
Lan-Yon Place
Mays Meadows
BRIDGE STREET
Mays Meadows
Street
BELFAST CENTRAL STATION
Stewart Street
Laganside Walkway
River Lagan
Ravenhill Reach
ORMEAU EMBANKMENT
Ormeau Park
D

People and horses throng the streets of Ballycastle at the Ould Lammas Fair in August

More than a drop of the hard stuff at the Bushmills distillery

BALLYCASTLE

349 G1 Sheskburn House, 7 Mary Street, Ballycastle, Co. Antrim, tel 028 2076 2024; Jul, Aug Mon–Fri 9–7, Sat 10–6, Sun 2–6; Sep–end Jun Mon–Fri 9–5.30

Retaining the appearance of an old-fashioned, Georgian seaside resort, Ballycastle makes a very convenient base for exploring the beautiful Antrim coast and glens. To get the most out of your explorations, you can learn all about the area's history and culture in the well-kept Ballycastle Museum (59 Castle Street, tel 0208 2076 2942; Jul, Aug Mon–Sat 12–6). Lammastide (the last Monday and Tuesday of August) is the best time to be here, for the Ould Lammas Fair. Held in the town since 1606, it is Ballycastle's great social event, with music, dancing, street entertainment, food markets and more. You're also guaranteed plenty of ritual tastings of two local delicacies: yellowman (a kind of toffee) and dulse, an edible seaweed–try it fresh or toasted.

BELFAST

See pages 166–173.

BELLEEK POTTERY

348 E3 • Belleek, Co. Fermanagh, BT93 3FY 028 6865 8501 Jul, Aug Mon–Fri 9–8, Sat 10–6, Sun 11–6; Apr–end Jun, Sep Mon–Fri 9–6, Sat 10–6, Sun 2–6; Nov–end Mar Mon–Fri 9–5.50 Visitor Centre free; tours: adult £4, child (under 12) £2
www.belleek.ie

Since Belleek Pottery began production in the late 1850s, the business has concentrated on high-quality products, especially white Parian ware, famous for its hard shiny surface and delicate shape. On the factory tour you see a fascinating process: beating the air out of a dough-like mixture of glass and clay with wooden paddles, teasing the material out and moulding it into plates, cups, vases and statuettes. You also get the chance to talk to the workers about what they are doing. These are very skilled people, working with tools they make themselves and hand down through the generations. The basket ware, a lattice of finely meshed clay strings, is probably the best-known of Belleek products. Hand-painting is another remarkable skill you can watch.

A Visitor Centre explains the history and technicalities, and there is a showroom where you can admire beautifully lit pieces before parting with your money. Belleek ware is expensive, and there are no 'seconds' for sale.

One story about the pottery's early days concerns a workman who slipped while helping to build the roof and tumbled about 10m (30 or 40ft) to the ground. Somehow he contrived to land on his feet. After a reviving tot of whiskey he went back up to the roof and carried on with his work. They're cool customers in Belleek.

Distinctive Belleek Pottery design

BUSHMILLS DISTILLERY

349 G1 • Distillery Road, Bushmills, Co. Antrim, BT57 8XH 028 2073 1521/3218 Apr–end Oct Mon–Sat 9.30–4, Sun 12–4; Nov–end Mar Mon–Fri 5 tours daily Adult £5, child (7–17) £2.50 Signposted off A2
www.bushmills.com

Bushmills is the oldest distillery in the world; it started production after gaining a licence in 1608, and has been distilling superb malt whiskeys ever since. The buildings, with their pagoda-style roofs, are a pleasure to look at. The tour takes you past the huge round mash tuns where the wash bubbles and ferments, and the great stills shaped like gleaming copper onions. In the cool gloom of the warehouse you inhale the faint, sweet smell of whiskey evaporating from the seams of the wooden barrels in which Bushmills matures. The guide tells you that this unreclaimable whiskey vapour is known as the 'angels' share'.

At the end of the tour you can sip a complimentary dram, buy a bottle of whiskey and reflect on the Bushmills mantra: 'Here's to health and prosperity, To you and all your posterity, And them that doesn't drink with sincerity, May they be damned for all eternity!'

CARRICKFERGUS CASTLE

349 H2 • Marine Highway, Carrickfergus, Co. Antrim, BT38 7VG 028 9335 1273 Jun–end Aug Mon–Sat 10–6, Sun 12–6, Apr, May, Sep Mon–Sat 10–6, Sun 2–6; Oct–end Mar Mon–Sat 10–4, Sun 2–4 Adult £3, child (under 16) £1.50, family £8 Carrickfergus

Carrickfergus is the southern gateway to the Antrim coast, and its great grey Norman stronghold makes

The ancient castle at Carrickfergus is a fine backdrop for the Irish National Mirra Championships on the water

Extensive grounds and gardens surround Castle Coole

an impressive introduction. Carrickfergus Castle was built on its shore promontory in 1180 by Sir John de Courcy to guard Belfast Lough. Its strategic position has always made it liable to attack and siege, but it has survived remarkably intact. Tableaux, effigies and explanatory plaques lay out its story for visitors, and there are sometimes visiting displays of armour and other attractions.

CASTLE COOLE

348 E3 • Co. Fermanagh, BT71 6JY 028 6632 2690 House: Jun–end Aug daily 12–6 (closed Tue in Jun); mid-Mar to end May, Sep Sat, Sun 12–6. Grounds: May–end Sep daily 10–8; Oct–end Apr daily 10–4 Adult £4.20, child (under 17) £2.10 (NT members free) Signposted on A4, 2.5km (1.5 miles) southeast of Enniskillen **www.**nationaltrust.org.uk.

Legend says that if the resident flock of greylag geese ever leaves the Castle Coole estate, so will the Earls of Belmore. The geese still live there, however, and so do the family who built the great Palladian mansion. One of Ireland's finest and grandest country houses, with its huge portico and long arcaded wings, Castle Coole was designed by James Wyatt and finished in 1798, the year after Armar Lowry-Corry was created first Earl of Belmore. The first earl never really enjoyed Castle Coole. Apart from his money worries (he died penniless in 1802), he was devastated when his wife—a dark-haired beauty—ran off and left him. Her portrait is one of the attractions of a tour round the interior, which contains most of its original furniture and fittings.

One other poignant fact: The gorgeously appointed State Bedroom, with its red and gold canopied bed, was created for a state visit by King George IV in 1821 that never actually took place. He was visiting one of his mistresses instead, and did not turn up.

CASTLE WARD

349 H3 • Co. Down, BT30 7LS 028 4488 1204 House and Wildlife Centre: mid-Apr to end Aug daily (closed Tue May, Jun); mid-Mar to mid-Apr, Sep, Oct Sat, Sun 1–6. Grounds: May–end Sep daily 10–8; Oct–end Apr 10–4 House and Grounds: adult £5, child (5–13) £2.30. Grounds only: adult £3.50, child (5–13) £1.50 (NT members free) Signposted on A25 between Downpatrick and Strangford **www.**nationaltrust.org.uk

Castle Ward is an intriguing monument to an ill-matched couple. Bernard Ward, first Viscount Bangor, and his wife Anne could not agree on the architectural style of the new house they were building in the 1760s on the southern shores of Strangford Lough. So Lord Bangor took one half and designed a severely restrained Classical frontage and set of front rooms, while his wife ordered a feast of exuberant Strawberry Hill Gothic to the back of the house. The result is both eccentric and delightful, from the austere symmetry of Bernard's music room to the frothy fan vaulting dripping down the walls of Anne's boudoir. Only in the entrance hall do whimsicality and classicism meet—for among the moulded fruits and figures of the stucco ornamentation are a genuine hat, basket and fiddle, dipped in plaster and stuck up amid all the artifice. Sadly, the odd couple stayed at odds, and soon separated.

In the grounds you'll find a farmyard with a sawmill, the original 16th-century fortified tower, the Strangford Lough Wildlife Centre (▷ 162–163), and a high-tech adventure playground.

Don't miss There are lovely walks through bluebell woods and along the lake.

CASTLEWELLAN FOREST PARK

349 H3 • Castlewellan, Co. Down, BT31 9BU 028 4377 8664 Daily 10–sunset £2 pedestrian, £4 car Entrance off Castlewellan's main street, on A25, 19km (12 miles) southwest of Downpatrick

This beautiful forest park occupies the estate of the Annesley family in the northern foothills of the Mountains of Mourne. Special features are the National Arboretum of rare trees and plants from all over the world, which surrounds an 18th-century garden; a long lake in which you can fish (you will need a permit and canoeing permission: telephone the Park Ranger); the Grange Yard, an early 18th-century farmstead; and many miles of footpaths.

CROM ESTATE

348 F3 • Co. Fermanagh, BT92 8AP 028 6773 8118 Jul, Aug daily 10–8; mid-Mar to end Jun, Sep 10–6 £4.50 car (pedestrians and NT members free) 5km (3 miles) west of Newtownbutler, signposted from A25 in the town **www.**nationaltrust.org

A great variety of woodland and the presence of Upper Lough Erne in so many of the views makes Crom Estate an ideal spot for walking at any time of the year, but especially in late autumn when the changing leaves reflected in the lake are at their most spectacular. Paths lead to Crom Old Church, and the ruin of Crom Old Castle of 1611. With luck you'll see some of the resident herd of deer, and the huge variety of bird life gives endless opportunities for birdwatching.

DERRY/LONDONDERRY

Northern Ireland's lively, friendly second city has the finest city walls walk in Ireland. Its monuments to hope in adversity, and the city's proudest Loyalist relics in St. Columb's Cathedral, reflect it's turbulent history.

It's easy to find your way around Derry, which is still referred to by its Loyalist population as Londonderry—the name given to the city in 1613 when James I and the livery companies of London established English and Scottish settlers here. To add further confusion for visitors, the official county name remains Londonderry. The wide River Foyle shapes the east boundary, while 'old Derry', the walled city, forms a neat rectangle whose four radiating streets—Shipquay Street, Butcher Street, Ferryquay Street and Bishop Street Within—converge on The Diamond or central market square. There's a good Craft Village within the angle of Butcher Street and Shipquay Street, where small workshops rub shoulders with cafés, wine bars and trendy eateries. The 'street of pubs' is Waterloo Street outside the western wall between Butcher's Gate and Waterloo Square; here you'll find great traditional and modern music in the bars.

WALKING THE WALLS

Derry's chief visitor attraction is undoubtedly the splendid city walls, built for defence between 1613 and 1618 by the trade guilds that had come from London to commercialize the old Celtic settlement. You can climb to the top and make the circuit of 1.6km (1 mile), with views over the old city and away to the hills. A Walls Walk starting at Shipquay Gate should begin with a visit to the eye-catchingly florid Guildhall (tel 028 7137 7335; Mon–Fri 9–5, Sat, Sun by appointment). Inside, fine stained-glass windows depict the city's history.

Numerous cannon stand on the walls, reminders of the great historic defence of Derry in 1688–89 when the Catholic army of King James II laid siege to the city. Before the siege was lifted, in April 1689, 7,000 of the 30,000 citizens had died. At Bishop's Gate you can descend from the walls to see St. Columb's Cathedral (tel 028 7126 7313; Mar–end Oct Mon–Sat 9–5; Nov–end Feb Mon–Sat 9–1, 2–4) and its treasured relics of the Great Siege. In the Tower Museum (tel 028 7137 2411) the history of Derry, including the dark, desperate days of the Troubles, is laid out in exemplary fashion. The museum's tower, a replica of a medieval round tower, was built by Paddy O'Doherty, as an article of faith and a pointer to better times to come.

RATINGS

Good for kids	●●●
Historic interest	●●●●
Photo stops	●●●
Walkability	●●●●

BASICS

348 F1

Derry Visitor and Convention Bureau, 44 Foyle Street, Derry, Co. Londonderry, BT48 6AT, tel 028 7126 7284; Jul–end Sep Mon–Fri 9–7, Sat 10–6, Sun 10–5; Oct–end Mar Mon–Fri 9–5; Apr–end Jun Mon–Fri 9–5, Sat 10–5

Derry (Londonderry Waterside)

www.derryvisitor.com
Attractive, easy to use, modern site, including downloadable maps.

TIPS

- **St. Columb's has the First Air Mail Letter—an iron mortar bomb fired into the city in 1689, with a note of the Jacobite surrender demands.**
- **St. Columb's has some wonderful Victorian stained glass.**

Derry is pleasant to explore (top). The uplifting Peace Statue *on the city walls (inset)*

Mussenden Temple, part of the Downhill Estate

This stone at Downpatrick may mark St. Patrick's burial place

Enniskillen Castle's water gate, on the River Fergus

DOWNHILL ESTATE

349 F1 • Co. Londonderry, BT51 4TW ☎ 028 7084 8728 Grounds: daily dawn–dusk. Mussenden Temple Jun–end Aug daily 11–7.30; Mar–end May Sat, Sun 11–6; Oct Sat, Sun 11–5 Car park £3.50 when Temple open (NT members free) Just east of Downhill, on A2 Coleraine–Limavady coast road
www.nationaltrust.org

The collection of buildings and ruins on the cliffs near Castlerock are all that remain of the 18th-century glories of the Downhill estate, laid out in 1783–85 by the red-blooded Protestant Bishop of Londonderry, Frederick Hervey, the fourth Earl of Bristol. He was a man who lived life to the full, with exotic foreign travels and a string of mistresses, one of whom was reputedly installed in the cylindrical Mussenden Temple. The ruin of the Bishop's Palace of Downhill, its walled garden and icehouse lie near the Lion Gate (topped with leopard sculptures) entrance.

DOWNPATRICK

349 H3 St. Patrick's Centre, 53a Market Street, Downpatrick, Co. Down, BT30 6LZ, tel 028 4461 2233; Jul, Aug Mon–Sat 9.30–6, Sun 2–6; Sep–end Jun Mon–Sat 9.30–5

Built on two hills, Downpatrick is a market and cathedral town. Down Cathedral (English Street, tel 028 4461 4922) stands on a site occupied by a cathedral since the sixth century, but the present building is mostly of the 18th and 19th centuries. Outside a massive stone slab, inscribed 'Patric', is usually bright with floral offerings; but whether Ireland's patron saint really does rest here is open to conjecture. Down County Museum (The Mall, tel 028 4461 5218), housed in the old jail, is in two parts: county history in the main building and an illuminating view of St. Patrick's story in the gatehouse. Families and railway buffs will enjoy the Downpatrick Railway Museum (Railway Station, Market Street, tel 028 4461 5779; guided tours Jun–end Sep Mon–Sat 11–2; running days Jul to mid-Sep Sat, Sun 2–5).

DUNGIVEN PRIORY

349 F2 • Dungiven, Co. Londonderry ☎ 028 7776 0307 Open access Free Signed off A6 Maghera road, south of Dungiven

The chancel of the 12th-century Augustinian Dungiven Priory holds one of the finest medieval tombs in Ireland, that of Cooey-na-Gal (*d*1385), a chieftain of the O'Catháin clan. His effigy, with sword and battleaxe, lies under a canopy of carved foliage. In niches under the tomb stand six guardians in the act of drawing their swords. Their pleated tunics may well be kilts, and they may be 'gallowglasses' or mercenaries from Scotland. It was evidently unwise to come upon their master without an introduction—his nickname means 'The Stranger's Bane'.

ENNISKILLEN

348 E3 Enniskillen Tourist Information Office, Wellington Road, Enniskillen, Co. Fermanagh, BT74 7EF, tel 028 6632 3110; Jul, Aug daily 9–7; Easter–end Jun Mon–Fri 9–5.30, Sat 10–6, Sun 11–5; Sep–Easter Mon–Fri 9–5.30; public holidays 10–5
www.fermanagh-online.com

Enniskillen is the bustling capital town of County Fermanagh. Attractions include Castle Barracks (tel 028 6632 5000; Mon 2–5, Tue–Fri 10–5, also May–end Sep Sat 2–5 and Jul, Aug Sun 2–5) with its regimental and county museums; the Cole Monument in Forthill Park, commemorating one of Wellington's generals (tel 028 6632 5050; Apr–end Sep, daily 1.30–3) from the top of which there's a splendid view over the town; and Blakes of the Hollow (tel 028 6632 2143), an old-fashioned pub with great traditional music.

FERNAGH CEILIDH HOUSE

348 F2 • Fernagh, Co. Tyrone, BT79 0XH ☎ 028 8077 1551 Occasionally, call for information Free 8km (5 miles) east of Omagh off A505 Cookstown road

Fernagh Ceilidh House is a beautifully restored former farmhouse where *ceilidhs*—evenings of home-made entertainment—take place at the stranger's behest or at locals' decision. All are welcome for the songs, dances, music, jokes and storytelling.

FLORENCE COURT

348 E3 • Co. Fermanagh, BT92 1DB ☎ 028 6632 8249 House: Jul, Aug daily 12–6; Jun Mon–Fri 1–6, Sat, Sun 12–6; mid-Mar to end May, Sep Sat, Sun 12–6. Grounds: May–end Sep daily 10–8; Oct–end Apr 10–4 Adult £4, child (under 12) £2, family £10 (NT members free) Signposted off A32 Swanlinbar road, 13km (8 miles) south-west of Enniskillen via A4 Sligo road
www.nationaltrust.org

The Cole family, later Earls of Enniskillen, built Florence Court early in the 18th century within sight of rugged 665m (2,180ft) Cuilcagh Mountain. The beauty of its wooded parkland looking to the mountains is still it's greatest asset. Inside you can admire superb plasterwork, antique Irish furniture, portraits of generations of red-haired Coles, and a Belleek chamberpot with a portrait of Victorian British Prime Minister William Gladstone, painted provocatively at the bottom. Gladstone supported Home Rule: the Coles family did not.

Giant's Causeway and the Antrim Coast

Northern Ireland's most dramatic coastline, with a UNESCO World Heritage Site.

The slipway at Ballintoy harbour on the Antrim coast

The precarious, swaying Carrick-a-Rede rope bridge

Dunluce Castle occupies a cliff-top spot near Portrush

RATINGS

Good for kids	●●●
Outdoor pursuits	●●●
Photo stops	●●●●●

BASICS

349 G1

Narrow Gauge Road, Larne, Co. Antrim, BT40 1XB, tel 028 2826 0088; Easter–end Sep Mon–Sat 9–5 (hours may be extended in peak season); Oct–Easter Mon–Fri 9–5

Sheskburn House, 7 Mary Street, Ballycastle, Co. Antrim, BT54 6QH, tel 028 2076 2024; Jul, Aug Mon–Fri 9.30–7, Sat 10–6, Sun 2–6; Sep–end Jun Mon–Fri 9.30–5

www.northantrim.com
Slick site with good information and some wonderful photographs. Covers the whole north Antrim region.

TIPS

- Though the new design of Carrick-a-Rede rope bridge makes it easier to cross, you still need both hands.
- To see the Giant's Causeway from above, walk until you are under the 'Organ Pipes'; here a path turns back towards the Visitor Centre, rising to the cliff tops for a fabulous kittiwake's-eye view of the Causeway.

SEEING THE GIANT'S CAUSEWAY AND ANTRIM COAST

The Antrim Coast is well served by its spectacular coast road, the A2, running north from Larne to hug the coast for the 40km (25 miles) to Cushendall. From here it bypasses Cushendun to take a 50km (30-mile) inland route over the moors to Ballycastle, then 2–3km (about 1.5 miles) inland of the basalt coast around Carrick-a-Rede and the Giant's Causeway. All these attractions are well signposted. There's an enjoyable, if slow and bumpy, 'Scenic Route' detour on the coast road, starting in Cushendun and winding for 19km (12 miles) round Torr Head, to rejoin the A2 at Ballyvoy.

HIGHLIGHTS

CLIFFS AND VILLAGES OF THE COAST

The Antrim Coast is especially striking for its cliffs, bluffs, headlands and glen mouths. Driving north you encounter white limestone cliffs around Carnlough Bay, beyond which dark red sandstone rises dramatically to 250m (820ft). Garron Point curves into Red Bay, where three of the Glens of Antrim (▷ 180) meet the sea around the great flat-topped promontory of Lurigethan, 350m (1,148ft). Farther north comes paler pudding-stone around Cushendun, before you swing west towards the basalt of the Giant's Causeway. Each of the villages has a particular charm: Glenarm, beautifully set at the foot of its glen; Carnlough, with sandy beach and harbour, and white limestone houses; Waterfoot or Glenariff, below the rampart of Lurigethan; Cushendall, the 'Capital of the Glens', with bright houses, sandstone Curfew Tower jail and a huddle of houses designed by Clough Williams Ellis.

CARRICK-A-REDE ROPE BRIDGE

800m (0.5 mile), including 161 steps, from parking area signposted on B15 between Ballycastle and Ballintoy 028 2073 1582/2076 9839 Jul, Aug daily 10–7.30; mid-Mar to end Jun, Sep daily 10–6 Adult £2.75, child £1.50
www.nationaltrust.org

Carrick-a-Rede rope bridge was originally a scary flywalk with a single guide-rope, slung 25m (80ft) in the air by salmon fishermen to reach their offshore fishing station. The National Trust has made it more stable, but it still sways enough to raise the hairs on your neck.

GIANT'S CAUSEWAY

44 Causeway Road, Bushmills, Co. Antrim, BT57 8SU Open access Free Visitor Centre: on B66 near Bushmills, tel 028 2073 1855; open daily £5 car, £1 audio-visual display
www.northantrim.com

A UNESCO World Heritage Site, the Causeway is a hump-backed promontory, formed of the wave-eroded stubs of 37,000 mostly hexagonal basalt columns created some 60 million years ago when lava from an undersea volcano cooled rapidly on contact with the cold sea water. Taller columns can be seen in the cliffs behind. Legend says that the hero-giant Fionn MacCumhaill laid down the Causeway as a stepping stone, so he could stride across the Sea of Moyle to his giant-ess girlfriend's cave in the Hebridean island of Staffa, where there are similar columns. You can catch a minibus, or walk down to the Causeway from the parking area in 10 minutes.

DUNLUCE CASTLE

87 Dunluce Road, Bushmills, Co Antrim, BT57 8UY 028 2073 1938 Apr–end Sep Mon–Sat 10–6, Sun 2–6 (Jul, Aug Sun 12–6); Oct–end Mar Tue–Sat 10–4, Sun 2–4 Adult £2, child (4–16) £1 Off A2 just west of Portballintrae

The poignant ruin of Dunluce Castle stands on the edge of the cliffs—so close that during a 1639 storm the kitchens fell into the sea and the kitchen workers were killed. Dunluce is associated with many stories—the most romantic concerns its recapture from the English in 1584 by the owner, Sorley Boy MacDonnell, whose men had been hauled 60m (200ft) up the cliffs in baskets.

The remarkable hexagonal columns of the Giant's Causeway (top)

Brave souls make their way across the chasm on the Carrick-a-Rede rope bridge (above)

BACKGROUND

The Antrim coast's complex geology includes rocks laid down more than 500 million years ago on an ancient ocean floor, pudding-stone that was a later desert floor, a belt of coal formed out of a swampy delta, salt trapped in the stone 200 million years ago, and mudstones and limestones from the time of the dinosaurs. The basalt that formed the Giant's Causeway comes from a volcano that dates from around 60 million years ago.

GLENS OF ANTRIM

Only a short drive away from the crowded Antrim coast you'll find peace and quiet amid beautiful scenery of basalt cliffs, green valleys and dense woodland. Waymarked walks for all tastes and abilities in Glenariff Forest Park take you past water in motion: fast mountain rivers, streams, rapids and waterfalls.

A stream tumbles down a rocky cleft in Glenariff Forest Park (top). Wild flowers cloak the slopes of Glenballyemon (above)

RATINGS	
Good for kids	●●●●
Outdoor pursuits	●●●●
Photo stops	●●●●●

BASICS

349 G1

Narrow Gauge Road, Larne, Co. Antrim, BT40 1XB, tel 028 2826 0088; Apr–Sep Mon–Fri 9–5, Sat 10–4; Oct–Mar Mon–Fri 9–5

Sheskburn House, 7 Mary Street, Ballycastle, Co. Antrim, BT54 6QH, tel 028 2076 2024; Jul, Aug Mon–Fri 9.30–7, Sat 10–6, Sun 2–6; Sep–end Jun Mon–Fri 9.30–5

www.northantrim.com (▷ 178)

TIPS

- **Don't ignore the glens on a wet day, especially Glenariff, where rain-swollen streams are spectacular.**
- **The narrow lane that climbs to Ossian's Grave is really too steep for a car, and there's nowhere sensible to park at the top. Walk up instead.**

The nine Glens of Antrim form one of Ireland's most beautiful landscapes. But because they are close to the spectacular basalt extravaganza of the Antrim coast, Northern Ireland's most popular (and most advertised) tourist attraction, the glens see less tourist activity than they might. That is good news for walkers, birdwatchers, photographers and other lovers of peace and quiet in the wide open spaces. Not that the glens are particularly wide. Great water-cut clefts in Antrim's coastal shelf, they tend to be U-shaped and high-sided, in some cases (notably Glenariff) with imposing cliffs forming their upper flanks. Iron ore was mined in the glens until the early 20th century, but now all is peaceful and green. Narrow roads wind up one glen and down the next, so that you can spend a very enjoyable day cruising the glens in low gear.

FROM SOUTH TO NORTH

The most southerly pair of glens are Glenarm, running down to Glenarm village, and Glencloy, the Glen of the Stony Dykes, which runs through its rocky defile to reach the harbour of Carnlough. North of these is Glenariff (see below), and then come four close together: wide Glenballyemon descending to Cushendall, and the threesome of Glendun, Glenaan and Glencorp. Glendun, the Glen of the Brown River, is spanned by a viaduct designed by the great architect Charles Lanyon; while at the foot of the Little Blue Glen, Glenaan, you'll find the sign-posted track to Ossian's Grave, a fine 'horned cairn' burial mound perhaps 5,000 years old. Legend says this is the resting place of bold Ossian, the warrior-poet son of the giant hero Fionn MacCumhaill. North again, Glenshesk and Glentaisie run down to Ballycastle.

Glenariff, sited between Glencloy and Glenballyemon, is the most spectacular glen, and the one most geared to tourism. Waymarked trails run from the Glenariff Forest Park Visitor Centre signposted on the A43 Cushendall–Ballymena road (tel 028 6675 8232; open all year). The Garden Trail (1km/0.5 miles) is a pleasant stroll. On the Glensway Nature Trail (2.5km/1.5 miles) you walk through woodland and beside the Inver River. The very popular Waterfall Trail (4.5km/3 miles) passes along the lovely waterfalls of the Glenariff River, while the slightly more demanding Scenic Trail of 9km (5.5 miles) goes by way of forest, moorland and river. Many of these paths and footbridges were laid out in Victorian times, giving the walks a period charm.

The ruins of Inch Abbey still hint at its former glory

Standing stones at Knockmany Cairn are well protected

The distinctively painted lighthouse at St. John's Point

GOSFORD CASTLE AND FOREST PARK

349 G3 • Co. Armagh, BT60 1GD 028 3755 1277 Daily 10–sunset Car £3; pedestrians: adult £1.50, child (under 12) £0.50 Signposted on A28 just west of Markethill

The Gosford estate, former seat of the Acheson family, has strong literary connections. Dean Swift used to visit the family in their former house on the site; his first visit in 1728 lasted eight months, as he humorously acknowledged in his poem *Lady Acheson Weary of the Dean*:
'The House Accounts are daily rising, So much his Stay does swell the Bills.'

The grand mock-Norman castle, built of grey granite in the 1820s–50s now stands empty. It features as 'Castlemallock' in *The Valley Of Bones*, Volume 7 of Anthony Powell's saga *A Dance to the Music of Time*. Today the estate forms the Gosford Forest Park with an arboretum and walled garden, and four waymarked trails through the paddocks and woods.

INCH ABBEY

349 H3 • Downpatrick, Co. Down, BT30 6LZ Open access Free Signed off A7, 1.5km (1 mile) north of town Tourist Information Office: St. Patrick's Centre, 53a Market Street, Downpatrick, Co. Down, tel 028 4461 2233; Jul, Aug Mon–Sat 9–6, Sun 2–6; Sep–end Jun Mon–Sat 9–5

Sir John de Courcy, whose wife, Affreca, founded Grey Abbey (⊳ 162), was a warrior—he led the Norman invasion of East Ulster in 1177—and also a spiritual man. He founded Inch Abbey in 1180 on its marshland site by the River Quoile as a Cistercian abbey, and until the Dissolution in the 1540s the monks proved their Anglo-Irish loyalties by rejecting all Irish applicants to join the monastery. The ruins have a beautiful site by the river.

IRISH LINEN CENTRE AND LISBURN MUSEUM

349 G3 • Market Square, Lisburn, Co. Antrim, BT28 1AG 028 9266 3377 Mon–Sat 9.30–5 Free Lisburn

Linen-making was once the Lagan Valley's biggest industry, and the Irish Linen Centre offers a window into the mystique and craftsmanship of the trade. You can try your hand at parts of the manufacturing process, learn about scutching, hackling and retting, look at the lives of Victorian linen workers, chat to a weaver working on a restored 19th-century hand loom, and visit the museum shop (tel 028 9266 0074). Local history is detailed in the Lisburn Museum alongside.

KNOCKMANY CHAMBERED CAIRN

348 F3 • Co. Tyrone Kept locked: arrange access with Peatlands Country Park, tel 028 388 51102 Free Signed off B83, 2.5km (1.5 miles) north of Clogher on A4 Dungannon–Enniskillen road Killymaddy Tourist Information Office, Ballygawley Road, Dungannon, Co. Tyrone, BT70 1TE, tel 028 8776 7259; May–end Aug Mon–Thu 9–6, Fri 9–7, Sat, Sun 9–5; Sep–end Nov Mon–Fri 9–5, Sat, Sun 10–4; Dec–end Apr Mon–Fri 9–5, Sat 11–3

At the end of your uphill walk from the parking area is an ugly modern structure, but it protects the Bronze Age passage tomb of Knockmany, its stones superbly incised with whorls, spirals and cupmarks. It's also adorned with graffiti cut over the centuries, hence the locked gate through which you are obliged to stare at them. However, you can climb to the roof skylight for a better view.

The vista from the hilltop is quite wonderful; it's said you can see seven counties from here.

LECALE PENINSULA

349 H3 Tourist Information Office, St. Patrick's Centre, 53a Market Street, Downpatrick, Co. Down, BT30 6LZ, tel 028 4461 2233; Jul, Aug Mon–Sat 9–6, Sun 2–6; Sep–end Jun Mon–Sat 9–5

Drive around the Lecale peninsula east of Downpatrick, and you'll find a quiet corner of countryside and coast that sees few tourists. From Downpatrick you go across country on the B176 to Killough, the port for the farm produce of Castle Ward (⊳ 175) in the 18th century. Turning east on the A2 you'll run through Ardglass, with its ancient fortifications around the harbour, to Kilclief. The 15th-century tower house here was the scene of a medieval scandal when the owner, the Bishop of Down, was caught with a married woman and was consequently defrocked.

LONDONDERRY

See page 176.

LOUGH ERNE

See pages 182–183.

LOUGH NEAGH

349 G2

This huge inland sea in the heart of Northern Ireland is the biggest lake in the British Isles, measuring 29km (18 miles) long and 18km (11 miles) wide. Of the six counties, only Fermanagh does not have a share of its shoreline. For birdwatching and an exhibition on Lough Neagh's natural history, visit Oxford Island Discovery Centre on the south shore (off Junction 10 of M1; tel 028 3832 2205; Apr–end Sep Mon–Sat 10–6, Sun 10–7; Oct–end Mar Wed–Sun 10–5).

Lough Erne

Woodland, marsh and moorland surround the two great contrasting lakes of Lower Lough Erne and Upper Lough Erne. Water sports are one attraction; lake islands with strange stone figures and the ruins of a monastery are another.

RATINGS	
Good for kids	●●●●
Historic interest	●●●●
Outdoor pursuits	●●●●●
Photo stops	●●●●●

BASICS

348 E3

Fermanagh Lakelands Centre, Wellington Road, Enniskillen, Co. Fermanagh, BT74 7EF, tel 028 6632 6932; Jul, Aug Mon–Fri 9–5.30, Sat, Sun 9–7; Mar–end Sep Mon–Fri 9–5.30, Sat 10–6, Sun 11–5

www.fermanagh-online.com. You can download an events guide from this well-designed site.

TIP

- Bring binoculars with you to Devenish to see what many visitors miss: the four little carved heads under the conical cap of the round tower.

Ruins of the 12th-century round tower on Devenish Island (top)

SEEING LOUGH ERNE

From Enniskillen, the hub of the Lough Erne system, you can circle Lower Lough Erne clockwise taking the A46 along the western shore to Belleek, returning down the east side of the lake on the A47 over Boa Island to Kesh, then on the A35 and B72 to Lisnarrick and B82/A32 back to Enniskillen. Upper Lough Erne, a maze of islets and small stretches of water, is flanked on the west by the A509, which becomes the N3 as it crosses the border into the Republic and reaches Belturbet. On the east, the A4 leaves Enniskillen; a turning to the B514 runs southeast to Lisnaskea and the A34 goes on to Newtownbutler, whence you steer south by minor roads for the border. Boating is a wonderful way to get to know the lakes.

HIGHLIGHTS

ISLANDS OF LOUGH ERNE

The monastery established by St. Molaise in the sixth century stands on Devenish Island just north of Enniskillen (ferry from Trory jetty, tel 028 6862 1588; or Erne Tours from Enniskillen, tel 028 6632 2882). Here you'll find a tall round tower, built by monks around 1120, the ruins of the beautiful little 15th-century abbey church and a fine High Cross. There's an explanatory exhibition, and you can climb the ladders inside the tower for a wonderful view over Lough Erne. On White Island (boat from Castle Archdale Marina, tel 028 6862 1333/1892) seven extraordinary stone carvings have been built into a wall: a grinning sheela-na-gig, a seated man with a book, another holding two gryphons, a warrior and a bishop, a King David figure and a morose face. In Caldragh cemetery on Boa Island, reached by causeways on the A47, stands the 'Janus Man', a stumpy figure, thought to be 2,000 years old, with two back-to-back faces, both with bulging eyes and pointed beards. Near him is his swollen-headed brother the 'Lusty Man'. It is uncertain what these figures represent, or their age.

On the causeway islands and shores of Upper Lough Erne are fine carvings of definite Christian tradition. Aghalurcher Old Church (signposted off the A43 just south of Lisnaskea), abandoned in 1484 after a murder at the altar, has elaborately carved skull-and-crossbones gravestones; so does the graveyard on Galloon Island (5km/3.5 miles southwest of Newtownbutler).

BOATING AND FISHING

Boating is the classic activity here, with boat rental on Lower Lough Erne from Manor House Marine Day Boats at Killadeas (tel 028 6862 8100), or Belleek Angling Centre (tel 028 6865 8181). Or you can take a trip on the *Lady of the Lake* (Inishclare Restaurant, Killadeas, tel 028 6862 2200) or MV *Kestrel* (Erne Tours Ltd., Enniskillen, tel 028 6632 2882). On Upper Lough Erne, try *Inish Cruiser* (Share Holiday Village, Lisnaskea, tel 028 6772 2122) or Belleek Charter Cruising (tel 028 6865 8027). For fly fishing on a lovely small lake, contact Rob Henshall at Coolyermer Lough Fishery (tel 028 663 41676).

COUNTRY PARKS AND COUNTRYSIDE ACTIVITIES

Lough Erne is wonderful for wildlife, with a good overview from ExplorErne's displays (Erne Gateway Centre, Belleek, tel 028 6865 8866; Jun–end Sep Wed–Sun 11–5). Three Country Parks around Lower Lough Erne provide lakeside and woodland walks. Castle Caldwell Forest Park (A47 near Kesh; all year) has good birdwatching, and at the entrance is the Fiddler's Stone, a violin-shaped memorial to drunken fiddler Denis McCabe who drowned in 1779. Castle Archdale Forest Park (A32 near Kesh; all year) has a boating marina, fine gardens, and an exhibition about the World War II flying boats based here (Jul, Aug Tue–Sun 11–7, Easter–end Jun Sun 11–7). At Lough Navar Forest (near Derrygonnelly; all year) an 11km (7-mile) scenic drive ends at the spectacular Cliffs of Magho viewpoint (▷ 253).

SHEELIN LACE MUSEUM

✉ Bellanaleck, Enniskillen, Co. Fermanagh, BT92 2BA ☎ 028 663 48041
⌚ Apr–end Oct Mon–Sat 10–6 (closed 1–2 for lunch); Nov–end Mar by appointment 🎫 Adult £2.50, child (4–16) £1

Ireland's best collection of antique lace is displayed here; some was made locally at Inishmacsaint, other pieces, from babies' caps to wedding dresses, have been collected from all over the country.

BACKGROUND

Lough Erne's shape has been likened to a leaping dolphin scattering a shower of broken water drops behind it. It measures some 80km (50 miles) in total. The surrounding soil is mostly clay and peat, poor land that has resisted agriculture and remained a beautiful mixture of moorland, forest and marsh.

Lough Erne is popular with pleasure cruisers (above)

One of the ancient carved figures in the ruined church on White Island

The Red Hand of Ulster in flowers at Mount Stewart (above). The stately house overlooks spectacular gardens (left)

MOUNT STEWART

This grand house retains an intimate, family atmosphere, and has the most delightful and eccentric gardens.

RATINGS	
Cultural interest	●●●●
Good for kids	●●●
Historic interest	●●●
Photo stops	●●●

BASICS

349 H2 • Portaferry Road, BT22 2AD 028 4278 8387 House: Jul–end Sep, daily 12–6; May–end Jun, Mon, Wed–Fri 1–6, Sat, Sun 12–6; (closed Tue in Sep); mid-Mar to end Apr, Oct Sat, Sun 12–6. Lakeside gardens: daily 10–dusk. Formal garden: May–end Sep, daily 10–8; Apr and Oct, daily 10–6; Mar Sat, Sun 10–4. Temple of the Winds: Apr–end Oct, Sat, Sun 2–5 Adult £4.95, child (5–18) £2.50 (NT members free) On A20 Newtownards–Portaferry road, 8km (5 miles) south of Newtownards

www.nationaltrust.org.uk
Detailed information and photographs of all National Trust properties.

TIPS

- If you have children with you, ask for the Children's Quiz/Trail.
- If your eyesight is impaired, ask to be shown the areas of scented plants.

Mount Stewart, on the eastern shore of Strangford Lough, is the home of the Stewart family, Marquesses of Londonderry. The Stewarts were major players in British and Irish politics, and the atmosphere in their 18th-century mansion is a nice mixture of the grand and the homely. A tour of the house starts in the pink and white galleried central hall. Look for the tail of the racehorse Hermit, which hangs beside his portrait here. Hermit won the Derby in 1867, causing the Marquis of Hastings, a deadly enemy of Hermit's owner Henry Chaplin, to lose £120,000. From here, you move through the richly appointed dining room, the study, the drawing room with its Aubusson carpets and huge pier glasses, the Rome Bedroom looking out over the terrace and Italian garden, a room full of copper pans and knife machines, the library with its signed volumes by Sean O'Casey, the sitting room lit by a ship-shaped crystal chandelier, and a wonderful music room with a floor whose inlay is mirrored by the pattern of the plaster ceiling. Between the sitting room and music room you'll find a charming feature—the door jamb against which the growing Stewart children measured their respective heights in the 1920s; you can see their progress, neatly ruled in pencil.

THE GARDENS

The estate is especially well known for its gardens, laid out between the 1920s and the 1950s with verve, imagination and more than a dash of eccentricity by Edith, Lady Londonderry, an early 20th-century Tory hostess with daringly tattooed legs and a circle of friends both great and raffish. Rare and beautiful plants thrive on all sides. In a pond in Lady Mairi's Garden there's a 'Mary, Mary, Quite Contrary' statue, surrounded, as in the nursery rhyme, by silver bells and cockle shells. The Dodo Terrace has freakish animal sculptures, and the Red Hand of Ulster is planted in red daisies and begonias. Water gardens, formal gardens, woods and dells lead on to the 'Land of the Fairies'; and also to the Temple of the Winds, a Georgian banqueting-hall on a hillock looking out over Strangford Lough.

The gentle, grassy slopes of the Mountains of Mourne

Rocky debris from above litters the coastline below Fair Head, which rises nearly 200m (655ft) above the sea

MARBLE ARCH CAVES

348 E3 • Visitor Centre, Marlbank, Florence Court, Co. Fermanagh, BT92 1EW ☎ 028 6634 8855 Jul, Aug daily 10–5; Mar–end Jun, Sep daily 10–4.30 Adult £6, child (5–18) £3 5km (3 miles) west of Florence Court (▷ 177), signed from Drumlaghy crossroads on A32
www.showcaves.com

Tours here start with the caving and mineral display in the Visitor Centre, then a spectacular underground route takes you by boat and on foot through the caverns, including the 'Moses Walk' through a subterranean river. Stalagmites, stalactites, glistening sheets of calcite and rock minerals are all revealed by lamplight and reflected in the water. It can get very busy, so call in advance and book onto a tour.

MOUNTAINS OF MOURNE

349 G3 Mourne Heritage Trust's Countryside Centre, 91 Central Promenade, Newcastle, Co. Down, BT33 0HH, tel 028 4372 4059; Mon–Fri 9–5; Newcastle Tourist Office, 10–14 Central Promenade, Newcastle, Co. Down, BT33 0AA, tel 028 4372 2222; Mon–Sat 10–5, Sun 2–6
www.mournelive.com
www.newcastletic.org

'…I'll wait for the wild rose that's waiting for me
Where the Mountains of Mourne sweep down to the sea.'
With these words the Victorian songwriter Percy French launched the Mountains of Mourne into the consciousness of the world's romantics. The Mournes are beautiful, a tight huddle of granite peaks that rise over 650m (2,100ft) from the southern coast of County Down. Most people have heard of these mountains, and many come to see them. But few bother to penetrate the narrow roads that lead up to the Silent Valley reservoir and through the spectacularly steep-sided Spelga Pass. Fewer still pull on walking boots for the walker-friendly paths, but those who do get up to the peaks are rewarded with some breathtaking views. Up here, too, is the extraordinary Mourne Wall, a granite drystone wall some 35km (22 miles) long, linking all the main summits. It stands as a memorial to the hungry, jobless men who built it early in the 20th century, trying to earn enough to put bread on their family's tables.

Birds of prey can be seen at Murlough Bay

MURLOUGH BAY

349 G1 • Signposted from Torr Head, on Cushendun–Ballyvoy scenic route off A2 (▷ 178); follow footpaths from first car park Ballycastle Tourist Information Office, Sheskburn House, 7 Mary Street, Ballycastle, Co. Antrim, tel 028 2076 2024; Jul, Aug Mon–Fri 9–7, Sat 10–6, Sun 2–6; Sep–end Jun Mon–Fri 9–5.30

You have to walk a section of the Ulster Way cliff path to reach the extremely beautiful and peaceful Murlough Bay, so it's rarely crowded. The curved bay is book-ended by Torr Head and Fair Head, with a mostly rocky shore beneath green slopes and woods. Sheltered by craggy cliffs, it has rich plantlife, from orchids to sea thrift, and birds such as peregrines and buzzards. There are remains of old lime kilns and of Drumnakill Church, where Independence activist Sir Roger Casement, executed in 1916 for his part in the Easter Rising (▷ 36–37), had asked to be buried. He is buried in Dublin, however, and all that's here is a commemorative inscription.

NESS WOOD COUNTRY PARK

348 F2 • Signposted off A6 Derry–Claudy road, 13km (8 miles) southeast of Derry, Co. Londonderry Open access Free

A beautiful wooded area with deep ravines thick with ferns, Ness Country Park has a spectacular walk from the parking area to where the River Burntollet makes a fine double leap of 9m (30ft) into a pool. Above, is the viewpoint of Shaun's Leap. Whether or not the famed 18th-century highwayman Shaun Crossan really escaped justice by leaping across this narrow gap, it's not a feat to try to emulate.

PORTSTEWART

349 G1 Tourist Information Offices: Town Hall, The Crescent, Portstewart, Co. Londonderry, tel 029 7034 4723; Jul, Aug. Railway Road, Coleraine, Co. Londonderry, BT52 1PE, tel 028 7034 4723; Mon–Sat 9–5
www.colerainebc.gov.uk

This trim little Victorian seaside resort sits on a gracefully curving waterfront. Its chief attraction is the sandy beach, stretching for 3km (2 miles) west of the town and cared for by the National Trust, who make a good job of keeping it clean, though, unfortunately, not car free. You can walk, fish, surf, swim or just make sandcastles and sunbathe on Portstewart Strand.

The view from O'Cahan's Rock in Roe Valley Country Park

This church and tower at Saul marks St. Patrick's landfall here

A rural scene within the Slieve Gullion Forest Park

PRESIDENT WILSON ANCESTRAL HOME

348 F2 • 28 Spout Road, Dergalt, Strabane, Co. Tyrone, BT82 8NB 028 7138 2204/8224 3292 Apr–end Sep daily 2–6 Free Signposted off B72 Strabane–Newtownstewart road, just east of Strabane

James Wilson was 20 years old when he emigrated to America from this little whitewashed cottage in 1807; his grandson, Woodrow Wilson, served as the 28th President of the United States from 1913–21. You can see the family's box beds, and furniture typical of the period, and you get the chance to chat to members of the Wilson family, who still live next door.

RATHLIN ISLAND

349 G1 • Off Ballycastle (A2 Antrim coast road) Caledonian MacBrayne tel 028 2076 9299; from Ballycastle, 45 min, adult £8.60 return, child (5–16) £4.30 Ballycastle Tourist Information Office, Sheskburn House, 7 Mary Street, Ballycastle, Co. Antrim, BT54 6QH, tel 028 2076 2024; Jul, Aug Mon–Fri 9–7, Sat 10–6, Sun 2–6; Sep–end Jun Mon–Fri 9–5.30
www.calmac.co.uk

Rathlin Island has a distinctive L-shape, and a reputation as one of the friendliest of Ireland's islands. It's a good idea to rent a bicycle (book in advance in peak season, tel 028 2076 3954) to explore the island, which measures 8km (5 miles) by 5km (3 miles). Out at the west end, the Kebble Cliffs National Nature Reserve is the largest and most remarkable cliff-nesting site in Northern Ireland. The cliffs are home to some quarter of a million seabirds during the nesting season (Apr–end Aug), and you don't need to be an expert to appreciate the numbers, the sights and the noise. For these months the hugely spectacular viewing point is open under the Warden's supervision (call first on 028 2076 3948 to make sure he/she is there). Rathlin also has an excellent small museum right on the harbour, the Boathouse Centre (tel 028 2076 3951/2024; open Jun–end Aug daily 10–5), run by the islanders.

ROE VALLEY COUNTRY PARK

349 F1 • Dogleap Road, Limavady, Co. Londonderry, BT49 9NN 028 7772 2074 Park: daily. Visitor Centre: Apr–end Sep daily 9–6; Oct–end Mar Mon–Fri 9–5, Sat, Sun 9–6 Free Signposted on B192 Limavady–Dungiven road, just west of Limavady

The River Roe runs red, hence its name, through the beautiful Roe Valley Country Park, a succession of gorges, and rapids interspersed with tranquil stretches running for 5km (3 miles). There are tree-lined paths by the river, remnants of old flax mills, and a stone shed which housed the plant of a Victorian hydroelectric scheme—a pioneering experiment which worked extremely well.

ROWALLANE GARDEN

349 H3 • Co. Down, BT24 7LH 028 9751 0131 May–end Sep daily 10–8; Oct–end Apr daily10–4 Mar–end Oct: adult £3.70, child (5–16) £1.70 (NT members free); Nov–end Feb free Signposted off A7 Belfast–Downpatrick road, 18km (11 miles) from Belfast at Saintfield

Rowallane Garden is testimony to the energy and imagination of one man, Hugh Armytage Moore, who during the first half of the 20th century laid out the walled garden's azalea display, the long sloping rhododendron walk (brilliant in late spring/summer) and the rock garden of various heathers, alpine plants and primulas. Nowadays, there are wild-flower meadows, too.

SAUL

349 H3 • Off A25 just east of Downpatrick, Co. Down
Downpatrick Tourist Information Office, St. Patrick's Centre, 53a Market Street, Downpatrick, Co. Down, BT30 6LZ, tel 028 4461 2233; Jul, Aug Mon–Sat 9.30–6, Sun 2–6; Sep–end Jun Mon–Sat 9.30–5

St. Patrick is said to have landed at Saul on his return to Ireland in AD432, and it is here he died in AD461. In 1932, to commemorate the 1500th anniversary of St. Patrick's arrival, a church and round tower were built here. You can learn of the saint's life in the church's exhibition, and climb the nearby hill of Slieve Patrick, up a path lined with Stations of the Cross, for a wonderful view.

SLIEVE GULLION FOREST PARK

349 G3 • Co. Armagh 028 4173 8284 Daily 10–dusk Free Signposted off B113 between Meigh and Forkhill

This lovely, partly wooded volcanic mountain has a scenic drive that runs for 13km (8 miles). A waymarked track leads on up to the summit at 573m (1,879ft), with views over South Armagh, a Bronze Age cairn and a dark little lake of enchanted waters—even Fionn MacCumhaill was transformed into a withered old man by their magic.

SPRINGHILL

349 G2 • 20 Springhill Road, Moneymore, Magherafelt, Co. Londonderry, BT45 7NQ 028 8674 8210 Jul, Aug daily 12–6; mid-Mar to end Jun Sat, Sun 12–6 Adult £3.90, child (under 12) £2.10, family £8.50 (NT members free) Signposted on the B18 Moneymore–Coagh road, 8km (5 miles) northeast of Cookstown

Springhill illustrates the style in which a family of prosperous

Extensive ruins of Scottish-style Tully Castle, amid lovely gardens

A steam locomotive forms the backdrop for a talk at the Ulster Folk and Transport Museum

'planters' lived. The Conynghams, who came from Scotland, built Springhill around 1690 and created a comfortable home. The ladderback chairs, tables and cabinets were made by estate workers from the Conynghams' own timber, and the Georgian library and gun-room, with historic weaponry display, retains its 18th-century wallpaper. In the former laundry is a collection of bygone costumes, and there are walks through the wooded grounds.

STRUELL WELLS

349 H3 • Downpatrick, Co. Down Open access Free Signed off the B1 Ardglass road, 3km (2 miles) east of town Downpatrick Tourist Information Office: St. Patrick's Centre, 53a Market Street, Downpatrick, Co. Down, BT30 6LZ, tel 028 4461 2233; Jul, Aug Mon–Sat 9–6, Sun 2–6; Sep–end Jun Mon–Sat 9–5

Each of the many springs in this green valley has a reputation for healing. During the 18th century Struell Wells became a major place of healing and of pilgrimage. Enthusiasm was spurred by the story that St. Patrick had spent a night in the freezing water of the drinking well known as The Tub. From The Tub, with its domed roof, the water flows through the Eye Well (said to cure eye diseases) to reach a pair of 19th-century bathhouses: a small, now roofless, one for women, and a larger house under a vaulted roof with male and female changing rooms. There's also a men's pool fed by a fall of water.

TULLY CASTLE

348 E3 • Co. Fermanagh 028 9023 5000 Apr–end Sep Sat, Sun, public holidays 10–6 Adult £1, child (under 18) £0.50 Signposted off A 46 Enniskillen–Belleek road, 5km (3 miles) north of Derrygonnelly

On the shore of Lower Lough Erne, the fortified house of Tully Castle was built around 1610 by Sir John Hume, who had moved here from Scotland. The defensive enclosure that surrounds the gaunt ruin of the house has been planted in the style of a 17th-century herb garden.

Tully Castle has a tragic and bloody history. During the 1641 rebellion, Roderick Maguire, whose family had lost all their land, besieged the castle. Lady Hume, trying to protect the 16 men and 69 women and children in the castle with her, negotiated safe conduct to Enniskillen in return for surrender. But as soon as he had possession, Maguire and his men stripped the women and shut them in the cellars, then tied up the male retainers and left them outside overnight. In the morning every man, woman and child was murdered; the castle was looted and burned.

ULSTER AMERICAN FOLK PARK

See page 188.

ULSTER FOLK AND TRANSPORT MUSEUM

349 H2 • 153 Bangor Road, Cultra, Holywood, Co. Down, BT18 0EU 028 9042 8428 Jul–end Sep Mon–Sat 10–6, Sun 11–6; Mar–end Jun Mon–Fri 10–5, Sat 10–6, Sun 11–6; Oct–end Feb Mon–Fri 10–4, Sat 10–5, Sun 11–5 For each museum: adult £5, child (5–18) £3; joint ticket £6.90, child £3.50 11km (7 miles) east of Belfast on A2
www.uftm.org.uk

This is an exemplary exhibition. The Folk Museum explores Ulster history and everyday life through reconstructed buildings, which include thatched cottages and farmhouses, a flax mill, a school and a rural Orange Hall. The Transport Museum consists of a number of galleries of beautifully maintained exhibits—gleaming steam locomotives, horse-drawn carriages, penny-farthings and racing bicycles, motorcycles and a horse-drawn tram.

Don't miss Ulster-built cars that are on show here include the fabulously stylish De Lorean (of *Back To The Future* fame), with its gorgeous but impractical gull-winged doors.

ULSTER HISTORY PARK

348 F2 • Cullion, 11km (7 miles) north of Omagh, Co. Tyrone on B48 028 8164 8188 Jul, Aug daily 10–6.30; Apr–end Jun, Sep daily 10–5.30; Oct–end Mar Mon–Fri 10–5 At the time of going to print, the Ulster History Park had just been sold. Call for further information.

At the Ulster History Park, the history of Ulster from the early Stone Age to the 17th-century 'plantations' is detailed with the help of re-created structures such as prehistoric tombs, a bark-roofed hut, a *crannóg* lake dwelling, a walled monastic settlement complete with a round tower standing 27m (88ft) high, and a medieval fortified house.

WELLBROOK BEETLING MILL

349 F2 • Co. Tyrone, BT80 9RY 028 8674 8210 Jul, Aug daily 12–6; mid-Mar to end Jun, Sep Sat, Sun 12–6 Adult £2.60, child (under 12) £1.60 (NT members free) Signed off A505 Omagh road at Kildress, 5km (3 miles) west of Cookstown,

Beetling (beating linen cloth smooth) played a vital part in Ulster's linen industry, and at the 18th-century Wellbrook Mill you can see the waterwheel and original machinery, learn about the industry in an enjoyable exhibition, and wince as the guide sets the beetles (wooden hammers) clattering.

RATINGS

Cultural interest	●●●●●
Good for kids	●●●●
Historic interest	●●●●●
Photo stops	●●●●●

BASICS

348 F2 • Co. Tyrone, BT78 5QY
028 8224 3292
Apr–end Sep Mon–Sat 10.30–4.30, Sun 11–5; Oct–end Mar Mon–Fri 10.30–3.30
Adult £4 .50, child £2.50
273 Belfast–Derry route
On A5 Omagh–Newtownstewart road, 8km (5 miles) north of Omagh

www.folkpark.com
Excellent, easy to navigate website with lots of information and a good interactive map.

TIPS

- Follow your nose as you enter the Mellon house: Fresh bread is often baked in the kitchen, and you may even be offered a share.
- The Park is extremely busy in school time, so it's worth arriving late in the day to avoid the school party crowds.

History is enthusiastically re-created at the Ulster American Folk Park

ULSTER AMERICAN FOLK PARK

A lively look at the lifestyle of 18th- and 19th-century Ireland, with a thought-provoking examination of poverty and emigration, and a tribute to the hardy Irish pioneers in America.

Just north of Omagh, the Ulster American Folk Park offers a multi-faceted experience. The site is divided into Irish and American areas, linked by a reconstruction of one of the ships in which Irish emigrants journeyed to the New World. Costumed guides work as their ancestors would have worked, and are always ready to explain and to answer questions. The Park came into being thanks to the generosity of the Mellon family of the United States, whose ancestor Thomas emigrated from the Omagh area with his family in 1818 when he was just five years old. Like so many Irish emigrants he prospered, becoming a judge; his son Andrew founded Pittsburgh's steel industry. The park's large collection of original buildings has been assembled from locations all over Northern Ireland and also from America.

IRISH AREA

In the Irish area you'll find the Mellon house, with its dark interior smelling of turf smoke, its cosy kitchen, and the ducks and hens in the yard outside. The family houses of other eminent Americans are here, too: The Hughes house, birthplace of John Joseph Hughes, the first Catholic Archbishop of New York and the McKinley house, ancestral home of William McKinley, US president from 1897 until his assassination in 1901. There's a simpler peasant cabin, too, with just a single room and a total lack of privacy, the state in which most Irish people were living back then. You'll also find a weaver's cottage complete with costumed spinner working at her wheel, and a blacksmith's forge where the fire often glows red and the sparks fly; also a Mass House from the era of the Penal Laws, and a splendid schoolhouse where visiting schoolchildren experience Victorian-style lessons.

ACROSS TO THE AMERICAN AREA

A replica of a 19th-century Ulster street leads to the dockside and the cramped, dark, frightening hold of a ship, similar to that in which emigrants made their dangerous and miserable three-month crossings of the Atlantic. On the far side is the American area with another replica of a street, this one in an American port. Beyond are the buildings encountered or built by the Irish in America: log cabins and barns, a smoke-house for preserving food, and the 18th-century house built by Samuel Fulton of Donegal Springs, Pennsylvania, with stones from his fields, exactly as he would have built it back home in his native Donegal.

This chapter gives information on things to do in Ireland other than sightseeing. It is divided into six regions, which are shown on the map on the inside front cover. Within each region, towns are listed alphabetically. Entries in the Dublin section are listed alphabetically by category.

What to Do

SHOPPING

Celtic jewellery, Ulster linen, Irish lace, Aran sweaters, Irish whiskey, Connemara marble, musical instruments, Waterford crystal—there are countless unique items you can buy in Ireland, and usually at considerably lower prices than you would pay outside the country. Many are available nationwide, though the best choice is naturally at the place of origin. Lots of shops display the 'Tax Free for Tourists' signs. Ask at any of them for details. Non-EU citizens can reclaim the VAT (currently 21 per cent) by presenting the refund forms at the airport on departure.

CLOTHES

Irish tweed is top quality and you can buy it as lengths of fabric or in ready-made items such as jackets, trousers, shirts, skirts and caps. Knitwear, especially Aran, is also good value. Plenty of the sweaters are factory made, but there are handmade ones too. You can usually tell by the price.

CRAFTS

Irish jewellery is exceptionally good, in particular the work of jewellers who incorporate traditional Celtic designs into rings, brooches, ear-rings and necklaces. Look for Claddagh rings, a design dating from the 17th century which incorporates a heart, a crown and two hands and is worn as a sign of fidelity. Celtic themes are also used by painters and print-makers—a welcome change from the ubiquitous landscape scenes, lovely as they are.

Belleek porcelain is uniquely Irish and appeals to those who like basketwork and floral designs. More modern styles of simple, but striking ceramics are produced by the increasing numbers of young potters.

Irish lace and Ulster linen are of exceptionally good quality if handmade, and if you just want a small souvenir you can find inexpensive items such as place-mats. Rugs are popular too, including ones made of tweed, and, like all bulky items, can be shipped.

FOOD

Smoked salmon is one of the most popular buys, but check that it is wild, not farmed salmon. The farmed variety can be fine but never tastes as good. If it doesn't say wild, assume it isn't. Irish cheeses are also worth seeking out. You only have to look at the green and healthy Irish landscape to know that they must be good. Whiskey-based products abound, including fruit cake, mustard and honey.

CHAIN STORES

NAME	Books, music and DVDs	Childrenswear	Cosmetics and toiletries	Crafts and jewellery	Food	Gifts and souvenirs	Household and electrical goods	Menswear	Toys	Womenswear	CONTACT NUMBER
Avoca		✔	✔	✔	✔	✔	✔	✔	✔	✔	01 677 4215
A-Wear										✔	01 671 7200
Blarney Woollen Mills	✔	✔	✔	✔		✔		✔		✔	021 451 6111
Debenhams		✔	✔	✔		✔	✔	✔		✔	01 878 1222
Dixons							✔				01 878 1515
Dunnes Stores		✔			✔		✔	✔		✔	01 671 4629
HMV	✔										01 679 5334
Mango										✔	01 805 0545
Miss Selfridge										✔	028 9023 5008
Monsoon		✔					✔			✔	01 671 7322
Mothercare		✔							✔	✔	01 478 4755
Next		✔	✔	✔			✔	✔		✔	01 674 3300
Quills				✔		✔		✔		✔	064 32277
Shaws		✔	✔				✔	✔		✔	050 221316
Waterstones	✔										01 679 1260

GLASS

Everyone knows the quality of Waterford Crystal, which is available all over the country and internationally, but there are other manufacturers of fine glassware too, such as Tyrone Crystal, and several regions have their own glassmakers so don't let your glass shopping start and stop with the name of Waterford.

MODERN STORES

Irish communities are smaller than in most other Western European countries, and chain stores are not as common, apart from the types you find anywhere, such as chemists, bookshops and department stores. There are some names you won't recognize, like the Avoca Handweaver shops and Blarney Woollen Mills. Dublin and Belfast are the best places for modern stores, with lively places such as Cork, Limerick and Galway not far behind.

MUSIC

Few can visit Ireland and not be touched at some point by the country's wonderful music. Its stars are famous around the world, including Van Morrison, The Chieftains, U2 and The Corrs, but there are many incredibly talented musicians whose fame has not necessarily spread beyond Ireland's shores, including local artists whose work you can only hear and buy in their own home region. Many produce their own tapes and CDs to sell when they're playing.

Musical instruments, too, are on sale everywhere, whether you know how to play them, aspire to play them, or simply see them as an attractive ornament. You don't need to spend the earth. Tin whistles are inexpensive and often come with tutorials. Much more costly are unique instruments such as the harp or *uillean* pipes (you may have to join a waiting list to buy one). The *bodhrán*, a hand-held drum traditionally covered in goatskin and beaten with a small stick, is in the mid-price range.

WINES AND SPIRITS

There are several brands of Irish whiskey (note the spelling, with an 'e'), which tastes different from Scotch—if you don't like Scotch, do at least try a sip of a good Irish brand such as Bushmills or Jameson's. You might be pleasantly surprised. The choice is less bewildering than the hundreds in Scotland. Do ask questions if you're thinking of buying, and tell the assistants what you like. They tend to know their product!

You can also buy whiskey-based liqueurs, the most popular being Bailey's Irish Cream, combining cream with whiskey, and a concoction called Irish Mist, a blend of whiskey, honey and heather.

In addition to countless individual boutiques and specialist shops, Ireland also has several chain stores. The chart below gives details of some of them, stating the number of branches each chain has in Ireland. You will find branches of these stores in shopping areas and malls in the Republic of Ireland, Northern Ireland or both.

NUMBER OF SHOPS	DESCRIPTION	WEBSITE
7	Original handweavings, fashion, toys, food, best Irish products	www.avoca.ie
20	Small chain of boutiques stocking Irish designer names	www.awear.ie
5	Irish gift items, good quality souvenirs	www.blarney.com
4	Smart department store, good for fashion and the home	www.debenhams.com
7	Major retailer of electrical goods and cameras	www.dixons.co.uk
110	Ireland's main nationwide store selling a wide range of goods	www.dunnesstores.com
25	Major outlet for records, CDs, videos, DVDs and books	www.hmv.com
5	Fashion stores for teens and early twenties	www.mango.es
19	Popular fashion store for teenage girls and young women	www.missselfridge.co.uk
15	Smart fashion stores, some stocking home and babywear	www.monsoon.co.uk
19	Specializing in maternity wear, baby and children's items	www.mothercare.com
16	Smart casual clothes for men, women and children and household items	www.next.co.uk
5	Family business with small stores across South and West Ireland	www.quillsireland.com
14	Family stores in southern Ireland selling clothes and household goods	www.shaws.ie
6	Smart bookstores with superb coverage in larger branches	www.waterstones.co.uk

Regional Shopping

While most goods that appeal to visitors can be bought nationwide, there are always local shops where you can find unique items, such as books, music, food, crafts and clothing, that are special to a particular town or region.

DUBLIN

The Republic's capital has the best choice of shopping, from old-fashioned food and flea markets to modern designer fashions. If you're only visiting Dublin you won't miss out on the chance to buy the best regional products too, as there are branches of stores such as Avoca, the Crafts Council of Ireland, Claddagh Records and the Kilkenny Shop, bringing the nation's best goods to the city. There are several shopping malls, including St. Stephen's Green and Powerscourt Townhouse, as well as traditional department stores Brown Thomas on Grafton Street and Arnotts on Henry Street.

Makula's is among Dublin's eclectic range of shops

THE EAST

There are two places of particular note if you are visiting the East. One is the Kilkenny Design Centre, in Kilkenny (www.kilkennydesign.com), one of the best places to buy the work of craftspeople from all over Ireland. It sells jewellery, clothing, glass, ceramics, metalwork and many other items. In Avoca in Wicklow is the original from which the chain of Avoca Handweavers shops sprang (www.avoca.ie). You can visit this, the oldest handweaving mill in Ireland, and buy products where they were originally made.

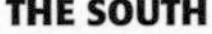

THE SOUTH

Waterford is the place for crystal—Waterford Crystal, of course. Glassmaking here goes back to 1783, and a tour of the factory is enlightening. Don't expect any bargains—anything that is even slightly flawed is destroyed. Cork and Kinsale are two of Ireland's main gourmet centres, so explore the local markets and food shops for the best regional produce.

THE WEST

Galway is the home of the Claddagh ring, and good jewellery stores in Galway City sell original rather than mass-produced examples. This is also a literary city, where you can browse second-hand bookshops for hard-to-find Irish titles. For Aran sweaters, there's no better place than the Aran Islands, off the west coast. Many are hand-knitted by local women operating cottage industries. You will pay more, but they will last much longer than lower-priced machine-made sweaters.

Just north of Galway City is Connemara, where Connemara marble is quarried. It's on sale everywhere in a huge range of items, and it's just as easy to find an inexpensive little souvenir as a costly gift.

Farther north, Donegal is the place to buy tweeds, especially in Donegal town itself. Tweeds here are made on traditional hand-looms and the quality is second to none. You can buy them elsewhere in Ireland, but a rewarding part of the shopping experience is buying items direct from the maker.

THE MIDLANDS

In this rural area of Ireland, woollen items are a good buy. Look for farm shops as you travel—you may find bargains buying direct from farmers' cottage industries that process fleeces as well as selling home-grown foodstuffs. The best shopping is in such towns as Athlone and Mullingar, although the range of local crafts is not as great as in other parts of Ireland.

There's a huge range of shops and merchandise in Belfast

NORTHERN IRELAND

Northern Ireland is home to Bushmills whiskey (you can tour the distillery) and Belleek Pottery, which has a Visitor Centre explaining how ceramics inspired by the Greek island of Paros, came to be made in an Irish village 150 years ago. The other great buys in this region are lace and linen. Lace is made in many parts of Ireland, but Ulster is noted for its linen—Belfast was at one time at the heart of the world's linen production.

ENTERTAINMENT

The Irish have a long and fine tradition in the performing arts, especially as musicians, dancers and storytellers. The great emphasis on the popular culture in the bars and on the streets should not detract from organized performances. You will find world-class theatre, dance and opera in Dublin and Belfast, and in regional artistic cities such as Galway and Cork (European Capital of Culture in 2005). Daily papers are the best sources of information, along with weekly listings magazines in the major cities.

THEATRE

Dublin is the major focus of contemporary and classical drama, with theatres such as the Abbey (opened 1904, www.abbeytheatre.ie) and Gate (opened 1929, www.gate-theatre.ie) of historical and cultural interest. Belfast has several theatres, and cities such as Galway, Limerick, Waterford and Cork have much to offer. The summer Galway Arts Festival is a major event, and there's a Theatre Festival in Dublin in September/October.

The violin is an integral part of traditional and classical music

CINEMA

There are few parts of Ireland where movies haven't been made–*The Quiet Man, In the Name of the Father, Braveheart, The Commitments, Michael Collins*–and the whole country has a huge interest in film. You will find several cinemas, including multiplexes, in the main cities, and at least one in most of the major towns, with just as much interest in art movies as in Hollywood blockbusters. There's also a film festival in Dublin in late February/early March, and another in Cork in October.

DANCE

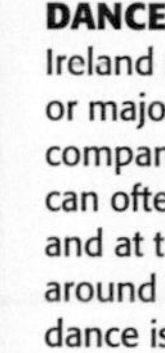

Ireland has no resident ballet or major contemporary dance company, but visiting groups can often be seen in the cities and at the major arts festivals around the country. Traditional dance is another matter. Boosted by the international success of *Riverdance*, Irish dancing is on a high and can be seen at traditional music festivals. The large hotels like Dublin's Arlington and Jury's put on shows for tourists.

OPERA

The major opera houses are in Belfast and Cork, while in Dublin opera fans can see occasional shows at the National Concert Hall, and at the Gaiety Theatre in April and November when the Dublin Grand Opera Society perform. The main event on the opera calendar is the Wexford Opera Festival in late October/early November, focusing on rarely performed works. The smaller Waterford International Festival of Light Opera is in late September/early October.

CLASSICAL MUSIC

In Dublin the National Symphony Orchestra appears at the National Concert Hall, while Belfast has its Ulster Hall for a variety of cultural events. One series not to miss is the June festival of Music in Great Irish Houses, with concerts in grand houses around the country. Bantry House in Cork hosts the West Cork Chamber Music Festival in June and July.

TRADITIONAL MUSIC

The best traditional music nights are the impromptu sessions in a bar. Ask around, and be guided by local advice. There are pubs in almost every town and city where music can be heard every night.

Traditional style is the hallmark of Belfast's Grand Opera House

BOOKING TICKETS

Most venues take credit card bookings over the phone, and an increasing number have facilities for online reservations. In Dublin, tickets can also be booked at the main Tourist Information Office on Suffolk Street. Around the corner is The Ticket Shop at 70 Grafton Street.

DRESS CODES

In Ireland, informal clothes are acceptable on most occasions. You may wish to wear smarter clothes for evening concerts, but only the grandest of events would require you to dress up in formal clothing.

NIGHTLIFE

There has never been any lack of good nightlife in Ireland, from the smallest village to the big cities. In the past it has mostly focused on music sessions in bars, a tradition that's as healthy as ever. However, there has been a big increase in the number of more sophisticated types of entertainment, particularly in Dublin, Belfast, Cork, Limerick, Galway and other major towns.

In smaller places, though, you might find that nightlife consists of the cinema or the pub, with the latter being as lively as you're likely to find anywhere else in the world.

If live music is on offer in one of the main bars, the musicians will usually just pass the hat round for a contribution. If it's in a separate bar for music only, you may have to pay a small entrance fee.

In early 2004, the Republic of Ireland banned smoking in all places of entertainment, including pubs, so if you want to smoke you will have to step outside.

Many of Belfast's bars offer a traditional Irish welcome

PUBS AND BARS

The old-fashioned pub is alive and well in Ireland, just as much in the big cities of Dublin and Belfast as in the smallest rural community, where it might double up as the village store. Few pubs are all-male domains, and women are welcome. Young children too, for the most part, but no-one under the age of 18 is allowed to stay after 9pm. In the Republic of Ireland pubs open at 10.30am (12.30 Sundays) until 11.30pm Monday–Thursday, till 12.30am Friday–Saturday and till 11pm on Sundays. In Northern Ireland the hours are 11.30am–11pm Monday–Saturday and 12.30pm–10pm Sundays. Those are official hours, but there are often extensions for live music sessions.

More stylish bars where trendy young people gather to see and be seen are also found in the big cities, especially Dublin. Here the bar at the Clarence Hotel (which is owned by members of the rock group U2) is a fashionable hang-out.

CLUBS

The club scene was slower to happen in Ireland than in many other European countries, but it is fast catching up in the big cities. Don't expect to find sophisticated nightclubs anywhere else, though. Clubs can stay open until 2am, with some of the more hardcore dance clubs such as Buck Whaleys in Dublin open until 5am. The Pod on Harcourt Street is a long-established and well-known club that draws Dublin's young movers and shakers.

CASINOS

Casinos are not big business in Ireland except in Dublin where there are several, including the Merrion Casino Club on Merrion Square (www.merrioncasinoclub.com) and the Mayfair Casino Club, 15 Harcourt Street (www.mayfaircasinoclub.com). The Club Oasis Casino on Westmoreland Street is the country's biggest casino. Opening hours vary, but are usually from about 6–9pm until 6am.

COMEDY

The Irish are known for their natural wit and ability to tell a tall tale, and comedy clubs in the major cities continue to enjoy huge popularity, in the wake of comedians such as Ed Byrne, Ardal O'Hanlon and Dylan Moran, who are leading lights on the international stand-up circuit.

The Milk Bar club in Belfast, with not a glass of milk in sight

GAY AND LESBIAN SCENE

Ireland was quite repressive until comparatively recently, and even now it is not considered acceptable to flaunt homosexuality in public. The atmosphere is more relaxed in Dublin, not surprisingly, and also in Belfast, Cork and Galway, where there are more open gay nightlife scenes. To tune in to what's happening, you can get a copy of the free monthly *Gay Community News*.

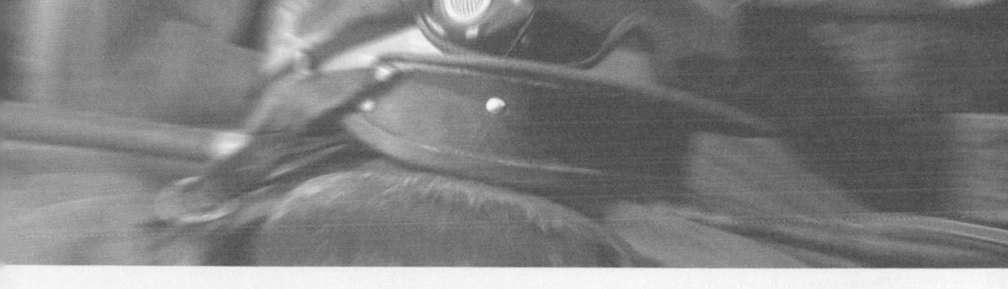

SPORTS AND ACTIVITIES

Ireland is a sports-mad nation, and anywhere in the country, at any time of year, there are sporting events, big and small, taking place. Try seeing one of the nation's home-grown sports, such as Gaelic football or hurling.

With its fabulous landscapes and small population, Ireland is justly popular with people who like to get out into the open for walking, bicycling, horseback riding, golf and almost any other sporting activity that can be enjoyed in the open air. Its waters also attract visitors who prefer fishing, kayaking, surfing and going to see, or swim with, dolphins. You have to be prepared for the weather, so take your waterproof gear, whatever you're doing. But wet or dry, everyone loves the active side of Irish life.

BICYCLING

There can be few countries better suited to bicycling than Ireland. Rural roads are generally quiet, although there can be as much traffic as anywhere else when you're bicycling in or near the big cities. Most drivers are respectful of bicyclists, however. The one drawback can be the weather, although that applies whatever you are doing in Ireland. Make sure you're equipped for the rain and cold.

Part of Ireland's appeal is that there are many places where the mountains sweep down to the sea, providing views of hills and ocean at the same time, though it does mean that you have to bicycle up those hills. The west and southwest areas are particularly good for bicycle routes, including outstandingly beautiful places such as the Dingle Peninsula, the Ring of Kerry and the Sheep's Head Peninsula.

Cruising Upper Lough Erne, part of the lovely Shannon waterway

CAVING

The opportunities to go caving are on the increase in Ireland, and the main places are in counties Clare, Cork, Kerry, Fermanagh, Leitrim and Sligo. For detailed information contact the Speleological Union of Ireland (www.cavingireland.org).

CRICKET

The summer game of cricket has never been as popular in Ireland as in its home country of England, but nevertheless it is widely played in Northern Ireland and increasingly in the south. A national side has recently been competing against some English county sides, and winning. There are currently eight grounds of international standard, two in Dublin and others in Belfast, Lurgan, Waringstown, Eglinton, Lisburn and Cork. Check in the local papers or the local tourist information office for details of fixtures.

CRUISING

While the beauty of Ireland's coastline is renowned, less appreciated are the delights of its inland waterways. Taking a small boat along its rivers and canals, and pulling up at night at a pub or restaurant where you might be the only visitors, is hard to beat. Not for nothing do they call it the Ireland of the Welcomes, and when you've arrived on the water you've earned your place at the bar or the table.

The River Shannon is the prime cruising location. It's the longest river in the British Isles at 354km (220 miles), and most of that distance is navigable. There are numerous companies offering boating trips, in craft ranging from basic to luxury. Almost as popular, and certainly just as beautiful, is Lough Erne and the waterways around it, known as the Lakes of Fermanagh. The Shannon–Erne Waterway which links them means you can enjoy both, and you can rent a boat to do a one-way trip if you wish.

Bicycle power on a sunny day near Lough MacNean

DOLPHIN-WATCHING

Few people can resist dolphins and there are opportunities to watch and swim with dolphins off the west coast of Ireland. These are concentrated in the West Clare area, and Dingle is another place with trips.

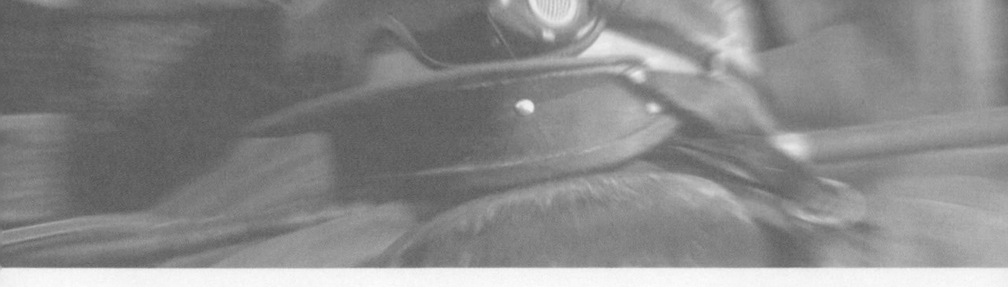

FISHING

Fishing attracts many visitors to Ireland, and is popular with locals too. In the Republic coarse fishing is permitted all year, but for other types of fishing such as salmon and trout you will need to check locally, as seasons vary within regions and sometimes even according to the specific river. Day permits (available from angling shops) are reasonably cheap, as are the licences which are necessary for salmon and sea-trout fishing. These can be bought in advance from some Irish Tourist Board offices overseas, or from Tourist Board and Fishing Board offices, from

A fisherman in County Mayo—fishing is very popular in Ireland

government-run fisheries and from angling shops within the Republic. In Northern Ireland rules do differ, so consult the Northern Ireland Tourist Board (www.discovernorthernireland.com) or a local angling shop, where you can buy permits.

For sea fishing the south and west coasts are the best, with Kinsale especially popular for several species, including shark. The Irish Tourist Board (www.ireland.travel.ie) publishes information for fishermen, as does the Central Fisheries Board (www.cfb.ie).

GAELIC FOOTBALL

The most watched sporting event in Ireland is the All-Ireland Football Final, held in September at the 80,000-seat Croke Park stadium in Dublin, the climax of a season that starts in February. The game is a very fast-moving cross between rugby and soccer.

GOLF

Ireland claims to have more golf courses per head of population than any other country in the world except Scotland. It is an incredibly popular pastime, and while its courses may not match Scotland's best in terms of their reputation, they can certainly match them for stunning settings and unique challenges. The Royal County Down (www.royalcountydown.org) and Royal Portrush in County Antrim (www.royalportrush.com) are two of the best. Costs remain comparatively inexpensive, and courses less busy, although in summer you would be advised to book ahead. You should also carry your handicap certificate. The Irish Tourist Board (www.ireland.travel.ie) and Northern Ireland Tourist Board (www.discovernorthernireland.com) both publish guides for golfers.

GREYHOUND RACING

Watching greyhound racing has been popular in Ireland since it was introduced to the country in 1927. There are 20 tracks all over the country, from Derry in the north to Cork in the south, with a concentration of courses in the south and east. Dublin has two courses, at Shelbourne Park and Harold's Cross. Details of all the stadia and fixtures are available from the Irish Greyhound Board (www.igb.ie).

HORSE-RACING

A day at the races is an incredibly popular pastime in Ireland, for all ages and for all walks of life, with 25 race tracks scattered around the country. Steeplechasing (also called National Hunt racing) takes place all year round, while the flat racing season is from March to November. There's great fun to be had at some of the smaller courses, but the big events are the Irish Grand National, held on Easter Monday at Fairyhouse, County Meath, and the Irish Classics run at the Curragh track in County Kildare.

HORSEBACK RIDING

The Emerald Isle is ideal riding country, and riding stables can be found almost everywhere. The Wicklow Hills south of

Thoroughbreds being exercised at the John Oxx Stables

Dublin are particularly good, and there are numerous places in Northern Ireland and on the west coast too. Contact the Irish Tourist Board (www.ireland.travel.ie) and Northern Ireland Tourist Board (www.discovernorthernireland.com) for specific information and lists of riding stables.

HURLING

Peculiar to Ireland, this immensely popular sport is an older version of both hockey and lacrosse, and is popular everywhere. The season is short, starting in summer and building up to the All-Ireland Hurling Final at Dublin's Croke Park at the start of September.

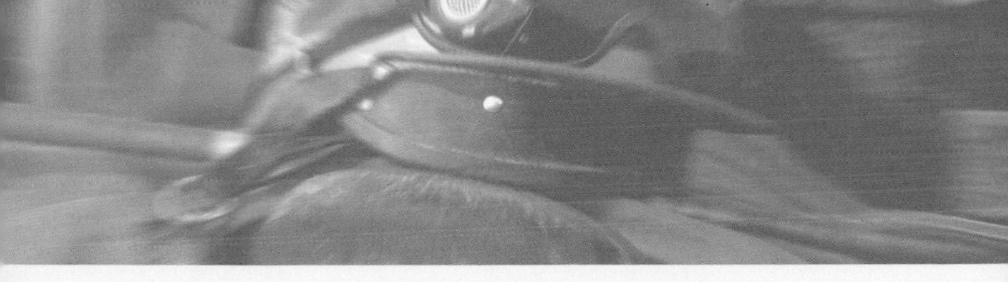

KARTING
There are karting tracks all over the country. The largest indoor track is Kylemore Indoor Karting in Dublin (tel 01 626 1444; www.kylemore-karting.com). You can try 15 minutes on its two tracks for €30.

RUGBY
If you are in Dublin in spring, you might be lucky enough to get a ticket for a home game in the Six Nations Championship at Lansdowne Road, in Dublin. Rugby is as popular here as in the rest of the British Isles, with games played weekly all over the country through winter into the early summer.

SAILING
There is hardly a part of Ireland's coastline where a sailing club cannot be found. It's an immensely popular pastime. To locate a club in any area contact the Irish Sailing Association (www.sailing.ie).

SOCCER
Soccer is almost as much of a passion in Ireland as in the rest of Europe. The Republic's national stadium is at Lansdowne Road, Dublin, and there are teams in virtually every town, with most games taking place on weekends. The season is now virtually all year round. Check local papers or at the local tourist information office if you would like to see a match.

SURFING
Hawaii it's not, but there are dozens of beaches where you can surf, most in the west and southwest, with some on the north coast. Conditions can be wild, however, and few beaches have tuition.

WALKING
Wherever you go in Ireland there's good walking, so it would be impossible to single out any regions in particular. Tourist information offices will be able to provide information.

There are many sailing clubs along the Irish coastline

Surfboards at the ready at White Rock Beach, Portrush

Rugby matches are played all over the country

HEALTH AND BEAUTY

Ireland might not be the first country people think of when they consider a health and beauty break, but it's fast catching up and new spas are opening all the time. Most of the major hotels feature health and beauty facilities, and there are retreats dedicated to personal pampering everywhere, often in some of the country's loveliest and most secluded and peaceful locations.

SPA TOWNS
There are only two spa towns in Ireland: Enniscrone in County Sligo and Lisdoonvarna in County Clare. The latter has Ireland's only working spa, the Spa Wells Health facility, although there are some other natural springs of the water, which has a strong mix of sulphur, iron and iodine. There are several Victorian bath-houses in Enniscrone, where a mix of seawater and seaweed is used to invigorate the visitor. A seaweed bath is something you will often find in hotel spas, especially in this corner of Ireland. Many of the larger hotels in Ireland offer a wide range of health and beauty treatments.

HEALTH FARMS
Some of the best health spas in Ireland, spread all over the country, have grouped together to promote themselves under the banner of the Health Farms of Ireland. Information about their facilities, and what to expect in Ireland these days, can be found on their website www.healthfarmsofireland.com.

FOR CHILDREN

There's no shortage of things for children to do in Ireland. Attractions, although not always highly sophisticated, certainly don't lack good, simple fun. There are numerous outdoor activities, as well as beaches to enjoy. You're more likely to find a farm to visit than a theme park but there's a warm welcome for children everywhere here.

BEACHES

Ireland may not have the best climate for a beach holiday, but it has many long golden beaches, usually with room for children to run and play, and explore rock pools. Look to the west coast, southwest and Donegal, but there are also excellent beaches in Antrim and Wexford, and some surprisingly close to Dublin too.

FESTIVALS AND FAIRS

In addition to many of the events listed below, children would particularly enjoy the old-fashioned fairs that travel the country and can turn up anywhere. There are also events like the Connemara Pony Show in Clifden, County Galway, where semi-wild ponies are sold and raced, and the Ould Lammas Fair in Ballycastle, County Antrim, both held in August.

FESTIVALS AND EVENTS

The Irish are renowned for getting the maximum enjoyment out of everyday life, but when a special day comes along they really celebrate, and it's a safe bet that music will be involved. In big towns and cities events are usually more organized than they tend to be in rural areas. Wherever you are, strangers are welcome to join in the fun. For Ireland's national holidays, see page 335.

Horse traders at the Ould Lammas Fair in Ballycastle, County Antrim

RELIGIOUS

St. Patrick's Day is of course celebrated everywhere on 17 March, with parades and parties sometimes eclipsing the religious element.

ARTS

Admirers of James Joyce come to Dublin on 16 June for Bloomsday, re-enacting parts of *Ulysses*, with a smaller celebration in Belfast too. Summer sees Galway's Arts Festival, while in Dublin there's a Theatre Festival in October/November and the Winter Opera Season in November/December. Music festivals abound: Jazz in Adare in March, classical in Dublin in April, closely followed by a Choral Festival in Cork and the 4-day Fleadh Nua of traditional Irish music in Ennis in County Clare at the end of May.

FOOD AND DRINK

Cork in the South is renowned for its food, with the Bantry Mussel Fair in May and the big Kinsale Gourmet Festival every October. September brings the International Oyster Festival in Galway.

TRADITIONAL

Romance plays a big part in traditional festivals, with an International Bachelor Festival in Ballybunion, the Rose of Tralee beauty pageant in County Kerry in summer, and the Matchmaking Festival at Lisdoonvarna in County Clare in September. Then there's food, music and fairgrounds in the Ould Lammas Fair held at the end of August in Ballycastle in County Antrim, which also hosts the old Horse Ploughing match on St. Patrick's Day. The Puck Fair at Killorglin in County Kerry in August is as traditional as they come, with a wild goat being crowned king.

DUBLIN

Dublin is not only the political capital of the Republic of Ireland, it is also the shopping capital, and Grafton Street is its senate, with designer names here and the small fashionable outlets that make shopping so much fun in side streets. Socializing and drinking are other capital pastimes; sometimes you may wish Dublin's reputation was less well known as you struggle to get to the bar in one of Temple Bar's many famous old pubs. It's worth seeking out one or two of the quieter ones for a pint of Guinness and a bit of *craic*. It won't take you long to realize another of this city's passions—sport. You can watch it on the TV in just about every bar, but for the real atmosphere go to a game—a hurling semi-final at Croke Park, a rugby international at Lansdowne Road, or a soccer game between the most successful local teams Shelbourne and Bohemians. For a more active experience, the county of Dublin excels at golf, with more than 20 courses ranging from the municipal to the exclusive championship variety. Dublin hosts its share of festivals, but the most impressive are St. Patrick's Day—all shamrocks and shindigs—and Bloomsday, uniquely celebrating the day depicted in Joyce's novel *Ulysses*.

KEY TO SYMBOLS

- **Shopping**
- **Entertainment**
- **Nightlife**
- **Sports**
- **Activities**
- **Health and Beauty**
- **For Children**

SHOPPING

BOOKS

DUBLIN WRITERS MUSEUM BOOKSHOP
18 Parnell Street North, Dublin 1
Tel 01 872 2077
www.writersmuseum.com
In a city that's world-renowned for its extraordinary literary output, it is hardly surprising that the Writers Museum should have an excellent bookshop. It covers all aspects of Irish writing from travel to poetry, including works by many of the writers featured in the museum.
Mon–Sat 10–5 (10–6 Jun–end Aug), Sun 11–5 10, 11, 11A, 11B, 13, 13A, 16, 16A, 19, 19A
DART Connolly, 20-min walk

EASON
O'Connell Street, Dublin 1
Tel 01 873 3828
www.eason.ie
Dublin's largest bookseller has 11 branches around the city, but the O'Connell Street outlet is the flagship. There is a good choice of Irish books, from travel guides to history and literature, as well as the latest blockbuster novels, general fiction and non-fiction titles.
Mon–Wed, Sat 8.30–6.45, Thu 8.30–8.45, Fri 8.30–7.45, Sun 1–5.45
Any O'Connell Street bus
DART Tara Street/Connolly

HODGES FIGGIS
56–58 Dawson Street, Dublin 2
Tel 01 677 4754
www.hodgesfiggis.ie
This famous old bookstore was established in 1768 and is particularly revered for its collection of works on Celtic and Irish history, culture, art and literature.
Mon–Fri 9–7 (Thu 9–8), Sat 9–6, Sun 12–6 Most cross-city buses
DART Tara Street/Pearse

DEPARTMENT STORES

ARNOTTS
12 Henry Street, Dublin 1
Tel 01 872 1111
www.arnotts.ie
A huge, long-established department store just off O'Connell Street, Arnotts is popular with Dubliners and visitors alike for fashion, sportswear and childrenswear as well as perfume, gifts and home furnishings. It also has a good selection of Irish crystal and other indigenous products.
Mon–Sat 9–6.30 (Thu from 9.30), Sun 12–6 Any O'Connell Street bus DART Connolly

BROWN THOMAS
88–95 Grafton Street, Dublin 2
Tel 01 605 6666
www.brownthomas.com
This elegant department store on Grafton Street specializes in household furnishings and fashion, gifts and wedding lists. A second store, BT2, is a little farther down Grafton Street and aims at a more youthful market, though the clothes are no less expensive.
Daily 9–6.30 (Thu until 9) Any cross-city bus DART Tara Street

CLERYS
18–27 Lower O'Connell Street, Dublin 1
Tel 01 878 6000
www.clerys.com
Clerys, one of Dublin's first department stores, has more than 70 departments, including Irish gifts, fashions, home furnishings and sportswear. It faces the Spire on Lower O'Connell Street.
Mon–Wed, Sat 9–6.30, Thu 9–9, Fri 9–8, Sun 12–6 Any O'Connell Street bus DART Tara Street/Connolly

GIFTS AND SPECIALIST CLOTHING

CELTIC WHISKEY SHOP
27–28 Dawson Street, Dublin 2
Tel 01 675 9744
www.celticwhiskeyshop.com
Boasting one of the best selections of Irish whiskeys in town, the Celtic Whiskey Shop also features a range of handmade chocolates and a rich assortment of wines and liqueurs.
Mon–Wed 10.30–8, Thu–Sat 10.30–9, Sun 12.30–8 Most cross-city buses DART Pearse

DESIGNYARD
12 East Essex Street, Temple Bar, Dublin 2
Tel 01 677 8453
Created as a platform for modern Irish design, DESIGNyard occupies a converted Victorian warehouse in Temple Bar. There is custom-made furniture, original jewellery, lighting and textiles.
Mon Sat 10–5.30 Most cross-city buses DART Tara Street

The Brown Thomas department store has a classy range of goods

KEVIN AND HOWLIN
31 Nassau Street, Dublin 2
Tel 01 677 0257
www.kevinandhowlin.com
Considered by many to be the best tweed shop in Dublin, Kevin and Howlin is certainly an outstanding place to buy a range of Donegal tweed clothing in both traditional and modern styles.
Mon–Sat 9.30–5.30 Most cross-city buses DART Tara Street/Pearse

KILKENNY
5–6 Nassau Street, Dublin 2
Tel 01 677 7066
www.christysirishstores.com
The Dublin branch of an Ireland-wide chain of stores specializing in Irish branded giftware. You'll find clothing, jewellery, crystal, pottery and ceramics, as well as a café and restaurant on the top floor.
Mon–Wed 8.30–6.30, Thu 8.30–8, Fri–Sat 8.30–6.30, Sun 11–6 10, 11, 13b, 14/A, 15/A/B/C, 20B, 27C, 46A/B, 84X, 127, 129 DART Tara Street

PATAGONIA
24–26 Exchequer Street, Dublin 2
Tel 01 670 5748
www.patagonia.com
The Patagonia shop is one of only four outlet stores in Europe (and the only one in the British Isles) for this iconic brand of eco-friendly outdoor wear.
Mon–Fri 10–6 (Thu 10–8), Sat 9.30–6, Sun 1–5 Most cross-city buses DART Tara Street

MARKETS AND MALLS

DÚN LAOGHAIRE FARMERS' MARKET
The Old Mail Boat, Carlisle Pier, Dún Laoghaire Harbour, Co. Dublin
www.irishfarmersmarkets.ie
With over 30 stalls, the Farmers' Market is the place to find organic vegetables, cheese and fruit, free-range meat, game, fish and poultry, not to mention home-made breads, relishes, chocolates and jam. The farmers in question come from all over Ireland, bringing traditional market sales back to the consumer.
Thu 10–5 From central Dublin: 7A, 46A, 746 DART Dún Laoghaire

GRAFTON STREET
Grafton Street, Dublin 2
Most cross-city buses pass close by DART Tara Street/Pearse
The premier shopping street in the Irish capital where you will find the grander designer outlets as well as gift, sports and fashion stores. Also home to Brown Thomas's department store and its funky designer cousin BT2, along with a host of main street stores familiar to anyone who has shopped in Britain. Buskers (street performers)

are an integral part of the whole Grafton Street experience and the side roads are full of interesting little boutiques and smaller independent stores.

MOORE STREET MARKET
Moore Street, off Henry Street, Dublin 1
Tel 01 605 7700
A Dublin tradition, Moore Street isn't just for fruit and vegetables. You'll find stalls selling just about anything, from giant bars of chocolate to dubious electrical goods. You'll need to observe commonsense precautions if you visit Moore Street, but do go there, not least to hear the banter of the traders.
Mon–Sat 9–5 Any O'Connell Street bus DART Connolly/Tara Street

POWERSCOURT TOWNHOUSE
59 South William Street, Dublin 2
www.powerscourtcentre.com
Tel 01 679 4144
A couple of minutes' walk from Grafton Street, this gracious 18th-century building has been converted to a smart shopping mall featuring 45 designer outlets, antiques, gift shops, craft galleries, bars and restaurants. Originally built for Lord Powerscourt in 1771, the building retains some fine stucco ceilings.
Most cross-city buses DART Tara Street

ST. STEPHEN'S GREEN SHOPPING CENTRE
Opposite St. Stephen's Green, at the top of Grafton Street, Dublin 2
Tel 01 478 0888
www.stephensgreen.com
Claiming to be 'where Grafton Street begins', the glittering St. Stephen's Green Shopping Centre is a spacious, light and airy mall with three floors of international names, gift and fashion outlets as well as several bars and restaurants.
Mon–Wed 9–7, Thu 9–9, Fri–Sat 9–7, Sun 11–7 Most cross-city buses DART Tara Street/Pearse

TEMPLE BAR MARKETS
Temple Bar, Dublin 2
www.templebar.ie
The bustling creative quarter has two weekly outdoor markets: Cow's Lane Market showcases Dublin's contemporary design and fashion scene, with everything from T-shirts to bags and jewellery. In winter it heads indoors to SS. Michael and John. Temple Bar Food Market fills Meeting House Square and specializes in the best international foods plus produce from nearby farms.
Cow's Lane: Sat 10–5; Temple Bar Food Market: Wed 11–3, Sat 10–5
Most cross-city buses
DART Tara Street

The lovely central courtyard of Powerscourt Townhouse

MUSIC

CLADDAGH RECORDS
Cecelia Street, Temple Bar, Dublin 2
Tel 01 677 0262
www.claddaghrecords.com
There is a great selection of music to be found in this little treasure trove, hidden away in a Temple Bar backstreet. It sells CDs and tapes from the countryfied sound of Irish dance bands to the archly traditional and contemporary. The shop is an offshoot of the roots-orientated recording label of the same name, and the staff know their stuff.
Mon–Fri 10.30–5.30, Sat 12–5.30
Most cross-city buses DART Tara Street

WALTONS WORLD OF MUSIC
2–5 North Frederick Street, Dublin 1 (also 69–70 South Great George's Street, Dublin 2)
Tel 01 874 7805
www.waltons.ie
Dublin brims over with music and musicians and Waltons World of Music supplies everyone from the wannabe rock stars to the stalwarts of the traditional scene with instruments, sheet music and accessories. They also manufacture tin whistles and *bodhráns* and publish Irish songbooks.
Mon–Sat 9–6 Most cross-city buses DART Tara Street/Pearse

ENTERTAINMENT

ARTS CENTRES

CIVIC THEATRE
Blessington Road, off Belguard Square East, Tallght, Dublin 24
Tel 01 462 7477
www.civictheatre.ie
The Civic is a community arts centre in the southwest suburbs of Dublin providing mainstream drama and classical music concerts, as well as some traditional and contemporary music. There is an art gallery upstairs and a small studio space, a popular café that's open during the day and a bar.
All year, box office: Mon–Sat 10–6
Varies 49/A, 50/X, 54A, 56A, 65/B/X, 77/A/B/X

THE HELIX
Dublin City University, Collins Avenue, Glasnevin, Dublin 9
Tel 01 700 7000
www.thehelix.ie
Opened in 2002, this complex at City University has three auditoria—the 1,260 capacity Mahony Hall, the 450-seat Theatre and the 150-seat Space—serving up a flexible mix of classical concerts, drama and mainstream rock and pop music.
All year, box office: 10–6 (to 8 on performance evenings) 13, 19, 83

SFX CITY THEATRE
23 Upper Sherrard Street, Dublin 1
Tel 01 855 4090
www.sfx.ie
An interesting venue, which has taken its role in the community seriously since the 19th century and now stages local drama, rock and wrestling.
All year, box office: Mon–Sat 10–6 Many, direction Drumcondra Drumcondra

CINEMA

IRISH FILM INSTITUTE
6 Eustace Street, Temple Bar, Dublin 2
Tel 01 679 3477
www.irishfilm.ie
A state-funded art-house cinema showing retrospectives of particular movie makers or actors, foreign language films (with subtitles) and the type of new works that are unlikely to make it to the multiplexes.
All year, subject to €2 membership fee payable 15 min before screening Varies Access to Cinema 1, shop and ticket office Most cross-city buses stop near by DART Tara Street

UGC
Parnell Street, Dublin 1
Tel 01 872 8444, info 01 872 8400
www.ugc.ie
With 17 screens, this huge northside multiplex, only 5 minutes' walk from the Millennium Bridge, shows a full range of current releases, from matinee G-rated performances for young children to late-night, 18-rated adult fare.
Varies Any O'Connell Street bus DART Connolly

CLASSICAL MUSIC, DANCE AND OPERA

BANK OF IRELAND ARTS CENTRE
Foster Place, College Green, Dublin 2
Tel 01 671 1488
www.boi.ie/artscentre
There are weekly daytime recitals of modern and standard classical music in this magnificent Georgian building that once housed the Irish parliament, across the street from Trinity College.
Free Most cross-city buses DART Tara Street Tours available, €3 (child €2) charge for special exhibitions only

NATIONAL CONCERT HALL
Earlsfort Terrace, Dublin 2
Tel 01 417 0000
www.nch.ie
Dublin's biggest classical music venue was built for the International Exhibition of Arts and Manufactures in 1865. As well as hosting the greatest visiting musicians of the day, it is home to the RTÉ National Symphony Orchestra.
All year Varies 10, 11, 13, 14/A, 15/A/B/C, 27C, 44, 46A/B, 48A, 86 DART Pearse

The stark, modernist exterior of Dublin's Abbey Theatre

CONTEMPORARY LIVE MUSIC

GAIETY THEATRE
South King Street, Dublin 2
Tel 01 677 1717
www.gaietytheatre.net
This is a big old-style theatre in the vicinity of the northwest corner of St. Stephen's Green. It's most famous for its winter pantomimes (children's fairytales given a vaudeville treatment), and also has a lively calendar of events, featuring a mixture of popular drama and music. It also hosts club nights and has a late bar.
All year; box office: 10–7 Varies Any passing St. Stephen's Green DART Tara Street

THE HUB
23–24 Eustace Street, Temple Bar, Dublin 2
Tel 01 670 7655
www.thehubmezz.com
An intimate Temple Bar venue for rock and pop gigs, attached to the Mezz nightclub. Local bands are popular here, with Battle of the Bands-style tryouts, DJ competitions and alternative/student nights. Gigs are followed by club sessions.
All year Most cross-city buses DART Tara Street

THE POINT
East Link Bridge, North Wall Quay, Dublin 1
Tel 01 836 6777
www.thepoint.ie
The Point is a huge music venue built in a former tram depot. Big-name performers here have included everyone from the Beach Boys and the Bolshoi Ballet to WWF and ZZ Top, via Frank Sinatra, Bob Dylan and the Kirov Ballet.
All year, box office times: Mon–Sat 10–6 53

TEMPLE BAR MUSIC CENTRE
Curved Street, Temple Bar, Dublin 2
Tel 01 670 9202
www.tbmc.ie
Here you're as likely to see big names in Irish traditional, folk and world music as contemporary rock acts. Popular salsa classes on Tuesday nights are open to beginners.
All year Most cross-city buses stop nearby DART Tara Street

WHELAN'S
25 Wexford Street, Dublin 2
Tel 01 478 0766
www.whelanslive.com
You'll see an eclectic line-up at this smaller rock and pop venue with late club bar from Wednesday to Saturday. Licensed to serve alcohol since 1772, renovation work in the early 1990s revealed the original wood and stonework, which is now a feature.
All year 16/A, 19/A., 65/B, 83 DART Pearse/Tara Street

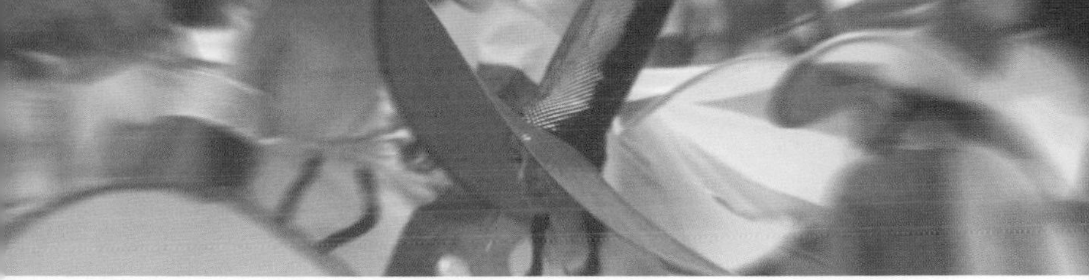

THEATRE

ABBEY THEATRE
26 Lower Abbey Street, Dublin 1
Tel 01 878 7222
www.abbeytheatre.ie
This purpose-built home of the National Theatre of Ireland dates from 1966. The main, fan-shaped auditorium seats 628, nearly 100 of which are in a shallow balcony.
All year, box office times: Mon–Sat 10–7 Varies DART Tara Street

ANDREW'S LANE THEATRE
9–17 St. Andrew's Lane, off Trinity Street, Dublin 2
Tel 01 679 5720
www.andrewslane.com
A small 220-seat theatre staging drama by Irish and international writers. The main theatre has more mainstream productions, while the smaller studio area hosts lesser known touring groups.
All year, box office: Mon–Sat 10.30–7 Varies Most cross-city buses DART Tara Street

GATE THEATRE
1 Cavendish Row, Parnell Square, Dublin 1
Tel 01 874 4045
www.gate-theatre.ie
One of Ireland's foremost theatres, staging new works and the standards in a beautiful Georgian-fronted building that has been a theatre since 1928. This was an early showcase for the likes of Orson Welles and James Mason.
All year, box office: Mon–Sat 10–7.30 Varies 3, 10, 11/A/B, 13/A, 16/A, 19/A, 38/A, 12, 121, 122 DART Connolly

PEACOCK THEATRE
26 Lower Abbey Street, Dublin 1
Tel 01 878 7222
www.abbeytheatre.ie
A tiny place beneath the foyer of the Abbey Theatre, dedicated to brand new works. The capacity is about 150 and there's a particularly intimate atmosphere.
All year Most cross-city buses stop nearby DART Tara Street

NIGHTLIFE

BARS AND CAFÉS

1780 BAR
The Old Jameson Distillery, Bow Street, Smithfield, Dublin 7
Tel 01 807 2355
www.whiskeytours.ie
The 1780 Bar takes its name from the year that Jameson's distillery was founded in Smithfield. It has a pleasant brick and timber finish inside and it's a popular meeting place, with bar food and an excellent range of Irish whiskeys, including Jameson's, of course.
Noon until it closes 25, 25A, 67, 67A (from Middle Abbey Street); 68, 69, 79 (from Aston Quay)

Fitzsimons in Temple Bar is buzzing every day of the week

CAPTAIN AMERICA'S COOKHOUSE AND BAR
44 Grafton Street, Dublin 2
Tel 01 671 5266
www.captainamericas.com
This is a lively American-style bar and diner that was established here in 1971. Since then it has amassed a huge collection of rock 'n' roll memorabilia. It also claims to be the only fully licensed bar that's actually on Grafton Street, and offers a great line in cocktails. Be prepared for crowds—this is a very popular place, especially on Saturdays.
Daily noon–midnight DART Pearse

DOHENY AND NESBITT
5 Lower Baggot Street, Dublin 2
Tel 01 676 2945
A distinguished old pub away from the usual tourist drinking spots, Doheny and Nesbitt attracts politicians and media people to its three floors and bars well-stocked with whiskeys and stouts. Its mirrored walls, high ceilings and intimate snugs betray its Victorian origins, over 130 years ago.
Daily, late nights Fri–Sat 10, 15X, 25X, 49X

FITZSIMONS
21–22 Wellington Quay, Temple Bar, Dublin 2
Tel 01 677 9315
www.fitzsimonshotel.com
With free traditional music and Irish dancing six days a week, bars on three floors and DJs every night, this bar complex is aimed at all-comers to the Temple Bar scene. Big, busy and bustling, it has a great atmosphere.
Daily 10.30am–2.30am

GUBU
7–8 Lower Capel Street, Dublin 1
Tel 01 874 0710
Just across the Grattan Bridge from Temple Bar, Gubu is a thriving gay bar, which attracts a friendly crowd both gay and straight. It gets very busy at weekends and there is live jazz during the week and on Sunday afternoons.
Mon–Wed 3–11, Thu–Sat 3–12.30, Sun 3–11

MCDAID'S
3 Harry Street, Dublin 2
Tel 01 679 4395
Just off Grafton Street, this is a traditional Dublin pub that has changed little since Brendan Behan and Patrick Kavanagh stood at the bar. It is cramped and noisy most nights of the week, but isn't that what you came for?
Mon–Thu 10.30am–11.30pm, Fri–Sat 10.30am–12.30am, Sun 12.30pm–11pm

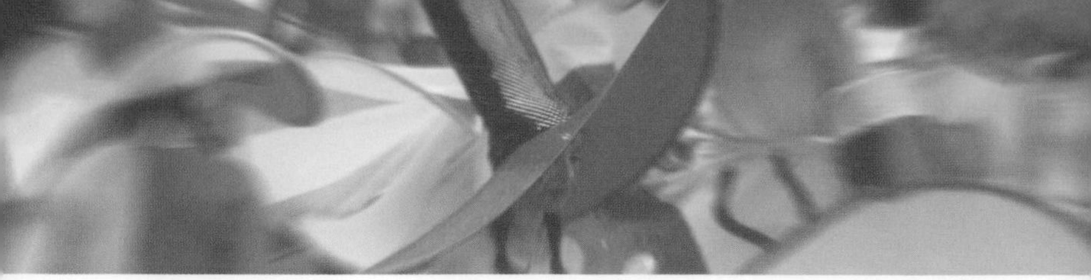

MULLIGANS
8 Poolbeg Street, Dublin 2
Tel 01 677 5582
www.mulligans.ie
A pub since 1820, Mulligans is a Guinness drinkers' institution. Retaining its Victorian mahogany furnishings, it has resisted change and would probably have looked the same when John F. Kennedy drank here, as a journalist, in 1947.
Sun–Fri 10.30am–11.30pm, Sat and evenings before a public holiday 10.30am–12.30am

O'NEILLS
2 Suffolk Street, Dublin 2
Tel 01 679 3656
www.oneillsbar.com
A licensed bar for over 300 years, this complex of snugs and alcoves is just across the road from the Tourism Office. It is believed to have been built on the site of the Norse parliament or 'thingmote'.
Mon–Wed 10.30am–11.30pm, Thu–Sat 10.30am–12.30am, Sun 12.30pm–11pm

THE PORTERHOUSE
16–18 Parliament Street, Dublin 2
Tel 01 679 8847
www.theporterhousebrewco.com
One of the few home brew pubs in Ireland. You can escape Guinness here and try their own brand of internationally acclaimed stout ale. Live music seven nights a week with afternoon sessions at the weekend.
Mon–Wed 11.30–11.30, Thu 11.30am–1.30am, Fri 11.30am–2am, Sat 12pm–2.30am, Sun 12.30–11

THE TEMPLE BAR
47–48 Temple Bar, Dublin 2
Tel 01 672 9286
With its huge selection of whiskeys, live traditional music sessions and crowds of party-minded drinkers, this is perhaps the epitome of tourists' Temple Bar, but the *craic* can be good and the layout of the interior means it is never overwhelming.
Mon–Thu 11am–12.30am, Fri–Sat 11am–1.30am, Sun 11am–12.30am

CLUBS

BREAK FOR THE BORDER
Lower Stephens Street, Dublin 2
Tel 01 478 0300
www.capitalbars.com
A huge all-round entertainment place on three floors, with downstairs gigs giving way to a nightclub after midnight. Many of Dublin's bands have cut their teeth playing here. The busy restaurant serves Tex-Mex-style food and steaks.
Mon–Wed 5–11.30, Thu–Sat 5pm–2.30am, Sun 4–11

The bright and beckoning frontage of the Temple Bar pub

EAMONN DORAN'S
3a Crown Alley, Temple Bar, Dublin 2
Tel 01 679 9114
A sprawling Temple Bar venue with a proper stage and dance floors as well as several bars. DJs mix anything from house to indie, midnight–2am. Live music includes occasional big names, young bands and traditional music.
12pm–3am

THE GEORGE
South Great George's Street, Dublin 2
Tel 01 478 2983
www.capitalbars.com
On the corner of Dame Street and South Great George's Street, the George is both a bar and a nightclub and has long been Dublin's main gay and lesbian venue.
Mon–Tue 12.30–11.30, Wed–Sat 12.30pm–2.30am, Sun 12.30pm–1am
Charge for nightclub after 10pm

THE MEZZ
23 Eustace Street, Temple Bar, Dublin 2
Tel 01 670 7655
www.thehubmezz.com
The Mezz is an eclectic music bar. The sounds cover everything from jazz and easy listening to funk and old fashioned rock 'n' roll.
Usually 6–12 but times may vary

THE VAULTS
IFSC (under Connolly Station), Dublin 1
Tel 01 605 4700
www.thevaults.ie
A busy mainstream nightclub in the International Financial Services Centre, where Friday is Smooth Grooves mixed up with some hip-hop and R'n'B, and Saturday nights are given over to R'n'B and '80s soul.
Mon–Thu 12pm–11.30pm, Fri–Sat 12pm–2.30am, Sun 12pm–11.30pm

SPORTS AND ACTIVITIES

BICYCLING

BELFIELD BIKE SHOP
UCD, Dublin 4
Tel 01 260 0749
www.cyclingsafaris.com
Dublin is perfect for bicycling. You can escape the crowded streets in Phoenix Park, or get out on the coast at Howth or Dalkey, or into the Wicklow Mountains. Main routes into the city have bicycle lanes, but you'll need at least two good locks to keep your wheels safe.
Daily 9–6 €18 per day

BUS TOURS

DUBLIN CITY TOUR
DublinBus Head Office, 59 Upper O'Connell Street, Dublin 1
Tel 01 873 4222
www.dublinbus.ie
Dublin City Tours are operated by DublinBus and run around the middle of Dublin all day.

There is live commentary, and tickets, which you can buy on board, are valid for 24 hours, so you can get on and off to visit the sights. The route takes in Phoenix Park, Collins Barracks (National Museum), the Dublin Writers Museum, Henry Street/GPO, Trinity College, the National Gallery, Dublin Castle and the Guinness Storehouse.
Daily 9.30–5 (every 10 min), 5–6.30 (every 30 min) Adult €12.50, child €6

CLIMBING

UCD CLIMBING WALL
UCD Sports Centre, UCD, Belfield, Dublin 4
Tel 01 716 2185
www.ucd.ie/sport
When the weather is too unpleasant to venture out of doors to the crags at Dalkey or into the Wicklow Mountains, an indoor wall is just the thing. Ropes, harnesses and belay devices can all be rented on site at this excellent facility.
Daily, but check for times €7 (visitors must complete a short competence test, only available Sat and Sun after 6pm) Buses go to UCD from all over town

WEST WOOD CLUB
Clontarf Road, Dublin 3
Tel 01 805 7827
www.westwood.ie
At 11m (36ft) the West Wood climbing wall claims to be the tallest in Ireland, though floor space and matting is a little limited, so there is not much space for bouldering. You can go all the way across the ceiling though. The four-day pass gives access to the club's fitness suite as well as the wall.
Mon–Fri 6am–11pm, Sat–Sun 8am–9pm €51 for a four day pass for non-members (free equipment hire) 130 DART Clontarf Road

FISHING

DUBLIN ANGLING INITIATIVE
Eastern Regional Fisheries Board, 15A Main Street, Blackrock, Co. Dublin
Tel 01 278 7022
www.fishingireland.net
Dublin presents some popular fishing opportunities: There is coarse fishing in the Liffey and the Royal and Grand canals, game fishing in the Liffey, the Tolka, the Dargle and the Dodder and excellent sea fishing all along the coast from Balbriggan to Bray. Beach fishing is popular at Dollymount Strand and inshore, self-drive boats can be rented at Bullock Harbour, Coliemore, Dún Laoghaire and Bray. The Eastern Regional Fisheries Board produces information leaflets explaining the opportunities and rules for each type of sport in the area.

A trip around Dublin on a tour bus is a fun way to see the city

GAELIC GAMES

CROKE PARK
Jones's Road, Dublin 3
Tel 01 819 2300
www.gaa.ie
There are dozens of teams all over County Dublin playing Gaelic football, hurling, camogie and handball. The easiest place to see football and hurling is in the Fifteen Acres area of Phoenix Park, where many of the local teams in these strictly amateur sports play. The headquarters of the Gaelic Athletic Association (GAA) is Croke Park (▷ 68) in north Dublin where the All-Ireland finals are played. You can only get tickets for these through contact with a local club, but semi-final games are also played at Croke Park and tickets are usually available in advance.
Match days are usually Sun
Varies (call for information)
3, 11, 11A, 16, 16A, 123, 51A
DART Connolly, 15-min walk

GOLF

LUTTRELLSTOWN CASTLE
Castleknock, Dublin 15
Tel 01 808 9988
www.luttrellstown.ie
This is a beautifully manicured parkland course in the grounds of a medieval castle on the western edges of the city. In addition to the golfing challenge, there are fine views over the Strawberry Beds and across to the Dublin Mountains.
Daily 8am–9pm Green fees from €30 for 9 holes, €50 for 18 holes

PORTMAROCK
Portmarnock, Co. Dublin
Tel 01 846 0611
www.portmarnock.com
Designed by Bernhard Langer, Portmarnock is one of Ireland's best links courses, attached to a luxury hotel.
Daily 9–6 Green fees €120 for non residents

ROYAL DUBLIN
Bull Island, Dollymount, Dublin 3
Tel 01 833 6346
www.theroyaldublingolfclub.com
Founded in 1885, this is Ireland's oldest golf club and the championship links course has hosted many important competitions. Access is from the central causeway across to Bull Island.
Mon–Fri and Sun for visitors, Sat members only Green fees from €120

STACKSTOWN
Kellystown Road, Rathfarnham, Dublin 16
Tel 01 949 1993
www.stackstowngolfclub.com
In the foothills of the Dublin Mountains this is a relaxed

18-hole parkland course with magnificent views across the city and Dublin Bay.
Best days for visitors are Mon, Thu, Fri and Sun Green fees from €30

HORSE-RACING

LEOPARDSTOWN RACECOURSE
Leopardstown Road (off the Stillorgan road), Foxrock, Dublin 18
Tel 01 289 3607
www.leopardstown.com
While most of the best racing near Dublin is in Co. Kildare (▷ 98–99), Leopardstown has a modern and popular course. The track is in the southern suburbs and there are one or two meetings a month, mostly National Hunt (steeplechase), but some flat racing too.
Once or twice per month (call or see press for details) From €12 63, 86, special buses run from Busáras on race days

RUGBY UNION

IRISH RUGBY FOOTBALL UNION
National Stadium, Lansdowne Road, Ballsbridge, Dublin 4
Tel 01 668 4601
www.irfu.ie; www.irishrugby.ie
The best rugby in Ireland is played in the Six Nations tournament, in which an all-Ireland side plays against England, Wales, Scotland, France and Italy.
Call or see press for fixtures Adult from €25, child from €7 5, 7/A, 45 DART Lansdowne Road

LEINSTER RUGBY UNION
55 Main Street, Donnybrook, Dublin 4
Tel 01 269 3224
www.leinsterrugby.ie
The next best thing to international rugby is one of the big regional tournaments, in which the Leinster Lions play. The cream of European rugby plays in the Heineken Cup, and Leinster play their fixtures at the national stadium. For the smaller Celtic League (regional teams from Ireland, Scotland and Wales), they play at their home ground in the southern suburb of Donnybrook.
Call or see press for fixtures From €15 Donnybrook is served by many cross-city buses DART Sandymount, 20-min walk

SOCCER

BOHEMIAN FOOTBALL CLUB
Dalymount Park, Phibsboro, Dublin 7
Tel 01 868 0923
www.bohemians.ie
Ireland's oldest soccer club was founded in 1890, but didn't turn professional until the late 1960s. Playing in their famous red and black stripes, they have won the Irish championship nine times and the cup six times.
Season runs Mar–end Nov 10, 19/A, 38/A/B/C, 83, 120, 121, 122 Drumcondra 25-min walk

A literary trail plaque displaying a quote from Joyce's Ulysses

SHELBOURNE FOOTBALL CLUB
Tolka Park, Richmond Road, Dublin 3
Tel 01 837 5536
www.shelbournefc.ie
Four times champions in recent years, Shelbourne is one of Ireland's most successful soccer clubs. The club was founded in 1895.
Season runs Mar–end Nov Adult €12, child €6 3, 11/A, 13A, 16/A, 33, 41/A/B/C, 746 Drumcondra

WALKING

HISTORICAL INSIGHTS
64 Mary Street, Dublin 1
Tel 01 878 0227
www.historicalinsights.ie
These historically themed walking tours of the city are led by knowledgeable history graduates from Trinity College. A 2-hour 'seminar on the street' includes Wood Quay in the heart of Viking Dublin, the Four Courts, Trinity College, Temple Bar, Christ Church Cathedral and, of course, Dublin Castle.
May–end Sep daily 11, 12, 3; Oct–end Apr Fri–Sun 12 Adult €10

JAMES JOYCE CULTURAL CENTRE
See page 75.
From here, walking tours are led around the various Bloomsday (▷ 207) locations and other sites associated with James Joyce.

HEALTH AND BEAUTY

DALKEY HEALTH AND BEAUTY CLINIC
19a Castle Street, Dalkey, Co. Dublin
Tel 01 284 0393
www.dalkeyhealthandbeauty.com
At the heart of this historic seaside suburb, this is a good place to come to wind down from the bustle of city life. There are three private rooms and treatments on offer include Reiki, reflexology, homeopathy and acupuncture. When you're nice and relaxed, you can spruce yourself up with manicures, pedicures and a range of beauty treatments, ready to head back to the city.
Sun–Mon 12–6, Tue–Wed, Fri–Sat 9–8, Thu 9–8.30 DART Dalkey

MADISON CLINIC AND DAY SPA
17 Upper Liffey Street, Dublin 1
Tel 01 872 5544
www.madisonclinic.ie
On the corner of Liffey Street and Henry Street, opposite Roches Stores, the Madison Clinic is particularly popular with hen (bachelorette) parties. There is a range of facials, manicures, pedicures and massages that makes the crowds outside seem less stressful.
Mon–Wed, Sat 9–6, Thu 9–8, Fri 9–7 Any O'Connell Street bus

FOR CHILDREN

THE ARK
11a Eustace Street, Temple Bar, Dublin 2
Tel 01 670 7788
www.ark.ie
This is a cultural venue especially for 4–14 year olds, located in the busy Temple Bar quarter of Dublin. It stages varied performances by children and for children in both the indoor theatre and outdoor amphitheatre, and there's a gallery space and workshops concentrating on arts and activities for young people.
Call for opening times and performances DART Tara Street

DUBLIN ZOO
Phoenix Park, Dublin 8
Tel 01 474 8900
www.dublinzoo.ie
Committed to conservation and education, this is a modern zoo housing over 700 animals. A recent development is the 'African Plains' area, where lions, giraffes and other animals from regions such as the Serengeti can roam with greater freedom.
Mar–end Sep Mon–Sat 9.30–6, Sun 10.30–6; Oct–end Feb Mon–Sat 9.30–dusk, Sun 10.30–dusk
Adult €12.50, child €8, family €35
Heuston

MALAHIDE CASTLE
See page 75.

NATIONAL WAX MUSEUM
See page 79.

PHOENIX PARK
See page 82.

VIKING SPLASH TOUR
64–65 Patrick Street, Dublin 8
Tel 01 707 6000
www.vikingsplashtours.com
An exciting trip in an ex-World War II amphibious vehicle tours Viking Dublin before driving into the Grand Canal.
Jun–end Oct Mon–Sat 10–12, 1.30–5, Sun 10.30–12, 1.30–5, tours every 30 min; mid-Feb to end May, Nov Tue–Sun 10–12, 1.30–3.30

FESTIVALS AND EVENTS

MARCH

ST. PATRICK'S DAY
Contact: St. Stephen's Green House, Earlsfort Terrace, Dublin 2
Tel 01 676 3205
www.stpatricksday.ie
The St. Patrick's Day parade in Dublin usually begins around noon near St. Patrick's and threads around the city to O'Connell Street. Merrion Square and Festival Square in Smithfield are full of street entertainers from all over Ireland, and each year it seems to get more ambitious.
17 March

St. Patrick's Day is not all shamrocks and leprechauns

JUNE

BLOOMSDAY
Contact: James Joyce Centre, 35 North Great George's Street, Dublin 1
Tel 01 878 8947
www.jamesjoyce.ie
James Joyce set his masterwork *Ulysses* on 16 June 1904, the day he met Nora Barnacle, his wife and muse. Every year Joycean enthusiasts and academics celebrate the man and his works with tours, readings and seminars.
16 June

AUGUST

DUBLIN HORSE SHOW
Contact: Royal Dublin Society, Ballsbridge, Dublin 4
Tel 01 668 0866
www.rds.ie/horseshow
First held in 1864, the Dublin Horse Show has become Ireland's largest equestrian event, with the third largest prize pool for showjumping in the world. The five-day event takes place at the RDS complex with entrants from all over the world.
First week in August

SEPTEMBER/OCTOBER

DUBLIN FRINGE FESTIVAL
Contact: 12 East Essex Street, Temple Bar, Dublin 2
Tel 01 677 8511
Since 1995 the Dublin Fringe festival has been celebrating performing arts, while the mainstream festival concentrates on more high-brow culture. Like its big sister in Edinburgh, it features comedy, music, cabaret and alternative theatre.

DUBLIN THEATRE FESTIVAL
Contact: 44 East Essex Street, Temple Bar, Dublin 2
Tel 01 677 8439
www.dublintheatrefestival.com
Dublin's theatrical tradition makes this is one of the most vibrant theatre festivals in Europe. Leading lights of the Dublin drama scene contribute to this celebration of contemporary Irish drama. Venues include the Abbey, Gate, Peacock and Project.
End September–early October

OCTOBER

ADIDAS DUBLIN MARATHON
Contact: Donore Harriers Sports Centre, Chapelizod, Dublin 20
Tel 01 623 2250 (open 9–5)
www.dublincitymarathon.ie
Around 10,000 competitors, over half from other countries, compete in this annual run around Dublin's Georgian streets, starting and finishing near the heart of the city.
Last week in October

THE EAST

On the whole, the east of Ireland has a gentle landscape, and so much of what you will find here reflects this gentleness. If you enjoy the arts, look for it mostly in the urban capitals of each county, where a municipal arts venue will show an eclectic mix of visual and musical forms. In Wexford, the opera festival in October attains international significance. You'll find countless traditional pubs, where fiddles, guitars, accordions and whistles are as likely to be heard as pop and rock tunes. The sea plays a big part in the life of eastern Ireland, particularly to the south, so boats feature on many people's itineraries, be that cruising down the Barrow River or bobbing up and down around the Saltee Islands.

The rolling green fields that dominate most of the eastern side of Ireland have made it perfect horse-breeding country. With horse-racing so popular here, it would be a shame not to take in a meeting at some stage, maybe at the famous Curragh or Punchestown courses. All that grass also makes for good golf courses, and some of Europe's best are within a couple of hours of Dublin.

KEY TO SYMBOLS
Shopping
Entertainment
Nightlife
Sports
Activities
Health and Beauty
For Children

ASHFORD

TIGLIN—THE NATIONAL MOUNTAIN AND WHITEWATER CENTRE

Near the Devil's Glen, Ashford, Co. Wicklow
Tel 0404 40169
www.tiglin.com

The foremost body in Ireland for developing outdoor skills, Tiglin provides courses in most outdoor disciplines, including canoeing, climbing, hillwalking and orienteering, from their headquarters in the Wicklow Mountains.

All activities must be booked and paid for in advance. Closed last week Jul and first week Aug, and 2 weeks around Christmas · Prices depend on activity

BRAY

AVOCA WEAVERS

Kilmacanogue, Bray, Co. Wicklow
Tel 01 286 7466
www.avoca.ie

In the grounds of the old Jameson whiskey estate in the foothills of the Wicklow Mountains, the headquarters of Avoca's retail network sells their lines of knitwear, home furnishings, children's clothing, separates and coordinates for men and women, plus a garden shop with a pleasant conservatory and a restaurant.

Daily 9–6 · Bus Éireann service from Dublin

MERMAID ARTS CENTRE

Main Street, Bray, Co. Wicklow
Tel 01 272 4030
www.mermaidartscentre.ie

Dance, drama and a wide range of musical performances have made the Mermaid a success as County Wicklow's arts centre. A good place to catch the big names in traditional music and professional theatre without paying Dublin prices.

All year, box office: Mon–Sat 10–6 (to 8 on performance evenings) · Varies · 45, 84 (from Eden Quay Dublin) · DART Bray

SEALIFE CENTRE
Bray, Co. Wicklow
Tel 01 286 6939
www.sealife.ie
The central feature of this all-weather attraction on the sea front in Bray is the 'Lair of the Octopus', a re-creation of the undersea world inhabited by these fascinating animals. Look, too, for sea-horses, sharks, moray eels and giant Japanese spider crabs.
Daily from 10am, call for display times Call for prices
45, 84 (from Eden Quay Dublin)
DART Bray

CARLINGFORD

MEMORIES
Tholsel Street, Carlingford, Co. Louth
Tel 042 937 3093
Cars are banned from the tiny street leading down to the Tholsel gatehouse, within the old town wall. A number of craft and gift outlets trade in the street's medieval buildings, selling Celtic and Irish designs.
Daily 10–6

CARLINGFORD ADVENTURE
Tholsel Street, Carlingford, Co. Louth
Tel 042 937 3100
www.carlingfordadventure.com
Carlingford Adventure arranges courses in sailing, windsurfing, kayaking and powerboating on the nearby lough, as well as climbing, hillwalking and orienteering on the hills of the Cooley Peninsula.
Closed 2 weeks around Christmas
Vary according to courses Bus Éireann from Newry (NI)

CARLOW

COUNTY CARLOW RUGBY FOOTBALL CLUB
Oak Park, Carlow, Co. Carlow
Tel 059 913 1218
www.leinsterrugby.ie
Outside Dublin, the only AIB National League Division One team is County Carlow. Leinster Lions represent the whole of the east of Ireland in the Heineken Cup and the Celtic League.
Call or check website for fixtures and ticket prices Bus Éireann service from Dublin Carlow

CAVAN

FARNHAM STREET
Cavan, Co. Cavan
Tourist Information Centre, Farnham Street, Cavan Town
Tel 049 4331942
www.cavantourism.ie
Despite the growth of out-of-town shopping near the bypass, Cavan still has much to attract shoppers to its narrow main street, where a number of brightly painted independent shops offer an interesting range of goods.
Individual shop times vary Bus Éireann service

Get caught up in the excitement of a fast-action game of rugby

ASTRA BOWL
Storm Cinema Complex, Townspark, Cavan, Co. Cavan
Tel 049 43 72662
www.astra-bowl.com
There are few bowling facilities in County Cavan, so these six lanes are very popular and it's a good idea to book in advance. There are also pool tables and arcade games.
Mon–Fri 12–11, Sat–Sun 10am–11pm From €3.70 per person per hour

DROGHEDA

CARBERRY'S
11 North Strand, Drogheda, Co. Louth
Tel 041 983 7409
Drogheda's best known pub for live traditional music has changed very little in the last 30 years and has built its reputation on serving good beer with no frills. Live music on Sunday afternoons, singers' night Wednesday.
Mon–Thu 8pm–11.30pm, Fri–Sat 8pm–12.30am, Sun 1.30–7.30 Bus Éireann services from Dublin
Drogheda

DROGHEDA UNITED FOOTBALL CLUB
United Park, Windmill Road, Drogheda, Co. Louth
Tel 041 983 0190
www.droghedaunited.ie
The only Leinster soccer team outside Dublin to have any lasting presence in the Eircom League of Ireland, Drogheda United was formed by a merging of two local clubs in 1975.
Mar–end Nov Call or check website for fixtures and ticket prices
Bus Éireann service from Dublin
Drogheda

ENNISCORTHY

CARLEY'S BRIDGE POTTERIES
Carley's Bridge, Enniscorthy, Co. Wexford
Tel 054 33512
Founded by two Cornish brothers in the 17th century, this pottery is still in the same family, making it one of Ireland's oldest businesses. Both modern and traditional designs are produced.
Mon–Fri 9–5.30, phone for weekend hours

ENNISKERRY

POWERSCOURT ESTATE
Enniskerry, Co. Wicklow
Tel 01 204 6000
www.powerscourt.ie
The Powerscourt Garden Centre has made a name for itself with horticulturalists in search of plants and garden equipment. In the entrance to the main house there are gift and furnishing outlets, too, which means some visitors never make it to the gardens.
Daily 9.30–5.30 44 from Dublin, 85 from Bray

POWERSCOURT SPRINGS HEALTH FARM
Coolakay, Enniskerry, Co. Wicklow
Tel 01 276 1000
www.powerscourtsprings.ie
Set in a large country estate on the edge of the Wicklow Mountains, this spa runs day sessions of stress release courses which include massages, mud and other skin treatments, hand and foot care, aromatherapy and reflexology.
Call for course details Day sessions from €120 44 from Dublin, 85 from Bray

GOWRAN

GOWRAN PARK RACECOURSE
Gowran Park, Mill Road, Gowran, Co. Kilkenny
Tel 056 772 6225
Gowran Park has made a name for itself as the place to see the up-and-coming young jump horses race in January and February. There are also some flat racing meetings.
16 meetings per year, call for fixtures From €8 Bus Éireann service

KILDARE

THE CURRAGH
Co. Kildare
Tel 045 441205
www.curragh.ie
The word Curragh may even derive from the Gaelic for racecourse, such is the pedigree of this famous flat racing venue. The headquarters for flat racing in Ireland, and its principal venue since 1741, there are five classic meets here every year and as many as 14 others between March and October.
Up to 19 meetings per year, call or check website for fixtures From €15 Bus Éireann service Kildare or Newbridge

KILKENNY

KILKENNY DESIGN CENTRE
Castle Yard, Kilkenny, Co. Kilkenny
Tel 056 772 2118
www.kilkennydesign.com
Drawing on the skills of more than 200 artisans from all over Ireland, this is a nationally recognized outlet for a wide range of crafts. The emphasis is on natural fibres and materials, be they linen, silk, wool or cashmere for clothing, silver and gold for jewellery, locally made, hand-blown Jerpoint glassware, or traditional and contemporary gifts from wood and porcelain. Upstairs there is an excellent café and restaurant overlooking the courtyard.
Mon–Sat 10–7, Sun 11–7. Closed Sun Jan–end Mar Bus Éireann service Kilkenny

The Curragh in County Kildare is Irelands's foremost racecourse

WATERGATE THEATRE
Parliament Street, Kilkenny, Co. Kilkenny
Tel 056 61674
www.watergatekilkenny.com
With a schedule of professional and amateur drama, contemporary, traditional and classical music, this is one of southeast Ireland's foremost arts complexes.
All year Prices vary depending on performance Bus Éireann services from Dublin Kilkenny

ANNA CONDA
Parliament Street, Kilkenny, Co. Kilkenny
Tel 056 777 1657
Just one of several vividly painted Irish pubs in Kilkenny offering live traditional music and the chance for amateurs to join in the session.
Mon–Thu 11am–11.30pm, Fri–Sat 11am–12.30am, Sun 11am–11pm Bus Éireann service Kilkenny

TYNAN WALKING TOURS
Depart from Kilkenny tourist office
Tel 087 265 1745
www.tynantours.com
The best way to get to know Ireland's medieval capital city is on foot with a knowledgeable guide. Explore its lanes and streets and discover where the best shops and pubs are.
Mar–end Oct Mon–Fri four times a day, Sun twice a day; Nov–end Mar Sat–Sun twice a day Adult €6, child €5.50 Bus Éireann services from Dublin Kilkenny

KILMORE QUAY

COUNTRY CRAFTS
Kilmore Quay, Co. Wexford
Tel 053 29885
With a good selection of paintings by local artists, pottery and crafts from around County Wexford, and some interesting collectables and general bric-à-brac, this is an interesting place to call in on the Hook Peninsula, overlooking the fishing port and marina.
May–end Sep daily 10–7; Oct–end Apr daily 11–5

PAUL BATES CHARTER BOAT SERVICES
Kilmore Quay, Co. Wexford
Tel 053 29831
Kilmore Quay is one of the best and most organized sea angling bases on the Irish coast. The inshore waters around the Saltee Islands have acquired an international reputation, with a wide range of species to be found.
All year Varies, call for details

MONAGHAN

THE MARKET HOUSE
Market Street, Monaghan, Co. Monaghan
Tel 047 38158
www.themarkethouse.ie

A mixed offering of classical, traditional and contemporary music is put on in the 18th-century market building, now an arts venue. Catch some famous names of the folk touring circuit as well as jazz and poetry.
All year Mon–Fri from 8.30pm
Varies depending on performance
Bus Éireann services from Dublin

NAAS

NAAS RACECOURSE

Tipper Road, Naas, Co. Kildare
Tel 045 897 391
www.naasracecourse.ie
Naas is one of two horse racing circuits near this small Kildare town. It's an important course for spotting this year's National Hunt hopefuls in February.
At least 14 meetings per year
From €12 Bus Éireann service
Sallins & Naas Station

PUNCHESTOWN RACECOURSE

Naas, Co. Kildare
Tel 045 897 704
www.punchestown.com
The Punchestown National Hunt horse-racing festival held in April/May draws racing people from all over Europe, and the course has been redeveloped to reflect this international popularity, with new stands and hospitality facilities.
19 meetings per year From €15
Bus Éireann service Sallins & Naas Station

KILLASHEE HOUSE HOTEL

Killashee Demesne, Naas, Co. Kildare
Tel: 045 981600
www.killasheehouse.ie
There are extensive spa facilities attached to this hotel in the Kildare countryside. You can choose from a variety of activities here, focusing on health, combating stress or other wellness issues, and the range of leisure facilities includes a gym, pool and children's pool.
All year round Call for details

NAVAN

MAGUIRE'S

Hill of Tara, Tara, Navan, Co. Meath
Tel 046 902 5534
www.tarahall.ie
Next to the parking area on the historic Hill of Tara, Maguire's specializes in gifts and craftwork in the Celtic/New Age tradition. There is also an excellent bookshop, with titles ranging from the academic to the bizarre, all relating to the rich archaeology of the area and beyond. If you're planning to visit the Loughcrew Cairns, you'll find books here explaining their scientific and New Age significance.
Daily 9–6

Gothic Slane Castle is now best known for mega concerts

NAVAN RACECOURSE

Proudstown, Navan, Co. Meath
Tel 046 902 1350
www.navanracecourse.ie
With about 14 meetings a year this is an important course for Irish horse trainers. The earlier ones in the year feature the young hopefuls.
14 meetings per year, check website or call for fixtures From €11 Bus Éireann service

NEWBRIDGE

RED HOUSE

Newbridge, Co. Kildare
Tel 087 685 2972
www.redhouse.ie
The Red Hot Music Club is a monthly gig at this country hotel between Newbridge and Naas. It's a good spot to see and hear some of the big names in Irish traditional music.
Varies according to performance
Bus Éireann services from Dublin
Newbridge

RIVERBANK ARTS CENTRE

Newbridge, Co. Kildare
Tel 045 448333
www.riverbank.ie
A modern complex for the arts in one of Kildare's fast-growing towns, the Riverbank promotes all forms of popular, classical and traditional music as well as staging plays and having gallery space.
Varies according to performance
Bus Éireann services from Dublin
Newbridge

SLANE

SLANE CASTLE

Slane, Co. Meath
Tel 041 988 4400
www.slanecastle.ie
A legendary venue, even though it stages only one big concert a year. In 2003 the Red Hot Chili Peppers set new records for their live album recorded here during the summer. Famous acts have included Madonna, the Rolling Stones, Bruce Springsteen, Oasis, REM, Robbie Williams and, of course, U2.
Concerts usually only once per year
Depends on who is playing Bus Éireann services from Dublin with extra services before and after annual concert

STRAFFAN

THE K CLUB

Straffan, Co. Kildare
Tel 01 601 7200
www.kclub.ie
A venue for the European Open and the 2006 Ryder Cup course, the K Club seldom drops out of the top ten Irish golf courses from the Irish Golf Institute. Established in 1991, this parkland course was designed by the Arnold Palmer team.
All year Green fees from €150

WEXFORD

GREEN ACRES

Relocating at time of going to print; call for details of new address
Tel 053 22975

A peculiar delicatessen-cum-art gallery with a good line in locally sourced breads and meats—great for buying picnic supplies. The building is interesting too; an inscription on the front from 1860 reads 'Bread is still the staff of life'.

Mon–Sat 9–6

WICKLOW

GLEN OF IMAAL BAR (FENTON'S)

Seskin, Co. Wicklow
Tel 045 404711

A legendary watering hole among outdoor enthusiasts, this remote bar attracts walkers, climbers and soldiers on manoeuvres in the nearby artillery range. Close by there's a memorial to Michael Dwyer, who returned to his native glen to wage a five-year guerrilla war against the Crown following the 1798 rebellion.

Hours vary, call for information

PADDY O'CONNORS

Abbey Street, Wicklow town, Co. Wicklow
Tel: 0404 61980

This is a traditional Irish music venue that is well-known throughout the southeast for its no-nonsense charm, good beer and convivial conversation.

Mon–Thu 10.30am–11.30pm, Fri–Sat 10.30am–12.30am, Sun 10.30am–11pm Bus Éireann services from Dublin Wicklow

THE EUROPEAN CLUB

Brittas Bay, Co. Wicklow
Tel 0404 47415
www.theeuropeanclub.com

This is one of the most enjoyable golf courses in Ireland, featuring elevated tees, seaside holes and other links features on its roller-coaster of a round.

All year Green fees: low season from €75, high season from €125

FESTIVALS AND EVENTS

MAY–JULY

WICKLOW GARDENS FESTIVAL

www.wicklow.ie

County Wicklow is proud of its reputation as the 'Garden of Ireland', and although some of the 30 venues open for the Gardens Festival are just outside the county, Wicklow still claims the lion's share. Joining the many gardens that are open to the public on a regular basis, the festival sees the temporary opening of such notable private ones as the Bay Garden at Comelin near Enniscorthy—a superb cottage garden—and the Avoca estate garden at Kilmacanogue.

JUNE

MURPHY'S CAT LAUGHS COMEDY FESTIVAL

Kilkenny, various venues
Tel 056 776 3837
http://thecatlaughs.com

Considered by many to be one of the best comedy festivals in the world, Cat Laughs features five days of stand-up, movies and improv, with a superb line-up. In recent years such home-grown talents as Ed Byrne, Dara O'Briain and Ardal O'Hanlon, British names like Jeff Green, Milton Jones and Boothby Graffoe, and transatlantic stars Dom Irrera, Rich Hall, Louis CK and Mike Wilmott have been on the bill.

Early June

JULY

ENNISCORTHY STRAWBERRY FAIR

Enniscorthy, Co. Wexford

What used to be a couple of weeks of funfairs, music and general celebration has distilled into a shorter traditional music festival, focused on the town's pubs and square, though there is still a funfair.

JULY-AUGUST

GREYSTONES ARTS FESTIVAL

Wicklow town, various venues
Tel 086 605 0771 or 832 9686
www.greystonesartsfestival.com

This is a weekend of recitals, drama, comedy, visual arts and workshops by performers from all over the world. It starts with a Friday evening Mardi Gras parade and ends on Monday evening with a fireworks display.

End July/early August

AUGUST

KILKENNY ARTS WEEK

9–10 Abbey Business Centre, Abbey Street, Kilkenny, Co. Kilkenny
Tel 056 776 3663
www.kilkennyarts.ie

Ten days are given over to a celebration of virtually every branch of the arts. There are visiting orchestras, quartets and bands, theatre workshops and performances, storytelling by children's authors and discussions on adult literature and poetry. The visual arts are represented, as is performance art. Jazz and traditional Irish music also feature in this renowned festival, which has been going for over 30 years.

OCTOBER

WEXFORD OPERA FESTIVAL

27 High Street, Wexford, Co. Wexford
Tel 053 22400
www.wexfordopera.com

Held in the town every October since 1951, the opera festival features three new operatic productions every year, plus exerpts from popular operas, classical concerts and lunchtime recitals by soloists. Singers and musicians come from all over the world and the whole town enters into the spirit with decorated shops and pubs and a popular antiques fair running at the same time.

THE SOUTH

There's plenty to do in the south, particularly in Cork, the Republic's second city after Dublin, and the best place for high-quality shopping, but also in the other main towns of Waterford, Killarney, Tralee and Limerick. In small towns, shops mainly serve local needs.

Sandy beaches stretch along this coastline, but currents can be strong and you should check locally about safe places to swim. Lifeguards operate at some of the most popular beaches, such as Inch Strand—a red and yellow flag means the lifeguard is on duty. Surfing and sailing are well served and golfers are spoiled for choice. Marshy coastal areas make for great birdwatching with the observatory on Cape Clear Island a noted spot for migrants. The mild climate of the south encourages semi-tropical plants to flourish, and many private gardens are open to visitors in summer. There are well signposted scenic drives, bicycle routes and long-distance walks, mainly on the peninsulas of the west coast—the Ring of Kerry, the Skellig Ring, the Valencia Ring and the Sheep's Head Way.

Cork and Limerick have some good clubs, but nightlife is largely based around pubs with live folk music and, if you're lucky, traditional set dancing.

KEY TO SYMBOLS

- **Shopping**
- **Entertainment**
- **Nightlife**
- **Sports**
- **Activities**
- **Health and Beauty**
- **For Children**

ADARE

CURRANS HERALDRY

Adare Heritage Centre, Adare, Co. Limerick
Tel 061 396961/362460
www.curransheraldry.com

For an unusual souvenir, check out your family coat of arms at this booth in the Heritage Centre, from their database of 120,000 worldwide. You can then buy or commission it as a mounted parchment, embroidery, a hand-painted plaque or perhaps a special piece of jewellery. Or buy a poster map featuring crests of American and European names.

Mar–end Oct daily 9–7 €15

SHANNA QUAY

Village Hall, Main Street, Adare, Co. Limerick
Tel 061 395861
www.shannaquay.com

You'll find this music shop in a 19th-century Tudor-style former village hall in the middle of town. It carries a good stock of Irish music CDs and tapes, but also traditional instruments, sheet music and song books

Mon–Sat 11–5

BANTRY

THE CRAFT SHOP

Glangarriff Road, Bantry, Co. Cork
Tel 027 50003

In a yellow-painted house in the north of town, this craft shop has a wide range of works by local artists—unusual pottery (including Nick Mosse's spongeware), willow baskets, driftwood mirrors and turned wood, silk scarves by Anne O'Leary, leatherwork, greetings cards and many items that you won't see elsewhere.

Mon–Tue, Thu–Sat 10–6

MCCARTHY SPORTS SHOP

Round Tower, Main Street, Bantry, Co. Cork
Tel 027 51133
www.bantrysports.com

'For all your sporting needs', announces the bright yellow shop front, and it's true. You can rent fishing tackle, get your live bait, and obtain salmon fishing and other permits. There's excellent brown- and sea-trout fishing in the area, as well as shore and sea fishing, and the owners are a mine of local information.
Daily 9–5.30

BLARNEY

BLARNEY WOOLLEN MILLS

Blarney, Co. Cork
Tel 021 438 5280
www.blarneywoollenmills.ie
After the castle, Blarney's second biggest attraction is this shop and visitor complex. The mill dates to 1824, and was originally Mahony's Mills. You'll find leather jackets and haute couture suits for ladies and men, high-quality goods in wool and silk, a gift shop with souvenirs, CDs and music, and household goods including crystal, china and linen. There's also an Irish food section. There are branches of Blarney Woollen Mills throughout the Republic of Ireland.
Mon–Sat 9.30–6, Sun 10–6

CAHER

CRAFT GRANARY

Church Street, Caher, Co. Tipperary
Tel 052 41473
For quality crafts, or just a cup of coffee, try this big shop in a converted granary, off the main square. You'll find turned and polished wood, Gallùnic soap, beaded jewellery, textiles and basketry, and edibles including fudge, and rhubarb and orange marmalade. There are temporary exhibitions to be found on the first floor.
Mon–Sat 10.30–6, also Feb–end Sep Sun 1–5

FLEURY ANTIQUES

The Square, Caher, Co. Tipperary
Tel 052 41226
www.fleuryantiques.com
Antiques don't come much grander than in this fascinating store on the main square, with its dark red front; expect to spend lavishly. The interior goes a long way back, and is a serious treasure house of quality furniture, mirrors, chandeliers, statues, marble fireplaces and paintings from the 18th and 19th centuries.
Mon–Sat 9–6

CASHEL

BRÚ BORÚ

Cashel, Co. Tipperary
Tel 062 61122
www.comhaltas.com
A sculpted trio of dancing figures announces this heritage and performance venue, in the shadow of the imposing and romantic Rock of Cashel. It serves as a base for Celtic and genealogical studies, as well as staging music, song, dance, storytelling and theatre. Evening banquets are held in the restaurant.
Mid-Jun to mid-Sep Tue–Sat 9am–11.30pm, Sun–Mon 10–5; mid-Sep to mid-Jun Mon–Fri 9–5 €15, child (over 12) €9

Fresh, home-made bread on sale at a Saturday market

CLONAKILTY

O'DONOVAN'S HOTEL

Pearse Street, Clonakilty, Co. Cork
Tel 023 33250
O'Donovan's is a family-run, central hotel that's full of character. There are three bars, two restaurants and a beer garden. In summer, traditional musicians play every night (and some weekends at other times, too) in the little An Teach Beag pub, in a 200-year-old cottage behind the hotel.

TIGH DE BARRA

55 Pearse Street, Clonakilty, Co. Cork
Tel 023 33381
www.debarra.ie
There's live music of some sort nearly every night at this lively pub; it might be folk and blues or funk and reggae—check out the website for upcoming gigs.

CLONMEL

OMNIPLEX CINEMA

Kickham Street, Clonmel, Co. Tipperary
Tel 052 27353
www.filiminfo.net
Mainstream films are the fare at this five-screen cinema on the edge of the Market Place shopping mall.
Daily 11–9 Adult €6.50, child €4, family €16

WHITE MEMORIAL THEATRE

Wolfe Tone Street, Clonmel, Co. Tipperary
Tel 052 23333
This little theatre, housed in a former Wesleyan chapel of 1843, seats an audience of just 225. It is named after James White, founder of the St. Mary's Choral Society, who perform here along with the Clonmel Theatre Group.
Mostly evening performances; times vary Varies, depending on what's on

CLONMEL RACE TRACK

Powerstown Park, Clonmel, Co. Tipperary
Tel 052 22611
www.powerstownpark.com
Horse-racing took place here for at least a century before the racecourse was properly enclosed in 1913. Around 120 horses will race at any meeting, and these take place most months (not July or August).
From €13, on the gate or on-line in advance, child (12–18) €8 In the Grandstand and Club Stand

COBH

INTERNATIONAL SAILING
East Beach, Cobh, Co. Cork
Tel 021 481 1237
www.sailcork.com
In these sheltered waters you'll see little sailboats and sailboards out at all times of the year—instructors come here in winter to train. Lessons, rental and charter are available from this well-established, family-run company, including dinghy sailing, canoes and powerboats. Novices and experts are welcome, and there's a multi-activity course for children.
Main sailing season May–end Sep
Varies depending on activity

TITANIC TRAIL
Departs from Commodore Hotel, Cobh, Co. Cork
Tel 021 481 5211
www.titanic-trail.com
You've seen the movie, hummed the tunes—now see some of the real sites associated with the *Titanic* and her first-and-last fateful voyage. This 90-minute walking tour of the town provides lots of information about Cobh's rich maritime and emigrant heritage, and there's a Ghost Trail on offer too.
Jun–end Aug daily at 10, 11 and 2; Sep–end May daily at 11 €7.50, child (4–12) €3.75

CORK

BUCKLEY BROTHERS
30 Oliver Plunkett Street, Cork, Co. Cork
Tel 021 427 2126
Behind an old-fashioned and unusual green art deco front, this tiny confectioner's shop specializes in hand-made chocolate and other sweets from all over Ireland. There's a small café squeezed in at the back, too. A little treasure.
Daily 10–4

LA GALERIE
32 Grand Parade, Cork, Co. Cork
Tel 021 427 7376
Original modern landscapes and seascape paintings of Ireland are on sale at this classy art gallery on Grand Parade.
Mon–Fri 9.30–1.30, 2.15–5.30, Sat 10–1.30, 2.30–5

IMB DESIGN
10a Paul Street, Cork, Co. Cork
Tel 021 425 1800/427 4912
Exquisite jewellery handcrafted in silver and gold is the pride of this tiny shop by the entrance to Paul Street Mall, off the west side of Patrick Street. One of the young owners is usually to be seen in the corner workshop. The results are beautiful, and understandably expensive.
Mon–Sat 10–5.30

The Titanic Bar in Cobh recalls the town's link with that vessel

MARTIN FAHERTY
Unit 3, Shandon Craft Centre, Shandon, Cork, Co. Cork
Tel 021 430 2368
Martin Faherty is a craftsman and instrument maker, and you'll see the bones of lutes, cellos, fiddles, guitars, mandolins and bouzoukis in every state of creation. The craft outlet is in the old butter market.
Mon–Fri 9–5

AN BODHRÁN
42 Oliver Plunkett Street, Cork, Co. Cork
Tel 021 427 4544
Live traditional music and occasional rock bands happen seven nights a week through most of the year at this lively pub. The outside is bright yellow and red, inside is wooden, snug and welcoming.
Mon–Wed 10.30am–11.30pm, Thu–Sat 10.30am–12.30am, Sun 10.30am–11pm

CORK OPERA HOUSE
Emmet Place, Cork, Co. Cork
Tel 021 427 0022
www.corkoperahouse.ie
Musical drama and family entertainment, from jazz concerts and pantomime (vaudeville-style fairy tales) to international touring ballet, set the scene at this modern, glass-fronted venue. The back stage door gives access to the Half Moon Theatre, with more experimental drama, live music and a nightclub.
Box Office: daily 9–7 From €11

EVERYMAN PALACE THEATRE
15 MacCurtain Street, Cork, Co. Cork
Tel 021 450 1673/450 3077
www.everymanpalace.com
A lively mixture of comedy, touring theatre and opera productions, with pantomime (vaudeville-style fairy tales) over the Christmas period, are staged in this Victorian building. Irish plays dominate the summer season.
Box office Mon–Sat 10–7.30
From €10

LE CHATEAU
93 Patrick Street, Cork, Co. Cork
Tel 021 427 0370
Established in 1793, this bright yellow pub is the perfect place to relax for a while when you're dropping from your shopping. Food is served all day, and you can also get hot drinks, including Irish coffee, hot whiskey and the traditional hot port.
Mon–Thu 10.30am–11.30pm, Fri–Sat 10.30am–12.30am, Sun noon–11pm

SCOTTS OF CAROLINE STREET
Caroline Street, Cork, Co. Cork
Tel 021 422 2779
www.scotts.ie

This is an elegant and streamlined bar, where glasses and bottles gleam in the soft lighting and tall bucket seats are gathered round the tables. There's a nightclub upstairs, open Thursday to Saturday; patrons under 21 must produce some form of photo-ID.
Lunch 12–3.30, Dinner 4–9; Bar Sun–Wed to 12.30am, Thu–Sat to 2am

CURRAHEEN PARK GREYHOUND STADIUM
Curraheen, Cork, Co. Cork
Tel 021 454 3095/1850 525575
Cork's state-of-the-art stadium is a modern temple to greyhound racing. It includes not only the excitement of 10 races a night, but also live music afterwards, not to mention the comforts of tote betting from your restaurant table. Curraheen Park offers a memorable and very Irish complete night out.
Racing Wed, Thu and Sat from 7.50, doors open 6.45 Adult from €7, child (4–16) from 50c Bus 8 from city; also free courtesy bus to city every 20 min between 10.30pm–12.30am Laurels Restaurant, advance booking essential, tel 021 493 3154

DINGLE PENINSULA

COMMODUM ART AND DESIGN
Main Street, Dingle, Co. Kerry
Tel 066 915 1380
www.commodum.ie
An eye-catching display of knitted sheep, in natural undyed wools, sets the scene at this high street craft shop. Within, there are superb etchings by a local artist that capture the essence of the Dingle in black and white, set out among the myriad hues of the range of mohair rugs, Avoca throws, woolly hats and ceramic Celtic brooches.
Jun–end Aug daily 9–8; Sep–end May daily 9–6

LISBETH MULCAHY
Green Street, Dingle, Co. Kerry
Tel 066 915 1688
www.lisbethmulcahy.com
Lisbeth Mulcahay is a weaver of great renown (as well as being the wife of the famous ceramic artist, Louis, featured below). Here she sells her beautiful wall hangings, scarves of the softest, silkiest lambswool, and the luxury throws made of wool mixed with alpaca, in natural greys and browns, or warm red and blue.
Summer Mon–Fri 9–9, Sat 9–6, Sun 10–6; winter Mon–Fri 9.30–6, Sat 10–6

LOUIS MULCAHY: POTADÓIREACHT NA CAOLÓIGE
Clogher, Dingle, Co. Kerry
Tel 066 915 6229
www.louismulcahy.com

This Dingle pub has welcomed many a famous name

The large, bright pots that are displayed on the grass beside a cluster of white buildings announces the workshop of Louis Mulcahy, one of Ireland's foremost ceramic artists. His imaginative decoration of such practical items as dishes, lampstands, jugs and other vessels utilizes a variety of shades and glazes that reflect the light and hues of the Dingle.
Jul, Aug daily 9–8; May, Jun daily 9–7; Sep–end Apr daily 9–6

DICK MACK'S
Green Street, Dingle, Co. Kerry
The pavement outside this blue pub, opposite St. Mary's Church, is set Hollywood-style with the names of the famous who have stopped by for a drink here. They include the Antarctic explorer Tom Crean, actors John Mills and Robert Mitchum, former taoiseach Charles Haughey and singer Christy Moore.
Opening times vary

JAMIE KNOX WATERSPORTS
The Maharees, Castlegregory, Co. Kerry
Tel 066 713 9411
www.jamieknox.com
Out towards the tip of the sandy spit that lies to the north of Castlegregory, Jamie Knox Watersports offers tuition in all kinds of watersports, including surfing, sailing, boardsailing, kitesurfing and waterskiing.
Apr–end Oct daily 9–5, Nov–end Mar five days a week 9–5 (call to confirm) Prices vary, depending on activity

LONGS HORSE RIDING AND TREKKING CENTRE
Kilcolman, Ventry, Co. Kerry
Tel 066 915 9034/087 225 0286
www.longsriding.com
If the idea of a canter along the sands has always held a particular appeal for you, this friendly riding centre to the west of Dingle town is the place to go. The emphasis here is on safety and fun, and activities on offer range from a short hack to a full day's trekking, and even a mounted pub crawl.
Mid-May to mid-Oct daily 10–6 Adult €25, child €25

DINGLE MARINE ECO TOURS
The Pier, Dingle, Co. Kerry
Tel 086 285 8802
www.dinglemarine.com
Enjoy the magnificent landscape and abundant sealife around the Dingle Peninsula from the sea, on an informative 2-hour cruise from Dingle harbour. Advance booking is essential.
Apr–Oct daily Adult €25 child (under 15) €10 Refreshments available on board

THE FRESHWATER EXPERIENCE
Emlagh, Lispole, Co. Kerry
Tel 066 915 1042
www.freshwaterexperience.com
There's lots to explore at this nature park on the Dingle Peninsula, from a reconstructed *crannóg* (medieval lake dwelling) to a wildfowl reserve. You can catch your own trout at the trout farm, and admire the otters, mink, foxes and wild boar in the wildlife park.
Mar–Oct Mon–Sat 10–6, Sun noon–6 (phone to check) Adult €3.81, child €3.17

KILLARNEY

KILLARNEY BOOKSHOP
32 Main Street, Killarney, Co. Kerry
Tel 064 34108
In the upstairs section of this great bookshop they have maps and guides, while downstairs is an excellent selection of Irish biographies, including all the best of the Blasket books—perfect holiday reading—as well as a good range of modern fiction.
May–end Sep Mon–Sat 9am–10pm, Sun 11–10; Oct–end Apr Mon–Sat 9–6, Sun 2–6

DANNY MANN
New Street, Killarney, Co. Kerry
Tel 064 31640
www.dannymann.ie
For the price of a pint you can enjoy live Irish music almost every night in this traditional old pub, easy to spot with its distinctive gold front and black trim. The food comes highly recommended, too, and you could even drop in for afternon tea in the comfortable lobby lounge.
Music starts at 9.30pm

GRAND HOTEL
Main Street, Killarney, Co. Kerry
Tel 064 31159
There's plenty of music in the front bar of this hotel, with rock bands taking over when the folk musicians stop. There's a nightclub, too, and Wednesday reverts to the traditional theme with a set dancing night.
Traditional music nightly 9–11, rock music 11.30pm–1.30am

KILLARNEY RIDING STABLES
Ballydowney, Killarney, Co. Kerry
Tel 064 31686
www.killarney-reeks-trail.com
This large equestrian establishment is located on the northwestern edge of town, on the N72 Killorglin road. It offers a wide range of trekking, hacking and trail riding, with excursions lasting from one hour to six days.
Daily from 8am From €25 for a one-hour ride, to €60 for 3 hours

Picturesque Kinsale rises above its harbour on Compass Hill

KINSALE

BOLAND
Corner Pearse and Emmet streets, Kinsale, Co. Cork
Tel 021 477 2161
www.bolandkinsale.com
In this pretty seaside town, Boland is a busy shop that stocks lots of unusual, high-quality craft items, including leather belts, ceramic birds and mirrors, traditional spongeware crockery by Nick Mosse, fine knitwear and jewellery, fun children's clothing in fleece and wool, and hand-painted silk ties. There's a range of good quality outdoor clothing, too.
Mon–Sat 9.30–6.30, Sun 10–6.30

GRANNY'S BOTTOM DRAWER
53 Main Street, Kinsale, Co. Cork
Tel 021 477 4839
If you're after the best in Irish linen and bedding, you'll probably find it here. Clothing by Inis Meáin of Aran, damask and linen tablecloths and napkins, and romantic bedding. Also woollen Foxford blankets.
Jun–end Aug Mon–Fri 9.30am–10pm, Sat–Sun 10–6; Sep–end May 10–6

HEATHER MOUNTAIN
Market Street, Kinsale, Co. Cork
Tel 021 477 3384
The modest exterior of this shop belies its spacious interior, which extends behind the building next door. It's piled high with Irish craftwork, from felt handbags, traditional shirts and designer knitwear to wooden mobiles and therapeutic soap products.
May–end Oct daily 9–9; Nov–end Apr daily 9–5

CRUISE OF KINSALE HARBOUR
Summercove, Kinsale, Co. Cork
Tel 021 477 3188
www.kinsaleharbourcruises.com
Enjoy a cruise of the harbour area aboard the *Spirit of Kinsale*. The boat takes you to the outer harbour, and up the River Bandon, with full commentary. There's also music, a bar and snacks on board.
Mon–Sat 2, 3, 4pm, Sun 12, 1, 2, 3, 4pm Adult €9, child (7–12) €4.50 (under 7 free)

LIMERICK

BELLTABLE ARTS CENTRE
69 O'Connell Street, Limerick, Co. Limerick
Tel 061 319866/315871
The city's premier theatre shows a wide selection of Irish and mainstream touring productions, and also hosts temporary art exhibitions. The arts cinema offers movies from as far afield as Spain, China, Russia and Norway.
Box office: daily 9.30–5.30, depending on shows From €12

WHAT TO DO

ANGELA'S ASHES WALKING TOURS
Tours leave from Tourist Office, Arthur's Quay, Limerick, Co. Limerick
Tel 061 327108/087 6353648
Explore the locations associated with Frank McCourt's moving memoir of poverty and childhood in the city, in the company of an expert guide and friend of the author. Tours take around 2 hours.
Daily at 11–2.30 Adult €10, child (4–16) €5

THURLES

LÁR NA PAIRCE
Slievenamon Road, Thurles, Co. Tipperary
Tel 0504 22702
www.tipperary.gaa.ie
Thurles was the birthplace, in 1884, of the Gaelic Athletic Association, and here you can find out all about hurling, football, camogie and handball. Displays include a lively 18-minute audio-visual show, and a Hall of Fame. See the real thing at Semple Stadium.
Apr–end Sep Mon–Sat 10–5, Oct–end Mar Mon–Fri 10–5 Adult €4, child €2

TIPPERARY

TIPPERARY EXCEL HERITAGE CENTRE
Mitchel Street, Tipperary, Co. Tipperary
Tel 062 80520
www.tipperary-excel.com
This community-driven development incorporates the intimate Simon Ryan Theatre, plus a cinema that screens the latest releases. There's also a café, art gallery and gift shop. The Visitor Centre here has interactive media to illustrate the town's past.
Mon–Sat 9.30–5.30. Theatre and cinema nightly

TRALEE

SIAMSA TÍRE THEATRE
Townpark, Tralee, Co. Kerry
Tel 066 712 3055
www.siamsatire.com
This striking modern building is home to the National Folk Theatre of Ireland. The company was set up in 1974, and through a highly accessible, entertaining schedule of drama, mime, dance and music it brings to life characters and tales of Irish folklore.
May–end Sep 8.30 Free

BLENNERVILLE WINDMILL
Blennerville, Tralee, Co. Kerry
Tel 066 712 1064
This white-painted windmill with red sails was built in 1780 by Roland Blennerhasset, and-has been restored to working order. It's the focus of a craft and Visitor Centre, which tells of Blennerville's role as an emigration port in the 19th century. The windmill is a mile from Tralee beside the N86, and a fun way to get there is by vintage steam train from the town (May–end Sep daily).
Apr–end Oct daily 10–6 Adult €5, children (5–14) €3, family €13

Killorglin's ancient Puck Fair is still enthusiastically supported

AQUA DOME
Dingle Road, Tralee, Co. Kerry
Tel 066 712 8899
www.aquadome.ie
You can enjoy water-based fun in all weathers here. There's a wave pool, water slides, rapids and geysers and a sauna for adults. Children under 8 must be accompanied, and wear inflatable armbands. Outside, there's a miniature golf course, and remote-control toys.
Jun–end Aug daily 10am–10pm; times vary rest of year, check on tel 066 712 9150 Adult €10, child (3–16) €5

WATERFORD

WATERFORD BOOK CENTRE
Roberts Square, Waterford, Co. Waterford
Tel 051 873823
Three floors of books, magazines, stationery and music are inside this gem of a bookshop. International newspapers are available here, and there's even an outlet for Leonidas handmade chocolate bars.
Mon–Thu 9–6, Fri 9–9, Sat 9–6, Sun 2–6

T&H DOOLANS
31–32 George's Street, Waterford, Co. Waterford
Tel 051 841504
A traditional pub with a wood-lined interior, bottle-glass windows, open fires and old-fashioned booths, Doolans is all the best of Irish pubs rolled into one, with live music every night. Food is served at lunchtime and on summer evenings.
Mon–Wed 10am–11.30pm, Thu–Sat 10am–12.30am, Sun 10am–11.30pm

THEATRE ROYAL
The Mall, Waterford, Co. Waterford
Tel 051 874402
The most prestigious of Waterford's three theatres, located in the City Hall behind a modern glass front. Hosts Irish and international drama productions and opera.
Box office: Mon–Fri 10–1, 1.30–5.30, Sat 10–1, 1.30–5 Prices vary

WALKING TOURS OF HISTORIC WATERFORD
Granville Hotel, Waterford, Co. Waterford
Tel 051 873711/851043
There are many layers of history to explore in Waterford, and lots of unusual and fascinating facts to discover. It's all revealed on a 1-hour guided walking tour.
Daily 11.45 and 1.45 €5

FESTIVALS AND EVENTS

MAY

BANTRY INTERNATIONAL MUSSEL FAIR
Bantry, Co. Cork
Tel 027 50360
www.bantrymusselfair.ie
This 3-day family extravaganza, celebrating the harvest of local mussels, was established in 1980s, when mussel farming first began in Bantry Bay. There's entertainment, and mussels are served in all the restaurants and bars.
Early May

JUNE/JULY

KILLARNEY SUMMERFEST
Killarney, Co. Kerry
Tel 064 71560
www.killarneysummerfest.com
This 10-day event only started in 2002 but looks set to become very popular, with indoor and outdoor activities for all ages—street performers, top bands, a fun run and a big parade.
Late June to early July

JULY

CORK YACHT WEEK
Royal Cork Yacht Club, Crosshaven, Co. Cork
Tel 021 4831179
www.fordcorkweek.com
One of the largest sailing events in Europe, this prestigious regatta takes place every 2 years (even dates). Events focus on the famous Yacht Club at Crosshaven.
Mid-July

IRISH COFFEE FESTIVAL
Foynes, Co. Limerick
Tel 069 65416
www.irishcoffeefestival.com
The World Irish Coffee Making Championships attract entries from all over the world, and there's street theatre and fashion, a huge parade on the Sunday and a firework display to round off events.
Mid-July

AUGUST

PUCK FAIR
Killorglin, Co. Kerry
066 976 2366
www.puckfair.ie
This is one of the biggest events in Kerry, and it has been going strong for some 400 years; it's believed to have its origins in a pre-Christian celebration. Today's festivities include open-air music concerts, lively parades, drinking, storytelling and lots of family events—and the highlight of it all is the crowning of King Puck, a billy goat.
10–12 August

Thousands flock to the Puck Fair to see a goat's coronation

WATERFORD SPRAOI STREET FESTIVAL
Waterford, Co. Waterford
Tel 051 841808
www.spraoi.com
Events are free at this huge weekend fiesta of street theatre and world music. With more than 300 shows by international performers, it's the biggest event of its kind in Ireland, and climaxes in a parade and fireworks.
August Bank Holiday

ROSE OF TRALEE INTERNATIONAL FESTIVAL
Rose of Tralee Festival Office, Ashe Memorial Hall, Denny Street, Tralee
Tel 066 712 1322
www.roseoftralee.ie
One of Ireland's best-loved festivals has 200,000 visitors, 5 days of partying and huge TV coverage. It began in 1959 and now has entries from across the world. The Rose, picked for character and personality, recalls a sentimental song by William Mulchinock.
End August

LIMERICK SHOW
Limerick Racecourse, Patrickswell, Co. Limerick
Tel 061 355298
www.limerickshow.com
Munster's biggest agricultural show takes place over a weekend and features show jumping, carriage driving, sheep and cattle judging, dog show and agility classes, horticulture, craft and trade stands and classic cars.
End August Adult €10, child (under 12) free

SEPTEMBER

CORK FOLK FESTIVAL
Cork, Co. Cork
021 431 7271
www.corkfolkfestival.com
Six days of folk music in bars and other venues all over the city, with top musicians from across Ireland, and traditional music from elsewhere in Europe.
Early September

OCTOBER

CORK JAZZ FESTIVAL
Event office: 20 South Mall, Cork, Co. Cork
Tel 021 427 8979
www.corkjazzfestival.com
Ireland's premier jazzfest, taking over some 75 venues around the city for four days. Up to 1,000 musicians from 25 countries take part, and 40,000 visitors are expected. And it's not all pricey concerts—many pub events are free.
End October

THE WEST

In the west of Ireland you'll find an enormous variety of things to do. Shoppers can look for traditional quality goods (tweed, knitwear and other woollens), and also for craft items such as gold and jewellery; few shoppers get out of Galway without at least one Claddagh ring! There are several craft complexes where you can see the items being made.

The West is the heartland of traditional music, and the pubs are the platform, from internationally renowned venues such as Matt Molloy's in Westport to tiny country pubs. Experienced players and singers will be in heaven, while a few places actively encourage novices to join in. You can enjoy the music in more polished surroundings in arts centres such as Ennis's Glór, too. Set dancing is big all over the West, and at the Crane in Galway city you can join in. There are dance clubs in most of the big towns and thousands of 'talking pubs' where you can get a bit of peace and quiet.

The West is great for outdoor activities. Swimming is wonderful from the clean sandy beaches, bicycling is good on quiet side roads, and golf courses abound. Walking is gaining popularity, especially on the 'waymarked way' long-distance footpaths. As for festivals, the West specializes in them and themes include music, dancing, horse fairs and oysters.

KEY TO SYMBOLS

- Shopping
- Entertainment
- Nightlife
- Sports
- Activities
- Health and Beauty
- For Children

BALLYCONNEELY

CONNEMARA SMOKEHOUSE

Bunowen Pier, Ballyconneely, Co. Galway
Tel 095 23739
www.smokehouse.ie

The Connemara Smokehouse beside Bunowen Pier is superbly sited on Bunowen Bay and the smoked salmon and trout that are produced and sold here make wonderful gifts (the Smokehouse also has a postal service). The marinated gravadlax is highly recommended, and you can buy some of their special marinades to enjoy at home.

Mon–Fri 9–1, 2–5 From Clifden, turn right off the R341 in Ballyconneely, and follow the road for 5 km (3 miles) to Bunowen Pier

AN TRÁ MHÓIR, THE GREAT BEACH

Creggoduff, Bunowen, Ballyconneely, Co. Galway

There is great swimming to be enjoyed in the sea all along the Connemara coast, provided you have sufficient knowledge of which beaches have gently shelving sand and are free of clogging seaweed. *An Trá Mhóir*, the Great Beach, below the Connemara Golf Club, is one that fits this bill exactly.

At Connemara Golf Club (tel 095 23502); open Mon–Sat From Clifden, turn right off the R341 in Ballyconneely, and follow the road for 5 km (3 miles); turn right just before reaching Bunowen Pier at a Connemara Golf Club sign and follow the lane across the golf course to the club house

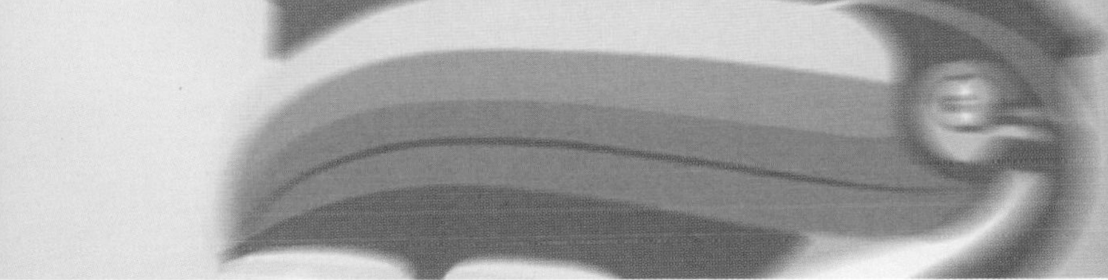

BALLYSHANNON

DONEGAL PARIAN CHINA

Ballyshannon, Co. Donegal
Tel 071 985 1826
www.donegalchina.ie

The showroom offers examples of fine Donegal Parian ware. This delicate, glossy china is available as vases, tea-sets such as the Irish Rose service, clocks, wildlife sculptures and figurines. Most coveted of all are the exquisite latticework baskets.

May–end Sep daily 9–5.30; Oct–end Apr Mon–Fri 9–5.30 On N15 Sligo road just outside Ballyshannon

BRUCKLESS

DEANE'S EQUESTRIAN CENTRE AND OPEN FARM

Darney, Bruckless, Co. Donegal
Tel 074 973 7160
www.northwestireland.travel.ie

The Deane family know how to make youngsters feel at home at this farm 19km (12 miles) from Donegal on the N56 Killybegs road. Children can feed, cuddle, stroke and walk a variety of animals including lambs, sheep, dogs and goats. There are trips in a venerable Land Rover, and pony or horse rides at the Equestrian Centre.

Equestrian Centre: daily 10–4. Open Farm: Easter–end Aug 10–4 Entrance: adult/child €4. Pony ride: €4

BUNRATTY

MEDIEVAL FEASTS AT BUNRATTY CASTLE

Bunratty, Co. Clare
Tel 061 360788
www.group-trotter.net

Feasting with your fingers while buxom maidens and courtly squires in medieval costume ply you with wine and song can seem like a wonderful way to have a bit of fun—if you are with like-minded friends and in the mood.

At 5.30 and 8.45 (subject to demand); pre-booking essential Adult €48.50, child (6–9) €24.25, (9–12) €36.40

CARRICK-ON-SHANNON

LEITRIM DESIGN HOUSE

Market Yard, Carrick-on-Shannon, Co. Leitrim
Tel 071 965 0550
www.leitrimdesignhouse.com

More than 40 Irish design studios and craft workshops supply Leitrim Design House with an eclectic range of original products: sculptures fashioned from recycled plastic and bog oak, modern and rustic furniture crafted in Irish wood, wrought-iron pieces, lamps made of recycled glass, fabric crafts such as cushions and hangings, jewellery and glasswork.

Mon–Sat 10–6, Sun 2–6

Pony trekking is a great way to enjoy the Irish countryside

GENE ANDERSON'S THATCH PUB

Elphin Road, Carrick-on-Shannon, Co. Leitrim
Tel 087 228 3288 or 071 962 0142
www.northwestireland.travel.ie

If you are shy about joining in a pub music session, you will be greatly reassured by spending an evening in this old thatched pub. The place is full of character, and local musicians and singers gently ease you into participation in an easy-going atmosphere.

Music 8.30 pm till late; pub hours Mon–Wed 10am–11.30pm, Thu–Sat 10am–12.30am, Sun 10am–11.30pm

MOON RIVER CRUISE

Main Street, Carrick-on-Shannon, Co. Leitrim
Tel 071 962 1777
www.moon-river.net

Float gently from Carrick Quay along the starlit Shannon with a drink in your hand, serenaded by the cream of local singers and bands.

Fri, Sat 11.30 pm–3 am from Carrick Quay From €12

CASTLEBAR

TWEED CENTRE

Main Street, Castlebar, Co. Mayo
Tel 094 902 1183
www.tweedcentre.com

A one-stop shop if you're looking for a keepsake or souvenir. The Tweed Centre stocks the Guinness range of clothes, toys and trinkets, as well as Aran sweaters and other Irish merchandise, with a Mayo bias.

Mon–Sat 10–6

MAYO LEISURE CYCLING

New Antrim Street, Castlebar, Co. Mayo
Tel 094 902 5220
www.mayocycling.ie

Peadar Leonard is a passionate and knowledgeable bicyclist, and will rent you a bike for the day (with the appropriate maps) or take you on a guided tour of some of the best bicycling country in Ireland. Pre-booking is essential.

Mon–Sat 9–6 Bicycle rental from €8 a day Packed lunch available on request

CROLLY

LEO'S TAVERN

Meenaleck, Crolly, Co. Donegal
Tel 074 954 8143
www.touchireland.ie

Leo's Tavern (▷ 268–269) is the 'home pub' of famous singing group Clannad and their sister, ambient star Enya. Celebrated singers and musicians are drawn to Leo's, and you never know who may turn up for a sing-song.

From 11am; music most nights from 9pm

WHAT TO DO

DONEGAL

MAGEE OF DONEGAL

The Diamond, Donegal, Co. Donegal
Tel 074 972 2660
www.mageeshop.com

Donegal tweed is famous the world over, and Magee's is the best-known and best-stocked shop in County Donegal for hand-woven tweeds and wool-mohair-cashmere. You can order a bolt of cloth, or buy jackets, skirts, caps, hats, scarves, ties and a whole range of other goods, all made from Magee's own cloth.

Mon–Sat 9.30–6

SCHOONER INN

Upper Main Street, Donegal, Co. Donegal
Tel 074 972 1671

The Schooner is a friendly pub decorated with old ship models and other nautical items. Music happens most nights in summer, more infrequently in winter. The traditional music is excellent, and there's ballad-singing and country tunes too.

From 11 am; music most nights from 9.30pm

DOOLIN

DOOLIN CRAFTS GALLERY

Doolin, Co. Clare
Tel 065 707 4309
www.doolincrafts.com

Husband-and-wife team Matt O'Connell and Mary Gray created the Doolin Crafts Gallery and the lovely split-level garden that surrounds it, and they still run things beautifully. Here you can browse carefully chosen items, some exclusive to the gallery, that include knitwear (from stoles to sweaters), leather bags and belts, pottery, jewellery, ornaments and *objets*.

Easter–end Sep daily 9–7, Oct–Easter Tue–Sat 10–6

MCGANN'S

Doolin, Co. Clare
Tel 065 707 4133

McGann's pub by the bridge can be just as jolly as O'Connor's, but here's where you'll find a more serious and quiet atmosphere, as players and listeners all concentrate on the wonderful music that locals and visitors create.

From 11am

O'CONNOR'S

Doolin, Co. Clare
Tel 065 707 4168

O'Connor's pub is an institution among singers and players of Irish traditional music; most of the great names have probably played here. These days it's a jolly, singalong sort of place, great for a night's music and chatter with some friends

From 11am

The west is the heartland of traditional Irish music

ENNIS

GLÓR IRISH MUSIC CENTRE

Friar's Walk, Ennis, Co. Clare
Tel 065 684 3103
www.glor.ie

A superb purpose-built concert venue, Glór has a mission to present the cream of Ireland's artists and performers and their work, especially in the field of traditional music. Performances feature the best Irish bands, individual musicians and singers, plus theatre, children's plays, film and dance. Exhibitions include paintings and photography.

Box office: Mon–Sat 9.30–5.30
Adult from €8 Mon–Sat 10-5

ENNISCRONE

KILCULLEN'S SEAWEED BATHS

Enniscrone, Co. Sligo
Tel 096 36238
www.destinationenniscrone.com

A traditional Irish west coast remedy is offered in this fine Edwardian bathhouse complete with its original fittings. Relax in an iodine-rich, silky-smooth seaweed bath, and you'll emerge feeling like a million dollars. Private rooms; no need to book.

May–end Oct 10–10; Nov–end Apr 12–8 Adult from €17; room with 2 baths, double occupancy €30

FOXFORD

FOXFORD WOOLLEN MILLS

Foxford, Co. Mayo
Tel 094 925 6756
www.foxfordwoollenmills.ie

Foxford Woollen Mills were established in 1892 to bring employment to a poverty-stricken area of Country Mayo. You can learn all about it on a Mill Tour before visiting the Mill Shop. Here excellent quality goods include mohair and merino rugs, tweed caps and vibrant rugs and throws, soft baby blankets, scarves and other clothing and furnishings.

May–end Oct Mon–Sat 10–6, Sun 12–6; Nov–end Apr Mon–Sat 10–6, Sun 2–6

GALWAY

CLADDAGH GOLD

1 Quay Street, Galway, Co. Galway
Tel 091 566365
www.claddaghring.ie

Thomas Dillon's Claddagh Gold shop near the foot of Quay Street is Ireland's longest-established jeweller's, and the oldest makers of the Claddagh Ring, that famous lovers' token with the two hands clasping a heart. Buy your ring here, and then take a tour of the shop's little museum dedicated to the history of the ring style.

Mon–Sat, 10–5.30, Sun 12–4 (summer only)

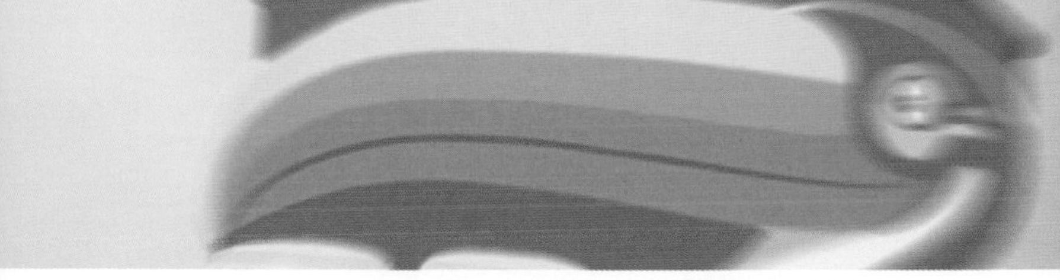

GALWAY MARKET
Market Street, Galway, Co. Galway
Visitor information: tel 091 537700
This is one of the liveliest street markets in the west of Ireland, a must for visitors to the city who want to see local life. Here you'll find everything from paintings and pottery to fruit and flowers, from local meat and cheeses to olives, toys, herbs and crafts—and a great helping of chat, too.
Sat–Sun, early morning till mid-afternoon

KENNY'S BOOKSHOP
High Street, Galway, Co. Galway
Tel 091 562739
www.kennys.ie
Kenny's is far more than just another family-run bookshop. It's an art gallery, an antiquarian's dream, a map fiend's delight, and heaven for those who love ramshackle, laid-back, 'interestingly' organized bookshops. You may find what you're looking for on a shelf or in a heap in an old basket.
Mon–Sat 9–6

JUDY GREENE POTTERY
Kirwan's Lane, off Cross Street, Galway, Co. Galway
Tel 091 561753
www.judygreenepottery.com
Judy Greene has been making her exquisite pottery for more than 20 years, and her delicate range of earthenware—hand-painted in the shop—has become extremely collectable. You can browse the goods in Cross Street, and also visit the workshop on Tuam Road, Galway, to see how the items are transformed from raw clay to the finished product.
Kirwan's Lane shop: Mon–Wed, Sat 9–6, Thu, Fri 9–7, Sun 12–6. Tuam Road workshop: Mon–Thu 9–5, Fri 9–2

THE CRANE
2 Sea Road, Galway, Co. Galway
Tel 091 587419
The Crane hosts Galway's best traditional music sessions and staff and musicians are friendly and knowledgeable. There's music every night ('Dusty Banjos' sessions of slow tunes for beginners, Monday 7–9), and Irish set dancing on Monday, Tuesday and Friday.
From 11am; music from 9.30pm

DRUID THEATRE
Chapel Lane, off Quay Street, Galway, Co. Galway
Tel 091 568 6617
www.druidtheatre.com
One of Ireland's best modern theatre companies, Druid is based in a refurbished former warehouse. This dynamic company puts on Irish classics, and also premières up-and-coming young playwrights.
Box office: 9–5.30 From €15

There's a terrific range of goods for sale in Irish street markets

GPO
21 Eglinton Street, Galway, Co. Galway
Tel 091 563073
www.gpo.ie
A really enjoyable club with a good mix of techno and hip-hop nights, R&B, established bands, local hopefuls and up-and-coming groups.
From around 9pm From €9

LETTERKENNY

AN GRIANÁN THEATRE
Port Road, Letterkenny, Co. Donegal
Tel 074 912 0777
www.angrianan.com
County Donegal's biggest and most versatile theatre, offering a varied schedule that includes new and classic plays, stand-up comedy, modern dance, children's plays and shows, musicals, and a wide range of music, from rock to jazz and from cabaret to crooners.
Box office: Mon–Sat from 10, Sun and public holidays from 2hr before performance Adult from €12, child €8 Before and after performances

LISDOONVARNA

BURREN SMOKEHOUSE
Lisdoonvarna, Co. Clare
Tel 065 707 4432
www.burrensmokehouse.ie
All kinds of smoked foods are on sale here, but its primarily fish. Delicious offerings include organic salmon, hot-smoked salmon, eels, trout and mackerel, and there are also smoked cheeses. Alongside all the smoked items are Irish chocolates and preserves, sheep and goat cheeses, Burren honey, wines, and gourmet foods, from oils and chutneys to mustards and speciality teas.
Visitor Centre: Jun–end Aug daily 9–7; Apr–end May, Sep–end Dec daily 9–5; Mar Sat, Sun 10–4

ROUNDSTONE

ROUNDSTONE MUSICAL INSTRUMENTS
IDA Craft Centre, Roundstone, Co. Galway
Tel 095 35808
www.bodhran.com
Malachy Kearns, known as 'Malachy Bodhrán' to one and all, is Ireland's Master Maker of *bodhráns,* or traditional goatskin drums. Since he established his workshop here in the old monastery buildings at Roundstone his fame has spread worldwide. You can buy a beautifully made *bodhrán* (Malachy's wife adds the lovely Celtic designs) or other musical instruments, and browse in the well-stocked gift and craft shop.
Jul, Aug daily 9–7; May, Jun, Sep, Oct daily 9.30–6; Nov-end Apr Mon–Sat 9.30–6

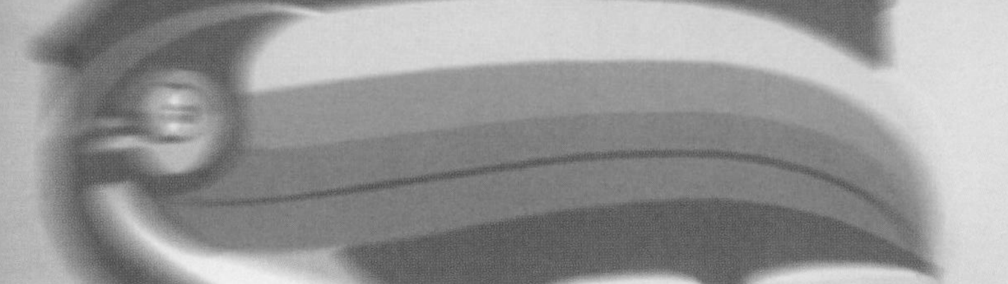

SHANNON AIRPORT

BALLYCASEY CRAFT AND DESIGN CENTRE
Ballycaseymore House, Airport Road (N19), Shannon Airport, Co. Clare
Tel 061 362105
The workshops of Ballycasey Craft and Design Centre are in the courtyard of the Georgian mansion, Ballycaseymore House. Before you buy you can watch the craftspeople at work producing jewellery, knitwear and clothing, forged ironwork, pottery and a range of delicious eatables.
Daily 10–5

SLIGO

FUREY'S, A.K.A. THE SHEELA-NA-GIG
Bridge Street, Sligo, Co. Sligo
Tel 071 914 3825
This is Sligo's Number One venue for traditional music. The pub is owned by well-known, world-travelling Sligo band Dervish; they frequently play here.
Mon–Sat noon–11.30pm, Sun noon–11. Traditional music Mon, Tue, Thu from 9.30pm, often at other times. Jazz on Wed

HAWK'S WELL THEATRE
Temple Street, Sligo, Co. Sligo
Tel 071 916 1518/1526
www.hawkswell.com
The Hawk's Well is a good quality provincial theatre that stages a big variety of events. They include classical concerts and gigs by well-known Irish bands; musicals; plays with local settings and international pieces; dance; singers and traditional musicians; comic plays and stand-up comedians.
Box office: Mon–Fri 10–6, Sat 2–6
Adult from €18, child €12

HARGADON'S
4 O'Connell Street, Sligo, Co. Sligo
Tel 071 917 0933
Hargadon's pub is a Sligo institution: The Victorian frontage, the dark old interior with its ranks of apothecary's shelves, the private little snugs and the long modern rooms at the back are all delightful. This is a soporific, soothing 'talking pub' for conversation-makers and readers of newspapers.
Mon–Sat 11–11.30, Sun 11–11

STRANDHILL GOLF COURSE
Strandhill, Sligo, Co. Sligo
Tel 071 906 8188
www.strandhillgc.com
Strandhill is one of the prettiest golf courses in Ireland; an 18-hole seaside links with a wonderful panorama over Ballysadare Bay and superb views of the mountain of Knocknarea.
From 9.30 Adult green fees Mon–Fri €40, Sat, Sun €50; child €10

Riverside Westport House has lots of attractions for children

WESTPORT

MATT MOLLOY'S
Bridge Street, Westport, Co. Mayo
Tel 098 26655
www.tradcentre.com
Matt Molloy plays flute with Ireland's best-known traditional band, The Chieftains. When he's at home he's usually found joining in the session in the bar of his own pub. Molloy's is generally jumping and crowded; if too busy, try Hoban's on The Octagon (tel 098 27249) or McHale's on Lower Peter Street (tel 098 25121) for excellent music.
Mon–Sat 11am–11.30pm, Sun 11–11. Traditional music from 9.30pm

JANUARY

CONNEMARA FOUR SEASONS WALKING FESTIVAL
Clifden, Co. Galway
Tel 095 21379
http://indigo.ie/~walkwest/cwc.html
Walk all day in and around the Twelve Bens and Maumturk mountains, then party as much of the night as possible in and around Clifden. Run by the Connemara Walking Centre, Clifden.
Early January (call to confirm)

FEBRUARY

ALL IRELAND DANCING CHAMPIONSHIPS
West County Hotel, Ennis, Co. Clare
Tel 01 475 2220
Experts from all over Ireland assemble to compete for the traditional dancing crown.
Early February

FESTIVAL OF WORDS AND MUSIC
Glór, Ennis, Co. Clare
Tel 065 684 3103
www.glor.ie
Irish writers and musicians, both local and national, are celebrated at Ennis's Glór Arts Centre.
Late February

MARCH–APRIL

WORLD DANCING CHAMPIONSHIPS
West County Hotel, Ennis, Co. Clare
Tel 01 475 2220
Irish dancers from all over the world converge on County Clare to compete in a dazzling display of expertise.
Late March to early April

APRIL

CÚIRT INTERNATIONAL FESTIVAL OF LITERATURE
Galway, Co. Galway
Tel 091 569777
www.galwayartscentre.ie
The most prestigious literary festival in Ireland, with local, national and international writers and events.
Late April

WHAT TO DO

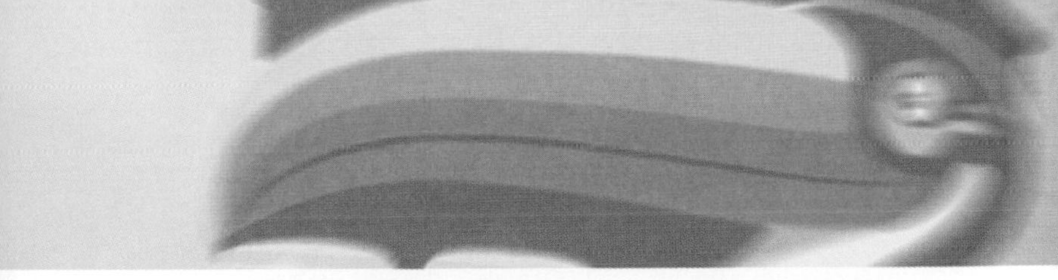

FESTIVALS AND EVENTS

MAY

FLEADH NUA
Ennis, Co. Clare
Tel 065 684 0406
www.fleadhnua.com
The county town plays host to Clare's great celebration of the very best in Irish traditional music, song and dance.
Late May

MAY–JUNE

SLIGO ARTS FESTIVAL
Sligo, Co. Sligo
Tel 047 169802
http://homepage.tinet.ie/~arts/
Celebrate summer's arrival with music and drama, traditional song and music sessions and exhibitions.
Late May to early June

JUNE

WESTPORT INTERNATIONAL SEA ANGLING FESTIVAL
Clew Bay, Co. Mayo
Tel 098 27297/27344
One of the best of its kind in Ireland, taking place in the sheltered and well-stocked waters of Clew Bay.
Late June

JULY

GALWAY FILM FLEADH
Galway, Co. Galway
Tel 091 751655
www.galwayfilmfleadh.com
Directors, actors and movie-goers descend for six days of talking, seeing and being seen.
Early July

GALWAY INTERNATIONAL ARTS FESTIVAL
Galway, Co. Galway
Tel 091 509700
www.galwayartsfestival.com
Music, plays, films and literary events, exhibitions, street parades and theatre are all part of this two-week festival.
Mid- to late July

CROAGH PATRICK PILGRIMAGE
Croagh Patrick mountain, near Westport, Co. Mayo
Join up to 60,000 other pilgrims on a climb to the summit of the holy mountain.
Last Sunday in July

JULY–AUGUST

MARY FROM DUNGLOE FESTIVAL
Dungloe, Co. Donegal
Tel 074 952 1254
www.maryfromdungloe.info
Ten days of music, singing and informal fun, leading up to the crowning of this year's 'Mary'.
Late July to early August

YEATS INTERNATIONAL SUMMER SCHOOL
Sligo, Co. Sligo
Tel 071 914 2693

Traditional dance performance at the Galway Oyster Festival

www.yeats-sligo.com
All a Yeats a fan could possibly crave, with talks, readings, excursions and lectures on the life of Ireland's 'national poet'.
Late July to early August

AUGUST

CRUINNIÚ NA MBÁD
Kinvara, Co. Galway
Tel 091 850687
www.kinvara.com
A festival dedicated to restored traditional sailing boats, with a great gathering of Galway hookers, Donegal Drontheims, Cork mackerel boats, Wexford cots and many more.
Early August

CONNEMARA PONY SHOW
Clifden, Co. Galway
Tel 095 21863
www.cpbs.ie
Where the adorable semi-wild Connemara ponies meet their public; festival-style fun, shows and sales.
Third Thursday in August

AUGUST–OCTOBER

LISDOONVARNA MATCHMAKING
Lisdoonvarna, Co. Clare
Tel 065 707 4005
www.matchmakerireland.com
A not-too-serious (if you don't want it to be) get-together, with dancing, singing, flirting and meeting up with lonely and not-so-lonely hearts from all over the world.
Late August to early October

SEPTEMBER

GALWAY INTERNATIONAL OYSTER FESTIVAL
Galway, Co. Galway
Tel 091 522066
www.galwayoysterfest.com
World Oyster-Opening Championship, selection of the 'Festival Pearl', Mardi Gras party, sailing, oyster eating and Guinness drinking.
Late September

OCTOBER

BALLINASLOE HORSE FAIR
Ballinasloe, Co. Galway
Tel 0905 42266
www.ballinasloe.com
Ireland's greatest horse fair has music, fireworks, entertainment, parades and thousands of horses to ride and buy.
First half of October

OCTOBER/NOVEMBER

SLIGO INTERNATIONAL CHORAL FESTIVAL
Sligo, Co. Sligo
Tel 071 917 0733
www.sligochoralfest.com
Choirs from across the world compete and perform.
Late October/early November

THE MIDLANDS

The green agricultural counties of central Ireland may sometimes lack the glamour of the rugged, tourist-orientated West, but you'll find they have much to offer. For shoppers in search of souvenirs, the gift and craft shops of Athlone and Mullingar will not disappoint. Hand-painted items from the Judy Green Pottery and copper figurines made by Genesis are much sought after. Mullingar's Arts Centre puts on a good variety of shows, and there's a lively clubbing scene—perhaps better for being a bit less frenetic than the Dublin hot spots—in towns such as Tullamore, Roscommon, Athlone and Mullingar. If you really want to join the locals in having a good time, go to the horse or greyhound racing for a loud and perhaps profitable bit of fun. Outdoor activities are largely based around the River Shannon and the huge number of lakes in the region. You can rent boats and canoes by the day or the week to explore them, or take a boat out for some of the fishing for which the area is justly famous. Young children can work off their energy on nature trails, at open farms or in children's activity centres, or there are more physically demanding activities at Lilliput on the shores of Lough Ennell. Midlands festivals go on all year round, many of them linked to agricultural shows, and offer a real chance to have fun among local people.

KEY TO SYMBOLS

- **Shopping**
- **Entertainment**
- **Nightlife**
- **Sports**
- **Activities**
- **Health and Beauty**
- **For Children**

ATHLONE

JUDY GREENE POTTERY

Paynes Lane, Golden Island Shopping Centre, Athlone, Co. Westmeath
Tel 090 647 7622
www.judygreenepottery.com

Judy Greene's range of hand-painted earthenware includes functional items for the kitchen, and fine *objets d'art,* from vases to decorative plates. Judy's inspiration comes from the wild flowers around her home in the West, and the beauty and delicacy of the designs has made her pottery highly sought after.

Mon–Sat 9–6, Sun 12–6

ATHLONE SPORTS CENTRE

Ballymahon Road, Athlone, Co. Westmeath
Tel 090 647 0975
www.athlonesportscentre.com

The best-equipped sports complex in the region, with a big swimming pool, children's pool, state-of-the-art gym, Jacuzzi and sauna. There are Over-50s and Adults-Only sessions, an activity club for children and a childcare facility.

Daily, Athlone Sports Academy (supervised indoor and outdoor sports and games): Sat 3–5 Swim: adult €5.50, child €3. Gym €5; gym-and-swim: €8.50. Over-50s sessions: gym €2.10 (Mon–Tue, Thu–Fri 2–3, Wed 11–12); gym-and-swim €2.50. Adults-only swim: €2.50 (Tue 3.30–4.15)

HODSON BAY WATER SPORTS CENTRE

Hodson Bay, Lough Ree, Co. Westmeath
Tel 090 649 2448

Fishing, power-boat driving, boat handling, boardsailing

and other water sports are available at the marina here. There's a golf club, too.
Daily Dublin–Galway route 8km (5 miles) north of Athlone via N6 Galway road and N61

ADVENTURE VIKING CRUISE
7 St. Mary's Place, Athlone, Co. Westmeath
Tel 086 262 1136
Dress up in full Viking gear and cruise the waters of the Shannon in a Viking longship, from The Strand in Athlone upriver into Lough Ree, or downstream to Clonmacnoise.
May–end Aug, 10, 12, 2, 4, 6, 8; Sep–end Apr by appointment Adult €9, child €6, family €27

TICKETY BOO!
Unit 6, Monksland Business Park, Tuam Road, Athlone, Co. Westmeath
Tel 090 644 4612
Parents can relax for a couple of hours with a cup of coffee while the kids go wild with slides, climbing frames, a bouncy castle and a ball-pool.
Mon–Thu 10–6, Fri–Sat 10–7, Sun 12–6 €6 (family rates available)

BANAGHER

SHANNON ADVENTURE CANOEING HOLIDAYS
The Marina, Banagher, Co. Offaly
Tel 0509 51411
www.iol.ie/~advcanoe/index.html
Being the master of your own craft is by far the best way to explore the Shannon and its lakes. Renting a two-person canoe gives you that freedom for an hour, a day, a weekend or a week.
Apr–end Oct daily 9–5 From €15 hourly, €50 day, €75 weekend, €120 week (€150 with camping equipment)

DRUM

GLENDEER OPEN FARM
Drum, Co. Roscommon
Tel 090 643 7147
www.glendeer.com
This family farm has cows, sheep, chickens, ostriches, emus, deer, peacocks and rabbits. Some of these can be stroked and cuddled. There is a special Christmas re-creation of 'Lapland'.
May–end Aug Mon–Sat 11–6, Sun 12–6; Easter–end Apr, Sep Sat 11–6, Sun 12–6; end Nov–23 Dec Mon–Fri 5–8, Sat, Sun 3–8 Farm: adult €6, child €6; Lapland (Dec) including gift from Santa, child €12 Off N6, 6.5km (4 miles) west of Athlone

EDENDERRY

IRISH PARACHUTE CLUB
Clonbullogue Airfield, near Edenderry, Co. Offaly
Tel 046 973 0103
www.skydive.ie
The ultimate adrenalin thrill, if you have the nerve. An hour's instruction is followed by the jump from a plane attached to an instructor. Then, as the old hands say, you'll know why the birds sing!
Sat, Sun and Bank Holidays 10–4; also midweek in summer Tandem jump €320 On R401, 11km (7 miles) south of Edenderry

A competitive swimming event at Athlone's Sports Centre

KILBEGGAN

KILBEGGAN RACE COURSE
Kilbeggan, Co. Westmeath
Tel 0506 32176
Irish National Hunt meetings are held on this 9-furlong track. The punters of Offaly and Westmeath turn out in force, and it's a great occasion.
Adult from €12, child (under 14) free

LOUGH ENNELL

LILLIPUT BOAT HIRE
Lilliput House, Lough Ennell, Mullingar Co. Westmeath
Tel 044 26167 or 086 828 6849
Lough Ennell is one of the Midlands' best fishing lakes, with plentiful trout, pike and perch as well as many other species. Rent a boat, either with an engine or with oars, and set out to see what luck you'll have. Fishing gear can be rented, too.
Mar–Oct, daily—telephone in advance for times Boat rental: €40 per day for boat with engine; €20 per day for boat without engine 8km (5 miles) southwest of Mullingar off N52

LILLIPUT ADVENTURE CENTRE
Lilliput House, Lough Ennell, Mullingar, Co. Westmeath.
Tel 044 26789
www.lilliputadventure.com
Children and young adults get their thrills under careful supervision at this activity centre. Day activities might include kayaking, abseiling, rock climbing, canoeing, pier jumping, gorge walking, orienteering, archery, hill walking and even a manhunt! There are residential courses, too.
Day and residential courses
Daily fee: adult €37.50 (with lunch), under 18 €30 (with lunch)
Follow signs from R390 and R391, 8km (5 miles) southwest of Mullingar

MULLINGAR

GENESIS GIFT GALLERY
The Downs, Mullingar, Co. Westmeath
Tel 044 44948
Here you can buy the collectable range of hand-painted, hand-crafted copper figurines produced by Genesis Fine Arts. The Gift Gallery is a great place to buy other quality Irish products such as Waterford crystal, Belleek china, Galway crystal, and Newbridge Silverware's jewellery and cutlery. Between Mullingar and Kinnegad.
Mon–Fri 9.30–6, Sat 10–6 5km (3.5 miles) from Mullingar on N4 Dublin road

MULLINGAR ARTS CENTRE

Mount Street, Mullingar, Co. Westmeath
Tel 044 47777
www.mullingarartscentre.com
Mullingar Arts Centre presents a wide variety of entertainment. There are regular exhibitions in its Art Gallery, art workshops, and a whole range of performance events that include clubbing dance nights, early music, plays, comedy, party nights and films.
Box office open 10.30–6.30
Adult €10–€35, child from €7.50

THE STABLES

Yukon Bar, Dominic Street, Mullingar, Co. Westmeath
Tel 044 40251
www.stableslive.com
Great evenings happen out of the blue at this club. There's a very eclectic bill—everything from straight rock and local cover bands to indie outfits, cheesy old handbag nights and more cutting-edge hip-hop.
From around 9 pm From €10

MULLINGAR GREYHOUND STADIUM

Ballinderry, Mullingar, Co. Westmeath
Tel 044 48348
www.mullingargreyhoundstadium.ie
The people of the Midlands adore their greyhound racing, and the Mullingar stadium makes a great night out. The emphasis here is on family fun and it's packed with humorous, knowledgeable punters.
Racing on Thu and Sat, doors open 7pm, racing starts at 8 Adult €7, child €1 Restaurant, food stalls, bars

MULLINGAR LEISURE CLUB

Mullingar Business Park, Mullingar, Co. Westmeath
Tel 044 40949
Mullingar Leisure Club offers activities for adults—a free-weights gym and a sauna—and for children—'Tons of Fun' play space with ball pools, climbing frames, slides and soft play.
Mon–Fri 9am–10.30pm; Sat 11–7, Sun 12–7 Adult €10, child (3–11) €4.40 per hour

FESTIVALS AND EVENTS

FEBRUARY

LANESBOROUGH HORSE FAIR
Lanesborough, Co. Longford
Tel 043 27070
www.loughree.com
Ancient horse fair, with shows and sales, carriage driving, Donkey Derby and a parade.
Mid-February

MARCH

MARIA EDGEWORTH LITERARY FESTIVAL
Edgeworthstown, Co. Longford
Tel 043 71801
A day of short story and poetry readings and competitions, workshops, music and performances.
Late March

The bodhrán *provides the driving rhythm of traditional music*

APRIL–MAY

FAIR OF BALLYCUMBER
Ballycumber, Co. Offaly
Tel 0502 22222
This weekend festival of music and fun is based around an agricultural show.
Late April/early May

MAY–JUNE

GOLDSMITH SUMMER SCHOOL
Ballymahon, Co. Longford
Tel 090 643 71448
Talks, tours, music and song to commemorate poet Oliver Goldsmith.
Late May/early June

JULY

BOYLE ARTS FESTIVAL
Boyle, Co. Roscommon
Tel 071 966 4069
www.boylearts.com
Classical, traditional, contemporary, jazz and world music plus art and storytelling.
Late July

JULY–AUGUST

FESTIVAL OF THE O'CAROLAN SUMMER SCHOOL IN TRADITIONAL MUSIC AND SONG
Keadue, Co. Roscommon
Tel 071 964 7204
Song, music, set dancing, concerts and *ceilidhs*, and a harping competition in a festival honouring the greatest harper Turlough O'Carolan.
End July–early August

AUGUST

NATIONAL TRACTION ENGINE STEAM RALLY
Stradbally, Co. Laois
Tel 0502 25444
www.irishsteam.ie
The behemoths of steam go through their paces in exhibitions of stone crushing, log hauling and threshing. Also tractors, fairground organs, sheepdog trials and more.
Early August

SEPTEMBER

KNOCKCROGHERY FAIR
Knockcroghery, near Roscommon town, Co. Roscommon
Tel 090 666 1110
A three-day sheep fair, plus pony trotting, puppet theatre, and vintage car rally.
Mid-September

NOVEMBER

BOYLE CHRISTMAS CRAFT FAIR
Boyle, Co. Roscommon
Tel 071 966 3242
Crafts of all kinds are sold in the striking surroundings of Kings House, with seasonal refreshments.
Late November

NORTHERN IRELAND

Northern Ireland offers an outstanding range of things to do. The province is well provided with large shopping malls, and most of the major retail chains have a presence here. Specialist shops carry designer labels in clothes and accessories, but the region is most famous for its linen. Follow the linen trail for exquisite table linen, shirts and dresses. Antiques shops have lots to offer, and Irish silver, glass and paintings are all collectable. A visit to a farmers' market will result in delectable home-produced goodies.

Golfers are spoiled for choice and most clubs, many of them in scenic locations, welcome visitors. Fishermen have equally abundant choices, and can enlist the help of a ghillie to get the best from a lough or river teeming with fish. Adrenalin junkies can partake of everything from microlight flying to caving, kayaking to abseiling, all in beautiful surroundings. There are good opportunities for walking, horseback-riding and birdwatching, and a network of marinas cater for a growing number of sailing enthusiasts.

Cultural life thrives in Northern Ireland, too. Summer is probably the least busy time for the theatres, but this is balanced by the chance to catch a big outdoor concert, a pipe band championship or an informal traditional music session in a pub. There are lots of local events throughout the summer months.

KEY TO SYMBOLS
- Shopping
- Entertainment
- Nightlife
- Sports
- Activities
- Health and Beauty
- For Children

ANTRIM

DAVID WOLFENDEN ANTIQUES

219B Lisnevenagh Road, Antrim, Co. Antrim, BT41 2JT
Tel 028 9442 9498
www.country-antiques-wolfenden.co.uk

This well-established specialist in fine antique furniture has a wide range of Irish pieces. Side tables with a distinctive raised frieze are a much prized item.
Mon–Sat 10–6

JUNCTION ONE

M2 Junction
Ballymena Road, Antrim, Co. Antrim
Tel 048 9442 9111

Northern Ireland's biggest outlet mall contains top-flight names like Estée Lauder, Ralph Lauren and Louis Feraud, plus chain-store brands like Next.
Mon–Wed 10–6, Thu–Fri 10–9, Sat 9–6, Sun 1–6 1km (0.5 miles) from J1 of M22

CLOTWORTHY ARTS CENTRE

Antrim Castle Gardens, Randalstown Road, Antrim, Co. Antrim, BT41 4LH
Tel 028 9442 8000
www.antrim.gov.uk

Set in a neo-Tudor courtyard, this centre offers exhibitions, lectures, drama and music in a range of galleries and a studio theatre. Garden historians are restoring the important surrounding parkland. Its formal avenues and canal date from the same period as Versailles.
Mon–Fri 9.30–9.30, Sat 10–5, Sun 2–5; children's shows in afternoon, performance 7.30 or 8.00 Free–£15

ANTRIM FORUM LEISURE COMPLEX
Lough Road, Antrim, Co. Antrim, BT41 4DQ
Tel 028 9446 4131
One of Northern Ireland's most important leisure complexes, regularly hosting international tournaments. Facilities include pools, gym, tennis courts and the Health Suite with full spa facilities.
Mon–Fri 8.15am–10pm, Sat 10–5, Sun 2–5.30 Adult swim £2.50

ARMAGH

THE SHAMBLES MARKET
Cathedral Road, Armagh, Co. Armagh, BT61 7AT
Tel 028 3752 1800
Everything from radishes to ribbons are sold at this traditional variety market, all day Tuesdays and Fridays. Try the car boot (trunk) sales on alternate Saturday mornings for a hidden treasure.

MARKET PLACE THEATRE AND ARTS CENTRE
Market Street, Armagh, Co. Armagh BT61 7BR
Tel 028 3752 1821
www.marketplacearmagh.com
This state-of-the-art facility for visual and performing arts has everything from set dancing to children's shows and serious theatre. Jazz features prominently and there's late-night bar entertainment on Fridays and Saturdays.
Box office: Mon–Sat 9.30–4.30; performance 7pm £5–£18

THE MET ARENA
109 Drumcairn Road, Armagh, Co. Armagh, BT61 8DQ
Tel 028 3751 1360
www.metarena.com
City sounds in a rural location, specializing in progressive uplifting trance and house. This is one of Ireland's most renowned clubs; you will need to dress smartly to get past door staff.
Sat 9pm–3am Details of special bus services from local towns are on website

PALACE STABLES
Palace Demesne, Armagh, Co. Armagh, BT60 4EL
Tel 028 3752 9629
www.visit-armagh.com
A perfect place for family outings, the old stable block of the Bishop's Palace has been converted to provide first-rate children's activities, some with historical themes. There are games for special occasions and an adventure playground. The stables also contain living history exhibits and an imaginative display on servant life. You can also visit the Bishop's Palace.
Mon–Sat 10–5, Sun 2–5 Adult £4.50, child (4–18) £2.50, family £9.50

Mellow brick and cobblestones of the Palace Stables in Armagh

BALLYCASTLE

THE HOUSE OF MACDONNELL
71 Castle Street, Ballycastle, Co. Antrim, BT54 6RN
Tel 028 2076 2975
www.houseofmacdonnell.com
Claiming to be the home of traditional music in County Antrim since 1766, this is a wonderful old pub with a great atmosphere. As for the music, there are traditional sessions here every Friday night and folk music concerts every Saturday night.
Apr–end Sep Mon–Thu from 4pm, Fri–Sat from noon, Sun from 8pm; Oct–end Mar Mon–Thu from 7pm, Fri–Sat from noon, Sun from 8pm

BALLYCASTLE TENNIS COURTS
Mary Street, Ballycastle, Co. Antrim, BT54 6QH
Tel 028 2076 3300
www.moyle.council.org
Pleasantly set on the seafront, these public authority tennis courts are used for local championships. All-weather courts, grass surfaces and floodlights ensure year-round play.
Tue–Fri 3pm–10pm, Sat 10–4 Floodlit courts £6 per hour

BALLYMENA

STORE STORE
12 Broadway Avenue, Ballymena, Co. Antrim, BT43 7AA
Tel 028 2565 1123
www.store-store.com
Within a traditional market town, this is a contemporary furnishing concept focusing on well-sourced 21st-century European style. Staff here can offer design ideas and gift suggestions, and there's a rather funky café.
Daily 9–5.30 (to 9pm Thu)

ECOS MILLENNIUM ENVIRONMENTAL CENTRE
Kerohans Lane, Broughshane Road, Ballymena, Co. Antrim, BT43 7QA
Tel 028 2566 4400
www.ecoscentre.com
In a 60ha (150-acre) park, this is an imaginative concept, with plenty of hands-on, fun activities for children. They can build a rainforest, discover the sad case of the ecos gonks, or explore the park with a rented electric bicycle.
Easter Sat–30 Sep Mon–Sat, 10.30–5, Sun 12–5; Oct–Good Friday Mon–Sat 12–5 Adult £4, child (4–16) £3, family £12.50

BALLYNAHINCH

COUNTRY MARKET
Leisure Centre, Windmill Street, Ballynahinch, Co. Down
A farmers' initiative provides the opportunity to buy fresh, local produce, hand-made goods, and home-baked fare direct from the producer.
Thu 10.30–noon

BANGOR

CAFÉ CEOL AND BOOM BOOM ROOM
17–21 High Street, Bangor, Co. Down
Tel 028 9146 8830
Upstairs is for hedonists, downstairs is funky at this top spot for young partygoers. Japanese themes portray 'a delightful weirdness' and it's a heady blend of zest and Zen.
Daily 7pm to late · Downstairs usually free, upstairs, £5

BANGOR CASTLE LEISURE CENTRE
Castle Park Avenue, Bangor, Co. Down, BT20 4BN
Tel 028 9127 0271
www.northdown.gov.uk
Four pools, a fully equipped health suite, a great range of the latest exercise classes and everything from trampolining to indoor bowling make this a good wet-weather option.
Mon, Wed, Fri 7.30am–10pm, Tue 7.30–6.30, Thu, Sat 9–6, Sun 2–6
Swim: adult £1.90, child (3–18) £1.40

GRANSHA EQUESTRIAN CENTRE
10 Kerrs Road, Six Roads End, Bangor, Co. Down, BT19 7QD
Tel 028 9181 3313
Horses and facilities for all equestrian pursuits. Experienced staff welcome novices who prefer a trek on County Down's country lanes.
1-hour trek £15

PICKIE FUN PARK
Marine Gardens, Pickie, Bangor, Co. Down
Tel 028 9127 4430
Family fun on the seashore, within a safe environment. Activities include rides on giant floating swans, the Pickie Puffer, mini karts and an adventure playground.
Swan boat rides £1.50

BELFAST

ARCADIA
378 Lisburn Road, Belfast, BT9 6GL
Tel 028 9038 1779
Crammed into this tiny delicatessen is a wonderful range of good things to eat, including a great variety of delicious Irish cheeses.
Mon–Sat 9–5.30 · Citybus 58

ARCHIVES ANTIQUES CENTRE
88 Donegall Pass, Belfast, BT7 1BK
Tel 028 9023 2383
Specialist collectors will have a heyday in this bulging antiques shop, full of pub memorabilia, militaria, coins, postcards and railway and shipping items. Saturdays are the best time to visit, when other stalls dedicated to particular collectables are also open.
Mon–Sat 10–5 · Citybus 82

Tempting treats are on offer at Belfast's Chocolate Room

THE BOOKSHOP AT QUEEN'S
91 University Road, Belfast, BT7 1NL
Tel 028 9066 6302
One of the few remaining independent bookshops, with helpful staff and a good selection, including Irish books.
Mon–Sat 9.30–5.30 · Citybus 69, 70, 71

CARTER
11 Upper Queen Street, Belfast, BT1 6NE
Tel 028 9024 3412
Carter clothes the city's most elegant business people, and the coolest young clubbers. Expert staff, chic accessories and stylish premises are the formula for its success.
Mon–Sat 10–5.30

THE CHOCOLATE ROOM
529 Lisburn Road, Belfast, BT9 7GS
Tel 028 9066 2110
An intoxicating aroma of cocoa beans heralds this shrine to chocolate, with seasonal treats and gift boxes made especially to order.
Mon–Sat 10–5.30 · Citybus 58

CRAFTWORKS
Unit 8, Bedford House, Bedford Street, Belfast, BT2 7FD
Tel 028 9024 4465
Within the Linen Conservation Area, and surrounded by refurbished warehouses, Craftworks stocks the best of local crafts, plus clothing and jewellery.
Mon–Sat 9.30–5.30, Thu until 8.30

FULTONS
Boucher Crescent, Belfast, BT66 8HT
Tel 028 3831 4600
In a retail park to the south of Belfast, this is one of the city's most exclusive furniture shops, also laden with designer soft furnishing, Irish modern crystal and lots of giftware. The coffee shop serves delicious home-made dishes.
Mon–Sat 9.30–5.30, Thu until 8
Citybus 58, 59

HARPER
406 Lisburn Road, Belfast, BT9 6GN
Tel 028 9068 1556
With gorgeous bags, bijou accessories for the home, and selective designer labels, this elegant shop is frequented by local style seekers. Harper for children is just down the road.
Mon–Sat 9.30–5.30 · Citybus 58, 59

LAMONT FACTORY SHOP
Stranmillis Buildings, Stranmillis Embankment, Belfast
Tel 028 9066 8285
Tucked away beside a roundabout (traffic circle) in the university area, this small factory shop specializes in textiles, with bargains in linens and seconds in luxury towel ranges.
Mon–Sat 9–4.45 · Citybus 69

WHAT TO DO

MICHELLE O'DOHERTY
7 Chichester Street, Belfast, BT1 4JA
Tel 028 9023 3303
Three floors of fabulous clothes and irresistible accessories fill this elegant Georgian town house. Michelle O'Doherty's own label sits beside some top international names, and special orders can be commissioned.
Mon–Sat 9.30–5.30 (to 7pm Thu)

OAKLAND ANTIQUES
135 Donegall Pass, Belfast, BT7 1DS
Tel 028 9023 0176
www.oaklandni.com
Irish furniture, curios, jewellery and well-chosen china fill this south Belfast emporium. Irish Georgian silver is very collectable and there's a big range of large and small items here.
Mon–Sat 10–5.30 Citybus 82

PARKS CLOTHING LIMITED
68–72 Great Victoria Street, Belfast, BT2 7DD
Tel 028 9024 2394
A converted warehouse makes a great setting for this coolest of cool shops selling the hottest labels for both men and women. Sharing the premises is one of Belfast's top hair stylists, a lingerie shop and a café.
Mon–Sat 9.30–5.30, Sun 1–5

ROSS'S AUCTIONS
May Street, Belfast, BT1 4NX
Tel 028 9032 5448
Thursday is auction day in this long-established auction house, which handles the best country-house furniture, silver, glass, porcelain and paintings. Look for bargains and items of local interest.
Auctions: Wed 9–5, Thu 9am–10pm. Last Thursday of month, specialist antiques sale

SMYTH & GIBSON, SHIRTMAKERS
Bedford House, Bedford Street, Belfast, BT2 7FD
Tel 028 9023 0388
Smyth & Gibson make the most beautiful shirts, following in a tradition of expertise from when Belfast craftsmen led the world of shirtmakers. Irish linen garments are a speciality.
Mon–Sat 8–5.30

ST. GEORGE'S MARKET
See page171.

SURF MOUNTAIN
12 Brunswick Street, Belfast, BT2 7GE
Tel 028 9024 8877
Outdoor sports fans head to this specialist in water sports, mountain sports and adventure travel for expert advice and the latest gear. Leading the field in Northern Ireland, the shop also has cool sunglasses, caps and more.
Mon–Sat 9.30–5.30

The Waterfront Hall in Belfast is a wonderful modern venue

GRAND OPERA HOUSE
See page 168.
Ticketline: 028 9024 1919 Box Office: Mon–Fri 8.30am–9pm, Sat 8.30–6. Performance: usually 7.30pm
£5–£40

THE LYRIC THEATRE
Ridgeway Street, Belfast, BT9 5FB
Tel 028 9038 1081
The Lyric began as a small company specializing in the plays of W. B. Yeats but it now puts on a varied calendar, still with an emphasis on Irish plays. The bars overlook the River Lagan.
Box office: Mon–Sat, 10–7, Performance: 8pm £8–£13.50

ODYSSEY
Queen's Quay, Belfast, BT3 9QQ
Tel 028 9073 9074
www.odysseyarena.com
Dozens of international eateries, bars, clubs, multiplex cinemas, ten-pin bowling and games rooms fill this riverside complex, Belfast's most popular nightspot for all ages. There's a sports arena, which doubles as the preferred venue for big music events.
Box office: Mon–Sat, 10–7
£12–£60

OLD MUSEUM ARTS CENTRE
7 College Square North, Belfast, BT1 6AR
Tel 028 9023 3332
www.oldmuseumartscentre.org
Belfast's most adventurous contemporary arts organization is housed in one of its finest buildings. The Old Museum Arts Centre presents creative fringe and cutting-edge events.
Box office: Mon–Sat 9.30–5.30
Adult £9, child £6

ULSTER HALL
Bedford Street, Belfast
Tel 028 9032 3900 (Ulster Orchestra Box Office: 028 9066 8798)
www.ulsterhall.co.uk
Stately Victorian architecture and great acoustics make this the preferred home of the Ulster Orchestra. Friday night concerts are popular with Belfast audiences, and the Mulholland organ adds great resonance to many occasions.
Box office: Mon–Fri 12–3 From £7

WATERFRONT HALL
Lanyon Place, Belfast, BT1 3WH
Tel 028 9033 4455
www.waterfront.co.uk
Even without its full calendar of major cultural events and pop concerts, it's worth going to this stunning 3,000-seat auditorium just to enjoy the views from the bars overlooking the River Lagan and Belfast Lough.
Box office: Mon–Sat 10–6
£10–£60

APARTMENT
2 Donegall Square, Belfast, BT1 6JA
Tel 028 9050 9777
www.apartmentbelfast.com
A funky, stylish bar/restaurant with hip décor, resident and guest DJs, attracting a sophisticated and stylish crowd. It's right in the middle of Belfast, and window tables give great views over the City Hall.
Daily 9am–1am Usually free

BAMBU BEACH CLUB
Odyssey, Queen's Quay, Belfast, BT3 9QQ
Tel 028 9046 0011
This huge, beach-themed club is popular with students. Clubbers may have to wait in line, but at least they can do so under cover in the Odyssey Arena. Music is mainstream, and the five bars on two floors offer a choice of cocktails.
Mon–Sat 8pm–1am £5–£10

EMPIRE
42 Botanic Avenue, Belfast, BT7 1JD
Tel 028 9024 9276
www.belfastpubs-n-clubs.com
Anything from salsa classes to stand-up comedy is staged at the Empire, distinctively set in a converted church in the university area.
Mon–Tue 11.30–11, Wed–Sat 11.30am–1am, Sun 7–12 £6–£13

KREMLIN
96 Donegall Street, Belfast, BT1 2JF
Tel 028 9031 6060
www.kremlin-belfast.com
Belfast's latest gay venue has regular racy features, together with resident and guest DJs, making it a top destination. The new Russian-inspired Tsar Bar is open from noon.
Tue, Thu–Sat 8pm–3am Tue £3, Thu £5, Fri £7 (free before 10pm), Sat £8 (free before 10pm)

M CLUB
23–31 Bradbury Place, Belfast, BT7 1RS
Tel 028 9023 3131
www.mclub.co.uk
Patrons lining the street mark the popularity of this club, with its large floor space, central position and choice of bars. Thursday is student night, theme parties are on Fridays, and Saturday is ultimate club.
Daily 9pm–1am Mon £2, Thu, Fri £5, Sat £8

ROTTERDAM BAR
54 Pilot Place, Belfast, BT1 3AH
Tel 028 9074 6021
Tucked between Belfast's old dock area and a prestigious office and residential development, the tiny Rotterdam is well known as a great place for live music. There are different styles on different nights—jazz, folk, reggae, rock and disco.
Daily 11am–1am, Thu sessions begin 9pm £3

The Belfast Giants play at the Odyssey Arena

CASEMENT PARK
Andersonstown Road, Belfast, BT11 9AS
Tel 028 9061 3661
In the west Belfast heartland, Casement Park is the top stadium for Gaelic games in Ulster
Sun 5.30 £8–£15 Citybus 12, 15

ODYSSEY ARENA
Queen's Quay, Belfast, BT3 9QQ
Tel 028 9073 9074
www.odysseyarena.com
The Belfast Giant's Ice Hockey team competes here in the National League. The matches are great family occasions, with full USA-style razzmatazz. It's also home to occasional indoor sports events and motorcycle shows.
Box office: Mon–Sat 10–6.45 Adult £13.25, child (4–16) £8, family £33

OZONE TENNIS CENTRE
Ormeau Embankment, Belfast, BT6 8LT
Tel 028 9045 8024
www.belfastcity.gov.uk
This indoor tennis arena provides the only public tennis courts in the city. It is in a park by the river, offers classes and lessons, and there's a climbing wall too.
Mon–Sat 9am–10pm, Sun 10–6 Tennis from £6 Citybus 78, 79

RAVENHILL
Ravenhill Park, Belfast, BT6 0DG
Tel 028 904 93111
www.ulsterrugby.com
From late summer to late spring the Ulster rugby teams bring top-class fixtures to Ravenhill. Witness the pride and passion of provincial sport, at a good family event.
Aug–end May Fri (home games only) 7.30 Adult £5–£15 Citybus 33

WINDSOR PARK
Donegall Avenue, Belfast, BT12 6LW
Tel 028 9024 4198
Home of the Northern Ireland international football team, Windsor Park welcomes some top European teams in the build-up to the World Cup.
Citybus 58, 59

BELFAST ZOO
Antrim Road, Belfast, BT36 7PN
Tel 028 9077 4625
www.belfastzoo.co.uk
Completely re-housed in the last decade, the zoo provides good facilities for its animals. It is set under the dramatic headland of Cave Hill, and has become a top visitor attraction, with plenty of activities especially designed for families.
Apr–end Oct 10–6; Nov–end Mar 10–3 Apr–end Oct: adult £6.70, child (4–16) £3.40, family £18.40; Nov–end Mar: adult £5.40, child (4–16) £2.80, family £14.50 Citybus 45, 46

DUNDONALD INTERNATIONAL ICE BOWL

Old Dundonald Road, Belfast, BT16 1XT
Tel 028 9080 9100
www.dondonaldicebowl.com

Dundonald's Olympic-size ice rink is part of a very popular complex that includes an indoor adventure playground and a 30-lane bowling alley.

Mon–Sat 10–11.30, Sun 10–10.45 Adult £4, family £18 (including skate rental) Citybus 16, 17

STREAMVALE FARM

Ballyhanwood Road, Gilnahirk, Dundonald BT5 7SN
Tel 028 9048 3244
www.streamvale.com

The dairy farmers who decided to open their farm some years ago knew exactly what children want to see and do, and Streamvale is perennially popular with families. There always seems to be a newborn lamb in need of a bottle-feed!

Jul, Aug Mon–Sat 10.30–6, Sun 2–6; Apr–end Jun, Mon–Fri, Sun 2–6, Sat 10–6 Adult £3.50, family £14.50 Citybus 77

W5

Odyssey, Queen's Quay, Belfast, BT3 9QQ
Tel 028 9046 7700
www.w5online.co.uk

The five Ws are who? what? when? where? why? Enquiring young minds find learning lots of fun here, and experts are always on hand to help out.

Mon–Sat 10–5.30, Sun 12–6 £6, child (3–16) £4, family £15

BELLEEK

BELLEEK POTTERY SHOP

See page 174.

CASTLEWELLAN

MOUNT PLEASANT TREKKING & HORSE RIDING CENTRE

15 Bannanstown Road, Castlewellan, Co. Down, BT31 9BG
Tel 028 4377 8651
www.mountpleasantcentre.com

Safe experienced horses, expert guides and beautiful scenery combine to make a memorable visit. All levels of expertise are catered for, but book in advance to make sure.

1-hour trek £12

COMBER

CLATTERINGFORD

51 Old Ballygowan Road, Comber, Co. Down, BT23 5NP
Tel 028 9187 4545
www.clatteringford.com

In a stone farmyard off a leafy lane, this store has an array of linen, moleskin, cashmere, alpaca, 'Titanic' tablecloths and fabulous sheets, the result of a dedicated mission to find all kinds of items made with natural fibres.

Mon–Fri 9–5

A budding rock star steps into the spotlight at W5

PURE DAY SPA

48a Ballybunden Road, Killinchy, Co. Down, BT23 6RF
Tel 028 9754 3000
www.puredayspa.com

Pure is a rural day retreat that offers a comprehensive range of relaxing treatments. The service is highly personalized.

Daily, strictly by appointment only Half day from £110

CUSHENDALL

MCCOLLAM'S BAR

Cushendall, Co. Antrim
Tel 028 2176 1291

The headquarters of the Antrim Glens Traditions Group, McCollam's has a Traditional Singers' Club (no guitars!) on the second Friday of the month in winter, and regular sessions in summer. Set dancing and traditional instrument master-classes are also organized.

Times vary

ARDCLINIS OUTDOOR ADVENTURE CENTRE

Cushendall, Co. Antrim, BT44 0NB
Tel 028 2177 1340
www.ardclinis.com

A thoroughly professional provider, offering everything from corporate team-building and solo challenges to family fun. Includes power-boating, windsurfing and abseiling.

Daily from 9am Day from £35

CROSSGAR

JAMES NICHOLSON, WINE MERCHANT

27a Killyleagh Street, Crossgar, Co. Down, BT30 9DQ
Tel 028 4483 0091

Connoisseurs travel a long way to sample James Nicholson's latest wine discoveries. His shop in a small village holds treasures from France, the rest of Europe and the new world.

Mon–Sat 10–7

DERRY

BOOKWORM

18–20 Bishop Street, Derry, Co. Londonderry, BT48 6PW
Tel 028 7128 2727

A bibliophile's delight, this well-established bookshop stocks a wide selection of local and Irish titles, and has an out-of-print search facility and a coffee shop.

Mon–Sat 9.30–5.30

THE CRAFT VILLAGE

Shipquay Street, Derry, Co. Londonderry
Tel 028 7126 0329

Craftspeople work in this imaginative historic project right in the heart of Derry. Visitors quickly sense the great atmosphere of creative activity. The Craft Village provides a welcome alternative to the multinational chains.

Daily 9–7

FALLER THE JEWELLER
12 Strand Road, Derry, Co. Londonderry BT48 7AB
Tel 028 713 62710
This family firm stocks Irish and European designer jewellery, but don't miss the 'Handmade in Derry' collection, produced in the Faller workshop.
Mon–Sat 9–5.30

OGMIOS
34 Great James Street, Derry, Co. Londonderry, BT48 7DB
Tel 028 7126 4132
www.gaelaras.ie
This specialist shop has an extensive range of Irish language books, cards, crafts and music items, including musical instruments.
Mon–Fri 10–5

THE GUILDHALL
Guildhall Square, Derry, Co. Londonderry, BT48 6DQ
Tel 028 7137 7335
Taking its name from historic ties with the Guilds of the City of London, Derry's neo-Gothic civic and cultural complex hosts a varied calendar of performances.
Tickets (and prices) for performances are advertised locally

MILLENNIUM FORUM
Newmarket Street, Derry, Co. Londonderry, BT48 6EB
Tel 028 7126 4455
www.millenniumforum.co.uk
This large theatre stages a variety of shows. The brand new performance arena attracts top international stars as well as local talent.
Box office: Mon–Sat 10–5, evenings of performance 7–9 £5–£30

THE NERVE CENTRE
Magazine Street, Derry, Co. Londonderry, BT48 6HJ
Tel 028 7126 0562
www.nerve-centre.org.uk
Cutting-edge music and film are major elements of this adventurous arts venue.
Box office: Mon–Fri 9.30–5.30, Sat 2–5 Price varies

CAFÉ ROC
125–139 Strand Road, Derry, Co. Londonderry, BT48 7PA
Tel 028 7136 0556
Derry's top club, attracting national DJs. Clubbers like to dress up here.
Bar daily from 12; club Fri–Sun 10.30pm–2.30am Tue £5, Sat £6

FOYLE INTERNATIONAL GOLF CENTRE
12 Alder Road, Derry, Co. Londonderry, BT48 8DB
Tel 028 7135 2222
An 18-hole par 72 course, a 9-hole par 3 course, indoor driving range and golf shop.
Mon–Fri 9–dark, Sat–Sun 8–dark
£14 (£17 weekends)

You can see all kinds of crafts in production at Derry's Craft Centre

FISHING
Tel 028 7134 2100
www.loughs-agency.org
The Foyle system is one of the best salmon rivers in the world. Contact the Loughs Agency for permits and licences.

FOYLE CRUISES
Harbour Museum, Harbour Square, Derry, Co. Londonderry, BT48 6AF
Tel 028 7136 2857
Enjoy views of Derry's walls and the shores of Lough Foyle from the water, and learn of its eventful history. Evening cruises have entertainment.
Daily cruises 2pm, evening sailings 8pm; phone to confirm Adult £5, child £3.50, family £15

LISNAGELVIN LEISURE CENTRE
Richill Park, Derry, Co. Londonderry, BT47 5QZ
Tel 028 7134 7695
A wave pool and water-based adventure play area makes this more than just a swimming pool. And there are spa facilities and a fitness room for adults.
Mon 2–9.40, Tue–Fri 10–9.40, Sat 10–5.40, Sun 12–4.40 Swim: adult £2.20, child (5–17) £1.60

DONAGHADEE

GRACE NEILL'S
33 High Street, Donaghadee, Co. Down, BT21 0AH
Tel 028 9188 4595
Some good jazz can be heard at this pub, one of many claiming to be the oldest in Ireland. The food is good, and some famous musicians have been known to join in a session.
Mon–Thu 11.30–11, Fri–Sat 11.30am–12.30am, Sun 12.30pm–6

DOWNPATRICK

DOWNPATRICK RACECOURSE
Ballydugan Road, Downpatrick, Co. Down, BT30 8SP
Tel 028 4461 2054
Flat and National Hunt horse racing are held at this undulating course, and racegoers flock to see the Ulster Grand National in March. It's small and slightly old-fashioned, but builds a great atmosphere.
Phone for details Adult £8, child £4

DUNAMANAGH

RASPBERRY HILL HEALTH FARM
29 Bonds Glen Road, Dunamanagh, Co. Londonderry, BT47 3ST
Tel 028 7139 8000
With treatments designed to ease stress and reduce weight, Raspberry Hill offers a full range of beauty products and spa facilities, plus indoor bowls, tennis and a gym. Guests are encouraged to spend the day here, and can choose whether to be active or relaxed.
Full day 9.30–8, £55 including meals; treatments extra

DUNGANNON

THE LINEN GREEN
Moygashel, Co. Tyrone, BT71 7HB
Tel 028 8775 3761
www.thelinengreen.com
Well designed and small in scale, the Linen Green has excellent designer shopping at discount prices. People come here for the Irish linens, fine Moygashel fabrics, and the factory shop of international designer Paul Costelloe.
Mon–Sat 10–5.30

TYRONE CRYSTAL
Killybrackey, Co. Tyrone, BT71 6TT
Tel 028 8772 5335
The shop at the home of Tyrone Crystal stocks a wide range of products, together with a few 'seconds'. For a small charge, visitors can get a guided tour of the factory.
Mon–Fri 9–5, tours at 11, 12, 2, 3 Sun 1–5 Adult £2, child free

DUNGANNON GOLF CLUB
34 Springfield Lane, Dungannon, Co. Tyrone, BT70 1QX
Tel 028 8772 2098
The home of international golf star Darren Clarke, this is a mature 18-hole parkland course. The best days for visitors are Monday, Thursday and Friday.
£20–£25, 24-hour advance booking required

ENNISKILLEN

THE BUTTERMARKET
Down Street, Enniskillen, Co. Fermanagh, BT74 7DU
Tel 028 6632 4499
The restored Buttermarket makes an ideal focus for local craft workers, who present a fascinating range of items, including Frankie McPhillips' classic salmon fly collection, wood-turning, textile designs, miniatures and knitwear.
Mon–Sat 10–5.30

ARDHOWEN THEATRE
Dublin Road, Enniskillen, Co. Fermanagh, BT74 6BR
Tel 028 6632 3233
www.ardhowentheatre.com
This lakeside theatre has a lovely setting and presents events of broad appeal, from local artists to drama festivals.
Box office: Mon–Fri, 10–4.30, 7–8.30, Sat 10–1, 2–5, plus 6–8 on performance evenings
£7–£15

BLAKES OF THE HOLLOW
6 Church Street, Enniskillen, Co. Fermanagh, BT74 7EJ
Tel 028 6632 2143
Catch traditional music sessions on Friday or Saturdays in this lovely old pub, which has been owned by the same hospitable family since the 1880s.
Mon–Sat 11–1

Fishing on Upper Lough Erne is popular and rewarding

FISHING AND CRUISING
Fermanagh has a huge selection of cruising opportunities on the Erne–Shannon waterway or loughs. Fishing is good, too, alone or with a ghillie for local expertise. The tourist office has full details.

LAKELAND CANOE CENTRE
Castle Island, Enniskillen, Co. Fermanagh, BT74 5HH
Tel 028 6632 4250
Everything for outdoor activities—sailboards, canoes, bicycles, caving equipment and residential facilities. Instructors are available, too.
£30 per day, including equipment and instruction

HILLSBOROUGH

CHESHIRE CAT
1 The Square, Hillsborough, Co. Down, BT26 6AG
Tel 028 9268 3031
This is a mine of fun things to buy, with lots of little toys within pocket-money range for the children.
Mon–Sat 9.30–5.30

HOLYWOOD

THE BAY TREE
118 High Street, Holywood, Co. Down, BT18 9HW
Tel 028 9042 1419
In an attractive courtyard, this pottery shop and gallery also has a restaurant and garden.
Mon–Sat 9.30–5.30

TESORO
37 Church Road, Holywood, Co. Down, BT18 0PN
Tel 028 9042 4494
Holywood is full of lovely specialist stores, but this one is a gem, packed with antiques, knick-knacks and pictures.
Mon–Sat 9.30–5.30

KESH

ALISON BRITTON BATIK
The Cow Shed, 13 High Street, Tullyhommon, Co. Fermanagh, BT93 8BD
Tel 028 6863 2289
Strong patterns in vivid hues define Alison Britton's work in batik. Her range includes wall hangings and greetings cards.
Daily 9–5, but phone before visiting in case preparing for craft fair

LARNE

CARNFUNNOCK COUNTRY PARK
Coast Road, Larne, Co. Antrim, BT40 2QG
Tel 028 2827 0541
www.larne.gov.uk/carnfunnock
A family-friendly park with a maze in the shape of Northern Ireland, a miniature railway and other activities, all overlooking the Irish Sea.
Reception: daily 10–5, Fri–Sat until 8. Activity Centre: 1–7, but check in off-season Maze free. Crazy golf £1.20. Table tennis £1.50. Miniature train £1.30

LISBURN

BALLINDERRY ANTIQUES

2 Lower Ballinderry Road, Ballinderry Upper, Lisburn, Co. Antrim, BT28 2EP
Tel 028 9265 1046
This multilevel stone shop is one of Ireland's largest antiques shops, with large and small items.
Mon–Sat 10–5

DOWN ROYAL RACECOURSE

Maze, Lisburn, Co. Down, BT27 5RW
Tel 028 9262 1256
www.downroyal.com
Home of the Ulster Derby, held in summer, this attractive racecourse is aspiring to become one of Ireland's top courses.
£8–£15

NEWCASTLE

ROYAL COUNTY DOWN GOLF CLUB

Golf Links Road, Newcastle, Co. Down, BT33 0AN
Tel 028 4372 3314
www.royalcountydown.org
Marvellously scenic, this championship course borders the Irish Sea, beneath the Mourne Mountains. One of the world's toughest golf challenges.
£12–£125 (telephone in advance)

TOLLYMORE MOUNTAIN CENTRE

Bryansford, Newcastle, Co. Down, BT33 0PT
Tel 028 4372 2158
www.tollymore.com
A full range of mountain-based activities, including climbing and white-water kayaking. Fortuitously, they offer first aid courses, too!
Introduction to kayaking £45

NEWTOWNARDS

SCUBA DIVING

DV Diving, 138 Mount Stewart Road, Newtownards, Co. Down, BT22 2ES
Tel 028 9146 4671
www.dvdiving.co.uk
Strangford Lough is a premier destination for divers of all abilities, who are drawn by wrecks, spectacular drop-offs and exhilarating drift dives.
All year Prices on application

ULSTER FLYING CLUB

Ards Airport, Portaferry Road, Newtownards, Co. Down, BT23 8SG
Tel 028 9181 3327
Flying lessons, scenic aerial tours and microlight flying trials are all available here.
Flying lessons £70–£100

PORTADOWN

CRAIGAVON WATERSPORTS

Lake Road, Craigavon, Co. Armagh, BT64 1AF
Tel 028 3834 2669
www.craigavon.gov.uk
Waterskiing, canoeing, banana boating or windsurfing. Tuition and equipment are provided.
Telephone in advance Canoe rental £13 for 2 hours

Royal Portrush uses the natural landscape to wonderful effect

PORTAFERRY

ARDMINNAN EQUESTRIAN CENTRE

15 Ardminnan Road, Portaferry, Co. Down, BT22 1QJ
Tel 028 4277 1321
Country lanes or unspoiled beaches, novice or expert, this family-run equestrian centre caters for all.
Open all year, book in advance
From £15

EXPLORIS

The Ropewalk, Portaferry, Co. Down, BT22 1NZ
Tel 028 4272 8062
www.ards-council.gov.uk/exploris
This aquarium, with hands-on activities, is popular with families. Expert guides tell of the enormous marine riches of Strangford Lough in an easy-to-understand way.
Mon–Fri 10–6, Sat 11–6, Sun 12–6
Adult £6, child (4–16) £3.50

PORTRUSH

LUSH@KELLYS COMPLEX

Bushmills Road, Portrush, Co. Antrim, BT56 8JQ
Tel 028 7082 3539
Nationally recognized as the top club in the north, Lush attracts crowds from all over the province, grabs major club awards and imports top DJs.
Wed and Sat 9–1.30 £10

ROYAL PORTRUSH GOLF CLUB

Dunluce Road, Portrush, Co. Antrim, BT56 8JQ
Tel 028 7082 2311
www.royalportrushgolfclub.com
One of the world's great courses, Royal Portrush regularly welcomes the Senior Masters for a competition of veteran style, skill and good humour. For green times for the championship Dunluce course, contact the Secretary in advance; access to the Valley Course is less restricted.
£32–£95

DUNLUCE CENTRE

Sandhill Drive, Portrush, Co. Antrim, BT56 8BF
Tel 028 7082 4444
www.dunlucecentre.co.uk
Interactive games, turbo rides and a treasure hunt make the Dunluce Centre a perfect refuge if the weather's bad.
Jul, Aug daily 10.30–6.30; Sep–end Mar Sat–Sun 12–5 Adult £8, family £23

TOOME

CROSSKEYS INN

40 Grange Road, Ardnaglass, Toome, Co. Antrim, BT41 3QB
Tel 028 7965 0694
One of Ireland's most famous traditional music pubs, with sessions on Saturdays, and impromptu music other nights.
Daily 11.30am–late

FESTIVALS AND EVENTS

MARCH

ST. PATRICK'S DAY
Tourist information: Belfast, tel 028 9023 9026; Derry, tel 028 7137 7577; Down, tel 028 4461 2233
www.discovernorthernireland.com
Throughout the province, events mark the day dedicated to Ireland's patron saint. Carnivals, concerts and parades in Belfast, Derry and Downpatrick, and religious services at Armagh and Saul.
17 March

APRIL/MAY

SONORITIES FESTIVAL OF CONTEMPORARY MUSIC
Queen's University, Belfast, BT7 1NN
Tel 028 9097 5337
www.sonorities.org.uk
One of the most important modern music festivals of its kind, Sonorities highlights electronic, acoustic and multimedia works from all over the world, and commissions new compositions from international artists.

MAY

BELFAST CITY MARATHON
Belfast
Tel 028 9027 0345
www.belfastcitymarathon.com
For over 20 years Belfast's marathon has taken competitors on an undulating course through the city. Traditionally held on the May Day holiday, it attracts serious athletes and fun-runners.
First weekend in May

BALLYCLARE HORSE SHOW
Tel 028 9334 1110
www.discovernorthernireland.com
Today this traditional horse fair has lots of street activities, music and carnival fun. Amid this atmosphere you can learn where the expression 'horse trading' arose.

THE LORD MAYOR'S SHOW
Belfast
Tel 028 9024 6609
www.belfastcity.gov.uk
The streets are full of floats, bands and carnival fun in this traditional civic parade.
End May

JUNE

GALWAY HOOKERS REGATTA AND FESTIVAL
Portaferry, Co. Down
Tel 028 9182 6846
www.ards-council.gov.uk
Portaferry is one of Ireland's most beautifully positioned coastal villages, and the annual visit of the traditional red-sailed hookers from Galway is celebrated with bands, *ceilidhs*, traditional music and yacht racing.
End June

Horse trading is an integral part of the Ould Lammas Fair

JULY

FEIS NA NGLEANN
Tel 028 2076 2225
www.moyle-council.org
The nine Glens of Antrim have a fabled beauty and a very distinctive culture. At Glenariff, a festival of Gaelic games and local arts and crafts brings this tiny seaside village to life.

JULY–AUGUST

ORANGEMEN'S CELEBRATIONS
Tel 028 9023 9026
www.discovernorthernireland.com
Marches (sometimes controversial) celebrating the Loyalist tradition take place throughout the summer. They range from the marches to commemorate the World War I Battle of the Somme to those remembering the Battle of the Boyne.

AUGUST

OULD LAMMAS FAIR
Ballycastle, Co. Antrim
Tel 028 2076 2024
www.moyle-council.org
Claiming to be Ireland's oldest traditional market fair, 'the Ould Lammas' fills the narrow streets of Ballycastle with horse traders, market stalls and street entertainment. Look out for the local delicacies 'dulse' (edible seaweed) and 'yellow man' (honeycomb confectionery).
Last weekend in August

SEPTEMBER

HILLSBOROUGH INTERNATIONAL OYSTER FESTIVAL
Hillsborough
Tel 028 9268 9717
www.hillsboroughoysterfestival.com
The traditional combination of Guinness and oysters seemed a good enough reason for the residents of the pretty Georgian village of Hillsborough to indulge in a celebration. Now it's an established festival in which quality food and great entertainment are on the menu.

OCTOBER/NOVEMBER

BELFAST FESTIVAL AT QUEENS
Belfast
Tel 028 9097 2626
www.belfastfestival.com
One of the biggest events of its kind in Europe, this arts festival (inaugurated by Queens University) attracts big names from all branches of the performing and visual arts. The schedule includes an eclectic range of events.

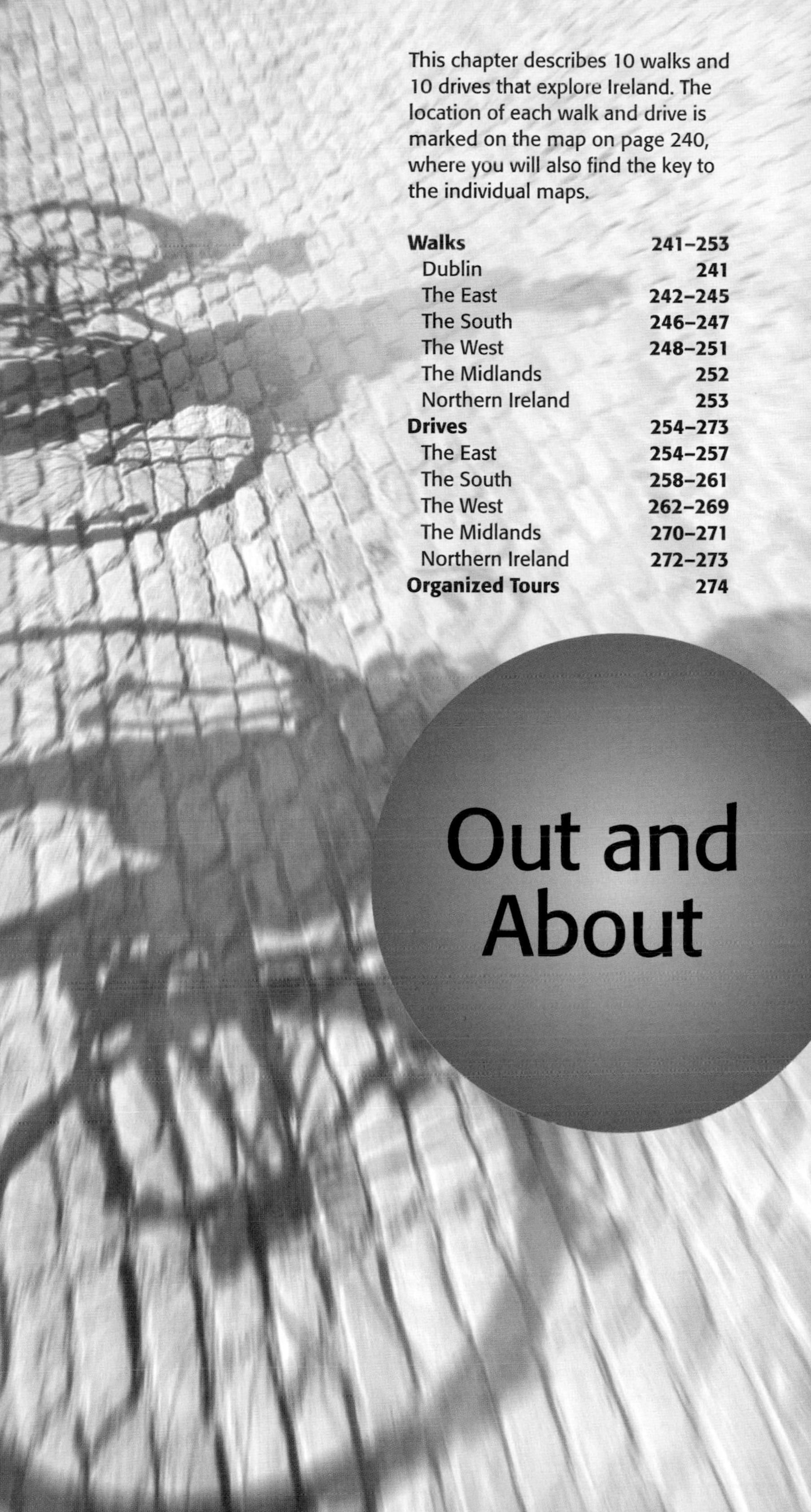

This chapter describes 10 walks and 10 drives that explore Ireland. The location of each walk and drive is marked on the map on page 240, where you will also find the key to the individual maps.

Out and About

LOCATION OF WALKS AND DRIVES

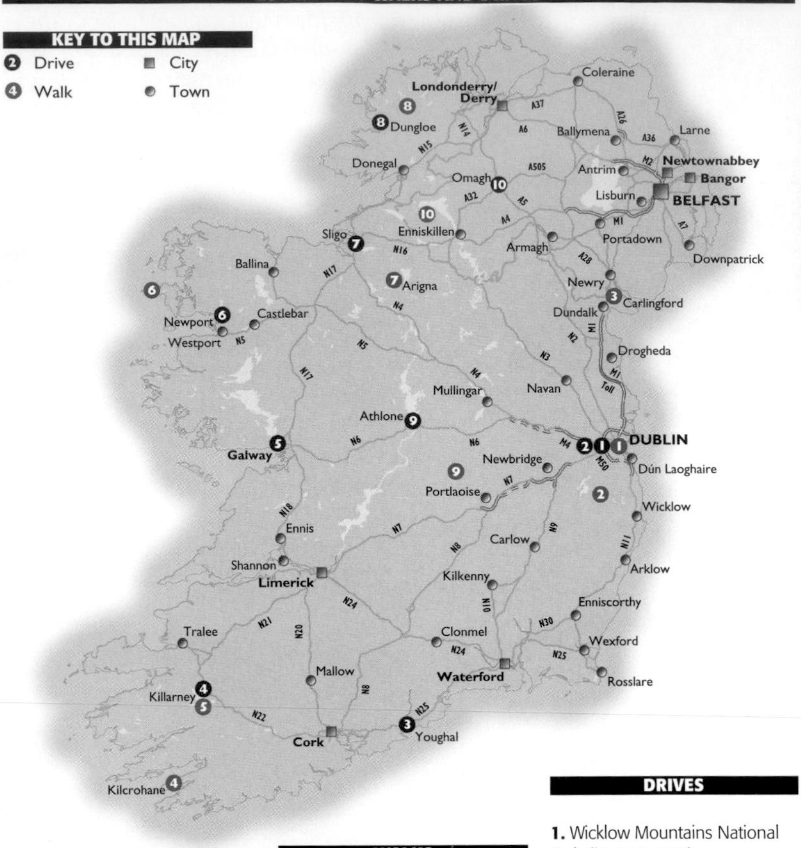

KEY TO THIS MAP

- ❷ Drive
- ❹ Walk
- ■ City
- ● Town

Londonderry/Derry, Coleraine, Dungloe, Ballymena, Larne, Donegal, Newtownabbey, Antrim, Bangor, Omagh, Lisburn, BELFAST, Enniskillen, Sligo, Portadown, Armagh, Downpatrick, Ballina, Arigna, Newry, Carlingford, Dundalk, Castlebar, Newport, Westport, Drogheda, Mullingar, Navan, Athlone, DUBLIN, Galway, Newbridge, Dún Laoghaire, Portlaoise, Wicklow, Ennis, Carlow, Shannon, Limerick, Kilkenny, Arklow, Enniscorthy, Tralee, Clonmel, Wexford, Mallow, Waterford, Rosslare, Killarney, Cork, Youghal, Kilcrohane

A37, A6, A26, A36, M2, A505, A32, A5, A4, M1, A7, A28, N14, N15, N16, N17, N4, N5, N3, N2, M1, Toll, M4, N6, M50, N7, N18, N9, N11, N8, N24, N21, N20, N10, N30, N25, N22

GENERAL INFORMATION

For the rural walks in this chapter you will need to have a good, general standard of fitness. You should wear sensible walking shoes or boots, and take waterproof clothing with you in case it rains. It is best to avoid doing the walks in bad weather. Before setting out on any of the walks or drives, it is advisable to buy a detailed map of the area.

KEY TO ROUTE MAPS IN THIS CHAPTER

- Start point
- Route
- Alternative route
- Route direction
- Walk start point on drive
- Featured sight along route
- Place of interest in Sights section
- Other place of interest
- Viewpoint
- 621 Height in metres

WALKS

DRIVES

1. WALK

GEORGIAN DUBLIN

Stroll back in time passing some of the grandest Georgian buildings in Dublin. You will see many of the best examples of town houses from this period set around the most famous squares in the city.

THE WALK

Distance: 3km (2 miles)

Allow: 1.5 hours

Start at: Bank of Ireland, College Green 67 E3

End at: Powerscourt Townhouse, William Street South 67 E3

HOW TO GET THERE

DART Tara Street, Cross-city buses

★ Starting outside the Bank of Ireland (1785) on College Green, a fine example of Georgian architecture, cross over the road and go through the archway into Trinity College.

❶ Trinity College contains some superb Georgian architecture. Within the first square, notice the Chapel (1798), the Dining Hall (1761) and the Examination Room (1791). Other important Georgian buildings of the college include the magnificent Old Library (1732) in Fellows' Square and the Provost's House (c1760).

Return to College Green and turn left into Grafton Street, a fashionable shopping street lined with four-floor Georgian buildings. At the end of the street turn left into St. Stephen's Green.

❷ St. Stephen's Green, originally common land where public executions and punishment beatings took place, is today a haven for visitors and office workers. In the 18th century wealthy Dubliners began to build elegant town houses around the green and had private access to it. Free entry to all was granted in 1877.

Continue past the splendid Georgian houses with their attractive doors, balconies and fanlights, passing the 18th-century Shelbourne Hotel into Merrion Row and turn left on Merrion Street Upper. You then pass the Natural History Museum and the rear entrance of the imposing Leinster House.

Dublin is famous for its many fine Georgian doorways

❸ When Leinster House was built in 1745 for the Earl of Kildare, this part of the city was almost open country. Within 20 years it became the most fashionable district of Dublin. In 1814 Leinster House was acquired by the Royal Dublin Society and was finally bought by the Irish Government in 1925 to become the seat of the national parliament. This view of Leinster House resembles a country estate.

Look across to Merrion Square South with its striking Georgian buildings. Continue up the square, past the Victorian National Gallery of Ireland (1859). To your right is Oscar Wilde House, on the corner of Merrion Square North, the first house to be built in the square in 1762. Turn left into Clare Street, then on to Leinster Street South taking the third left into Kildare Street, past the National Library on the left; stop to admire the main façade of Leinster House.

❹ Seen from this side, Leinster House looks like a large town house and is flanked by the later buildings of the National Library and National Museum.

From here, cross the road to Molesworth Street with some fine Georgian houses including three early ones with huge chimneys known as the Dutch billies. At the end of the street turn left into Dawson Street; St. Anne's Church is on your left.

❺ The striking church of St. Anne's was founded in 1707, and ministered to the rapidly growing Georgian suburbs. The façade was added in 1868.

Continue down Dawson Street to admire the Mansion House on your left, official residence of the Lord Mayor. Turn right into St. Stephen's Green North then left down the west side of the green to the Royal College of Surgeons on your right.

❻ A striking building, the Royal College of Surgeons is one of the city's best Georgian houses. Designed by Edward Park in 1806, the college has a neoclassical granite façade and distinctive round-headed windows.

Return to the corner of St. Stephen's Green and turn left into King Street South. Bear right into William Street South and walk up the hill where, on the right, you will find the Georgian Dublin Civic Museum (closed at time of writing) and Powerscourt Townhouse.

❼ The attractive 1774 Powerscourt Townhouse is now a shopping mall but still features the original grand staircase and finely detailed plasterwork.

WHEN TO GO

A pleasant morning stroll or alternatively in the evening when several of the buildings are illuminated.

WHERE TO EAT

There is lots of choice in the Powerscourt Townhouse Shopping Centre, or try one of the many pubs.

2. WALK

GLENDALOUGH AND THE WICKLOW WAY

Glendalough, the valley of the two lakes, lies at the very heart of the Wicklow Mountains National Park. A walk up this peaceful glen, by the lough sides and into the mountains, reveals the ruins of its monastic past, amid woodlands and waterfalls.

THE WALK

Distance: 8km (5 miles)

Allow: 3 hours

Start/end at: Glendalough Visitor Centre parking area, Glendalough

1:50,000 OSI Discovery Series, map 56

Grid reference 312 196

HOW TO GET THERE

Glendalough is about 40km (25 miles) southeast of Dublin; the R757 leaves the Wicklow Gap road 1.6km (1 mile) or so west of Laragh.

INFORMATION

Pick up the walks leaflets from the Visitor Centre. The colour-coded one is free and there is also a general map of the valley at 1:25,000 scale for €0.50.

★ From the parking area, head to the left of the buildings across a picnic area to a bridge over the Glenealo River, following a Wicklow Way marker.

1 The Wicklow Way is Ireland's oldest long-distance trail. It is well waymarked throughout and it takes about five days to walk its 131km (81 miles) south from the suburbs of Dublin to Clonegall, near Bunclodyin County Wexford.

Cross the bridge and turn right, following the sign marked 'Green Road to Upper Lake'. The main monastic site is through the trees across the river on your right. Ignore any turnoffs to the right and follow the broad track past the lower lake, eventually following a sign to the information office, still on the Wicklow Way. At the next junction bear right, ignoring a path rising to the left. About 50m (55yards) past the information office, cross the wooden bridge on your left. Now follow the signs up to Poulanass Waterfall.

2 The track rises fairly steeply, following the edge of the gorge that Poulanass Waterfall leaps, but it is well fenced. There are viewing areas and an interpretative panel explaining the brook's significance.

The Wicklow Way footpath passes through Glendalough

Continue up the hill, now joining a forest road coming in from the right. When the track forks, bear right, leaving the Wicklow Way, and follow the forest road, which curves round to the right, heading back towards the valley initially and then bending sharply left. Ignore the markers pointing to your right. Instead follow the blue arrow pointing up the glen.

3 These arrows mark the Spinc Walk and lead you up the glen.

The walk sometimes goes through plantations, sometimes in clear-felled areas, where the tops of the mountains are visible.

4 Glendalough was naturally wooded until about 1,000 years ago, when climate change and felling timber for charcoal-making began to take its toll. Coppices were managed and much of what you see now is the product of deliberate planting. The oaks, larches and Scots pines on the lower slopes date from the 19th century, when there was a heavy demand for pit props. Higher up you'll see later sitka and Norwegian spruce, initially planted in the early 20th and still felled commercially.

At the next junction bear right with the arrow and head up the track for about 100m (110 yards). Now a blue arrow directs you into the forest on your right, up a steep and at times muddy path. A warning sign suggests danger, but the risks are the same as they were lower down. Towards the top, daylight shines through a narrow tunnel of trees and you emerge on a heathered ridge above the Upper Lake.

5 Across the Upper Lake, on the far side of the glen, and to your left, conspicuous mine tailings bleed down the scree and crags to the road. These are remnants of the Glendalough lead and silver mines that flourished here in the 19th century.

Take a moment to enjoy the view down and up the glen before turning right, along the ridge. You continue on a non-slip boardwalk, which not only protects the vegetation around the path, but also enables you to proceed at a reasonable speed. At the end of the undulating ridge the route drops steeply back to the Poulanass Brook. It does this in a long cascade of wooden steps; it is only polite to let those struggling up to pass.

Eventually you come back onto the forest road you walked on earlier. Turn briefly left before following the sweeping bend back down to the right. At the intersection keep left, heading down the hill, and ignore the turnoff back to the waterfall on your right. Follow the forest road down to a bend where a sign indicates a viewpoint. Leave the forest road here and descend steeply, eventually to the intriguing remains of the Reefert Church.

6 Reefert Church, an 11th-century Romanesque building, was the burial place of the O'Toole clan. The ruined nave and chancel can be seen along with many ancient gravestones.

Beyond the church, cross the little bridge, and head for the

Glendalough's Lower Lake is a good place for quiet contemplation

lakeshore. Walk along the road, with the Upper Lake to your left. Go through the barrier and across the wooden bridge. Now turn right down the road, passing the upper parking area on your right, to a track that drops down from the road on the right. Take it and then turn left, joining the wide boardwalk down the valley below the road. Follow this past the Lower Lough and across the river to rejoin the Green Road. Turn left to return to the Visitor Centre or to view the main monastic site.

WHERE TO EAT

The Glendalough Hotel
Glendalough
Tel 0404 45135
www.glendaloughhotel.ie
The restaurant serves Irish and mainstream world food.
Closed Dec–end Jan

PLACES TO VISIT

Glendalough Visitor Centre and Monastic Site
▷ 94–95.

Glendalough (right) is one of Ireland's foremost monastic sites

The Vale of Glenmacnass in the Wicklow Mountains (below)

CARLINGFORD AND THE TAIN TRAIL

This walk starts from a medieval town hardly touched by development since the 18th century, then ascends Carlingford Mountain. Far-reaching views unfold across Carlingford Lough to the Mountains of Mourne, before you return to the town to explore its ruined Norman castle.

THE WALK

Distance: 8km (5 miles)
Allow: 3 hours
Start/end at: parking area by Visitor Centre, Carlingford, Co. Louth
1:50,000 OSI Discovery Series, map 36
Grid reference 318 311

HOW TO GET THERE

Carlingford is on the north side of the Cooley Peninsula 17km (10.5 miles) from Dundalk on the R173.

★ From the parking area by the Visitor Centre, walk into town, past Taafe's Castle and the memorial to Thomas D'Arcy Magee (1835–68), a local man who was one of the founders of modern Canada.

❶ Taafe's Castle is a fortified merchant's house from the 16th century. It takes its name from a prominent local family.

Turn left opposite the general store and then bear left down the pedestrianized street when you get to the corner, and go on to the Mint.

❷ The Mint is another fortified 16th-century house, now used as a base for outdoor activities. Look for the fine stone carved mullions with patterns distinctive of this period of the Celtic Renaissance. The gateway is known as the Tholsel. It once stood higher, being the tollgate through the 15th-century walls, where taxes would be collected. The town's corporation would also meet here, and in the 18th century it served as a prison.

Past the Mint, go through the gatehouse, and turn right into the churchyard to the Church of the Holy Trinity.

❸ The Church of the Holy Trinity can trace its origins to the 13th century, but most of the building we see today is a result of the renovations of 1804. The crenallated tower was built in the 16th century, but the oldest tombstone is from 1703. Inside, the church is still used for worship, and the Heritage Exhibition explains the development of the town, the trading links of its heyday and its subsequent decline.

Leave the churchyard on the far side and turn right. At the junction turn left and follow the old main road past the remains of the priory on the left and the modern Catholic church on the right.

❹ The Dominican priory was established by Richard de Burgo in 1305 to work with the town's poor. It was similar to most 14th-century monastic foundations, with cloister, refectory, chapter-house and church, but of these buildings only the church and east range of the domestic quarters remain. The violence of the late Middle Ages is indicated by the priory's need to fortify itself in 1423. It was dissolved in 1539.

Turn right now, following the Tain Trail signposts. Walk up the road which bears left, past a ruined cottage on the right; a Tain Trail sign lurks on the left-hand side. It directs you right again, up the hill. Follow this winding lane up the hill, with waymarks at the prominent points.

Ruined King John's Castle still dominates the loughside village of Carlingford

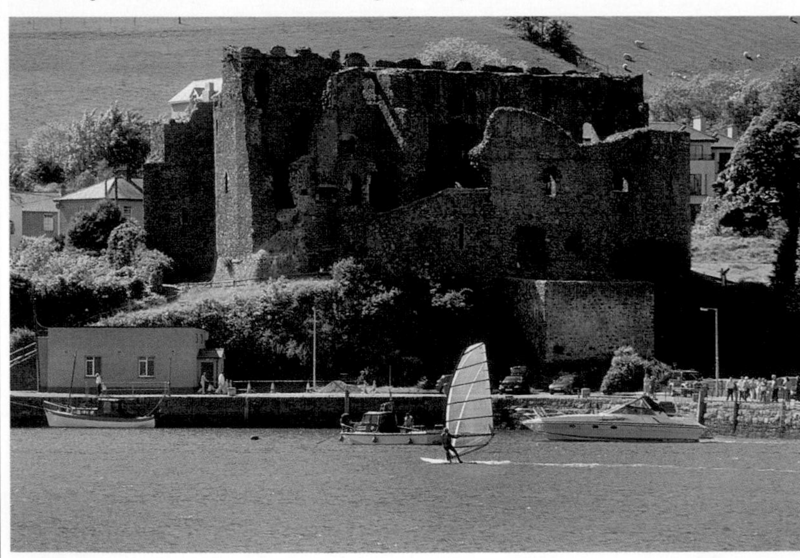

5 The Tain Trail is a walking and bicycling route covering 40km (25 miles) that commemorates one of Ireland's most enduring Iron Age legends, that of the Tain Bo Cuailgne (the Cattle Raid of Cooley). Queen Maeve of Connaught from Rathcroghan in County Roscommon was jealous because her husband was richer than she was. To even the score she set out with a vast army to capture the famous Brown Bull of Cooley. The Ulstermen's defence was led by Cúchulainn, the greatest of all the Irish heroes. He was slain in the battle but, inspired by his bravery, his men repulsed the invaders.

Eventually a waymark points you to the right, off the road through a gap in the gorse. This path leads up, fairly steeply at first, to a gate. Go through this and follow the signs as the Tain Trail bears around to the right, with views of the town and its harbour emerging below you. Follow the well-signposted green track as it traverses the hillside, rising steadily. As it meets an eastern spur of Carlingford Mountain it veers left, back across the face of the slope, gently rising to the col between Carlingford Mountain and Barnavave.

6 Walk a few paces over the col to look down into the valley of the Big River on the other side. Slievenalogh rises beyond and the eastern coast stretches away past Dunany Point. Experienced walkers may choose to continue to the rocky summit of Slieve Foye, the mountain's highest point, 587m (1,925ft), though this part of the walk is not signposted and involves some rougher terrain.

Retrace the path back into Carlingford. To visit King John's Castle, carry straight on when you get to Taafe's Castle, passing the Garda station on your left, and the road will take you up a bank to the castle entrance.

7 King John's Castle, founded by Hugh de Lacy in the 12th century, has a commanding view of the lough and shows how important Carlingford was to the Anglo-Normans. The castle suffered in the wars of the 17th century and stayed in a ruined state until restoration was started in the 1950s.

To return to the parking area from here, retrace your steps and turn left at Taafe's Castle.

Carlingford Harbour has a working fishing fleet (right). Ancient buildings line the streets of Carlingford, which is a good base for outdoor activities (below)

WHERE TO EAT

There are several bistro-style restaurants in Carlingford, among them Ghan House (tel 042 937 3682) and The Oystercatcher (tel 042 937 3922), where Cooley lamb and Carlingford mussels and oysters feature.

PLACES TO VISIT

Holy Trinity Heritage Centre
Carlingford
Tel 042 937 3454
Mon–Fri 9.30–12.30, 2–4.30
Adult €2, child €1

4. WALK

THE SHEEP'S HEAD PENINSULA

This walk through farmland around Kilcrohane takes in part of the Sheep's Head Way, a spectacular long-distance footpath of 88km (55 miles) that encircles the peninsula and is one of the great walks of Ireland.

THE WALK

Distance: 5km (3 miles)
Allow: 2 hours. Good boots required: lots of stiles, two small streams to ford, and some muddy fields to cross
Start/end at: Kilcrohane village
1:50,000 OSI Discovery Series, map 88
Grid reference 081 037
Parking: Kilcrohane main street

HOW TO GET THERE

Take the R591 from Bantry.

★ Kilcrohane is on the minor road which runs down the south side of the Sheep's Head peninsula in the far west of County Kerry. Bantry Bay spreads on the northern shores of the peninsula, and to the west, the next land is North America.

Walk west from the main street of Kilcrohane, along the pavement (sidewalk) beside the main road. Keep along the road, past a children's playground on the left. Ignore a turning to the left, signed Kilcrohane Pier, and keep straight on. Soon you pass a pink cottage on the right; a gushing stream passes under the road, tumbling towards the sea. Soon after this turn left, following the direction of a yellow waymarker painted on a stone. Immediately cross a cattle grid, and follow the rough gravel road, heading down towards the sea.

❶ As you walk down here, behind and to the left is the peak of Seefin, 345m (1,132ft), with Rosskerrig Mountain in front of it. The high pointy peak on the Mizen Peninsula opposite is Knocknamaddry.

Follow the gravel track as it curls away from the village. Go through the white posts of a gateway into a farmyard. Just before the farm buildings, turn left through a field gate and bear right, down to a gap in the wall at the bottom of the field. Follow a path which leads round to the left, ford a small stream, and bear right towards the little shingle

Distinctive signs mark the path of the Sheep's Head Way

beach. Cross a high wooden stile over a fence, following the yellow marker. On the other side, look for a waymarker to your right, and bear right along the fence.

❷ Stay alongside this fence, which is between you and the sea. Black fingers of rock poke into the next little bay along; look for black and white oystercatchers on the shingle.

Pass a waymarker and cross the next high stile. Ford a small stream on the other side, and continue ahead across the grass. Towards the other side of this bay, look for another waymarker. Now bear left along the edge of the field, with fence, wall and drainage ditch on your right. Look for another waymarker on a post in the corner of the field, and cross a low wooden stile there. Continue straight ahead across pasture towards a metal field gate, with scattered houses up on the left. Cross the stone stile beside the field gate, and continue ahead with the waymarkers, following a rough track. Go through a field gate and keep straight on, with the stream broadening to your right.

❸ From here, look right to see waves crashing on the reef to the west of Carbery Island.

The track becomes stony just before another field gate. Climb the stone stile to the left of the gate, cross the stream, and walk straight ahead on the minor road. A gateway gives grand views on the right. Walk through a little hamlet, past ruined farmhouses and between fuchsia hedges. Go between two white houses, and keep straight ahead over a stone stile beside a field gate. Immediately bear left up an overgrown path, passing one of the white houses to your left. Turn sharp left over a stone stile by a gate, and right, following the arrow, up the edge of a field. At the corner continue straight ahead, up a short lane. Cross a mossy stone stile and continue up the rough lane between low stone walls. The stone stile at the end takes you into a private garden. Cross the grass and bear left round a building, following the yellow waymarker. Pass through a narrow gap in the wall, descend rough stone steps, cross a big slab bridge to reach a road and turn right.

❹ The road leads past the village graveyard, with roofless remains of the old church, and down to the quay at the end.

Return to the last slab bridge and turn right through a private gateway. Cross the area in front of a garage and go straight ahead up stone steps, with a waymarker. Go through a small field gate, bear left through a stone gateway, waymarked, and almost immediately bear right through a field gate. Walk up the fenced grassy path towards farm buildings. Turn right before them over a stile into a field. Keep left across the top of the field. At the far corner cross the stone stile and continue straight ahead over the next field. Cross a stone stile at the end and bear left up the tarmac road back to Kilchrohane.

WHERE TO EAT

There's no café on the route, but the old-fashioned village store and post office sell most goods and basic supplies for a picnic.

5. WALK

A CIRCUIT OF MUCKROSS LAKE

The beautiful woods and mountain scenery in the heart of Killarney National Park make a wonderful backdrop for a walk.

THE WALK

Distance: 11km (8 miles)
Allow: 3–4 hours
Start/end at: At the lower parking area at Muckross House
1:50,000 OSI Discovery Series, map 78
Grid reference 096 085

HOW TO GET THERE

Muckross is signed from the N71, 5.5km (3.5 miles) south of Killarney.

★ Leave the parking area by the path signed Lake Shore and Nature Trails. Bear right where it says 'Jaunting Cars for Hire', with Muckross House to your left. Note that you could catch a jaunting car to this point from Killarney.

❶ Muckross House, a Tudor-style 19th-century mansion, houses the Kerry Folklife Museum. Within the Muckross Estate lie the ruins of 15th-century Gothic Muckross Abbey.

Keep left across the yard where the jaunting cars wait, and walk straight on down the tarmac road towards the lake, passing Muckross House to your left. Stay on the road as it bends sharp left, signed to the Torc Waterfall. Continue along the tarmac road with the lake on your right. Pass Dundag Bay. Torc Mountain 535m (1,755ft) is ahead. The route runs through mixed woodland, with rhododendrons dominating the undergrowth. Ignore a turning marked Boathouse Trail and keep straight on the road. This section is part of the Kerry Way long-distance footpath. Walk ahead through an iron gate, and stay on the road across a more open section of ground. This is the bottom end of Lough Leane, flat meadowland picturesquely studded with old pine trees. Ahead are the wooded slopes of Torc Mountain, and to the left, beyond a fence, is the footpath which leads to the Torc Waterfall.

❷ Torc Waterfall drops 18m (60ft) and a path climbs up beside it. From the top there's a good view over Macgillycuddy's Reeks, the mountains to the west.

Where the road meets the trees, veer right onto a footpath which leads up over an old stone bridge. Stay with this gravel path as it bears right of a wooden gateway and climbs uphill, leaving a house to your left. For some distance this path runs parallel to the road above, with good views between the trees to the lower end of the lake. The path ends unceremoniously at the N71 road. Turn right and walk along the side of the road, high above the edge of the lake. After about 1.5km (1 mile) bear right onto an unsigned road, across a parking space. The narrow tarmac road is signed to the Meeting of the Waters and Dinis Cottage, and leads quickly downhill to the level of the lake again.

❸ At the Meeting of the Waters, a noted beauty spot, Lough Leane, Middle Muckross Lake and a river come together in a picturesque setting with abundant trees and shrubs.

The undulating road now goes through open woodland, with views to the left of Purple Mountain 757m (2,483ft), Tomies Mountain 735m (2,411ft) and Shehy Mountain 571m (1,873ft), to reach lake level again at Bog Bay. Cross a wooden bridge, where part of the river that drains from an upper lake runs into this lower one. Pass Dinis Cottage (no public access) on the left. After a reed bed on your left, the next lake, Lough Leane, starts to appear. Continue over the arched Brickeen Bridge, where the waters of the two lakes form a steady current.

❹ The views of Lough Leane get better and better as you go along, framed by trees and with a series of coves.

After about 1.5km (1 mile), take a rough track off to your left, by a signpost for Dinis Cottage. (If you prefer to avoid this path, which is muddy after rain and includes a short scramble up a bank, stay on the tarmac.) This leads through the beech and oak woods. Note a number 14 by the path, and soon after a number 15. The path turns inland and rises sharply to meet a metal field gate. Turn right before the gate (there's a white arrow), and follow the grassy path around the edge of the field, keeping the fence to your left. Pass a number 16 and continue. The track descends, and there are views through the trees to water on your right—not the big lake, but a little secret one, the Doo Lough.

❺ Doo Lough is hidden away among the trees and offers a tranquil place to stop for a while.

Continue beside a stream, and scramble up a short bank. At a metal field gate on the left, turn right down the stony track, and follow it to the road. Turn left and go through an ancient gateway, then through an open pole-gate, and soon you will see a house on your left. At the junction ahead, keep to the right, passing a pink cottage on your left. A sign points the way to Muckross House (400m/436 yards). At a crossing of tracks, turn right and walk towards Muckross House. In front of the house, bear left through the jaunting-car parking area and retrace your steps back up the path to where you started.

WHERE TO EAT

Muckross Visitor Centre
Tel 064 31440
The bright, modern Garden Restaurant at the Muckross Visitor Centre serves coffee, teas and lunches.
Open all year

PLACES TO VISIT

Muckross Estate ▷ 121.

6. WALK

AROUND KEEM BAY, ACHILL ISLAND

County Mayo is rugged, mountainous and breathtakingly beautiful. This walk, set around Keem Bay at the western end of Achill Island, starts with a short, stiff climb, negotiable by anyone reasonably fit and wearing shoes with grip in the soles. The climb gets you high up on the cliffs, with spectacular views all around. The return passes an abandoned village, the ruin of a house once owned by Ireland's most notorious landlord, and the poignant Mass Rock.

THE WALK

Distance: 8km (5 miles)
Allow: 3 hours
Total ascent: 374m (1,227ft)
Start/end at: Keem Bay
1:50,000 OSI Discovery Series, map 30
Grid reference 056 304
Parking: Keem Bay parking area

HOW TO GET THERE

Keem Bay is at the western end of the R319 from Achill Sound.

★ The walk starts from the south side of the beach.

❶ **Keem Strand lies in a deep green-sided bay overlooked by Croaghaun (664m/2,178ft), a mountain of quartzite. Amethysts have been found in this southern flank of Croaghaun, and if you're exceptionally sharp-eyed (and lucky) you may spot one on the beach.**

From the beach, follow the ridge of an old boundary wall as it rises steeply 200m (655ft) up to the ruined watchtower on the summit of Moyteoge Head. After this climb, the worst is already behind you!

❷ **The watchtower on the summit of Moyteoge Head, now in ruins, was constructed up here during World World II to give observers a bird's-eye view of the movement of shipping off the Mayo coast. The views from Moyteoge Head more than justify the climb up from Keem Strand. Northeast stands the bulk of Croaghaun, with huge cliffs falling from its seaward shoulder, and the cap of Slievemore (672m/2,204ft) to the east. Turning southward the view opens out along the mighty Minaun Cliffs, with the Nephin Beg Mountains standing along the skyline beyond, round to Clew Bay, the cone of Croagh Patrick, the sleeping otter hump of Clare Island, and the low-lying shapes of the islands of Inishturk, Inishbofin and Inishshark out to sea.**

When you have gazed your fill, bear right (northwest) along the clifftop track which rises and falls for 1.5km (1 mile) until it climbs to the top of Benmore (332m/1,090ft), the summit of the cliff ridge and the highest point of this walk. Continue along the cliffs until you are nearly level with the landward end of Achill Head.

❸ **From here there is a wonderful view down to your left over Achill Head, a narrow promontory shaped like a dinosaur's back, whose steep, rocky flanks project at a sharp right-angle into the sea from the cliffs of Benmore. The view to the right is memorable, too, as the great cliffs behind Croaghaun come into view.**

Now turn right and make a steep descent from the clifftops, aiming for the ruins of Bunowna booley village, 150m (490ft) in the valley below.

❹ **Bunowna was one of the 'booley villages': In the rural Ireland of the past, the young men and women would herd the cattle into the hills in spring and look after them all summer, milking them and making butter and cheese, in special seasonal settlements known as booley villages, a name derived from the Irish word for milk. Along the banks of the stream in the valley below Benmore you can make out the shapes of the 17 roughly built, circular stone houses and the cattle pens of long-abandoned Bunowna booley village.**

Cross the stream and turn back right along its east bank towards Keem Bay, picking your way carefully through peat and boggy parts, until after 1.5km (1 mile) you reach the ruin of Captain Boycott's house.

❺ **Captain Charles Boycott gained his notoriety at Ballinrobe on the mainland in the 1870s, when his unreasonable overcharging of rents led to his social ostracism and the withholding of his tenants' labour and rent—the famous 'boycott' that immortalized his name. But it was here at Keem in 1857 that he first leased land. The substantial house he built was later burned, and now stands as a gloomy ruin.**

Just beyond the house you'll pass a large altar, built on the site of a Mass Rock.

❻ **During the 18th century, when the Penal Laws outlawed Catholic practices, it was at isolated open-air sites such as this that Mass was celebrated.**

Walk down from the altar to Keem Bay parking area.

WHERE TO EAT

Buy picnic materials from Lavelle's Foodstore (tel 098 43107) in Dooagh, 5km (3 miles) from Keem; or eat at Dooagh's pub, which is called simply 'The Pub' (tel 098 43109).

PLACES TO VISIT

Bunowna booley village
Open access
Free

Captain Boycott's house (ruin)
Open access
Free

Mass Rock
Open access
Free

OUT AND ABOUT

7. WALK

ARIGNA AND THE MINER'S WAY

Few people associate the gritty, grimy business of coal mining with rural Ireland but Arigna on the shores of Lough Allen was until recently the hub of the small Irish coal industry. This walk, much of it waymarked as 'The Miner's Way', passes through some of the now greened-over pit sites, but there's nothing grimly industrial about it, as you cross moorland, and pass ancient sauna houses and a prehistoric cairn. But there is a proper mine to explore!

THE WALK

Distance: 8km (5 miles)
Allow: 3 hours
Total ascent: 150m (490ft)
Start/end at: The Miner's Bar, Derreenavoggy Bridge, Arigna
1:50,000 OSI Discovery Series, map 26
Grid reference 193 314
Parking: By the Miner's Bar

HOW TO GET THERE

Arigna is signposted from the R280 Drumshanbo–Drumkeeran road just north of the junction with the R285 Keadew road, 4km (2.5 miles) from Drumshanbo.

★ The Miner's Bar is adorned outside and inside with murals and photographs depicting the coal and iron-mining industries that were the lifeblood of Arigna and its surrounding area until the last coal mine closed in 1990. There's almost certain to be an ex-miner to chat to in the bar.

From the Miner's Bar bear right up the hill. On your left is the factory of Arigna Fuels Ltd.

❶ Arigna Fuels produces coal briquettes, Arigna's sole connection with the mining trade these days.

Just past the factory a brown 'Arigna Mining Experience' sign points left up the road, but keep straight ahead here along a narrow lane which in 275m (300 yards) leads to a crossroads. Keep ahead up the hill in front of you for 0.75km (0.5 miles) to pass a lane on your right. In another 92m (100 yards) look over the hedge on the right to see a pair of sweathouses built into the bank.

❷ From early times, until modern medicine made them redundant, sweathouses were used to treat many ailments from insanity to rheumatism. Two or more adults were packed inside the tiny subterranean chambers, already preheated. The door was sealed and the sufferers left to sweat it out, before being extracted and plunged into an ice-cold stream.

The Miner's Bar is at the starting point of the Miner's Way

In another 184m (200 yards) a 'Miner's Way' fingerpost on the left points you to the right up stone steps, over a stile and on up a steep, narrow sunken path. At the top a right turn (arrow) leads past another fine sweathouse. Continue following marker posts and yellow blobs on rocks; then turn left again over a stile onto a green path over stony moorland. In 0.5 km (0.25 miles) a rough sign 'Mega Tomb' points left to a big cairn on the skyline of Kilronan Mountain.

❸ This cairn may well hide an early Stone Age grave. From it you have stunning views, east over Lough Allen to the long humpback shape of Slieve Anierin (585m/1,920ft), highest point on the Iron Mountains, named for the iron ore that was mined there, and west over the twin loughs of Meelagh and Skean.

Return by turning left along the main track. In 0.5km (0.25 miles) a yellow arrow points right (northeast) along a path making straight for Lough Allen. On the edge of the escarpment the path swings left, marked by yellow arrows, and goes over stiles and through gates. In 0.75km (0.5 miles) you reach a 3-finger 'Miner's Way' post. 'Arigna' points downhill; don't follow this, but continue ahead, now northwest, for 1km (0.6 miles) through old colliery sites, now green and grassy. Pass a curlicued cast-iron bracket stamped 'Pooley & Son, Birmingham'; cross the stile after this, and in 18m (20 yards) turn right downhill, following yellow arrows to the road. Turn right toward Arigna. In 1.25km (0.75 miles) turn right up a road to the Arigna Mining Experience.

❹ After you have visited the Arigna Mining Experience, an ex-miner will take you on an underground tour through the damp, cramped workings—an object lesson in how men can survive the toughest of jobs.

Back on the lane below Arigna Mining Experience, turn right. In 0.4km (0.25 miles) bear left down a lane to return to the Miner's Bar.

WHERE TO EAT

The Miner's Bar offers good hot food; there's also a café at the Arigna Mining Experience.

PLACES TO VISIT

The Miner's Bar, Arigna
Tel 071 964 6007
Daily 9.30am–11.30pm

Sweathouses at Crosshill
Open access Free

Kilronan Mountain cairn
Signed 'Mega Tomb' off the track on Kilronan Mountain
Open access Free

Arigna Mining Experience
Tel 071 964 6466
Apr–end Sep daily €8, child €6

8. WALK

GLENVEAGH NATIONAL PARK

After more than a century of being managed as a sporting estate, Glenveagh National Park was acquired by the Irish nation in the 1970s and '80s. Its mountains and loughs retain something of the atmosphere of a carefully preserved private demesne. This is a walk of contrasts, from pine forests and wild moorland to the shores of Lough Beagh and the immaculately maintained gardens round Glenveagh Castle.

The park's entrance sign

THE WALK

Distance: 8km (5 miles)
Allow: 2.5 hours
Start/end at: Glenveagh National Park Visitor Centre
1:50,000 OSI Discovery Series, map 6
Grid reference 204 423
Parking: Visitor Centre

HOW TO GET THERE

Signposted on the R251 Gweedore–Letterkenny road, 16km (10 miles) east of Dunlewy.

★ From the Visitor Centre, you set off for Glenveagh Castle by turning left along the tarmac drive, passing to the left of the National Park headquarters, then bending right between entrance gateposts of the castle. A pair of stone deer with real antlers stare mournfully at each other across the entrance. On your right the waters of Lough Beagh come into view, and the road runs right along the lough shore with fine views across to the Derryveagh Mountains. Follow the road for 2.5km (1.5 miles) to reach the gates to the castle grounds.

❶ The gardens of Glenveagh Castle were mostly laid out in the mid-20th century by American owner Henry McIlhenny, with a pleasing blend of native woodland and exotic trees, lawns and sunken dells, flower beds, an Italian terrace and a pretty little hedged kitchen garden.

Go into the gardens and follow the paths towards the castle.

❷ Glenveagh Castle was built of granite in Scottish baronial style in 1870–73 by one of the harshest of all Irish landlords, John Adair, to house himself and his new American wife, Cornelia. It was she who was responsible for introducing the rhododendron thickets that bloom brightly in spring around the castle. Tours of the interior show that the keep, so stark on the outside, conceals a comfortable Victorian country house, with drawing room, music room and oval bedrooms inside the castle tower.

Return along the lakeside road to the parking area once more. Opposite the entrance booth turn left between two boulders onto a path that descends through the trees. Go through a gate and follow the path through a wood of Scots pines. Emerging from the wood through a forest gate, you are greeted by a stunning view over open moorland and the waters of Lough Beagh to the mountains beyond.

❸ There is every chance here of sighting Glenveagh's red deer, the largest herd in Ireland. It was Cornelia Adair who introduced them to the estate, when she took over after John Adair's death in 1885 and established herself as a society hostess. Local people grew to like her as much as they had disliked her husband, a high-handed, arrogant landowner. The creation of a grand estate was more important to him than the well-being of his tenants, and he had notoriously evicted 244 of them at the end of the harsh winter of 1861 so that he could incorporate their land.

Go through the gate and 27m (30 yards) on, turn left along a path. In another 92m (100 yards) it forks; don't take the rough track that climbs straight ahead, but bear right along the lower, grassy track into a sedgy hollow.

❹ This part of the walk follows one of the trails detailed in Glenveagh National Park Visitors' Guide, available from the Visitor Centre. Numbered posts direct your attention to examples of blanket bog, broad-leaved woodland and other good habitat for wildlife of all sorts.

The gravel path steepens to climb through a little wood and run east across the moor to meet a fence. Bear right along the fence; then, halfway to the trees ahead, turn left through a deer gate in the fence to reach a road, where you turn right to return to the Visitor Centre parking area.

WHERE TO EAT

Glenveagh National Park (tel 074 913 7090) has a tea room at the castle (open Easter and Jun–end Sep) and a restaurant at the Visitor Centre (open mid-Mar to early Nov)

PLACES TO VISIT

National Park Visitor Centre
Tel 074 913 7090
Mid-Mar to mid-Nov, daily 10–5
Free

Glenveagh Castle and Gardens
Tel 074 91 37262/37090
Castle: mid-Mar to early Nov daily 10–6.30; castle interior by tour only
Tour: adult €2.75, child (over 6) €1.25, family €7

The castle and gardens are in a stunning location (right). Rocky Poison Valley (below)

GRAND CANAL, TULLAMORE

The Grand Canal was a typically ambitious Georgian idea—a great water highway across the waist of Ireland, connecting the Irish Sea and the Atlantic Ocean. Refurbished for pleasure cruising, the canal now has a new lease of life and its towpath gives mile after mile of level walking through the green farming country and the great bogs of the Midlands. This stroll into the countryside west of Tullamore shows you a couple of fine old castles, some handsome canal architecture, and waterside wildlife in peaceful rural surroundings.

THE WALK

Distance: 8km (5 miles)
Allow: 2 hours
Start/end at: Tullamore Dew Heritage Centre
1:50,000 OSI Discovery Series, map 48
Grid reference 233 225
Parking: Tullamore Dew Heritage Centre

HOW TO GET THERE

Signposted from William Street, Tullamore's main street, just south of Kilbeggan Bridge.

★ The Tullamore Dew Heritage Centre is a hands-on exhibition housed in the distillery's handsome Victorian bonded warehouse. Here you can shovel barley and fill bottles before a tasting session, and also learn about the town. From the early 19th century onwards, Tullamore was famous for producing fine whiskey, notably Tullamore Dew, and also for Irish Mist, a smooth liqueur blend of whiskey, honey and herbs. These days, however, both Dew and Mist are made elsewhere. The Heritage Centre also contains an exhibition on how Tullamore flourished when the Grand Canal reached the town from Dublin in 1798. Eastwards, Tullamore was linked to the capital, and on via the Irish Sea to the ports and markets of the British mainland; westwards to the River Shannon and the Atlantic trade.

Leave the Tullamore Dew Heritage Centre and turn west along the quay and follow the Grand Canal towpath as it heads out of town. You pass Lock 27 and cross the next bridge, Cox's Bridge, to the north bank of the canal. A brown 'Grand Canal Way' fingerpost points you to the left down Rahan Way. Soon the canal passes under a road bridge and then a rail bridge, before emerging round a right bend into

A lock gate on the Grand Canal

open countryside. On your right rises the gaunt ruin of Srah Castle (not open to the public).

❶ Srah Castle was built in 1588 by John Briscoe, 'an officer of rank and merit who served the Crown in the wars of Queen Elizabeth'. Local stories say that the garrison was armed with a blunderbuss so heavy that one man could hardly lift it. That didn't deter the Irish chief O'Neill from arriving in force at Srah to challenge the aged Briscoe. The English officer recognized O'Neill, which caused the Irishman to spare him. When O'Neill's band rode away, they took with them Briscoe's daughter Eleanor, tied on horseback to one of the men, and she was subsequently forcibly married to O'Neill's nephew Hugh McManus.

Continue along the towpath for 2km (1.25 miles), passing Srah Bridge, until you meet a road which you follow for 0.5km (0.25 miles) to reach the ruin of St. Brigid's Church on the right.

❷ All that is left of St. Brigid's Church, founded in the late eighth or early ninth century, are two ivy-hung gables and a mass of higgledy-piggledy gravestones. It was destroyed in the late 17th or early 18th century at the start of the Penal era, when Catholics could no longer use their churches but had to celebrate the outlawed Mass at secret locations. During the Great Famine of 1845–49 the churchyard was still in use to bury the dead.

Continue past Lock 29 to Ballycowan Bridge, beyond which stands the ruin of Ballycowan Castle (not open to the public).

❸ Tall chimneys and mullioned windows are the most notable features of Ballycowan Castle, a four-floor fortified house built in 1626 by Sir Jasper Herbert on the site of a former stronghold of the O'Melaghlin clan.

Cross Ballycowan Bridge and turn left along the south bank of the Grand Canal for the 4km (2.5-mile) walk back to Tullamore.

WHERE TO EAT

Bridge House Inn
Bridge Street, Tullamore
Tel 0506 21704
Excellent hot lunches.

Tullamore Dew Heritage Centre (▷ below) has a coffee shop, restaurant and pub.

PLACES TO VISIT

Tullamore Dew Heritage Centre
Bury Quay, Tullamore
Tel 0506 25015
May–end Sep Mon–Sat 9–6, Sun noon–5; Oct–end Apr Mon–Sat 10–5, Sun noon–5 Tour and tasting: adult €5, child (4–18) €3.20

St. Brigid's Church
Kilbride, north bank of canal 0.75km (0.5 miles) east of Ballycowan Bridge
Open access Free

TOURIST INFORMATION

Tullamore
Bury Quay, Tullamore
Tel 0506 52617

10. WALK

CLIFFS OF MAGHO AND LOWER LOUGH ERNE

An opportunity to enjoy one of the very best views in Ireland, and to earn your enjoyment too! There's a stiff climb to start with, helped by handily placed flights of steps, from the south shore of Lower Lough Erne to the rim of the Cliffs of Magho and that amazing view. Then you make a damp detour (wear strong shoes or boots) over heather moorland and through pine woods to a secret lake, before returning by way of forest roads and the cliffs once more.

Sunrise at Lough Erne

THE WALK

Distance: 4.5km (2.5 miles)
Allow: 2 hours
Total ascent: 250m (820ft)
Start/end at: Car parking area on the A46 Enniskillen–Belleek road, 13km (8 miles) east of Belleek.
1:50,000 OSNI Discoverer Series, map 17
Grid reference 206 358

★ From the parking area follow the 'viewpoint' sign into the wood on a path that soon steepens and begins to zigzag up through the trees by flights of steps.

❶ **In the damp woods grow hart's tongue and broad buckler ferns, bracken, horsetails, mosses and pale green lichens that only flourish where the air is unpolluted.**

It's a short, steep climb. Near the top pass a little well, and emerge at a parking place where you can stop and admire the view.

❷ **Ireland is a country packed full of good views, but this is among the best. The waters of Lower Lough Erne stretch out to the north, with tumbled green country beyond. In the distance rise the Blue Stack Mountains of County Donegal, and beyond those, some 65km (40 miles) away, the pale cone of Mount Errigal (▷ 145). To the northeast roll the round-backed Sperrin Hills of County Tyrone, while out to the west lie the waters of Donegal Bay. Some 55km (34 miles) away the mighty cliffs of Slieve League rise above the bay to the north, and to the southeast in County Sligo the unmistakable ship's-prow shape of Benbulbin, W. B. Yeats's favourite mountain, stands out 526m (1,726ft) tall.**

After gazing your fill, turn right (west) along the cliff-edge path for 0.5km (0.25 miles) until you reach a wooden fence guarding the drop on your right. Beside the sixth upright of this fence, bear inland (south) on a faint path to a double post with yellow arrows, and follow the arrows in the same direction across moorland and up a gap between blocks of coniferous woodland.

❸ **You are now in Lough Navar Forest, with blocks of conifers interspersed with heather moorland and patches of sphagnum moss. The moors support a great variety of wildlife, including red deer, feral goats, hares, peregrines, hen harriers and owls; crossbills and woodcock are among less common woodland birds.**

Reaching little Finnauan Lough, bear right along its bank; then turn left at a post with a yellow arrow at the west end of the lake, walking south towards the trees.

❹ **Try jumping up and down here, and you can feel the earth move! You are walking on a bog of spagnum moss which holds many times its own weight of water. Its floating surface is knitted together by marsh cinquefoil roots.**

Enter the trees beside a post whose yellow arrow points left. Follow it to the left inside the fringe of the trees on a path that soon bears right and emerges from the trees. Head south on this narrow path between more blocks of trees to a forest road and turn left for 92m (100 yards), then left again on another forest road which leads you back to the viewpoint parking area on the Cliffs of Magho.

❺ **Two war memorial stones stand at the side of the car parking place: One remembers the crew of a Sunderland flying boat that sank in Lough Erne in November 1943 with the loss of three lives; the other is dedicated to the eight crewmen who died when their Catalina crashed at Lough Anlaban a year later.**

Follow the steep path back down to the lower parking area.

WHERE TO EAT

There are no facilities on the walk itself. In Enniskillen, stock up for a picnic at Forthill Fine Foods delicatessen in Forthill Street. After the walk, enjoy tea and cakes in Johnson's Jolly Sandwich Bar at 3 Darling Street, or Maud's on Shore Road.

PLACES TO VISIT

Cliffs of Magho viewpoint
229m (750ft) above and due south of parking area on the A46
Open access; Free

OUT AND ABOUT

WICKLOW MOUNTAINS NATIONAL PARK

From Dublin, escape to the mountains, where rebels and saints once hid away, and where today hydroelectric and water supply schemes have created a new, but still beautiful landscape.

THE DRIVE

Distance: 113km (70 miles)
Allow: 4 hours
Start/end at: Dublin

★ Leave Dublin on the N11, which becomes the M11 briefly on the edge of Bray. As the N11 again it reaches Kilmacanoge under the Great Sugar Loaf, where you turn off on the R755.

1 **Great Sugar Loaf and its companion Little Sugar Loaf look like children's drawings of volcanoes, but they are not volcanic. Their summits are very hard quartzite, left standing when the surrounding rocks were weathered away by water, wind and glacier. You can see the same rocks in the Rocky Valley, which follows a fault line. It's an energetic scramble to the summit of Great Sugar Loaf, the last part requiring hands as well as feet. Its relatively low elevation of 501m (1,644ft) doesn't qualify it as a proper mountain, but its isolated position means the views on a clear day are unsurpassed on this coastline.**

As you ascend the Rocky Valley, bear right on the R760 through Ballybawn, then turn left on a minor road signposted to Roundwood. Follow this road as it skirts the hillside, ignoring any turnings until you reach a crossroads with the R759. Turn right here and stay with this spectacular mountain road as it ascends to Sally Gap. Lough Tay appears far below you on the left.

2 **Sally Gap breaks the ridge of the Wicklow Mountains. After the failed rising of 1798, many rebels fled to the hills, and succeeded in evading capture for several years. The British army realized it would have to pacify the Wicklow Mountains so built a road from Rathfarnham on the edge of Dublin, winding for 69km (43 miles) through the mountains to Aghavannagh. It took nine years to complete, with barracks at Glencree, Laragh, Drungoff and Aghavannagh. By the 1830s many of these had been abandoned, but the road became a miners' route. Not surfaced properly until the 1950s, it's now a popular drive.**

At Sally Gap, turn left again on to the R115, and follow the winding high-level Military Road across the heather moors and down Glenmacnass into Laragh. Turn right in the village, then right again to enter Glendasan on the R756.

3 **Glendasan, which stretches due west of Laragh, was once an important mining area. Lead was discovered by Thomas Weaver, an engineer working on the Military Road. Mining began in 1809 and was moderately productive throughout the century, extending workings into the next valley of Glendalough. Work ceased after World War I but flourished again briefly in the mid-1950s, only to stop for good in 1963.**

Continue on the R756. After 1.6km (1 mile) turn left to visit Glendalough.

4 **St. Kevin established a monastic settlement at Glendalough, the valley of the two loughs, in the sixth century. The ruins of his cathedral church, round tower and other buildings lie scattered around this lovely mountain valley. There is a Visitor Centre at the entrance to the main monastic site, explaining the context of the valley, its history and wildlife.**

There is no way out of this valley so you will have to return to the R756 to carry on. From the Glendalough road end, turn left and continue up Glendasan. The road takes you high up into the mountains again, to the Wicklow Gap, before dropping down into the remote valley of the King's River.

5 **The Wicklow Gap, a high pass through the Wicklow Mountains, was once used by pilgrims on their way to Glendalough. The mountains stretch high either side of the road, Tonelagee (817m/2,680ft) to the north and Camaderry (698m/2,290ft) to the south. Hidden away in the hills here, Lough Nahanagan is supposed to be inhabited by a monster. If it's still there it is very tolerant; the corrie lough has been converted into a reservoir for a pumped-storage hydroelectric scheme deep inside the mountain.**

About 9.6km (6 miles) from the Wicklow Gap summit, take the right turn towards Valleymount and Blessington on the R758. Two causeways and bridges carry you over the waters of the Pollaphuca Reservoir.

6 **This three pronged lake (sometimes known as the Blessington Lakes) was created in 1940, by the building of the Pollaphuca Dam across the Liffey Gorge near Ballymore Eustace. It takes its name from a dramatic waterfall, now somewhat reduced, the hiding place of the mischievous water sprite Pooka. Despite its artificial origins, the lake is now an important and beautiful haven for wildlife, and a circuit of its perimeter makes a popular drive. The forest planting began in 1959 and is mostly sitka spruce and Japanese larch for commercial felling.**

Geologists have shown that there was a large glacial lake here until about 10,000 years ago, which perhaps accounts for the modern lake's natural feel.

Continue north on the R758. At the T-junction on the N81, turn right to return to Dublin.

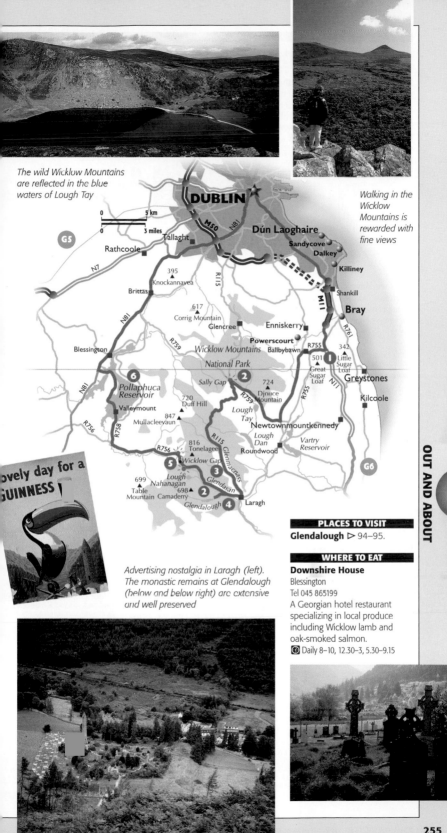

The wild Wicklow Mountains are reflected in the blue waters of Lough Tay

Walking in the Wicklow Mountains is rewarded with fine views

Advertising nostalgia in Laragh (left). The monastic remains at Glendalough (below and below right) are extensive and well preserved

PLACES TO VISIT

Glendalough ▷ 94–95.

WHERE TO EAT

Downshire House
Blessington
Tel 045 865199
A Georgian hotel restaurant specializing in local produce including Wicklow lamb and oak-smoked salmon.
Daily 8–10, 12.30–3, 5.30–9.15

THE BOYNE VALLEY

Driving out from Dublin on the M1 you are soon in the rolling countryside of 'Royal Meath'. Here you'll find the seat of the High Kings of Ireland, a 5,000-year-old passage tombs to rival the pyramids, superb Norman castles and a 17th-century battlefield site that can still raise tempers in modern Ireland.

THE DRIVE

Distance: 162km (100 miles)
Allow: One day
Start/end at: Dublin

★ Leave central Dublin on the N1, then join the M1, heading north for about 32km (20 miles). Leave the M1 at the intersection for Drogheda (south) before the start of the toll section. Follow the R132 signs into the town.

❶ As you drive in, the Millmount, with its Martello tower, is up to your left and the town's central area is over the bridge to your right.

Don't drive into the town, but stay on the R132 as it crosses the Boyne, then turn left on the N51. Cross the motorway and in about 1km (0.5 miles) turn left to cross over the River Boyne by the battlefield observation area.

❷ The Battle of the Boyne has gained iconic status in modern Irish history. In 1690 the Protestant army led by William III defeated the Catholics under James II. It wasn't the decisive battle of the campaign but the presence of the two monarchs on the battlefield that gave it extra resonance.

Pass the parking area for battlefield tours and bear right to Donore. Drive through the village and turn right following the signposts for Brú na Bóinne.

❸ Brú na Bóinne (Palace of the Boyne) is the collective name given to over 50 important archaeological sites. Of these the most impressive are the passage tombs of Dowth, Knowth and Newgrange. These 5,000-year-old structures are the core of a UNESCO World Heritage Site. Dowth's mound is visible across the valley to your right, followed by the Visitor Centre and the distinctive Newgrange. Lastly the Knowth site comes into view.

Sheep now graze where Ireland's High Kings once held court

Continue on this road until you meet the N2. Turn right into Slane.

❹ The Hill of Slane stands to the north of the village, on a side road from the N2. The legend goes that St. Patrick lit a symbolic fire here to announce the arrival of Christianity in Ireland to the pagan Kings of Tara, whose ceremonial site is visible to the south. You can see the remains of a medieval monastery on the hill. Slane is better known today for its huge rock concerts; U2 recorded the *Joshua Tree* album at Slane Castle.

At the crossroads in Slane turn left along the N51 to Navan. Leave Navan on the N3 and 5.5km (3.5 miles) after crossing the Boyne again, turn right on a minor road signed to Tara.

❺ The Hill of Tara was the traditional coronation place of the High Kings of Ireland. The site is mostly grassed-over earthworks, but the views are magnificent and there is a small seasonal Visitor Centre and a café.

When you get to the ancient site, turn right, in front of the parking area, and head down the hill. Turn left at the next two intersections, then take a right turn down a winding minor road. At a T-junction, turn left and then right at the Bective Inn. Cross the bridge and Bective Abbey is across the fields to your right.

❻ Bective Abbey, a Cistercian establishment, was founded in 1147 and dissolved in 1536, later becoming a stately home before being abandoned in the 18th century.

Continue to the intersection with the R161 and turn left towards Trim. Turn left as you approach the first housing estate, signed 'Newtown'. A lane takes you down to the Boyne again. The Cathedral of SS. Peter and Paul is on your right and the Hospital ruins are across the ancient bridge on your left. Cross the bridge and turn right, into Trim.

❼ Trim is best-known for its superb Anglo-Norman castle, one of the biggest and best preserved in Ireland. The nave and chancel survive from the 13th-century cathedral of SS. Peter and Paul, and across the river the ruins of the Hospital of St. John the Baptist date from a similar time. The hospital was established by Simon de Rochfort for the Crusader Order of Crutched Friars. Facing the castle, the Yellow Steeple is all that remains of St. Mary's Abbey.

Leave Trim on the R158 and drive through Summerhill to Kilcock and pick up the R148 on the other side, which follows the Royal Canal into Maynooth.

❽ Maynooth is dominated by its 13th-century castle, home of the Kildare FitzGeralds. From here the family became one of the most powerful in Ireland and Garret Mór, the Great Earl of Kildare, governed the whole country for the English Crown at the end of the 15th century. Today the castle is cared for by the state.

From Maynooth you can take the M4 back into Dublin.

The battle that had a lasting impact is commemorated by a mural on this cottage wall near Drogheda

St. Patrick's College in Maynooth

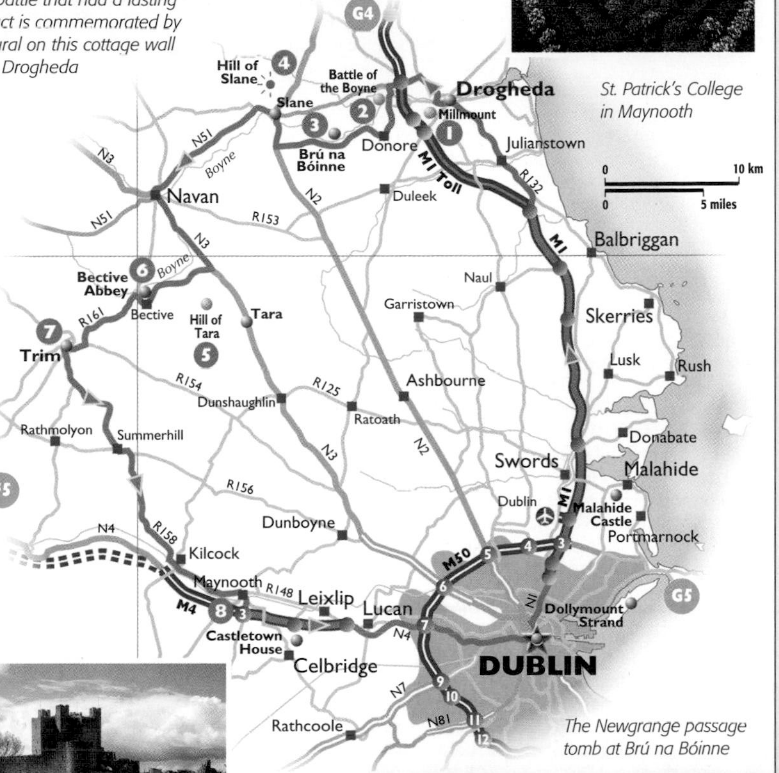

The Newgrange passage tomb at Brú na Bóinne

Trim Castle, by the River Boyne

PLACES TO VISIT

Millmount ▷ 89.

Brú na Bóinne ▷ 90–93.

Bective Abbey ▷ 88.

Maynooth Castle
Tel 01 628 6744
Jun–end Sep Mon–Fri 10–6, Sat, Sun, public holidays 1–6; Oct Sun, public holidays 1–5
Adult €1.50, child (6–18) €0.75

WHERE TO EAT

Navan, Trim and Maynooth are all well supplied with pubs and eateries. The Ardboyne Hotel is a good place to eat:

Ardboyne Hotel
Dublin Road, Navan
Tel 046 902 3119

This ancient inscribed stone is a feature of the Newgrange tomb

THE BLACKWATER VALLEY

From Youghal, this loop drive starts inland up the Blackwater River valley, goes through the little town of Lismore and up, over moorland, to the high point of the Vee. You descend via Clonmel to Dungarvan and back along the coast.

THE DRIVE

Distance: 156km (97 miles)
Allow: One day
Start/end at: Tourist Office, Market Square, Youghal

★ From the tourist office in Youghal, head north through the town along North Main Street.

Youghal is a thriving port and resort. Its historical significance is shown by the massive town walls, still standing in places.

At a roundabout (traffic circle) as you leave the town go straight on, signed N25 and Rosslare. The Blackwater Estuary is to the right.

❶ The Blackwater Estuary provides feeding grounds for waders, wildfowl and marsh birds. Look for little egrets, widgeon and reed buntings in the marshy reserve of Foxhole.

At the next roundabout turn right onto the N25 for Rosslare. After about 1.5km (1 mile) take the next turning left onto a minor road, by the sign for the River Blackwater. Follow this narrow road through woodland, with the river on your right. After 3km (2 miles), you pass the gateway to Ballynatray House and Demesne.

❷ The grounds of Ballynatray House shelter the ruins of the 13th-century Molana Abbey.

Continue on this road, and at an unsigned fork bear right uphill between houses and through trees. At another unsigned intersection keep right. Where the road turns back on itself keep left, signed Scenic Route. The road climbs, with open farmland on the left, the Knockmealdown Mountains ahead. At Knockanore continue ahead downhill. After 0.75km (0.5 miles) you reach a T-junction where you turn right, again signed as a Scenic Route. Continue downhill, through two sharp bends, and after 2.5km (1.5 miles) turn right at a T-junction. In another 0.75km (0.5 miles) turn right, signed Lismore and Cappoquin, at a three-way intersection. Cross a bridge over the river. After a sharp left bend, the road runs beside the river again, with a forward view of mountains. At the next junction keep straight on for Lismore, and at the T-junction turn left to enter the town.

❸ Lismore Castle on its bluff above the river is an imposing 19th-century mock Tudor edifice, built around the remains of the 12th-century original.

In the town turn right downhill, passing the castle. Cross a bridge and take the R668, the second turning left, signed Clogheen. Follow this road as it ascends through woods and onto moorland. At a junction keep ahead, signed to the Vee. The parking area is 3km (2 miles) farther on.

❹ The Vee is a natural cleft between two hills, with views north over the patchwork plains of the Galtee Valley to the Galtee Mountains.

Follow the road downhill around two hairpin bends. Descend through woods, and after 7km (4.5 miles), on the edge of Clogheen, take the turning right, signed Newcastle. Drive east across farmland and go through Goaten Bridge village. Continue ahead beside the River Tar. After 4km (2.5 miles) keep left, signed Clonmel, and pass through Newcastle village. Keep ahead, signed Dungarvan. Cross the Tar and at a crossroads turn left, signed Clonmel. Soon afterwards you reach a major intersection and turn left onto the R671. Go through Kilmanahan and at the T-junction turn right. After half a mile reach a roundabout. Turn left here to explore Clonmel.

❺ On the northern bank of the River Suir, Clonmel was a stronghold of the important Butler family, the Earls and Dukes of Ormond.

Leaving Clonmel turn right down an unsigned road. At a junction follow the road keeping the River Suir on your left. At a roundabout turn right onto an unsigned road and go past a sports club, then a golf club. Pass a waterfall at a left bend, and 0.75km (0.5 miles) later turn sharp right onto a minor road, signed Hanora's Cottage, that turns back on itself uphill. After a hairpin bend look for a viewpoint on the left. Cross a cattle grid and go over the high moorland tops. Descend through conifers, and at an intersection keep straight on. Continue down, cross a bridge and keep right on the main road through the Nire Valley. At the T-junction in Ballymacarbry turn left onto the R671. Keep straight ahead for Dungarvan on the R672, passing through horse country. Descend towards Dungarvan, to the bypass. Turn left onto the N72, and almost immediately keep straight on on the R672, signed Dungarvan. After 3km (2 miles), at a roundabout intersection with the N25, go straight over for Dungarvan.

❻ Dungarvan is a busy market town, with a big central square and a lovely sandy beach. The mudflats of the bay attract a variety of migrant wading birds in winter.

Leave Dungarvan on the N25, following signs to Cork. As you approach the top of the ridge pull in to the viewpoint on the left for a great view back along the coast. Still on the N25, you can see Knockadoon Head, with Capel Island off the end. After about 26.5km (16.5 miles) you will cross the Old Youghal Bridge, and stay on the N25. At the roundabout turn left to return to Youghal.

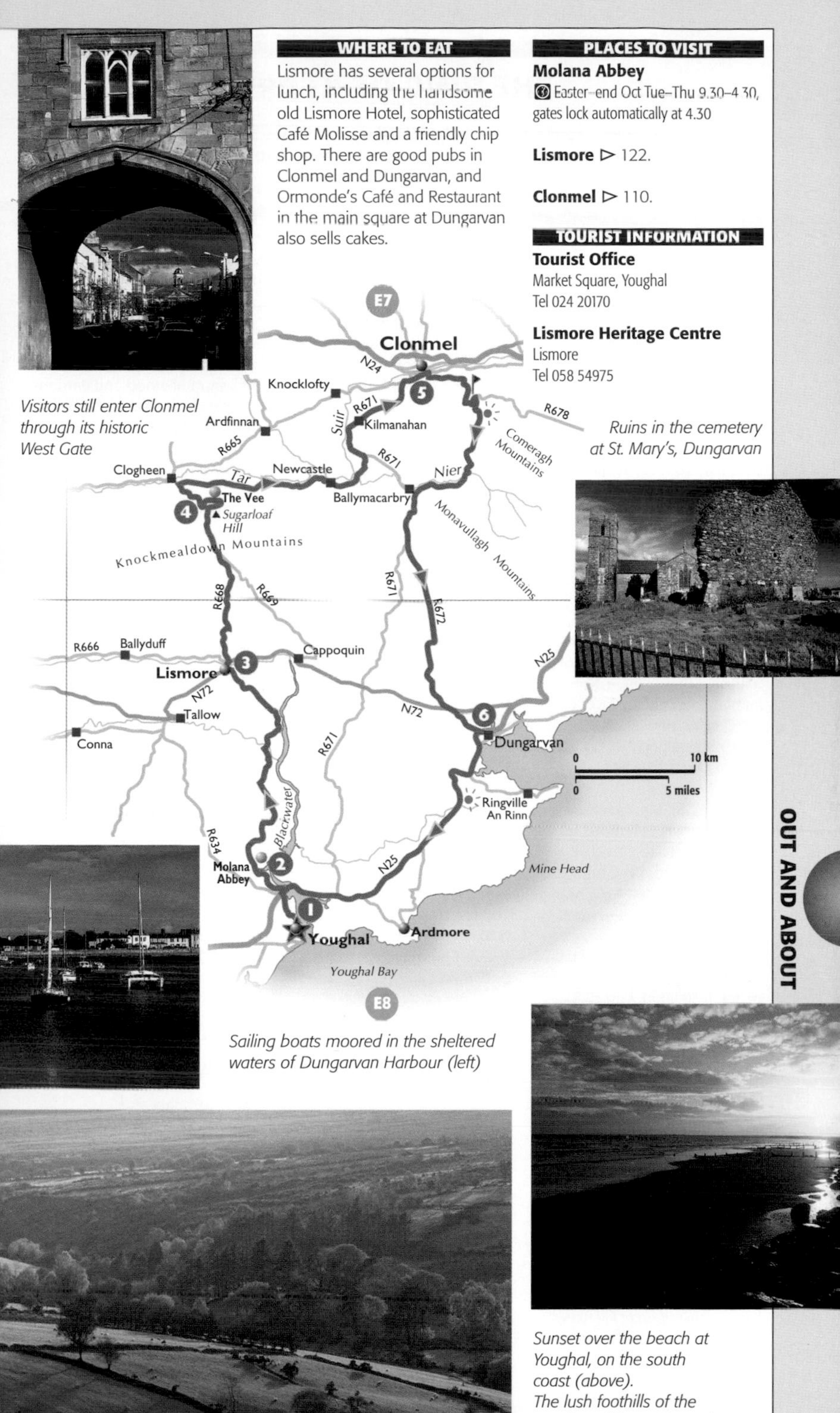

WHERE TO EAT

Lismore has several options for lunch, including the handsome old Lismore Hotel, sophisticated Café Molisse and a friendly chip shop. There are good pubs in Clonmel and Dungarvan, and Ormonde's Café and Restaurant in the main square at Dungarvan also sells cakes.

PLACES TO VISIT

Molana Abbey
Easter–end Oct Tue–Thu 9.30–4.30, gates lock automatically at 4.30

Lismore ▷ 122.

Clonmel ▷ 110.

TOURIST INFORMATION

Tourist Office
Market Square, Youghal
Tel 024 20170

Lismore Heritage Centre
Lismore
Tel 058 54975

Visitors still enter Clonmel through its historic West Gate

Ruins in the cemetery at St. Mary's, Dungarvan

Sailing boats moored in the sheltered waters of Dungarvan Harbour (left)

Sunset over the beach at Youghal, on the south coast (above).
The lush foothills of the Knockmealdown Mountains, astride the borders of counties Tipperary and Waterford (left)

THE RING OF KERRY

The most famous scenic drive in Ireland begins at Killarney and encircles the Iveragh Peninsula. Spectacular mountain scenery on one side contrasts with the unspoiled coastline on the other.

THE DRIVE

Distance: 214km (134 miles) plus diversions
Allow: 1–2 days
Start/end at: Killarney

★ Killarney is the foremost tourist town in western Ireland, mainly because it is a superb starting point for excursions to some famous landscapes.

Leave Killarney on the N72, signed Ring of Kerry, passing the cathedral on the right. As you leave the town, turn left at a roundabout, signed Dingle and Killorglin. Continue through Fossa, with the peaks of Macgillycuddy's Reeks to the left. Pass the turning to Kate Kearney's Cottage, with the Gap of Dunloe clearly visible to the south. Continue across farmland, beside the River Laune, to Killorglin. Turn left into the town and veer right at the bottom of the high street.

❶ Killorglin, a prosperous farming town, is famous for its August Puck Fair (▷ 219). Before you cross the bridge to the town, look left for a bronze statue of King Puck—a goat.

Leaving Killorglin, at the roundabout follow signs to Glenbeigh, on the N70. After 3km (2 miles), look for a sign right to Cromane beach—a sandspit that runs inland of Inch (▷ 118). Continue past a peat bog, with stacks of drying turfs. A haze of blue peat smoke heralds Kerry Bog Village on the right.

❷ Kerry Bog Village preserves a long-gone scene, a township of thatched 18th-century cottages.

Return to the N70 and after 3km (2 miles) enter Glenbeigh, perhaps diverting right to the glorious sands of Ross Behy beach. Continue on the N70, crossing narrow stone bridges, and after 8km (5 miles) there are viewing points with telescopes trained on the Dingle.

❸ The Dingle Peninsula is a dramatic sight. On its northern edge stands Mount Brandon, the second highest peak in Ireland. The large number of ancient stones on the Dingle, some from the early Christian period, indicate its importance in Ireland's early history.

Stay on the N70 above the pretty bay of Kells, go over a pass, then along the inlet to Cahersiveen.

❹ Cahersiveen is superbly set on the estuary of the Valencia River. Note the bronze memorial on the right as you enter the town depicting four monks in a boat. The Heritage Centre is a square keep with odd baronial towers and a crowstep gable, looking towards the harbour and the remains of Ballycarbery Castle.

Leave Cahersiveen on the N70, and after 3km (2 miles) look for the turning to Valencia Island, an excellent diversion from the Ring.

❺ The bridge to Valencia Island goes from Portmagee, 10.5km (6.5 miles) west of N70. The Skellig Experience Visitor Centre is just over the bridge on Valencia.

Return to the N70 and continue across the broad tip of the Iveragh peninsula. After 10.5km (6.5 miles) enter Waterville.

❻ Waterville, a seaside town, stands on Ballinskelligs Bay, with Lough Currane behind. Movie actor Charlie Chaplin (1889–1977) holidayed here for many years, and a memorial to him stands in the green park by the sea front.

Continue on the N70 over the high Commakesta Pass, with views to Deenish and Scariff islands, and the Beara Peninsula. Below are the sands of Derrynane Bay. The road winds down to Caherdaniel. Make a detour here to Derrynane.

❼ Follow signs to Derrynane House, passing an Ogham stone (▷ 27), to enter Derrynane National Historic Park. A small Georgian house with a castellated, slate-covered square tower is the focus of 120ha (296 acres) of beautiful woodland gardens on the shore. It was the home of Daniel O'Connell (1775–1847), the great political reformist.

Return to the main road and continue round the rugged point, passing prehistoric Stake Fort, and through Castle Cove to Sneem.

❽ The houses in Sneem are painted in rainbow shades. Look for the odd stone sculptures by the churchyard, and a memorial on the triangular village green to former French president, Charles de Gaulle.

Keep on the N70, signed Ring of Kerry. The road now follows the bank of the Kenmare River. After 17.5km (11 miles) a sign points to Blackwater Pier for a diversion onto the shore. Continue on a narrow bridge over the Blackwater River, and pass through Templenoe. On the outskirts of Kenmare, turn right on the N71 to visit the town.

❾ A compact and handsome old town, painted in rich, warm tones, Kenmare is famous for lacemaking. Learn more at the Heritage Centre in the Visitor Centre.

Leave Kenmare on the N71, signed to Killarney. This is a spectacular stretch of mountain road, passing over Moll's Gap, with views to the south side of the Gap of Dunloe. Ladies View is just one of the viewpoints in the Killarney National Park. Pass the turning to Muckross Estate and return to Killarney.

Jaunting cars are popular tourist transport around Killarney

Macgillycuddy's Reeks rise behind Killarney's Upper Lakes

Inch Strand is one of Ireland's most famous beaches (left)

Traditional-style cottages at the Kerry Bog Village (above)

WHERE TO STAY

Cahersiveen, Waterville and Caherdaniel have plenty of hotel and bed-and-breakfast accommodation. Valentia View guesthouse, Cahersiveen, is an old farmhouse overlooking Valencia Island (tel 066 972227).

Butler Arms Hotel
Waterville
Tel 066 94 74144
Apr–end Oct

WHERE TO EAT

Red Fox Inn by Kerry Bog Village promises snacks and Irish coffee; for chargrilled seafood, try QC's restaurant at 3 Main Street, Cahersiveen; the Bridge Bar in Portmagee serves crab; Sneem has several cafés, including the Riverside Coffee Shop.

TOURIST INFORMATION

Killarney
Beech Road, Killarney
Tel 064 31633

Kenmare
The Square, Kenmare
Tel 064 41233

PLACES TO VISIT

Killarney ▷ 120–121.

Dingle Peninsula ▷ 116–119.

Valencia Island ▷ 128.

Derrynane House
Caherdaniel
Tel 066 94 75113
House: May–end Sep Mon–Sat 9–6, Sun 11–7; Nov–Mar Sat, Sun 1–5; Apr, Oct Tue–Sun, 1–5. Gardens: all year

Heritage Centre
The Square, Kenmare
Tel 064 41233
Easter–end Sep

LOUGH CORRIB AND LOUGH MASK

This leisurely circuit of two of Ireland's most attractive large lakes is a beautiful expedition from Galway city on surprisingly unfrequented roads, up the eastern side of Lough Corrib by way of Ross Errilly Abbey to Cong, a handsome small town with another striking medieval abbey. Moving north, you pass from County Galway into County Mayo to circle Lough Mask. The return runs beside the untamed bogs of Iar-Connacht, down side roads close to the west shore of Lough Corrib, and back to Galway.

THE DRIVE

Distance: 200km (125 miles)
Allow: 5 hours
Start/end at: Galway city

★ Leave Galway city north along the N84 Headford and Ballinrobe road. Three kilometres (2 miles) north of the city you'll see on your right the tower of Ballindooley Castle.

❶ Ballindooley Castle, a fine, if grim, medieval castle, was a stronghold of the Burke clan. In a ruinous condition not so long ago, it has been restored and is now a private residence once more (no public access).

Continue north on the N84 to Cloonboo, where you turn left on a minor road for 8km (5 miles) to reach the ruin of Annaghdown Priory next to a graveyard ('Annaghdown Pier' sign) beside Lough Corrib.

❷ The ruins of medieval Annaghdown Priory are blunt, weathered and massive, contrasting the fine architecture you'll see later in the tour. St. Brendan the Navigator founded this nunnery, and it was here that his sister Brigid nursed him through his final illness to his death in AD577. The shell of 15th-century Annaghdown Cathedral, the size of a modest parish church, is adjacent; one of its windows is richly carved with animal heads, monsters, trees, flowers and shamrocks.

Return to the N84, where you turn left for 8km (5 miles) to Headford. Signs here point left along a minor road to Ross Errilly Abbey.

❸ Ross Errilly Abbey, a well-preserved Franciscan friary, consists of a tight cluster of plain, dignified 14th- and 15th-century buildings. Though the

Oughterard's Aughnanure Castle has suffered from river erosion

empty buildings stand in a lonely position out among the fields beside the Black River, the domestic details—bread ovens, vast fireplaces, water spouts, fuel chutes—summon up shades of the bustling monastic community that lived here. Note also the elaborately carved tomb of Hugh O'Flaherty under the east window of the church.

Turn left on the R334 for 6.5km (4 miles), crossing the county boundary from Galway into Mayo. At Cross bear left on the R346 for 5km (3 miles) to Cong.

❹ Cong's great abbey tells of the past importance of the town and is the main reason to stop here, but the town itself is a delightful place.

From Cong take the R345 Ballinrobe road for 4km (2.5 miles) to Neale, where you turn left on the R334 for 6.5km (4 miles) to Ballinrobe.

❺ The parish church in Ballinrobe has wonderful stained-glass windows by master-craftsman Harry Clarke (1889–1931). If you're here in late July, you'll see the town at its moment of annual glory during Ballinrobe Races, the archetype of all Irish country race meetings in their energy, fun and good humour.

Follow the N84 Castlebar road north out of Ballinrobe, passing the racecourse on your left and continue for 10km (6 miles) to Partry. Turn left here on the R330 Westport road, then in 1km (0.5 miles) bear left to Srah, where you turn left onto a minor road.

❻ This scenic road skirts the west bank of Lough Mask, and it's worth stopping every now and then to enjoy the wonderful views.

Follow the road for 21km (13 miles) by way of Toormakeady before you turn sharp left on the north shore of Lough Nafooey along the Clonbur road. Another 13km (8 miles), through Finny and across the spectacular narrows at Ferry Bridge, brings you back across the border into Galway and on to Clonbur between Lough Mask and Lough Corrib. Follow the R345 Maum road from Clonbur for 14km (9 miles), and on the outskirts of Maum turn left on the R336 to Maam Cross. Here you bear left on the N59 for 16km (10 miles) through magnificent bogland scenery to Oughterard. Continue on the N59 for 2.5km (1.5 miles) beyond the town, then turn left on a signposted road to Aughnanure Castle.

❼ Built in the 16th century, Aughnanure Castle is the best preserved medieval castle on the lakes. The O'Flaherties built it six floors high within strong walls, gave it a lookout tower and filled it with secret chambers and murder holes in true fairy-tale castle tradition.

From Aughnanure weave your way via Carrowmoreknock through a maze of lanes beside Lough Corrib, to meet the N59 again at Moycullen. Or you can return from the castle directly to the N59, and turn left for 24km (15 miles) back to Galway city.

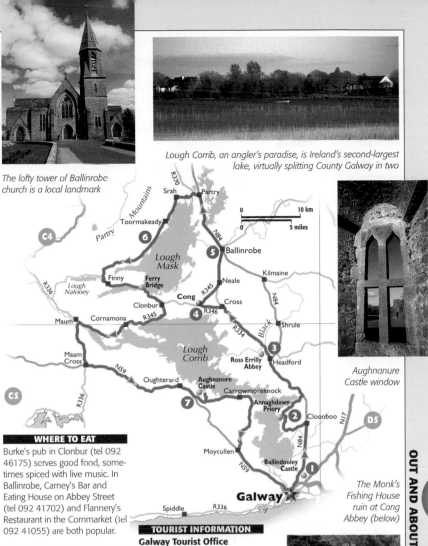

The lofty tower of Ballinrobe church is a local landmark

Lough Corrib, an angler's paradise, is Ireland's second-largest lake, virtually splitting County Galway in two

Aughnanure Castle window

The Monk's Fishing House ruin at Cong Abbey (below)

WHERE TO EAT

Burke's pub in Clonbur (tel 092 46175) serves good food, sometimes spiced with live music. In Ballinrobe, Carney's Bar and Eating House on Abbey Street (tel 092 41702) and Flannery's Restaurant in the Cornmarket (tel 092 41055) are both popular.

PLACES TO VISIT

Annaghdown Priory
Off N84, 8km (5 miles) south of Headford
Open access
Free

Ross Errilly Friary
Signed from R334 at Headford
Open access
Free

Cong Abbey ▷ 136.

Aughnanure Castle
Oughterard
Tel 091 552214
Mid Jun–end Sep daily; May to mid-Jun and Oct weekends
Adult €2.55, child (under 12) €1.25

The golden glow of dawn lights up lovely Lough Corrib (right)

TOURIST INFORMATION

Galway Tourist Office
Forster Street, Galway
Tel 091 537700
Daily 9–5.45 (closed Sun Oct–Mar)

Cong Tourist Office
Abbey Street, Cong
Tel 094 954 6542
Jul, Aug daily 9.30–7; Sep–end Nov, mid-Mar to end Jun daily 10–6

6. DRIVE

NORTHWEST MAYO

You'll see some of Ireland's most bleakly beautiful landscape on this drive into the heartland of County Mayo's western bogs and mountains. It's not all melancholy moodiness, however: There are stunning golden beaches on the Mullet peninsula, abbey ruins and gaunt old castles to stimulate the imagination, and some hidden villages that are as friendly as they are remote.

THE DRIVE

Distance: 257km (160 miles)
Allow: 5 hours
Start/end at: Newport

★ Newport is a neat Georgian town with some elegant old houses. If you fancy stretching your legs before spending the day in the car, try a stroll over the former railway viaduct that forms a backdrop to Newport.

Set off westward from Newport on the N59 towards Mulrany. In 2.5km (1.5 miles) turn left down a signposted minor road to Burrishoole Abbey.

1 Burrishoole Abbey stands right on the Shromore estuary. The tower and ruined walls remain, its east window still containing stone tracery. It was here that 'Iron Dick' Burke, the unfortunate second husband of Grace O'Malley (see Rockfleet Castle, below), spent the last years of his life.

Return to the N59 and turn left for 4km (2.5 miles); bear left on a signposted minor road to Rockfleet (formerly Carrigahowley) Castle.

2 Rockfleet Castle, a Tudor-era fortified tower, presses even closer to the water than Burrishoole Abbey. It was once occupied by Clare Island's famous pirate queen Grace O'Malley, otherwise known as Granuaile. In 1567 she divorced her second husband, 'Iron Dick' Burke, by slamming the door of Rockfleet Castle against him. During their single year of marriage, she had put her own supporters in control of every one of Iron Dick's castles, so he was left without houses or land.

Return to the N59 and turn left. Continue for 11km (7 miles), with the mountains of Achill Island growing steadily larger ahead, to Mulrany (*An Mhala Raithní*, 'the ferny hilltop'). From here the N59 runs north for 32km (20 miles) past the Mayo bogs to Bangor Erris.

3 The bleak, brown, magnificently moody landscape of the Mayo bogs rises to the Nephin Beg Mountains on your right along this road, making a striking contrast with the green of the Achill Island mountains and mainland shores to the left.

At Bangor Erris (*Baingear Iorrais*, 'the pointed hill of Erris') turn left on the R313 for 19km (12 miles) to Belmullet (*Béal an Mhuirthead*, 'mouth of the Mullet peninsula'). From here continue along the R313 to the end of the Mullet peninsula, enjoying the superb coast and sea views, and back again to Belmullet (43km/27 miles). Return along the R313 towards Bangor Erris for 4km (2.5 miles), then bear left onto the R314. Follow this road for 45km (28 miles) through more wild bogland to Ballycastle, with two detours north to the coast. For the first detour turn left by Barnatra post office, 6km (4 miles) after joining the R314. The road loops for 16km (10 miles) round a stubby peninsula.

4 Halfway around the peninsula you pass the Bronze Age stone circle at Dooncarton. Don't pick the flowers, or the fairies, so it's said, will rig you out with a pair of horns while you're asleep! Return through Pollatomish village.

Turn left on the R314 for 1.5km (1 mile), then make a second detour by taking the first left to Portacloy and Porturlin.

5 Portacloy and Porturlin, two remote villages, both have tiny harbours; the one at Portacloy is almost shut in by high cliffs. Off shore are the 97m-high (318ft) rock stacks known as the Stags of Broad Haven.

Return to the R314 and turn left for 27km (17 miles) passing through lonely, wild bog country. After Belderg you pass the entrance to the archaeological site of Céide Fields before reaching Ballycastle, a charming village with a slanting main street. Bear left just beyond Ballycastle on a signposted road through Gortmore to the parking area at Downpatrick Head.

6 Downpatrick Head itself can be reached by a footpath from this parking area. The high cliff promontory of the Head has Doonbristy ('the broken fort'), a sea stack 46m (150ft) high, standing majestically offshore. Just inland of the cliff edge you'll pass a wide gash in the ground. This is Poll na Seantainne, a blowing hole which connects via a cave with the sea. You can generally hear the sound of waves rising from the chasm, and on stormy days the gash sends up a fine spout of water—so beware! In 1798 a force of Frenchmen landed at nearby Killala Bay to assist an Irish uprising against the English; the locals who supported them, and who were subsequently massacred while hiding in the Poll na Seantainne caves, are commemorated on a monument near the blowing hole.

Return to Ballycastle and follow the R315 south for 19km (12 miles) through Crossmolina. Continue for 4.5km (3 miles) beyond Crossmolina then turn right on the R316 to Derreen, where you turn left on the R312 Castlebar road for 6.5km (4 miles). Just before Beltra turn right on the R317 for 14km (9 miles) back to Newport.

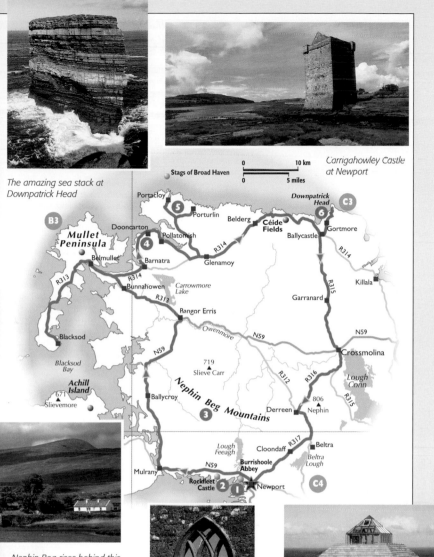

The amazing sea stack at Downpatrick Head

Carrigahowley Castle at Newport

Nephin Beg rises behind this lonely cottage (above)

The Céide Fields Interpretive Centre has a striking design (above).
A graceful window at Moyne Abbey (left)

WHERE TO EAT

Mary's Bakery and Tea Rooms
Main Street, Ballycastle
Tel 096 43361
Excellent home-baking and teas.
Mar–end Sep daily 10–6; Oct–end Feb Mon–Sat 10–4 (Closed Jan 1–22)

PLACES TO VISIT

Burrishoole Abbey
Off N59, 1.5km (1 mile) west of Newport
Open access Free

Rockfleet Castle
Off N59, 6.5km (4 miles) west of Newport
Open access Free

Nephin Beg Mountains and Mullet Peninsula ▷ 145.

Dooncarton Stone Circle
3km (2 miles) northwest of Pollatomish
Open access Free

Céide Fields ▷ 133.

Downpatrick Head Sea Stack and Blowing Hole
Off R314 at Ballycastle
Open access Free

TOURIST INFORMATION

Tourist Office
James Street, Westport
Tel 098 25711

'YEATS COUNTRY' AND LOUGH ALLEN

The spirits of poet William Butler Yeats and his painter brother Jack fill the landscape of sandy coasts and flat-topped, dramatic hills around Sligo town where the brothers grew up. Starting from Sligo you skirt the shores of lovely Lough Gill, crossing from County Sligo into County Leitrim. Then you travel farther east and south to make a circuit of Lough Allen's calm water, before exploring the peninsulas and beaches of Sligo and Drumcliff bays.

THE DRIVE

Distance: 170km (106 miles)
Allow: 3.5–4 hours
Start/end at: Sligo town

★ Head eastward out of Sligo town along the Manorhamilton road (N16), turning right after 0.75 km (0.5 miles) down the R286 to skirt the upper shore of Lough Gill. In 13km (8 miles) you pass the eye-catching pile of Parke's Castle.

❶ Parke's Castle, built on the site of an O'Rourke tower in 1609 by Captain Robert Parke, has been superbly restored after centuries of dereliction, with Irish oak roofs pegged together in traditional style.

In another 3km (2 miles) bear right along the R288 for 4.5km (3 miles) towards Dromahair; just before reaching the village, you'll see the ruins of Creevelea Friary by the road.

❷ Creevelea Friary, founded in 1508, was the last friary to be established in Ireland before the Dissolution some 30 years later. It's now a handsome ruin with tower, nave and choir remaining, plus one transept of the church and extensive remains of the cloisters. There are some fine carvings, notably the two depicting St. Francis of Assisi.

Continue on the R288 into Dromahair, and follow R287 signs for Manorhamilton. Just before leaving the village, look for the 17th-century mansion of Old Hall on a bend of the Bonet River

❸ Old Hall was built in 1626 on the site of Breffni Castle, an O'Rourke stronghold from which 44-year-old Dervorgilla O'Rourke eloped in 1152 with Dermot MacMurrough, King of Leinster. This set the chieftains against MacMurrough, so that in 1166 he had to beg help from the English King Henry II. Henry sent Richard de Clare, known as Strongbow, to subdue the natives—the start of 750 years of British involvement in Ireland.

Turn right 2.5km (1.5 miles) beyond Dromahair onto the R289. In 6.5km (4 miles), bear right along the R280 through Drumkeeran and down Lough Allen's western shore towards Drumshanbo.

❹ Lough Allen is a beautiful, tranquil stretch of water shaped like an arrowhead, its tip pointing south to spill the infant River Shannon towards the Irish Midlands.

Turn right off the R280 for 2.5km (1.5 miles) to visit Arigna, a former coal-mining village (▷ 249, walk 7). Then return to the R280 and turn right to Drumshanbo, in 4km (2.5 miles).

❺ The Sliabh an Iarainn Visitor Centre in Drumshanbo has an audio-visual presentation and other displays on the area's history: the sweat-houses, traditional healing places, that you can find dotted across this region; the restored steam-powered Cavan and Leitrim Railway; and the coal mines.

From Drumshanbo the R207 runs north for 18km (11 miles) up the east side of Lough Allen to Dowra, where you turn left on the R200 to return to Drumkeeran and then take the R289 to Dromahair. Bear left here on the R287 for 16km (10 miles), skirting the lower shore of Lough Gill to reach the N4, 3km (2 miles) south of Sligo. Turn left for 3km (2 miles) to Belladrihid, where you bear right to follow the R292 on its 19km (12-mile) circuit of the Strandhill peninsula. Just before you reach the sand dunes and wild, pebbly shore at Strandhill, turn right on sign-posted roads to the parking area under Knocknarea hill.

❻ From the summit of Knocknarea at 327m (1,072ft) you get a great view: seaward over the sands and channels of Sligo Bay, landward to the flat-topped Benbulbin. Yeats loved both mountains, and often included them in his poems. Queen Medb ('Maeve' to W. B. Yeats), the first-century warrior queen of Connacht, is said to be buried under the cairn.

The R292 continues through Strandhill, to return to Sligo. Take the R291 west, and follow to the Rosses Point peninsula.

❼ The sandy beaches at Rosses Point were the setting for several of Jack Yeats's paintings, including his ghostly masterpiece *Leaving The Far Point* (1946).

Go back along the R291 and turn left at Cregg for the N15, where you turn left for 1.5km (1 mile) to Drumcliff.

❽ Drumcliff churchyard is a place of pilgrimage for W. B. Yeats' enthusiasts, for the poet's grave lies here under a plain limestone headstone.

Continue on the N15 and in another mile bear left on a sign-posted road to Lissadell House.

❾ Lissadell House also has Yeats connections; the poet stayed with the Gore-Booth family who owned it and wrote about the two lovely daughters of the house.

Returning to the N15, turn right for 8km (5 miles) to return to Sligo town.

OUT AND ABOUT

The setting sun casts a fiery glow over the waters of Sligo Bay

W. B. Yeats statue in Sligo town

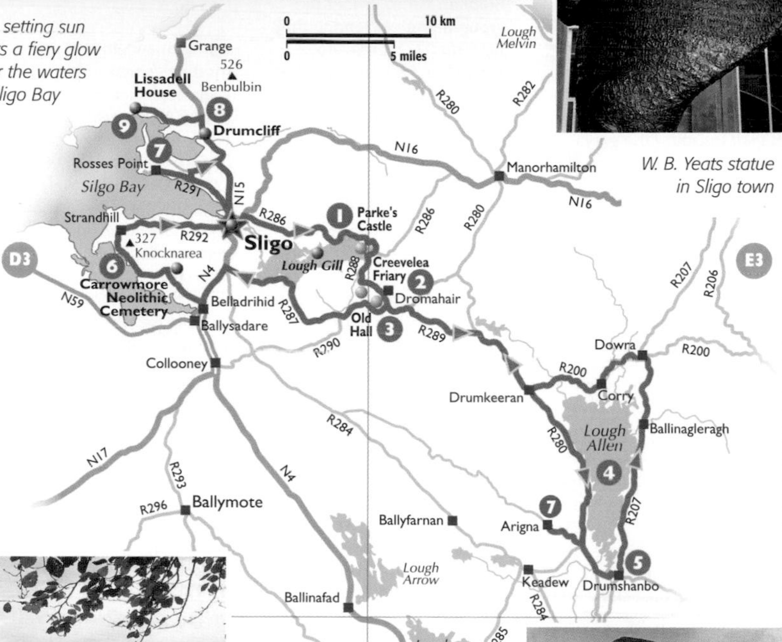

Wading in the reedy shallows of Lough Gill (above). The ornate gallery of Lissadell House (below)

Exploring on horseback in front of the distinctive Benbulbin

WHERE TO EAT

Stanford's Inn, Dromahair (tel 071 64140) is a cheerful place serving good food all day; The Miner's Bar by the bridge in Arigna (tel 071 964 6007) has mining murals and displays.

PLACES TO VISIT

Parke's Castle ▷ 144–145.

Creevelea Friary
Dromahair (beside the R288 Sligo road)
Open access
Free

Lough Gill ▷ 144–145.

Queen Medb's Tomb
Knocknarea, '*Meascán Meadhba*' (off Sligo–Strandhill–Ballysadare road)
Open access
Free

TOURIST INFORMATION

Aras Reddan
Temple Street, Sligo
Tel 071 91 61201
Apr–end Sep daily 9–5.30; Oct–end Mar Mon–Thu 9.30–5.30, Fri 9.30–5 (times may vary, phone to confirm)

Sliabh an Iarainn Visitor Centre
Drumshanbo
Tel 071 964 1522
Apr–end Oct Mon–Sat 10–6, Sun 2–6
€1.50

THE ROSSES TO THE DERRYVEAGH MOUNTAINS

A tour through Donegal's wild western landscapes moves from rugged Atlantic coasts and the county's highest mountain into a dramatically beautiful national park. An intriguing lakeside gallery of modern art provides a change of tone before the homeward run through the mountains.

THE DRIVE

Distance: 112km (70 miles)
Allow: 2 hours
Start/end at: Dungloe

★ **Dungloe is often spelled 'Dunglow', and you will also see it rendered in Irish as *An Clochán Liath* ('the grey stepping stones'). Many place names in Ireland have slight spelling variations. Each July in Dungloe, local beauties compete for the title of 'Mary from Dungloe', a modern competition named after a hit single. The town is the southern gateway to The Rosses—the wildest region in Donegal.**

Leave Dungloe on the R259 Burtonport road. After 6.5km (4 miles) on the R259 turn left on the R260 into Burtonport.

❶ **Burtonport (*Ailt an Chorráin*, 'ravine of the curve') is a thriving little fishing and fish-processing port. You can have a look at the trawlers and chat to the fishermen before treating yourself to some fresh seafood.**

Return to the R259 and turn left to continue the drive. In 5km (3 miles), on the outskirts of Kincaslough (*Cionn Caslach*, 'head of the inlet'), bear left and over a bridge onto Cruit Island.

❷ **A narrow, winding road runs beside the rocky shores, salt marshes, reed beds and sand flats of Cruit Island, whose inhabitants have made bright gardens of the hardy rock plants that can survive the salty winds.**

Return to the R259 and turn left crossing bleak moorland scenery for 11km (7 miles), through Kincaslough and Annagary. After 1.5km (1 mile) turn left (signed '*Tábhairne Leo*/Leo's Tavern'); the tavern is 100m (110 yards) on the left.

❸ **Leo's Tavern is the home base of the music-making Brennan family. Under the group name of Clannad they have many records and awards to their credit and one of the sisters, Enya, is a huge star of the ambient music world in her own right. Photos, press clippings and gold, silver and platinum discs adorn the walls of the pub, where you can sometimes catch live music.**

Return to R259 and turn left to the N56, where you bear left to Gweedore (*Gaoth Dobhair*, 'water inlet'). In another 3km (2 miles), with the white quartzite cone of Mount Errigal straight ahead, fork right on the R251, signposted Dunlewy (*Dún Lúiche*, 'Lughaidh's Fort'), passing to the south of the mountain. Opposite Dunlewy post office turn right to Dunlewy Lakeside Centre.

❹ **Dunlewy Lakeside Centre offers weaving displays, boat trips with a storyteller on Dunlewy Lough, children's outdoor and indoor play areas, a shop and café.**

Return to the R251 and turn right. If you would like to climb Mount Errigal, the best path ascends from a pull-off on the left in 4km (2.5 miles).

❺ **The climb to the summit of Mount Errigal, 752m (2,467ft) high, is fine for any walker with a good level of fitness. At the top a narrow ridge connects the twin summits, from which on a fine day you can enjoy an enormous prospect over almost all of County Donegal's lakes, mountains and coasts.**

Continue along the R251 in a northeasterly direction for 11km (7 miles), following Letterkenny signs over a high pass in very wild and beautiful mountainous country, until you come to the gates of Glenveagh National Park on your right.

❻ **Moorland, forests and mountains make up Glenveagh National Park (▷ 250–251, walk 8), with the elongated Lough Veagh as a feature of the park's 9,667ha (23,887 acres). In lovely rhododendron gardens on the lake shore you'll find 19th-century Glenveagh Castle. From the footpaths that run through the National Park you have an excellent chance of seeing red deer. The Visitor Centre has displays on the wildlife and land formations of the National Park.**

Continue on the R251 for 10km (6 miles) to Gartan Bridge, where a right turn (signposted) takes you to the Glebe House and Gallery.

❼ **Glebe House (guided tours only) is decorated in late Victorian Arts and Crafts style, with rustic furniture, William Morris wallpaper and paintings of 'naïve' artists of the Tory Island school (▷ 148). English artist Derek Hill bought this former rectory in 1953, and the Derek Hill collection displays the work of modern artists from Ireland (including Jack B. Yeats) and farther afield (Augustus John, Pablo Picasso and others).**

Return to the R251 and bear right. In 1km (0.5 miles) bear right again onto an unclassified road to join the R254. Keep ahead for 26km (16 miles) in magnificent mountain scenery through Glendowan to Doocharry (*An Dúchoraidh*, 'the black weir'). Here you turn right on the R252. In 9km (5.5 miles) turn right on the N56 to return to Dungloe.

Riding along the deserted sands at Dungloe beach

Owey Island, as viewed from nearby Cruet Island

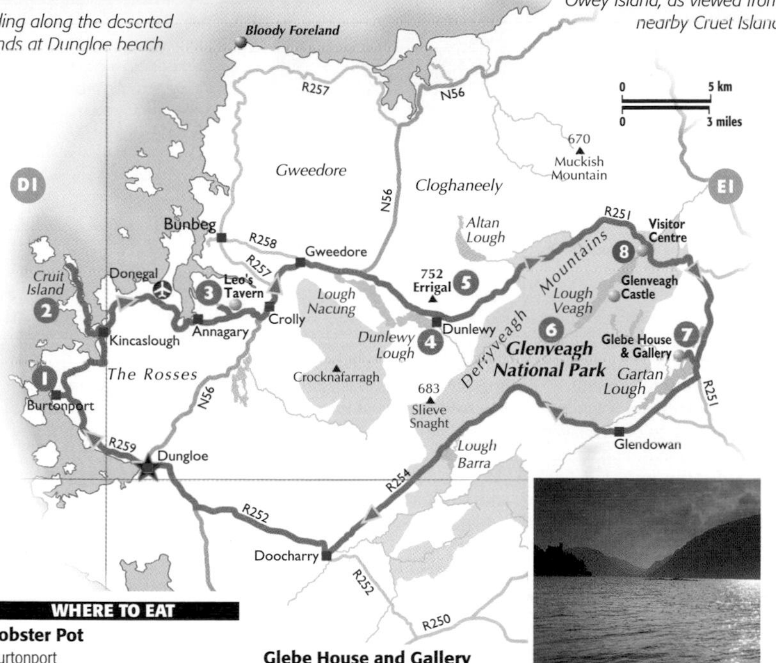

WHERE TO EAT

Lobster Pot
Burtonport
Tel 074 954 2012
Locally caught seafood.
Daily noon 10pm

Leo's Tavern
Meenaleck, Crolly
Tel 074 954 8143
Soup and sandwiches.
Daily 1–8.30pm

Glenveagh National Park
Glenveagh, Letterkenny
Tel 074 91 37090
Castle tea room: Easter, Jun–end Sep. Visitor Centre restaurant: mid-Mar to early Nov

PLACES TO VISIT

Dunlewy Lakeside Centre
Dunlewy, Letterkenny
Tel 074 953 1699
Easter–end Oct Mon–Sat 10.30–6, Sun 11–8 (Nov, Dec open Sat, Sun)

Glebe House and Gallery
Churchill, Letterkenny
Tel 074 913 7071
Daily 11–6.30
Adult €2.75, child (4–12) €1.25

Glenveagh Castle and National Park ▷ 143.

TOURIST INFORMATION

Tourist Office The Quay, Dungloe
Tel 074 952 1297
Apr–end Sep or Oct, daily 9–5; weekends only in winter

Glenveagh Castle, on a promontory above Lough Beagh (above). A view towards Mount Errigal from Dunlewy (below)

9. DRIVE

FROM ATHLONE TO CLONMACNOISE

This drive takes a wide swing through the contrasting landscapes of the Irish Midlands: green dairying country, and vast expanses of bogland. It includes two very different monastic sites—the little ancient church and holy well at Lemanaghan, and the world-famous monastery at Clonmacnoise with its round tower and many churches overlooking the River Shannon.

THE DRIVE

Distance: 96km (60 miles)
Allow: 2 hours
Start/end at: Athlone

★ Leave Athlone on the N6 Dublin road, and just outside the town bear right onto the N62, running south for 26km (16 miles) through Ballynahown to Ferbane. Turn left here on the R436 Clara road, and in 5.5km (3.5 miles) you'll reach the signposted site of St. Manchan's Church and Holy Well in Lemanaghan.

❶ Lemanaghan graveyard and the well-restored 12th-century church have yielded many ancient crosses and other carved stones, to be displayed in an exhibition (being planned at the time of writing) in the old school across the road. Just east of the church you'll find St. Manchan's Well, set in a keyhole-shaped surround with steps leading down to gently dimpling water. The presence of many religious statuettes, a *bullaun* stone (prehistoric quern), and a guardian ash tree festooned with strips of prayer rags demonstrates that this is a holy well still very much in use. St. Manchan (died AD664) founded his monastery at Lemanaghan, and is still venerated in these parts. One legend tells how St. Manchan's cow was stolen by rival monks, butchered, put in a pot and boiled. But St. Manchan managed miraculously to restore her to full health (all but one of her thigh bones), and she continued to be an excellent milker.

Opposite the church turn left off the R436 beside the old school, down a winding lane that loops round the back of Lemanaghan. In 457m (500 yards), where the lane bends back on itself, bear left over a hump and turn right along a long, straight bog road.

Clonmacnoise has revealed the skills of medieval craftsmen

In 1.25km (0.75 miles) turn left on another rough road running northwest out into the heart of the bog.

❷ This is classic machine-cut bog, a wide dark wasteland of raw peat harvested for commercial purposes by Bord na Móna, the Irish Peat Board (▷ 152). It is interspersed with vast tracts of uncut bog, a sombrely beautiful expanse of heather and ragged stands of pine trees and scrub, full of glinting bog pools, wild flowers, butterflies, dragonflies and songbirds.

After 1.5km (1 mile) you meet the track of an old industrial railway with a farm beyond, surely one of the loneliest farms in Ireland. Turn round here and return to the bog road crossroads, where you keep ahead to turn left on the R436 for 3km (2 miles). On the outskirts of Ballycumber turn left by Flynn's Bar along a minor road (signed 'Athlone'). In 0.75km (0.5 miles) you pass a Church of Ireland church with its tall tower on your right; in another 1.25km (0.75 miles) you reach the Catholic church of Boher on the right.

❸ Boher Church displays a treasure: the astonishing 12th-century Shrine of St. Manchan. The box of yew wood contains the bones of the founder of Lemanaghan monastery, and is lavishly decorated with gold, bronze and enamelling in the form of human figures, stylized animals and patterns, and two big crucifixes.

Continue along the road for 2km (1.25 miles) to a crossroads. Turn left (signed 'Ferbane') for 5.5km (3.5 miles). At a 'Yield' sign bear left, then turn right along the N62. At the first crossroads turn left (signed 'Endrim'); in 1.25km (0.75 miles) keep ahead over a crossroads, and in another 1.25km (0.75 miles) bear right at a T-junction and continue on this country lane as it circles right round Endrim Hill for 3km (2 miles).

❹ The landscape here, contrasting with the bog, is just as typical of the Irish Midlands: flattish, intensely green fields of dairy cows with plenty of hedges and patches of woodland.

Continue over the crossroads, and in another 2.5km (1.5 miles) bear left to a T-junction on the western outskirts of Ferbane. Turn right, and in 1.5km (1 mile) right again (signed 'Glebe Church' and 'Clonmacnoise 14'). Follow the Clonmacnoise signs along this road for 10km (6 miles) to the R444. Turn left and then right. to reach the historic monastic site.

❺ In the sixth century, Clonmacnoise was one of the most important monasteries in Ireland, if not in the whole of Europe, but it suffered severely from Viking raids. The large number of ruins still standing 1,500 years later shows what a huge complex it was.

From Clonmacnoise return to the R444, where you bear left; in 0.75km (0.5 miles) turn left again onto the 'Pilgrim's Road' and follow this minor road for 11km (7 miles) to Ballynahown. Here you turn left on the N62 to return to Athlone.

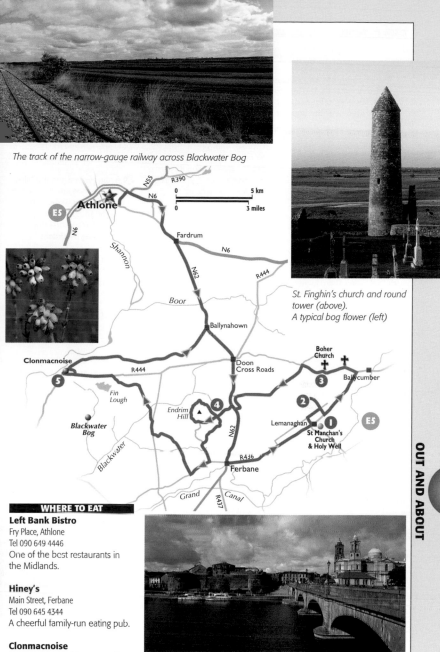

The track of the narrow-gauge railway across Blackwater Bog

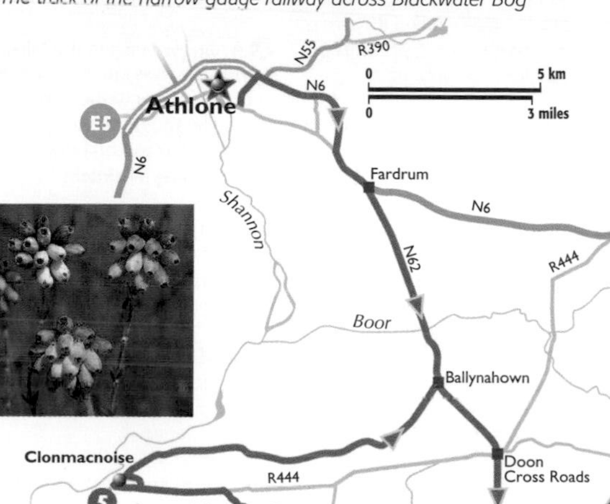

St. Finghin's church and round tower (above).
A typical bog flower (left)

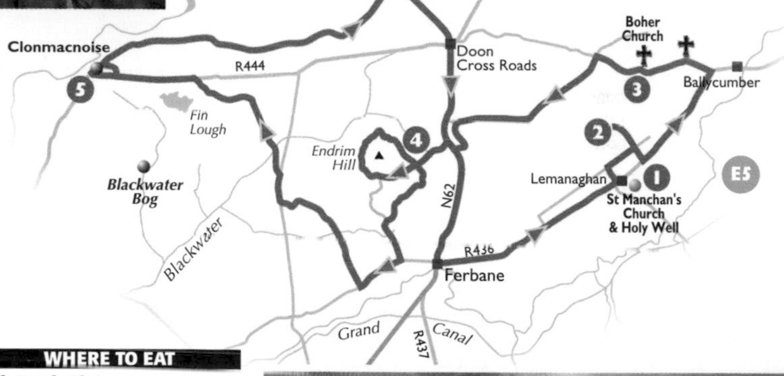

WHERE TO EAT

Left Bank Bistro
Fry Place, Athlone
Tel 090 649 4446
One of the best restaurants in the Midlands.

Hiney's
Main Street, Ferbane
Tel 090 645 4344
A cheerful family-run eating pub.

Clonmacnoise
On R444, signposted from N62, 13km (8 miles) south of Athlone
Tel 0905 74195
Coffee shop.

PLACES TO VISIT

Athlone ▷ 150.

St. Manchan's Church and Holy Well
Lemanaghan on the R436, 5.5km (3.5 miles) east of Ferbane
Open access Free

Athlone Castle, once a significant stronghold on the River Shannon

St. Manchan's Shrine in Boher Church
On country road between Ballycumber and Doon crossroads (N62), 3km (2 miles) west of Ballycumber
During daylight hours
Free

Clonmacnoise ▷ 154–157.

TOURIST INFORMATION

Athlone Castle
Tel 090 649 4630
Mon–Fri 9.30–1, 2–5.30 (call to confirm times)

Clonmacnoise
Shannonbridge
Tel 090 967 4134
For hours ▷ 155

HILLS AND GLENS OF TYRONE

The wild uplands and valleys of the Sperrin Mountains of County Tyrone make a superb half-day car tour. Starting to the south of the Sperrins you travel through boglands rich in archaeological remains, cross through the scenic Barnes Gap into the lovely Glenelly Valley, then over the highest part of the range, before winding your way back to Omagh.

THE DRIVE

Distance: 130km (80 miles)
Allow: 3 hours
Start/end at: Omagh

★ **Omagh, a quiet market town, blazed into the headlines on 15 August 1998 when a huge bomb exploded, planted by a dissident group calling itself the Real IRA, killing 29 people and injuring 200 more. The horror was such that rather than derail the peace process, as it was most likely intended to do, it probably helped it on its way.**

Leave Omagh on the A505 Cookstown road. After 7km (4 miles) bear right on the Drumnakilly–Carrickmore road, and in 137m (150 yards) turn left along the bog road to Milltown. In 1km (0.7 miles) you'll pass Fernagh Ceilidh House. Continue for another 2km (1.5 miles), then bear right at an intersection for 3km (2 miles) to Milltown. Turn left here, and keep on for 1.5km (1 mile) to Loughmacrory Wedge Tomb.

❶ **Loughmacrory Wedge Tomb is said to be guarded by a fairy tree, so no one has disturbed its great capstones that still stand supported by their massive edging stones as they have done for 4,000 years.**

Return to Milltown and turn left on the Carrickmore road, bearing left in 1.5km (1 mile) on the road towards Kildress and Drumshanbo Glebe. Cross the B46 Carrickmore–Creggan road, and in another 2.5km (1.5 miles) turn left at a crossroads for 3km (2 miles) to the A505, where you turn right for the An Creagán Visitor Centre.

❷ **An Creagán Visitor Centre's exhibition tells how the great blanket bogs grew, and of the rich archaeological treasures they contain.**

Return 3km (2 miles) to the crossroads and continue straight over on the Pomeroy road for 1.5km (1 mile) to find the signposted path to Creggandevesky Court Tomb on your right.

❸ **Lying in a beautiful position overlooking Lough Mallon, Creggandevesky (c3,500BC) is one of Ireland's best examples of a court tomb. Its huge hillock of stones contains three burial chambers, with the curved wings of the ceremonial court facing the lake.**

Back at the crossroads turn right and continue for 7km (4.5 miles) to the A505. Turn right for 3km (2 miles) if you want to visit Wellbrook Beetling Mill.

❹ **The Wellbrook Beetling Mill, still powered by water, shows the last stage in the production of linen, one of Ireland's renowned products. At this museum you can watch a beetling machine at work.**

Continue by turning left along the A505. In 2.75km (1.75 miles) turn right to cross the Ballinderry River and pass through Dunnamore. Cross a stream and take the next right across the bogland north for 3km (2 miles) to the signposted Beaghmore Stone Circles.

❺ **Beaghmore Stone Circles consist of dozens of stone alignments, dating from 2000–1200BC. In this bleak bog landscape, stone circles stand in pairs and solo, along with many round cairns, and several stone rows or avenues. Hundreds more may lie unexcavated beneath the bog.**

Continue north for 4km (2.5 miles), over a crossroads, towards the Sperrin Mountains. At a T-junction turn left for 6.5km (4 miles) to another intersection, where you turn right for 8km (5 miles) along the Gortin road, through Glenhull to Scotch Town. Turn right here into the hills, crossing the Barnes Gap pass.

❻ **A narrow crack in the hills, Barnes Gap has stunning views over the valleys of the two rivers, the Faughan and the Glenelly, that run on either side of Sawel Mountain.**

Descend into the Glenelly Valley. Turn right here on the narrow road along the south side of the valley, and in 5.5km (3.5 miles) bear left to reach the B47 beyond Oughtboy Bridge. Turn right and drive for 1.5 km (1 mile) to reach the Sperrin Heritage Centre.

❼ **You are now deep into the beautiful Sperrin Mountains, and the Sperrin Heritage Centre will give you an insight into the life and history of this range of moorland hills, indented with deep fertile valleys.**

Continue for 2.5km (1.5 miles) to Sperrin village. Turn left up the mountain road through the heart of the northern Sperrins for 11km (7 miles) to Park village. Turn left through Park village and on via Carnanreagh and Craig for 16km (10 miles) to the B48, where you turn left for Omagh by way of Plumbridge and Gortin. Gortin Glen Forest Park lies just off the B48 5km (3 miles) south of Gortin.

❽ **There's a lovely drive running for 8km (5 miles) through the forest, as well as numerous footpaths through the coniferous woods of Gortin Glen Forest Park.**

Continue for 11km (7 miles) back to Omagh.

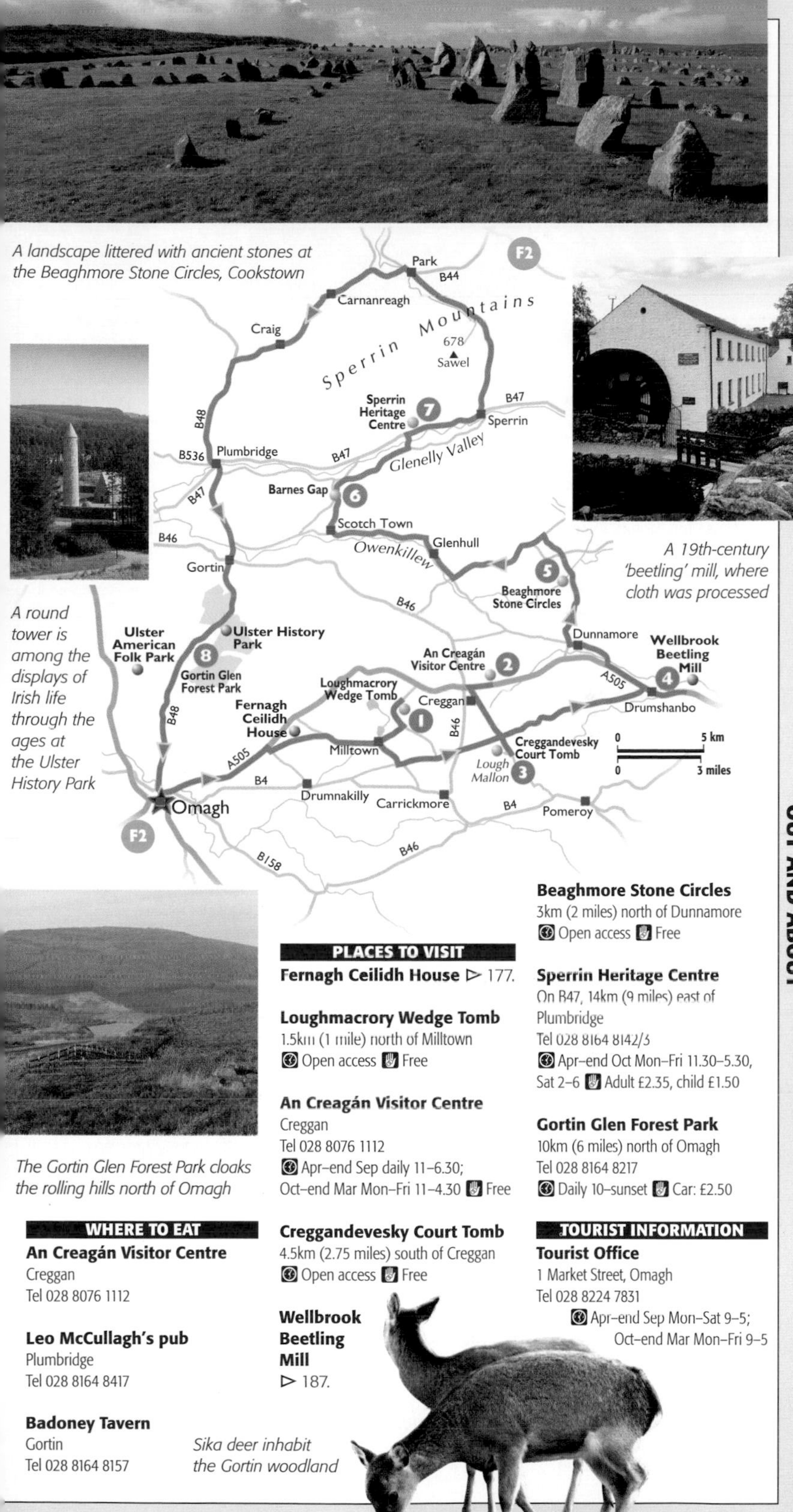

A landscape littered with ancient stones at the Beaghmore Stone Circles, Cookstown

A round tower is among the displays of Irish life through the ages at the Ulster History Park

A 19th-century 'beetling' mill, where cloth was processed

The Gortin Glen Forest Park cloaks the rolling hills north of Omagh

Sika deer inhabit the Gortin woodland

PLACES TO VISIT

Fernagh Ceilidh House ⊳ 177.

Loughmacrory Wedge Tomb
1.5km (1 mile) north of Milltown
Open access · Free

An Creagán Visitor Centre
Creggan
Tel 028 8076 1112
Apr–end Sep daily 11–6.30; Oct–end Mar Mon–Fri 11–4.30 · Free

Creggandevesky Court Tomb
4.5km (2.75 miles) south of Creggan
Open access · Free

Wellbrook Beetling Mill ⊳ 187.

Beaghmore Stone Circles
3km (2 miles) north of Dunnamore
Open access · Free

Sperrin Heritage Centre
On B47, 14km (9 miles) east of Plumbridge
Tel 028 8164 8142/3
Apr–end Oct Mon–Fri 11.30–5.30, Sat 2–6 · Adult £2.35, child £1.50

Gortin Glen Forest Park
10km (6 miles) north of Omagh
Tel 028 8164 8217
Daily 10–sunset · Car: £2.50

WHERE TO EAT

An Creagán Visitor Centre
Creggan
Tel 028 8076 1112

Leo McCullagh's pub
Plumbridge
Tel 028 8164 8417

Badoney Tavern
Gortin
Tel 028 8164 8157

TOURIST INFORMATION

Tourist Office
1 Market Street, Omagh
Tel 028 8224 7831
Apr–end Sep Mon–Sat 9–5; Oct–end Mar Mon–Fri 9–5

ORGANIZED TOURS

Tours with a guide can help you get even more out of a visit to Ireland, where the guides not only add to your knowledge but more often than not are great ambassadors for their country. The tours below include a wide range of options, each appropriate to the region.

DUBLIN

DUBLIN LITERARY PUB CRAWL
Starts at the Duke Pub, 9 Duke Street
Tel 01 670 5602
www.dublinpubcrawl.com
Dublin's literary greats and its best pubs are brought together on a 2-hour guided tour that combines fun, books, history, scholarship and good beer. Tickets can also be bought at Dublin Tourism, Suffolk Street.
Apr–end Nov nightly at 7.30 plus noon on Sun; Dec–end Mar Fri–Sun at 7.30pm Adult €10

HISTORICAL WALKING TOURS OF DUBLIN
64 Mary Street, Dublin 1
Tel 01 878 0227
www.historicalinsights.ie
These 2-hour tours are given by history graduates of Trinity College. They walk you around the city making Ireland's complicated history come alive.
Apr–end Sep daily 11 and 3, Oct–end Mar Fri–Sun 12 only Adult €10, child (under 14) free

THE EAST

CELTIC EXPERIENCE
33 Kinahan Steet, Dublin 7
Tel 01 838 6128
www.overthetoptours.com
These tours are an ideal way to see the best Celtic sights, such as the magnificent Hill of Tara in Meath.
Day-long tours depart from Dublin Tourism Offices: Suffolk Street at 9am and O'Connell Street at 9.20am
Adult €26, child (12 and under) €18

IRISH CYCLING SAFARIS
Bellfield Bike Shop, University College Dublin
Tel 01 260 0749
www.cyclingsafaris.com
See the best of Wicklow on a 3-night cycling weekend from Dublin, with Saturday night entertainment and cycling in the mountains on Sunday.
Apr–end Sep, various dates; advance booking required Phone for details

THE SOUTH

SEAFARI
Reenkilla, Lauragh, Killarney
Tel 064 83171
www.seafariireland.com
Cruises into Kenmare Bay, renowned for its seals but you'll see plenty of land-based creatures too. Amusing comments from the captain, and Irish music, make it a fun family outing. Booking is advised.
Daily (weather permitting). Times vary, phone to confirm Adults €20, child (12–17) €12.50, under 12 €10

SKELLIG EXPERIENCE SEA CRUISE
Skellig Experience Centre, Portmagee
Tel 066 947 6306
www.skelligexperience.com
A 2-hour tour around the Skellig islands giving a close-up look at the seabirds (27,000 pairs of gannets alone!). You might also see dolphins, seals, minke whales and basking sharks.
Apr–end Oct daily 3pm (weather permitting) Adult €21.50, child (12 and under) €10.70

THE WEST

DOLPHINWATCH CARRIGAHOLT
Carrigaholt, Co. Clare
Tel 065 905 8156
www.dolphinwatch.ie
Operating in the mouth of the Shannon where over 100 bottlenose dolphins have made their home, Dolphinwatch offers up to five 2-hour boat trips daily to see them.
Apr–end Oct daily (phone for times) Adult €18, child €9, under 3 free

SHANNON RIVER CRUISES
The Spirit of Killaloe, Killaloe Marina, Co. Clare
Tel 086 814 0559
www.killaloe.ie/whelans
An hour-long cruise on the Shannon to its largest lake, Lough Derg, with commentary on the historic sites.
May to mid-Sep daily, times vary
Adult €7.50, child (under 16) €4

THE MIDLANDS

VIKING CRUISES
7 St. Mary's Place, Athlone, Co. Westmeath
Tel 090 647 3383
www.iol.ie/wmeathtc/viking/
Travel on a Viking longship and explore the Viking heritage on Lough Ree or take a longer trip to the monastic site of Clonmacnoise, both with a crew dressed as Vikings.
May–end Aug daily; Sep–end Apr phone to confirm Adult €9 or €15, child (under 18) €6 or €9, babies free

BLACKWATER BOG RAILWAY TOURS
Clonmacnoise and West Offaly Railway, Shannonbridge, Co. Offaly
Tel 090 967 4450
www.bnm.ie
Intriguing and unusual 9km (6-mile) rail tour into a peat bog, stopping to see a demonstration of turf cutting and to learn about the archaeological finds.
Apr–early Oct daily 10–5, tours on the hour; Oct–Mar Mon–Fri by request only Adult €6, child (under 12) €4.10

NORTHERN IRELAND

DRUMGOOLAND EQUESTRIAN CENTRE
29 Dunnanew Road, Seaforde, Downpatrick, Co Down
Tel 028 4481 1956
www.horsetrek-ireland.com
Drumgooland offers 2-, 4- and 7-night trekking holidays, with forest rides and rides along the unspoiled beaches of Antrim.
All year; advance booking is required Prices vary; 2-night holiday including accommodation: £245

This chapter lists places to eat and stay, broken down by region, then alphabetically by town. Entries in the Dublin section are listed alphabetically.

Eating and Staying

EATING OUT IN IRELAND

Ireland has some of the world's finest natural food resources, but for many years didn't seem to know what to do with them. The land is fertile, the air is healthy and the seas and rivers are clean and pure. Yet for centuries the diet was mainly potatoes, meat and vegetables. Bread and cheese were always good, but now a demand for finer foods has brought out the best in Irish chefs and you can dine as well here as anywhere in the world.

Famous Galway oysters (left). There's an art to pouring a pint (middle). Renowned Irish cheeses (right)

CURRENT TRENDS
Styles are slow to change in the countryside, although there is an awareness that more diverse eating options are needed, such as healthy eating, vegetarian and vegan choices and more sophisticated dishes. The major cities follow European trends, whether it be for fusion cooking or tapas bars, and new twists on native Irish dishes—New Irish Cuisine—remain popular.

SMOKING BAN
A strict law prohibiting smoking in the workplace was introduced in the Republic of Ireland in 2004. This includes all bars and restaurants, though outdoor areas may be set aside for smokers.

PRICING
Ireland is not an especially expensive country, and restaurant prices are broadly similar to those in most of western Europe. It is expensive by American standards, but less so in rural areas, and cities have such inexpensive options as cafés and pubs, where bar food can be a good bargain.

MEALTIMES
Breakfast may be served any time from 7 until 10am, depending on the establishment, with lunch from about noon until 2 or 2.30pm. An increasing number of places stay open all day, and some pubs serve food all day, but this isn't the norm. Dinner is served quite early, from about 6pm, and might stop by 10pm, or even earlier in rural districts, In the cities, places will be open later, notably Indian and Chinese restaurants.

RESERVING
Ireland is a casual country and reserving isn't usually necessary, unless you're planning to dine in one of the finer restaurants. In smaller towns it might be advisable to check in advance, simply because there may not be other options nearby.

DRESS CODE
As with most things in life, the Irish take a very laid-back approach to dress codes. Casual attire is fine in all but the most expensive restaurants and some of the smarter hotel restaurants.

LICENSING LAWS
In the Republic of Ireland pubs are open from 10.30am to11.30pm Monday to Thursday, 10.30am to 12.30am Friday and Saturday and 12.30pm to 11pm on Sunday. In winter they close 30 minutes earlier. In Northern Ireland pubs may open at any times, but are only permitted to sell alcohol from 11.30am to 11pm Monday to Saturday and from 12.30pm to10pm on Sunday. Extensions may be granted for special occasions.

The minimum drinking age is 18, and 18–20s must carry proof of age. Under 17s are banned from licensed premises after 9pm, unless attending a private function with a substantial meal. At other times under 15s must be with an adult.

VEGETARIAN
Being vegetarian in Ireland isn't easy but is far from impossible. The Irish diet has traditionally been meat-based, but hosts are more aware of the needs of vegetarians, and suitable options will often be available. If staying and dining in a small or country house hotel, you might find it helpful to call ahead with any specific dietary needs.

MORE INFORMATION
Look for a copy of *Dining in Ireland*, a free publication by the Irish Tourist Board.

A GUIDE TO IRISH FOOD AND DRINK

BREAKFAST
The traditional breakfast, in Northern Ireland known as an Ulster Fry, consists of fried bacon, sausages, tomatoes, eggs, black pudding, white pudding and perhaps several kinds of bread (frequently home-made). Lighter options are always available, though.

LUNCH
If you indulge in the full fry-up, you might feel the need for a lighter lunch. Picnic supplies include the very tasty and unusual Irish breads and local cheeses, which are two of the country's best products. Pub lunches are often excellent value. It may not be gourmet cuisine, but it is usually good, simple fare like fish and chips.

SNACKS
It's an Irish tradition to feed people well, and in some places, particularly guesthouses, you'll be faced with a plate of scones or sandwiches and a cup of tea or coffee, whenever you walk through the door, be it in the middle of the afternoon or late at night, when you have probably just returned from having dinner.

DINNER
Dinner itself can be anything you want it to be. The big cities offer everything from expensive restaurants to inexpensive ethnic cafés. Choice will be more restricted in smaller towns, but standards have improved vastly in the last 10 years or so, and Ireland has food to be proud of.

ALCOHOLIC DRINKS
Ireland is famous the world over for several of its alcoholic beverages, and also for the part played by the local pub in the social culture.

Irish whiskey is popular everywhere and can be drunk anytime, not merely as a post-dinner tipple. Many prefer it to Scottish whisky, and Bushmills, Powers and Jamesons are popular brands. Ireland has one vineyard, the most northerly in the world, near Mallow in County Cork, but Californian, Australian and European wines are widely available.

There isn't as much variety in beer as there is in some countries, as the Irish tend to prefer dark stouts over lager or bitter beers, and generally call them porters rather than stouts. These beers can be too heavy for some, but no one should go home without drinking a glass of Guinness, or its rival Murphy's. Guinness is said to get better the closer you are to the River Liffey, and therefore at its best in Dublin. Remember to order it in good time, as barmen take great pride in knowing how to pour a Guinness: very slowly and with a pause halfway through.

WHERE TO EAT

PUBS
Ireland hasn't yet quite had the explosion of so-called 'gastro-pubs' (pubs priding themselves on their restaurant-quality food) as has happened in mainland Britain, but nevertheless the standards of pub food in Ireland have increased immensely in recent years. In some instances they can provide a way of getting restaurant-type food at less expensive prices, and in other cases the pub is simply a place to find a good, hearty and affordable meal.

Some pubs in the main cities will serve food just about all day, but the vast majority will serve hot meals from around noon to 2 or 3pm, and again in the evenings from about 6 until around 9 or 10pm. At other times you may be able to get a basic bar snack, such as a sandwich.

A number of pubs do have proper restaurant areas in addition to their bar food, so make enquiries about what the eating options are. In the restaurant area you may get a wider menu than if you eat in one of the bars—and slightly higher prices.

In rural areas the food on offer probably won't be quite as sophisticated, or the menus as wide, though that's not to say it won't be good. The dishes on offer are more likely to be traditional Irish recipes rather than cutting-edge cuisine. The hours it's available may be shorter too, but it's not unknown for a landlord or landlady to rustle up a meal for visitors outside of the stated hours, if they're not too busy.

FAST FOOD
There is as much variety of fast food to be had in Ireland as anywhere else in the western world. Few places are without a fish and chip shop, a Chinese or Indian takeaway, or somewhere selling kebabs, fried chicken or burgers. In the cities you may find that some streets will have all these and more.

Various ethnic cuisines are popular in Ireland, and for an inexpensive and quick meal you should seek out one of the numerous Indian, Chinese, Italian or Mexican restaurants.

TEA AND COFFEE SHOPS
In Ireland the café, like the pub, is often a place to meet as well as eat. In the cities you will find a wide variety to choose from and, depending on the establishment, you'll be able to enjoy a range of meals and snacks from all-day breakfasts to cakes and other delicacies. Some cafés also open in the evenings when they might serve more elaborate meals.

There are still plenty of the old-fashioned working men's cafés around, known as the 'greasy spoon' from the greasy fried food they traditionally serve, but these days in the main cities there are just as many sophisticated continental-style cafés, too. In the smaller towns and rural areas it is more likely to be the old-fashioned kind you will find, which are fine for a quick cup of tea or coffee, or a cheap and filling plate of fried food if you're really hungry.

MENU READER

Bacon and cabbage: usually boiled ham rather than fried bacon, served with cabbage and potatoes. A hearty, country dish
Barm brack: a fruit loaf with a very doughy, yeasty texture
Black pudding: pork, pigs' blood, oatmeal, breadcrumbs and other ingredients producing something like a sausage, which tastes better than it might sound
Drisheen: a County Cork version of black pudding, using mutton instead of pork
Dublin Bay prawns: huge, slightly sweet and highly sought-after prawns, which are the same as langoustines, or scampi
Dublin coddle: potatoes and onions slowly cooked with meat, usually ham, bacon and/or sausage, which is traditionally
Potato cake: Not quite bread, not quite potato, made from a mixture of flour, butter and mashed potatoes
Poteen: an illegal home-distilled strong liquor, usually made from potatoes
Soda bread: bread, which can be white or brown, raised with bicarbonate of soda instead of yeast

Black and white pudding (left), fresh soda bread (middle) and fruits of the sea (right)

Boxty: potato cakes, sometimes served stuffed with meat, fish or vegetables
Brown bread: infinite varieties, made from wholemeal flour and sometimes buttermilk
Champ: potatoes puréed with butter, milk and spring onions
Colcannon: cabbage and scallions (spring onions) mixed into mashed potatoes. Leeks and kale might be used instead
Crubeens: pigs' feet, usually slowly cooked in stock
served late on a Saturday night
Irish coffee: a mix of coffee, a double whiskey, sugar and cream, the proportions varying according to the maker. You can always ask for a weak one, or one without sugar
Irish stew: a casserole of chunks of lamb with onions and parsley, topped with sliced potato
Porter cake: a very filling cake made with dried fruit such as sultanas and raisins, a porter, usually Guinness, and spices
Soda cake: a little like soda bread, but with raisins
Soda farl: a cross between a bread and a cake, made with soda and buttermilk
Struisín Gaelach: Gaelic for Irish stew
Uisce Beatha: Gaelic phrase from which the word 'whiskey' derives, meaning 'water of life'
Wheaten bread: Northern Irish version of brown soda bread
White pudding: Black pudding without the blood

RESTAURANT CLASSIFICATIONS

The AA's restaurant inspectors award ❀ rosettes to restaurants annually on a rising scale from one to five. These awards are based purely on the quality of food on the plate. The following give an indication of the levels of quality to be expected:

❀ Excellent local restaurants serving food prepared with care, understanding and skill, using good-quality ingredients.

❀❀ The best local restaurants, which aim for and achieve higher standards, better consistency and greater precision in the cooking. There will be obvious attention to the selection of quality ingredients.

❀❀❀ Outstanding restaurants that demand recognition well beyond their local area. The cooking will be underpinned by the selection and sympathetic treatment of the highest quality ingredients. Timing, seasoning and the judgement of flavour combinations will be consistently excellent, supported by other elements such as intelligent service and a good wine list.

❀❀❀❀ Among the very best restaurants in the British Isles and the Republic of Ireland. These restaurants exhibit ambition, excellence, superb technical skills and remarkable consistency. They combine appreciation of culinary traditions with a desire for further exploration and improvement.

❀❀❀❀❀ The finest restaurants in the British Isles and the Republic of Ireland, where the cooking stands comparison with the best in the world. These restaurants will have highly individual voices, exceptional culinary skills and set the standards to which others aspire.

The restaurants, cafés and pubs in the listings that do not have a rosette rating have not been inspected by the AA and are not part of its classification scheme.

DUBLIN

The thriving city of Dublin has many excellent restaurants, with Restaurant Patrick Guilbaud, L'Ecrivain and Thornton's (in The Fitzwilliam hotel, ⊳ 306) among the best. There are many other top quality restaurants, and numerous more affordable places still serving good cuisine.

Dubliners like to have fun, though, not just to worship at gastronomy temples, and places that flourish tend to be lively as well as providing tasty and innovative food. If you want to sample Irish food at its hearty best, then restaurants such as Gallagher's Boxty House in Temple Bar and many of the city's fine old pubs will provide just that. Dublin also has a thriving ethnic eating scene, including especially good Italian and Mexican places, with Indian, Chinese, Japanese and others too. You could spend a year in Dublin and not grow tired of the variety.

PRICES AND SYMBOLS

The restaurants are listed alphabetically (excluding The, Il and Le). The prices given are for a two-course lunch (L) and a three-course dinner (D) for two people, without drinks. The wine price is for the least expensive bottle.
For alternative places to eat, see pages 199–207.

For a key to the symbols, ⊳ 2.

IL BACCARO

Diceman's Corner, Meeting House Square, Dublin
Tel 01 671 4597

An Italian eatery in a 17th-century cellar; you step down into two tiny barrel-shaped rooms with curving ceilings made completely of red brick. It has the rustic informal atmosphere of a traditional Italian *osteria* where young Italian staff serve authentic regional dishes from a weekly changing menu. Il Baccaro faces a pedestrianized square in Temple Bar where outdoor seating is available in summer.

Sun–Fri 6–11, Sat 12–11
L €44, D €56, Wine from €18.40
Cross-city buses
DART Tara Street

BAD ASS CAFÉ

9–11 Crown Alley, Dublin
Tel 01 671 2596

Bad Ass first opened its doors in 1983 serving what it's best at: affordable burgers, pizza, barbecued chicken wings and coffee. Not a lot has changed at this warehouse-style diner where singer Sinéad O'Connor once worked as a waitress but, although maybe a bit uncool, it hasn't lost its edge as a meeting place for Dublin's youth. The café's heritage is retained in the overhead mechanical pulley that was used to whisk your order to the kitchen and through memorabilia posted on the walls.

Mon–Wed 12–9, Thu 12–10, Fri, Sat 9am–11pm, Sun 10–9
L €30, D €30
Cross-city buses
DART Tara Street

BOTTICELLI

3 Temple Bar, Dublin
Tel 01 672 7289

Situated in the heart of Temple Bar, this authentic Italian restaurant is run by Italians. Dependable traditional dishes—pasta, pizza, meat and fish dishes, plus delicious ice cream for dessert—are made from fresh and imported Italian ingredients. The fairly plain interior has paintings of Italian landscapes on the walls. You can choose to sit overlooking buzzing Temple Bar or, if you book early, facing the river.

Daily 12.30–midnight
L €17.60, D €46, Wine from €17
Cross-city buses
DART Tara Street

BROWNES BRASSERIE

22 St. Stephen's Green North, Dublin
Tel 01 638 3939
www.brownesdublin.com

In a Georgian town house facing St. Stephen's Green in the heart of Dublin, Brownes provides romantic dining at its best. The spectacular dining room boasts chandeliers and Italian-style friezes and is considered one of the most stylish in the city. Head chef Steven O'Connor's continental fare includes sumptuous dishes like the house special, pan-fried loin of venison with Irish cabbage, celeriac purée and seared foie gras.

Daily 12.30–2.30, 6.30–10; closed L Sat
L €60, D €92, Wine from €21
Cross-city buses
DART Pearse

CAFÉ MAO

2–3 Chatham Row, Dublin
Tel 01 670 4899
www.cafemao.com

Bold hues and Warhol pictures of Chairman Mao, are the theme at this trendy restaurant, which brings a fresh approach to oriental cooking. Asian fusion dishes combine Malaysian, Thai, Vietnamese and Indonesian tastes, cooked to perfection. Dishes such as chilli squid, Thai fish cakes, *nasi goreng* and Indonesian tiger prawns, plus vegetarian options, appear on the changing menu. Close to fashionable Grafton Street, Mao draws a young crowd at all times of the day.

Daily 12–11
L €54, D €54, Wine from €16.95
Cross-city buses
DART Pearse

CHAPTER ONE

18–19 Parnell Square, Dublin
Tel 01 8732266
www.chapteronerestaurant.com

Chapter One, in the basement of the Dublin Writers Museum, puts a modern twist to consistently excellent classic French cooking, which includes grilled skate with creamed leeks, roast salsify, red wine butter and boulangère potato or lasagne of crab, shellfish and fennel velouté. The walls are hung with fine art, and the subtle tones of the interior give an air of sophistication to the dining room. For wine lovers, a look at the impressive stocks of the wine cellar is a must. The restaurant is very popular with theatregoers, who come here for the pre-show meal served between 6 and 7.

Tue–Fri 12.30–2.30, Tue–Sat 6–11
L €50, D from €90, Wine €20
1, 2, 46
DART Connolly
To the north of the city hub

SPECIAL

BRAZEN HEAD

20 Lower Bridge Street, Dublin 8
Tel Restaurant: 01 677 9549
Bar: 01 679 5186
www.brazenhead.com

Ireland's oldest pub dates back 800 years and remains the archetypal Irish pub, with a lively atmosphere, good music, food and beer. The Courtyard Restaurant attached to the pub serves a mix of traditional Irish and international cuisine, accompanied by a good range of wines. Patrons can choose the bar they prefer by the live music being played in them: traditional Irish music in one and a variety of styles in the other. The pub's literary connections must not be overlooked either; the Brazen Head was frequented by James Joyce, who mentioned it in *Ulysses*.

Mon–Wed 11–11, Thu–Sat 11am–midnight
L (carvery) €40, D from €50, Wine from €18
DART Tara Street
Short walk from the heart of the city on the left-hand side of Bridge Street, just before the bridge

CLARION HOTEL DUBLIN IFSC ❀

North Wall Quay, International Financial Services Centre (IFSC), Dublin 1
Tel 01 433 8800
www.clarionhotelifsc.com

The Sinergie restaurant at the Clarion serves interesting food flavour combinations based on a modern Irish theme. Glass walls feature throughout, creating a light and spacious atmosphere.

Daily 6–midnight, Mon–Fri 12–2.30
L €26, D €49, Wine from €19.50
DART Connolly
In the city heart, past Custom Quay

DAVY BYRNE'S

21 Duke Street, Dublin 2
Tel 01 677 5217
www.davybyrnespub.com

Since 1889, when Davy Byrne first hung his name over the door of the premises in Duke Street, the pub has had a loyal following and went on to become a meeting place for writers including James Joyce, who featured the pub and its owner in *Ulysses*. Today, the pub, with its long marble counter, polished wood columns and bright domed ceiling, attracts many visitors for food and drink as well as for its literary connections. The menu has a range of salads and hot dishes, or you can just have a sandwich, or try a plate of oysters accompanied by a pint of Guinness.

Mon–Wed 11.30–11.30, Thu–Fri 11am–12.30am, Sat 10.30am–12.30am, Sun 12.30–11
Hot bar food from €9.45
7
DART Pearse
A short walk from Grafton Street in the middle of Dublin

L'ECRIVAIN

109a Lower Baggot Street, Dublin
Tel 01 661 1919
www.lecrivain.com

Diners can enjoy fine French cuisine and admirable wines at this minimalist, contemporary-style restaurant, with its large windows and modern art hung high on the walls. Chef Derry Clarke uses fresh local produce to create some outstanding dishes such as his signature one, seared Clonakilty black pudding, the notable crisp duck confit, or pan-seared ray wing with buttered asparagus wrapped in cured ham. A good selection of wines is available to complement your meal.

Mon–Fri 12.30–2, Mon–Sat 7–10.30
L €60, D €120, Wine from €21
7, then short walk
DART Pearse
From St. Stephen's Green North, go east to Baggot Street, then Lower Baggot Street. Restaurant is on south side of street, which is a divided highway; if driving, telephone for directions

EDEN

Meeting House Square, Dublin
Tel 01 670 5372
www.edenrestaurant.ie

Sleek and chic, Eden is in an ideal spot overlooking a busy square in Temple Bar. Contemporary food with a distinctive Irish taste is served in a spacious stark white space with huge picture windows and a relaxed atmosphere. Among the innovative dishes are pan-roasted guinea fowl with celeriac mash, glazed shallots, garlic and thyme jus, or vegetarian choices such as wild mushroom parcel with spinach, feta and cashew nuts.

Daily 12.30–3, 6–10.30
L €38, D €80, Wine from €22
Cross-city buses
DART Tara Street

FINNSTOWN COUNTRY HOUSE ❀

Newcastle Road, Dublin
Tel 01 601 0700
www.finnstown-hotel.ie

The restaurant in this beautiful old country house hotel offers a surprising choice of international dishes including roast crispy duckling with a fruit stuffing, pan-fried medallions of fillet beef with shallot mash, Bordeaux jus and Café de Paris sauce. For dessert lovers, finish with the chocolate and orange cheesecake with fruit coulis or a Finnstown sticky toffee pudding with a whiskey and caramel sauce. The accurately cooked dishes are beautifully

presented and are created from sound local produce. There's also a children's menu.

Mon–Sat 12.30–2.30, 7.30–9.30
L €38, D €72, Wine from €16.25
25A from Quays, then a short walk
From M1 take the first exit onto M50 southbound. First exit after Toll Bridge. At roundabout (traffic circle) take third exit left (N4 W) and continue over next two roundabouts. Hotel with restaurant is on the right

LES FRÈRES JACQUES
74 Dame Street, Dublin
Tel 01 679 4555
www.lesfreresjacques.com
In a great position by the Olympia Theatre, Les Frères Jacques offers French classic cooking with an emphasis on seafood. The home-cured salmon and toasted brioche with an anchovy and lemon mayonnaise is superb, as is the steamed sea trout in a basket of wild rice with a cider cream sauce. Desserts complement the subtle flavours of the main courses and include pear and frangipane bake with a honey and caramel chew ice cream.
Mon–Sat 12.15–2.30, 7.15–10.30
L from €34, D from €44, Wine from €18.50
10, 19
DART Pearse
Opposite City Hall

GALLAGHERS BOXTY HOUSE
20 Temple Bar, Dublin
Tel 01 677 2762
www.boxtyhouse.ie
Much hyped restaurant in Temple Bar, but it does have the feel of a traditional country kitchen—chunky wooden tables, open fires, wood beams and brass lanterns. The menu combines the best Irish cooking with individual touches, based on a unique tradition, the boxty—a potato pancake with a range of fillings such as boiled bacon and cabbage, various meats, or fish in a tasty sauce.
Mon–Fri 9am–11pm, Sat–Sun 10am–11.30pm
L €46, D €46, Wine from €18
Cross-city buses
DART Tara Street

HALÓ RESTAURANT ❀❀
The Morrison Hotel, Lower Ormond Quay, Dublin
Tel 01 887 2400
www.morrisonhotel.ie
This newly built hotel was designed by the renowned John Rocha and Douglas Wallace. Wood, stone and natural fabrics are combined with vibrant hues to create a relaxing environment that follows through to the dining room. The contemporary menu offers sophisticated, beautifully presented dishes along the lines of ballotine of foie gras with spiced pineapple compote and toasted brioche, and organic duck breast, sweet potato and celeriac gnocchi with spiced plum and garlic greens. Desserts are equally delicious and there is a very good wine list.
Daily 7pm–9.30pm
D €76, Wine from €20.95
7
DART Tara Street
On the north bank of the River Liffey, opposite Temple Bar

JACOB'S LADDER
4 Nassau Street, Dublin
Tel 01 670 3865
www.jacobsladder.ie
This light and airy restaurant spreads over two floors and is in a great position on Nassau Street with views of Trinity College. Chef/patron Adrian Roche creates punchy modern food with dishes such as marinated salmon with leek quiche, fried oyster and grain mustard and fillet of mackerel and red mullet with noodle cakes. Desserts find inventive uses of fruit such as iced lemon parfait with marinated strawberries gratinéed with almond sauce. The wine list has a good selection of wines from around the globe as well as champagne and port.
Tue–Fri 12.30–2.30, 6–10, Sat 12.30–2, 7–10
L €40, D €90, Wine from €21
7
DART Pearse
Follow signs for Trinity College and then turn into Nassau Street and park at Satanta Place car park

JOHNNIE FOX'S PUB
Glencullen, The Dublin Mountains, Co. Dublin
Tel 01 295 5647
www.jfp.ie
Known as Ireland's 'highest' pub, Johnnie Fox's enjoys a lovely position nestled in the Dublin Mountains. The bar has retained its old-world charm yet the atmosphere is lively and friendly. Every night of the week you can hear live Irish music, and on the pub's famous hooley nights Irish dancing, traditional music and a four-course meal make the evening special. À la carte meals are served in the restaurant area of the pub and feature a good range of Irish classics using the best of local produce.
Mon–Sat 10.30am–11.30pm, Sun 12.30–11
L from €50, D from €60, Wine from €19.50
44B
Take N11 south; at Donnybrook turn left on R117 to Kilternan then turn right to Glencullen; about a 30-min drive from Dublin

MERIDIAN RESTAURANT ❀
Marine Hotel, Sutton Cross, Co. Dublin
Tel 01 839 0000
www.marinehotel.ie
On the road from Dublin to the fishing village of Howth, this smart hotel restaurant is set in 1.6ha (4 acres) of gardens with views of Dublin Bay. The Irish- and French-inspired food shows a commitment to old preferences along with more fashionable tastes, specializing in local fish and seafood. Rocket leaf salad might share the starter menu with oven-roast quail, or warm smoked trout fillets while main courses could include ostrich steak, grilled black sole and roast duckling with smoked garlic and spring onion jus. Smart dress is preferred.

Daily 12.30–2.30, 6.30–10.30
L €51, D €65, Wine from €18.50
31, 31B
8km (5 miles) from city on Dublin Bay, on the road to Howth

MONTY'S OF KATHMANDU
28 Eustace Street, Dublin
Tel 01 670 4911
www.monty's.ie
This is the only Nepalese restaurant in Dublin. Located in Temple Bar, it draws people from far and wide to sample the exceptional cooking. Intriguing dishes using secret ingredients include deep-fried chicken or prawns with onions, capsicum, tomatoes and green chillies. The ethnic-style dining room over two floors is modest and unassuming with white-painted woodwork,

paintings of Nepal and dark furniture. Friendly waiters are happy to give advice about the food.
Mon–Sat 12–2.30, 6–11.30, Sun 6–11
L €34, D €70, Wine from €17
Cross-city buses
DART Tara Street

NUDE
21 Suffolk Street, Dublin
Tel 01 677 4804
An eco-friendly café with a commitment to 'Fairtrade' and recycling based on social concerns about protecting the environment. Their own range of organic products, such as wraps, salads, soup, low-fat desserts, smoothies and juices are free from additives and contain ingredients like ginseng and bee pollen. These healthy options can be taken away or eaten at the pinewood refectory tables set against lime green paintwork and milk crates, lined up waiting for the empties.
Mon–Fri 8am–9pm, Sat 10–9, Sun until 7pm
L €5, D €14
Cross-city buses
DART Pearse

NUMBER 10 ❀❀
Longfields Hotel, Lower Fitzwilliam Street, Dublin
Tel 01 676 1367
www.longfields.ie
At this restaurant you'll find fine contemporary dining with a dash of Irish humour. Friendly and chatty staff serve modish combinations in the intimate, elegant dining room. Typical dishes on the good value, set-price menu created by chef Kevin Arundel might be roasted pepper and tomato soup with parmesan and basil or cannelloni of goat's cheese, roasted red peppers, Puy lentils and salsa verde. The food is accompanied by a choice of very good wines.
Mon–Sat 12.30–2.30, 7–10.30; closed L Sat, Dec
L €28, D €34, Wine from €19
7, 10, 45
DART Pearse
From St. Stephens Green turn into Baggot Street and then turn left into Lower Fitzwilliam Street just before Larry Murphy's Pub

ONE PICO
5–6 Molesworth Place, School House Lane, Dublin
Tel 01 676 0300
The distinctive warm, yellow tones of the exterior are continued through to the dining area and along with the soft tones of the wood floor and comfortable, upholstered chairs, create a feeling of warmth and relaxation. The cooking makes the most of local produce, with dishes such as seared scallops and boudin noir with mousseline potato and horseradish foam or mignon of Irish Angus beef fillet with mushroom duxelles, braised root vegetables and truffle jus. A carefully selected range of wines complements the food.
Mon–Sat 12.30–2.30, 6–10.30
L €44.50, D €70, Wine from €25
7, 45
DART Pearse
Between the Mansion House and the National Museum

OSBORNE ❀❀
Portmarnock Hotel, Strand Road, Portmarnock, Co. Dublin
Tel 01 846 0611
www.portmarnock.com

Overlooking the sea, the smart Osborne restaurant allows diners to enjoy coastal views while they eat. A comprehensive carte of well-conceived classical dishes is executed with flair and imagination, typified by baked loin of rabbit on a bread and butter pudding with wild mushrooms or medallion of venison served with blackcurrant and parsley topping.
Tue–Sat, dinner only
D €120, Wine from €19.75
32A, 32B, 32X, 102, 105, 230
Take M1 north from city; at junction with R601 take turn towards Malahide. After 3km (2 miles) turn left at T-junction, go through Malahide and the hotel is 3.5km (2.2 miles) on the left

SPECIAL

RESTAURANT PATRICK GUILBAUD ❀❀❀❀
Merrion Hotel, 21 Upper Merrion Street, Dublin
Tel 01 676 4192
www.restaurantpatrickgilbaud.ie
The contemporary-style dining room is generously sized and flooded with natural light, while a particularly fine collection of modern Irish paintings (including *Frying Pan, Funnel, Eggs & Lemons* by William Scott which features on the menu cover) hangs on the walls. Service is impeccable. 'Modern classic cuisine using Irish produce in season' is the stated philosophy here, and although technique may be firmly rooted in the French tradition, there's plenty of flair and innovation. Enormous, sweetly caramelized scallops, for instance, might appear with a 'cake' of sliced apple and a dressing of wine vinegar, apple juice and almond oil, while a delicate ravioli of lobster is served with a coconut scented cream and kari (curry) oil. A signature dish of crubeen (pig's trotter) is particularly impressive, the trotter boned and stuffed with a very fine dice of trotter meat, carrot, morels and truffle, then finely sliced and presented carpaccio style with an intriguing Meaux mustard ice-cream. Desserts, along the lines of ravioli of pineapple with exotic fruits, spiced jelly and a coconut ice cream are simply superb. Great value lunch menu.
Tue–Sat 12.30–2.15, 7–10.15; closed 1st week Jan
L €60, D from €180, Wine from €28
7
DART Pearse
At the top of Upper Merrion Street on the left, beyond the Government buildings on the right

THE PAVILION ❀❀
Herbert Park Hotel, Ballsbridge, Dublin
Tel 01 667 2200
www.herbertparkhotel.ie
The Pavilion restaurant, decorated with murals and contemporary abstract art by

artists such as Cliona Doyle, has fabulous views over parkland. Shuttered glass doors open onto a terrace for fine-weather dining. The carte is essentially Irish but with international influences. Fresh Irish produce is to the fore, notably seafood from Howth and Wicklow lamb. Jazz buffet lunches and afternoon teas are especially good.

Daily 12.30–2.30, 5.30–9.30; closed D Sun and public holidays

L €40, D €90, Wine from €21

DART Pearse

7

A 5-min drive from the middle of the city. South over canal into Northumberland Road to Ballsbridge. Turn right and cross the bridge in Ballsbridge then take the first right down Anglesea Road

QUEEN OF TARTS

4 Cork Hill, Dame Street, Dublin

Tel 01 670 7499

Behind the quaint shop window of this tea shop are glass cookie jars, cake stands and wicker baskets that display the goodies that the owners bake themselves. Good breakfast options are followed by lunch choices such as hot savoury tarts and sandwiches made from home-baked breads. With your afternoon tea you can indulge in giant cookies, home-made cakes, fruit crumbles or what has got to be the best carrot cake in town.

Mon–Fri 7.30–6, Sat 9–6, Sun 10–6

B €12, L €14, afternoon tea €10. No credit cards

Cross-city buses

DART Tara Street

RESTAURANT 23 ❀

The Gresham Hotel, 23 Upper O'Connell Street, Dublin

Tel 01 874 6881

www.gresham-hotels.com

Light wood and glass fittings feature at this contemporary restaurant which is spread over two floors. Dinner fare is French and Irish. Traditional Irish dishes including Wicklow lamb and Irish salmon are created using a modern approach, and there is a good choice of signature dishes and daily specials.

Mon–Sat 5.15–10.30

D €46, Wine from €27.50

DART Connolly

Close to the GPO

ROLY'S BISTRO

7 Ballsbridge Terrace, Dublin

Tel 01 668 2611

www.rolysbistro.ie

This popular and lively bistro provides robust retro cooking, for example the parsnip and apple soup with curry cream or the roast pumpkin risotto with parmesan cheese shavings. Popular dishes such as warm chocolate brownie and vanilla ice cream with nutty chocolate sauce grace the dessert menu. The bistro is renowned for its homemade breads including Colin's gluten-free bread which can be bought at reception.

Daily 12–2.45, 6–9.45

L €37, D from €50, Wine from €28

5, 7, 45

DART Lansdowne Road

A 5- to 10-min drive south of the city on Northumberland Road; close to Herbert Park

LA STAMPA

35 Dawson Street, Dublin

Tel 01 677 8611

www.lastampa.ie

In a prime spot close to St. Stephen's Green, La Stampa combines an intimate atmosphere with superb modern European cooking, which delivers such treats as sevruga caviar with crème fraiche and toast followed by whole roast monkfish tail with pepperonata and Serrano ham. The elegant 19th-century dining room is adorned with rich fabrics, mirrors, fine artwork and candles, and is popular with a well-heeled crowd. Book well ahead.

Mon–Thu 6–12, Fri–Sat 6–12.30

D €100, Wine from €25

Cross-city buses

DART Pearse

WINTER GARDEN RESTAURANT

Red Cow Moran's Hotel, Red Cow Complex, Naas Road, Dublin

Tel 01 459 3650

www.moranhotels.com

Modern Irish cuisine is a feature of the daily changing menu in the Winter Garden Restaurant. Starters are deliciously light, such as the tian of smoked salmon with cream cheese set on a bed of lolla rossa leaves and drizzled with a house dressing, followed by classics such as beef stroganoff with a julienne of sautéed vegetables and flamed with brandy, bound in an onion and mushroom cream and served with pilaff rice. Traditional desserts include crème caramel and pecan tart.

Mon–Sat 12.30–3, 5.30–10, Sun 12.30–10.30

L €72, D from €80, Wine from €20

51, 69

At junction of M50 (ring road) and N7 Naas road, on the city side of the ring road

SPECIAL

THE TEA ROOM RESTAURANT ❀❀

The Clarence Hotel, 6–8 Wellington Quay, Dublin

Tel 01 407 0813

www.theclarence.ie

The Tea Room Restaurant can be found in this classic hotel, which dates from 1852 and has been given a fabulous contemporary look by rock band U2's Bono and the Edge. The restaurant is bathed in natural light from its floor to ceiling windows that look out over bustling Temple Bar. Flexible menus, offering Irish and French cuisine, include Sunday brunch, a speedy lunch-hour option and an eight-course tasting menu with wine.

Mon–Fri 12.30–2.30, 6.30–10.30, Sat 6.30–10.30, Sun 12.30–2.30, 6.30–9.30

L €35, D €70, Wine from €24.50

25, 66

DART Tara Street

On the south bank of the River Liffey in the Temple Bar area

THE EAST

With its easy access to Dublin, and its popularity for short breaks with both locals and visitors, the East can sustain a variety of good eating options, from country house hotels to the more rustic fare of traditional pubs. It has a long sea coast, so fresh fish is readily available, while the more rural areas inland are definitely farming country. The food here may not always be sophisticated, but if you stick to the local fish, beef, lamb and vegetables you'll eat well. Also local is Smithwick's bitter, made in Kilkenny, and the most common beer in the Republic. It has a very different taste to the more popular porters such as Guinness, and is well worth trying.

ARKLOW

HOWARD'S DINING ROOM ❀

Arklow Bay Hotel, Ferrybank, Arklow, Co. Wicklow
Tel 0402 32309
www.arklowbay.com

Diners can enjoy panoramic views of Arklow Bay from Howard's, and light, subtle decoration and candles placed around the room and in unlit fireplaces add to the charm. The carte emphasizes the commitment to quality and freshness with the likes of confit of duckling with Clonakilty pudding, and caraway roast halibut steak with celeriac mash.

Mon–Fri 6–10, Sat–Sun 6–9
L €40, D €58, Wine from €17.95
Come off the N11 at the by-pass for Arklow. After 2km (1 mile) turn left and the premises can be found 200m (210 yards) on the left

BALLYCONNELL

CONALL CAERNACH RESTAURANT ❀

Slieve Russell Hotel, Ballyconnell, Co. Cavan
Tel 049 952 6444
www.quinnhotels.com

Chef Peter Denny is the inspiration behind this bistro-style restaurant, which leans towards international dishes using Irish ingredients. Professional service is coupled with warm hospitality. The fixed-price dinner menu offers such combinations as mango and papaya salad with ginger and coriander and crispy duckling with plum glaze.

Daily 12.30–2.15, 7–9.15
L €30, D €80, Wine from €19.95
On the left, approximately 9km (6 miles) from Belturbet on N87 west towards Ballyconnell

CARRICKMACROSS

NUREMORE HOTEL ❀❀

Carrickmacross, Co. Monaghan
Tel 042 966 1438
www.nuremore-hotel.ie

The elegant, spacious, split-level dining room overlooks parkland and a golf course.

PRICES AND SYMBOLS

The restaurants are listed alphabetically (excluding The, Il and Le). The prices given are for a two-course lunch (L) and a three-course dinner (D) for two people, without drinks. The wine price is for the least expensive bottle.
For alternative places to eat, see pages 208–212.

For a key to the symbols, ▷ 2.

Head chef Raymond McArdle specializes in classic French and contemporary Irish dishes, with exceptional sauces. The poached and grilled squab pigeon from Bresse with a blanquette of vegetables is delicious, and the colcannon of local spring lamb with baked lamb tourte, creamed artichokes, savoy cabbage and lamb jus is another superb example from the well-conceived menu.

Daily 12.30–2.30, 6.30–9.45; closed L Sat
L €39, D €85, Wine from €18
3km (2 miles) south of Carrickmacross on N2 Dublin road

GOREY

MARLFIELD HOUSE ❀❀❀

Gorey, Co. Wexford
Tel 055 21124
www.marlfieldhouse.com

Dating from around 1830, this mansion has an ornate conservatory restaurant with frescoed walls and high ceilings. Fine local produce and trendy ingredients blend in classically based, uncomplicated dishes with hints of the Mediterranean. The kitchen garden at Marlfield House supplies most of the vegetables and herbs. Dress restrictions: jacket and tie preferred.

Mon–Sat 7–9, Sun 12.30–1.45, 7–9
L €76, D €116, Wine from €25
1.5km (1 mile) outside Gorey town on the Courtown Road, R742

SPECIAL IN KILKENNY

RIVERSIDE RESTAURANT ❀

Kilkenny River Court Hotel, The Bridge, John Street, Kilkenny, Co. Kilkenny
Tel 056 772 3388
www.kilrivercourt.com

This is a spacious restaurant with a black and white marble floor, crystal chandeliers and huge windows which flood the restaurant with natural light and give lovely views of the River Nore and Kilkenny Castle. The chefs pride themselves on the extensive international dinner menu, with dishes such as a warm trio of handmade local farmhouse cheeses, with raspberry tagliatelle, together served with a strawberry vinaigrette followed by tian of monkfish and cod with Parma ham, roasted tomatoes and a rocket pesto, baked in crepinette. Sunday lunch can be a full-blown meal or just a sandwich, all made using fresh local produce.

Mon–Sat 6–9.30, Sun 12.30–2.30, 6–9.30
L €44, D €48, Wine from €21.50
The hotel is opposite Kilkenny Castle (on the River Nore side of the castle)

LEIGHLINBRIDGE

THE LORD BAGENAL

Leighlinbridge, Co. Carlow
Tel 059 972 1668
www.lordbagenal.com

On the banks of the River Barrow, this country pub has grounds stretching down to its marina, and diners in the restaurant can enjoy lovely garden views. The restaurant menu is innovative and uses good quality ingredients complemented by a choice of fine wines. There is also a crèche.

Carvery: daily 12.30–2.30, all day Sun. Restaurant: Mon–Sat 6–10, Sun 6–9
L from €25, D €50, Wine from €14.50
In middle of village

LEIXLIP

THE BRADAUN RESTAURANT

❀❀

Leixlip House Hotel, Captains Hill, Leixlip, Co. Kildare

Tel 01 624 2268

www.leixliphouse.com/bradaun.html

The restaurant in this quiet country hotel has a pleasing atmosphere that encourages guests to linger. The accomplished modern Irish cooking is given an occasional imaginative twist toward the Mediterranean. Typical dishes include crab-meat profiteroles, sesame-seed crust, apple and lime chutney, cassoulette of rabbit with *forestière jus* and tarragon, and bread and butter pudding with toffee ice cream and apricot coulis.

Mon–Sat 12–2, 7–10, Sun 12–4, 7–8.30

L €50, D from €60, Wine from €18.50

From Dublin follow the N4 and take the Leixlip slip road exit into Leixlip Town. Take a right turn onto Captain's Hill and the hotel is the first on the left

MACREDDIN

THE STRAWBERRY TREE ❀❀

Brooklodge Hotel, Macreddin, Co. Wicklow

Tel 0402 36444

www.brooklodge.com

The elegant restaurant at this unique private village is for discerning diners. Only organic, wild and free range produce is used, and fixed-price menus offer light and fresh summer dishes, and earthy, gamey ones in the winter: breast of wood pigeon with chocolate Shiraz sauce, smoked salmon paté with citrus cream and winter herb gnocchi with basil and wild mushrooms.

Mon–Sat 1.30–4, 7–9, Sun 1.30–4, 6.30–8

L €70, D €96, Wine from €21

From N11, take R752 to Rathdrum, then R753 to Aughrim and follow signs for Macreddin 3km (2 miles) from Aughrim village

MAYNOOTH

MOYGLARE MANOR ❀❀

Moyglare, Maynooth, Co. Kildare

Tel 01 628 6351

www.moyglaremanor.ie

This beautiful 18th-century Georgian house is filled with antiques and conjures up the ultimate country house atmosphere. Food is prepared in true country house style; fruit and

vegetables from the gardens and orchards are used, along with quality local meats and fresh fish. Crab claws and prawns on a potato galette might be followed by tender roast breast of duckling, or baked turbot with an aromatic cream and bay leaf sauce.

Tue–Sun 12.30–2, 7–10; closed L Sat

L from €25, D €110, Wine from €26.95

From the main street turn left but keep to the right lane. Turn left at the church and continue for 2km (1.5 miles); go over a humpback bridge and take the first turning on the left

NAAS

THE TURNER RESTAURANT

❀❀

Killashee House, Kilcullen Road, Naas, Co. Kildare

Tel 045 879277

www.killasheehouse.com

Decked out in scarlet and gold, with high ceilings and crystal chandeliers, this room has an air of natural elegance and overlooks the beautiful Fountain Garden. A lengthy menu offers plenty of choice and some creative options, such as roasted rack of lamb with pepper and aubergine (eggplant) caviar, *pomme fondant*, tian of vegetables and a madeira and thyme jus. Interesting desserts include caramelized banana bavarois with peanut-butter crisps and coriander toffee sauce.

Daily 1–3, 7–9.45

L €60, D €90, Wine from €35

1.5km (1 mile) from Naas on old Kilcullen Road, on the left past the Garda (police station)

NEWBRIDGE

KEADEN HOTEL ❀❀

Curragh Road, Newbridge, Co. Kildare

Tel 045 431666

www.keadenhotel.kildare.ie

The finest ingredients go into the various fixed-price menus and bistro carte: From the latter expect several pasta and fish choices, as well as prime Irish beef in various guises. From the set dinner menu consider Swiss cheese crêpe with rocket salad, and duck leg confit to start, followed by pan-seared ostrich fillet, veal loin cutlet with onion soubise or braised lamb shank.

Daily 12.30–2, 7–10

L €30, D €45, Wine from €16

Towards the southwestern outskirts of Newbridge on the Curragh Road

RATHNEW

THE BRUNEL RESTAURANT ❀

Tinakilly Country House & Restaurant, Rathnew, Co. Wicklow

Tel 0404 69274

www.tinakilly.ie

Sea views and stunning scenery add to the experience at this charming country house restaurant. The modern cooking blends classical French cuisine with up-to-the-minute culinary ideas and might feature roast quail on beetroot couscous, Thai-spiced chickpeas with mizuna and parfait of duck livers on toasted brioche. Smart dress required.

Tue–Sat 7pm–9pm

D €55, Wine from €24

Take R750 towards Wicklow to Rathnew, entrance to the hotel is approximately 500m (550 yards) from the village on the left

ROSSLARE

LA MARINE BISTRO ❀❀

Kelly's Resort Hotel, Rosslare, Co. Wexford

Tel 053 32114

www.kellys.ie

The stylish, intimate restaurant features original art from the hotel's renowned collection. There is an emphasis on local produce including vegetables and fresh fish from Kilmore Quay, Wexford beef and the hotel's own lamb. Grilled lamb's liver with tossed green salad may be a lunch choice followed by summer fruit crumble and fresh cream while the grilled Wicklow steak with wild mushroom and Madeira jus or roast Barbary duckling with sauce Curaçao may feature on the dinner menu.

Daily 12.30–1.45, 7–9; closed L Sat, mid-Dec to end Feb

L €44, D €80, Wine from €12.50

Turn off the N25 Wexford–Rosslare Harbour road. Hotel is 6km (4 miles) from the ferry harbour

STRAFFAN

BYERLEY TURK ❀❀❀

The Kildare Hotel, Straffan, Co. Kildare
Tel 01 601 7200
www.kclub.ie

This magnificent establishment has two distinct dining experiences. The sumptuous Byerley Turk has high ceilings, ornate chandeliers, lavish furnishings and magnificent garden views. The inspired French cuisine with a unique Irish interpretation uses vegetables, fruit and herbs grown in the hotel's own walled garden. A gateau of fresh crab served with a citrus emulsion might be followed by roast guinea fowl with braised leg, accompanied by black pudding and grilled hazelnuts. Legends Restaurant, in the K Club, offers an extensive lunch menu of fine European cuisine. Smart dress code.

Daily 7pm–9.30pm

D €130, Wine from €24

From Dublin take N4, at start of M4 turn left on R403. After 11km (7 miles) turn left on R406 for Straffan. The hotel is just outside the village on the right

THOMASTOWN

LADY HELEN DINING ROOM ❀❀

Mount Juliet Conrad Hotel, Thomastown, Co. Kilkenny
Tel 056 777 3000
www.kilrivercourt.com

On one of the loveliest estates in Ireland, renowned for the food served in the Lady Helen Dining Room. The formal room has an understated elegance with high ceilings and floor-to-ceiling windows with views of the River Nore and the sweeping landscape beyond. From

the extensive choice of main dishes expect truffled breast of corn-fed chicken with liver hash brown, spinach and wild mushroom sauce, or breast of duck seasoned with anise and cinnamon. Fresh vegetables and herbs come from the kitchen gardens.

Daily 7pm–9.30pm

D €133, Wine from €27

From Thomastown follow signs to Mount Juliet Conrad Hotel

SPECIAL IN STRAFFAN

BARBERSTOWN CASTLE ❀❀

Clan Celdridge Road, Straffan, Co. Kildare
Tel 01 628 8157
www.barberstowncastle.ie

Dining here is a candlelit and atmospheric occasion in the original 13th-century castle keep. In this classic country-house ambience the modern French and Irish cooking comes as a rewarding surprise. From a confident carte come rosemary prawn kebabs with chilled pipérade and a well-judged saffron dressing, or perhaps asparagus salad with persillade of lamb's sweetbreads and a hazelnut dressing, while stylish main dishes might include an imaginatively composed confit and roast Gressingham duck, or baked wild salmon with pan-fried oysters.

Daily 12–2.30, 7.30–9.30; closed L Sat, 2nd–3rd week Jan

L €58, D €100, Wine from €22.50

On the Clan Celdridge Road just outside Straffan

VIRGINIA

THE PARK HOTEL ❀

Ballyjamesduff Road, Virginia, Co. Cavan
Tel 049 854 6100
www.parkhotelvirginia.com

The elegant dining room in this 18th-century hunting lodge looks out over Lough Ramoor and the beautiful gardens.

The classic country-house cooking here produces delicious starters such as crispy poppy seed parcel of mild goat's cheese and galatine of pig's trotter. Main courses to look for include a tender pan-roast fillet of beef on a bed of horseradish mashed potato, with a pesto crust and served with a red wine and thyme jus. To accompany these delights, there's a substantial wine list with many excellent choices.

Daily 6pm–9pm

D €60, Wine from €17.50

From the N3 northwest in town, turn down Ballyjamesduff Road; the Photel is 480m (500 yards) on the left just past the garden centre

WOODENBRIDGE

REDMOND RESTAURANT ❀

Woodenbridge Hotel, Woodenbridge, Co. Wicklow
Tel 0402 35146
www.woodenbridgehotel.com

Original art from the hotel's renowned collection adorns the walls at this intimate restaurant. There is an emphasis on regional produce including locally grown vegetables, fresh fish landed at Kilmore Quay, Wexford beef and the hotel's very own lamb. Game also makes a showing in such dishes as grilled Wicklow venison steak with wild mushroom and Madeira jus.

Daily 7–9, also Sun 12.30–3

L €36, D €64, Wine from €20

In the middle of town

EATING

THE SOUTH

True food lovers should head straight for the South of Ireland, for this region regards itself as the food capital of Ireland, whatever Dubliners might say. For a start it's the home of Ballymaloe in County Cork, the revered restaurant and cooking school run by Myrtle Allen, one of the nation's best-known star chefs. There are also other cooking schools, reflecting a great enthusiasm for food, and plenty of fine restaurants in the region.

Kinsale in County Cork has its own Gourmet Festival each October, with a big emphasis on the delicious local seafood, and there's a Bantry Mussel Fair too. Cork is also one of the best regional cities for eating out, as well as being the home of Murphy's, the big rival to Guinness in the bars of Ireland.

ADARE

MAIGUE RESTAURANT ❀❀

Dunraven Arms, Main Street, Adare, Co. Limerick
Tel 061 396633
www.dunravenhotel.com

Antiques and open fireplaces give charm to this friendly country inn that dates back to 1792, while large bay windows overlook the thatched cottages of one of Ireland's prettiest villages. The Maigue Restaurant majors on modern cuisine with the odd French influence. A well-balanced menu has some tempting options: You might start with a coarse country terrine, and then try sea bass with pak choi, beetroot and coriander salsa.

Daily 7–10, also Sun 12.30–1.30
L €54, D €100, Wine from €25
In the middle of town

BALLYLICKEY

SEA VIEW HOUSE HOTEL ❀

Ballylickey, Co. Cork
Tel 027 50073
www.seaviewhousehotel.com

The soft greens and gold hues of the restaurant reflect the lovely gardens surrounding the hotel. The food lives up to the promise of these stylish surroundings, with some classical ideas sharing menu space with more modern interpretations. Fresh Bantry Bay crab salad twinned with scallop mousse with vermouth sauce, and warm goat's cheese salad with blackberry compote make interesting starters before roast rack of lamb, or brill in a light wine sauce.

Daily 7–9.30; also Sun 12.30–1.45; closed Nov–end Mar
L €30, D from €44, Wine from €16
5km (3 miles) north of Bantry towards Glengariff, 70m (75 yards) off main road

PRICES AND SYMBOLS

The restaurants are listed alphabetically (excluding The, Il and Le). The prices given are for a two-course lunch (L) and a three-course dinner (D) for two people, without drinks. The wine price is for the least expensive bottle.
For alternative places to eat, see pages 213–219.

For a key to the symbols, ▷ 2.

BALTIMORE

THE BALTIMORE ROOM ❀

Casey's of Baltimore, Baltimore, Co. Cork
Tel 028 20197
www.caseysofbaltimore.com

Beloved of locals, this simply decorated restaurant, with its polished wooden floor and pine tables and chairs, boasts stunning sea views. Not surprisingly, the accent is on seafood, especially mussel and lobster dishes. The seafood comes from the catches of the Baltimore fishing fleet and the restaurant has a mussel farm to provide fresh mussels. All dishes are simply cooked to accentuate the tastes and make good use of fresh local farm produce.

Daily 12.30–2, 6.30–9
L €34, D €50, Wine from €18
Overlooking the harbour

CASHEL

THE BISHOPS' BUTTERY ❀

Cashel Palace Hotel, Main Street, Cashel, Co. Tipperary
Tel 062 62707
www.cashel-palace.ie

This Queen Anne property, with vaulted ceilings and huge fireplaces, has beautiful views of the surrounding countryside. Superb Irish cooking uses locally sourced produce as well as organically grown vegetables and herbs from the hotel's garden. To complement the neatly presented food there is a wide choice of wines from around the world. Service is friendly and professional.

Daily 12–3, 6–10
L €50, D €70, Wine from €17
On the N8, near the traffic lights in Main Street in the heart of town

CHEZ HANS

Moor Lane, Cashel, Co. Tipperary
Tel 062 61177

At this former Wesleyan chapel, familiar French dishes are listed beside modern Irish ones, and both are carefully cooked.

Tue–Sat 6.30pm–10pm
D €48, Wine from €15
Just off the N8, near Rock of Cashel

CASTLECONNELL

ACORN RESTAURANT

Castle Oaks House, Dublin Road, Castleconnell, Co. Limerick
Tel 061 377666
www.castleoaks.ie

The sumptuous surroundings and wonderful views over the River Shannon make the Acorn Restaurant an ideal place to stop and relax. Dishes might include pan-fried black sole on a prawn and leek fondue, oven-baked Barbary duck breast with an orange and kumquat glaze, and for dessert a tiramisú or sablé biscuit with seasonal fruit.

Daily 7–9, also Sun 12.30–2.30
L €46, D €70, Wine from €16.95
From Limerick City take the N7 to

Castleconnell. The hotel is on the left just as you enter the village

CHEEKPOINT

MCALPIN'S SUIR INN

Cheekpoint, Co. Waterford
Tel 051 382220
www.mcalpins.com

McAlpin's is a 16th-century inn beside the river in a pretty village, 11km (7 miles) to the east of Waterford. It has been owned and run by the McAlpin family for more than 30 years and is well known for its excellent seafood and dining in general. The food is hearty fare and the menu may feature crab bake: white crabmeat in fennel sauce with crusty breadcrumb topping. The atmosphere is friendly and the location is superb.

Tue–Sat 6pm–9.45pm
D €52, Wine from €16
In Cheekpoint village

CLONMEL

SLIEVNA MON ❀

Minella Hotel, Coleville Road, Minella, Clonmel, Co. Tipperary
Tel 052 22388
www.hotelminella.ie

Friendly staff welcome diners into the comfortable dining room, decorated in warm tones with red chairs and a red carpet, and an open fire to complete the setting. The menu offers traditional choices based on accomplished cooking of fresh produce; warm smoked chicken salad, oven-baked fillet of cod provençale, and apple pie with crème anglaise are all noteworthy.

Daily 12.30–2.30, 6.30–9.30
L €52, D €72, Wine from €22
Just outside town beside the river

COBH

JACOB'S LADDER RESTAURANT

Waters Edge Hotel, Yacht Club Quay, Cobh, Co. Cork
Tel 021 481 5566
www.watersedgehotel.ie

The brightly painted exterior of this waterfront hotel hides a chic modern restaurant in tones of sage and terracotta with tall windows and wooden floors. Irish continental cuisine dominates the menu with dishes such as chargrilled salmon fillet with a mango and lime salsa for lunch or Atlantic hot seafood platter for dinner. Ditherers be warned—the Waters Edge has a lengthy list of specials to complement an even lengthier carte. Smart casual dress required.

Daily 12.30–3, 6.30–10
L €48, D €70, Wine from €19.95
On the waterfront, follow signs for Cobh Heritage Centre & Fota Golf Club

CORK

GALLERY RESTAURANT ❀

Rochestown Park Hotel, Rochestown Road, Douglas, Co. Cork
Tel 021 489 0800
www.rochestownpark.com

The Gallery Restaurant offers a wide choice from simple fish dishes (pan-fried sole with lemon and parsley butter) to more complex carnivorous fare (sautéed pheasant, braised cabbage, lardons and red wine jus). Or you could plump for

steak with onions, mushrooms and french fries if you're in the mood for something more down to earth.

Daily 12.30–2.30, 6.30–10
L €25.20, D €65, Wine from €23.50
From central Cork take south link road. Take the third exit at the roundabout (traffic circle) for Rochestown. At the small roundabout take the third exit into Rochestown Road

CAFÉ PARADISO

16 Lancaster Quay, Western Road, Cork, Co. Cork
Tel 021 427 7939
www.cafeparadiso.ie

A lively vegetarian restaurant in a great spot just a 5-minute walk from University College Cork. The imaginative lunch menu offers choices such as feta, pinenut and couscous cake with lemon and cumin wilted spinach, while the dinner menu may list sage-grilled portobello mushrooms with tomato and glazed walnut dressing with red onion jam, smoked gubeen mash and braised cannellini beans. The wine list emphasizes Italian and New Zealand wines.

Tue–Sat 12–3, 6.30–10.30
L from €44, D from €72, Wine from €20
Follow Washington Street in the direction of Universtiy College Cork, opposite the entrance to Jurys Hotel

JACOBS

30a South Mall, Cork, Co. Cork
Tel 021 425 1530
www.jacobsonthemall.com

The high ceilings and contemporary furnishings give Jacobs a light, airy feel, a modern oasis in the bustling financial district of the city. Add to that the skilful, creative menus using top-notch ingredients, it is no wonder that this restaurant is ever popular. Lunch might be duck confit potato cakes with spinach, caramelized onion and green peppercorn jus followed by a milk chocolate and caramel brulée with strawberries. The dinner menu has such choices as crispy salmon with couscous served with marinated grilled vegetables and harissa, expertly presented. There is a good selection of dessert wines and port to finish your meal.

Mon–Sat 12.30–2.30, 6.30–10
L from €38, D from €62, Wine from €19
In the heart of the city

DINGLE

HALF DOOR

3 John Street, Dingle, Co. Kerry
Tel 066 915 1600

In the attractive village of Dingle, this popular restaurant serves excellent fresh fish dishes and traditional Irish fare. You can choose a dish of the day, or select from the interesting menu. Starters may include baked crab au gratin and the main menu has dishes such as crispy monkfish fillets with tomato and basil sauce pasta gratin.

Mon–Sat 12.30–2, 6–10
L €40, D €72, Wine from €20
In the heart of the village

FERMOY

CASTLEHYDE HOTEL ❀❀

Castlehyde, Fermoy, Co. Cork
Tel 025 31865

Old and new blend charmingly in the split-level restaurant at this carefully restored 18th-century hotel. The stylish room, complete with exposed stone arched entrance and log fire,

overlooks the gardens and woodland. The carte shows the kitchen's dedication to fresh seasonal produce: a delicately flavoured terrine of ham and duck foie gras with a gutsy texture to start perhaps, followed by a medley of seafood from nearby Ballycotton Bay, enhanced by a light lime and dill pancake filled with pineapple and passion fruit.
Daily 12.30–3, 7.30–9.30
L from €40, D from €62, Wine from €19
3km (2 miles) west of Fermoy on the Mallow Road

KENMARE

LA CASCADE ❀❀

Sheen Falls Lodge, Kenmare, Co. Kerry
Tel 064 41600
www.sheenfallslodge.ie

Dramatic views of the floodlit Sheen waterfalls are the backdrop to your meal while the resident pianist plays softly in the background at this exclusive hotel restaurant. The food isn't outdone by the views—fresh local produce and home-grown herbs contribute to dishes full of taste and panache. The sommelier knows his wines, and the choice is extensive. The Lodge catches and smokes its own salmon. Smart dress required.
Daily 7.15pm–9.30pm; closed 3 weeks Christmas and 2 Jan–1 Feb
D €130, Wine from €41.50
From Kenmare take N71 towards Glengariff. Take first left after suspension bridge

LIME TREE

Shelbourne Street, Kenmare, Co. Kerry
Tel 064 41225
The Lime Tree is in a charming stone building and is a bustling, seasonally inspired restaurant. The food is impeccably served and the Kenmare Bay seafood pot pourri, made of four types of fish cooked in parchment, is popular.
Daily 6.30–10; closed Nov–end Mar
D €70, Wine from €17
At the top of the town

SPECIAL IN KENMARE

PARK HOTEL KENMARE ❀❀❀

Kenmare, Co. Kerry
Tel 064 41200
www.parkkenmare.com
The period dining room of this renowned hotel looks out on gardens that sweep down to the water's edge. The finest produce from the neighbouring sea and the Kerry hills is used in an enticing carte of traditional dishes with a strong streak of creativity; perhaps pan-fried foie gras on Sneem black pudding, with rhubarb chutney, Granny Smith sorbet and truffle jus. Lunch is served in the lounge. Smart dress required in the restaurant.
Daily 11–6, 7–9; closed Nov–end Apr (open Christmas and New Year)
L from €30, D €96, Wine from €39.50
In Kenmare, take R569 past the golf club and continue on through the town where the hotel is on the left, at the top of the main street

PACKIE'S

Henry Street, Kenmare, Co. Kerry
Tel 064 41508
Good local ingredients are treated with care and intelligence at this busy bistro run and owned by Maura. The daily fish catch appears in a mix of Irish, European and American influenced dishes. The menu reflects this variety of food with dishes such as traditional lamb stew alongside sole and prawns with a brandy cream sauce.
Jun–end Sep Mon–Sat 6–10; Mar–end May Oct–end Dec Tue–Sat 6–10; closed Jan, Feb
D €70, Wine from €16.50
In the middle of town near the Park Hotel

KILLARNEY

FREDERICK'S ❀❀

Aghadoe Heights Hotel, Lakes of Killarney, Co. Kerry
Tel 064 31766
www.aghadoeheights.com
A stylish, modern restaurant where every table has magnificent views of Killarney's lakes and national park. Long acknowledged as one of Ireland's finest restaurants, Frederick's draws inspiration from the surrounding natural environment (loin of Kerry lamb, mélange of local seafood) and from classical French cuisine. An extensive, varied wine list complements the balance and taste of the food.
Daily 6.30–9.30, also Sun 12.30–2
L €30, D €90, Wine from €25.50
5km (3 miles) north of Killarney. Signed off the N22 Tralee road

THE GARDEN ROOM RESTAURANT ❀

Great Southern Hotel, Killarney, Co. Kerry
Tel 064 45122
www.gshkillarney.com
Diners can feast on the magnificent setting as well as the cuisine at this elegant restaurant. The ceiling is delicately carved with detail picked out in gold leaf. Leek and crabmeat roulade with lime and herb cream, Châteaubriand carved at the table, tournedos of venison Rossini, and pan-fried black sole fillets and scallops with turmeric sauce are typical of the carte. Warm plum pudding makes a lovely end to a meal.
Daily 7pm–9pm
D €76, Wine from €22
In the heart of the town

THE HERBERT ROOM ❀

Cahernane House Hotel, Muckross Road, Killarney, Co. Kerry
Tel 064 31895
www.cahernane.com
Expect the odd international influence to the cuisine offered at this subtly decorated dining room. Local produce is skilfully used by the master chef to give a good range of Irish traditional and international dishes including a selection of vegetarian ones. There is an extensive wine list.
Daily 7pm–9.30pm; closed Dec, Jan
D €78, Wine from €23.50
From Killarney follow signs for Kenmare, then from Muckross Road go over the bridge and the hotel is signposted on the right

THE BLUE POOL RESTAURANT
Muckross Park, Muckross Village, Killarney, Co. Kerry
Tel 064 31938
www.muckrosspark.com

The elegant dining room overlooks the gardens at this traditional country house. The serious approach to food is evident from a carte devoted to seasonal Kerry produce: stuffed crab's toes with salmon mousse, hot-smoked salmon smokies, and pan-fried black sole from the nearby sea, plus roast duck breast and tender rack of lamb. Try dark chocolate Grand Marnier parfait for a delicious conclusion.
Daily 7pm–9.30pm
D €80, Wine from €18
4km (2.5 miles) from Killarney within the Killarney National Park

KINSALE

FISHY FISHY CAFÉ
Guardwell, Kinsale, Co. Cork
Tel 021 477 4453
Run by Martin and Marie Shanahan, this is a treasure trove of great seafood served any number of ways by helpful, friendly staff. All the food provided here is good, but a popular choice is the warm salad of chilli seafood which comprises a mixture of fish including monkfish, salmon and prawns with a sweet chilli sauce on a bed of mixed leaves. Lunch only.
Daily 12pm–3.45pm
L €40, Wine from €19.50
Opposite St. Multose Church

JIM EDWARDS
Market Quay, Kinsale, Co. Cork
Tel 021 477 2541
www.jimedwardskinsale.com
On the roadside in Market Quay, it is difficult to miss Jim Edwards with its cream walls and bright blue window shutters decorated with ships' anchors. The nautical theme continues into the restaurant, which serves a varied menu based on local produce such as fish and seafood. The lobster could not be any fresher, taken from a tank inside the restaurant, and there's a variety of lamb, beef and duck dishes to choose from.
Daily 12.30–3, 6–10
L from €40, D from €35, Wine from €19
Market Quay

SAVANNAH WATERFRONT RESTAURANT ❀
Trident Hotel, Worlds End, Kinsale, Co. Cork
Tel 021 477 2301
www.tridenthotel.com
An attractive harbourside restaurant in one wing of a 17th-century corn store. As well as friendly service, diners can enjoy superb views across to Scilly and Summercove. The best of local produce from land and sea is used to create dishes with a modern edge. There is a wide range of desserts.
Mon–Sat 7–9, Sun 1–2.30, 7–9
L €46, D €70, Wine from €17
At end of Pier Road, along the waterfront

THE SPANIARD INN
Scilly, Kinsale, Co. Cork
Tel 021 477 2436
Sitting at the top of Scilly and known throughout Ireland and abroad, The Spaniard Inn is a welcoming traditional Irish inn where good food, beer and the *craic* can be found in abundance. Patrons Pat and Mary O'Toole have run the pub since 1989 with the help of their friendly and cheerful staff. Meals tend to be in the Irish tradition: bacon and cabbage, and oysters and smoked Bandon salmon. The Spaniard is also renowned for its traditional music evenings.
Mon–Thu 10.30am–11pm, Fri–Sat 10.30am–12.30am, Sun 12.30–11.30
Bar lunch from €14, D €60, Wine from €18
In Scilly, 1km (0.7 miles) out of town

THE VINTAGE RESTAURANT
Main Street, Kinsale, Co. Cork
Tel 021 477 2502
Friendly staff welcome you to this traditional restaurant where the food reflects the wealth of the local sea and land harvests. Interesting starters and main courses include oysters, sea bass and other locally caught fish as well as Irish red deer and wild duck. A good selection of wines complements the food and the desserts maintain the high standard.
Apr–end Oct daily from 6.30pm; Nov–end Mar call for opening hours
D €87, Wine from €19
In the middle of town

LIMERICK

MCLAUGHLIN'S RESTAURANT ❀
Castletroy Park, Dublin Road, Limerick, Co. Limerick
Tel 061 335566
www.castletroy-park.ie
Probably the only restaurant in the world named after the inventor of hydroelectric power, McLaughlin's offers a contemporary menu that incorporates both international and local influences. The walls are hung with art and native crafts and wood features in the restaurant. Light snacks are available from the hotel pub.
Tue–Sat 6–9.30, Sun 12.30–2.30
L €48, D €76, Wine from €27
5-min east from Limerick on the N7

LISMORE

BALLYRAFTER HOUSE ❀
Lismore, Co. Waterford
Tel 058 54002
The relaxed atmosphere of this delightful country house appeals to locals and visitors, especially anglers because it has its own salmon fishing.

Expect modern Irish food along the lines of tasty crab claws served with a kirsch and fresh orange juice sauce, a symphony of white fish including cod, brill, turbot and lemon sole with dill butter, followed by fresh cherries with a brandy chocolate sauce. Much is made of the local fresh and smoked Blackwater salmon, and home-produced honey

EATING

and local cheeses are also served.

Daily 1–2.30, 7.30–9.30; closed D Mon, 31 Oct–17 Mar

L €56, D €88, Wine from €22.50

1km (0.5 miles) out of town, opposite Lismore Castle

MACROOM

CASTLE HOTEL ❀

Main Street, Macroom, Co. Cork
Tel 026 41074
www.castlehotel.ie

This establishment has been run by the Buckley family for over 50 years. The dining room is an attractive mix of modern and traditional with some exposed brick walls and some painted with muted tones, dark wood tables and high-backed chairs. Steps lead up from the main dining to a snug of extra tables. The menu combines international and more traditional dishes, all made from the freshest of local ingredients.

Daily 12–2.30, 6–9

L €50, D €70, Wine from €18.95

On N22, 37km (23 miles) west of Cork

WATERFORD

THE MUNSTER DINING ROOM ❀❀

Waterford Castle, The Island, Ballinakill, Co. Waterford
Tel 051 878203
www.waterfordcastle.com

The Munster Dining Room in the castle on its river island is inviting, wood-panelled and furnished with antiques. A resident pianist often plays through dinner. The seasonal menus, created by chef Michael Quinn, place an emphasis on Irish specials as well as international cuisine, so Dublin Bay prawns may come as kebabs with roast garlic, basil and cherry tomatoes, while skate au poivre has a sauce lie de vin. Main courses range from Moroccan spiced beef to roast breast of chicken stuffed with foie gras and morels. Dress code: no denim or trainers (sneakers).

Daily 7–8.45, also Sun 12.30–1.45; closed early Jan

L €50, D €116, Wine from €28

5km (3 miles) east of the city, then ferry. Telephone for directions

SPECIAL IN MALLOW

THE PRESIDENTS' RESTAURANT ❀❀❀

Tel 022 47156
Longueville House, Mallow, Co. Cork
www.longuevillehouse.ie

Dinner is served in various places in the House throughout the year, including the restored Turner conservatory, with candlelight, white drapes and delicate flowers. A talented team, led by chef William O'Callaghan, offers a blend of modern and classical French cuisine, based largely on produce from the hotel's own farm, river and gardens. The carefully

selected wine list encompasses European and New World wines. Smart dress preferred.

Oct–end Mar daily 12.30–1.45, 6.30–9; closed Nov–end Feb

L €70, D €100, Wine from €36

5km (3 miles) west of Mallow via N72 towards Killarney, turn right at Ballyclough junction, the hotel is 200m (220 yards) on the left

THE NEW SHIP RESTAURANT ❀

Dooley's Hotel, 30 The Quay, Waterford, Co. Waterford
Tel 051 873531
www.dooleys-hotel.ie

A friendly, family-run bright restaurant with an inviting ambience. The menu has an international appeal, with dishes such as chicken liver paté on a bed of fresh leaves, roasted lemon-scented monkfish with leeks, and perhaps a traditional apple pie with cinnamon cream to finish. There is also a good value 'early-bird' menu. Every Wednesday night there is traditional Irish music and on Friday and Saturday nights diners are entertained by live music.

Mon–Sat 6–9.30, Sun 12.30–2.30, 6–9

L €38, D €50, Wine from €18.50

Along the quay, a 5-min walk from the heart of the town

WATERVILLE

FISHERMAN'S RESTAURANT ❀❀

Butler Arms Hotel, Waterville, Co. Kerry
Tel 066 947 4144
www.butlerarms.com

The Huggard family and their staff extend a warm welcome to guests at this traditional hotel restaurant. Locally caught fish prevails on the menu, including salmon cooked simply with lemon parsley butter, and fresh Ballinskelligs Bay lobster. There is an excellent wine list to complement the beautifully presented meals.

Daily 7.30pm–9pm; closed 31 Oct–4 Apr

D €50, Wine from €20

On the waterfront in the middle of Waterville

THE WEST

The land can be surprisingly barren in many parts of the West of Ireland, so people here have often depended on the sea for their food—and the sea certainly provides it. Galway in particular is noted for its oysters: Its annual Oyster Festival began in September 1954 and has been celebrated every year since then, but if you want to visit in late September you must plan well ahead. It's a city you can eat well in all year round, though, and because of its big student population there are numerous good-value choices. The whole area is very popular with overseas visitors, and this helps support the restaurants of towns such as Sligo and Donegal.

BALLINROBE

FLANNERY'S TAVERN

Cornmarket, Ballinrobe, Co. Mayo
Tel 094 9541055

This is fishing country; the many lakes include Lough Corrib, with abundant fish stocks, especially brown trout. Flannery's Tavern is a haven for anyone looking for somewhere to get a decent pint and good wholesome Irish food, as well as international cuisine. Customers are looked after well by the friendly and courteous staff, and on fine days there are picnic tables set outside for patrons.

Mon–Sat 10.30am–11pm, Sun 12.30–11
L €10, D €18, Wine from €15.50
In middle of town

PRICES AND SYMBOLS

The restaurants are listed alphabetically (excluding The, Il and Le). The prices given are for a two-course lunch (L) and a three-course dinner (D) for two people, without drinks. The wine price is for the least expensive bottle.
For alternative places to eat, see pages 220–225.

For a key to the symbols, ▷ 2.

BALLYBOFEY

LOOKING GLASS RESTAURANT

Kee's Hotel, Stranorlar, Ballybofey, Co. Donegal
Tel 074 913 1018
www.keeshotel.ie

Dinner in the Looking Glass Restaurant is a relaxed but elegant affair at this hotel run by the Kee family for four generations. Formally dressed tables are complemented by candlelight and fresh flowers, and tapestries worked by Grandmother Kee, two generations back, decorate the restaurant walls. The traditional cooking has been touched by European influences. Lighter snacks are also available in the Gallery Bistro.

Daily 1–2.45, 6.30–9.30; weekends only in winter
L €34, D €74, Wine from €21.50
2km (1 mile) northeast on the N15, in Stranorlar village

BALLYVAUGHAN

GREGAN'S CASTLE ❀❀

Ballyvaughan, Co. Clare
Tel 065 707 7005
www.gregans.ie

The full-length windows in the dining room of this country house in the heart of The Burren make the most of the evening light. In this semi-formal setting, where staff are renowned for their personal service, the modern French cooking takes some beating: Warm salmon mousse stuffed with a wild mushroom velouté, or salad of smoked chicken and pistachio might open the short menu, with pan-seared medallions of local beef with a creamy whiskey sauce, or baked cod wrapped in organic smoked salmon to follow.

Daily 7pm–8.30pm; closed Nov–end Mar
D €99, Wine from €25
6km (4 miles) south of Ballyvaughan on N67

BUNRATTY

DURTY NELLYS

Bunratty, Co. Clare
Tel 061 364861
www.durtynellys.ie

This fine old pub has two restaurants serving different styles of food. The pub itself reflects days gone by with its stone floor, old wood settles and bygones on the walls. Traditional Irish songs ring out and add to the atmosphere. Upstairs is the Loft Restaurant, which offers international cuisine in an informal setting. The Oyster Restaurant on the lower ground floor serves traditional Irish fare such as bacon, cabbage and potatoes, in a romantic atmosphere.

Mon–Thu 10.30am–11.30pm, Fri–Sat 11.30am–12.30am, Sun 12.30–11
L from €30, D from €40, Wine from €16.90
Right next to the castle

PJ'S

Tel 061 361177
Fitzpatrick Bunratty Hotel, Bunratty, Co. Clare

This friendly, bistro-style restaurant is decorated with striking contemporary artwork. The comprehensive menu shows a selection of modern dishes, and may feature chowder, wantons, pan-fried chicken breast or salmon with sweetcorn and rice cakes. The chef's choice of the day is always a sure bet, especially if it is the crab and salmon dish with chilli oil dressing.

Daily 7pm–10.30pm
D €58, Wine from €19.50
Next to Bunratty Castle

CASHEL

CASHEL HOUSE ❀❀

Cashel, Co. Galway
Tel 095 31001
www.cashelhouse.ie

A large conservatory overlooking the garden houses the semi-formal restaurant at this country-house hotel by the sea. The dining room is thoughtfully built on three levels which descend towards

the windows. Excellent ingredients such as Connemara lamb and fresh fish bless the area, and with them the chef produces an array of well-balanced dishes with clear tastes

EATING

and good textures. Smart casual dress.

Daily 12.30–2.30, 7–8.30; closed 6 Jan–6 Feb

L €22.50, D €45, Wine from €21

Turn south off N59 on to R340 1.5km (1 mile) west of Recess and the hotel is well signposted

SPECIAL IN CLIFDEN

ROCK GLEN COUNTRY HOUSE ❀❀

Clifden, Co. Galway

Tel: 095 21035

www.connemara.net/rockglen-hotel

Comfort abounds at this 19th-century former shooting lodge set in lovely gardens beside the Atlantic. The delightfully converted restaurant epitomizes the elegance and grace of Victorian style. The well-constructed modern Irish cooking, with hints of the Pacific Rim and classical French, uses freshly caught seafood and free-range meat in dishes such as warmed bruschetta of Thai chicken,

or risotto of fresh salmon and crabmeat, with a choice of soup (perhaps spring pea or chilled gazpacho) or sorbet, then duck breast roulade with forest mushrooms and veal sweetbreads, or roast lamb with spiced polenta cake. Old-fashioned desserts like bread and butter pudding are offered alongside white and dark chocolate mousse with brandy snap disc and espresso crème Anglaise. The wine list has some fine examples. Smart casual dress (no shorts).

Daily 7pm–9pm; closed 2 Nov–14 Feb

D €87.40, Wine from €21.50

From Clifden take the Ballyconneely road for 3km (1.5 miles); hotel is signposted on right

ZETLAND COUNTRY HOUSE ❀❀

Tel 095 31111

Cashel Bay, Co. Galway

www.zetland.com

The kitchen at this peaceful country house overlooking Cashel Bay makes good use of local produce, including herbs and vegetables grown in the hotel gardens.

Daily 7.30pm–8.30pm; closed Sun Sep–end Nov

D €95, Wine from €32

Turn south off N59 after Recess on to R340; after approximately 6.5km (4 miles) turn left onto R341, and the hotel is on the right

DONEGAL

HARVEY'S POINT COUNTRY HOTEL ❀❀

Lough Eske, Co. Donegal

Tel 074 972 2208

www.harveyspoint.com

Enjoy an aperitif in front of the peat fire as the pianist plays, before being seated in the elegant, split-level dining room. A four-course dinner menu of accomplished French cuisine presents some interesting taste combinations. The lunch menu may have poached salmon fillet with mashed potato and fennel chips while the dinner menu might include tournedos of beef fillet on pommes dauphines, with shallot cream and bordelaise sauce. To end your meal there are desserts such as a tulip of marinated fruit with lemon sorbet on raspberry coulis or a selection of Irish and French cheese. Not surprisingly, the wine list includes some very good wines.

Daily 12.30–2.30, 6.30–9.30; closed D Sun Nov–end Feb, also Mon–Tue Nov–Easter

L €55, D €96.80, Wine from €20

From Donegal take the N56 west, then take the first right signed Lough Eske/Harveys Point. The hotel is about a 10-minute drive from Donegal

ENNIS

JM'S BISTRO ❀

Tel 065 682 3300

Temple Gate Hotel, The Square, Ennis, Co. Clare

www.templegatehotel.com

In this Gothic-themed former convent, the dining room has painted wood panels, luxurious drapes and chandeliers all of which contribute to its elegant charm. An international menu is served by friendly, helpful staff. Shrimps might be followed by oriental stir-fry. Booking is strongly recommended at this extremely popular restaurant.

Daily 12.45–3, 7–10.15

L €20, D €58, Wine from €22.55

Follow signs for the Tourist Office; the hotel is on the same square

ENNISCRONE

BEACHWOOD RESTAURANT

Atlantic Hotel, Enniscrone, Co. Sligo

Tel 096 36119

Enjoy sea views while you dine at this friendly family restaurant in the coastal village of Enniscrone. The menu includes chilli con carne, pasta carbonara and vegetarian stir-fry as well as traditional Irish dishes such as bacon and cabbage and fresh monkfish. There is also a children's menu. The staff are friendly and helpful, making dining here a relaxed and enjoyable experience.

Daily 6–9; closed Sep–end Jan

D €40, Wine from €16.75

Along the main street next to the beach

GALWAY

COUCH POTATAS

40 Upper Abbeygate Street, Galway, Co. Galway

Tel 091 561664

You can fill up for very little money at Couch Potatas, hence its popularity with students, as long as you like potatoes! There are many fillings to choose from and the servings are generous. The cheerful interior reflects the attitude of the staff and the relaxed atmosphere makes this a great place to take a break.

Mon–Thu 12–9, Fri–Sat 12–10

From €10

In the middle of Galway

PARK ROOM RESTAURANT ❀
Tel 091 564924
Park House Hotel, Forster Street, Eyre Square, Galway, Co. Galway
www.parkhousehotel.ie
An original 19th-century grain store houses this celebrated restaurant, where paintings of old Galway help to keep the past alive. Classical French cuisine with Italian and Chinese additions inspires dishes such as honey-glazed

breast of duckling with an orange jus, grilled veal sirloin with Madeira, and ostrich fillet with garlic potato and glazed shallot.
Daily 6pm–10pm
D €39.50, Wine from €17.50
In the heart of the city, off Eyre Square

PIERRES RESTAURANT
8 Quay Street, Galway, Co. Galway
Tel 091 566066
www.pierresrestaurant.com
A little piece of France in Galway town. Pierre's is a popular French bistro in the middle of town which serves traditional French cooking using fresh Galway ingredients. The atmosphere is informal and fun, and the knowledgeable staff are friendly and helpful. The fixed-price menu may include steamed mussels with garlic and white wine or brochette of salmon, monkfish and tiger prawns with saffron pilaf rice. A varied wine list accompanies the uncomplicated food. An early bird menu is available between 6 and 7.
Mon–Sat 6–10.30, Sun 6–10
D €47.80, Wine from €17.90
In the middle of the city

KINVARA

KEOGH'S BAR AND RESTAURANT
The Square, Kinvara, Co. Galway
Tel 091 637145
www.kinvara.com/keoghs
Keogh's is a traditional bar, well worth the half-hour drive round Galway Bay from Galway city. A menu of simple, Irish fare made using fresh local produce is served, featuring popular dishes such as seafood chowder and mussels—pub food at its best.
Mon–Sat 10.30am–11pm, Sun 12.30–11
L €17, D €34, Wine from €15
30-min drive south of Galway

LETTERKENNY

CASTLEGROVE COUNTRY HOUSE ❀
Ballymaleel, Letterkenny, Co. Donegal
Tel 074 915 1118
www.castlegrove.com
The restaurant at this hotel offers accomplished cooking on a wide-ranging menu. Local produce is very much to the fore, using fresh fish caught nearby and vegetables grown in the hotel's own kitchen garden. The dining room itself is a picture of sophistication and elegance; tables laid with crisp white linen topped by sparkling glasses and vases of fresh flowers, drenched in natural sunlight from the long windows which look out onto beautifully landscaped gardens. Staff are friendly and helpful and there is an extensive wine list.

Mon–Sat 6.30pm–9.30pm
D €70, Wine from €16
7km (4.5 miles) northeast of Letterkenny off R245, Ramelton road

NEWMARKET-ON-FERGUS

DROMOLAND CASTLE ❀❀
Newmarket-on-Fergus, Co. Clare
Tel 061 368144
www.dromoland.ie
Dinner is served in the very grand Earl of Thomond room with its Venetian silk wall hangings, Irish linen and crystal chandeliers. The superior, yet relaxed, setting is reflected in the food served and is world renowned. A sizeable carte is complemented by a

four-course fixed-price menu, both designed by chef McCann with simplicity and freshness in mind. The comprehensive wine list is also first class. Dress code: jacket and tie.
Mon–Sat 10–6, 7–9.30, Sun 12.30–1.30
L €70, D €122, Wine from €24
2.5km (1.5 miles) northeast of Newmarket-on-Fergus; signed off N18; 13km (8 miles) from Shannon Airport, 27km (17 miles) from Limerick City

PONTOON

HEALY'S RESTAURANT & COUNTRY HOUSE ❀
Tel 094 925 6443
Pontoon, Co. Mayo
www.healyspontoon.com
Traditional fare is served in the Lough Cullin dining room which has large picture windows affording beautiful lake views. Succulent breast of chicken kiev or grilled fillet of Atlantic salmon hollandaise may feature on the *table d'hôte*, followed by tropical fresh fruit salad or Healy's House gateau. The Sunday lunch choices may include roast stuffed leg of lamb with rosemary jus or prime rib of beef accompanied by fresh seasonal vegetables. Smart dress is required.
Daily 6–10, also Sun 12.30–4.30
L €42, D €76, Wine from €25
From Ballina go south on N26 for 1.5km (1 mile), then bear right on R310 to Pontoon between loughs Conn and Collin

RATHMULLAN

FORT ROYAL
Fort Royal, Rathmullan, Co. Donegal
Tel 074 915 8100
www.fortroyalhotel.com
The hotel enjoys a fine and deserved reputation for good food. The short menus pay tribute to Ireland's outstanding

natural larder. Fish is well represented on the four-course dinner menu: Expect Donegal salmon mayonnaise, followed by grilled monkfish, fillets of Killybeg plaice, and whole Dover sole, along with roast rack of Donegal lamb, sirloin steak with Bordelaise sauce, and roast loin of pork with roast apples and a port and thyme jus. Desserts might include lemon and lime cheesecake, or a robust banana split.

7.30–9.45; closed Nov–end Mar
D €80, Wine from €13.50
Take R247 through Rathmullan and continue north for 1.5km (1 mile); hotel signposted

RECESS

LOUGH INAGH LODGE HOTEL ❀❀

Inagh Valley, Recess, Co. Galway
Tel 095 34706
www.loughinaghlodgehotel.ie

The Turk Mountains form a dramatic backdrop to this intimate restaurant which overlooks Lake Inagh. Seafood and wild game dishes are specialties here, and the freshly baked breads are a treat. From the fixed-price dinner menu come terrine of chicken with blue cheese and peppernut sauce; succulent fresh prawns tossed in butter with a hint of garlic, accompanied by a side dish of crisp vegetables and cinnamon parfait with apple sauce. Inspired wine choices complement the food perfectly.

Daily 7pm–9pm; closed mid-Dec to mid-Mar
D €80, Wine from €21
Turn right off N59 after Recess on R344 towards Kylemore Abbey and go up the Inagh Valley

ROSSNOWLAGH

SEASHELL RESTAURANT ❀❀

Sand House Hotel, Donegal Bay, Rossnowlagh, Co. Donegal
Tel 071 985 1777
www.sandhouse-hotel.ie

The plush red restaurant is elegantly furnished with antiques and original artwork, and is in a relaxing setting overlooking Donegal Bay at the edge of the Atlantic Ocean. Cooking incorporates the finest produce, including locally landed seafood, prime beef and lamb, and Irish cheeses. Special dishes include sea trout, Donegal Bay salmon and Fresh Bay oysters. The cuisine style has classical roots but acknowledges contemporary trends.

Daily 7–8.30pm, also Sun 1–2; closed Nov–end Feb
L €45, D €90, Wine from €21
From the coast road, N15, south of Donegal, turn off on R231 to Rossnowlagh

WESTPORT

ARDMORE COUNTRY HOUSE

The Quay, Westport, Co. Mayo
Tel 098 25994
www.ardmorecountryhouse.com

A luxurious little family-run hotel with wonderful views. The menu offers soup, warm or cold starters and a good selection of main courses. Chef, and patron, Pat Hoban has introduced a comprehensive menu. Fish comes fresh from Clew Bay, the vegetables are grown nearby and are organic for the most part, while meats include local lamb and Irish beef. There is a good range of wines to choose from, including some fine ones, and the locally made cheese should not be missed.

Daily 7pm–9.30pm; closed Jan to mid-Mar
D €68, Wine from €18.50
1.5 km (1 mile) west from Westport on coast road, R335

THE LEMON PEEL

The Octagon, Westport, Co. Mayo
Tel 098 26929
www.lemonpeel.ie

In the middle of Westport, this buzzy bistro-style restaurant is just the place for a good night out. The menu reflects influences from around the world with delights such as Cajun blackened shrimp, paillard of chicken breast and home-made seafood ravioli. The staff are helpful and the food is beautifully presented. The wine list includes new world wines alongside classic French and Italian labels. There is also a good early bird menu.

Tue–Sat 6pm–10pm
D from €70, Wine from €15
In the middle of town, at the end of Shop Street

THE OLD RAILWAY HOTEL ❀

The Mall, Westport, Co, Mayo
Tel 098 25166
www.theoldrailwayhotel.com

Convivial hospitality and 19th-century grandeur combine in this antiques-filled building with its Conservatory Restaurant. Local ingredients are used to create a good spread of simple but effective dishes. Lobster, salmon, mussels and oysters feature highly as does lamb and there are fish specials on offer most days. The restaurant has a relaxed atmosphere and the service is excellent.

Daily 6.30pm–9.30pm
D €70, Wine from €19.95
Overlooking the Carrowbeg River in the middle of town

SPECIAL IN WESTPORT

BLUE WAVE RESTAURANT ❀❀

The Atlantic Coast Hotel, The Quay, Westport, Co. Mayo
Tel 098 29000
www.atlanticcoasthotel.com

Take your seat in the top-floor Blue Wave Restaurant and enjoy the stunning West Coast views across the shores of Clew Bay. The food's as modern as the setting. Main courses might include duck on Thai noodles in a zesty teriyaki marinade, or celeriac and garlic risotto or tempura prawns with mango and chilli salsa, hoisin sauce and sesame oil. To finish you may be offered a light and dark chocolate tower with spiced apricot compote. Classic wines are stocked alongside New World wines.

Daily 6.30pm–9.30pm
D €72, Wine from €18.50
1 km (0.75 miles) west from Westport on coast road, R335

EATING

THE MIDLANDS

Surrounded as it is by excellent eating options on all sides, the Midlands could be seen to suffer in comparison but it isn't that there is no good food to be had, just that fine restaurants are harder to find. In fact in some places you may have to settle for a hearty pub meal and a good atmosphere—not that there's anything wrong with that.

If you do your homework, though, there are some exceptional places to be found, often serving local produce such as lamb and game. Good quality restaurants in the region include Wineport Lodge near Athlone, which calls itself Ireland's first wine hotel and specializes in Atlantic seafood, or the L'Escale Restaurant in the Hodson Bay Hotel in Athlone on the shores of Lough Ree. Great places do exist, and part of the pleasure is in tracking them down.

ATHLONE

LEFT BANK BISTRO

Fry Place, Athlone, Co. Westmeath
Tel 090 649 4446
www.leftbankbistro.com

Close to Athlone Lock on the River Shannon, this stylish, architect-designed restaurant within an old building is light and airy, with modern furniture. The Australian chef provides an eclectic choice of imaginative dishes from around the world, such as Thai spiced chicken, baked salmon on smoked bacon mash with basil oil, and chargrilled beef fillet with Dijon mustard and Shiraz butter. A loyal clientele provides a lively atmosphere.

Tue–Sat 12–5, 5.30–9.30
L €28, D €70, Wine from €19

SPECIAL IN ATHLONE

L'ESCALE RESTAURANT

Hodson Bay Hotel, Hodson Bay, Athlone, Co. Westmeath
Tel 090 644 2000
www.hodsonbayhotel.com

Dishes in the hotel's L'Escale restaurant are inspired by the finest produce, with fresh fish delivered daily. Head chef Kevin Ward runs a tight ship with an experienced team, and waiting staff are friendly and courteous. The standard and presentation of the food, especially the fresh lobster which is available from a tank each day, is impressive. You may find it hard to choose from the delicious selection of desserts.

Daily 12.30–2.30, 7–9.15
L €39, D €76, Wine from €18.50
From Athlone take the N61 8km (5 miles) towards Roscommon and turn right to Lough Rea

PRICES AND SYMBOLS

The restaurants are listed alphabetically (excluding The, Il and Le). The prices given are for a two-course lunch (L) and a three-course dinner (D) for two people, without drinks. The wine price is for the least expensive bottle.
For alternative places to eat, see pages 226–228.

For a key to the symbols, ▷ 2.

BALLYLYNAN

PEDIGREE CORNER

Ballylynan, Co. Laois
Tel 059 862 5120

Where the N80 Carlow–Portlaoise road crosses the N78 from Athy to Kilkenny, you'll find this famous pub, which is justly popular for its good beer, good food and good entertainment. The menu features traditional Irish and European cuisine, and popular choices include the succulent roast beef and the seafood specials.

Mon–Sat 12.30–4, Sun 12–6
L €16–20, Wine from €12.95

BIRR

THE THATCH

Crinkle Bar, Birr, Co. Offaly
Tel 0509 20682

A characterful Irish pub in the heart of the Irish countryside, where the welcome is friendly and the food and the drink are good. Relax and enjoy the hearty food while listening to a yarn from a local or enjoy one of the many evenings of Irish music held here.

Mon–Sat 12.30–2.30, Tue–Sat 7–9.15
L €42, D €80, Wine from €19
1.5km (1 mile) from Birr in Crinkle village

GLASSAN

GROGAN'S PUB

Glassan, Co. Westmeath
Tel 090 648 5158

Just 10km (6 miles) north of Athlone on the N55, Glassan is in the heart of Oliver Goldsmith Country (the village is said to be the *Sweet Auburn* of his famous poem). This ancient pub, established in 1750, serves good bar food year-round, including steaks and seafood. There's also traditional music in the bar every Wednesday and Sunday night.

Mon–Sat 12–9, Sun 1–8
L €30, D €40, Wine from €14.95

LONGFORD

EDWARD J. VALENTINE

65–66 Main Street, Longford, Co. Longford
Tel 043 45509 or 043 48704
www.edwardjvalentine.com

This distinctive building on Main Street, with flowers cascading from its many window boxes, houses a great pub. Though it's only been open since 1990, it has the furnishings and the ambience of a traditional town pub. It serves standard pub fare for lunch, such as steak burgers, cajun chicken wraps, and fish and chips, which are well cooked and in generous portions.

Mon–Thu 10.30am–11.30pm, Fri–Sat 10.30am–12.30am, Sun 12.30pm–11pm
L €15, Wine from €4.75 (only quarter bottles available)

MULLINGAR

BELFRY RESTAURANT

Ballynegall, Mullingar, Co. Westmeath
Tel 044 42488
www.belfryrestaurant.com

SPECIAL IN GLASSAN

WINEPORT LODGE ❀

Glassan, Co. Westmeath
Tel 090 6439010
www.wineport.ie

Customers can arrive by land or water and dine on the deck overlooking Lough Rea or in the attractive dining room. Chef Feargal O'Donnell serves innovative food, made with the best local produce. The menu changes regularly and there is a daily special. A good selection of desserts and a comprehensive wine list complement the excellent main meals. Service is friendly and the setting is superb, making this a very relaxing place to dine. Light snacks only are available at lunchtime.

Daily 6pm–10pm
D €110, Wine from €15
Take N55 north of Athlone for 9km (6 miles); turn left at the Dog and Duck pub. Wineport Lodge is about 2km (1 mile) on the left hand side

Housed in a magnificently converted church with a tall spire, the Belfry has a beautiful wooden ceiling, original pillars and windows, and a stylish new mezzanine bar. Top-quality local produce, including Mullingar beef and lamb and organic vegetables, are crafted into imaginatively presented traditional and modern dishes. Reservations are advised as people come from all around to eat here.

Wed–Sat 6–9.30, Sun 1–3.30
L €27.50, D €40, Wine from €21
6km (4 miles) north of Mullingar on the R384 Castlepollard road

PORTLAOISE

LEMON TREE RESTAURANT

Main Street, Portlaoise, Co. Laois
Tel 0502 62200

Opposite the historic Court House and the Laois Arts Centre, Grellan Delaney's pub complex, one of the largest in Ireland, has four bars, meeting rooms and this excellent restaurant. Beige walls, burgundy carpeting and pine furniture create a relaxing atmosphere, and the menu features modern European cuisine, including seafood, steaks and game.

Tue–Sun 6pm–10pm
D €60–€70, Wine from €15

TREACY'S PUB

The Heath, Portlaoise, Co. Laois
Tel 0502 46539

Dating from 1780, this pub is said to have been owned by the same family for longer than any other in Ireland, and it is Tom and Marie Treacy who offer the renowned hospitality today. In the shadow of the Rock of Dunamaise, it's about as authentic as you will find, and has beautifully mellow pine panelling—a lovely setting in which to enjoy the traditional Irish cooking. If you go on the weekends, you can also join in the singalong sessions in the bar.

Mon–Fri 7am–9.45pm, Sat 7am–8.45pm, Sun 12–8.45
L €25, D €40, Wine from €15
4.5km (3 miles) east of Portlaoise on the N80 Stradbally road

ROSCOMMON

DURKINS

The Square, Ballaghaderreen, Co. Roscommon
Tel 094 9860305
www.durkins.org

Durkin's is a large rambling pub which has two bars, each with a traditional long counter and wooden bar stalls and warmed by an open fire. Durkin's Lounge is a separate area for those who want to sit in comfort, and then there is the restaurant serving a selection of Irish and international cuisine. On the main Dublin to Westport route, this is a great place to stop.

Mon–Sat 10–9 (Durkins Bar also 9.30pm–2am), Sun 12.30–2
L€30, D €40, Wine from €15
In the middle of town

THE MANSE RESTAURANT

Gleeson's Townhouse, Market Square, Roscommon, Co. Roscommon
Tel 090 662 6954
www.gleesonstownhouse.com

Gleeson's Townhouse Hotel is on Roscommon's historic town square, right next to the museum, and is a convenient place to drop in for a snack in the café or, better still, a full meal in the formal restaurant. The dinner menu has Irish, European and Oriental influences in dishes such as the Irish Salad appetizer (with black pudding, smoked bacon, poached egg and Béarnaise sauce), wild Atlantic salmon and the 'Manse Stir-Fry'.

Mon–Thu 12–3, 6.30–9, Fri–Sat 12–3, 6.30–10, Sun 12–3, 6–9
L €30, D €65, Wine from €15

TARMONBARRY

KEENAN'S

Tarmonbarry, Co. Roscommon
Tel 043 26052
www.keenans.ie

In the heart of the village, on the banks of the River Shannon, Keenan's is a lovely family-run traditional pub with a dark-wood interior, a great atmosphere, patrons telling fishing stories and excellent food. You can get just a sandwich here, or choose from the varied menu (available in the bar or the restaurant). Seafood chowder is a signature dish, and main courses include salmon, steaks, mussels and roast chicken—or perhaps fillet of ostrich. For dessert, try the brown bread, Guinness and honeycomb ice cream.

Mon–Sat 12.30–8.30, Sun 12.30–7.30
L €15–€30, D €40, Wine from €17.50

NORTHERN IRELAND

Northern Ireland has its own regional dishes, such as champ (▷ 278), and its own beer too, from Caffrey's of Belfast. With its numerous loughs and long coastline, fresh fish and seafood is just as good here as it is anywhere else on the island. The province recently opened its first cooking school, of which there are at least eight in the Republic, showing that although it may have been lagging behind, it is now intent on catching up.

Belfast has several top-class restaurants such as the Restaurant Michael Deane and Shu. One of the country's top celebrity chefs, Paul Rankin (▷ 13), whose name appears regularly in books and on TV, owns the Cayenne restaurant in the city. There are also many excellent restaurants to be found outside of the capital, including Shanks in County Down.

BALLYCASTLE

WYSNER'S

16 Ann Street, Ballycastle, Co. Antrim, BT54 6AD
Tel 028 2076 2372

On Ballycastle's main street, this is an elegant little French-style café serving delicious food throughout the day, with a more sophisticated upstairs restaurant open in the evenings. It serves an interesting range of modern Irish cuisine, using local seafood and produce. Head chef Jackie Wysner's Bushmills malt cheesecake is legendary.

Mon–Sat 9–5, 7–9.30
L £15, D £40, Wine from £10.45
Ballycastle is on the A2, on the north Antrim coast

BANGOR

OLD INN ❀❀

15 Main Street, Crawfordsburn, Co. Down, BT19 1JH
Tel 028 9185 3255
www.theoldinn.com

Brass chandeliers and 17th-century oak panelling might suggest grand dining on an impersonal level, but candlelight and eager-to-please staff turn on the warmth. Hints of the Pacific rim are detectable in a menu that fuses the modern and classical. Roasts and grills appear alongside crispy duck confit with hoi sin sauce and wasabi, and slow-roasted duck breast with pak choi and honey five-spice jus.

Mon–Sat 12.30–2.30, 7–9.30, Sun 12.30–2.30
L £52, D £52, Wine from £11.50
5km (3 miles) past Holywood on the A2 there is a sign for the Old Inn and 100m (110 yards) past this sign, turn left at the traffic lights; the hotel is on the left in the village

PRICES AND SYMBOLS

The restaurants are listed alphabetically (excluding The, Il and Le). The prices given are for a two-course lunch (L) and a three-course dinner (D) for two people, without drinks. The wine price is for the least expensive bottle.
For alternative places to eat, see pages 229–238.

For a key to the symbols, ▷ 2.

BELFAST

ALDENS ❀❀

229 Upper Newtownards Road, Belfast, BT4 3JF
Tel 028 9065 0079
www.aldensrestaurant.com

The purple-canopied, frosted glass frontage gives a striking first impression of this sophisticated restaurant close to the city ring road. The interior uses a contemporary blue, grey and purple palette, with large, polished hardwood tables, a stripped oak floor and halogen downlighters. Cooking is crisp, clear and technically advanced, providing a wide-ranging menu with many luxury ingredients. Lunch specials may include warm potato salad with feta, capers and parma ham, or wild boar, leek and garlic sausages with mint butter colcannon. Excellent home-made ciabatta and rolls.

Mon–Thu 12–2.30, 6–10, until 11 Fri–Sat
L £34, D £40, Wine from £14.50
B6, B5
3km (2miles) east of city on A20 towards Newtownards

SPECIAL IN BANGOR

SHANKS ❀❀❀

150 Crawfordsburn Road, Bangor, Co. Down, BT1 9GB
Tel 028 9185 3313
www.shanksrestaurant.com

Part of the Blackwood golf complex, Shanks has earned a widespread reputation thanks to talented husband and wife owners, the Millars. Designed with the help of Sir Terence Conran, the restaurant is sleek and warm, with polished wood flooring, red bench seating and views of the hills through the large windows. Chef Robbie Millar travels widely and plenty of unusual influences are evident in his cooking. Portavogie prawns might appear in a gratin with fragrant rice and a Café de Paris butter, while pork belly is given spectacular treatment in a dish comprising oats, honey, chilli, cauliflower purée and Lexia raisin jus. There is a great value set lunch.

Tue–Fri 12.30–2.30, Tue–Sat 7–10; closed 1–21 Jul
L £34, D £76, Wine from £20
Section; no pipes or cigars
From A2 (Belfast–Bangor), turn right onto Ballysallagh road 3km (2 miles) before Bangor, then take first left after 1km (0.5 miles) to the Golf Centre on the right

BEATRICE KENNEDY ❀

44 University Road, Belfast, BT7 1NJ
Tel 028 9020 2290
www.beatrice-kennedy.co.uk

Rich hues, lazy colonial ceiling fans and a backing of tinny 1930s big band jazz conspire to create a brasserie atmosphere. Books are placed around the restaurant as a reminder of its location, near to Queen's University. Expect familiar themes and ingredients, enhanced by some big

EATING

bold tastes and an occasional whiff of the Orient. Chef/owner Jim McCarthy has created dishes with influences from around the world. Good value express menu served from 5–7.
Tue–Sat 5–10.30, Sun 12.30–2.30, 5–10.30; closed Easter
L £24, D £50, Wine from £11.95
71, 69
Adjacent to Queen's University on the main University road, A55

BOURBON ❀
60 Great Victoria Street, Belfast, BT2 7BB
Tel 028 9033 2121
www.bourbonrestaurant.com
The quirky interior combines Victorian Gothic with a feel of the American Deep South, and touches of Spanish colonial architecture. Food influences come from America, the Far East and Britain. By keeping things simple the chef is able

to focus on freshness and taste in dishes such as delicious jumbo sumo chips or the smoked haddock, mustard and leek gratin. Luscious desserts include double chocolate truffle cake and apple and plum crumble served with vanilla ice cream.
Mon–Fri 12–3, 5–11, Sat 5–11
L from £30, D £50, Wine from £11.95
Opposite Great Victoria Street Bus Station

MCHUGHS BAR AND RESTAURANT
29–31 Queen's Square, Belfast, BT1 3FG
Tel 028 9050 9999
www.mchughsbar.com
The traditional exterior of McHughs belies its contemporary interior, where you can relax and just have a drink or go through to the restaurant and have a meal. The stylish restaurant has clean lines, iron work and polished wood floors. The lunch menu incorporates anything from Irish stew and wheaten bread to a sizzling selection from the wok station. Reservations essential.
Restaurant: Mon–Fri 12–3, 5–10.30, Sat 5–10.30, Sun 5–9
L from £20, D from £30, Wine from £11.95
Section
On the corner of Queen's Square and Princes Street

THE METRO BRASSERIE ❀
The Crescent Townhouse, 13 Lower Crescent, Belfast, BT7 1NR
Tel 028 9032 3349
www.crescenttownhouse.com
Slick and modern, The Metro Brasserie displays a trendiness not normally associated with hotel restaurants. The split-level dining areas are bright and cheerful, as are the staff. Some flashes of brilliance are detectable together with a commitment to simplicity. Good 'early bird' menu option.
Mon–Thu 5.45–9.30, Fri–Sat 5.45–10, Sun 5–9
D from £55, Wine from £12
No pipes
74, 76
South towards Queen's University; the hotel is on corner of Botanic Avenue and Lower Crescent, opposite Botanic Train Station

RESTAURANT MICHAEL DEANE ❀❀❀
34–40 Howard Street, Belfast, BT1 6PF
Tel 028 9033 1134
www.michaeldeane.co.uk
He may be a celebrity but Michael Deane is still a 'hands on' chef, floating between his vibrant downstairs brasserie and the more staid upstairs restaurant. The setting is opulent, and there's real theatre to the experience: Chefs work in full view of the guests, and meals are brought out on huge trays. Prepare to be smitten by the perfection of dishes that sound quite simple on the menu: perhaps local scallops, foie gras and potato bread or a main course of pan-fried turbot and velouté of artichoke.
Wed–Sat 7pm–9.30pm; closed 2 weeks Jul
D £77, Wine from £18.50
Section in bar
In the middle of the city, just west of City Hall

SPECIAL IN BELFAST

SHU ❀❀
253 Lisburn Road, Belfast, BT9 7EN
Tel 028 9038 1655
www.shu-restaurant.com
Were the ancient Egyptian god of the atmosphere to pay a visit, he'd be pleased with his namesake. Shu's minimalist ambience—warm chocolate brown, reds and creams, with suede seats and leather banquettes—provides the perfect background for the discreet,

lazy jazz soundtrack. The eclectic menu (foie gras terrine sits alongside sausages and mashed potatoes) takes a loose fusion line, and fashionable ideas make their mark, but all is executed with a light touch. Freshness and seasoning in seared salmon, bacon and crab risotto with shellfish vinaigrette are beyond reproach.
Mon–Sat 12.30–2.30, 6–10; closed 12–14 Jul
L £23, D £27, Wine from £13.50
Section
58, 59
From the middle of the city take Lisburn road, A1, for 1.5km (1 mile) southwest

BUSHMILLS

BUSHMILLS INN
Bushmills, Co. Antrim, BT57 8QG
Tel 028 2073 2339
www.bushmillsinn.com
The restaurant of this famous inn, close to the Giant's Causeway and Bushmills Distillery, is a beautiful conversion of the former stables and wine cellar. It still has exposed brick, ancient timbers and whitewashed walls, and overlooks a lovely courtyard. Prime Ulster meat, fish and vegetables are used in creative dishes such as lamb loin with maple and lavender cream and fresh

blueberries, or salmon with a dulse-butter sauce. Baked rhubarb and elderflower cheesecake is a popular dessert choice.

Mon–Sat 12–6.45, 7–9.30, Sun 12–6, 7–9

L £28, D £50, Wine from £11.95

On the A2, east of Portrush, just south of the Giant's Causeway

COOKSTOWN

OTTER LODGE WINE BAR AND RESTAURANT

26 Dungannon Road, Cookstown, Co. Tyrone, BT80 8TL
Tel 028 8676 5427
www.otterlodge.co.uk

Between Lough Neagh and the Sperrin Mountains, this is a lovely riverside wine bar and restaurant. With an interior as warm as the welcome, it offers good-value meals, including such dishes as pork fillet with roast apples, honey-glazed duck, beef with peppercorn sauce and chicken kiev.

Mon–Thu 12–2, 5.30–9.30, Fri–Sat 12–2, 5.30–10, Sun 12–2.30, 5–9.30

L £20, D £40, Wine from £5.95

On the A29 17km (11 miles) north of Dungannon

CREGGAN

AN CREAGÁN VISITOR CENTRE

Omagh, Co. Tyrone, BT79 9AF
Tel 028 8076 1112
www.an-creagan.com

In the very south of Northern Ireland, this visitor complex (▷ 272) includes an interpretative exhibition, a craft shop, holiday homes and this lovely bar-restaurant. The lofty and spacious room has picture windows, flagstone floors and a mellow ambience. The sizeable menu has seafood, steak and grills, chicken and duck, and vegetarian options, and some evenings there's music, singing and storytelling.

Mon–Tue 10–3, Wed–Sun 10–11

L £28, D £30, Wine from £8.95

20km (12.5 miles) east of Omagh on A505

DERRY

BEECH HILL COUNTRY HOUSE ❀

32 Ardmore Road, Derry, Co. Londonderry, BT47 3QP
Tel 028 7134 9279
www.beech-hill.com

Just 3km (2 miles) from Derry, this rural retreat displays the finest tradition of country house elegance and sophistication. The restaurant has creative menus and friendly service, and glorious woodland views set the scene. Sharp, direct cooking uses clever combinations to woo diners. Try pan-fried belly pork with foie gras in a puff pastry casing, or summer lamb with creamy black beans and rosemary jus. The wine list offers good value for money.

Daily 12.30–2.30, 6–9.45

L £29.90, D £55.90, Wine from £12.50

Section; no pipes or cigars

Take the A6 Derry–Belfast road and turn off at Faughan Bridge and continue for 1.5km (1 mile). The hotel is opposite Ardmore Chapel

DUNDRUM

THE BUCKS HEAD

77–79 Main Street, Dundrum, Co. Down, BT33 0LU
Tel 028 4375 1868

The Buck's Head serves up a wonderful traditional roast at a bargain price; regular customers come from far and wide every weekend for the culinary treat. The rest of the week, this 100-year-old pub offers a good variety of dishes, including seafood straight from Dundrum Bay. The wood-panelled dining room has an open fire in winter and there's also a pleasant conservatory and a beer garden.

Daily 12–2.30, 5–9.30 (Sun until 8.30)

L £24, D £49, Wine from £11.90

Section

9.5km (6 miles) north of Newcastle on the A2, on an inlet of Dundrum Bay

ENNISKILLEN

BAR M

33 Darling Street, Enniskillen, Co. Fermanagh, BT74 7DP
Tel 028 6632 2059

Just a short walk from Enniskillen's main jetties, this pub is brimming with rustic charm and a lively clientele, and there's live music three times a week. The lunch menu includes such dishes as stuffed sausages wrapped in bacon, and the different dinner menu might include pan-fried chicken with green peppercorn sauce.

Food served 12–8

L £20, D £30, Wine from £6.95

GILFORD

ORIEL OF GILFORD ❀❀

2 Bridge Street, Gilford, Co. Armagh, BT63 6HF
Tel 028 3883 1543
www.orielrestaurant.com

A modest interior belies the powerful and accomplished cooking served up at this modern restaurant in a quiet little village. Barry Smyth's stunning food impresses with its depth and quality; starters like terrine of chicken, rabbit and duck layered with shiitake mushrooms, fillet of beef with caramelized pig's trotter, and baked chocolate pudding with pistachio ice cream are all stamped with the same pedigree. A fixed lunchtime menu on Sunday provides fusion themes.

Tue–Sat 6.30–9.30, Sun 12.30–2.30; closed 1 week Jan, 1 week Jul

L £42, D £57.80, Wine from £13.95

Section; no pipes or cigars

From Bainbridge take Tandragee road straight through town, over the mini-roundabout (traffic circle), and the restaurant is 140m (150 yards) farther on up the hill

GLENAVY

MCGEOWN'S

22 Main Street, Glenavy, Co. Antrim, BT29 7LW
Tel 028 94422467
www.mcgeowns.co.uk

Owner Gabriel McGeown is always on hand at this friendly, popular place that has snug corners with open fires as well as spacious bar areas. The restaurant here serves high-quality food, with choices such as lobster or medallions of fillet steak with courgettes (zucchini) and aubergines (eggplant). Desserts are of the same high quality and there is an excellent wine list. The guestbook attests to the pub's many celebrity guests.

Mon–Sat 12–9, Sun 12–9.30

L from £20, D from £30, Wine from £8.95

In the middle of Glenavy

KILLYLEAGH

DUFFERIN ARMS

35 High Street, Killyleagh, Co. Down, BT30 9QF
Tel 028 4482 1182
www.dufferinarms.com

Standing in the shadow of Killyleagh Castle, off the main street, this lively pub is well known for its good food and

its good music. It has been in operation for more than 200 years and has a traditional pub atmosphere. The Kitchen Restaurant is in country style, with pine furniture and potted plants, and the regularly changing menu features such appetizers as seafood chowder and game paté with wheaten bread and redcurrant glaze. Main courses might include grilled sea bass on roast leeks or pan-fried venison on garlic champ. There's also an extensive bar menu.
Daily 12.30–3, 5.30–8.30 (Fri–Sat to 9.30)
L £20, D £48, Wine from £9.35
Section
Killyleagh is on the western shore of Strangford Lough, 8.4km (5.5 miles) north of Downpatrick on the A22

LIMAVADY

THE LIME TREE ❀

60 Catherine Street, Limavady, Co. Londonderry, BT49 9DB
Tel 028 7776 4300
www.limetreerest.com

A small, owner-run restaurant where Stanley Matthews cooks and Maria Matthews manages. A simple cooking style is used to great effect and the meals are complemented by a good selection of wine. Signature dishes include seafood chowder using fresh market fish, and oven-baked supreme of salmon with roasted vegetables and a balsamic dressing. Desserts could include steamed banana and ginger sponge with custard. There is an 'early bird' menu for budget dining which can be a two- or three-course option.
Tue–Sat 6–9.30; closed 1 week Nov, 1 week Feb/Mar, 1 week Jul
L £13.90, D £25.90, Wine from £15
No pipes or cigars
Entering Limavady from the Derry side, the restaurant is on the right on a small slip road

MAGHERA

ARDTARA COUNTRY HOUSE ❀❀

8 Gorteade Road, Upperlands, Co. Londonderry, BT46 5SA
Tel 028 7964 4490
www.ardtara.com

An original hunting scene frieze dominates the dining room of this 150-year-old country house, while a high lantern ceiling lets in plenty of natural sunlight. A carefully balanced menu focuses on the best of Ulster dishes and the freshest of local produce. Ravioli of lobster and basil on a bed of spinach and basil foam shows striking use of colours, while sirloin of beef with a wild mushroom sauce is a robustly flavoured main dish. Vegetarian dishes by request.
Tue–Sat 7–9, Sun 12.30–2.30
L £23, D £55, Wine from £12.95
Section, no pipes or cigars
From Maghera take the A29 towards Coleraine. After 3km (2 miles) take the B75 for Kilrea through the Upperlands. Pass the W. M. Clark & Sons sign and take the next left

NEWTOWNABBEY

CORR'S CORNER

315 Ballyclare Road, Co. Antrim, BT36 4TQ
Tel 028 9084 9221
www.corrscorner.com

This friendly place offers a long menu that can be enjoyed in the informal Lady R Bar or in the more intimate surroundings of the Corriander Room Restaurant. There are lots of salads, burgers and sandwiches for a quick lunch, plus grills, fish and chips, and international dishes such as a Thai stir-fry, curries, or syrup-glazed spare ribs with the chef's own barbecue sauce.
Mon–Sat noon–9.45pm, Sun noon–8.45pm
L £25, D £40, Wine from £8.95
11km (7 miles) from Belfast

PORTAFERRY

THE NARROWS

8 Shore Road, Portaferry, Co. Down, BT22 1JY
Tel 028 4272 8148

With its sunny yellow exterior, The Narrows stands out on the quay at Portaferry and the food in the restaurant stands out for the superb standard of cooking. Portaferry mussels with tomato, basil and garlic sauce are a popular starter, and main courses might include a succulent rack of lamb with Lyonnaise potatoes and red wine jus, or pan-fried salmon fillet with roast peppers. The lunch menu also has the mussels, along with baguettes, prime beef burgers and scampi.
Mon–Sat 12–2.30, 7–8.30, Sun 12–3, 7–8.30
L £20, D £45, Wine from £10.95
Take the A20 to Portaferry and continue down to the shore; turn left to The Narrows

PORTAFERRY HOTEL ❀

10 The Strand, Portaferry, Co. Down, BT22 1PE
Tel 028 4272 8231
www.portaferryhotel.com

A popular venue right on the quayside, with a stunning view of Strangford Lough. Seafood from nearby Portavogie and Ardglass is prominent on the interesting menu, with an emphasis on prawns, scallops, lobster and mussels, but there are plenty of meat dishes too, based on local produce. Dress code: Men must have their shoulders covered.
Daily 7–9, also Sun 12.30–2.30
L £35, D £65, Wine from £13.50
No pipes or cigars
On the quayside

SPECIAL IN PORTRUSH

RAMORE WINE BAR ❀

The Harbour, Portrush, Co. Antrim, BT56 8BN
Tel 028 7082 4313
www.theramore.fsnet.co.uk

This hugely popular restaurant thrives on providing cosmopolitan dishes with flair and creativity. The second-floor quayside location blends with a modern, funky interior and busy lunchtimes swing to a smooth jazz soundtrack. The views over the harbour are stunning and the large menu has something for all tastes. There is even a children's menu.
Mon–Sat 12.15–2.15, 5–10, Sun 12.30–3, 5–9
L from £18, D from £22, Wine from £8.50
On the harbour in Portrush

STAYING IN IRELAND

In Ireland you can stay in anything from a castle to a horse-drawn caravan. The variety of accommodation is tremendous, and there's something to suit every budget. But whether you choose a manor house or a working farm, a city hotel or a country cottage, you'll receive a warm welcome and hospitality second to none. Most local tourist information offices will have a bed-booking service or can advise on accommodation.

Hodson Bay Hotel, Athlone; Gresham Hotel, Dublin; Duvane Farm, Clonakilty (left to right)

BOOKING

It's always a good idea to book ahead, especially for Dublin and if you're visiting in peak season or during holidays. Prices are listed either as a room rate, usually without breakfast, or as bed-and-breakfast (B&B) per person based on two people sharing a room. Single supplements are often charged. Always ask what is included if you're not sure. Prices are quoted in euros for the Republic and in pounds sterling for Northern Ireland.

Within Ireland, tourist information offices offer a nationwide booking service, charging a small fee to cover phone calls and a 10 per cent non-refundable deposit. You can also book online through the Bord Fáilte website www.ireland.ie. The booking services below cover a wide range of accommodation around the island in all price brackets. You may pay a small fee per booking.

Gulliver operates an accommodation and car rental reservations system throughout the Republic and Northern Ireland. All properties are approved by the Irish Tourist Board. You can book on-line at www.goireland.com or via the following toll-free numbers: within Ireland: 1-800 668 668; from the UK: 0800 783 5740; from Europe: 00800 668 668 66; from the US: 1-888 827 3028. Lines are open Monday to Friday 9am to 8pm.

The Irish Hotels Federation (tel 01 497 6459) publishes *Be Our Guest*, a directory of approved hotels and guesthouses in the Republic, available at tourist offices or by calling 0800 039 7000. Or you can book online: www.irelandhotels.com. The Northern Ireland Hotels Federation (tel 028 9035 1110) publishes a free guide to every hotel and guesthouse in Northern Ireland, available at tourist offices or from the Northern Ireland Tourist Board, 59 North Street, Belfast BT1 1NB, tel 028 9023 1221. Or book online at www.nitb.com.

HOTELS

Hotels range from elegant castles and manor houses, to country houses and village inns, to modern chain hotels in both cities and the countryside. Properties which display the shamrock symbol have been inspected and approved by the Irish Tourist Board or Northern Ireland Tourist Board.

Prices average around €80 for a two-star hotel, €145 for three-and four-star, and €225 for five-star. Some of the large chain hotels in major cities which cater for business clientele during the week may offer discounted rooms at the weekend. Others may offer special packages.

In resort areas, four- and five-star hotels may have swimming pools, golf courses and other sports and leisure facilities. In smaller towns, a hotel with a good bar, restaurant and entertainment may be the hub of social activity for the locals as well as visitors. Our listings indicate where hotels have extra facilities or activities available.

Throughout Ireland, castles have been converted into luxury accommodation. Like manor houses and country house hotels, they are generally set in beautiful rural surroundings and offer sophisticated dining, some of the finest in the country. Activities such as fishing or horseback riding may also be available.

Hidden Ireland (tel 01 662 7166, www.hiddenireland.com) is a collection of private houses with great character and fascinating history. Guests often dine with their hosts and enjoy an intimate experience of Irish life.

Ireland's Blue Book (tel 01 676 9914, www.irelands-blue-book.ie) gives details of some of the top castle hotels, manor houses and country house hotels in the country.

Manor House Hotels and Irish Country Hotels (tel 01 295 8900, www.cmvhotels.com) have accommodation in castles, manor houses and family-owned country hotels with a relaxed atmosphere.

Most hotels charge dearly for drinks and snacks from the mini-bar. You will also pay high rates for using the telephone line in your room for making calls or using the internet. International calls can be exorbitant. Check the rates in advance if they are not already posted in your room.

Tipping is not generally expected, even at the larger hotels. Services such as carrying bags to your room or serving drinks are considered part of the hospitality. The exception is hotel restaurants: Unless a service charge is added to the bill, waiters should be tipped the usual 10 to 15 per cent as you would in any eating establishment.

Riverside Park Hotel, Enniscorthy

GUESTHOUSES

Guesthouses may be located in family homes, in handsome Victorian or Georgian residences, or in newer, modern buildings. They have more rooms than a B&B, but the atmosphere is friendly and informal, with an emphasis on personal attention. The hosts may or may not live on the premises. You'll often be served afternoon tea and scones on arrival, and a generous Irish breakfast is assured.

Prices are higher than a B&B, which reflect a higher level of comfort and amenities. Elegant or historic properties can be as expensive as a top hotel.

Associations with properties of character include Premier Guest Houses of Ireland (tel 01 205 2826, www.premierguesthouses.com) and Irish Country Inns (tel 01 660 7975, www.tourismresources.ie/fh).

BED-AND-BREAKFAST

Bed-and-breakfast accommodation is in family homes, with generally one to four private rooms reserved for guests. Furnishings are simple, but rooms are clean and pleasant and usually have private bathrooms. Although they are inexpensive, the real attraction is the chance to mingle with an Irish family. There are B&Bs in nearly every town and village, and while advance booking is always wise, another attraction is that accommodation can usually be found for those visiting without a fixed schedule. Average B&B prices are €28.50 per person, including a full Irish breakfast. Many close for a period during the winter.

Farmhouse B&Bs are particularly popular in Ireland. They are an excellent way to experience the countryside at first hand and make contact with local people. Good fresh food and a warm welcome are an added feature. Prices start at €26 per person, including breakfast.

Associations specializing in B&B include: Family Homes of Ireland (tel 091 552 000, www.family-homes.ie); the Town and Country Homes Association (tel 071 98 22222, www.townandcountry.ie); Irish Farmhouse Holidays (tel 061 400 700, www.irishfarmholidays.com); and the Northern Ireland Farm & Country Holidays Association (tel 028 8284 1325; www.nifcha.com).

HOSTELS

For those on a budget, there are more than 200 hostels in both cities and the countryside. Many are affiliated with international hostelling associations, others are privately run. In addition to dormitory beds, most now have private rooms, including family rooms, some with private bathrooms. Many offer meals and activities.

Prices range from €10–€25 for dormitory beds and €10–€60 for private rooms.

For affiliated hostels, contact An Óige, the Irish Youth Hostel Association (tel 01 830 4555; www.anoige.ie) or Hostelling International Northern Ireland (tel 048 90 315 435; www.hini.org.uk). Private hostels are listed with the tourist boards.

SELF CATERING

Self catering is a good option for those who like to set their own hours. You can rent traditional houses, cottages, chalets, apartments (or even a castle with butler and housekeeping staff), usually on a weekly basis. Cooking utensils and bed linen are generally supplied, though you may want to bring extra towels. Prices range from €100–€700 per week (£65–£455 in Northern Ireland) and vary according to season. You often pay extra for electricity and heat and the use of other facilities.

Gulliver (▷ 302) lists over 2,500 approved properties. In the Republic, contact Irish Self Catering Federation (tel 1890 201 268, www.iscf.ie) or Irish Cottages and Holiday Homes Association (tel 01 475 7596; www.irishcottageholidays.com). In Northern Ireland try Northern Ireland Self-Catering Association (tel 028 9077 6174; www.nischa.com) or Rural Cottage Holidays (tel 028 9024 1100; www.cottagesinireland.com).

CAMPING AND CARAVANNING

There are more than 200 camping and caravan parks in Ireland, many in scenic locations. They range from family-run parks to large sites with many amenities for families, to basic sites in quiet, more remote surroundings. Many sites have motor homes that can be rented by the week. Prices range from €6–€15 for a small tent and from €6–€22 for a motor home, but these vary according to location and season.

The Irish Camping and Caravan Club (tel 01 495 1303; www.camping-ireland.ie) lists parks throughout the Republic on its website. In Northern Ireland, contact the tourist board for a list of approved sites. You can obtain permits for camping in forest areas from the Northern Ireland Forest Service (tel 028 9052 4480; www.forestserviceni.gov.uk).

HORSE-DRAWN CARAVANS

For a slow but adventurous journey through the countryside, you can rent a horse-drawn caravan. Wagons can accommodate four to five people, and you spend the nights in the country or on the grounds of a rural pub or country house. A short break costs between €330 and €600 in the off season, while a week in the peak season starts at €700. You'll pay around €12–€18 for overnight parking. Riding horses can also be rented; www.horsedrawn.in-ireland.net has information.

CABIN CRUISING

Ireland's navigable waterways provide an unusual option for a group or family holiday in the countryside. You can rent a barge or cruiser sleeping between two and ten people, don't need a licence to operate it, and will be given instructions on handling the boat. Cruisers are usually rented on a weekly basis and prices range from €750 in low season to €2,200 or more in high season, and vary according to size and specifications. The Irish Tourist Board can provide more information and a list of operators, or contact Waterways Ireland (www.waterwaysireland.org) or Inland Waterways Association of Ireland (www.iwai.ie).

TIPS

- Check to see if your visit coincides with a local festival, cultural or sporting event. If so, book well ahead. Accommodation will fill quickly, especially in the lower price ranges.
- Be sure to ask about special offers when booking. Some hotels, particularly chains, have special midweek or weekend rates at certain times of the year.
- If you arrive without a reservation, the local tourist office may be able to help you find accommodation. If they are closed, ask at a local pub.
- Seaside resorts and other popular destinations are crowded during summer, holiday and school holiday periods. An off-season visit may be cheaper and more enjoyable.
- In remote areas some lodging facilities close for the winter.
- Country house hotel dining rooms often have set menus only. Unless they can handle special requests, you may have to go out if you want something lighter or à la carte.

HOTEL AND BED-AND-BREAKFAST CLASSIFICATIONS

HOTELS

All hotels recognized by the AA should have the highest standards of cleanliness, proper records of booking, give professional service, assist with luggage on request, accept and deliver messages, provide a designated area for dinner (if available) and breakfast, with drinks available in a bar or lounge, and provide an early morning call on request.

A guide to some of the general expectations for each star classification is as follows:

★ A relatively informal yet competent style of service and an adequate range of facilities, including a television. The majority of bedrooms have a private bath. At least one designated eating area for breakfast and dinner (if available).

★★ As above plus professional management, with at least one restaurant or dining room for breakfast and dinner. Last orders for dinner no earlier than 7pm.

★★★ As above plus direct dial telephones, remote control television, private bath or shower and toilet, a wide selection of drinks in the bar and last orders for dinner no earlier than 8pm.

★★★★ As above plus a range of high-quality toiletries and private bath with fixed overhead shower and toilet. Uniformed, well-trained staff with additional services, a night porter and a serious approach to cuisine. Well-appointed public areas. Last orders for dinner no earlier than 9pm.

★★★★★ These are the most luxurious hotels, offering extra facilities and services, top-quality rooms and a full concierge service. A wide selection of drinks, including cocktails, is available in the bar, and the restaurant's menu and food should reflect the quality of the hotel. Last orders for dinner no earlier than 10pm.

THE TOP HOTELS

These hotels, identified by open stars (☆), stand out as the very best hotels in Ireland and range from large luxury hotels to small country inns.

BED-AND-BREAKFAST

Bed-and-breakfast (B&B) and guesthouse accommodation is rated for the quality of its operation. This quality is rated with a diamond symbol (♦) on a rising scale from one to five. The criteria for a higher rating is guest care and quality rather than the choice of extra facilities.

At all grades, guests can expect:

- a prompt and professional check in and out
- comfortable accommodation equipped to modern standards
- regularly changed bedding and towels
- a sufficient hot water supply at all times
- adequate storage, heating, lighting and comfortable seating
- a full English or continental breakfast
- evening meals may or may not be available.

OPEN DIAMOND RATING ◇

To help readers seeking accommodation, the very best establishments in each of the top three quality ratings (five, four and three diamonds) are identified with open diamonds.

DUBLIN

Accommodation fills quickly in the capital, so always book ahead. Although there are many good hotels, and new ones being built, they tend to be at the upper end of the market and there is a shortage in the lower price brackets, though there's cheaper accommodation outside the heart of the city (look for one near a DART station or bus route). The Dublin Tourist Board publishes the *Dublin Accommodation Guide*, listing all types of lodging in the capital, with photographs. It costs €3.50 and can be purchased online (www.visitdublin.com) or in the tourist offices. The Dublin Tourism Centre on Suffolk Street (tel 01 605 7777; e-mail information@dublintourism.ie) has an accommodation service. For a small fee they will help you find something in your price range, in the capital and elsewhere in Ireland.

A budget option if you're visiting between June and September is to stay in student accommodation at Trinity College or University College Dublin (UCD). Trinity has standard rooms, rooms with private bathrooms and apartments on campus, with continental breakfast (tel 01 608 1177; e-mail reservations@tcd.ie; www.tcd.conferences/visitor2.htm). University College Dublin has self-catering apartments with three or four single bedrooms on campus (tel 01 269 7111; e-mail ucd.village@kinlaygroup.ie; www.ucdvillage.ie).

ABBERLEY COURT ★★★
Belgard Road, Tallaght, Dublin
Tel 01 459 6000
www.abberley.ie

Next to an excellent complex of shops, restaurants and a cinema, this smart hotel includes a lounge bar that serves food all day and the first-floor Court Restaurant.

Closed 24 Dec–2 Jan
Double €118–€124
40 (8 non-smoking)
49, 65, 65B, 77
Opposite The Square at the junction of Belgard Road and the N81

ARIEL HOUSE ♦♦♦♦♦
50–54 Lansdowne Road, Ballsbridge, Dublin
Tel 01 668 5512
www.ariel-house.net

This gracious Victorian house is in a southeastern suburb, near the rugby ground. Luxurious premier rooms and more contemporary standard rooms are available, and healthy and vegetarian options are on offer at breakfast. Staff are friendly and there are professional aromatherapy and reflexology treatments, plus secure parking.

Closed 23–27 Dec
Double €89–€150
37 (non-smoking)
7, 45
DART Lansdowne Road
From Merrion Square, take Northumberland Road to Ballsbridge. Turn left at Jurys Hotel and Ariel House is on left past the traffic lights

BEWLEY'S BALLSBRIDGE ★★★
Merrion Road, Ballsbridge, Dublin
Tel 01 668 1111
www.bewleyshotels.com

This comfortable hotel is near the RDS Showgrounds. It offers good value, and its casual restaurant serves interesting dishes. The spacious lounges on the lower floor are a popular meeting place. Some parking is available (nominal fee); it should be requested on making a reservation.

Double €99
304
7, 7A, 45
DART Sandymount
Close to the heart of the city, at junction of Simmonscourt and Merrion roads. Entrance on Simmonscourt Road

PRICES AND SYMBOLS

Prices are for a double room for one night. Breakfast is included unless noted otherwise. All the hotels listed accept credit cards unless otherwise stated. Note that rates vary widely throughout the year.

For a key to the symbols ▷ 2.

BROWNES TOWNHOUSE & BRASSERIE ◇◇◇◇◇
22 St. Stephen's Green, Dublin
Tel 01 638 3939
www.brownesdublin.com

A gracious Georgian town house on Dublin's most prestigious square. Bedrooms are luxurious and there is a comfortable sitting room and meeting room. Reservations are advisable at the popular brasserie.

24 Dec–3 Jan
Double €200–€255
11
15, 45
DART Pearse
On the north side of St. Stephen's Green beside the Shelbourne Hotel

SPECIAL

BLAKES TOWNHOUSE ♦♦♦♦♦
50 Merrion Road, Ballsbridge, Dublin
Tel 01 668 8324
www.halspinsprivatehotels.com

A luxurious town house which has been completely refurbished to a high standard. Some of the spacious, air-conditioned bedrooms have four-poster beds, others have balconies overlooking the gardens, plus all the expected facilities. Parking available.

Double €119–€149
13
7, 45
DART Sandymount
Take Merrion Road south to Ballsbridge where you will find Blakes opposite the RDS Convention Centre

BUSWELLS ★★★
23–25 Molesworth Street, Dublin
Tel 01 614 6500
www.quinnhotels.com

One of Dublin's 18th-century Georgian town houses, Buswells is convenient for the main shopping and cultural attractions. Bedrooms are well equipped and attractively

decorated. Public areas include an elegant lobby lounge and restaurant, and the club-style bar is a popular meeting place.
Closed 25–26 Dec
Double €220
69
10
DART Pearse
On the corner of Molesworth Street and Kildare Street, opposite Dáil Éireann (Government Buildings)

THE CARNEGIE COURT ★★★
North Street, Swords Village, Swords, Co. Dublin
Tel 01 840 4384
www.carnegiecourt.com
This modern, tastefully built hotel is just off the N1, close to Dublin airport. The air-conditioned bedrooms are comfortable and many are spacious. Public areas include a residents' lounge, contemporary Courtyard Restaurant, the dramatic Harp Bar and conference and banqueting facilities.
Closed 24–26 Dec
Double €140–€155
36 (7 non-smoking)

41
Malahide Station then bus 230

CASSIDYS HOTEL ★★★
Cavendish Row, Upper O'Connell Street, Dublin
Tel 01 878 0555
www.cassidyshotel.com
This family-run hotel with modern bedrooms is in a red-brick Georgian terrace at the top of O'Connell Street. Grooms Bar is warm and friendly, Cassidy's is in traditional style, and Restaurant 6 is contemporary and stylish. There are conference facilities, but parking spots are limited.
Double €115–€200
88 (23 non-smoking)
7, 10, 45
DART Tara Street

CHARLEVILLE LODGE ♦♦♦♦
268–272 North Circular Road, Phibsborough, Dublin
Tel 01 838 6633
www.charlevillelodge.ie
In a northern suburb, near Phoenix Park, this elegant Victorian terrace has been beautifully restored. Lounges are welcoming, and a choice of breakfasts is available in the smart dining room. Bedrooms are very comfortable, and there's secure parking.
Closed 21–26 Dec
Double from €69
30 (4 ground floor)
10
Near to St. Peter's Church

SPECIAL

THE CLARENCE ☆☆☆☆ ❀❀
6–8 Wellington Quay, Dublin
Tel 01 407 0800
www.theclarence.ie
The Clarence is at the heart of Dublin City, on the banks of the River Liffey, within walking distance of the shopping areas, museums and galleries. This is a very individual hotel, where contemporary design is tastefully incorporated into the original features of the 1850 building. The unobtrusive professional staff have a keen interest in guest care.
Double from €315–€2,100
50 (4 non-smoking)
7, 10, 45
DART Tara Street
From O'Connell Bridge, go west along quays, and the hotel is 500m (550 yards) beyond the first set of lights (at the Ha'Penny Bridge)

THE FITZWILLIAM HOTEL ★★★★ ❀❀
St. Stephen's Green, Dublin
Tel 01 478 7000
www.fitzwilliamhotel.com
In a central position on St. Stephen's Green, this friendly hotel is a pleasing blend of contemporary style and good traditional standards of hotel-keeping. Bedrooms, many of which overlook an internal rooftop garden, have thoughtful extras. Eating options include the informal Citron, and Thornton's, which offers a truly fine dining experience.
Double €340
130 (90 non-smoking)
7, 45
DART Pearse
Next to the top of Grafton Street

THE GRESHAM ★★★★❀
23 Upper O'Connell Street, Dublin
Tel 01 874 6881
www.gresham-hotels.com
Friendly staff remain a strength here, and refurbishment has given a smart new look to the popular lounge and brasserie, where there's an emphasis on quality seasonal produce. Bedrooms come in a variety of styles, and there are extensive corporate facilities.

Double €150–€300
288 (248 non-smoking)

7, 45
DART Connolly
Close to the GPO

HARDING HOTEL
Cooper Alley, Fishamble Street, Christchurch, Dublin
Tel 01 679 6500
www.hardinghotel.ie
In the lively and fascinating Temple Bar area, this friendly hotel offers good-value accommodation. Its interesting Peruvian-style bar and Fitzers Restaurant are popular meeting places.
Closed 23–26 Dec
Double €89–€96
53
7, 45
DART Connolly
Top of Dame Street beside Christ Church Cathedral

JURYS HOTEL DUBLIN ★★★★ ❀
Pembroke Road, Ballsbridge, Dublin
Tel 01 660 5000
www.jurysdoyle.com
The flagship of the Jurys chain incorporates Jurys Hotel and The Towers at Jurys. The first is large and popular, with several restaurants and bars and good conference and leisure facilities. The Towers offers discreet luxury, with spacious bedrooms and private suites.
Double €126–€320
403 (140 non-smoking)
Indoor and outdoor
7
DART Lansdowne Road
South of city via Merrion Road, at junction with Northumberland Road

KILRONAN HOUSE ♦♦♦♦
70 Adelaide Road, Dublin
Tel 01 475 5266
www.dublinn.com

Rose and Terry Masterson welcome guests to this fine period town house near the National Concert Hall. Bedrooms are well-appointed and there is a

smart dining room and guest-lounge. Parking at the rear.
Double from €120
12
7, 45
DART Pearse
A 5-min walk from St. Stephen's Green

LONGFIELDS HOTEL ★★★
Lower Fitzwilliam Street, Dublin
Tel 01 676 1367
www.longfields.ie
Longfields has a warm, hospitable feel. Staff are focused toward guest care in an informal, yet professional, manner. Rooms vary in size but are very

comfortable. A serious attitude to food is evident in Kevin Arundel's cooking at No. 10 restaurant.
Double €215–€255
26
10
DART Pearse
From St. Stephens Green turn into Baggot Street and then turn left just before Larry Murphy's Pub

MARINE HOTEL ★★★ ❀
Sutton Cross, Co. Dublin
Tel 01 839 0000
www.marinehotel.ie
This nicely decorated hotel is in attractive gardens on the north shore of Dublin Bay. Public areas are comfortable, and the restaurant specializes in seafood. There is also a business suite.
Closed 24–27 Dec
Double €165–€235
48
Indoor
31, 31B
DART Sutton
8km (5 miles) from city on the road to Howth

MERRION HALL ◆◆◆◆◆
54–56 Merrion Road, Ballsbridge, Dublin
Tel 01 668 1426
www.halpinsprivatehotels.com
An elegant town house in Ballsbridge, convenient for all local amenities. The reception rooms are spacious and the

breakfast room overlooks the gardens. The large bedrooms are air-conditioned, and some have balconies.
Double €119–€149
28
45
DART Sandymount
Ballsbridge is approximately 1.5km (1 mile) along the main route from Dublin to Dun Laoghaire Port. Hotel is between the British and US embassies

THE MERRION HOTEL
☆☆☆☆☆ ❀❀❀❀
Upper Merrion Street, Dublin
Tel 01 603 0600
www.merrionhotel.com
This terrace of gracious Georgian buildings, reputed to have been the birthplace of the Duke of Wellington, has

undergone many changes of use through more than 200 years. Spacious bedrooms offer deep comfort and a wide range of extra facilities, lounges retain the charm and opulence of past times, while the Cellar Bar area is ideal for a relaxing drink. The choice of dining options includes Dublin's finest: Restaurant Patrick Guilbaud.
Double from €130
145 (65 non-smoking)
Indoor
7, 10, 45
DART Pearse
At the top of Upper Merrion Street on the left, beyond the Government buildings on the right

MOUNT HERBERT HOTEL ★★★
Herbert Road, Lansdowne Road, Ballsbridge, Dublin
Tel 01 668 4321
www.mountherberthotel.ie
Near to local places of interest, this hotel has comfortable public rooms, well-equipped bedrooms and a friendly atmosphere. There is a spacious lounge, a TV room, a cocktail bar and a lovely, good-value restaurant, overlooking the floodlit gardens. There is also a children's playground.
Double €133–€200
185
10, 45
DART Lansdowne Road (200m/220 yards)
Close to rugby stadium

NO. 66 TOWNHOUSE ◆◆◆◆
Northumberland Road, Ballsbridge, Dublin
Tel 01 660 0333/660 0471
www.66townhouse.com
This imposing house has eight comfortable bedrooms, all fully equipped to a high standard. There's a dining room and two lounges, one in a lovely conservatory. It's convenient for Lansdowne Road and the RDS showgrounds.
Double from €120
8
7, 8, 45
DART Lansdowne Road
Opposite Czech Republic Embassy, 1.5km (1 mile) south of Trinity College

THE PARLIAMENT HOTEL ★★★
Lord Edward Street, Dublin
Tel 01 670 8777
www.regencyhotels.com

An attractive hotel, near to the Temple Bar area and Dublin Castle, where the staff offer a friendly welcome. Bedrooms are decorated in a modern style, and there's a popular bar and a separate restaurant.
Double from €240
63
123
DART Pearse
Adjacent to Dublin Castle

THE PLAZA HOTEL ★★★★
Belgard Road, Tallaght, Dublin
Tel 01 462 4200
www.plazahotel.ie
A contemporary hotel near to the Tallaght complex. It has spacious public areas, good corporate facilities and a secure underground parking. The Vista Café and Olive Tree Restaurant enjoy views of the

Wicklow Mountains. There's informal dining in the traditional Grumpy McClaffertys bar.
Closed 24–30 Dec
Double €105–€175
122 (61 non-smoking)
77
On the ring road, a 30-min drive southwest of the city on the N81

RADISSON SAS ST. HELEN'S
Stillorgan Road, Dublin
Tel 01 218 6000
www.radissonsas.com
This 18th-century mansion is now a fine hotel, with many original features in the public rooms of the main house. Comfortable bedrooms and suites are in a purpose-built block. Diners can eat in the informal Orangerie bar, the Italian Talavera trattoria or Le Panto restaurant.
Double €285
151 (75 non-smoking)
46A, 46, 700
DART Blackrock
On left side of N11, 4km (2.5miles) south of the city towards Wicklow

RED COW MORANS ★★★★
Red Cow Complex, Naas Road, Dublin
Tel 01 459 3650
www.redcowhotel.com
This smart complex is built around the original Red Cow Inn, with extensions providing excellent conference facilities. Publicareas are striking and

spacious bedrooms are stylish and well equipped.
Double €190–€250
123 (63 non-smoking)
51B, 68, 69
At intersection of M50 (ring road) and N7 Naas road, on the city side of the motorway

ST. AIDEN'S ♦♦♦
32 Brighton Road, Rathgar, Dublin
Tel 01 490 2011
A fine Victorian house in a tree-lined residential road just 15 minutes south of the city. The reception rooms are comfortable and relaxing, and include a hospitality trolley. Bedrooms vary in size from spacious family rooms to snug singles, but all have TVs and telephones.
Double €90–€110
8
15, 15A, 15B
Off M50 junction 11 towards city. St. Aiden's is the third premises on the left after the traffic lights in Terenure Village

THE SHELBOURNE ★★★★
27 St. Stephen's Green, Dublin
Tel 01 663 4500
www.shelbourne.ie
A Dublin landmark since 1824, the rare and timeless elegance of this hotel has strong literary and historical links. It has gracious reception rooms, a choice of restaurants, a leisure suite and popular bars. Bedrooms are smart and comfortable, many with beautiful views of St. Stephen's Green.
Double €210–€391
190
Indoor
7, 45
DART Pearse
Go south across O'Connell Bridge to pass Trinity College, then go left into Nassau Street and right into Kildare Street; the hotel is on the left

STILLORGAN PARK ★★★★
Stillorgan Road, Dublin
Tel 01 288 1621
www.stillorganpark.com
Attractive and striking interior design is a feature of this hotel on the southern outskirts. Bedrooms are smart and

modern, and there's a contemporary restaurant and inviting bar. The air-conditioned banqueting and conference suite has all the latest technology, and there's plenty of parking.
Double €145–€170
125 (54 non-smoking)
46A
DART Blackrock (15-min walk from hotel)
Take N11 south, signed Wexford, pass RTE Studios on left, then after the next five traffic lights hotel is on the left

TEMPLE BAR ★★★
Fleet Street, Temple Bar, Dublin
Tel 01 677 3333
www.towerhotelgroup.com
This stylish hotel is right in the heart of old Dublin and is in a good position for experiencing the cultural life of the city. Comfortable, well-equipped bedrooms are competitively priced, and good food is served throughout the day. Guests can take advantage of reduced rates at nearby leisure facilities.
Closed 24–25 Dec
Double from €190
129
7, 45
DART Tara Street/Pearse
From Trinity College, go north towards O'Connell Bridge up Westmorland Street and take first left onto Fleet Street; hotel is on the right

THE EAST

Drogheda is the largest city in the Boyne Valley and makes a good base for touring the region, with several good restaurants and other tourist facilities. Accommodation ranges from manor house hotels to B&Bs. Smaller towns, such as Trim and Kells, are equally delightful, and village or farmhouse B&Bs or self-catering cottages put you in touch with this ancient countryside.

Accommodation in County Kildare is heavily booked during horse-racing events, so make reservations well ahead of your visit. County Wicklow has a range of atmospheric options, from lodges with mountain views to old coaching inns and manor houses. A mountain base is great for outdoor activities such as hiking along the Wicklow Way or visiting the pretty Vale of Avoca.

The east coast has fine sandy beaches, and resort hotels here often have health clubs and other leisure facilities. Wexford and Kilkenny are the largest towns in this region. With their historic areas and attractions, they are usually busy, particularly during major events such as the Wexford Opera Festival.

PRICES AND SYMBOLS

Prices are for a double room for one night. Breakfast is included unless noted otherwise. All the hotels listed accept credit cards unless otherwise stated. Note that rates vary widely throughout the year.

For a key to the symbols ▷ 2.

ARKLOW

ARKLOW BAY ★★★ ❀

Ferrybank, Arklow, Co. Wicklow
Tel 0402 32309
www.arklowbay.com

This hotel, including many of its well-appointed bedrooms, enjoys panoramic views of Arklow Bay. The public areas are in a contemporary style, and include a spacious lobby lounge and a comfortable bar with casual dining. Howard's restaurant is more formal.

Double €130–€150
92 (72 non-smoking)
Indoor
Turn off the N11 at the Arklow bypass. After 1.5km (1 mile) turn left and the hotel is 200m (210 yards) on the left

BALLYCONNELL

SLIEVE RUSSELL HOTEL GOLF AND COUNTRY CLUB ★★★★ ❀

Ballyconnell, Co. Cavan
Tel 049 952 6444
www.quinnhotels.com

This imposing hotel and country club stands in 120ha (300 acres) , with an 18-hole PGA championship golf course and a 9-hole par 3 course. Public areas include a range of lounges, choice of restaurants and extensive leisure and banqueting facilities. Bedrooms are tastefully furnished and equipped to a high standard. Other amenities include tennis courts, a snooker table, sauna and a hair and beauty salon.

Double from €230
159 (135 non-smoking), (27 ground floor); 60 new rooms under construction
Indoor
On left, about 9km (6 miles) west of Belturbet on the N87 Ballyconnell road

SPECIAL IN ASHFORD

BALLYKNOCKEN HOUSE AND COUNTRY COOKERY SCHOOL ◊◊◊◊

Glenealy, Ashford, Co. Wicklow
Tel 0404 44627
www.ballyknocken.com

In the foothills of the Wicklow Mountains, this farmhouse offers great hospitality, very good food and excellent accommodation. The refurbished bedrooms have elegant private bathrooms, some with Victorian-style tubs, and are equipped with TV, tea- and coffee-making facilities, and direct-dial telephone. Two relaxing sitting rooms overlook beautiful gardens and countryside. Dinner reservations are necessary. The cookery school here uses garden produce and local suppliers for its carefully prepared meals.

Double €90–€110
7 (all non-smoking)
From Dublin: turn right after the Texaco garage in Ashford (N11). The house is 5km (3 miles) from Ashford on the right

BETTYSTOWN

NEPTUNE BEACH HOTEL AND LEISURE CLUB ★★★★

Bettystown, Co. Meath
Tel 041 9827107
www.neptunebeach.ie

Overlooking the sea, with access to a sandy beach, the Neptune also offers such leisure facilities as swimming pool, children's pool, sauna and Jacuzzi. Public areas include an inviting lounge and attractive winter garden, and many rooms enjoy sea views.

Double from €130
38 (16 non-smoking)
Indoor
Just off the N1, Dublin–Belfast road

BLESSINGTON

DOWNSHIRE HOUSE ★★★ ❀

Main Street, Blessington, Co. Wicklow
Tel 045 865199
www.downshirehouse.com

Renowned for its friendly atmosphere, this family-run Georgian house is relaxing and inviting. Bedrooms, in a variety of sizes, are comfortable, and cooking is in traditional country-house style. There is a tennis court, croquet lawn and table tennis, and the hotel is set amid lovely scenery.

Closed 22 Dec–6 Jan
Double from €166.50
25 (11 in annexe)
On the N81 in middle of the village

BRAY

ROYAL ★★★

Main Street, Bray, Co. Wicklow
Tel 01 286 2935
www.regencyhotels.com

The Royal Hotel stands near to the seafront and just a few miles from the Dun Laoghaire ferryport. It has well-equipped

leisure facilities, including sauna, solarium and whirlpool spa, and there's a massage and beauty clinic.
Double from €120
91 (14 non-smoking)

Going south on the N11. take the first exit for Bray. At roundabout (traffic circle) take the second exit and go through two sets of traffic lights. Cross the bridge and the hotel on the left

WOODLAND COURT HOTEL
Southern Cross, Bray, Co. Wicklow
Tel 01 276 0258
www.woodlandcourthotel.com
In a beautiful setting opposite Kilruddery House and its famous gardens, this is an ideal place to stay for touring Dublin and Wicklow. The attractive hotel has spacious, modern bedrooms, an open-plan lobby lounge with bar, a cosy restaurant and corporate facilities.
Closed 23–27 Dec
Double from €110
65
Take the third exit off the N11 after the Loughlinstown turning, then take the turn off for Bray/Greystones

CARLOW

DOLMEN HOTEL ★★★
Kilkenny Road, Carlow, Co. Carlow
Tel 059 9142002
www.dolmenhotel.ie
Surrounded by 8ha (20 acres) of landscaped grounds, the Dolmen enjoys a peaceful setting next to the river. Guests can relax in the grounds or take advantage of the free coarse fishing. Spacious public rooms include a large bar and restaurant and a luxurious boardroom that doubles as an additional lounge.
Double €70–€160
81, 12 lodges

1.5km (1 mile) south of town on N9

SEVEN OAKS HOTEL ★★★
Athy Road, Carlow, Co. Carlow
Tel 059 913 1308
www.sevenoakshotel.com
Staff are friendly and helpful at this hotel, which has undergone extensive refurbishment. The lounge is spacious and there are comfortable bedrooms and a good leisure club. The popular restaurant is also being extended and there is a relaxing bar.
Closed 25–26 Dec, restricted service Good Fri
Double €130–€190
60
Indoor
From Dublin, drive into Carlow on the N9, go straight on at the first roundabout (traffic circle), turn right at the second and left at the third. The hotel is on the left

CARRICKMACROSS

NUREMORE HOTEL ★★★★
Carickmacross, Co. Monaghan
Tel 042 966 1438
www.nuremore-hotel.ie
Overlooking the golf course and the lakes, this is a quiet retreat with excellent facilities. There are spacious public areas and chef Ray McFardle's imaginative cooking continues to impress. There's a variety of

leisure and sporting facilities, including sauna, solarium, golf, snooker, tennis and fishing.
Double €210–€300
72 (some non-smoking)
Indoor
3km (2 miles) south of Carrickmacross on N2 Dublin road

CAVAN

KILMORE ★★★
Dublin Road, Cavan, Co. Cavan
Tel 049 433 2288
www.quinnhotels.com
Set on a hillside outside Cavan, this comfortable hotel features spacious public areas. Guests returning from fishing, golf, windsurfing or boating, which are all available nearby, appreciate the good food served in the Annalee Restaurant.
Double €98–€120
39

3km (2 miles) from Cavan on the N3

COURTOWN HARBOUR

BAY VIEW ★★★
Courtown Harbour, Co. Wexford
Tel 055 25307
www.bayview.ie
This comfortable, refurbished waterfront hotel overlooks the marina. The lounge has a sea view, the McGarry family are attentive and excellent cuisine is served in the restaurant.
Closed 30 Nov–14 Mar
Double from €130
17

From the N11 turn left before Gorey and follow signs to Courtown. The hotel is in the main square

DELGANEY

GLENVIEW HOTEL ★★★★
Glen O' the Downs, Delgany, Co. Wicklow
Tel 01 287 3399
www.glenviewhotel.com
In a lovely hillside location overlooking terraced gardens, the hotel provides luxurious lounges, a restaurant and a conservatory bar with delightful views. The bedrooms are well equipped and there are good leisure facilities, including an aerobics studio.
Double €120–€230
70
Indoor
Take the N11/M11 south from Dublin for 32km (20 miles) past Bray, turning left to Delganey

DROGHEDA

BOYNE VALLEY HOTEL AND COUNTRY CLUB ★★★
Stameen, Dublin Road, Drogheda, Co. Louth
Tel 041 983 7737
www.boynevalleyhotel.ie
This mid-Victorian mansion stands in 6.5ha (16 acres) of gardens and woodlands on the southern outskirts of town. The emphasis is on good food, attentive service and high standards of comfort. There are extensive leisure amenities.
Double €145–€160
73 (all non-smoking)
Indoor
On the M1 north from Dublin, on right, just before Drogheda

ENFIELD

JOHNSTOWN HOUSE ★★★★
Enfield, Co. Meath
Tel 046 954 0000
www.johnstownhouse.com
Built around a Georgian mansion in 32ha (80 acres) of parkland and gardens, this fine hotel offers up-to-date conference facilities, comfortable bedrooms and suites,

restaurants and bars. The reception hall and library exude 18th-century elegance. Fishing is available for guests.
Closed 24–25 Dec
Double €170–€235
82 (40 non-smoking)
Indoor
On the N4, on outskirts of Enfield.

ENNISCORTHY

RIVERSIDE PARK HOTEL ★★★

The Promenade, Enniscorthy, Co. Wexford
Tel 054 37800
www.riverparkhotel.com
Set beside the picturesque River Slaney, this hotel is painted in distinctive terracotta and blue. The foyer is equally dramatic, and public areas all take advantage of the riverside

views, including the Mill House pub. The spacious bedrooms have every modern comfort.
Double €160–€170
60 (30 non-smoking)
Indoor
800m (a half-mile) from New Bridge in Enniscorthy, on the N11 Dublin to Rosslare road

GOREY

ASHDOWN PARK HOTEL ★★★★ ❀

The Coach Road, Gorey, Co. Wexford
Tel 055 80500
www.ashdownparkhotel.com
Overlooking Gorey, this modern hotel has excellent health and leisure facilities, a choice of bars and an attractive first-floor restaurant. Bedrooms match the overall high standards. Leisure facilities include steam and therapy rooms, a beauty salon and a sauna and solarium.
Closed 24–25 Dec
Double €150–€190
60 (40 non-smoking)
Indoor
Take the N11 south towards Gorey where you take the first left turn before the bridge. The hotel is on the left

SPECIAL IN GLENDALOUGH

THE GLENDALOUGH HOTEL ★★★

Glendalough, Co. Wicklow
Tel 0404 45135
www.glendaloughhotel.ie
Forest and mountains provide the setting for this long-established hotel, beside the famous Glendalough monastic site. The hotel has been refurbished and extended, and guests can enjoy good bar food or eat in the pleasant restaurant overlooking the river and forest.
Closed Dec–end Jan
Double from €150
44
Take the N11 to Kilmacongue, right onto the R755 and carry straight on at Caragh before turning right onto the R756

KILKENNY

KILKENNY RIVER COURT HOTEL ★★★★ ❀

The Bridge, John Street, Kilkenny, Co. Kilkenny
Tel 056 772 3388
www.kilrivercourt.com
With its private courtyard, riverside restaurant and bar and lovely views of Kilkenny Castle, this is a great place to stay. Attentive staff serve good food, and there's a friendly feel here.
Closed 24–26 Dec
Double €120–€400
90 (45 non-smoking)
Indoor
On the River Nore side of the castle

LANGTONS HOUSE ★★★

69 John Street, Kilkenny, Co. Kilkenny
Tel 056 776 5133
Langton's has long had a reputation as an entertainment venue and bar, which is now complemented by a range of comfortable accommodation. The restaurant is popular with visitors and locals.
Closed Good Fri and 25 Dec
Double €100–€220
14, plus 16 in annexe
Coming from Dublin, on the outskirts of Kilkenny turn left; Langtons is 500m (550 yards) on the left

NEWPARK HOTEL ★★★

Castlecomer Road, Kilkenny, Co. Kilkenny
Tel 056 776 0500
www.newparkhotel.com
A friendly hotel with an impressive foyer lounge, a bar/bistro and conference suites. A purpose-built bedroom wing offers a choice of rooms, decorated and equipped to a high standard.
Double €145–€185
130 (some non-smoking)
Indoor
1km (0.5 miles) outside the city

KILTEGAN

BARRADERRY HOUSE ♦♦♦♦♦

Kiltegan, Co. Wicklow
Tel/fax 059 647 3209
www.barraderrycountryhouse.com
A granite stone gateway marks the entrance to this restored Georgian house. Light evening meals are available if booked in advance. The bedrooms are in period style and all have private bathrooms.
Closed mid-Dec to mid-Jan
Double €80–€90
4 (all non-smoking)
Follow the N81 Dublin to Baltinglass road, turn left on to the R747 for 7km (4.5 miles) to Barraderry House on right

MACREDDIN

BROOKLODGE AT MACREDDIN ★★★★ ❀❀

Macreddin Village, Co. Wicklow
Tel 0402 36444
www.brooklodge.com
Brooklodge is a real find, where comfort predominates among restful lounges and sumptuous bedrooms. The Strawberry Tree restaurant specializes in organic and wild ingredients, and the hotel also has a microbrewery, smoke house and shop.
Double from €210
40
From N11, take R752 to Rathdrum then R753 to Aughrim and follow the signs to Macreddin, 3km (2 miles)

RATHNEW

TINAKILLY COUNTRY HOUSE & RESTAURANT ★★★★ ❀

Rathnew, Co. Wicklow
Tel 0404 69274
This fine hotel is high at the end of a tree-lined avenue, with superb views of the Irish Sea and Broadlaugh bird sanctuary. It is full of Victorian charm, but has every modern facility.
Closed 24–26 Dec
Double €204–€630
51
On R750, 500m (550 yards) north of the village

THE SOUTH

This region contains some of the most popular tourist areas in the country, so it is important to book in advance if you've set your sights on particular places to stay. Shannon International Airport is Ireland's western gateway city and nearby Limerick offers a full range of places to stay. Historic Waterford, with its famous crystal factory, is highly popular and the attractive towns of the Blackwater Valley offer a nearby alternative, as do the coastal villages, with some lovely country house hotels. The Waterford coast has several resorts with beaches and sports facilities. Cashel is another place buzzing with visitors, but the surrounding Tipperary towns and countryside are quieter and have many good hotels and country houses.

Cork and Kerry are two of Ireland's most visited counties. Cork city will be particularly busy in 2005 as European Capital of Culture, with events and attractions throughout the year. As bases for the popular Ring of Kerry, Killarney and Kenmare hotels fill quickly in peak season, but small coastal towns and villages have guesthouses and B&Bs. Tralee is the main base for the Dingle Peninsula, but there are small hotels, pubs and B&Bs in the villages on the peninsula itself.

ADARE

DUNRAVEN ARMS ★★★★
❀❀
Ferrybank, Adare, Co. Limerick
Tel 061 396633
www.dunravenhotel.com

This lovely hotel, in the heart of one of Ireland's prettiest villages, was established in 1792. A traditional country inn in both style and atmosphere, it has comfortable lounges and bedrooms, attractive gardens, leisure and beauty facilities and good food.

Double from €190
74 (all non-smoking)
Indoor
In the middle of town

ARDMORE

ROUND TOWER ★
Ardmore, Co. Waterford
Tel 024 94494

Round Tower is a large, friendly country house set in its own grounds in a pretty fishing village. There's a comfortable lounge, panelled bar and a conservatory, and the menu features local seafood.

Double from €80
12
In the middle of the village

BALTIMORE

BALTIMORE HARBOUR RESORT HOTEL AND LEISURE CENTRE ★★★ ❀
Lifeboat Road, Baltimore, Co. Cork
Tel 028 20361
www.baltimoreharbourhotel.ie

This smart, friendly hotel is in a delightful position overlooking the harbour. The spacious public areas include a restful lounge with deep sofas and a turf fire, and the bar and garden room open onto the patio and gardens. Fresh local ingredients feature on menus. The bedrooms are well appointed and all have sea views.

Closed Jan
Double €116–€168
64
Indoor
From Skibbereen, take the R595 for 13km (8 miles) to Baltimore

PRICES AND SYMBOLS

Prices are for a double room for one night. Breakfast is included unless noted otherwise. All the hotels listed accept credit cards unless otherwise stated. Note that rates vary widely throughout the year.

For a key to the symbols ▷ 2.

BANDON

GLEBE COUNTRY HOUSE ♦♦♦♦
Ballinadee, Bandon, Co. Cork
Tel 021 477 8294
http://indigo.ie/glebehse/

This lovely old guesthouse stands in well-kept gardens and is run with great attention to detail. Antique furnishings predominate and the breakfast menu offers unusual options, and a country-house style dinner is available by reservation.

Closed 21 Dec–3 Jan
Double €80–€100
4
Turn south off N71 at Innishannon Bridge, signed Ballinadee, for 8km (5 miles) along the river bank, turn left after village sign

BANTRY

WESTLODGE HOTEL ★★★
Bantry, Co. Cork
Tel 027 50360
www.westlodgehotel.ie

Superb leisure and good children's facilities make this hotel popular with families, and it's it an ideal base for touring west Cork and south Kerry. The staff are friendly and helpful, and the bedrooms and public rooms are decorated to a high standard.

Closed 23–27 Dec
Double €130–€170
90 (20 non-smoking)
Indoor
N71 to west Cork

CAHER

CAHIR HOUSE HOTEL ★★★
The Square, Caher, Co. Tipperary
Tel 052 42727
www.cahirhousehotel.ie

In the heart of town, this hotel has been extending hospitality to visitors since the days of the famous Bianconi horse-drawn coaches. It offers modern comforts in well-equipped and tastefully furnished rooms and maintains traditional standards.

Closed 25 Dec
Double €100–€120
41 (17 non-smoking)
On the town square, with parking at the rear

CLONAKILTY

DUVANE FARM ♦♦♦♦
Ballyduvane, Clonakilty, Co. Cork
Tel/fax 023 33129
www.duvanefarm.com

Well kept and decorated in cheerful shades, this comfortable guesthouse includes one room with a four-poster bed, and two on the ground floor, sharing a bathroom—ideal for family groups. There's a guest sitting room, and a wide choice at breakfast.

Closed Nov to mid-Mar
Double from €70
4
1.5km (1 mile) southwest on N71

THE LODGE AND SPA AT INCHYDONEY ISLAND ★★★★ ❀❀

Clonakilty, Co. Cork
Tel 023 33143
www.inchydoneyisland.com

Steps from this modern coastal hotel lead down to two long sandy beaches. The bedrooms are prettily decorated in warm tones and have modern facilities. Guests can eat in the third-floor Gulfstream restaurant or the more casual Dunes bar and bistro. There's a sauna and thalassotherapy spa.

Closed 24–26 Dec
Double €260–€310
67 (17 non-smoking)
Indoor
From the N71, at the entry roundabout (traffic circle) in Clonakilty, take the second exit and follow the signs

COBH

WATERS EDGE HOTEL ★★★

Yacht Club Quay, Cobh, Co. Cork
Tel 021 481 5566
www.watersedgehotel.ie

This delightful hotel has spectacular harbour views, notably from the Jacob's Ladder Restaurant. Spacious bedrooms are furnished to a high standard, most overlook the waterfront and the ground-floor rooms have private balconies. Secure parking.

Closed 23–28 Dec and 1–4 Jan
Double €110–€200
19 (6 non-smoking)
On the waterfront, follow the signs for Cobh Heritage Centre

CORK

GARNISH HOUSE ♦♦♦♦

1 Aldergrove, Western Road, Cork, Co. Cork
Tel 021 427 5111
www.garnish.ie

Rooms here are tasteful, and some have a private Jacuzzi. The breakfast menu provides a huge choice. It's convenient for the ferry and airport, and has

24-hour reception. Five minutes walk to the heart of the city.

Double €60–€100
13
Opposite Cork University College

SPECIAL IN CASHEL

CASHEL PALACE ★★★★ ❀

Main Street, Cashel, Co. Tipperary
Tel 062 62707
www.cashel palace.ie

The Rock of Cashel, floodlit at night, is a dramatic backdrop to this 18th-century former bishop's palace. An elegant drawing room has garden access and bedrooms in the main house are luxurious. Those in the adjacent mews are ideal for families or groups. A private path leads to the Rock.

Closed 23–27 Dec
Double €254
23 (5 non-smoking)
Near traffic lights in the middle of the town

GRESHAM METROPOLE ★★★

MacCurtain Street, Cork, Co. Cork
Tel 021 450 8122
www.gresham-metropole.com

This city hotel has good conference facilities with natural daylight and air conditioning. Bedrooms very in size but are well equipped and comfortable. There is a leisure suite, waterside restaurant and a café. Ask reception for car parking information.

Double from €140
113 (26 non-smoking)
Indoor
In the middle of the city

HAYFIELD MANOR ☆☆☆☆ ❀❀

Perrott Avenue, College Road, Cork, Co. Cork
Tel 021 484 5900
www.hayfieldmanor.ie

Part of a grand estate with lovely gardens in its 1ha (2.5 acres) of grounds, this fine secluded hotel has every modern amenity and a tranquil

atmosphere. Bedrooms offer high levels of comfort, with many thoughtful extras. Elegant public rooms have fine furnishings and real fires.

Double €345
88
Indoor
Take N22 towards Killarney, in 2km (1 mile) turn left at University Gates off Western Road. Turn right into College Road, then left into Perrott Avenue

FERMOY

BALLYVOLANE HOUSE ◇◇◇◇◇

Castlelyons, Fermoy, Co. Cork
Tel 025 36349
www.ballyvolanehouse.ie

An Italianate country house, built in 1728, in a magnificent setting of parkland and gardens (open to the public in May). The Greens are exceptionally welcoming hosts. Comfortable bedrooms overlook the park, where one of the three lakes is stocked with brown trout. Dinner is served around one fine table.

Closed 23–31 Dec
Double from €130–€170
6 (all non-smoking)
From N8, take R628 and follow signs to Ballyvolane House

GOUGANE BARRA

GOUGANE BARRA ★★

Gougane Barra, Macroom, Co. Cork
Tel 026 47069
www.gouganebarra.com

Its lakeside location makes this hotel very popular. The restaurant, bedrooms and bathrooms all have lovely views.

Closed 13 Oct–13 Apr
Double from €110
27
Turn off N22 onto R584 and continue west for 32km (20 miles)

INNISHANNON

INNISHANNON HOUSE ★★★ ❀

Innishannon, Co. Cork
Tel 021 4775121
www.innishannon-hotels.ie

This attractive 1720 house has lovely gardens running down to the River Bandon. Public areas are comfortable and there's a relaxed atmosphere.

Closed 22–26 Dec
Double €130–€170
12
Off N71 Kinsale road, at the eastern end of the village

KILLARNEY

AGHADOE HEIGHTS ☆☆☆☆ ❀❀

Lakes of Killarney, Co. Kerry
Tel 064 31766
www.aghadoeheights.com

Superbly located overlooking Loch Lein, this hotel has a first-floor restaurant that enjoys the same mountain and lake views as the stylish bedrooms. There is a spacious lounge, cocktail bar and conference suite. The staff are extremely friendly.

Closed 30 Dec–27 Jan
Double €310–€786
75 (10 non-smoking)
Indoor
5km (3 miles) north of Killarney, signed off the N22 Tralee road

ARBUTUS ★★★ ❀

College Street, Killarney, Co. Kerry
Tel 064 31037
www.arbutuskillarney.com

This smart hotel has been run by the friendly Buckley family since 1926. There's a comfortable lounge, guest sitting room, traditional bar and restaurant.

Closed 12 Dec–30 Jan
Double from €140
35
In the middle of town

GLENEAGLE HOTEL ★★★

Muckross Road, Killarney, Co. Kerry
Tel 064 36000
www.gleneaglehotel.com

Excellent facilities for both leisure and corporate guests are provided in this large family-run hotel. Comfortable bedrooms, many for families, are well equipped.

Double from €180
250 (20 non smoking)
Indoor
1.5km (1 mile) from Killarney on the N71 Kenmare road

SPECIAL IN KENMARE

SHEEN FALLS LODGE ☆☆☆☆☆ ❀❀

Kenmare, Co. Kerry
Tel 064 41600
www.sheenfallslodge.ie

This former fishing lodge has been developed into a beautiful hotel on the banks of the Sheen River. The cascading Sheen Falls are floodlit at night, forming a romantic backdrop to the enjoyment of the outstanding cuisine in

the La Cascade restaurant. Bedrooms are comfortably appointed, many being particularly spacious. There's a leisure suite and beauty therapy facilities.

Closed 2 Jan–1 Feb
Double €260–€395
66 (10 non-smoking), two 2-bedroom cottages
Indoor
From Kenmare take the N71 Glengariff road, then first left after suspension bridge

KINSALE

ACTONS HOTEL ★★★ ❀

Pier Road, Kinsale, Co. Cork
Tel 021 477 2135
www.actonshotelkinsale.com

In waterfront gardens, this hotel has a bar and bistro and the Captain's Table restaurant. The lounge is luxurious, bedrooms are all of a good standard, and staff are friendly.

Closed 24–27 Dec
Double €140–€225
73
Indoor
Overlooking Kinsale harbour, close to the Yacht Club Marina

MACROOM

CASTLE HOTEL ★★★ ❀

Main Street, Macroom, Co. Cork
Tel 026 41074
www.castlehotel.ie

The Castle Hotel contains a leisure centre and some fine bedrooms. Service is excellent and really makes you feel at home. There is a pleasant lounge, and the food in the restaurant and bar is carefully cooked and nicely presented.

Closed 24–28 Dec
Double €129–€155
60
Indoor
Central Macroom, across from the Briery Gap Theatre

ROSSCARBERY

CELTIC ROSS HOTEL ★★★

Rosscarbery, Co. Cork
Tel 023 48722
www.celticrosshotel.com

Overlooking a lagoon on the edge of the village, this is a luxurious and striking hotel. Inside, it's all rich fabrics and polished wood. There is a cocktail bar and a pub with a lunch carvery.

Closed mid-Jan to mid-Feb
Double €140–€190
66 (10 non-smoking)
Indoor
From the N71 Bandon–Clonakilty road, follow signs for Skibbereen and you'll find the hotel on main road

THE WEST

Galway city is the largest city in the West, and a popular base for touring the region. It has stylish modern hotels, historic conversions, guesthouses and B&Bs as well as seaside resort hotels outside the city at Salthill. Be sure to book well ahead for a stay here during the International Oyster Festival in September. Sligo Town is another lively city base with good nightlife. But the main attraction in the West is the scenery, and whether you're staying in a castle or a country house, you are likely to have a good view.

For such a remote region there is a surprising range of accommodation, from lavish castles to comfy cottages. Smaller towns such as Ennis in County Clare, Clifden in the Connemara and Donegal Town offer a good range of mid-price options. The coastal villages are very popular in summer, but in remote areas lodging is generally closed during the winter.

ACHILL ISLAND

ACHILL CLIFF HOUSE ★★★

Keel, Achill Island, Co. Mayo
Tel 098 43400
www.achillcliff.com

This whitewashed family-run hotel in the old fishing village of Keel has spacious bedrooms with large bathrooms. The restaurant specializes in local seafood. No children under 10 years.

Closed 23–26 Dec
Double €70–€140
10 (all non-smoking)
In Keel village

BALLYBOFEY

KEE'S HOTEL ★★★

Stranorlar, Ballybofey, Co. Donegal
Tel 074 913 1018
www.keeshotel.ie

The fourth generation of the Kee family run their hotel with warm hospitality. Its Gallery Bistro is popular with locals, and fine dining is available in the Looking Glass restaurant at weekends and during the holiday season.

Double €93–€105
53
Indoor
1.5km (1 mile) northeast on the N15

CASHEL

CASHEL HOUSE HOTEL

☆☆☆ ❀❀

Cashel, Co. Galway
Tel 095 31001
www.cashel-house-hotel.com

A mid-19th century house, at the head of Cashel Bay, in the heart of Connemara, Cashel House is set in superb gardens with woodland walks. The attentive service comes with a perfect balance of friendliness and professionalism from the McEvily family and their staff. The comfortable lounges have turf fires and antiques. The restaurant serves local produce, including Connemara lamb and fish straight from the sea.

Closed 4 Jan–4 Feb
Double €160–€338
32 (10 non-smoking)
Turn south off N59, on to R340 1.5km (1 mile) west of Recess and the hotel is well signposted

SPECIAL IN BALLYVAUGHAN

GREGANS CASTLE ☆☆☆

❀❀

Ballyvaughan, Co. Clare
Tel 065 707 7005
www.gregans.ie

At the foot of Corkscrew Hill in the heart of The Burren, Gregans Castle has splendid views towards Galway Bay. The Hayden family and welcoming staff offer a high level of personal service,

in which hospitality, good food and relaxation are high on the agenda. Bedrooms are sumptuous and are individually decorated (but do not have TVs), and superior rooms and suites offer the ultimate in comfort. Some of these are at ground level.

Closed Nov–end Mar
Double from €198
22
6km (4 miles) south of Ballyvaughan on N67

CLIFDEN

ARDAGH HOTEL ★★★ ❀❀

Ballyconneely Road, Clifden, Co. Galway
Tel 095 21384
www.ardaghhotel.com

Att the head of the Ardbear Bay, this family-run hotel makes full use of the spectacular views. The restaurant is renowned for its cuisine, which is matched by friendly and knowledgeable service. Rooms are individually decorated, with great attention to detail.

Closed Nov–end Mar
Double €165–€185
19 (all non-smoking)
Take the N59 to Clifden and then follow the signs for Ballyconneely

PRICES AND SYMBOLS

Prices are for a double room for one night. Breakfast is included unless noted otherwise. All the hotels listed accept credit cards unless otherwise stated. Note that rates vary widely throughout the year.

For a key to the symbols ▷ 2.

ROCK GLEN COUNTRY HOUSE

★★★ ❀❀

Clifden, Co. Galway
Tel 095 21035/21393
www.connemara.net/rockglen-hotel

The pretty clematis- and creeper-framed façade of this house is but an introduction to the comfort that lies inside. The hospitality of the Roche family and their staff makes a visit to this hotel relaxing and very pleasant. Many of the bedrooms have views of the gardens and the bay.

Closed Nov–early Mar
Double €177–€214
26
Take the Ballyconneely road from Clifden for 3km (1.5 miles); hotel is signposted on right

DOOLIN

ARAN VIEW HOUSE ★★★

Coast Road, Doolin, Co. Clare
Tel 065 707 4061/707 4420
www.aranview.com

Surrounded by 40ha (100 acres) of rolling farmland and panoramic views of the Aran

SPECIAL IN DONEGAL

HARVEY'S POINT COUNTRY HOTEL ★★★ ❀❀
Lough Eske, Co. Donegal
Tel 074 972 2208
www.harveyspoint.com
In a clearing beside Lough Eske is this distinctive hotel where comfort, quality, good cuisine and attentive service are top priorities, and where only the wildlife disturbs the tranquillity. Comfortable bedrooms are in the adjacent Swiss-style building. Junior suites are available.
Double from €180
20
From Donegal take the N56 west, then first right signed Lough Eske/ Harvey's Point. The hotel is about a 10-minute drive from Donegal

Islands, this Georgian house offers attractive and comfortable accommodation. Staff are welcoming, the atmosphere is convivial, and there's traditional music in the bar three times a week.
Closed Nov–end Mar
Double €110–€140
13 + 6 annexe
On the R453 north of Doolin

ENNIS

WOODSTOCK
Shanaway Road, Ennis, Co. Clare
Tel 065 684 6600
This secluded modern hotel overlooks an 18-hole golf course. Public areas include an impressive lobby and comfortable lounges with welcoming log fires. Modern Irish cuisine is served in Spikes Brasserie, which has spectacular views. Spacious bedrooms offer comfort and individuality. The hotel has extensive health, leisure and conference facilities available.
Double €200–€230
67 (47 non-smoking)
Indoor
From Ennis take N18 and at roundabout (traffic circle) take N85 Lahinch road. After 800m (half a mile) turn left for Woodstock; hotel is 800m (0.5 mile) on

GALWAY

ATLANTIC HEIGHTS ♦♦♦♦
2 Cashelmara, Knocknacarra Cross, Salthill, Co. Galway
Tel 091 529466/528830
www.galway.net/pages/atlantic-heights
Enthusiastic hosts, Robbie and Madeleine Mitchell, take great pride in their home, a fine balconied house overlooking Galway Bay. Bedrooms have TV, tea- and coffee-making

facilities, telephone, hairdryer and many thoughtful extras. An extensive breakfast menu, served late if required, features home baking. Laundry service.
Closed Nov–end Mar
Double €60–90
6
1km (0.5 miles) from Salthill Promenade in Upper Salthill on R336. Turn right after Spinnaker House Hotel, just before the junction

GALWAY BAY HOTEL CONFERENCE & LEISURE CENTRE ★★★★ ❀
The Promenade, Salthill, Galway, Co. Galway
Tel 091 520520
www.galwaybayhotel.net
This hotel is in a spectacular location overlooking Galway Bay and most bedrooms, lounges and the restaurant enjoy sea views. Dining options include fine dining in the Lobster Pot and more casual meals in the less formal Café Lido. The conference and leisure facilities are impressive.
Double from €150
153 (24 non-smoking)
Indoor
On the promenade in Salthill on the coast road to Connemara.

THE HARBOUR ★★★
The Harbour, Galway City, Co. Galway
Tel 091 569466
www.harbour.ie
This contemporary hotel is beside the redeveloped harbour in the heart of Galway. The large lobby lounge has generous seating and open fires, while Krusoes café bar and restaurant offers modern cuisine. Bedrooms are smartly furnished and well equipped. Guests have the benefit of complementary secure car parking at the rear.
Double €118–€300
96 (34 non-smoking)
Follow signs for Galway City East, at roundabout (traffic circle) take the first exit to Galway City. Follow signs to the docks and the hotel is 1km (half a mile) from the roundabout, on the left

QUALITY HOTEL GALWAY RYAN
Dublin Road, Galway, Co. Galway
Tel 091 753181
www.choicehotelsireland.ie
This modern hotel on the southeastern outskirts of the city provides good leisure facilities including tennis and a sports hall. The bedrooms are

well equipped and comfortable. Food, including a carvery lunch, is served all day in Toddy's Bar.
Double from €150
96 (20 non-smoking)
Indoor
Follow signs to Galway City East off the N6, N18, N17, past Galway Crystal factory on the left and the hotel is 2km (1 mile) on the right

KILKEE

HALPIN'S ★★
Erin Street, Kilkee, Co. Clare
Tel: 065 905 6032
www.halpinsprivatehotels.com
The finest tradition of hotel service is offered at this family-run hotel which has a commanding view over the old Victorian town. The attractive bedrooms are comfortable.
Closed 16 Nov–14 Mar
Double €89–€109
12 (8 non-smoking)
In the middle of town

KNOCK

KNOCK HOUSE HOTEL ★★★
Ballyhaunis Road, Knock, Co. Mayo
Tel 094 938 8088
www.knockhousehotel.ie
Next to the Marian Shrine and Basilica, this creatively designed limestone-clad

building is set in landscaped gardens. Facilities include comfortable lounges, a dispense bar, conference rooms and a restaurant. Six bedrooms are adapted for wheelchairs, which can also be provided.
Double €102–€136
68
Just outside Knock on Ballyhaunis Road

LETTERKENNY

CASTLE GROVE COUNTRY HOUSE ★★★ ❀

Castlegrove, Ballymaleel, Letterkenny, Co. Donegal
Tel 074 915 1118
www.castlegrove.com

This elegant Georgian house, set in a sheltered position and reached by a long avenue through parkland, enjoys spectacular views of Lough Swilly. Family owned, the hotel offers true Irish hospitality. The dining room serves dishes using local produce. Bedrooms are spacious, equipped with modern

necessities and furnished with some fine antiques. Ideal for touring northwestern Ireland. No children under 14 years.
Double from €150
15 (3 non-smoking)
7km (4.5 miles) northeast of Letterkenny off R245, Ramelton road

RECESS

BALLYNAHINCH CASTLE ★★★★ ❀❀

Recess, Co. Galway
Tel 095 31006
www.ballynahinch-castle.com

Open log fires and friendly professional service are just some of the delights of staying at this 16th-century castle, set among 142ha (350 acres) of woodland, rivers and lakes. Many of the suites and rooms have stunning views, as does the restaurant.
Closed 17–27 Dec, 30 Jan–end Feb
Double €180–€400
40 (4 non-smoking)
From Recess take the Roundstone left turn, then turn off in 4.5km (3 miles)

ROSSNOWLAGH

SAND HOUSE HOTEL ★★★

Rossnowlagh, Co. Donegal
Tel 071 985 1777
www.sandhouse-hotel.ie

Beside a crescent of golden sand, 8km (5 miles) north of Ballyshannon, this hotel is well known for its hospitality, food and service. Many rooms have

sea views and a there's a relaxing conservatory lounge.
Closed Dec, Jan
Double €160–€280
55 (27 non-smoking)
From the N15 south of Donegal turn off on R231 to Rossnowlagh

SHANNON

SHANNON COURT ★★★

Ballycasey, Shannon, Co. Clare
Tel 061 364588
www.irishcourthotels.com

This friendly hotel is conveniently close to Shannon Airport and near Bunratty Castle. There's a comfortable bar, themed restaurant and meeting rooms, as well as contemporary style bedrooms.
Closed 24–26 Dec
Double €79–€129
54 (8 non-smoking)
On the western edge of Shannon village, 5km (3 miles) from the airport

SPANISH POINT

BURKES ARMADA ★★★

Spanish Point, Co. Clare
Tel 065 7084110
www.burkesarmadahotel.com

On the coast overlooking the breaking waves and golden sands, this hotel is in a natural, unspoiled environment. Public areas have stunning views, especially the restaurant and patio. Bedrooms, most facing the sea, are spacious.
Double €80–€150
61
From N18 in Ennis take N85 to Inagh, then R460 to Miltown Malbay. Follow signs for Spanish Point

WESTPORT

ARDMORE COUNTRY HOUSE

The Quay, Westport, Co. Mayo
Tel 098 25994
www.ardmorecountryhouse.com

A pretty country house hotel, above the quay and within walking distance of the middle of town. The attractive restaurant and lounges overlook Clew Bay, with Croagh Patrick in the background. Individually styled bedrooms are spacious and most have spectacular views. No children under 12 years.
Double € 170–€ 250
13 (all non-smoking)
1.5km (1 mile) west from Westport on coast road, R335

THE OLDE RAILWAY HOTEL ★★ ❀

The Mall, Westport, Co. Mayo
Tel 098 25166/25605
www.theolderailwayhotel.com

Set on a tree-lined mall overlooking the river, this classic coaching inn offers a welcoming atmosphere with blazing turf fires. There's a variety of bedroom sizes, with some very spacious rooms. Public areas include an attractively furnished bar, a comfortable lounge and a conservatory restaurant with access to the patio and barbecue area.
Double €120–€180
24 (all non-smoking)
Overlooking the Carrowbeg River in the middle of town

THE MIDLANDS

The Midlands generally offer good value accommodation. Even a night in some of its historic manor houses won't break the bank. Athlone is the largest town and handy for the region's main attraction, Clonmacnoise. To the south, the lovely town of Birr with its magnificent castle gardens also makes a fine base for exploring the region. Country villages such as Fore, where you'll find friendly B&Bs set in beautiful countryside, are an excellent option here.

PRICES AND SYMBOLS

Prices are for a double room for one night. Breakfast is included unless noted otherwise. All the hotels listed accept credit cards unless otherwise stated. Note that rates vary widely throughout the year.

For a key to the symbols ▷ 2.

ABBEYLEIX

ABBEYLEIX MANOR HOTEL

★★★

Cork Road, Abbeyleix, Co. Laois
Tel 0502 30111
www.abbeyleixmanorhotel.com

This modern hotel is on the outskirts of town, handy for the N8. Bedrooms are spacious and furnished to a high standard. Public areas are comfortable with a lobby and conservatory and a themed bar where food is served all day.

Closed 25 Dec
Double from €110
23 (all non-smoking)
On the N8 just south of Abbeyleix

ATHLONE

RIVERVIEW HOUSE ♦♦♦♦

Galway Road, Summerhill, Athlone, Co. Westmeath
Tel 090 649 4532
www.riverviewhousebandb.com

Modern accommodation in attractively decorated bedrooms is provided at this pleasant house. There's a comfortable lounge and a breakfast room that opens on to the garden. Nearby Lough Ree attracts anglers.

Closed 18 Dec–1 Mar
Double €60–€70
4
On N6, 1.5km (1 mile) west of town

ROYAL HOEY ★★

Mardyke Street, Athlone, Co. Westmeath
Tel 090 647 2924

In an enviable location on the shores of the inner lakes of Lough Rea. Guests can arrive by road or water, and dine on the deck or in the attractive dining room. The cuisine is wholesome and innovative, using the best local produce. There are 10 luxurious lakeshore bedrooms, each with a balcony.

Closed 25–27 Dec
Double from €110
38 (10 non-smoking)
6.5km (4.5 miles) northwest of Athlone via N61

SPECIAL IN ATHLONE

HODSON BAY HOTEL

★★★

Hodson Bay, Athlone, Co. Westmeath
Tel 090 648 0500
www.hodsonbayhotel.com

Close to the River Shannon and right on the shore of Lough Rea, this hotel has been reconstructed and extended to provide up-to-date accommodation. With a golf course to the rear and a marina to the front, most of the bedrooms have excellent views. Public areas include a sun lounge, two restaurants, a bar, and conference and banqueting facilities.

Double €150–€220
133 (15 non-smoking)
Indoor
From Athlone take the N61 8km (5miles) towards Roscommon and then turn right to Lough Rea

BALLINLOUGH

WHITEHOUSE HOTEL

Ballinlough, Co. Roscommon
Tel 0907 40112
www.white-house-hotel.com

The staff are friendly at this comfortable and appealing hotel with spacious bedrooms. Facilities include a TV lounge, restaurant, cheerful bars and a well-equipped conference/banqueting suite. The hotel is convenient for Lough O'Flynn and Knock Airport.

Closed 25 Dec
Double from €99
19 (13 non-smoking)
Between Castlerea and Ballyhaunis

BIRR

COUNTY ARMS HOTEL ★★★

Birr, Co. Offaly
Tel 0509 20791
www.countyarmshotel.com

This fine Georgian house has comfortable bedrooms, all furnished and decorated to a high standard. The rooms overlook the meticulously kept walled Victorian gardens, which supply fruit, vegetables and herbs to the hotel kitchens. There is a choice of two restaurants, a bar and a lounge.

Double from €130
24 (2 non-smoking)
Take N62 north to Birr, the hotel is on the right, just before the church

DRUMLISH

LONGFORD COUNTRY HOUSE

♦♦♦♦

Drumlish, Co. Longford
Tel 043 23320
www.longfordcountryhouse.com

An hospitable, Tudor-style house. The parlour has a wrought-iron stairway to the library loft, as well as a snug sitting room with turf fire and a dining room where dinner is served by prior arrangement.

Other facilities include a games room and pitch-and-putt course. Self-catering cottages are also available.
Double €35–€140
6 (all non-smoking)
From the second roundabout (traffic circle) of the N4 Longford bypass, take the R194 north for 5km (3 miles). After the Old Forge pub, turn left at the crossroads and it's the second house on the right

HORSELEAP

WOODLANDS FARM ♦♦♦

Streamstown, Horseleap,
Co. Westmeath
Tel 044 26414
A delightful farmhouse set in 49ha (120 acres) of rolling countryside. The spacious sitting and dining rooms are relaxing, and a new addition is the hospitality kitchen, where

tea and coffee are available at all times. Dinner is served by prior arrangement.
Double from €60
6 (all non-smoking)
Take the N6 through Kilbegan to Horseleap, turn right at the filling station, and the farm is 4km (2.5 miles) farther on

MULLINGAR

CROOKEDWOOD HOUSE

Crookedwood, Mullingar,
Co. Westmeath
Tel 044 72165
As charming as its name, this beautifully restored old rectory overlooks Lake Derravaragh and offers exceptionally comfortable bedrooms. There is also an inviting lounge where tea is served and a bar for drinks before dinner. The evening meals are the highlight of a stay here and have earned much praise for chef/patron Niall Kenny.
Closed 25 Dec
Double €120–€150
8
Take R394 off the Mullingar bypass to Crookedwood, turn right at the Wood Pub and continue for 2km (3miles) to reach Crookedwood House

SPECIAL IN MULLINGAR

HILLTOP COUNTRY HOUSE ♦♦♦♦

Delvin Road, Rathconnell, Mullingar,
Co. Westmeath
Tel 044 48958
www.hilltopcountryhouse.com
This is a lovely country house in glorious gardens, where flowers and shrubs fill every available space. Public areas and bedrooms are well furnished and the breakfast menu is excellent with an extensive choice. Dinner is by advance reservations only. Dymphna and Sean Casey will do everything possible to ensure happy visits to their home. No children under 15 years.
Closed Dec–Jan
Double €68
5
From the Mullingar bypass (N4) take the N52 towards Delvin. Hilltop sign is a short drive from the exit roundabout (traffic circle)

PORTLAOISE

IVYLEIGH HOUSE ♦♦♦♦♦

Bank Place, Church Street, Portlaoise,
Co. Laois
Tel 0502 22081
www.ivyleigh.com
This refurbished Georgian town house, just off the main street and close to the railway station, is an oasis of calm and luxury. The elegant drawing rooms are complemented by a fine dining room where Dinah Campion's superb breakfasts are served. Particularly comfortable beds are dressed with excellent cotton in well-appointed bedrooms. No children under 8 years.
Closed 20 Dec–4 Jan
Double from €115
6
Opposite the multi-level parking in the middle of town

O'SULLIVAN ♦♦♦

8 Kelly Ville Park, Portlaoise, Co. Laois
Tel 0502 22774
This period semi-detached house on the outskirts of town is family run, and has a nice home-from-home atmosphere. Bedrooms are comfortable and all have private bathrooms. Secure parking is available.
Double €78
6
Opposite the County Hall parking

ROSCOMMON

ABBEY HOTEL

Galway Road, Roscommon,
Co. Roscommon
Tel 090 662 6240
www.abbeyhotel.ie
Set in its own grounds just outside Roscommon, this fine manor house dates back over 100 years. The bedrooms are individually decorated, with a choice of period style rooms in the original part of the house and more contemporary rooms in the newer wing. The hotel has a friendly atmosphere.
Closed 24–26 Dec
Double €140–€150
50
Indoor
In Roscommon town, take the Galway Road and the hotel is the first left after the library

STRADBALLY

TULLAMOY HOUSE ♦♦♦♦

Stradbally, Co. Laois
Tel 059 862 7111
This pleasant limestone farmhouse was built in 1871, and is just south of Stradbally on the Carlow Road. Caroline and Pat Farrell and their children welcome guests and offer tea and home-baking, served beside the fire in the sitting room. Local produce and home-produced beef are served at dinner, available on request. Attractively decorated bedrooms vary in size and are comfortably furnished. Credit cards not accepted.
Closed Nov–end Feb
Double from €64
3
Just off N80, 5km (3 miles) south of Stradbally

NORTHERN IRELAND

Northern Ireland has the same range of accommodation options as the Republic, from luxurious country houses to friendly B&Bs. Belfast has smart, modern hotels catering for business clientele as well as more traditional options. The capital also has sophisticated bars and restaurants and entertainment, making it an enjoyable place to stay.

Enniskillen is a good base for exploring the lakeland region of County Fermanagh. Accommodation in historic Derry ranges from B&Bs to fine country house hotels outside the city hub. Several resort towns with beach facilities make good bases for touring the scenic north coast. The east coast also has pleasant resorts, handy for the Ards Peninsula and the Mountains of Mourne.

AGHADOWEY

BROWN TROUT ★★

209 Agivey Road, Aghadowey,
Co. Londonderry, BT51 4AD
Tel 028 7086 8209
www.browntroutinn.com

Set alongside the Agivey River and featuring its own 9-hole golf course, this welcoming inn offers a choice of accommodation. Spacious and attractively furnished bedrooms are situated around a courtyard area while the cottage suites also have comfortable lounge areas. Home-cooked meals are served in the restaurant; lighter fare is offered in the character lounge bar. Game fishing is available for guests.

Double £70–£90
15

At the junction of the A54/B66 on the road to Coleraine

ARMAGH

CHARLEMONT ARMS ★★★

57–65 English Street, Armagh,
Co. Armagh, BT61 7LB
Tel 028 3752 2028
www.charlemontarms.com

Centrally placed for all of this historic city's principal attractions, the Charlemont Arms has been under the same family ownership for almost 70 years and offers a choice of dining styles and bars. The mostly spacious bedrooms have been refurbished in a contemporary style and provide all of the facilities that you would expect to find.

Closed 25 Dec
Double from £65
30 (all non-smoking)
In the heart of the city, a 5-min walk from the cathedrals

BALLYGALLEY

BALLYGALLY CASTLE

Coast Road, Ballygally, Co. Antrim,
BT40 2QZ
Tel 028 2858 1066
www.hastingshotels.com

This is a stylish, welcoming hotel, occupying a fine 17th-century castle. A large part of the attraction is the panoramic sea view from the lounge and many bedrooms. Most bedrooms are in a modern wing, but all are comfortable. The lounges are spacious and roaring log fires are lit in cooler months. Diners in the Garden Restaurant can select from creative menus.

Double £115
44 (some non-smoking)
Some 6.5km (4 miles) north of Larne on the Antrim coast road

PRICES AND SYMBOLS

Prices are for a double room for one night. Breakfast is included unless noted otherwise. All the hotels listed accept credit cards unless otherwise stated. Note that rates vary widely throughout the year.

For a key to the symbols ⊳ 2.

SPECIAL IN BALLYMENA

GALGORM MANOR ★★★★ ❀

Ballymena, Co. Antrim, BT42 1EA
Tel 028 2588 1001
www.galgorm.com

Standing in 34ha (84 acres) of private woodland and sweeping lawns beside the River Maine, this 19th-century mansion offers spacious and comfortable bedrooms. Public areas include a welcoming cocktail bar and elegant restaurant, as well as Gillies, a lively and atmospheric locals' bar. Horseback riding is available from the estate's stables.

Double £119
24
2km (1 mile) outside Ballymena on the A42, between Galgorm and Cullybackey

BANGOR

CLANDEBOYNE LODGE ★★★ ❀

10 Estate Road, Clandeboyne,
Co. Down, BT19 1UR
Tel 028 9185 2500
www.clandeboynelodge.co.uk

Just west of Bangor, Clandeboyne Lodge sits in delightful landscaped and

wooded grounds. The hotel provides high quality accommodation with a bright, open-plan foyer and attractive lounge as well as extensive conference, banqueting and wedding facilities.

Closed 24–26 Dec
Double £80–£90
43 (some non-smoking)
From A2 turn right at sign for Blackwood Golf Centre & Lodge. 500m (545 yards) along the Ballysallagh Road, turn left and take Crawfordsburn Road, where the hotel is 200m (220 yards) on the left

MARINE COURT HOTEL ★★★

The Marina, Bangor, Co. Down,
BT20 5ED
Tel 028 9145 1100
www.marinecourthotel.net

Overlooking the marina, Marine Court offers a good range of leisure and conference facilities suited to both the business and leisure guest. There are extensive public areas, including the first-floor restaurant and cocktail bar. Alternatively, the popular Nelson's Bistro/Bar is more relaxed and there is also the lively restyled Bar Mocha.

Closed 25 Dec
Double £75–£110
52 (some non-smoking)
Indoor
Take A2 through Hollywood to Bangor, follow the main street and then go left for the seafront

OLD INN ★★★ ❀❀
15 Main Street, Crawfordsburn, Co. Down, BT19 1JH
Tel 028 9185 3255
www.theoldinn.com
This delightful hotel, dating from 1614, enjoys a peaceful, rural setting just a short drive from Belfast. The popular bar and intimate restaurant offer a variety of creative menus and staff throughout are keen to please. Individually styled bedrooms, many with feature beds, offer comfort and modern facilities.
Double from £90
31 (7 on ground floor)
5km (3 miles) past Holywood on the A2 there is a sign for the Old Inn and 100m (110 yards) past this sign, turn left at the traffic lights; the hotel is on the left in the village

ROYAL HOTEL ★★★
Seafront, Bangor, Co. Down, BT20 5ED
Tel 028 9127 1866
www.royalhotelbangor.com
This substantial Victorian hotel enjoys a delightful seafront location, overlooking the marina. The bedrooms are comfortable and practical, and the traditional public areas include a choice of bars and a popular brasserie.
Closed 25 Dec
Double £70–£80
50
Take A2 through Hollywood to Bangor. Follow the main street and go left for the seafront. Turn right for 300m (330 yards) to the hotel

BELFAST

BALMORAL HOTEL
Blacks Road, Dunmurry, Co. Antrim, BT10 0NF
Tel 028 9030 1234
www.balmoralhotelbelfast.com
A modern, refurbished hotel just south of the city in the village of Dunmurry. Bedrooms here vary in size and offer practical furnishings and amenities. There is a choice of contrasting bars, one of which provides an informal alternative to the main restaurant.
Closed 25 Dec
Double £50–£85
40 (4 non-smoking)
530
Take the M1 and after 4.5 km (3 miles) take the exit at Suffolk slip road. Turn right and the hotel is about 300m (330 yards) ahead

THE CRESCENT TOWNHOUSE ★★★ ❀
13 Lower Crescent, Belfast, BT7 1NR
Tel 028 9032 3349
www.crescenttownhouse.com
This stylish, smartly presented Regency town house is close to the Botanic Gardens and railway station. The popular Bar Twelve and Metro Brasserie are found on the ground floor; the reception and well-equipped bedrooms are on the upper floors.

Closed 25–27 Dec and part of Jul
Double £69–£145
17 (2 non-smoking)
South towards Queen's University; the hotel is on corner of Botanic Avenue and Lower Crescent, opposite Botanic Train Station

EXPRESS BY HOLIDAY INN
106a University Street, Belfast, BT7 1Hp
Tel 028 9031 1909
www.exhi-belfast.com
A modern hotel ideal for families and business people. Fresh and uncomplicated, the spacious bedrooms include satellite TV, power shower and tea- and coffee-making facilities.
Double £59–£69
114
Behind Queen's University in the south of the city. Turn left at the lights on Botanic Avenue onto University Street where the hotel is 500m (550 yards) farther on left

JURYS BELFAST INN ★★★
Fisherwick Place, Great Victoria Street, Belfast, BT2 7AP
Tel 028 9053 3500
www.jurysdoyle.com
Central for most sights and shops, this hotel makes a good base for seeing Belfast. The public areas include a lounge, a bar and a stylish restaurant. The spacious bedrooms are smartly decorated, with good facilities, including satellite TV.
Closed 24–26 Dec
Double from £75
190 (76 non-smoking)
At junction of Grosvenor Road and Great Victoria Street, by Opera House

MALONE LODGE HOTEL ★★★
60 Eglantine Avenue, Belfast, BT9 6DY
Tel 028 9038 8000
www.malonelodgehotel.com
In the leafy suburbs of the university area of south Belfast, this stylish hotel forms the focal point of an attractive Victorian terrace. The unassuming exterior belies a pleasant interior with a smart lounge, popular bar and elegant restaurant.
Double £79–£99
51
71 (to Malone Road)
South of the city, turn right onto Lisburn Road, then left onto Eglantine Avenue, where the hotel is on the left

RAMADA BELFAST ★★★★
117 Milltown Road, Shaws Bridge, Belfast, BT8 7XP
Tel 028 9092 3500
www.ramadabelfast.com
Within Laggan Valley Regional park, this modern conference and leisure hotel caters for all markets. The bedrooms are stylish and furnished in bright, eye-catching designs. The LA Fitness club is well equipped, and the Grand Ballroom hosts top events. The Belfast Bar and Grill serves innovative Irish cuisine, while the trendy Suburbia Bar offers a lighter alternative.
Double £80–£100
120 (some non-smoking)
13
Indoor
South from the city, follow Malone Road to the roundabout (traffic circle) and signs for Barnett Demesne. Turn left on Milltown Road; hotel is on left

CARNLOUGH

LONDONDERRY ARMS ★★★ ❀
20 Harbour Road, Carnlough, Co. Antrim, BT44 0EU
Tel 028 2888 5255
www.glensofantrim.com

Originally built in the mid-19th century as a coaching inn by Lady Londonderry, the building was owned at one time by her grandson, war-time British Prime Minister Winston Churchill. The hotel has a prime location in this pretty fishing village.
Double from £85
35
Go north from Larne on the coast road, A2, for 22km (14 miles)

CARRICKFERGUS

DOBBINS INN HOTEL ★★

6–8 High Street, Carrickfergus,
Co. Antrim, BT38 7AP
Tel 028 9335 1905
www.dobbinsinnhotel.co.uk
Bright window boxes adorn the front of this popular inn, near the ancient castle and the waterfront. Public areas are furnished to modern standards without compromising the historic character. Bedrooms vary in size and style but all provide modern comforts. The staff are friendly and helpful.
Closed 25–26 Dec, 1 Jan
Double from £65
15
From Belfast take the M2, keep right at the roundabout (traffic circle) and follow the A2 to Carrickfergus; turn left opposite castle

DERRY

BEECH HILL COUNTRY HOUSE ★★★ ❀

32 Ardmore Road, Derry,
Co. Londonderry, BT47 3QP
Tel 028 7134 9279
www.beech-hill.com
Dating back to 1729, Beech Hill is an impressive mansion, standing in 13ha (32 acres) of glorious woodlands and gardens. Traditionally styled day rooms provide deep comfort and ambitious cooking is served in the attractive dining room. The splendid bedroom wing provides spacious bedrooms, in addition to the more classically decorated bedrooms in the main house. The beautiful grounds are perfect for walking and there is a tennis court for the more energetic.
Closed 24–25 Dec
Double £95–£120
27
Take the A6 Derry–Belfast road and turn off at Faughan Bridge and continue for 1.5km (1 mile). The hotel is opposite Ardmore Chapel

SPECIAL IN DERRY

CITY HOTEL ★★★★

Queens Quay, Derry,
Co. Londonderry, BT48 7AS
Tel 028 7136 5800
www.gshotels.com
This busy, contemporary hotel overlooks the River Foyle and appeals to both business and leisure guests. The executive rooms are spacious and have good facilities, including internet access. The open-plan ground floor is conducive to relaxation and the restaurant provides modern style food.
Closed 24–27 Dec
Double from £85
145 (66 non-smoking)
Indoor
The hotel is in the middle of the city on the waterfront adjacent to the Guildhall

HASTINGS EVERGLADES

Tel 028 7132 1066
Prehen Road, Derry, Co. Londonderry, BT47 2NH
www.hastingshotels.com
This purpose-built hotel situated on the edge of the city, offers comfortable bedrooms, with family and interconnecting rooms also available. There are 20 bedrooms on the ground floor. Stylish open-plan day rooms include a relaxing lounge and Library bar leading into the bright Sachmo restaurant. Outside, guests can put in some golf practice on the putting green.
Double £79–£110
64 (20 non-smoking)
On the A5, Omagh to Derry road, 2km (1 mile) from the city

TOWER HOTEL DERRY ★★★★ ❀

Off the Diamond, Derry,
Co. Londonderry, BT48 6HL
Tel 028 7137 1000
www.towerhotelgroup.com
A stylish hotel that's proving to be a big hit with tourists and corporate guests alike. Modern bedrooms are furnished with flair and style and those on the upper floors enjoy super views of the city. The minimalist day rooms include a popular bistro and the staff in the contemporary bar provide friendly Irish hospitality.
Closed 24–27 Dec
Double £60–£110
93 (12 non-smoking)
From the Craigavon Bridge drive into the middle of the city, to Carlisle Road, where the hotel is straight ahead

QUALITY HOTEL DAVINCIS ★★★

15 Culmore Road, Derry,
Co. Londonderry, BT48 8JB
Tel 028 7127 9111
www.davincishotel.com
This hotel is convenient, yet far enough from the city hustle and bustle. The well-designed bedrooms are spacious and stylish and all have two double beds and satellite TV. The public areas include Da Vinci's bar and restaurant offering light snacks and an innovative à la carte menu.
Closed 25 Dec
Double £49.95–£80
67 (26 non-smoking)
From the city take Strand Road for 1.5km (1 mile) north and turn onto Culmore Road; hotel is on the right

WHITE HORSE HOTEL ★★★

68 Clooney Road, Campsie,
Co. Londonderry, BT47 3PA
Tel 028 7186 0606
www.whitehorsehotel.biz

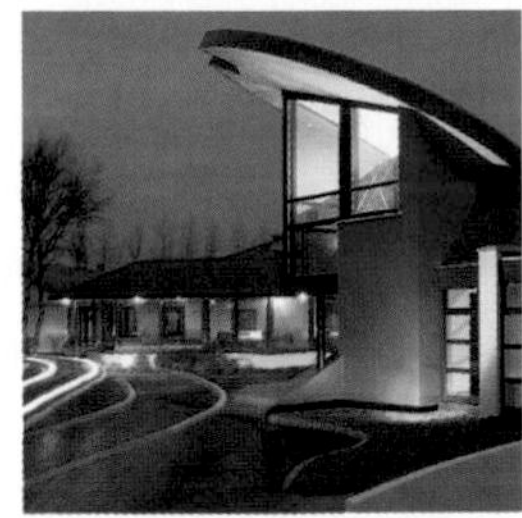

The stylish exterior of this privately owned hotel and leisure complex indicates the excellent state of the interior. The modern bedrooms include full suites, family rooms and interconnecting rooms. All are spacious, well designed and well equipped. Equally as smart are the bright, modern and spacious public areas. The leisure and fitness suite has everything you need to work out and there is a beauty salon, sauna and solarium.
Double £60–£80
57 (14 non-smoking)
Indoor
The hotel is on the A2, 5km (3 miles) from the city and 800m (half a mile) from Derry City Airport

DUNGANNON

GRANGE LODGE ◇◇◇◇◇

7 Grange Road, Dungannon, Co. Tyrone, BT71 7EJ
Tel 028 8778 4212

Nestling in 8ha (20 acres) of well-tended grounds, Grange Lodge dates back to 1698 and sets the highest of standards. Award-winning cooking is served in the bright and airy

dining room, and guests can enjoy home-baked afternoon teas in the sumptuous drawing room.

Closed 21 Dec–9 Jan
Double £70–£78
5 (non-smoking)
Turn off M1 at junction 15 on A29 Armagh road for 1.5km (1 mile). Follow sign for 'Grange' then take the first right; Grange Lodge is first on the right

ENNISKILLEN

WILLOWBANK HOUSE ♦♦♦♦

60 Bellevue Road, Enniskillen, Co. Fermanagh, BT74 4JH
Tel 028 6632 8582
www.willowbankhouse.com

Peacefully set in attractive grounds just outside the town, Willowbank House has all its bedrooms at ground level, some suitable for families. There is a comfortable lounge and substantial breakfasts are served in the conservatory dining room, overlooking the lakes. Dinner by arrangement.

Closed 21 Dec–9 Jan
Double £50
5 (non-smoking)
From Enniskillen take the A4 Belfast road. Turn right 500m (550 yards) after Killy Hevlin Hotel and follow signs for Upper Lough Erne and Willowbank House; hotel is 3km (2 miles) on left

IRVINESTOWN

MAHONS HOTEL ★★

Mill Street, Irvinestown, Co. Fermanagh, BT94 1GS
Tel 028 6862 1656
www.mahonshotel.co.uk

This family-run hotel has been in the same ownership and has offered friendly hospitality for over 100 years. Public areas, especially the bar, have a wealth of character. In the restaurant, the menu offers a wide range of dishes. The prettily decorated bedrooms come in a variety of sizes. There is a tennis court for guests' use.

Closed 25 Dec
Double £70
25
On the A32 midway between Enniskillen and Omagh, beside the town clock in the heart of town

LIMAVADY

RADISSON SAS ROW PARK RESORT ★★★★ ❀

Limavady, Co. Londonderry, BT49 9LB
Tel 028 7772 2222
www.radissonrowpark.com

This impressive hotel has its own golf resort. The spacious, modern bedrooms are well equipped and many have excellent views of the fairways. The Greens Restaurant provides a refreshing dining experience and the Coach House brasserie offers a lighter menu. Leisure options include fishing and bicycle rental as well as golf tuition and a floodlit driving range.

Double £80–£110
118 (76 non-smoking)
Indoor
Take the A2 Derry to Limavady road. The hotel is 2km (1 mile) outside Limavady along this road

MAGHERA

ARDTARA COUNTRY HOUSE ★★ ❀❀

8 Gorteade Road, Upperlands, Co. Londonderry, BT46 5SA
Tel 028 7964 4490
www.ardtara.com

Ardtara is a charming Victorian country house with extensive mature grounds. The stylish public rooms include a choice of lounges and a conservatory. The elegant dining room has period furnishings and is a perfect setting in which to enjoy the skilfully prepared cuisine. Bedrooms vary in style and size but all are tastefully decorated. Within the lovely grounds there is a hard tennis court that guests may use.

Closed 25–26 Dec
Double £100–£150
8 (2 non-smoking)
From Maghera take the A29 towards Coleraine and after 3km (2 miles) take the B75 for Kilrea through the Upperlands. Pass the W. M. Clark and Sons sign and take the next left

PORTAFERRY

THE NARROWS ♦♦♦♦

8 Shore Road, Portaferry, Co. Down, BT22 1JY
Tel 028 4272 8148
www.narrows.co.uk

This is a delightful quayside hotel on the shores of Strangford Lough. Some of the bedrooms have sea views but all are comfortable with facilities that include TV, tea- and coffee-making provisions and direct dial telephones. The contemporary public areas

include an appealing restaurant and the Ruffians bar. There is also a function room that enjoys panoramic views of the harbour and the ocean beyond.

Double £90
13 (all non-smoking)
Take the A20 to Portaferry and continue down to the shore; turn left to The Narrows

PORTAFERRY HOTEL ★★★ ❀

10 The Strand, Portaferry, Co. Down, BT22 1PE
Tel 028 4272 8231
www.portaferryhotel.com

Portaferry is a smart, popular hotel in a lovely position on the waterfront, where it benefits from a superb panorama of Strangford Lough. The bedrooms vary in size and style and are particularly well equipped. Day rooms include a comfortable lounge and split-level dining room, while snacks can be enjoyed in the informal bar. Hospitality here is especially warm and the staff demonstrate a real eagerness to please.

Closed 24–25 Dec
Double from £90
14
Opposite the ferry terminal

MAJOR HOTEL CHAINS

Company logo	Description	Number of hotels	Telephone number and website
Best Western	Independently owned and managed hotels, modern and traditional, in the two-, three- and four- star markets. Many have leisure facilities and many have rosette awards.	19	08457 73 73 7 3 www.bestwestern.co.uk
DE VERE HOTELS	In Ireland De Vere Associate hotels specialize in leisure stays, golf and conferences.	2	0870 606 3606 www.devereonline.co.uk
GRESHAM HOTELS	Part of the Ryan Hotels group, Gresham is a collection of four-star properties, all in central city positions in the Republic of Ireland.	2	01 878 7966 www.gresham-hotels.com
Holiday Inn HOTELS · RESORTS	This internationally known group offers a wide range of hotels.	7	0800 40 50 60 www.holidayinn.co.uk
ibis	Ibis is a growing chain of modern travel accommodation.	3	0870 609 0963 www.ibishotel.com
IRELAND'S BLUE BOOK	An association of owner-managed establishments across Ireland.	41	01 676 9914 www.irelandsbluebook.com
IRISH COUNTRY HOTELS	Friendly and informal in style, Irish Country Hotels is a collection of 30 individual family owned and run hotels, located throughout the country.	30	01 295 8900 www.irishcountryhotels.com
JURYS DOYLE HOTELS	This Irish company has a range of three- and four-star hotels in the UK and the Republic of Ireland.	13	01 607 0070 www.jurysdoylehotels.com
MANOR HOUSE HOTELS	Located throughout Northern Ireland and the Republic, Manor House Hotels is an independent group comprising Georgian manors, country houses, castles and four-star guesthouses.	26	01 295 8900 www.manorhousehotels.com
Marriott HOTELS · RESORTS · SUITES	This international brand offers four-star hotels in primary locations. Most are modern and have leisure facilities; some have a focus on golf.	3	0800 699 996 www.marriott.com
Radisson SAS HOTELS & RESORTS	A recognized international brand offering high-quality four-star hotels in key locations.	8	0800 37 44 11 www.radisson.com
RELAIS & CHATEAUX.	An international consortium of rural, privately owned hotels, mainly in the country house style.	5	01 457 296 50 www.relaischateaux.com
SMALL LUXURY HOTELS OF THE WORLD	Part of an international group of mainly privately owned hotels, often in the country house style.	10	00800 525 48000 www.SLH.com
THE INDEPENDENTS	A consortium of independently owned, mainly two- and three-star hotels.	13	0800 88 55 44 www.theindependents.co.uk
Travelodge	Good-quality, modern, budget accommodation. Almost every lodge has an adjacent family restaurant, often a Little Chef, Harry Ramsden's or Burger King.	7	08700 850 950 www.travelodge.co.uk

Planning

BEFORE YOU GO

WHEN TO GO

• Although Ireland is temperate, there are several factors which can help you to decide when to go. In winter some visitor attractions close and don't reopen until spring, and it gets dark early, so be prepared for total darkness by 4pm if you travel in December. This is an important consideration if you are planning on doing a lot of driving while you are there.

• In July and August it doesn't get completely dark until about 11pm, although the roads will be busier as this is the main tourist season. For the best chance of sunny weather, come in May or June, and for the highest temperatures, July and August, though these two months are the height of the tourist season which means that you should book ahead for accommodation and that the volume of traffic on the roads will be greater.

• Dublin and Belfast are great cities to visit at all times of the year with attractions open all year round.

WEATHER STATIONS

CLIMATE

• Ireland does not have extremes of temperature owing to the influence of the Atlantic Ocean and the Gulf Stream. Temperatures of below 32°F (0°C) or above 86°F (30°C) are rare. The average daily temperature is about 50°F (9°C) across the country. The coldest months are January and February with a mean temperature between 39° and 44°F (4° and 7°C), and the warmest months are July and August, although even then average inland temperatures are only between 64° and 66°F (18° and 20°C). In terms of sunshine, the sunniest months are May and June, while December has the fewest hours of sunshine.

• The main weather factor likely to affect your day is the rain, because despite being mild, Ireland is a very wet country. Irish skies are completely covered by cloud approximately half of the time. You can, and should, expect rain at all times of the year, although the summer is generally not as wet as winter. The parts of the country that receive most rainfall are the west and the hills. In terms of wind, the north and west coasts are two of the windiest areas in Europe.

WEATHER REPORTS

• For weather forecasts, look up www.met.ie (The Irish Meteorological Service Met Éireann), which gives regional forecasts for the island. The Meteorological Office in the UK (www.metoffice.com) also gives forecasts for the Republic and Northern Ireland. The BBC website (www.bbc.co.uk/weather) gives 5-day weather forecasts, which are useful if your plans are weather-dependent.

• *The Irish Times*, *Irish Independent*, The *Belfast Telegraph* and *Evening Herald* newspapers all have detailed weather forecasts.

PASSPORTS

• When planning your trip to Ireland, remember that the Republic of Ireland and Northern Ireland (which is part of the UK) may have different passport and visa requirements. For this reason, you should check what applies to you before you leave your home country.

• Take a photocopy of the relevant pages of your passport to carry around with you, so you can leave your actual passport in your hotel safe. It is also a good

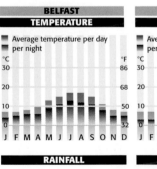

BELFAST
TEMPERATURE

Average temperature per day
per night

°C 30 20 10 0 · °F 86 68 50 32

J F M A M J J A S O N D

CORK
TEMPERATURE

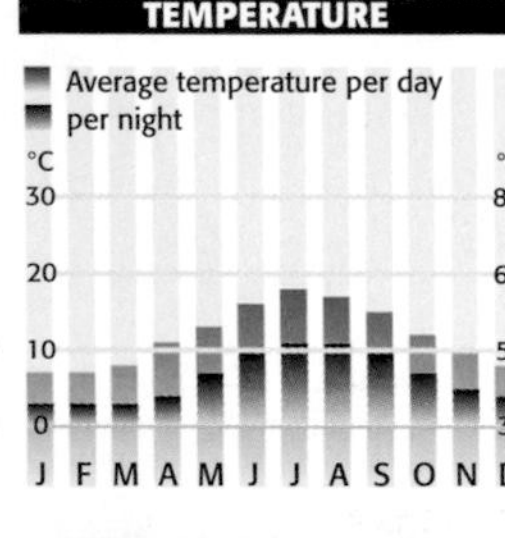

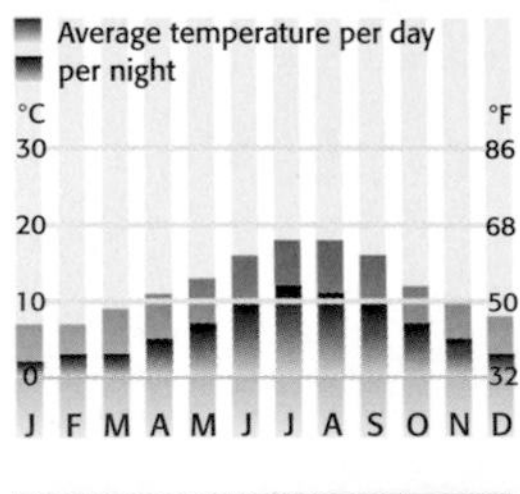

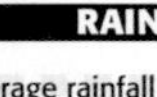

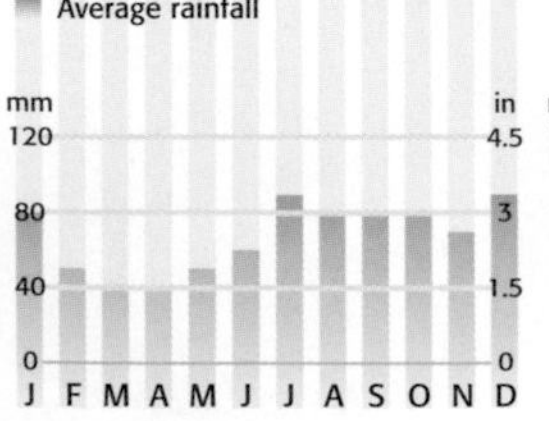

RAINFALL

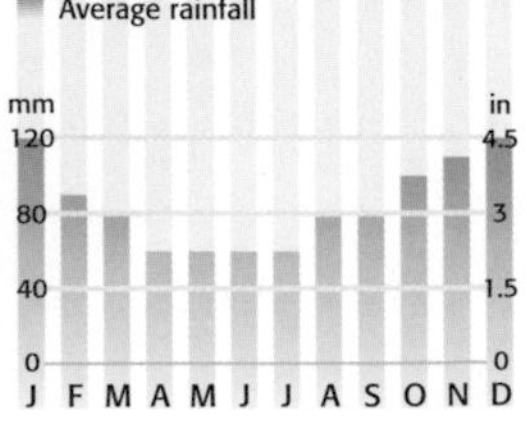

RAINFALL

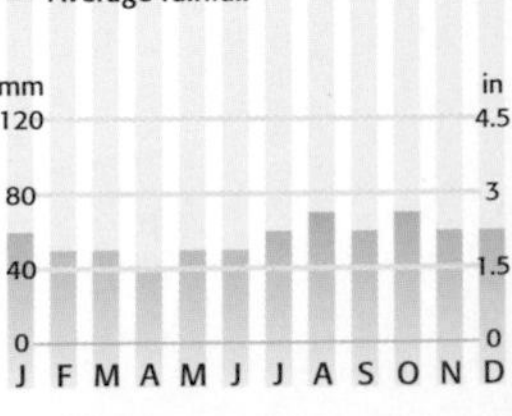

TIME ZONES

The Republic of Ireland and Northern Ireland are both on Greenwich Mean Time (GMT), and for daylight saving, clocks are put forward one hour in mid-March and back one hour at the end of October.

CITY	TIME DIFFERENCE	TIME AT 12 NOON GMT
Amsterdam	+1	1pm
Auckland	+10	10pm
Berlin	+1	1pm
Brussels	+1	1pm
Chicago	-6	6am
Dublin	0	noon
Johannesburg	+2	2pm
Madrid	+1	1pm
Montréal	-6	6am
New York	-5	7am
Paris	+1	1pm
Perth, Australia	+8	8pm
Rome	+1	1pm
San Francisco	-8	4am
Sydney	+10	10pm
Tokyo	+9	9pm

CUSTOMS

From another EU country

The following are guidelines for the quantity of goods you can take into Ireland without paying further taxes or duties, provided you accompany the goods and they are for personal use.

- **3,200 cigarettes**
- **400 cigarillos**
- **200 cigars**
- **3kg smoking tobacco**
- **110 litres of beer**
- **10 litres of spirits**
- **90 litres of wine (of which only 60 litres can be sparkling wine)**
- **20 litres of fortified wine (such as port or sherry)**

For the purposes of visitors' allowances, the Canary Islands, Gibraltar and the Channel Islands are regarded as non-EU countries.

Note: Limits for tobacco products are lower if you are travelling from some EU countries. Check before you travel.

From a country outside the EU

- **200 cigarettes or 100 cigarillos or 50 cigars or 250g of smoking tobacco**
- **60cc/ml perfume**
- **250cc/ml eau de toilette**
- **2 litres of still table wine**
- **1 litre of spirits or strong liqueurs over 22% volume; or 2 litres of fortified wine, sparkling wine or other liqueurs**
- **Up to €175 worth of all other goods per adult**

GALWAY TEMPERATURE

Average temperature per day
per night
°C °F
30 86
20 68
10 50
0 32
J F M A M J J A S O N D

RAINFALL

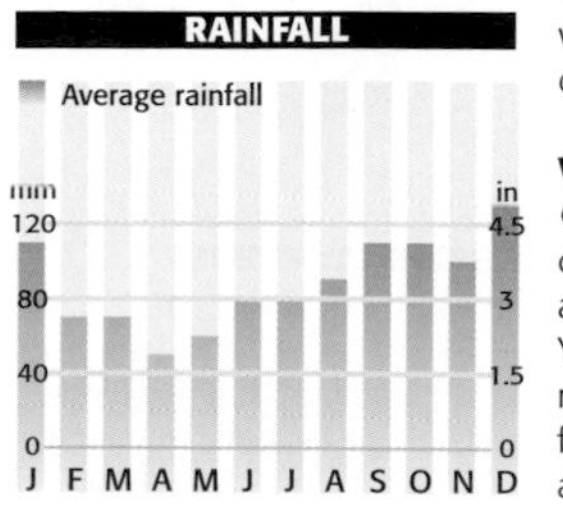

idea to have details of your passport number in case you lose it. If you do lose your passport, contact your embassy without delay.

Northern Ireland

- Foreign visitors must have a passport that is valid for at least six months at the date of entry into Northern Ireland. UK nationals can enter the country without a passport, but will need photographic identification. You are strongly advised to take your passport as identification anyway, because ferry companies and airlines each have their own rules as to what constitutes an acceptable form of 'photographic identification'. If you are at all uncertain, get clarification from your travel agent, airline or ferry operator.

Republic of Ireland

- EU nationals should take a valid passport.
- Non-EU nationals must have a valid passport or national identity card as appropriate.

VISAS

- Entry requirements differ depending on your nationality and are also subject to change. You should always check the requirements prior to a visit and follow news events that may affect your situation.

Republic of Ireland

- EU citizens and nationals from the US, Australia, Canada, New Zealand and South Africa do not need a visa. Visitors from all other countries should contact their local Irish Embassy/Consulate before visiting the Republic. The website of the Irish Department of Foreign Affairs (ww.irlgov.ie/iveagh) is useful.

Northern Ireland

- If you have a passport from the US, Canada, Australia, New Zealand or South Africa, you do not need a visa for stays of up to six months. You must have enough money to support yourself without working or receiving money from public funds. Those who wish to stay longer than six months and nationals of certain countries require a visa. To check this see the UK government's website: www.ukvisas.gov.uk

TRAVEL INSURANCE

- Insurance is recommended for loss or theft of your personal possessions and for medical costs. If you are robbed, report it to the police and keep all receipts for expenses. Make sure your insurance covers any high-risk sports you plan to do. For details of health insurance, ▷ 332.

CUSTOMS

Visitors to Ireland from the UK and other EU countries do not need to make a customs declaration on arrival. However, certain goods are restricted or prohibited for environmental and health reasons—restricted goods include meat and poultry.

VAT REFUNDS

Value Added Tax is generally included in the price of goods and services in Ireland. If you are from a country outside the EU, you can obtain a VAT refund on goods you purchase to take home. Some department stores will deduct the VAT (from large purchases) at the point of sale when your purchases are to be shipped overseas. Otherwise, get a tax refund form from the store and keep your receipts. When you leave the country go to the Customs Office to have your receipts stamped and the goods inspected before you check in. You will need your passport or other identification in order to do this.

PRACTICALITIES

If you forget to take something, you should be able to buy most things you may need in Ireland.

CLOTHES

The amount of rainfall in Ireland, makes an umbrella and rainwear essential. For city visits an umbrella may be enough, but in windy coastal areas and the hills an umbrella won't be much use so be sure to pack a waterproof jacket. The weather can change quickly so pack sweaters as well as lighter clothes, whatever the time of the year. It is not necessary to dress up for a visit to the pub, or for any but the top-end restaurants.

ADAPTORS

The standard electricity supply is 240 volts AC in Northern Ireland and 230 volts AC in the Republic of Ireland. Sockets take 3-square-pin plugs, as used in the UK, so visitors from Europe and the US will need an adaptor for any electrical equipment that they bring. A plug adaptor is necessary to convert 2-pin plugs to 3-pin plugs and can be bought at electrical stores and airports.

OTHER ITEMS TO PACK

- Details of emergency contacts and friends.
- Driving licence or International Driving Licence (if your licence is not in English).
- First aid kit.
- Glasses or contact lenses and solution, and prescription details or a spare set.
- Photocopies of passport and travel insurance (or send scanned versions to an email account such as Hotmail that you can access while you are away).
- Travellers' cheques and/or credit cards (preferably more than one card), and some cash in euros (Republic) or sterling (Northern Ireland).
- Credit card numbers and registration numbers of mobile phone, camera and other expensive items in case of loss.

CONVERSION CHART

FROM	TO	MULTIPLY BY
Inches	Centimetres	2.54
Centimetres	Inches	0.3937
Feet	Metres	0.3048
Metres	Feet	3.2810
Yards	Metres	0.9144
Metres	Yards	1.0940
Miles	Kilometres	1.6090
Kilometres	Miles	0.6214
Acres	Hectares	0.4047
Hectares	Acres	2.4710
Gallons	Litres	4.5460
Litres	Gallons	0.2200
Ounces	Grams	28.35
Grams	Ounces	0.0353
Pounds	Grams	453.6
Grams	Pounds	0.0022
Pounds	Kilograms	0.4536
Kilograms	Pounds	2.205
Tons	Tonnes	1.0160
Tonnes	Tons	0.9842

MEASUREMENTS

Officially Ireland uses the metric system, but it is not used all over the country.

Distance	measured in both kilometres and miles
Food	sold in both kilograms and pounds
Drinks (pubs)	sold in pints and half pints
Petrol	sold in litres

CLOTHING SIZES

Use the clothing sizes chart below to convert the size you use at home.

UK	Metric	USA	
36	46	36	SUITS
38	48	38	
40	50	40	
42	52	42	
44	54	44	
46	56	46	
48	58	48	
7	41	8	SHOES
7.5	42	8.5	
8.5	43	9.5	
9.5	44	10.5	
10.5	45	11.5	
11	46	12	
14.5	37	14.5	SHIRTS
15	38	15	
15.5	39/40	15.5	
16	41	16	
16.5	42	16.5	
17	43	17	
8	36	6	DRESSES
10	38	8	
12	40	10	
14	42	12	
16	44	14	
18	46	16	
20	46	18	
4.5	37.5	6	SHOES
5	38	6.5	
5.5	38.5	7	
6	39	7.5	
6.5	40	8	
7	41	8.5	

PUBLIC LAVATORIES

As with many European countries, hygiene standards in public lavatories vary. If you don't want to use the facilities in older buildings, go to a department store or a train or bus station. Redeveloped and newer buildings such as the Laganside Bus Station in Belfast, have lavatories for men, women, people with physical disabilities and a separate parents' room for changing babies. Some signs may be in Irish only. *Mná* means 'women' and *fir* means 'men'.

LAUNDRY

It may be worth checking when you reserve accommodation whether the hotel or guesthouse has a laundry service and how much this costs. Otherwise, if you prefer to do your own washing, most towns have self-service laundrettes. Look under 'Laundries' or 'Dry cleaners' in Golden Pages (Republic of Ireland) or the Yellow Pages (Northern Ireland).

PLACES OF WORSHIP

One thing Ireland is not short of is churches. Tourist Information Offices can advise you on places of worship in their area; listed below are places of worship in Dublin and Belfast.

Dublin

Christ Church Cathedral, Christchurch Place, tel 01 677 8099; www.cccdub.ie
Sunday: 11am Sung Eucharist and sermon, 3.30pm Choral Evensong, 5pm Eucharist in Irish on 4th Sunday of the month.
Weekdays: 10am Morning Prayer, Noon Peace Prayers, 12.45 The Eucharist, 5pm (Mon, Tue, Fri) Evening Prayer, 6pm Choral Evensong.

St. Patrick's Cathedral, St. Patrick's Close, tel 01 475 4817; www.stpatrickscathedral.ie
You can listen to the choir at a service, Mon–Fri 5.45.

St. Mary's Pro-Cathedral, Marlborough Street, tel 01 874 5441
Mass: Sat evening 6pm, Sun 10, 11, 12.45, 6.30, weekdays 8.30, 10, 11, 12 .45, 5.45.
Confessions: Mon–Fri after 8.30 and 12.45 Mass.
Wheelchair access in entrance by Cathedral Street.

Dublin Jewish Progressive Synagogue, tel 01 490 7605.

Islamic Cultural Centre of Ireland, 19 Roebuck Road, Clonskeagh, Dublin 14, tel 01 208 0000.

Belfast

The Cathedral Church of St. Anne, Donegall Street; www.belfastcathedral.com
Sunday Services: 10am, 11am, 3.30pm. Weekday Services: Mon–Sat 1pm. Holy Communion: Holy Days, Saint's Days and Wed 1pm. Healing Service, Fri 1pm.

St. Peter's Roman Catholic Cathedral, St. Peter's Square, tel 028 9032 7573.

Belfast Islamic Centre, 38 Wellington Park, BT9 6DN, tel 028 9066 4465; http://belfastmosque.tripod.com

Belfast Synagogue, 49 Somerton Road, tel 028 9077 5013.

LOCAL WAYS/ETIQUETTE

Talking to strangers

Irish people are very friendly, and will spontaneously chat to you in a pub or at a bus stop. If you look as if you are lost, someone may come up to try and help you, without you even asking. In a social situation, unless you are directly asked for your opinion, it's wise to listen rather than opine when politics and/or religion are on the agenda. Sensitivities can run close to the surface and you don't want to cause offence. It is also best not to bring these subjects up.

Buying your round

There is a tradition in Ireland (and also in Britain), that if you are with a group of friends in a pub, each person in the group takes a turn in buying drinks for the others in the group. This is called buying a round. If you find yourself in this situation, it is better to offer to buy drinks for your companions rather than to be prompted with the phrase 'It's your round!' If you are not sure, ask 'Whose round is it?'

A friendly bar in Belfast (top). There's a widespread smoking ban in the Republic (above)

Joining in with music

In pubs, particularly in rural areas, people may pull out a fiddle, *bodhrán* or penny whistle for an impromptu musical session. This can be a wonderful experience and you may be invited to join in if you have an instrument with you. As long as you feel comfortable and confident in your musical ability, play along.

Smoking

Early in 2004 a law came into effect in the Republic of Ireland, prohibiting smoking in all public places including hotels, restaurants and pubs. The law came about despite a legal challenge mounted by hotel, restaurant and pub owners.

MONEY

When you are planning a visit to Ireland, remember that the Republic of Ireland uses the euro, while Northern Ireland (which is part of the United Kingdom) has pounds sterling as its currency. Pounds are not accepted in the Republic, although occasionally some establishments in Northern Ireland (particularly in Belfast) accept euros. For example, in Belfast some telephone booths accept pounds and euros. However, you should not rely on this, and plan to take pounds sterling to the North, or change money when you get there.

THE EURO

The euro was introduced as the unit of currency in the Republic of Ireland on 1 January 2002. Euro notes are identical across the euro zone, while euro coins have one side dedicated to their country of origin. For some reason, Irish euro coins have become quite collectable and many are bought for higher than their real value by collectors!

BANKS

Ireland has no shortage of banks, with downtown Dublin and Belfast particularly well served. Many have a foreign exchange desk where you can change money; look for bureau de change signs. Standard opening hours in the Republic and Northern Ireland are 9.30 or 10am to 4pm Monday to Friday, although some banks also stay open until 5pm one day a week (often Thursday). Banks are closed on Saturdays, Sundays and on public holidays.

AUTOMATIC TELLER MACHINES (ATMS)

These are widely available across the country and accept most credit and debit cards. Remember that your credit card issuer may charge you a fee for a cash advance by credit card.

CREDIT CARDS AND TRAVELLERS' CHEQUES

Visa, MasterCard and American Express are widely accepted in Ireland. You'll see credit card symbols displayed in the windows of many shops, hotels, restaurants, car rental companies and fuel stations. If you have another credit card, ask in advance if it is acceptable. You can cash travellers' cheques at most banks and bureau de change offices in Ireland. Remember to bring some identification with you.

CHANGING MONEY

Larger branches of major banks have money-changing facilities and there are many bureau de change kiosks, for example at airports, at the Busáras bus station in Dublin and in the Belfast Welcome Centre on Donegall Place. The commission charged at bureaux de change, which have longer opening hours than banks, may be high so shop around.

One option in Northern Ireland is to change your money at a post office, although only larger branches offer this service. The post office does not charge any commission, although the exchange rate may not be as competitive as that offered at banks. You can pay by cheque, cash, Visa, MasterCard, Switch/Maestro, Delta, Solo or Electron and you may be asked for identification, so bring your passport. The post office also has the advantage of opening on Saturdays.

WIRING MONEY

In an emergency, money can be wired from your home country, but this can take a few days and is expensive. You can send and receive money using Western Union (www.westernunion.com) or MoneyGram (www.moneygram.com). You can do this at Busáras bus station in Dublin and also at the bureau de change kiosk in the Dublin Tourism Office on Suffolk Street.

VAT REFUNDS

See page 328 for VAT refunds.

TIPPING

In restaurants, check to see if a service charge has been made. If it hasn't, add 10–15 per cent if you are satisfied with the service. You don't have to tip taxi drivers, but if you do, about 10 per cent of the fare is probably about right. For hotel porters about 75 cents (Republic) or 50p (NI) per bag is the norm.

PRICES OF EVERYDAY ITEMS

ITEM	EUROS (Republic)	POUNDS STERLING (Northern Ireland)
Pint of Guinness (pub)	4.00	2.00
The Irish Times	1.50	0.75
Postcard	0.40	0.30
Stamp for postcard to England	0.60	0.28
Cup of tea or coffee	2.00–2.70	1.50–2.00
Packet 20 cigarettes	6.00	4.50-5.00
Litre of unleaded petrol	0.88	0.79
Bottle of water (in café)	2.00–2.25	1.70–2.50
Takeout sandwich	3.00–3.50	2.00–2.50
1 hour city parking (Dublin/Belfast)	2.50	1.20

MAJOR BANKS

These banks have many branches across Ireland. Some main branches in Dublin and Belfast are listed.

NAME OF BANK	ADDRESS AND TELEPHONE NUMBER	WEBSITE
Bank of Ireland	6 Lower O'Connell Street, Dublin; tel 01 878 7870	www.bankofireland.ie
	4–8 High Street, Belfast, BT1 2BA; tel 028 9024 4901	
National Irish Bank	66 Upper O'Connell Street, Dublin; tel 01 873 1877	www.nib.ie
Allied Irish Bank	37 Upper O'Connell Street, Dublin; tel 01 873 1188	www.aib.ie
Ulster Bank	11–16 Donegall Square East, Belfast, BT1 5UB; tel 028 9024 4112	www.ulsterbank.com

BANKNOTES AND COINS IN THE REPUBLIC OF IRELAND

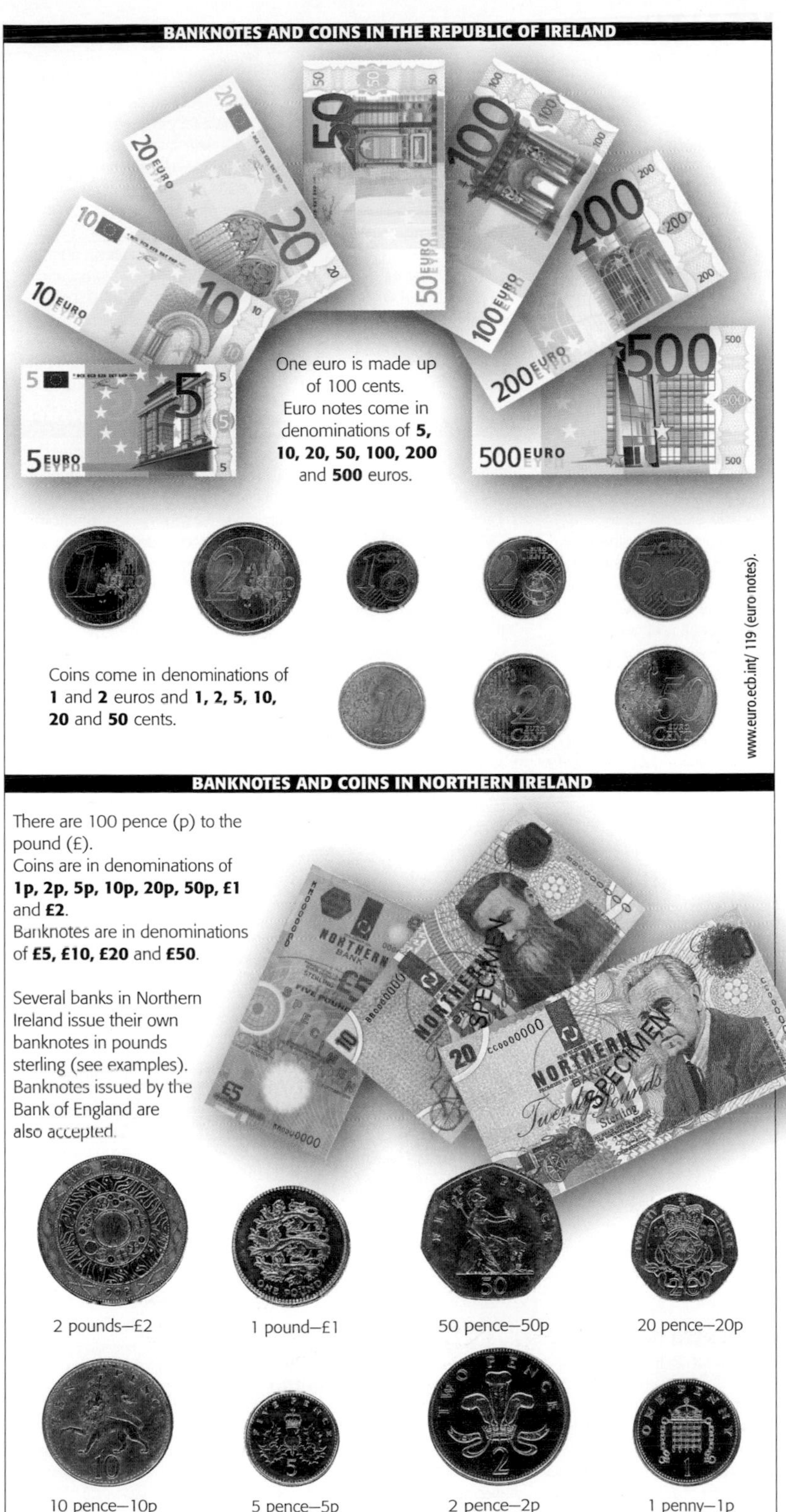

One euro is made up of 100 cents. Euro notes come in denominations of **5, 10, 20, 50, 100, 200** and **500** euros.

Coins come in denominations of **1** and **2** euros and **1, 2, 5, 10, 20** and **50** cents.

www.euro.ecb.int/ 119 (euro notes).

BANKNOTES AND COINS IN NORTHERN IRELAND

There are 100 pence (p) to the pound (£).
Coins are in denominations of **1p, 2p, 5p, 10p, 20p, 50p, £1** and **£2**.
Banknotes are in denominations of **£5, £10, £20** and **£50**.

Several banks in Northern Ireland issue their own banknotes in pounds sterling (see examples). Banknotes issued by the Bank of England are also accepted.

2 pounds–£2

1 pound–£1

50 pence–50p

20 pence–20p

10 pence–10p

5 pence–5p

2 pence–2p

1 penny–1p

HEALTH

The Republic and Northern Ireland both have a national health service which works alongside the private sector.

BEFORE YOU GO

- Make sure you have full health and travel insurance.
- British visitors to the Republic of Ireland should bring an E111 form (EHIC card from 2006), which entitles them to free urgent medical treatment, from a public hospital or from a doctor participating in the General Medical Service Scheme. In Northern Ireland, you are entitled to receive medical treatment as if you were in mainland Britain.
- If you are from another EU country (not Britain), you may be entitled to a certain amount of free health care, including hospital treatment. You must complete all the necessary paperwork before you travel.
- If you are visiting Ireland from a non-EU country, private medical insurance is essential; bring the policy document and a photocopy with you.
- Australia has a reciprocal agreement with Ireland, which entitles Australian passport holders to receive emergency public hospital treatment. However, they still have to pay a nightly in-patient charge and an Accident and Emergency fee.

WHAT TO TAKE WITH YOU

- If you are taking any medication, bring enough for the length of your stay.
- If you wear glasses, bring a spare set.
- A first-aid kit is always a good thing to pack. It should include plasters (Band Aids), sterile dressings, cotton wool, antiseptic cream, pain relief tablets, remedies for constipation and diarrhoea, antihistamine tablets, wet wipes and bandages.

IF YOU NEED TREATMENT

- Admission to hospital in Ireland is usually arranged by a doctor. However, in an emergency, call 999 or 112 for an ambulance or go to the casualty department (emergency room) of a hospital.
- The following hospitals in Dublin have an accident and emergency department:
Beaumont Hospital, Beaumont Road (tel 01 809 3000)
Mater Hospital, Eccles Street (tel 01 803 2000)
James Connolly Memorial Hospital, Blanchardstown (tel 01 821 3844)
St. James Hospital, James Street (tel 01 410 3000)
St. Vincents Hospital, Elm Park (tel 01 269 4533)
- In Belfast there are several hospitals with an accident and emergency department:
The Belfast City Hospital Trust is on Lisburn Road (tel 028 9032 9241)
Mater Hospital is on Crumlin Road (tel 028 9074 1211)
The Royal Hospitals are in the west of the city, on Grosvenor Road (tel 028 9024 0503)
Ulster Hospital is east of the city in Dundonald (tel 028 9048 4511).

HEALTHY FLYING

- Visitors to Ireland from as far as the US, Australia or New Zealand may be concerned about the effect of long-haul flights on their health. The most widely publicized concern is Deep Vein Thrombosis, or DVT. Misleadingly called 'economy class syndrome', DVT is the forming of a blood clot in the body's deep veins, particularly in the legs. The clot can move around the bloodstream and could be fatal.
- Those most at risk include the elderly, pregnant women and those using the contraceptive pill, smokers and the overweight. If you are at increased risk of DVT see your doctor before departing. Flying increases the likelihood of DVT because passengers are often seated in a cramped position for long periods of time and may become dehydrated.

To minimize risk:
Drink water (not alcohol)
Don't stay immobile for hours at a time
Stretch and exercise your legs periodically
Do wear elastic flight socks, which support veins and reduce the chances of a clot forming

EXERCISES

1 ANKLE ROTATIONS

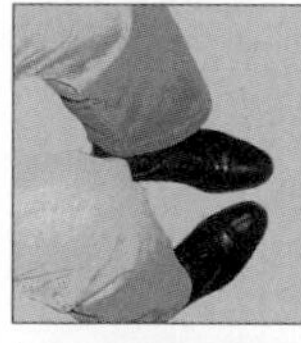
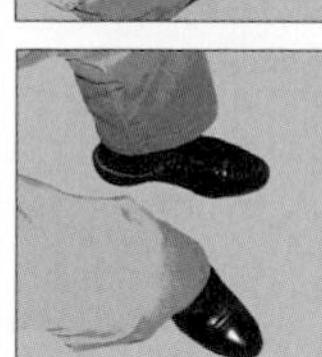

Lift feet off the floor. Draw a circle with the toes, moving one foot clockwise and the other counterclockwise

2 CALF STRETCHES

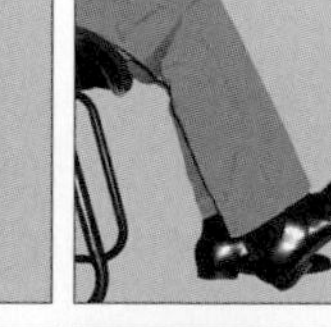
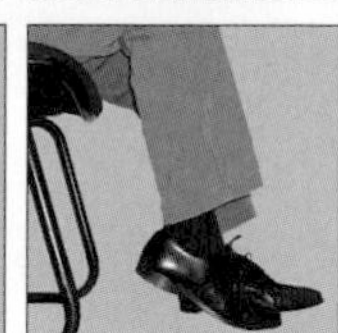

Start with heel on the floor and point foot upward as high as you can. Then lift heels high, keeping balls of feet on the floor

3 KNEE LIFTS

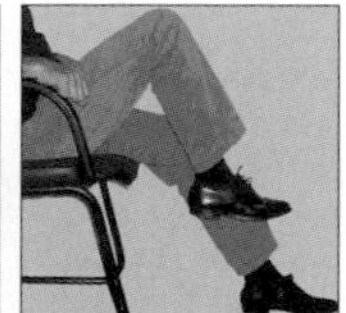
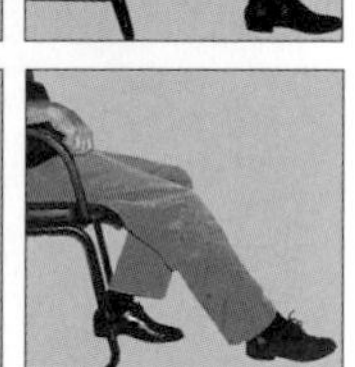

Lift leg with knee bent while contracting your thigh muscle. Then straighten leg, pressing foot flat to the floor

Other health hazards for flyers are airborne diseases and bugs spread by the plane's air-conditioning system. These are largely unavoidable but if you have a serious medical condition seek advice from a doctor before flying.

PHARMACIES

- For minor ailments, it is often worth consulting a pharmacist before speaking to a doctor Many pharmacies in Ireland have a flashing green cross outside and most are open Mon–Sat 9–5.30 or 6. In Dublin, several city branches of the O'Connell's chain stay open until 10pm. In Belfast, some pharmacies stay open until 9pm on Thursdays.

DENTAL TREATMENT

- Dentists are listed in telephone directories or, for Northern Ireland, use the British Dental Association's online service at www.bda.findadentist.org.uk
- Check that your health insurance policy covers dental treatment.

OPTICIANS

- If you wear glasses or contact lenses, pack a spare set and bring your prescription in case you lose or break them. Opticians are listed in the Yellow Pages (NI) and Golden Pages (Republic), including such chains as Vision Express (RI and NI), Boots (NI) and Specsavers (NI).

WATER

- Tap water is safe to drink.
- Mineral water is widely available.

PHARMACIES IN DUBLIN AND BELFAST

CITY	PHARMACY	CONTACT DETAILS
Dublin	O'Connell's	55 Lower O'Connell Street, tel 01 873 0427 There are several branches in the city and they all stay open late
Belfast	Boots	10-16 Castle Place, BT1 1GB, tel 028 9024 6085; www.boots.com

OPTICIANS IN DUBLIN AND BELFAST

CITY	OPTICIAN	CONTACT DETAILS
Dublin	Vision Express	Ilac Centre, Henry Street, Dublin 1 tel 01 873 2477; www.visionexpress.com
Dublin	Insight Opticians	Jervis Street Shopping Centre, Jervis Street, Dublin 1 tel 01 878 1188
Belfast	Boots Opticians	35–47 Donegall Place, Belfast, BT1 5AW tel 028 9032 5450; www.boots.com
Belfast	Specsavers	36–40 Ann Street, Belfast, BT1 4EG tel 028 9031 1999; www.specsavers.co.uk
Belfast	Optical Express	32 Donegall Place, Belfast, BT1 5BB tel 028 9043 7768A

ALTERNATIVE TREATMENT

Most types of alternative medicine are available in Ireland, including homeopathy and osteopathy. These treatments are not free for visitors. The organizations listed below are a starting point and local telephone directories will have more details. Try the Golden Pages (Republic) or Yellow Pages (NI).

NAME	TELEPHONE NUMBER
Chiropractic Association of Ireland (RI)	071 914 7976
Irish Osteopathic Association (RI)	01 269 5281
The Irish Society of Homeopaths (RI)	091 565040
Association of Reflexologists (NI)	0870 567 3320
British Osteopathic Association (NI)	01582 488455

FINDING HELP

PERSONAL SECURITY

- In general, crime rates are fairly low in Ireland, although you should be particularly careful in Dublin and Belfast, as you would in any other capital city and take the normal precautions.
- If possible, keep valuables in your hotel safe.
- If you are visiting as a couple or in a group, split the money between you.
- Make a note of the numbers on any travellers' cheques and keep it separate from the cheques.
- Park your car in an official, covered car park and keep the ticket that you are issued with.
- Never leave valuable items in your car and think twice about leaving anything on view in your car.
- Avoid walking in deserted streets at night.

EMERGENCY PHONE NUMBERS

Police, fire, ambulance, mountain rescue, cave rescue

Republic
999 or 112
Northern Ireland
999

- Be aware of who is standing behind you when you are withdrawing money from an ATM.
- Keep a tight hold of your handbag or shoulder bag, particularly in crowded streets, restaurants and on buses and trains.

POLICE

Republic of Ireland

- The national police force in the Republic of Ireland is the Garda Siochána, known as Garda or Gardaí. Police officers wear dark blue uniforms, peaked caps and have the word 'Garda' on the back of their jackets. The Gardaí offers a Tourist Victim Support Service (TVSS) which aims to provide emotional support and practical assistance to tourists who are victims of crime while in the Republic. TVSS is

The friendly face of the police in Cork

PLANNING

based in Dublin but can provide assistance anywhere in the country. The service includes use of telephone, fax and email facilities and help with language difficulties, replacing stolen travel tickets and cancelling credit cards. The service does not include financial assistance or legal advice. If you are a victim of crime, contact Tourist Victim Support Service, Garda HQ, Harcourt Square, Dublin 2; tel 01 478 5295; email info@touristvictimsupport.ie; www.touristvictimsupport.ie. It's open Monday to Saturday 10–6 and on Sunday and national holidays 12–6.

Northern Ireland

- The Police Service of Northern Ireland (PSNI) is the police force. If you are a victim of crime in Northern Ireland, contact the local police station by calling 999 or 028 9065 0222. Once the PSNI have taken details of the crime, they will refer you to the nearest tourist information office, where staff will try to help you. www.psni.police.uk

CALLING AN EMERGENCY NUMBER

- You should only call the emergency numbers 112 and 999 in a genuine emergency. State clearly which service you need and wait to be connected to that service. When you are connected, say where you are and what the problem is.

LOST PROPERTY

Republic

- For lost property in Dublin contact the Garda (police) or tel 01 666 0000. For items lost on buses contact Dublin Bus, Earl Place, Dublin 1, tel 01 703 1321, Mon–Fri 8.45–5; www.dublinbus.ie

Northern Ireland

- The Lost Property Office in Belfast is at Musgrave Police Station, Ann Street, tel 028 9065 0222 extension 26049.

LOSS OF PASSPORT

- Always keep a note of your passport number and a photocopy of the relevant pages.
- Before you leave home, scan the pages of your passport, then email them to yourself at an account that you can access anywhere, for example www.hotmail.com
- If you lose your passport, contact your embassy. See the chart for contact details for some embassies in Ireland. If your passport is stolen, you should also report the theft to the police.

A police patrol car in the Republic of Ireland

EMBASSIES IN DUBLIN

If you lose your passport or are arrested, contact your embassy.

COUNTRY	ADDRESS	CONTACT DETAILS
Australia	2nd Floor, Fitzwilton House, Wilton Terrace, Dublin 2	Tel 01 664 5300; www.australianembassy.ie
Britain	29 Merrion Road, Dublin 4	Tel 01 205 3700; www.britishembassy.ie
Canada	4th Floor, 65–68 St. Stephen's Green, Dublin 2	Tel 01 417 4100; www.canada.ie
New Zealand	The Embassy of New Zealand for Ireland is in London. See chart below for details.	
South Africa	2nd Floor, Alexandra House, Earlsfort Centre, Earlsfort Terrace, Dublin 2	Tel 01 661 5553
US	42 Elgin Road, Ballsbridge, Dublin 4	Tel 01 668 7122; www.usembassy.ie

EMBASSIES IN BELFAST AND LONDON

COUNTRY	ADDRESS	CONTACT DETAILS
Australia	Australian High Commission, Australia House Strand, London, WC2B 4LZ	Tel 020 7379 4334; www.australia.org.uk
Canada	Canadian High Commission, Macdonald House 1 Grosvenor Square, London, W1K 4AB	Tel 020 7258 6600 (general enquiries) Tel 020 7258 6699 (immigration and visa info)
New Zealand	New Zealand House, 80 The Haymarket, London SW1 4TQ	Tel 020 7930 8422; www.nzembassy.com
South Africa	High Commission for the Republic of South Africa, South Africa House, Trafalgar Square, London, WC2N 5DP	Tel 020 7451 7299; www.southafricahouse.com
US	US Consulate General, Danesfort House 223 Stranmillis Road, Belfast, BT9 5GR	Tel 028 9038 6100; www.usembassy.org.uk

OPENING TIMES AND TICKETS

OPENING TIMES		
Banks	Mon–Fri 9.30 or 10–4	Some banks are open until 5pm one day a week, although the day varies from town to town (in Dublin and Belfast this is Thursday). Banks are closed on Saturday and Sunday and on public holidays.
Shops	Mon–Sat 9–5.30	In villages and towns there is often a grocery store which stays open until 10pm. In Dublin most shops are open until 6pm Monday to Saturday and late-night opening (until 8 or 9) in Dublin and Belfast is Thursday. Shopping malls often open Sunday 12–5 or 6. See www.ulstershopper.co.uk for Northern Ireland.
Pubs	In the **Republic** closing time is 11.30pm midweek, about 12.30am from Thu–Sat and 11pm on Sun	There's half an hour drinking up time. Pubs shut on Good Friday and Christmas Day. Nightclubs and late-night bars serve drinks until 2.30am.
	In **Northern Ireland** when a pub closes depends on its licence	Many close at 11pm Monday to Saturday, 10pm on Sunday, although some Belfast bars close at midnight during the week and at midnight or 1am on Friday and Saturday. Nightclubs close at about 3am, although owing to a legal anomaly, you can't buy an alcoholic drink after 1am.
Post offices	Mon–Fri 9–5.30	Some post offices also open on Saturday 9–1. In Dublin the main post office on O'Connell Street is open until 8pm Monday to Saturday and until 6.30pm Sunday. In Belfast the main post office on Castle Place is open Monday to Saturday 9–5.30.
Pharmacies	Pharmacies are generally open from 9–5.30 or 6	In Dublin, several central branches of O'Connell's stay open until 10pm. In central Belfast no pharmacies open late, except on Thursday, when some stay open until 9pm.

TICKET CONCESSIONS

Student and youth cards

International Student Identity Cards (ISIC cards) entitle students to concessionary rates of admission to museums and visitor attractions as well as discounted transport tickets (▷ 58). A Euro Under 26 card is available to visitors who are under the age of 26, but who are not necessarily students, and provides similar discounts to the ISIC card. These cards can be obtained from student travel agencies and youth hostels.

NATIONAL HOLIDAYS	
1 January	New Year's Day
17 March	St. Patrick's Day
March/April	Good Friday (Northern Ireland)
March/April	Easter Monday
May (first Monday)	May Holiday
May (last Monday)	May Holiday (Northern Ireland)
June (first Monday)	June Holiday (Republic)
12 July	Orangeman's Day (Northern Ireland)
August (first Monday)	August Holiday (Republic)
August (last Monday)	August Holiday (Northern Ireland)
October (last Monday)	October Holiday (Republic)
25 December	Christmas Day
26 December	St. Stephen's Day/Boxing Day

Good Friday is not a public holiday in the Republic, but many businesses observe it, so expect to find some offices, restaurants and pubs closed on this day.

Seniors

Senior citizens, usually those aged over 60 or over 65, can benefit from reduced rates at a number of attractions and places of interest as well as on public transport. You will need to carry some form of identification with a date of birth as proof of age.

Heritage Cards

The National Trust (in Northern Ireland) and Dúchas (in the Republic of Ireland) are both heritage organizations which manage such properties as stately houses and gardens, prehistoric sites, cathedrals and national parks. Admission to these is free to holders of an annual ticket, and this can save you money as long as you are doing a lot of sightseeing. Annual tickets are available at any of the sites managed by the relevant organization: membership of the National Trust (www.nationaltrust.org.uk) costs £62.50 for a family and £34 for an adult. A Dúchas Heritage Card (www.heritageireland.ie) costs €50 for a family and €20 for an adult.

Joining in a St. Patrick's Day parade

COMMUNICATION

INTERNATIONAL DIALLING CODES	
Australia	00 61
Canada	00 1
Germany	00 49
Italy	00 39
New Zealand	00 64
Spain	00 34
UK	00 44
US	00 1

AREA CODES WITHIN THE REPUBLIC OF IRELAND	
Cork	021
Dublin	01
Galway	091
Limerick	061
Sligo	071
Waterford	051

USEFUL TELEPHONE NUMBERS		
WITHIN:	**NORTHERN IRELAND**	**THE REPUBLIC**
Emergency	999	999 or 112
Directory enquiries	118 500	11850 or 11811
International directory enquiries	118 505	11818
Talking Pages to find a number	0800 600 900	1 618 8000
(Yellow Pages directory in NI and Golden Pages directory in the Republic)		

TELEPHONES

The main phone company in the Republic is Eircom (www.eircom.ie) and in Northern Ireland, British Telecom (ww.bt.com/ni). Both companies are efficient with reasonably priced calls and a large number of phone boxes (phone booths) across the area they cover.

PUBLIC PHONE BOXES (PHONE BOOTHS)

Republic of Ireland

Eircom call boxes are the most widespread. Some accept coins only (minimum €0.50), while others accept coins, Eircom call cards and credit cards including American Express, Diners, Visa and Eurocard/MasterCard. The display instructions are in a choice of languages (English, German, Irish, French and Spanish) and if you need assistance, dial the free number 1800 799 099. You can buy €4, €7 or €15 Eircom call cards in newsagents, shops and post offices.

Northern Ireland

British Telecom (BT) is the national phone company and BT call boxes are widespread. To call within Northern Ireland or other places in the UK costs 11p per minute (but the minimum charge is 20p) and call boxes accept cash (coins only), credit cards (Eurocard/Mastercard, Diners, Visa, American Express), debit cards (Delta) and BT chargecards. There are no longer any prepaid phonecards, as BT has withdrawn them. It's worth remembering that call boxes accept incoming calls. For free operator assistance dial 100 (UK) or 155 (international). www.bt.com/payphones

MOBILE TELEPHONES

If you want to use your cell phone in Ireland, only phones with GSM subscriptions and a roaming agreement will work. Check with your phone provider before you leave home.

CALLING IRELAND

- To call the Republic from abroad or from Northern Ireland, dial 00 353, then the area code (without 0), followed by the local number.
- For internal calls within the Republic, dial the area code (including the first 0), followed by the local number.
- To call Northern Ireland from abroad, dial 00 44 then the area code (without 0) then the local number.
- To call Northern Ireland from the Republic of Ireland, dial 048 then the area code (without 0) then the local number.
- Calling Northern Ireland from the UK or from within Northern Ireland is the same. Dial the area code including the first zero, then the local number.
- All codes within Northern Ireland are 028.

POST OFFICES

- AnPost (www.anpost.ie) runs mail services in the Republic and post boxes here are bright green. Royal Mail (www.royalmail.com) covers Northern Ireland and their post boxes are red.
- The main post office in Dublin is in a beautiful neoclassical building on Lower O'Connell Street and is open 8am–8pm Mon–Sat and also 10–6.30 on Sun and holidays, but only for stamps and

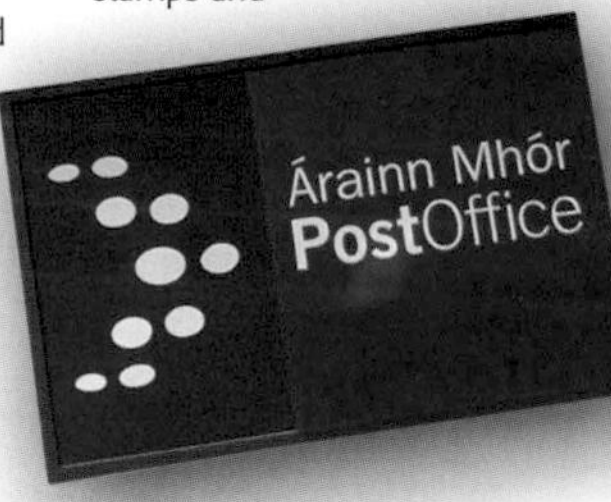

Post office sign (right) and old-style mailbox (below)

MAILING RATES		
FROM THE REPUBLIC OF IRELAND		
The prices below are all for a letter or postcard which weighs up to 50g		
Priority to Britain		€0.60
Economy to Britain		€0.50
Priority to Europe		€0.65
Economy to Europe		€0.55
Priority to rest of the world		€0.65
Economy to rest of the world		€0.55
FROM NORTHERN IRELAND		
First class within the UK	up to 60g	£0.28
Second class within the UK	up to 60g	£0.20
Airmail Europe	postcard	£0.38
	letter 60g	£0.69
Airmail USA, Canada,	postcard	£0.42
South Africa, Middle East	letter 60g	£1.42
Australia	postcard	£0.42
	letter 60g	£1.56

bureau de change. The main post office in Belfast is on Castle Place and is open from 9–5.30 Mon–Sat. You can change money at both.

- Post offices across the country are generally open from 9–5.30 Mon–Fri; some open 9–noon or 1 on Sat. You can buy stamps here or at newsagents and shops.
- Postal codes in Northern Ireland are a combination of letters and numbers, for example, BT1 5AD (The Belfast Welcome Centre); the Republic doesn't have a postal code system. Dublin has a simple numbering system, with numbers 1 and 2 indicating the middle of the city.

INTERNET CAFÉS

DUBLIN

easyInternetcafé
37–39 Wellington Quay, Dublin 2, beside Ha'penny Bridge, tel 01 672 9593
Open 7 days a week from 8am and the cost varies depending on demand, from as little as €0.50 an hour, although you are more likely to pay from €2+ for an hour. You pay by putting coins in a machine and the café doesn't give change, so come with coins.

Global Internet Café
8 Lower O'Connell Street, Dublin 1, tel 01 878 0295; www.globalcafe.ie
Here you can make international calls, surf the internet, scan documents and burn CDs.

BELFAST

Revelations Café
27 Shaftesbury Square, Belfast, BT2 7AB, tel 028 9032 0337; www.revelations.co.uk

Belfast Welcome Centre
47 Donegall Place, Belfast, BT1 5AD; www.gotobelfast.com
There is a small internet café here which charges £1 for 15 minutes, £2 for 30 minutes and £3 for an hour.

BT phone booths
In Donegall Square there are some BT phone booths which also have a keypad for internet access, but it is an expensive way to log on as the charge is per minute.

TOURIST INFORMATION

There are various organizations which promote tourism in Ireland. Tourism Ireland (which covers Northern Ireland and the Republic), promotes Ireland abroad, while Fáilte Ireland is Ireland's main tourist authority. The Northern Ireland Tourist Board covers Northern Ireland including Belfast, while Dublin Tourism promotes the capital of the Republic.

TOURIST INFORMATION OFFICES

IN THE REPUBLIC OF IRELAND

Aran Islands
Kilronan, Inishmore, Co. Galway
tel 099 61263, fax 099 61420

Cork
Áras Fáilte, Grand Parade, Cork City
tel 021 425 5100, fax 021 425 5199;
www.corkkerry.ie

Dublin City
Dublin Tourism Centre, Suffolk Street, Dublin 2, tel 01 605 7700;
www.visitdublin.com

Donegal Town
Quay Street, Donegal Town
tel 074 972 1148, fax 074 972 2762;
www.irelandnorthwest.ie

Galway
Áras Fáilte, Forster Street, Eyre Square, Galway, tel 091 537700, fax 091 537733;
www.irelandwest.ie

Kilkenny
Shee Alms House, Rose Inn Street, Kilkenny, tel 056 775 1500,
fax 056 776 3955;
www.southeastireland.com

Limerick City
Arthur's Quay, Limerick City
tel 061 317522, fax 317939;
www.shannonregiontourism.ie

Northern Ireland Tourist Board
16 Nassau Street, Dublin 2
tel 01 679 1977;
www.discovernorthernireland.com

Sligo
Áras Reddan, Temple Street, Sligo
tel 071 916 1201, fax 071 916 0360;
www.irelandnorthwest.ie

Waterford
41 The Quay, Waterford City
tel 051 870800, fax 051 876720;
www.southeastireland.com

Wexford
Crescent Quay, Wexford
tel 053 23111, fax 053 41743;
www.southeastireland.com

IN NORTHERN IRELAND

Belfast
Belfast Welcome Centre, 47 Donegall Place, BT1 5AD
tel 028 9024 6609, fax 028 9031 2424;
www.gotobelfast.com

Fáilte Ireland, 53 Castle Street, BT1 1GH
tel 028 9026 5500, fax 028 9026 5515;
www.discoverireland.com

Derry
44 Foyle Street, BT48 6AT
tel/fax 028 7126 7284

TOURISM IRELAND OFFICES ABROAD

Australia
Tourism Ireland, 5th level, 36 Carrington Street, Sydney, NSW 2000
tel +61 2 9299 6177,
fax +61 2 9299 6323;
www.tourismireland.com.au

Canada
Tourism Ireland, 2 Bloor Street West, Suite 1501, Toronto, M4W 3E2
tel +1 416 925 6368,
fax +1 416 925 6033;
www.tourismireland.com

New Zealand
Tourism Ireland, 6th floor, 18 Shortland Street, Private Bag 92136, Auckland 1
tel +64 9 977 2255, fax +64 9 977 2256;
www.tourismireland.com.au

UK
Tourism Ireland, Britain Visitor Centre, 1 Lower Regent Street, London, SW1Y 4XT
tel 0800 039 7000, fax 020 7493 9065;
www.tourismireland.com

US
Tourism Ireland, 345 Park Avenue, New York, NY 10154
tel +1 212 418 0800, fax +1 212 371 9052;
www.tourismireland.com

MEDIA

TELEVISION

- National television and radio stations in the Republic are operated by Radio Telefís Éireann (RTÉ). RTÉ has five radio and two TV channels, funded by a licence fee and advertising.
- In Northern Ireland, the British Broadcasting Corporation (BBC) has BBC1 and BBC2, both non-commercial channels. The main commercial channel is UTV which has a similar schedule to ITV1 in England. There are also some independent regional channels such as Channel 9 (C9TV) which broadcasts in the Derry area.

TERRESTRIAL CHANNELS	
IN THE REPUBLIC	
RTÉ 1	Similar to BBC1 in Britain, although unlike the BBC, it has advertisements. Soaps including British *Eastenders* and the Dublin-set *Fair City*; main evening news at 9pm. The *Late Late Show* is a popular chat show. www.rte.ie
RTÉ 2	Mostly showing films, documentaries, Australian soaps and *The Simpsons*. www.rte.ie
TV3	National independent commercial station showing mostly American talk shows *(Oprah, Rikki Lake)* and British soaps such as *Emmerdale* and *Coronation Street.* www.tv3.ie
TG4	Irish language channel. www.tg4.ie
IN NORTHERN IRELAND	
BBC1	Soaps, chat shows, shows for children, drama and documentaries. The main evening news shows are at 6pm and 10pm, with regional news and weather reports immediately afterwards. www.bbc.co.uk
BBC2	This channel has documentaries, comedy and cultural/arts shows. www.bbc.co.uk
UTV	This commercial channel has children's shows in the afternoon and soaps, drama, movies and entertainment shows in the evenings. www.utvinternet.com
Channel 4	Some American shows, such as *Will and Grace* and repeats of others, including *Friends* and *Sex and the City*, documentaries, quality movies and comedy; news at 7pm Mon–Fri. www.channel4.com
Five	Lots of movies, Australian soaps; news at 5.30pm and 7pm Mon–Fri. www.five.tv

RADIO

There are several independent, regional radio stations in Ireland.

- The national independent radio station in the Republic is Today FM (100–100.3 FM). It has music and talk shows www.todayfm.com
- For Irish speakers, there is the RTÉ channel Radio na Gaeltachta (92.5–96 FM).
- RTÉ Radio 1 (88–90 FM) has music, news and chat shows.
- 2FM (90.4–97FM) plays pop music.
- Lyric FM (96–99FM) plays classical music.
- BBC Radio Ulster (92–95.4 FM) has news, weather reports and travel bulletins.
- Radio Foyle (93.1 FM) has news, sports and talk shows with phone-ins.

NEWSPAPERS

In the Republic

There are four daily papers available in the morning in the Republic:

- *Irish Independent* (www.independent.ie) the biggest selling daily paper in Ireland.
- *The Irish Times* (www.ireland.com).
- *The Irish Examiner* (www.irishexaminer.ie).
- *The Star.*

The Republic's evening papers are:

- *The Evening Echo* (www.eecho.ie).
- *Evening Herald.*

There are also several Sunday papers. The two weekly newspapers in Irish, are *Lá* and *Foinse* (www.foinse.ie).

In Northern Ireland

- The *Irish News* (www.irishnews.com) has a nationalist slant.
- *News Letter* has a Unionist perspective.
- The capital's main 'evening' paper, *The Belfast Telegraph* (www.belfasttelegraph.co.uk), has two editions, one of which comes out in the morning.

British newspapers

- There are also plenty of British papers to choose from in Ireland, some of which are available in Irish editions. Some examples are quality broadsheets such as

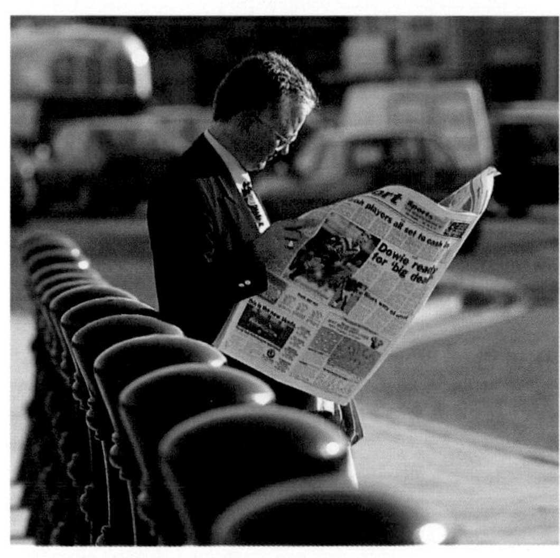

Keeping up with the daily news in Belfast

The Daily Telegraph (www.telegraph.co.uk), *The Times* (www.thetimes.co.uk) and *The Guardian* (www.guardian.co.uk). There are also tabloids such as *The Daily Mail* (www.dailymail.co.uk) and *The Daily Mirror* (www.mirror.co.uk).

MAGAZINES

- The main British magazines are available across Ireland. *RTÉ Guide* is the most popular TV and radio listings magazine (although daily newspapers also contain TV and radio schedules). There are also What's On guides (some of which are free), which list the current range of things to see and do.
- Dublin Tourism produces several guides to the city, although they are not free. These include *Where to Stay in Dublin, Top Visitor Attractions and Tours, Where to Eat* and *Rock 'n' Stroll-Music Walking Trail*. You can buy all of these guides at Dublin Tourism on Suffolk Street., O'Connell Street and the airport
- Belfast has *Inside+Out* an annual guide to arts, entertainment, shopping and eating, which costs £3.95.
- The best music magazine in Ireland is *Hot Press* (www.hotpress.com) which covers traditional, folk, pop, rock and dance music in Ireland and beyond. It comes out every two weeks.

BOOKS AND FILMS

BOOKS

Ireland has a long literary history and a list of the world's best-known writers would surely include several Irish names. To get you in an Irish frame of mind before you go, read from the selection below.

- James Joyce's literary masterpiece *Ulysses* (1922) is set in Dublin on one day in 1904 and provides an insight into Ireland and its people, although it is long and can be confusing. Other works by Joyce include *Finnegans Wake* (1939) and *Portrait of the Artist as a Young Man* (1916). Jonathan Swift (1667–1745) was Dean of St. Patrick's Cathedral in Dublin and his best known work is probably *Gulliver's Travels* (1726). If you prefer poetry, try any work by Sligo poet W. B. Yeats.
- Ireland has also produced many noted playwrights. Oscar Wilde's wit is legendary and some of his best-known plays include *The Importance of Being Earnest* (1899) and *An Ideal Husband* (1899). George Bernard Shaw, who won the Nobel Prize for Literature in 1925, wrote *Pygmalion*, and the best-known play by Samuel Beckett (1906–89) is the absurdist *Waiting for Godot*.
- Ireland has also produced its fair share of women writers. Novelist Edna O'Brien's trilogy of *The Country Girls* (1960), *The Lonely Girl* (1962) and *Girls in their Married Bliss* (1964), paints a picture of life in the countryside of West Ireland. Iris Murdoch (1919–99) won the Booker Prize for her novel *The Sea, The Sea* (1978).
- For something more recent, try a collection of poems by County Derry poet Seamus Heaney, (who won the Nobel Prize for Literature in 1995), such as *The Spirit Level* (1996). Two of Roddy Doyle's novels *The Commitments* (1987) and *The Van* (1991), which are set in working class Dublin, have been made into films. Frank McCourt's gritty depiction of his childhood in Limerick in his novel *Angela's Ashes* (1996), won him a Pulitzer Prize, and the book was made into a film in 1999. If you prefer travel writing, read County Waterford-born Dervla Murphy's account of her journeys around Northern Ireland by bicycle, *A Place Apart* (1980).

FILMS

- Several recent films have been made about well-known Irish figures. *Michael Collins* (1996) depicts his cause, an independent Ireland. *Nora* (2000) is about James Joyce and his wife Nora's exile in Italy, with Ewan McGregor in the title role. *Iris* (2001) is about the writer Iris Murdoch's life, focusing on her loving relationship with her husband John Bayley.
- For a whimsical look at Irish ingenuity, watch *Waking Ned* (1998). It's the story of a village's attempt to collect the lottery winnings of a man who had a winning lottery ticket, but died before he could collect his money. For lovers of soul music *The Commitments* (1991) is a must. It's the tale of a group of working class Dubliners who decide to form a band.
- The Troubles in Northern Ireland are the background to *Some Mother's Son* (1996), which stars Helen Mirren. *In the Name of the Father* (1993), which stars Daniel Day Lewis, tells the true story of the perpetrators of an IRA bombing in England.
- Though not about Ireland, *Braveheart* (1994) and *Saving Private Ryan* (1997) merit a mention as they were both filmed on the island. To find out where a movie was filmed, look up www.movie-locations.com
- Many Irish actors have made it big in Hollywood. A few well-known names are Pierce Brosnan (James Bond movies), Liam Neeson (*Rob Roy, Schindler's List*), Colin Farrell (*Minority Report*) and Gabriel Byrne (*The Usual Suspects*).
- There are film festivals in Cork (October), Galway (July), Dublin (March) and Belfast (March; see www.belfastfilmfestival.org).

A scene from Gulliver's Travels *on a Dublin plaque recalls author Jonathan Swift*

USEFUL WEBSITES

The internet is invaluable for pre-departure planning; the websites below are a good place to start.

AIR TRAVEL
www.aer-rianta.com
Information on Dublin, Cork and Shannon airports
www.aerlingus.com
www.ryanair.com
www.aerarann.com
www.easyjet.com

BUSES, TRAINS AND FERRIES
www.dublinbus.ie Timetables and prices for Dublin buses
www.buseireann.ie Long-distance buses in the Republic
www.irishrail.ie Train timetable and fares for the Republic
www.irishferries.com Ferries to Ireland
www.translink.co.uk
Information on all public transport in Northern Ireland

CYCLING
www.ctc.org.uk Cyclists' Touring Club of Northern Ireland
www.sustrans.org.uk Maps of Northern Ireland
www.cyclingsafaris.com
Accompanied cycling holidays

DRIVING
www.aaroadwatch.ie Up to the minute traffic reports
www.aaireland.ie Automobile Association of Ireland
www.trafficwatchni.com Traffic bulletins for Northern Ireland, particularly Belfast
www.theAA.com Become a member, buy motor insurance or order maps, atlases and travel guides

GENEALOGY
www.groireland.ie Office of the Registrar General for information on births, deaths and marriages in the Republic
http://proni.nics.gov.uk Public Records Office, for help in tracing ancestry in Northern Ireland
www.nli.ie For the National Library's Genealogy Service
www.irishgenealogy.ie The origins of Irish surnames

GENERAL INFORMATION
www.anpost.ie The site for the postal service in the Republic.
www.postoffice.co.uk Postal services in Northern Ireland/UK
www.goldenpages.ie Business directory for the Republic
www.yell.com Yellow Pages Business directory for Northern Ireland

HERITAGE
www.nationaltrust.org.uk The Trust owns many grand houses and gardens in Northern Ireland
www.heritageireland.ie Dúchas, Irish heritage service responsible for protecting historic sites, castles, houses and national parks
www.heritagetowns.com A directory of Heritage Towns, listed for their architecture

HORSE DRAWN CARAVANS
www.horsedrawn.in-ireland.net
www.horsedrawncaravans.com

NEWS AND SPORT
www.ireland.com Website for *The Irish Times* newspaper
www.belfasttelegraph.co.uk
Belfast's evening newspaper
www.bbc.co.uk News, weather reports and TV listings for all BBC TV channels and radio stations

REGIONAL TOURIST BOARDS
www.southeastireland.com
www.corkkerry.ie
www.irelandwest.ie
www.irelandnorthwest.ie
www.eastcoastmidlandsireland.com
www.shannonregiontourism.ie
www.derryvisitor.com
www.kingdomsofdown.com
www.causewaycoastandglens.com
www.fermanaghlakelands.com

TOURIST INFORMATION
www.failteireland.ie
www.tourismireland.com
www.visitdublin.ie
www.gotobelfast.com
www.discovernorthernireland.com

VISITORS WITH DISABILITIES
www.nda.ie National Disability Authority in the Republic of Ireland
www.disabilityaction.org
Information for Northern Ireland

WALKING
www.irelandwalkingcycling.com
www.walkireland.ie

WEATHER
www.met.ie
www.metoffice.com

KEY SIGHTS QUICK WEBSITE FINDER

SIGHT/TOWN	WEBSITE	PAGE
Aran Islands	www.visitaranislands.com	131
Ards Peninsula and Strangford Lough	www.northdown.gov.uk	162–163
Belfast	www.gotobelfast.com	166–173
Blarney Castle	www.blarneycastle.ie	111
Brú na Bóinne	www.meathtourism.ie	90–93
Bunratty	www.shannonheritagetrade.com	132
The Burren	www.theburrencentre.ie	134–135
Connemara	www.westireland.travel.ie	138–141
Cork	www.cork-guide.ie	112–113
Derry	www.derryvisitor.com	176
Dingle Peninsula	www.dingle-peninsula.ie	116–119
Dublin Castle	www.dublincastle.ie	70–71
Galway	www.irelandwest.ie	142
Kildare	www.kildare.ie/tourism	98–99
Kilkenny	www.southeastireland.com	100–101
Killarney	www.killarney.ie	120–121
Limerick	www.limerick.com	123
Lough Erne	www.fermanagh-online.com	182–183
National Museum	www.museum.ie	80–81
Powerscourt	www.powerscourt.ie	104–105
Sligo	www.irelandnorthwest.ie	146–147
Strokestown Park and Famine Museum	www.strokestownpark.ie	158–159
Trinity College Library	www.tcd.ie/library/	84–86
Ulster American Folk Park	www.folkpark.com	188
Waterford	www.waterfordtourism.org	126–127

IRISH LANGUAGE

Irish is the official first language of the Republic of Ireland. Spoken everywhere on the island until the early 19th century, it was subsequently relegated to the fringes until its revival in the 20th century. And while English–the official second language– is the dominant tongue today, the Irish language is an important symbol of national identity. All official documents are printed in both languages, making Ireland a bilingual nation. And with the Hibernian gift of eloquence, it could also be said that nobody speaks English quite like the Irish.

A CELTIC TONGUE

Irish is the purest of the Celtic family of languages which once ranged throughout Europe. It was introduced by the first Celtic migrations to the island during prehistoric times. Irish is the correct name for the language, though it is often called Gaelic, as it is related to, but different from, Scottish Gaelic, Breton and Welsh. Old Irish is the earliest of the Northern European languages in which extensive writings still exist.

Irish bards took the language to poetic heights, and the Norman aristocracy adopted it as their own. Until the early 16th century, the country remained Irish speaking. But with the English conquests and plantations, and the ascendancy of the English ruling classes, Irish culture was systematically destroyed. English became the language of government and town, though Irish continued to be spoken in rural areas. Death and emigration during the Famine years took a heavy toll on the Irish-speaking community, and it became further associated with poverty. By 1891, more than 85 per cent of the people only spoke English.

REVIVAL

In the late 19th century, two forces spawned an Irish language revival: literature and nationalism. Writers such as W. B. Yeats and J. M. Synge found inspiration in the old Irish storytelling tradition. Douglas Hyde founded the Gaelic League in 1893 and promoted the return of Irish lessons in schools. It became associated with the rise of the republican spirit.

Today, Irish is a compulsory subject in schools in the Republic, and a requirement for university entrance. Figures vary, but some 35 per cent of adults claim to have a knowledge of Irish. English remains the official language of Northern Ireland.

THE GAELTACHT

Areas where Irish is spoken as the main tongue are called the Gaeltacht. They are largely rural regions on the western seaboard, in counties Galway, Mayo, Donegal, Cork, Kerry and pockets of Waterford, separated from each other. People from other parts of the country send their children to board with Gaeltacht families during summer holidays to learn Irish. But the Gaeltacht regions are largely remote with poor economic prospects compared to the rest of the country, and as a result young people tend to move away, so the number of Irish speakers is threatened. People in the Gaeltacht are bilingual, although the road signs are in Irish only. For visitors, these regions are a place to hear the native tongue and enjoy traditional music and culture.

PLACE NAMES

For visitors, Irish is most noticeable in place names, which are often based on ancient terms for natural features or landmarks. Here are some you are likely to come across, with their Irish root, English meaning and a relevant place name:

IRISH ROOT	ENGLISH MEANING	IRISH PLACENAMES
ar, ard	height	Ardmore, Ardgroom
áth, atha	ford	Athlone, Athy
bal, baile, ballya	town	Ballycastle, Ballyhack
beg, beag	small	Beaghmore Stone Circles, Lough Beg
carrig, carrick	rock	Carrick-on-Shannon
cashel	castle	Rock of Cashel
drom, drum	a ridge	Drombeg Stone Circle, Drumsna
dun, dún	a fort	Dundalk, Dún Laoghaire
glen, gleann	a valley	Glenveagh, Glencree
innis, ennis	island	Enniskerry, Enniscorthy
kil, kill, cil	a church	Killarney, Glencolumbkille
knock, cnoc	a hill	Knocknarea Mountain, Knockferry
lis, liss, lios	a ring fort	Listowel, Lisdoonvarna
mor, mór	big or great	Aranmore, Lismore
rath	a ring fort	Rathfarnham, Rathdrum
slieve	a mountain	Slieve Bloom, Slieve League
tra, trá, tráigh	a beach or strand	Tramore, Tralee
tul, tulagh	small hill	Tullamore, Tullynally Castle

SPEAKING IRISH

The Irish language is difficult for the beginner. Words are often pronounced quite differently from the way they are written. Most vowels are short, not long. The 'craic' is pronounced 'crack' and 'fáilte' is pronounced 'fawl-ch'. There are many unfamiliar combinations and silent letters; for example, 'bh' is usually pronounced as 'v', as in the name Siobhan ('Sh-vawn') and 'sidhe' is pronounced 'she', with the 'dh' silent. 'Si' or 'se' is pronounced as 'sh', while the combination 'gh' is pronounced as an 'h', as in Gallagher ('Gal-a-her'). To complicate matters, there are different Irish dialects and spellings in different regions.

Here are a few basic words you may find useful:

fáilte	welcome
tá/sea	yes
níl/ní hea	no
le do thoil	please
go raibh maith aguth	thank you
oscailte	open
dúnta	closed
gardaí	police
leithreas	toilet
fir	men
mná	ladies
an lár	middle of town
óstán	hotel
oifig an phoist	post office

PLANNING

GLOSSARY FOR THE US VISITOR

anticlockwise	counterclockwise
aubergine	eggplant
bank holiday	a public holiday
bill	check (at restaurant)
biscuit	cookie
bonnet	hood (car)
boot	trunk (car)
busker	street musician
caravan	house trailer or RV
car park	parking lot
carriage	car (on a train)
casualty	emergency room (hospital department)
chemist	pharmacy
chips	french fries
coach	long-distance bus
coaching inn	pubs or hotels dating from 17th–19th centuries, located on main travel routes
concessions	reduced fees for tickets, often available to students, children and elderly people
courgette	zucchini
crèche	day care
crisps	potato chips
directory enquiries	directory assistance
dual carriageway	two-lane highway
en suite	a bedroom with its own private bathroom; may also just refer to the bathroom
football	soccer
full board	a hotel tariff that includes all meals
garage	gas station
garden	yard (residential)
GP	doctor
half board	hotel tariff that includes breakfast and either lunch or dinner
handbag	purse
high street	main street
hire	rent
inland	within the UK
jelly	Jello™
jumper, jersey	sweater
junction	intersection
layby	rest stop, pull-off
level crossing	grade crossing
lorry	truck
licensed	a café or restaurant that has a license to serve alcohol (beer and wine only unless it's 'fully' licensed)
lift	elevator
main line station	a train station as opposed to an underground or subway station (although it may be served by the underground /subway)
nappy	diaper
note	paper money
off-licence	liquor store
pants	underpants (men's)
pavement	sidewalk
petrol	gas
plaster	Band-Aid or bandage
post	mail
public school	private school
pudding	dessert
purse	change purse
pushchair	stroller
return ticket	roundtrip ticket
rocket	arugula
roundabout	traffic circle or rotary
self-catering	accommodation including a kitchen
single ticket	one-way ticket
stalls	orchestra seats (in theatre)
surgery	doctor's office
tailback	traffic jam
takeaway	takeout
taxi rank	taxi stand
ten-pin bowling	bowling
tights	panty-hose
T-junction	an intersection where one road meets another at right angles (making a T shape)
toilets	restrooms
torch	flashlight
trolley	cart
trousers	pants
underpass	subway
way out	exit
windscreen	windshield (car)

IRISH FLOOR NUMBERING

In Ireland the first floor of a building is called the ground floor, and the floor above it is the first floor. So an Irish second floor is a US third floor, and so on. This is something to watch for in museums and galleries in particular.

PILGRIMAGE SITES IN IRELAND

Pilgrimage to Ireland has been in high profile since the opening of Knock's international airport in 1986 to deal with the massive annual influx to the shrine at the town of Knock. This amazing County Mayo site draws a massive 1.5 million (approximately) pilgrims every year. The story began on the evening of 21 August 1879, when 15 people witnessed for 2 hours a clear and detailed apparition on the gable of the church featuring the Virgin, St. John the Evangelist and St. Joseph. As a result, this is now an international pilgrimage site, has a new Church of Our Lady, Queen of Ireland (dedicated 1976) with a capacity for 10,000 people, and was visited by Pope John Paul II in 1979.

There is evidence of pilgrimage to Irish religious sites since at least the 12th century, when a European knight called Owen is known to have visited St. Patrick's Purgatory on an island in Lough Derg, County Donegal. Here devout pilgrims—about 3,000 every year—go through an austere regime of fasting and barefoot penance over three days at the place St. Patrick is said to have visited for prayer more than 400 times.

Croagh Patrick mountain (▷ 136) in County Mayo, is where St. Patrick is said to have fasted for 40 days and nights in AD441. Thousands of people come to climb to the top—many in bare feet—during the summer, but the big day is the last Sunday in July, when more than 20,000 make the ascent.

KEY FIGURES IN IRISH LITERATURE

Samuel Beckett (1906–89)
Born in Foxrock, near Dublin, Beckett was one of the late 20th century's most influential dramatists. He won the Nobel Prize for Literature in 1969, one of four Irish writers to do so. His best-known work is *Waiting for Godot*, summed up by one critic as 'nothing happens, twice'. Like James Joyce (for whom he once worked as secretary), he achieved his fame in exile, in Beckett's case in Paris, where he is buried.

Brendan Behan (1923–64)
Dublin-born and as famous for his personal life as for his writing, Behan joined the IRA at the age of 13. His later experiences in reform school and prison produced work such as *Borstal Boy* and *The Quare Fellow*.

Roddy Doyle (1958–)
Probably the most prominent of contemporary Irish writers, Doyle's background growing up in, and teaching in, one of the poorer parts of Dublin helped to shape novels such as *The Commitments* (later filmed by Alan Parker) and *Paddy Clarke Ha Ha Ha*, which won the prestigious British Booker Prize for Fiction.

Séamus Heaney (1939–)
Born in County Londonderry, the son of a farmer, Heaney is a well-liked and well-respected poet. He lectured at Queen's College, Belfast, before achieving the highest accolade for his craft, when he received the Nobel Prize for Literature, in 1995. He has also taught at Oxford and at Harvard. His work often deals in subtle ways with his rural childhood, Irish mythology and the modern political situation in Ireland.

James Joyce (1882–1941)
Joyce was born in Dublin but wrote his greatest works when he was living in self-imposed exile, in Switzerland, Italy and France. He first achieved fame with his 1916 novel, *A Portrait of the Artist as a Young Man*, a semi-autobiographical account of his early life in Dublin, but it was the two later monumental works which confirmed his place as one of the leading novelists of the 20th century: *Ulysses* (1922) and *Finnegans Wake* (1939).

Edna O'Brien (1932–)
Born in County Clare, Edna O'Brien qualified as a pharmacist in Dublin. Her first novel *The Country Girls*, published in 1960 after she had moved to London, became the first in a trilogy following the lives of two Irish girls. The trilogy was among several of her books that were banned in Ireland for their sexually explicit passages. She has also produced a play about Virginia Woolf (1981), a biography of James Joyce (1999) and the non-fiction *Mother Ireland* (1976). She has won several awards, such as the Kingsley Amis Award for fiction in 1962 and the Los Angeles Times Book Prize in 1990.

George Bernard Shaw (1856–1950)
Dublin-born Nobel Prizewinner (in 1925), Shaw was one of those writers seemingly blessed with boundless energy. He wrote more than 50 plays for the stage, thousands of letters, a few novels, a vast amount of journalism and became regularly embroiled in political matters. He was an early vegetarian, a campaigner for women's rights, a naturist and an advocate for, among many other things, the simplification of English spelling. His plays include *Mrs Warren's Profession*, *Arms and the Man*, *Man and Superman*. His best-known work, *Pygmalion* was adapted into the stage and film musical, *My Fair Lady*.

Bram Stoker (1847–1912)
Born in Dublin, Stoker worked for a time as a civil servant at Dublin Castle, and only turned to writing in later life, though it was a long-held dream. He is best known for *Dracula* (1897). Less well known is his volume of children's fairy tales, *Under the Sunset* (1882) and several other works of fiction that failed to match *Dracula* in popularity.

Jonathan Swift (1667–1745)
Like Oscar Wilde two centuries later, Swift was born in Dublin, studied at Trinity College and went on to outrage society—though not for quite the same reasons. Swift came from an eminently respectable family, and after an English education he returned to Dublin and took holy orders. He also began writing, and became known as one of the sharpest satirists of his day. His suggestion that the Irish poor sell their children as food to the rich was not always seen in the savage way it was intended. His great work, *Gulliver's Travels*, was another satire on the society of his time. In 1713 he became Dean of St. Patrick's Cathedral, where he is buried.

Oscar Wilde (1854–1900)
Wilde was born in Dublin and studied there at Trinity College, before moving to Oxford in England, where his Bohemian nature and his literary talents began to manifest themselves. He is as much remembered today for his lifestyle and his wit ('I have nothing to declare except my genius,' he is said to have told a New York immigration official) as his writing, but he wrote several successful plays, including *Lady Windermere's Fan* (1892), *A Woman of No Importance* (1893) and *The Importance of Being Earnest* (1895), as well as his only novel, *The Picture of Dorian Gray* (1891). He was persecuted and jailed for his homosexuality, and died in exile in Paris.

W. B. Yeats (1865–1939)
Yeats was the first Irish writer to win the Nobel Prize for Literature, in 1923, and one of the many fine writers to have been born in Dublin. His interest in philosophy, religion, Irish legends and the occult influenced his poetry enormously. He also wrote plays and short stories. He was a great promoter of Irish literature, and was manager of the Abbey Theatre for several years, as well as helping found the theatre and Dublin's National Literary Society. Some of his best-known poems include *Easter 1916*, about the Easter uprising, *The Lake Isle of Innisfree* and *Under Ben Bulben*. The poet is buried in a graveyard in the shade of Ben Bulben mountain, in County Sligo, where he spent much of his childhood.

TRACING YOUR ANCESTORS

After the mass exodus of the Famine years, the Irish diaspora spread throughout the world. But emigrant ties to the old country have always remained strong, passing down the generations to the present day. People of Irish descent are proud of their roots—witness the exuberant St. Patrick's Day celebrations in America—often to the point of nostalgia, and it's no wonder that tracing ancestors has become a popular pursuit among visitors to Ireland.

STARTING YOUR SEARCH

Every Irish person is descended from an old family sept, or clan, and even if you can't go further back than your grandfather, it's fun to learn the archaic spelling of your family name and whether your ancient kin were bards, warriors or high kings. Many books and websites can tell you the regions where particular names were prevalent. However, you will need to know more than your surname if you're serious about tracing your roots. Do some basic research at home before your visit, so you can make the most of your time in Ireland.

First, pinpoint where your ancestors lived, not only the county but preferably the name of the parish or townland (an ancient land division, unique to Ireland, and now the smallest recognized sub-division). Build up a profile of each ancestor you want to trace: the year he or she emigrated, the age, marital status, names of spouse (including maiden name), any children, and their port of arrival. Knowing their religion and occupation can also be useful in deciding the parish registers, directories and legal records to consult. If you can't find out from relatives or family records, you can search various public records such as marriage and death records or passenger lists.

PLANNING

RESEARCH IN IRELAND

In Ireland, a good place to start is the Genealogical Office in the National Library in Dublin (tel: 01 603 0200; www.nli.ie). Staff here can help you to access the library's many information sources, including Catholic parish registers, land valuation records, estate records, newspapers, and trade and social directories. The service is free and especially helpful for beginners. There is also a list of genealogists who will undertake research for a fee. The Genealogy Service is open Monday to Friday 10am–4.45pm and Saturday 10am–12.30pm. No appointment is necessary.

Every county has a genealogical or Heritage Centre. These are listed on www.irishroots.net. Although the available data and search facilities vary, these places should be able to help you access parish rosters and other local records. General advice is usually given free, but professional researchers will charge a fee for their services, so always ask before you begin a search. The Irish Tourist Board publishes a booklet, available at tourist offices, listing resources for tracing ancestors in Ireland. To trace ancestors in Northern Ireland, contact the Public Record Office (tel: 028 9025 5905; http://proni.nics.gov.uk). Admission is free and the website gives advice on using its records to trace your family tree. The Centre for Migration Studies at the Ulster American Folk Park (▷ 188, tel 028 8225 6315; www.qub.ac.uk/cms/) is another excellent resource. Its Irish Emigration Database has primary source documents on emigration to North America, including letters, newspaper articles and family papers as well as records.

Unfortunately many census records and Church of Ireland parish registers were destroyed when the national public records office in Dublin was burned in 1922. But many Roman Catholic parish registers have survived, as have other sources. The Office of the Registrar General (tel: 01 635 4000; www.groireland.ie) is the central archive for records of births, marriages and deaths in the Republic. Check online for samples of records held and how to read them. You can also search records in the National Archives (tel 01 407 2300; www.nationalarchives.ie). In Northern Ireland, contact the General Register Office (tel: 028 9025 2000). In addition to civil records, clues can be found in census, church and property records.

ANCESTOR HUNTING ON THE WEB

With the development of the internet, genealogical research has become infinitely easier and more accessible. Many types of public records are now available online, and there are a number of websites which offer advice on how to trace your ancestors. They also have links to sources in your home country where you can access data and start your background research. Many of these services are free. The following is a list of useful websites to get you started:

www.genuki.org.uk
This self-styled virtual reference library has excellent advice for beginners in how to get started in researching your family history; it gives recommended publications, books and other sources for tracing your Irish roots from abroad.

www.ireland.com/ancestor
Part of *The Irish Times* website, this site has basic surname and ancestor information to whet your appetite, and for a fee you can access their database searches.

www.genealogy.com
A wealth of practical articles on researching your family history, some specific to Irish ancestry; also free online lessons in tracing your ancestors.

www.genealogy.about.com/cs/ireland/
Useful site with online Ireland databases, articles, tips, lessons and documents for tracing your Irish ancestors.

www.familysearch.org
The Church of Latter Day Saints in Salt Lake City, Utah, keeps the largest family history library in the world; the website gives advice on searching their vast collection of records.

http://genealogy.allinfoabout.com/countries/ireland.html
Information and links to many other useful websites.

www.ancestry.com
Online collection of US and UK databases including passenger and immigration lists, census data, newspapers, periodicals, civil and other records.

www.irelandseye.com/articles/features/tracing.shtm
Good advice on beginning your genealogical research.

Giant's Causeway
Coleraine
Londonderry/ Derry
Glens of Antrim
Strabane
Larne
Ballymena
NORTHERN IRELAND
Antrim
Newtownabbey
Donegal
Ulster American Folk Park
Omagh
BELFAST 172-173
Bangor
Lower Lough Erne
Lisburn
Mount Stewart
Portadown
Strangford Lough
Ards Peninsula
Enniskillen
Armagh
Sligo
Upper Lough Erne
346-347
348-349
Downpatrick
Ballina
Newry
Achill Island
Dundalk
Castlebar
Strokestown Park & Famine Museum
Brú na Bóinne
Drogheda
Connemara
Mullingar
Navan
REPUBLIC OF IRELAND
Athlone
DUBLIN 66-67
Galway
Clonmacnoise
Dún Laoghaire
Aran Islands
The Burren
Birr
Kildare
Powerscourt
Portlaoise
Ennis
Glendalough
Wicklow
Bunratty Castle & Folk Park
Shannon
Carlow
Arklow
Limerick
350-351
Adare
Kilkenny
352-353
Enniscorthy
Rock of Cashel
Dingle Peninsula
Tralee
Wexford
Clonmel
Mallow
Waterford
Killarney
Blarney Castle
Cork
Cobh
Bantry House

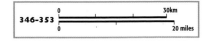

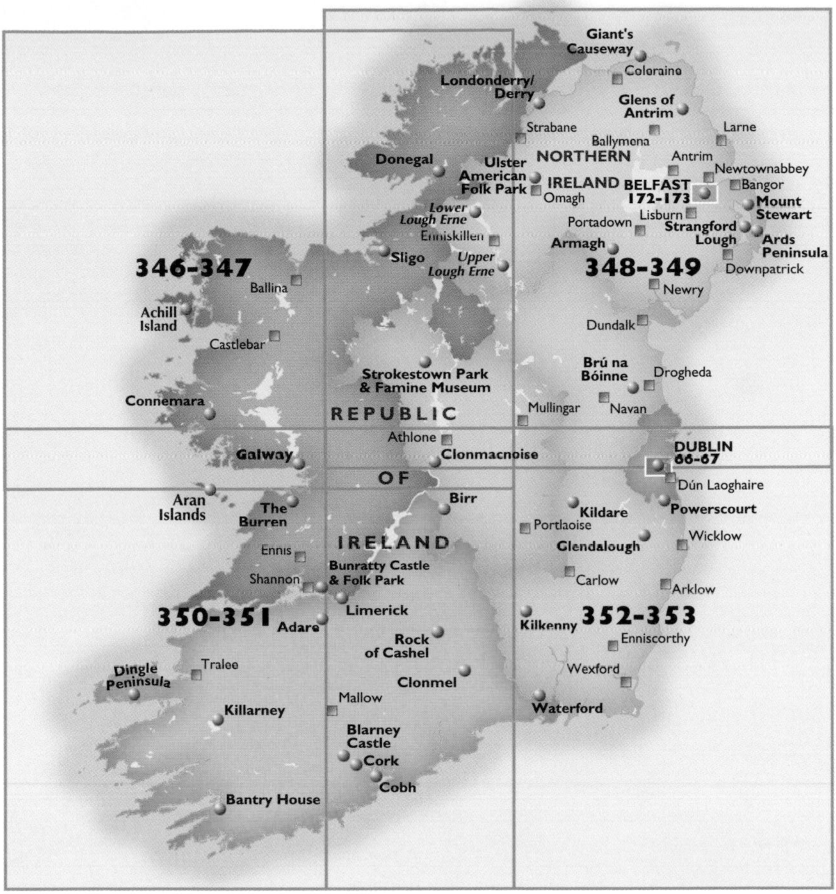

- Toll motorway (Turnpike)
- Motorway (Expressway)
- Motorway junction with and without number
- Main road
- Other road
- Railway
- International boundary
- County boundary
- City / Town
- Built-up area
- National park
- Featured place of interest
- Airport
- 621 Height in metres
- Viewpoint

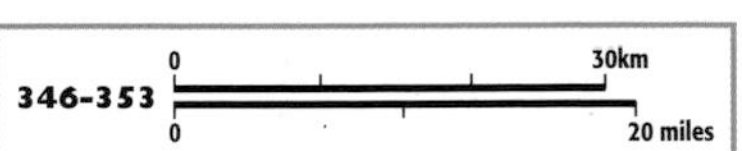

Maps

A
B
C
1
2
3
4
5
Erris Head
Broad Haven
Mullet Peninsula
Belmullet
Béal an Mhuirthead
R314
Bunnahowen
Carrowmore Lake
Inishkea North
R313
Bangor Erris
Inishkea South
719
Duvillaun More
Blacksod Bay
671
Nephin Beg Mountains
MAYO
Achill Head
Slievemore
N59
R319
Keel
Achill Island
Lough Feeagh
Mulrany
Newport
Clare Island
Clew Bay
Westport
762
Louisburgh
R335
Croagh Patrick
Inishturk
Caher Island
Inishbofin
R335
Killary Harbour
N59
673
Inishshark
Leenaun
Letterfrack
Connemara National Park
R344
R336
Clifden
Cornamona
Mannin Bay
Connemara
Ballyconneely
R341
N59
R342
Slyne Head
Roundstone
R340
Glinsk
Glinsce
R340
R336
Croaghnakeela Island
Kilkieran
Gorumna Island
R336
350
Inishmore

D
E
Tory Island
Tory Sound
Fanad Head
Horn Head
1
Rosapenna
Dunfanaghy
Bloody Foreland
N56
Carrickart
Carraig Airt
R245
Gola Island
Creeslough
Milford
Bunbeg
752
Mount Errigal
R251
Donegal International
Aran Island/ Arranmore
Kilmacrenan
Crolly
Croithli
Glenveagh National Park
Dungloe
An Clochán Liath
R252
R254
Letterkenny
N56
Gweebarra Bay
R250
R252
Raphoe
R236
R253
Stranorlar
N15
R261
Glenties
676
Ardara
R262
DONEGAL
Ballybofey
Rossan Point
Glencolumbkille
Lough Eask
N15
2
Castlederg
Malin More
Carrick
An Charraig
N56
595
Slieve League
Killybegs
Mount Charles
Donegal
Lough Derg
B50
Dunkineely
B72
R232
Ballintra
St John's Point
Donegal Bay
Pettigo
B4
Kesh
Ballyshannon
Bundoran
A47
Lower Lough Erne
A35
Belleek Pottery
Tully Castle
Inishmurray
N15
Kinlough
Cliffony
B52
Derrygonnelly
A46
Grange
Lough Melvin
Garrison
526
Downpatrick Head
Lissadell House
Benbulbin
FERMANAGH
Drumcliff
R280
R282
R281
Ballycastle
Rosses Point
N16
B52
Enniskillen
Killala Bay
Easky
Sligo Bay
Manorhamilton
Strandhill
Belcoo
A4
Dromore West
Sligo
Blacklion
Lisbellaw
R314
R297
Carrowmore Neolithic Cemetery
R286
348
A32
3
Inishcrone
Lough Gill
Marble Arch Caves
Killala
Skreen Churchyard
N59
Dromahair
Florence Court
A509
Upper Lough Erne
R315
R207
R206
Ballysadare
Dowra
Ox Mountains
Collooney
R290
SLIGO
Swanlinbar
Ballina
Drumkeeran
R280
Crossmolina
Bunnyconnellan
R293
R284
R200
N17
N4
R294
Ballymote
Lough Allen
R207
Lough Conn
R310
N26
Tobercurry
Lough Arrow
R202
N87
R226
Ballyfarnan
R205
R295
Drumshanbo
Ballinamore
Foxford
Curry
R294
R293
Keadew
Lough Key
R208
R199
R315
N58
Ballinafad
R204
Charlestown
Lough Key Forest Park
Fenagh
Carracastle
R294
Boyle
Leitrim
LEITRIM
Killashandra
Lough Cullin
Swinford
Lough Gara
R361
Carrick-on-Shannon
R201
Knock International
N5
Carrigallen
Turlough
N5
R320
R325
Ballaghaderreen
Mohill
N61
R368
R198
Castlebar
Kiltamagh
Frenchpark
N4
Arvagh
R322
Kilkelly
Lough Boderg
N84
R324
Loughglinn
R369
Elphin
Farnaght
N83
N17
R293
Lough Gowna
Balla
N60
Knock
Clonalis House
R361
ROSCOMMON
Roosky
Ballyhean
R323
Ballyhaunis
Castlerea
Tulsk
Strokestown Park & Famine Museum
Drumlish
4
Claremorris
N60
N60
Scramoge
Newtown Forbes
Ballinlough
R367
Castleplunket
Lough Carra
R331
R327
Ballintober
R368
N5
Cloondara
Longford
Lisryan
Ballymoe
R371
N4
Ballindine
R360
N60
R364
N61
N63
Killashee
R393
Edgeworthstown
R328
Ballinrobe
LONGFORD
Kilmaine
N17
Dunmore
Glenamaddy
Fuerty
Roscommon
Rathowen
Neale
N83
R362
R392
Keenagh
Cong
Shrule
R328
R364
Athleague
Knockcroghery
R393
R332
R362
N61
Ballymahon
Lough Corrib
R334
R333
Tuam
Ballygar
R357
Lough Ree
R392
Moyvore
R322
R363
N55
Tang
Headford
Ballymore
N63
Mount Bellew
Dysart
Curraghboy
Glassan
R390
Oughterard
N84
GALWAY
Caltra
R363
WESTMEATH
R347
R339
Athlone
Moate
N6
Monivea
Ahascragh
R358
N59
R357
N62
N80
R359
N6
N17
Galway
R348
Doon
5
Galway
Athenry
Kilconnell
Ballinasloe
Clonmacnoise
R348
351
R436
Ballycumber
Oranmore
Suck
Shannonbridge
Grand Canal
R350
R355
347
Spiddle
An Spidéal
N6
N6
Clonfert Cathedral
Blackwater Bog
Charleville Forest Castle
Craughwell
D
E
R357
Kilcolgan

D
E
F
I
2
3
4
5
Malin Head
Tory Island
Fanad Head
Horn Head
Tory Sound
Malin
Culdaff
Clonmany
Carndonagh
Inishowen
Dunfanaghy
Rosapenna
Bloody Foreland
N56
Carrickart
Carraig Airt
R245
R246
Lough Swilly
R238
R240
Moville
Gola Island
Creeslough
Buncrana
Carrowkeel
Milford
Rathmullan
Lough Foyle
Bunbeg
Donegal
752
Mount Errigal
R251
Muff
City of Derry
Aran Island
Arainn Mhór
Kilmacrenan
Rathmelton
Crolly
Croithlí
Glenveagh National Park
Eglinton
N13
A2
Dungloe
An Clochán Liath
Londonderry/ Derry
NessWood Country Park
R252
R254
Letterkenny
N14
New Buildings
N56
Gweebarra Bay
R250
Raphoe
Claudy
A6
B48
B49
R236
Lifford
President Wilson Ancestral Home
B44
R253
Stranorlar
N15
Strabane
Sperrin Mountains
Ardara
R261
Glenties
676
Ballybofey
Plumbridge
DONEGAL
R262
Sion Mills
B47
Glencolumbkille
Gleann Cholm Cille
Lough Eask
Castlederg
Newtownstewart
Malin More
Carrick
An Charraig
B164
Gortin
595
Mount Charles
Donegal
Ulster History Park
B46
Killybegs
Slieve League
Lough Derg
B50
B84
Ulster American Folk Park
A5
B48
Fernagh Ceilidh House
Dunkineely
B72
Omagh
B4
R232
Drumquin
St John's Point
Carrickmore
Ballintra
Donegal Bay
Pettigo
B4
Beragh
A32
Kesh
Ballyshannon
Bundoran
Dromore
Seskinore
A47
TYRONE
Lower Lough Erne
A35
A32
B83
A5
Belleek Pottery
B52
Tully Castle
Irvinestown
Fintona
Inishmurray
N15
Kinlough
Ballygawley
Grange
Cliffony
Garrison
Knockmany Chambered Cairn
Lough Melvin
Derrygonnelly
A46
B46
Augher
526
Ballinamallard
B122
Clogher
Lissadell House
Benbulbin
FERMANAGH
Drumcliff
R280
R282
R281
B107
Aughnacloy
Rosses Point
Enniskillen
Castle Coole
A4
Sligo Bay
N16
B52
Fivemiletown
Manorhamilton
Dromore West
Strandhill
Belcoo
A4
Lisbellaw
Emyvale
Sligo
347
R280
Blacklion
Maguiresbridge
Carrowmore Neolithic Cemetery
Lough Gill
B514
R186
Skreen
Marble Arch Caves
A32
Dromahair
R207
Florence Court
A509
Upper Lough Erne
Lisnaskea
Rosslea
Monaghan
Ballysadare
R206
Collooney
R290
Dowra
Swanlinbar
A34
Derrylin
Smithborough
R189
R188
SLIGO
Clones
Drumkeeran
R284
R280
R200
Newtownbutler
N4
R293
Lough Allen
Crom Estate
MONAGHAN
N17
Ballymote
R207
R202
N87
Newbliss
Lough Arrow
Belturbet
Rockcorry
Tobercurry
R296
Ballyfarnan
N3
N54
R293
R295
Drumshanbo
Ballinamore
R205
Cootehill
Curry
R294
Keadew
Lough Key
R208
R199
Butler's Bridge
Ballinafad
Ballyhaise
Charlestown
Lough Key Forest Park
R204
R192
Carracastle
R294
Boyle
Fenagh
Killashandra
R188
R165
Lough Gara
Leitrim
LEITRIM
N5
R361
Carrick-on-Shannon
R201
Carrigallen
Cavan
R191
R325
Ballaghaderreen
Stradone
N61
CAVAN
R368
Mohill
R165
Frenchpark
N4
Lough Boderg
R198
Arvagh
Bellananagh
Kilkelly
Baillieborough
Loughglinn
R369
Elphin
Farnaght
Lough Gowna
R154
Kilnaleck
N83
R293
N55
R361
ROSCOMMON
Roosky
R194
Ballyjamesduff
Clonalis House
Strokestown Park & Famine Museum
Drumlish
Ballyhaunis
Castlerea
Tulsk
Virginia
R154
Lough Ramor
Ballinalee
Scramoge
Ballinlough
N60
Newtown Forbes
R367
Castleplunket
Granard
R394
Oldcastle
N3
R368
N5
Loughcrew Cairns
Cloondara
Longford
Lisryan
R396
Ballymoe
Ballintober
R371
N4
R195
R360
N60
N61
N63
Killashee
Edgeworthstown
Tullynally Castle
Crossakeel
R364
R393
Fore
LONGFORD
Lough Derravaragh
Castlepollard
Dunmore
Glenamaddy
Fuerty
Rathowen
Clonmellon
R362
Roscommon
R392
Athboy
N83
R328
Keenagh
R395
N51
R364
Athleague
Knockcroghery
R393
Crookenwood
Delvin
Lough Owel
N52
Ballygar
R357
R362
Ballymahon
R392
Moyvore
N61
Lough Ree
Mullingar
Ballivor
R363
N55
Tang
Ballymore
N4
N63
Mount Bellew
Curraghboy
Glassan
R390
Killucan
GALWAY
Caltra
Dysart
R363
R391
Belvedere House
R400
Kinnegad
R161
R347
R339
WESTMEATH
Lough Ennell
N52
N6
Athlone
Moniyea
Ahascragh
R358
Moate
N6
Tyrrellspass
R359
R357
N6
N62
N80
352
R400
Kilconnell
R348
Ballinasloe
Clonmacnoise
Edenderry

G
H
1
2
3
4
5
Rathlin Island
Inishowen Head
Giant's Causeway
White Park Bay
Murlough Bay
Portrush
Portstewart
Castlerock
Bushmills Distillery
Ballycastle
Downhill Estate
Coleraine
Dervock
Armoy
Limavady
Roe Valley Country Park
Ballymoney
Glens of Antrim
Cushendall
Red Bay
Garron Point
Dunloy
Garvagh
Rasharkin
Carnlough
Glenarm
Dungiven
Kilrea
ANTRIM
Swatragh
Culleybackey
Broughshane
Ballygalley
Ballymena
Maghera
Larne
Island Magee
LONDONDERRY
Ahoghill
Moorfields
Tobermore
Draperstown
Bellaghy
Kells
Ballynure
Ballycarry
Whitehead
Randalstown
Magherafelt
Ballyclare
Moneymore
Ballyronan
Carrickfergus
Antrim
Newtownabbey
Springhill
Coagh
Belfast International
Bangor
Cookstown
Ardboe High Cross
Ulster Folk & Transport Museum
Donaghadee
Crumlin
Belfast City
Lough Neagh
Dunmurry
Newtownards
Stewartstown
Coalisland
Irish Linen Centre & Lisburn Museum
BELFAST
Mount Stewart
Ballywalter
Dungannon
Lisburn
Carryduff
Comber
Greyabbey
Ballygowan
Ards Peninsula
Kircubbin
Moy
Lurgan
Hillsborough
Saintfield
Strangford Lough
Portavogie
Ardress House
Craigavon
The Argory
Benburb
Portadown
Rowallane Garden
Ballynahinch
Killyleagh
Dromore
Armagh
Gilford
Portaferry
Caledon
Tandragee
Banbridge
DOWN
Castle Ward
Strangford
Glaslough
Gosford Castle & Forest Park
Loughbrickland
Inch Abbey
Saul
Struell Wells
Middletown
Markethill
Castlewellan Forest Park
Clough
Downpatrick
Lecale Peninsula
Keady
ARMAGH
Rathfriland
Castlewellan
Dundrum
Ardglass
Killough
St John's Point
Newtownhamilton
Hilltown
Newcastle
Newry
Mourne Mountains
Castleblayney
Slieve Gullion Forest Park
Warrenpoint
Annalong
Crossmaglen
Rostrevor
Kilkeel
Kilcurry
Carlingford
Dundalk
Carrickmacross
Dundalk Bay
Kingscourt
LOUTH
Castlebellingham
Ardee
Dunleer
Dunany Point
Monasterboice
Collon
Termonfeckin
Mellifont Abbey
Kilberry
Slane
Brú na Bóinne
Drogheda
Navan
Julianstown
Duleek
M1 Toll
Bective Abbey
Balbriggan
Boyne
Skerries
Naul
Tara
Garristown
Dunshaughlin
Lusk
Rush
Rathmolyon
Ratoath
Ashbourne
Lambay Island
Summerhill
Donabate
Swords
Enfield
Dublin
Malahide Castle
Kilcock
Dunboyne
Portmarnock
Maynooth
Leixlip
Toll
Dollymount Strand
Howth Head
353
KILDARE

A
B
C
5
6
7
8
9
346
Glinsk
Glinsce
R340
R336
Kilkieran
Gorumna Island
Inishmore
Aran Islands
Inishmaan
Inisheer
South Sound
Cliffs of Moher
Liscannor
Hags Head
Mal Bay
Milltown Malbay
Mutton Island
Donegal Point
Doonbeg
Cooraclare
Kilkee
N67
R483
R487
Kilrush
Killimer
Loop Head
Tarbert
R551
Ballylongford
Ballybunion
R553
R552
Ballyduff
Kerry Head
Causeway
Listowel
Ballyheige
R555
Ardfert Cathedral
R556
N69
Ballyheige Bay
Abbeyfeale
Rough Point
Abbeydorney
357
Ardfert
Brandon Bay
Tralee Bay
Tralee
N21
950
Brandon Mountain
824
Beenoskee
R560
Camp
852
Baurtregaun
Castleisland
Sybil Point
R559
Dingle Peninsula
N86
N70
N23
R577
Anascaul
R561
Castlemaine
Farranfore
Scartaglin
Great Blasket Island
Dingle
An Daingean
Inch
Milltown
Kerry County
Slea Head
Killorglin
N72
R563
KERRY
Dingle Bay
Glenbeigh
Laune
Beaufort
N22
Killarney
Lough Leane
Muckross
Macgillycuddy's Reeks
1039
Carrauntoohil
Killarney National Park
Muckross Estate
837
Mangerton Mtn
Poulgorm Bridge
Doulus Head
Valencia Island
Cahersiveen
Iveragh
R565
R566
R568
Kilgarvan
Kenmare
R569
Little Skellig
Waterville
Sneem
Skellig Michael/ Great Skellig
Bolus Head
Parknasilla
R571
N71
Caherdaniel
Lauragh
705
Knockboy
R584
Kenmare River
Scariff Island
Ardgroom
Glengarriff
Beara Peninsula
R574
R575
685
Adrigole
Cod's Head
R572
Garinish Island
Bantry
Allihies
Castletown Bearhaven
Bantry House
Drimoleague
Bear Island
Bantry Bay
Sheep's Head Peninsula
R586
Durrus
Dursey Island
R591
R594
R593
Muntervary/ Sheep's Head
Dunmanus Bay
Mizen Peninsula
407
Ballydehob
R592
Toormore
Skull
Skibbereen
Goleen
Roaringwater Bay
R595
Mizen Head
Crookhaven
Baltimore
Clear Island

GALWAY
D
347
Monivea
Ahascragh
WESTMEATH
Athlone
E
Galway
Athenry
Kilconnell
Ballinasloe
Clonmacnoise
Doon
Ballycumber
Spiddle
An Spidéal
Oranmore
Craughwell
Shannonbridge
Ferbane
Charleville Forest Castle
Clonfert Cathedral
Blackwater Bog
Grand Canal
Suck
Kilcolgan
Loughrea
Eyrecourt
Cloghan
Banagher
Kinvarra
Killimor
Shannon
OFFALY
Kilcormac
Cadamstown
Coole Park
Thoor Ballylee
368
The Burren
Gort
Birr
Slieve Aughty Mountains
Portumna
Kinnitty
Lisdoonvarna
Kilmacduagh Monastic Site
Woodford
Carrigahorig
Slieve Bloom Mountains
Kilfenora
Lough Cutra
Lough Graney
Borrisokane
Shinrone
Mountrath
Corrofin
Crusheen
Feakle
Lough Derg
Roscrea
Scarriff
Mountshannon
Cloughjordan
Borris in Ossory
CLARE
Tulla
Tuamgraney
Portroe
Nenagh
Moneygall
Ennis
Craggaunowen Project
533
462
Clarecastle
Broadford
Killaloe
Ballina
Toomyvara
Rathdowney
Newmarket on Fergus
Sixmilebridge
Silvermines
Templemore
Clonmore
Templetouhy
694
Shannon
Bunratty Castle & Folk Park
Cloonlara
Borrisoleigh
Johnstown
Newport
NORTH TIPPERARY
Limerick
Thurles
Urlingford
Foynes
Cappamore
Holy Cross Abbey
Loghill
Askeaton
Patrickswell
Doon
Clonoulty
Kilmanagh
Adare
Caherconlish
Pallas Grean (New)
Ballingarry
Lough Gur Stone Age Centre
Ardagh
Rathkeale
Croom
Oola
352
Cashel
Killenaule
Callan
LIMERICK
Herbertstown
Golden
SOUTH TIPPERARY
Newcastle West
Ballingarry
Bruff
Tipperary
Kilmeedy
Bruree
Hospital
Athassel Priory
Fethard
719
Bansha
Slievenaman
Maigue
Charleville
An Ráth
Kilmallock
Galbally
919
Broadford
Ballylanders
Caher
409
Galty Mountains
Clonmel
Dromcolliher
517
Freemount
Mitchelstown Cave
Knocklofty
Carrick-on-Suir
Ardfinnan
Liscarroll
Mitchelstown
Newmarket
Buttevant
Clogheen
Knockmealdown Mountains
Kildorrery
Ballyporeen
793
792
Kanturk
Doneraile
Glanworth
727
Kilmacthomas
Castletownroche
WATERFORD
Banteer
Blackwater
Mallow
429
Fermoy
Ballyduff
Cappoquin
Lemybrien
Millstreet
Lismore
Bunmahon
Rathcormack
Conna
646
Boggeragh Mountains
Burnfort
Tallow
Dungarvan
Carriganimmy
CORK
Watergrasshill
Clashmore
Ringville
An Rinn
Blarney Castle
Jameson's Old Midleton Distillery
Dungourney
Mine Head
Macroom
Dripsey
Youghal
Midleton
Ardmore
CORK
Passage West
Ovens
Inchigeelagh
Crookstown
Fota Wildlife Park
Youghal Bay
Cork
Cloyne
Kilmichael
Ballinhassig
Ringaskiddy
Cobh
Ballycotton
Whitegate
Carrigaline
Crosshaven
Bandon
Inishannon
Dunmanway
Enniskean
Dunderrow
Belgooly
Timoleague Abbey
Kinsale
Timoleague
Ballinspittle
Clonakilty
Courtmacsherry
Ross Carbery
Old Head of Kinsale
Drombeg Stone Circle
Clonakilty Bay
Galley Head
5
6
7
8
9
D
E

D
E
F
5
6
7
8
9
348
351
352
WESTMEATH
Athlone
Monivea
Ahascragh
Kilconnell
Ballinasloe
Clonmacnoise
Shannonbridge
Doon Cross Roads
Clara
Kilbeggan
Tyrrellspass
Edenderry
Kinnegad
Ballycumber
Grand Canal
Daingean
Tullamore
Clonbullogue
Bog of Allen
Craughwell
Clonfert Cathedral
Blackwater Bog
Ferbane
Charleville Forest Castle
Killeigh
Geashill
Rathangan
Loughrea
Eyrecourt
Cloghan
Kilcormac
Banagher
Killimor
OFFALY
Cadamstown
Clonaslee
Portarlington
Thoor Ballylee
Birr
Monasterevin
Kildare
Slieve Aughty Mountains
Portumna
Kinnitty
Mountmellick
Emo Court
LAOIS
Woodford
Carrigahorig
Slieve Bloom Mountains
Portlaoise
Rock of Dunamase
Fontstown
Lough Graney
Borrisokane
Lough Derg
Shinrone
Mountrath
Stradbally
Athy
Feakle
Scarriff
Mountshannon
Roscrea
Cloughjordan
Timahoe
Ballylynan
Ballyroan
Tuamgraney
Portroe
Borris in Ossory
Abbeyleix
Heywood House Gardens
Nenagh
Moneygall
Ballycolla
Castledermot
Killaloe
Ballina
Toomyvara
Rathdowney
Ballinakill
Durrow
Clogh
Silvermines
Templemore
Clonmore
Templetouhy
Carlow
Castlecomer
Cloonlara
Borrisoleigh
Ballyragget
Freshford
Newport
NORTH TIPPERARY
Johnstown
Urlingford
Dunmore Cave
CARLOW
Bagenalstown
Muine Bheag
Thurles
KILKENNY
Holy Cross Abbey
Kilkenny
Cappamore
Doon
Pallas Grean (New)
Clonoulty
Kilmanagh
Gowran
Goresbridge
Caherconlish
Lough Gur Stone Age Centre
Rock of Cashel
Ballingarry
Croom
Oola
Killenaule
Callan
Dungarvan
Herbertstown
Cashel
SOUTH TIPPERARY
Stonyford
Graiguenamanagh
Tipperary
Golden
Jerpoint Abbey
Thomastown
Bruff
Hospital
Athassel Priory
Bruree
Bansha
Fethard
Slievenaman
Kilmaganny
Ballyhale
Kilmallock
Galbally
Caher
Ahenny High Crosses
Ballylanders
Galty Mountains
Clonmel
Rosbercon
New Ross
Mitchelstown Cave
Knocklofty
Carrick-on-Suir
Mullinavat
Glenmore
Mitchelstown
Ardfinnan
Clogheen
Mooncoin
Buttevant
Kildorrery
Ballyporeen
Knockmealdown Mountains
Waterford
Doneraile
Kilmeadan
Arthurstown
Glanworth
Kilmacthomas
Castletownroche
WATERFORD
Passage East
Ballyduff
Kill
Waterford
Fethard
Mallow
Fermoy
Cappoquin
Lemybrien
Tramore
Lismore
Bunmahon
Annestown
Dunmore East
Rathcormack
Conna
Hook Head Peninsula
Burnfort
Tallow
Dungarvan
Watergrasshill
Blackwater
Clashmore
Ringville An Rinn
Blarney Castle
Jameson's Old Midleton Distillery
Dungourney
Mine Head
Youghal
Ardmore
Midleton
Youghal Bay
CORK
Passage West
Fota Wildlife Park
Cloyne
Cork
Cobh
Ringaskiddy
Whitegate
Ballycotton
Carrigaline
Crosshaven
Inishannon
Belgooly
Kinsale
Ballinspittle
Old Head of Kinsale
Shannon
Suck
Suir
Nore
Barrow
Maigue
N6
N4
N52
N80
N62
N7
N8
N77
N78
N9
N10
N76
N24
N74
N20
N73
N72
N25
N28
N71
N65
N66
M7

349
G
H
5
6
7
8
9
Summerhill
Enfield
R156
Kilcock
Dunboyne
Swords
Donabate
Island
Malahide Castle
Portmarnock
Dollymount Strand
Howth Head
M4
Maynooth
Leixlip
Toll
KILDARE
Celbridge
Castletown House
DUBLIN
M50
Clane
Dún Laoghaire
Rathcoole
Tallaght
Sandycove
Dalkey
Sallins
N7
Killiney
Naas
Brittas
R115
R116
M11
Bray
M7
N81
Blessington
Enniskerry
Kilcullen
Pollaphuca Reservoir
Powerscourt
Kilmacanoge
Greystones
Ballymore Eustace
847
R759
R755
N11
Kilcoole
N9
Mullaghcleevaun
Dunlavin
R412
R756
Roundwood
Newtownmountkennedy
R764
Wicklow Mountains
Ashford
Mount Usher Gardens
Glendalough
Rathnew
R747
925
Laragh
Wicklow
Lugnaquillia
R755
R752
Baltinglass
Glenealy
Wicklow Head
National Park
Rathdrum
Kiltegan
WICKLOW
R750
Brittas Bay
Rathvilly
Hacketstown
R753
R752
R754
Aughrim
Avoca
R727
Mizen Head
Tullow
Tinahely
R747
Woodenbridge
Arklow
R725
Ballon
Shillelagh
R748
Carnew
Kilmichael Point
Myshall
Kildavin
R746
Gorey
Bunclody
R725
Courtown
Clohamon
N11
R746
Ballycanew
Ferns
R741
Kiltealy
Cahore Point
WEXFORD
Enniscorthy 1798 Centre
Enniscorthy
R742
R744
N11
Slaney
R730
Blackwater
Oilgate
R735
Castlebridge
Curracloe
Wexford Bay/ North Bay
Irish National Heritage Park
Wexford Wildfowl Reserve
Taghmon
Wexford
Johnstown Castle
Rosslare
R733
R738
Rosslare Harbour
Bridgetown
Duncormick
Ballyteige Bay
Kilmore Quay
Carnsore Point
Saltee Islands

Page numbers in **bold** indicate the main reference.

A

B

C

D

ACKNOWLEDGMENTS

Abbreviations for the credits are as follows:
AA = AA World Travel Library, **t** (top), **b** (bottom), **c** (centre), **l** (left), **r** (right), **bg** (background)

UNDERSTANDING IRELAND

4 AA/S McBride; **5cl** AA/S Hill; **5c** AA/G Munday; **5cr** AA/J Blandford; **6cl** Northern Ireland Tourist Board; **6c** AA/S Hill; **6cr** AA/M Diggin; **8t** AA/S Day; **8ct** AA/L Blake; **8cl** AA/M Short; **8cr** Irish National Stud and Japanese Gardens; **8bl** AA/S McBride; **8/9** AA/J Blandford; **9t** AA/P Aithie; **9cl** AA/G Munday; **9cr** AA/C Hill; **9b** AA/S McBride; **10t** Belfast Visitor and Convention Bureau; **10cl** AA/S McBride; **10ctr** AA/M Short; **10cbr** Northern Ireland Tourist Board; **10b** AA/S Day

LIVING IRELAND

11 AA/S Day; **12/3bg** AA/S Day; **12tl** AA/C Coe; **12c** AA/S Day; **12cr** AA/C Coe; **12b** Northern Ireland Tourist Board; **13tl** AA/S Day; **13c** Getty Images; **13cb** AA/S Day; **13cbr** Rex Features Ltd; **14/5bg** Belfast Visitor and Convention Bureau; **14tr** AA/S McBride; **14cl** Stockbyte; **14cr** Getty Images; **14b** AA/S McBride; **15t** Britain on View; **15cl** Northern Ireland Tourist Board; **15cr** Mayo Naturally; **16/7bg** Mayo Naturally; **16tc** AA/C Coe; **16tr** AA/C Coe; **16cl** AA/S Day; **16cr** AA/A Stonehouse; **16b** Mayo Naturally; **17ltl** Mayo Naturally; **17tl** Stockbyte; **17tc** Northern Ireland Tourist Board; **17tr** Mayo Naturally; **17rtr** Mayo Naturally; **17cl** AA/S McBride; **17cr** AA/S McBride; **17b** AA/C Coe; **18/9bg** AA/C Coe, **18l** AA/S Day; **18r** AA/C Coe; **18b** © Geray Sweeney/Corbis; **18/9** AA/C Coe; **19t** AA/C Coe; **19cl** Rex Features Ltd; **19cr** AFP/Getty Images; **20/1bg** AA/S McBride; **20tl** Dublin Theatre Festival; **20tr** AA/S McBride; **20cl** Dublin Theatre Festival; **20cr** AA/M Diggin; **20b** AA/S Day; **21tl** Hell's Kitchen; **21tr** Dublin Theatre Festival; **21cl** FSG Publicity; **21c** Dublin Theatre Festival; **21cr** Beacon Communications/20th Century Fox/The Kobal Collection; **22/3bg** AA/S Hill; **22tl** Stockbyte; **22tc** AA/S McBride; **22cl** Stockbyte; **22cr** Stockbyte; **22b** AA/C Hill; **23t** AA/S Hill; **23cl** AA/S Day; **23c** AA/S Hill; **23cr** Stockbyte; **24bg** AA/M Diggin; **24l** AA/M Diggin; **24r** Cork – European Capital City of Culture 2005

THE STORY OF IRELAND

25 AA/M Short; **26/7bg** AA/S McBride; **26cl** AA/M Diggin; **26cr** AA/C Coe; **26bl** Mayo Naturally; **26bc** Mary Evans Picture Library; **26/7** AA/M Trelawney; **27cl** AA/C Coe; **27c** Mary Evans Picture Library; **27cr** AA; **27b** AA; **28/9bg** AA; **28cl** AA; **28bl** MS 57 fol.21v The Man, symbol of St. Matthew the Evangelist, introductory page to the Gospel of St. Matthew, Irish, from Durrow, County Offaly (vellum), The Board of Trinity College, Dublin, Ireland/Bridgeman Art Library; **28br** AA; **28/9** AA/S Hill; **29cl** AA; **29c** AA/M Short; **29cr** Mary Evans Picture Library/Edwin Wallace; **29b** AA; **29br** AA/S Hill; **30/1bg** AA; **30c** AA/M Short; **30bl** AA; **30bc** AA; **30/1** AA/C Coe; **31cl** AA; **31c** AA/M Short; **31cr** AA; **31b** AA; **32/3bg** AA; **32c** AA; **32bl** AA/S Day; **32/3c** AA; **32/3b** Mary Evans Picture Library; **33cl** AA; **33c** AA; **33br** AA; **34/5bg** AA/S Day; **34c** AA/S Day; **34bl** AA/G Munday; **34/5** AA; **35cl** AA; **35c** AA/M Diggin; **35bc** AA; **35cr** AA/S Whitehorne; **35br** Mayo Naturally; **36/7bg** AA; **36c** AA/S Day; **36cr** AA; **36bl** AA/M Short; **36bc** AA/S Day; **36/7** AA; **37tl** AA/M Short; **37c** AA; **37tr** Illustrated London News; **37cb** AA/S Day; **37br** Illustrated London News; **38/9bg** AA/M Diggin; **38tr** Mary Evans Picture Library; **38c** AA/C Coe; **38cl** AA/S Whitehorne; **38b** AA/C Coe; **38/9** Mary Evans Picture Library; **39cl** Mary Evans Picture Library; **39c** AA/C Coe; **39cr** Rex Features Ltd; **39b** AA/C Coe; **40bg** AA/C Coe; **40cl** Belfast Visitor and Convention Bureau; **40cr** © Paul Mcerlane/Reuters/Corbis; **40bc** © Reuters/Corbis; **40br** AA/C Coe

ON THE MOVE

41 AA/S Whitehorne; **42** Digital Vision; **43t** Digital Vision; **43c** Digital Vision; **44t** Digital Vision; **44b** easyJet Airline Company Limited; **45t** AA/C Jones; **45c** Stena Line Ferries; **46t** AA/C Jones; **46b** AA/C Jones; **47t** Digital Vision; **47c** AA; **48** Digital Vision; **49** Digital Vision; **50t** Digital Vision; **50c** Belfast Visitor and Convention Bureau; **50b** Belfast Visitor and Convention Bureau; **51** Digital Vision; **52** Digital Vision; **53t** Digital Vision; **53c** Irish Road Signs from the Traffic Signs Manual with permission from the Department of Transport, Ireland. UK Traffic Signs © Crown Copyright. Crown Copyright material is reproduced with the permission of the Controller of HMSO and the Queen's Printer for Scotland; **54** Digital Vision; **55t** Digital Vision; **55b** Irish Rail; **56** Digital Vision; **57t** Digital Vision; **57c** Translink Trains; **58** AA/C Jones; **59t** Aer Arann; **59c** Aer Arann; **60t** AA/C Jones; **60c** AA/J Blandford; **61t** Photodisc; **61c** AA/M Diggin; **62** Irish Rail

THE SIGHTS

63 Belfast Visitor and Convention Bureau; **65ct** AA/S Day; **65c** AA/Slide File; **65cb** AA/S Whitehorne; **68tl** AA/S Day; **68tr** AA/S Day; **68b** AA/S Day; **69tl** AA/S Whitehorne; **69tr** AA/G Munday; **70t** AA/M Short; **70cl** AA/S Day; **70/1** AA/S Whitehorne; **71t** AA/Slide File; **71c** AA/M Short; **71b** The Caliph Ma'mun (813-833) Bathing, Khusrau and Shirin Khamsah by Nizami, 1529 (936 Hijra) (vellum), © The Trustees of the Chester Beatty Library, Dublin/Bridgeman Art Library; **72tl** AA/S Day; **72tr** AA/S McBride; **72b** AA/S Day; **73tl** AA/S Day; **73tr** Guinness Storehouse; **73b** Guinness Storehouse; **74tl** AA/M Short; **74tc** Hugh Lane Gallery; **74tr** Irish Museum of Modern Art, Dublin; **75tl** AA/S Day; **78tc** AA/Slide File; **75tr** AA/S Whitehorne; **75b** AA/M Short; **76t** AA/S McBride; **76cl** AA/S McBride; **76c** AA/S Whitehorne; **76/7** AA/S McBride; **77t** AA/S McBride; **77c** AA/S Whitehorne; **77b** AA/S McBride; **78tl** AA/S Day; **78tc** AA/S Day; **78tr** AA/Slide File; **78b** AA/S Day; **79tl** AA/S Day; **79tc** AA; **79tr** AA/S Whitehorne; **80t** The Tara Brooch (cast silver), Celtic, (8th century), National Museum of Ireland, Dublin, Ireland/Bridgeman Art Library; **80c** AA/S Day; **81c** AA/S Day; **81cr** AA/S Whitehorne; **81b** The Ardagh Chalice, early 8th century (silver with silver gilding, enamel, brass and bronze) Celtic, (8th century), National Museum of Ireland, Dublin, Ireland, Boltin Picture Library/Bridgeman Art Library; **82tl** AA/S Whitehorne; **82tc** AA/Slide File; **82tr** AA/Slide File; **83tl** AA/S Day; **83tc** AA/Slide File; **83tr** AA/S Day; **84t** MS 58 fol.291v Portrait of St. John, page preceding the Gospel of St. John, Irish (vellum), The Board of Trinity College, Dublin, Ireland/Bridgeman Art Library; **84cl** AA/S Day; **84c** AA/S Day; **84cr** AA/L Blake; **85** AA/Slide File; **86t** MS 58 fol.291v Portrait of St. John, page preceding the Gospel of St. John, Irish (vellum), The Board of Trinity College, Dublin, Ireland/Bridgeman Art Library; **86b** AA/M Short; **88tl** AA/C Jones; **88tr** AA/M Short; **89tl** AA/M Short; **89tc** AA/M Short; **89tr** AA/M Short; **89b** AA/C Jones; **90t** AA/M Short; **90c** AA/P Zoiller; **91main** AA/M Short; **91inset** AA/C Jones; **92** AA/C Coe; **93cl** AA/C Jones; **93c** AA/P Zoiller; **93cr** AA/C Jones; **93b** AA/C Coe; **94t** AA/M Short; **94cl** AA/M Short; **94/5** AA/C Jones; **95t** AA/Slide File; **95cr** AA/C Jones; **95b** AA/C Jones; **96tl** AA/M Short; **96tc** AA/M Short; **96tr** AA/P Zoiller; **97tl** AA/M Short; **97tc** AA/M Short; **97tr** AA/M Short; **97b** AA/P Zoiller; **98t** AA/S McBride; **98c** AA/M Short; **98/9** AA/S McBride; **99t** Irish National Stud and Japanese Gardens; **99c** AA/M Short; **99b** AA/M Short; **100t** AA/M Short; **100c** AA/C Jones; **101t** AA/C Jones; **101ct** AA/M Short; **101c** AA/P Zoiller; **101cb** AA/S McBride; **102tl** AA/C Jones; **102tc** AA/J Johnson; **102tr** AA/C Jones; **103tl** AA/C Jones; **103tc** AA/M Short; **103tr** AA/C Hill; **103b** AA/C Jones; **104/5** AA/L Blake; **104c** AA/M Short; **105tc** AA/M Short; **105bc** AA/M Short; **106tl** AA; **106tc** AA/S Day; **106tr** AA/M Short; **108tl** AA/S Hill; **108tr** AA/C Jones; **109tr** AA/C Jones; **109tc** AA/S Hill; **109tr** AA/M Diggin; **110t** AA/C Jones; **110c** AA/S Hill; **110b** AA/S Hill; **111t** AA/S Hill; **111ct** AA/S Hill; **111cb** AA/S McBride; **112t** AA/S Hill; **112c** AA/S McBride; **112b** AA/C Jones; **113t** AA/C Jones; **113c** AA/C Jones; **114t** AA/D Forss; **114b** AA/C Jones; **115tl** AA/C Jones; **115tc** AA/S Hill; **115tr** AA/J Blandford; **116t** AA/C Jones; **116cl** AA/J Blandford; **116c** AA/J Blandford; **116cr** AA/C Jones; **117** AA/C Jones; **118t** AA/M Diggin;

118ct AA/C Jones; 118cb AA/C Jones; 118b AA/J Blandford; 119t AA/J Blandford; 119ct AA/C Jones; 119c AA/C Jones; 119b AA/C Jones; 120t AA/S McBride; 120c AA/J Blandford; 121t AA/S McBride; 121c AA/S McBride; 122tl AA/S McBride; 122tc AA/J Blandford; 122tr AA/D Forss; 123t AA/P Zoiller; 123c AA/S Hill; 123b AA/C Jones; 124tl AA/J Blandford; 124tc AA/J Blandford; 124tr AA/C Jones; 125t AA/S McBride; 125c AA/S McBride; 126t AA/C Jones; 126cl Waterford Crystal Visitor Centre; 126c AA/C Jones; 126cr AA/C Jones; 127t Waterford Crystal Visitor Centre; 127c Waterford Crystal Visitor Centre; 128tl AA/D Forss; 128tc AA/S Hill, 128tr AA/M Diggin; 130tl AA/L Blake; 130tr AA/C Jones; 131t AA/S Hill; 131c AA/S Hill; 132t AA/P Zoiller; 132c AA/S Hill; 132b AA/S Hill; 133tl AA/C Coe; 133tr AA/S Hill; 133b AA/M Diggin; 134t AA/S Hill; 134c AA/M Diggin; 134b AA/S McBride; 135t AA/C Coe; 135c Nature Photographers (Brinsley Burbidge); 135b AA/C Coe; 136tl AA/C Jones; 136tc AA/L Blake; 136tr AA/L Blake; 136c AA/L Blake; 137tl AA/C Hill; 137tr AA/C Hill; 137b AA/C Hill; 138t AA/C Jones; 138c AA/D Forss; 138b AA/C Jones; 139main AA/L Blake; 139l AA/C Jones; 139c AA/C Jones; 139r AA/C Jones; 140l AA/C Jones; 140r Nature Photographers; 141 AA/C Jones; 142t AA/S McBride; 142c AA/S McBride; 143tl AA/I Dawson; 143tc AA/M Diggin; 143tr AA/S Day; 144tl AA/C Jones; 144tc AA/C Coe; 145tl AA/I Dawson; 145tr AA/C Coe; 146t AA/C Hill; 146cl AA/C Hill; 146c © Greg McAteer; 146/7 AA/I Dawson; 147c AA/C Coe; 147t AA/C Hill; 148tl AA/S McBride; 148tr AA/L Blake; 150tl AA/P Zoiller; 150tc AA/L Blake, 150tr AA/C Jones; 150c AA/L Blake; 151t AA/C Jones; 151c AA/C Jones; 152tl AA/C Jones; 152tc AA/L Blake; 152tr AA/S McBride; 152c AA/S McBride; 153tl AA/L Blake; 153tr AA/C Jones; 153b AA/L Blake; 154 AA/C Coe; 155t AA/C Coe; 155cl AA/S McBride; 155c AA/L Blake; 155cr AA/M Short; 156 AA/C Coe; 157cl AA/M Short; 157cr AA/C Coe; 157b AA/S McBride; 158t Strokestown Park and Famine Museum; 158cl Strokestown Park and Famine Museum; 158c Strokestown Park and Famine Museum; 158cr Strokestown Park and Famine Museum; 159 Strokestown Park and Famine Museum; 160tl AA/L Blake; 160tc AA/M Short; 160tr AA/M Short; 162t AA/D Forss; 162c AA/I Dawson; 162b Nature Photographers; 163t AA/I Dawson; 163ct AA/G Munday; 163cb AA/M Diggin; 163b AA/I Dawson; 164tl AA/I Dawson; 164tc AA/G Munday; 164tr AA/G Munday; 165l Northern Ireland Tourist Board; 165tr AA/G Munday; 165cr AA/I Dawson; 166t AA/G Munday; 166cl AA/I Dawson; 166c AA/C Coe; 166cr AA/G Munday; 166b Belfast Visitor and Convention Bureau; 167 Belfast Visitor and Convention Bureau; 168cl Belfast Visitor and Convention Bureau; 168c Belfast Visitor and Convention Bureau; 169cl AA/C Coe; 169c AA/C Coe; 169cr AA/I Dawson; 169b Belfast Visitor and Convention Bureau; 170cl Belfast Visitor and Convention Bureau; 170c Belfast Visitor and Convention Bureau; 171cl AA/I Dawson; 171c Belfast Visitor and Convention Bureau; 171cr AA/I Dawson; 174tl Northern Ireland Tourist Board; 174tr AA; 174b AA/C Coe; 175tl Northern Ireland Tourist Board; 175tr AA/C Coe; 176t Northern Ireland Tourist Board; 176c AA/C Coe; 177tl AA/G Munday; 177tc AA/I Dawson; 177tr AA/G Munday; 178t Northern Ireland Tourist Board; 178cl Northern Ireland Tourist Board; 178c AA/G Munday; 178cr AA/M Diggin; 179t Northern Ireland Tourist Board; 179c Northern Ireland Tourist Board; 180t Northern Ireland Tourist Board; 180c AA/I Dawson; 181tl AA/I Dawson; 181tc AA/M Diggin; 181tr AA/I Dawson; 182/3 AA/G Munday; 182c AA; 183c AA/C Coe; 183b AA; 184t AA/G Munday; 184c AA/G Munday; 185tl AA/G Munday; 185tr AA/M Diggin; 185b Nature Photographers; 186tl AA/J Johnson; 186tc AA/I Dawson; 186tr AA/I Dawson; 187tl AA/M Diggin; 187tc Northern Ireland Tourist Board; 188 Northern Ireland Tourist Board

WHAT TO DO

189 Belfast Visitor and Convention Bureau; 190 AA/S Whitehorne; 191 AA/S Whitehorne; 192t AA/S Whitehorne; 192cl AA/S Whitehorne; 192cr Belfast Visitor and Convention Bureau; 193t AA/Slide File; 193cl AA/Slide File; 193cr Belfast Visitor and Convention Bureau; 194t Northern Ireland Tourist Board; 194cl AA/S Hill; 194cr Belfast Visitor and Convention Bureau; 195t AA/S McBride; 195cl Northern Ireland Tourist Board; 195cr Northern Ireland Tourist Board; 196t AA/S McBride; 196cl Mayo Naturally; 196cr AA/S McBride; 197t AA/S McBride; 197cl Mayo Naturally; 197c Northern Ireland Tourist Board; 197cr Belfast Visitor and Convention Bureau; 198t Northern Ireland Tourist Board; 198c Northern Ireland Tourist Board; 199t AA/S Day; 199c AA/S Day; 200t AA/S Day; 200c S Whitehorne; 201t AA/S Day; 201c AA/M Short; 202t AA/S Day; 202c AA/S Day; 203t AA/S Day; 203c AA/S Day; 204t AA/S Day; 204c AA/S Day; 205t AA/S Day; 205c AA/S Day; 206t AA/S Day; 206c AA/M Short; 207t AA/S Day; 207c AA/S Day; 208t AA/C Coe; 208c AA/L Blake; 209t AA/C Coe; 209c Photodisc; 210t AA/C Coe; 210c AA/C Coe, 211t AA/C Coe; 211c AA/P Zoiller; 212t AA/C Coe; 213t AA/S Day; 213c AA/P Zoiller; 214t AA/S Day; 214c AA/S Day; 215t AA/S Day; 215c AA/C Jones; 216t AA/S Day; 216c AA/S Hill; 217t AA/S Day; 217c AA/J Blandford; 218t AA/S Day; 218c Puck Fair Festival; 219t AA/S Day; 219c Puck Fair Festival; 220t AA/M Diggin; 220c AA; 221t AA/M Diggin; 221c AA/R Ireland; 222t AA/M Diggin; 222c AA/C Coe; 223t AA/M Diggin; 223c AA/C Hill; 224t AA/M Diggin; 224c AA/L Blake; 225t AA/M Diggin; 225c AA/S McBride; 226t AA/S Day; 226c AA/P Zoiller; 227t AA/S Day; 227c Photodisc; 228t AA/S Day; 228c AA/M Short; 229t Belfast Visitor and Convention Bureau; 229c Belfast Visitor and Convention Bureau; 230t Belfast Visitor and Convention Bureau; 230c AA/I Dawson; 231t Belfast Visitor and Convention Bureau; 231c Photodisc; 232t Belfast Visitor and Convention Bureau; 232c Belfast Visitor and Convention Bureau; 233t Belfast Visitor and Convention Bureau; 233c Belfast Visitor and Convention Bureau; 234t Belfast Visitor and Convention Bureau; 234b Belfast Visitor and Convention Bureau; 235t Belfast Visitor and Convention Bureau; 235b Northern Ireland Tourist Board; 236t Belfast Visitor and Convention Bureau; 236c Northern Ireland Tourist Board; 237t Belfast Visitor and Convention Bureau 237c Northern Ireland Tourist Board; 238t Belfast Visitor and Convention Bureau; 238c Northern Ireland Tourist Board

OUT AND ABOUT

239 Belfast Visitor and Convention Bureau; 241 AA/S Whitehorne; 242 AA/C Jones; 243t AA/C Jones; 243c AA/M Short; 243b AA/M Short; 244 AA/I Dawson; 245c AA/I Dawson; 245b AA/I Dawson; 246 AA/C Jones; 249 AA/I Dawson; 250 AA/I Dawson; 250/1 AA/I Dawson; 251 AA/G Munday; 252 AA/S Day; 253 Nothern Ireland Tourist Board; 255tl AA/C Jones; 255tr AA/C Coe; 255c AA/C Coe; 255bl AA/M Short; 255br AA/C Jones; 256 AA/P Zoiller; 257tl AA/P Zoiller; 257tr AA/S Day; 257cl AA/C Jones; 257cr AA/P Zoiller; 257b AA/M Short; 259l AA/S McBride; 259ct AA/S Day; 259c AA/S Day; 259bl AA/S McBride; 259br AA/D Forss; 261tl AA/J Blandford; 261tr AA/J Blandford; 261cl AA/C Jones; 261cr AA/J Blandford; 262 AA/S Day; 263tl AA/C Jones; 263tr AA/C Jones; 263c AA/C Jones; 263cb AA/M Diggin; 265b AA/C Jones; 265tl Mayo Naturally; 265tr Mayo Naturally; 265cl AA/C Coe; 265c Mayo Naturally; 265cr Mayo Naturally; 267tl AA/C Coe; 267tr AA/C Hill; 267cl AA/C Hill; 267cr AA/C Hill; 267b AA/C Hill; 269tl AA/I Dawson; 269tr The Irish Image Collection; 269c AA/G Munday; 269b The Irish Image Collection; 270 The Irish Image Collection; 271tl The Irish Image Collection; 271tr AA/M Short; 271c Nature Photographers; 271b AA/Liam Blake; 273t The Irish Image Collection; 273ctl AA/G Munday; 273ctr AA/M Diggin; 273c AA/M Diggin; 273b AA/J Johnson

EATING AND STAYING

275 Belfast Visitor and Convention Bureau; 276cl AA/S McBride; 276c AA/C Coe; 276r AA/S Day; 278l AA/M Short; 278c AA/M Short; 278r AA/S Hill; 280 AA/S Day; 287 Bord Bia, the Irish Food Board; 279tr Bord Bia, the Irish Food Board; 301 Bord Bia, the Irish Food Board

PLANNING

328 AA/S Whitehorne; 329t Belfast Visitor and Convention Bureau; 329c AA/I Dawson; 331t www.euro.ecb.int/; 331b Northern Bank notes reproduced with the permission of Northern Bank; 333 AA/C Jones; 334 AA/I Dawson; 335 AA/S Day; 336c AA/I Dawson; 336b AA/G Munday; 338 Belfast Visitor and Convention Bureau; 339 AA/S Day

Project editor
Cathy Hatley

Interior design
David Austin, Glyn Barlow, Kate Harling, Bob Johnson,
Nick Otway, Carole Philp, Keith Russell

Additional design work
Katherine Mead, Nautilus Design, Mike Preedy, Jo Tapper

Picture research
Vivien Little

Cover design
Tigist Getachew

Internal repro work
Susan Crowhurst, Michael Moody, Ian Little

Production
Lyn Kirby, Helen Sweeney

Mapping
Maps produced by the Cartography Department of AA Publishing

Main contributors
Chris Bagshaw, Donna Dailey, Lyn Gallagher, Mike Gerrard, Sheila Hawkins,
Marilynne Lanng, Marie Lorimer, Isla Love, Daniel Mccrea, Penny Phenix,
Christopher Somerville, Jackie Staddon, Ann Stonehouse, Hilary Weston, Nia Williams

Copy editor
Josephine Perry

See it Ireland ISBN 1-4000-1513-8

Published in the United States by Fodor's Travel Publications and simultaneously in Canada by Random House of Canada Limited, Toronto. Published in the United Kingdom by AA Publishing.

Fodor's is a registered trademark of Random House Inc, and Fodor's See It is a trademark of Random House, Inc. Fodor's Travel Publications is a division of Fodor's LLC.

Color separation by Keenes, Andover, UK
Printed and bound by Leo, China

A01611

Important Note: Time inevitably brings changes, so always confirm prices, travel facts, and other perishable information when it matters. Although Fodor's cannot accept responsibility for errors, you can use this guide in the confidence that we have taken every care to ensure its accuracy.

Dear Traveler

From buying a plane ticket to booking a room and seeing the sights, a trip goes much more smoothly when you have a good travel guide. Dozens of writers, editors, designers, and cartographers have worked hard to make the book you hold in your hands a good one. Was it everything you expected? Were our descriptions accurate? Were our recommendations on target? And did you find our tips and practical advice helpful? Your ideas and experiences matter to us. If we have missed or misstated something, we'd love to hear about it. Fill out our survey at www.fodors.com/books/feedback/, or e-mail us at seeit@fodors.com. Or you can snail mail to the See It Editor at Fodor's, 1745 Broadway, New York, New York 10019. We'll look forward to hearing from you.

Tim Jarrell
Publisher